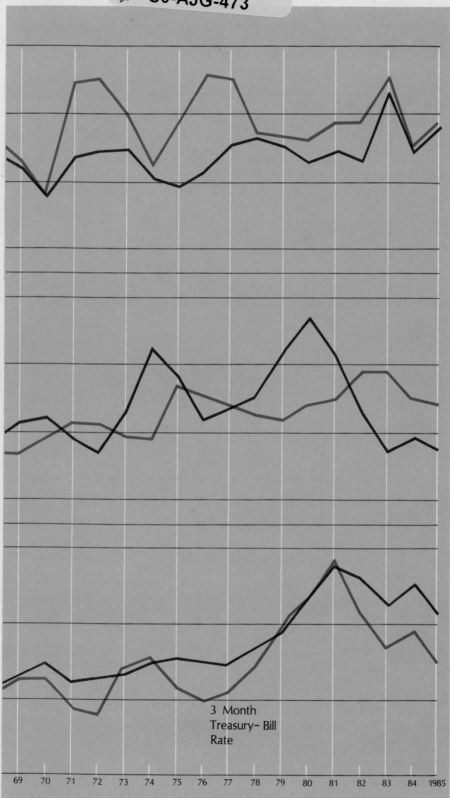

3 Month
Treasury– Bill
Rate

69   70   71   72   73   74   75   76   77   78   79   80   81   82   83   84   1985

MONEY, BANKING, AND THE ECONOMY

THIRD EDITION

Thomas Mayer, *University of California, Davis*

James S. Duesenberry, *Harvard University*

Robert Z. Aliber, *University of Chicago*

W. W. NORTON & COMPANY
New York · London

Copyright © 1987, 1984, 1981 by W. W. Norton & Company, Inc.
ALL RIGHTS RESERVED.
PRINTED IN THE UNITED STATES OF AMERICA.

Library of Congress Cataloging-in-Publication Data

Mayer, Thomas, 1927-
  Money, banking, and the economy.

  Includes bibliographies and index.
  1. Money—United States. 2. Banks and banking—United States. 3.
Monetary policy—United States.
I. Duesenberry, James Stemble, 1918-   . II. Aliber, Robert Z. III. Title.
HG540.M39 1987   332.1′0973   86-33160

ISBN 0-393-95557-5

W. W. Norton & Company, Inc., 500 Fifth Avenue, New York, N.Y. 10110
W. W. Norton & Company Ltd., 37 Great Russell Street, London WC1B 3NU

1 2 3 4 5 6 7 8 9 0

CONTENTS

CHAPTER 11: BANK RESERVES AND RELATED MEASURES   175

PART 3: MONEY, NATIONAL INCOME, AND THE PRICE LEVEL   187

CHAPTER 12: THE DETERMINANTS OF AGGREGATE DEMAND   189

CHAPTER 13: THE INTEREST RATE   207

CHAPTER 14: THE DEMAND FOR MONEY   225

PREFACE

Our aim in this Third Edition remains the same as in the first two: to give a concise, up-to-date, and well-balanced picture of financial institutions, theory, and policy. That this edition looks substantially different from its predecessors reflects both continuing change in the field of money and banking and suggestions for improvement that have arisen from widespread class use of this text. We had three goals: to cut the length of the book, to clarify the presentation of theory, and to take account of all the relevant changes that have occurred in the last three years.

Length is an important concern. Money and banking courses hardly suffer from a dearth of material to be covered, but choices have to be made. As a disciplinary device, we set ourselves a goal in this edition of no more than 500 pages, a length we have found to be a realistic limit to the amount of material that can be covered in most courses.

The issue of length brought us smack up against a critical question: how much space to allocate to institutional description as opposed to monetary theory and policy. Behind that question was our awareness of the "class struggle" that sometimes arises between instructors who prefer to stress theory and policy and a class that prefers to learn about bank management, capital markets, and the operations of the Federal Reserve. This conflict is less severe than it once was. With stresses and strains in the financial system often front-page news, policy debates involve both the functioning of institutions and the theories that influence the actions of monetary authorities. So, without skimping on strictly institutional material, our book does more than describe the activities of banks, financial intermediaries, the central bank, and regulatory agencies; it pays greater attention than most other texts to the impact policy measures have on the financial sector.

The book has the following shape. Parts 1 and 2, roughly the first third, deal with financial institutions, the creation of money and bank reserves, and the measurement of money. Part 3 takes up monetary theory and inflation. The development of aggregate supply, aggregate demand, and the wage-price spiral provides a bridge to Part 4, on monetary policy. The text ends with a full part on international money and finance.

Those familiar with earlier editions will find major changes in the theory chapters, Part 3, which have been thoroughly reworked in the interests of brevity and clarity. We now focus on those parts of macroeconomic theory that relate more directly to money. Chapter 12 summarizes the income-expenditure approach and shows that the interest rate is one of the variables determining aggregate demand. Chapter 13 deals with factors determining interest rates. One of these, important in the short run, is the demand for money, which is the topic of Chapter 14. Finally, a brief chapter, Chapter 15, pulls the analysis together by means of IS-LM analysis. We have tried to demystify the IS-LM diagram by showing both its power in summarizing Keynesian analysis and its limits with respect to changes in the price level.

Having set forth the income-expenditure approach in Chapters 12–15, we examine the quantity theory and monetarism in Chapter 16. Since teachers vary in the amount of time they spend on monetarism we have moved some of this material into an appendix to that chapter. Chapter 17 then sets the two schools in perspective, summing up the points at issue between monetarists and Keynesians. A slimmed-down version of Chapter 18, dealing with inflation, closes the theory section.

Throughout the theory chapters, we continue to stress an intuitive understanding of basic principles rather than the pyrotechnics of diagrams and equations that students tend to forget the moment the last exam is taken. Simply put, we have tried to show students how economists think about macroeconomics.

Innovations in the financial sector, new regulations on financial institutions, and new Fed policies combine to make regular updating essential. Major developments, such as the Depository Institutions Decontrol and Monetary Control Act of 1980 and the Depository Institutions (Garn–St. Germain) Act of 1982 discussed in the Second Edition, became established history a few years later. New concerns arise, such as the problem of deposit insurance and the FSLIC, the rise of "nonbank banks," and the speed with which state compacts on interstate banking will change.

As for updates in the policy area, the classic debate about whether the Fed should choose the money supply or long-term interest rates as its target has now been largely replaced by the choice between the money supply and GNP. We have therefore substantially expanded our discussion of the GNP target. The difficulty of predicting velocity brings up the question of whether the Fed should pay attention to a money target, or should instead simply accommodate changes in the demand for money, and led us to add a section on accommodative policy in Chapter 21.

In addition, without being trendy, we have tried to make the book reflect recent discussions in the professional journals. Rational expectations, no longer a new development but still much discussed, receives expanded attention in this edition. We continue to integrate this topic into the theory and policy discussions, in Chapters 13, 22, and 23. The proposal by some economists that we return to a system where private banks issue their own money may rank low on lawmakers' agendas, but it raises interesting questions about money creation and inflation. We cover it in Chapter 25.

Finally, in the interest of keeping our readers abreast of new developments in regulations and policy, we will continue to issue the *Newsletter* twice yearly. This popular supplement, available from W. W. Norton, gives us a chance to continue the updating process even without writing whole new editions.

As important as touching on recent developments is our attempt to anticipate them. In our rapidly changing financial system, one thing is certain: students will emerge from school to face innovations and regulations that did not exist when they took the money and banking course. We therefore provide a chapter on the evolution of both the financial structure and its regulation. This chapter, Chapter 8, largely rewritten for this edition, should help students understand future changes as they occur.

A final comment on the distinctive features of our text. At one time international finance could be treated very briefly, since it had little direct impact on domestic monetary institutions and policy. But this is no longer the case. The United States has become a much more open economy in recent years, and monetary policy is now influenced to a much larger extent by international considerations. Accordingly, after covering the evolution of the international payments system and operations of the foreign exchange market, we conclude with whole chapters on the structure of international banking and the most recent developments in the international monetary system.

This book is organized to permit flexible use in the classroom. In general, we have tried to write chapters so that they will stand independently. This requires occasional recapitulation, but has the advantage that some chapters can readily be shifted around or omitted. For example, some instructors may want to take up the tools of monetary policy along with Part 1, or shift the chapter on Fed organization from Part 1 to Part 3. Some instructors may prefer to skip most of Chapter 24 dealing with the history of Fed policy, but assign the last part that deals with the Fed's current procedures. A short course, stressing institutions, might well omit Chapters 11 (from page 175 to 181), 13–18, and 25–26, while a course that focuses on monetary theory and policy might want to omit Chapters 3–6, 8, and 11 (from page 175 to 181), or assign them as outside reading.

A Study Guide by Steven Beckman and Janet Wolcutt of Wichita State University contains highlights, exercises, and problems for each chapter. An Instructor's Manual, prepared by us, contains a battery of multiple-choice test questions. The test questions are also available on computer diskette.

We are deeply indebted to those whose comments and suggestions have helped shape this book. For this edition, Steven Beckman of Wichita State University, Peter Frevert of the University of Kansas, Jack Gelfand of the State University of New York at Albany, Richard C. Harmstone and Peter Olsheski of Pennsylvania State University, Worthington-Scranton Campus, and Joseph Lo of the University of California at Los Angeles offered detailed critiques based on their classroom experience.

Earlier editions benefited from the comments of George Bentson, University of Rochester; William Brainard, Yale University; Philip Brock, Duke University; Karl Brunner, University of Rochester; Jonathan Eaton, Princeton University; Wilfred J. Ethier, University of Pennsylvania; Milton Friedman, Stanford University; Beverly Hadaway, University of Texas at Austin; Thomas Havrilesky, Duke University; Arnold Heggestad, University of Florida, Gainesville; Robert S. Holbrook, University of Michigan; Walter Johnson, University of Missouri, Columbia; David Laidler, University of Western

Ontario; Edmund S. Phelps, Columbia University; James L. Pierce, University of California, Berkeley; William Poole, Brown University; Uri M. Possen, Cornell University; and John Rutledge, Claremont Men's College.

Donald S. Lamm at W. W. Norton did much more for this book than any author has a right to ask of an editor. And Drake McFeely and Debra Makay, editor and manuscript editor, respectively, of the Third Edition, did a sterling job. Finally, we owe a debt to Marguerite Crown and to Ann Frischia for excellent secretarial services.

T. M.	Davis, California
J. S. D.	Cambridge, Massachusetts
R. Z. A.	Chicago, Illinois

January 1987

PART ONE

THE FINANCIAL STRUCTURE

CHAPTER 1

Introduction

It would certainly be an exaggeration to say that *all* economic problems are the result of malfunctions in the monetary system, but some of the most important ones are. Inflation is a monetary problem in the obvious sense that it means that our monetary unit, the dollar, is losing value. It is also a monetary problem in a much less obvious way: substantial and sustained inflations have occurred only when the quantity of money has risen at a fast rate. Hence, in one sense of the much abused term *cause*, one can say that major inflations are "caused" by a rapid rise in the supply of money. Unemployment, while it has many nonmonetary aspects, is also closely connected with changes in the money supply. If the supply of money rises at a faster than expected rate, this lowers unemployment temporarily, while a sharp decrease in the quantity of money usually increases unemployment temporarily. While one may well argue about which one is cause and which is effect, most recessions since 1908 have been associated with a decline in the growth rate of the money supply. And, as we shall show, the relative growth rates of the money supply in various countries are a major factor in determining the exchange rates of their currencies.

Obviously, **monetary theory**, the theory that *deals with the relation between changes in the quantity of money, interest rates, and changes in money income*, is an important topic, and so is **monetary policy**, which is concerned with *how the quantity of money and interest rates should be managed.*

But to understand how money and monetary policy affect the economy one must know something about banks and other depository institutions. This is so because they create the major part of our money stock. In addition, financial institutions are the main providers of credit. Beyond this, there is the fact that all of us have day-to-day dealings with financial institutions and we should therefore know something about how they operate. But first a few words about money and what it does.

DIFFERENT USES OF THE WORD "MONEY"

We have used the word *money* as though it were obvious what it means, but this is far from the truth. Actually, a major reason why students often have difficulty in money and banking courses is that they forget that *money* has a very specific meaning in economics. By contrast, in everyday conversation the term *money* is used to mean many many different things. One of these is just currency, as in the phase, "Do you have any money with you?" But in modern economics money is never defined solely as currency, because currency and checking deposits do the same thing: they pay for goods and services. In fact, only a small proportion of the dollar value of purchases, probably around 1 percent or so, is paid for with currency. Hence, if we were to define money as just currency we would have great difficulty in relating money to the bulk of all purchases that are made. And it is the very fact that money is related to total purchases that makes money interesting. Since currency and deposits on which checks can be written do the same thing, and since we are interested in what money does, we must include checkable deposits along with currency in the definition of money.

One obvious objection to treating deposits as money just like currency is that one cannot make some small payments, such as a bus fare, by check, and that even for larger payments checks are sometimes not accepted. This is perfectly true. But it is also true that if someone buying, say, $10 million of securities tried to pay by currency the deal would look suspicious and probably fall through. Besides, if we were to exclude checking deposits from the definition of money because checks are not accepted for small payments, should we also exclude some currency notes, such as $1,000 bills? In fact, it helps to think of money as essentially deposits, and of currency as the small change of the system. Although peasants like us use currency for a large proportion of our payments, this is not so for large transactors. They use mainly wire transfers, that is, telex messages or telegrams to transfer money. While no recent data are available, one study estimated that in 1978 currency payments accounted for less than 1 percent of the value of total payments, checks about one-quarter, and wire transfers roughly three-quarters. By contrast, families in 1984 used currency for 36 percent of their expenditures, checks for 57 percent, and credit cards for 6 percent.

While the popular definition of money as currency is too narrow to be useful in economics, there is another popular definition of money that is too broad. This definition treats money as a synonym for wealth. Saying "she has a lot of money" means that she is wealthy. If this particular usage were followed in economics, thus merging money with real estate, stocks, bonds, and all other types of wealth, we would be ignoring the distinctive features of money.

A third popular definition of money is as income, by asking, for example, "How much money does he earn?" But defining money as income can be most confusing if we want to discuss, as we later will, whether changes in the money supply bring about equivalent changes in income. Moreover, money is a *stock*, which means that it is a certain amount at any one moment in time, while income is a *flow* over time. If you are told that someone's income is, say, $5,000, you do not know whether he has a high or low income until you are told whether the $5,000 is income per year or per week. But someone who carries $3,000 of currency in his pocket certainly has a large stock of currency.

Instead of defining money either so narrowly as just currency or so broadly as to include all wealth, economists define money by its functions. Anything that functions as a *medium of exchange*, as a *standard of value*, or as an extremely liquid *store of wealth* is considered **money**. These functions of money need explaining.

THE FUNCTIONS OF MONEY

Money acts as (1) a medium of exchange, (2) a standard of value, (3) a standard of deferred payments, and (4) a store of wealth. The first two of these functions are the ones that are unique to money.

Medium of Exchange

The medium of exchange function is obvious; we use money as an intermediary in exchange. We exchange goods and services for money, and then exchange this money for those goods and we want to acquire. Such a roundabout system of exchange avoids the great disadvantage of barter, the need for a so-called **double coincidence of wants.** What this rather stuffy phrase means is that to effect barter we have to find someone who wants to obtain the goods and services we have to offer *and*, at the same time, can provide the goods and services we want to obtain in exchange.

In a primitive society with little division of labor, such a person may not be so hard to find, since only a few types of goods are being exchanged and much of the trading is ceremonial and governed by tradition. But in an advanced society with a myriad of commodities it is a different matter. A seller of steel who wishes to exchange it for, say, vanilla ice cream would have to look around a long time before finding someone who has extra vanilla ice cream and, at the same time, wants steel. By contrast, in an economy with money this exchange process is broken into two parts. He first locates someone who wants steel and then someone who has ice cream to sell. It is much easier to locate two such people than to locate a person who just happens to combine both of these characteristics. Another problem with barter is the indivisibility of many goods. For example, a manufacturer of cars could hardly give a farmer, say, one-thousandth of a car in exchange for a pound of butter.

The inefficiency of *direct* barter then leads to the possibility of replacing it with *indirect* barter, that is with a system in which some people exchange their goods not directly for the goods they desire, but for the goods they believe are wanted by those who have the goods they want. The more a product is employed for indirect barter, the more useful it becomes, hence the greater is the willingness of people to accept it. Ultimately it may be used primarily to effectuate exchange and thus become "money."

Despite the great advantage of "money" over simple barter we do find simple barter used occasionally in a modern economy. Barter may reappear to some extent when the monetary system breaks down into a gigantic inflation, with prices doubling, say, every day. In this case money is such a poor store of value that even the very short period of time that must elapse between receiving and spending money is too long to hold it, so that some, though not all, transactions are best conducted by barter.

A more common reason for barter is that prices are not allowed to adjust to equilibrium. There may be price control, and demand may substantially exceed supply at the controlled prices. In this case sellers may be reluctant to sell their goods at controlled prices, that is, for less money than they are worth, but they may be willing to exchange them for other goods. An example of this type of barter was seen during the Allied occupation of Germany after World War II, when prices were controlled:

> "Everybody knows that to get cement you must offer coal," said the city fathers of Stuttgart, and they bought liquor brewed in the surrounding countryside, shipped it to the French zone [of occupation] in exchange for cigarettes, shipped the cigarettes to a Ruhr mine and swapped them for coal, brought the coal back to a cement plant in Württemberg, and thus got the cement for reconstruction work.[1]

Another situation where barter is sometimes used is when there are laws setting a minimum price, or if sellers with market power can keep their prices from falling when supply exceeds demand. For example, a country may set a minimum price for a commodity it exports, but then cannot sell all its output at that price. One solution is to barter this commodity with another country that is in the same fix. Then neither country has to admit that its commodity is not worth all that it claims on the market.

Barter also occurs to a limited extent under more normal circumstances, for example, in trading a car. Apparently barter arrangements have also become significant in countries with very high tax rates, such as Britain and Sweden, as a way of evading taxes.[2]

Standard of Value and Deferred Payment

The second function of money is to act as a standard of value, which simply means that we use money as a way of comparing worth. We think of, and express, the values of goods and services in terms of money, so that money is the measuring rod of value the same way as a mile is a measure of distance. Obviously, a modern economy requires continual comparisons of value; buyers have to compare the offers of numerous sellers, and this would be hard to do if different sellers denominated their prices in different goods; for example, if one store demands two pounds of butter for a pound of beef, and another store demands ten pencils for a pound of beef, which store is cheaper? A similar problem would arise in deciding whether to buy, say, beef or fish, if the price of beef is expressed in terms of butter and the price of fish

[1] Horst Mendershausen, "Prices, Money and Distribution of Goods in Postwar Germany," *American Economic Review* 39 (June 1949):656.

[2] There are "barter clubs" in the United States that allow members to swap goods and services. However, most of this activity involves the use of script as a medium of exchange, and dollars are, of course, used as a standard of value. Hence these transactions are not really barter transactions but are merely transactions in an informal currency. Presumably, a major advantage of this arrangement is that it facilitates income-tax evasion.

in terms of typewriter ribbons. To make rational decisions we would have to know the ratios at which any one good exchanges for all the others.

Suppose that we have a very simple economy with only five commodities, A, B, C, D, and E. If there is no standard of value, and we want to know the exchange ratios of these five commodities in terms of each other, we have to learn ten different exchange ratios (A—B, A—C, A—D, A—E, B—C, B—D, B—E, C—D, C—E, D—E). But if we use one of these five commodities, say A, as our standard of value, we can express the prices of the other four goods in terms of it, and thus we have to learn only four exchange rates (A—B, A—C, A—D, A—E). In general, with N commodities, if there is no standard of value, we have to learn $(N - 1)N/2$ exchange rates between them. The first part of the expression is $N - 1$ because the exchange rate of a commodity with itself is obviously unity, so that we have to discover the exchange rates of only $N - 1$ commodities. For each of these commodities we have to know its exchange rate with every other one, so we have $(N - 1)N$ exchange rates. But if we know the exchange rate of A with B we already know the exchange rate of B with A and for this reason we divide by 2.

But if we use one of these commodities as the standard of value, there are only $N - 1$ ratios. Hence, a standard of value allows us to achieve an immense economy of effort. Assume, for example, that someone is concerned with 201 items, hardly an outlandish number. Given a standard of value he or she has to ascertain only 200 prices in terms of this standard of value. But in the absence of a standard of value, there are 20,100 exchange ratios.

Another great advantage of a standard of value is that it simplifies bookkeeping. Imagine trying to manage an accounting system in which the entries in the books consist of the physical quantities of thousands of commodities. Try to see whether you made a profit or loss.

One particular function of a standard of value is to act as a standard of deferred payment, that is, a standard in which debts are expressed. This use of a standard of value creates serious problems because, as unfortunately we have all found out, the value of money varies over time; the dollar you lent last year will not buy as much when you receive it back this year. In this respect, money is a poor standard of value.

Store of Wealth

The final function of money is to serve as a store of wealth. Although this function of money is no more important than the other ones, we will discuss it in more detail because it needs more explaining.

Money has several peculiarities as a store of wealth. One is that it has no, or only trivial, transaction costs. People who decide to hold any other asset as a store of wealth must take the money they receive as income and buy this asset. Later on, when they want to obtain goods or other assets in place of this asset they have to exchange it for money. Both of these transactions, from money into this asset and, later on, from this asset back into money, involve a cost. For example, suppose that someone saves $10,000 to buy a car next year and decides to put the $10,000 into common stock in the meantime. She now has to take the time and trouble to decide which stock to buy, and to call a broker and pay a brokerage fee as well. Then, next year she has again to go to the trouble of calling the broker and paying another brokerage fee. In contrast, by holding the $10,000 as a demand deposit instead, she could have avoided (at the cost of foregoing any potential yield on the stock) both the brokerage costs and the implicit costs represented by the time and trouble required to buy the stock. This is a unique characteristic of money, and in this respect it is superior to all other assets.

A second characteristic of money as a store of wealth is that, quite obviously, its value in terms of money is fixed. This is important because debts are normally stated in money terms. Hence money has a fixed value in terms of debts and certain commitments, such as rental payments. Those who want an asset that will allow them to pay off a debt have a definite incentive to hold money. To be sure, money is not the only asset that has this convenient characteristic; a bond that matures when the debt is due has it too, but buying and selling a bond involve transactions costs.

The absence of significant transactions costs and the fixity of its value in terms of debts are the two basic characteristics of money as a store of wealth. Two other, but less basic, characteristics are that the value of money fluctuates relative to goods and services, and that some types of money (e.g., currency) have no explicit yield.[3] Hence, if someone wants an asset that will have stable purchasing power over goods and services rather than over debts, money is certainly not the ideal one. Since most of us use money primarily to buy goods it may seem that money is not as good a store of wealth as are assets whose money prices vary. While there is certainly some truth to this contention, it is subject to a major qualification. The prices of various assets and of goods and services do not fluctuate in unison. Hence, people who hold, say, common stocks or inventories of commodities may find that, despite inflation, they are even worse off than they would have been had they held money instead. Certainly, despite the inflation since 1970, someone who bought seemingly sound Penn Central stock that year, just before the company went bankrupt, would have lost more purchasing power than someone who held money instead. Unfortunately, a really good inflation hedge does not exist.

Interaction of the Functions of Money

In the United States a single monetary unit, the dollar, fulfills all four functions of money. A dollar bill for example, is a medium of exchange and a store of wealth, while prices are stated in dollars. But it is not always the case that all functions of money are fulfilled by the same monetary unit. For example, in colonial America many merchants used the British pound as their standard of value in which they kept their books, but Spanish coins were a more common medium of exchange since there were more of them around. Similarly, in Britain, until recently, prices of certain high-status goods, for example, expensive clothes, were stated in terms of guineas, a guinea equaling one pound plus one

---

[3] An explicit yield is a yield that is paid in money, and typically expressed as an interest rate. By contrast, an implicit yield can consist of free services and convenience.

shilling. But guineas were no longer in circulation and the customer paid for these goods with the medium of exchange, pounds and shillings.[4]

Usually the same unit performs all functions of money. This is so because it would be inconvenient to use different units as the medium of exchange and the standard of value. For example, suppose that the medium of exchange consists of silver coins, but that the standard of value in which prices are stated is a gold coin. Then at every purchase one would have to do a bit of mental arithmetic to calculate how many silver coins to give the merchant to meet the price set in terms of gold coins. And, as we just pointed out, as a store of wealth the advantage of money is precisely that it is the same unit as the medium of exchange (thus avoiding transactions costs) and as the standard of value (thus having a fixed value in terms of debts). And this requires that all functions be fulfilled by the same monetary unit.

M-1

When it comes to defining money, not in a theoretical sense by pointing to its functions, but by specifying the particular *measurable* items that are included in it, some difficulties arise. Most economists emphasize the medium of exchange function, and hence include in money only those items that can be used as a medium of exchange, that is, currency and checkable deposits. This is called *M-1* or "narrow money." But some economists believe that whether checks can, or cannot, be written against a deposit is not so important as long as depositors can quickly and costlessly take funds out of their deposits. They therefore define money in a broader way than *M-1* by including such items as savings deposits. We will discuss both definitions of money in some detail in Chapter 11. For the time being, just think of money as *M-1*, that is, as consisting of the public's holdings of currency and checkable deposits.

TYPES OF MONEY

There are various types of money. **Full-bodied commodity money** is *money that has a value as a commodity fully equal to its value as a medium of exchange.* An obvious example is a gold coin with its value as gold, if sold on the gold market, equal to its face value. A frequently more convenient form of money is representative full-bodied money. This is a monetary unit, such as paper money, that has little intrinsic worth, but can be redeemed in full-bodied money.

If money does not itself have value as a commodity fully equal to its monetary value, and cannot be redeemed in such commodity money, it is called **credit money.** All U.S. money is credit money.

Currency is **legal tender.** This means that *it has to be accepted in payment of*

---

[4] The guinea was originally a gold coin while the pound was a silver coin. Dealing in gold rather than silver coinage indicates superior social status, hence the use of guineas for prices of prestige goods. There is an extensive history of the use of different types of money by various social classes. The lower classes were sometimes paid in copper while the aristocracy dealt in gold. In ancient Greece, for example, the use of gold by the common people was prohibited at one time because gold could be used to bribe the gods, and this was not something the lower classes were supposed to do. Currently we still have one remnant of this tradition of "high" and "low" money—one should not leave pennies as part of the tip.

a debt unless the debt instrument itself specifically provides for another form of payment, such as, for example, the delivery of commodities. But a deposit is not legal tender. A creditor does not *have* to accept a check and can demand to be paid in currency instead. However, whether or not something is legal tender is *not* the criterion of whether it is money. As long as it is generally accepted in exchange, or used as a standard of value, we call it money.

Nature of Credit Money

Credit money economizes on scarce resources. Instead of using gold or silver, items with a high cost of production, we use items with trivial production costs, entries on a bank's books, paper, or, in the case of coins, some base metals. Money is a token entitling the bearer to draw on the economy's goods and services, and what makes *us* willing to accept it is that *other people* are willing to accept it in exchange for their goods and services. It does not need to have any value as a commodity in its own right any more than the admission ticket to a concert has to be capable of producing music.

This is not to foreclose the issue of whether or not full-bodied money, such as gold coins, or representative full-bodied money is preferable to credit money. While the quantity of a commodity money is governed by the availability of the commodity, the government controls the quantity of credit money. Opinions can reasonably differ on whether it is better to have the quantity of money controlled by accidents such as the discovery of new gold fields, or by governments.[5] Some believe that governments, unrestrained by a gold standard or some other rule, tend to increase the quantity of money too fast, which results in inflation. They do this because in the short run raising the quantity of money rapidly has very pleasant results: unemployment falls and so does the interest rate.

Credit money requires considerable sophistication. People have to grasp the idea that something is valuable if other people will treat it as valuable, despite the fact that it has no value in direct use as a commodity. Not surprisingly, credit money is therefore a relatively recent innovation. While there had been episodes of credit money before, in 1930 most of the developed countries were on a gold standard, though credit money in the form of checks did circulate. In general, as one would expect, the evolution of money has been from concrete objects to abstract symbols, that is, from precious metals traded by weight, through coins made of precious metals, to paper money redeemable in precious coins, and to irredeemable paper money and bank deposits. But evolution has not followed a straight line. For example, goldsmiths' deposits, which were essentially checks, were used as a means of payment in seventeenth-century England at a time when paper money was not yet acceptable.

---

[5] Thus Houston McCulloch has responded to the argument that a commodity standard wastes resources with the following analogy: "A similar argument could be made for bicycle locks and chains. If metal locks could be replaced with symbolic paper locks, resources would be released that could be used productively elsewhere. As long as thieves honor paper locks as they would metal locks, your bike will be perfectly secure. Surely hardened steel and phosphor bronze shackles are evidence of irrationality on the part of those who insist on them" (Houston McCulloch, *Money and Inflation.* New York: Academic Press, 1975, p.78).

THE CASHLESS SOCIETY

Has the evolution of money run its course, or will it go on? There is a wide-spread belief that not only will it continue, but that a substantial further step is close at hand. There is much concern now about the rapid growth in the volume of checks to be cleared each year, and the cost that this involves. Moreover, check clearing is a relatively slow process. Not surprisingly, computer-based innovations have been introduced. These innovations take many forms. One is automated clearinghouses that clear checks cheaply between banks. Another more visible one, is automatic teller machines in many banks that allow customers to make withdrawals and deposits twenty-four hours a day without the intervention of a human teller. These machines need not be installed in the bank itself but can be installed, when the law permits, even in places like shopping centers, thus obviating the need for a branch bank. Moreover, similar machines, called point-of-sale (pos) terminals, can be installed at checkout counters in supermarkets and other stores, so that customers can pay by having their accounts debited automatically.

One can allow one's imagination to roam beyond such relatively mundane devices and imagine a completely automated payments system. Income and other receipts would be credited automatically to a person's account by computer. When making purchases the buyer would offer an account number, which the seller would punch into a computer terminal. The payment would thus be automatically transferred to the seller's account. Recurrent payments, such as mortgage payments and utility bills, would be automatically subtracted from the payer's account, as, in fact, is already done in some cases.

However, there are still many obstacles to such a system. In some experiments that have been undertaken the public has been less than enthusiastic about electronic payments, in part because such a system does not provide the choice of delaying payment of bills when an account is low. Eventually we will probably move to a widespread electronic payments system, but we are not likely to do so soon. However, most large payments, that is, payments of many thousands of dollars, are already made by wire, and not by check, to avoid delays in the mail. Throughout this book when we refer to transfer by checks we will also mean such wire transfers.

To see one problem with an electronic transfer system consider the following story. Some colonists in a new land were familiar with a monetary system, but had not brought any money with them. Being without a medium of exchange they could still benefit from their familiarity with money by using money as a unit of account. They bartered goods, but they expressed the values of the goods they brought to the market in terms of the standard of value. But, even with a unit of account, barter is cumbersome, so they decided to use a medium of exchange. Since they did not want to tie up valuable goods by using them as a medium of exchange they hit upon the idea of using a credit system. Each colonist was given a line of credit, and one of them served as a clerk who recorded all the transactions, crediting the account of the seller and debiting the account of the buyer. But although this was a great improvement over barter even this system was cumbersome; the clerk was kept busy recording all the transactions and thought that recording very small transactions was a great nuisance. So he suggested that each colonist be given pieces of paper denoting small amounts to be credited to his or her account. They could then pass these pieces of paper to each other to make purchases. This would save a lot of bookkeeping. Only those who accumulated more pieces of paper than needed would turn them in to the clerk who would then credit their accounts. The colonists accepted this scheme and lived happily ever after. They had reinvented currency.

MONEY, NEAR-MONEY, AND LIQUIDITY

Since monetary systems change over time, the assets that are considered money change too. As a result the distinction between money and "other things" is not clear-cut. At any particular time there may be some items that are just halfway in the process of becoming money. The line of distinction between money and nonmoney is therefore blurry. Where we want to draw this line depends, in part, on what our purpose is, that is, what particular function of money is the most relevant for the problem at hand. For example, if we focus on the medium of exchange function, we want to define money as just those items that generally function as a medium of exchange.

But suppose that we stress the store of wealth function instead. If so, we want to include in the definition of money those assets that are extremely liquid, since it is its liquidity that differentiates money from other stores of wealth.

The liquidity of an asset depends on (1) how easily it can be bought or sold, (2) the transactions cost of buying or selling it, and (3) how stable and predictable its price is. Narrow money, at one end of the scale, has perfect liquidity. Since it already is money there is no cost and trouble in selling it, that is, in turning it into money, and the price of a dollar is constant at one dollar. Toward the other end of the scale there are items like real estate, which may take quite some time to sell, involve a substantial brokerage cost, and may have to be sold at less than the anticipated price. We can rank all items by their liquidity, that is, by their degree of *moneyness*.

This raises the question of where along this spectrum of liquidity and moneyness one should draw the line between money and nonmoney. There is no point at which one can draw an obvious and clear-cut line. Regardless of how broadly or narrowly one defines money there are always some assets that, while excluded from the definition of money, are very close to the borderline. Moneyness is a continuum. We therefore call *items that are excluded from the definition of money, but are quite similar to some items that are included,* **near-monies.**

These near-monies are items that are highly liquid, but not *quite* as liquid as money. Admittedly, this is rather vague, and it is not clear exactly what items should be included. At one end of the spectrum this depends on the definition of money that is used. The other end of the spectrum, where one draws the line between near-monies and those assets that are not liquid enough to be considered near-monies, is rather arbitrary. While stock in corporations is definitely not a near-money, it is not clear whether, say, a government security that matures within one or two years should be considered a near-money.

SUMMARY

1 The term "money" should not be confused with currency, income, or wealth.
2 The bulk of all payments (measured in dollar terms) is made by wire transfers.
3 Money functions as a medium of exchange, as a standard of value, as a standard of deferred payments, and as a store of wealth. As a medium of exchange money avoids the double coincidence of wants required under simple barter. As a standard of value money simplifies the comparison of values and facilitates bookkeeping. As a store of wealth, money is characterized by the virtual absence of transactions costs and by fixity of its value in terms of most debts. Usually the same unit serves all the functions of money.
4 In terms of measurable quantities the term "money" is used in this book to mean M-1, that is, checkable deposits plus currency held by the public.
5 All U.S. money is credit money. The value of credit money is based on the fact that it is generally accepted.
6 There is a trend toward a cashless society in which most transfers are by electronic book entries. But there are still many advantages to using checks and currency.
7 Near-monies are items that are not quite as liquid as money, but are highly liquid. Moneyness is a matter of degree.

QUESTIONS AND EXERCISES

1 Define and distinguish between the following:
   a. currency
   b. money
   c. income
   d. wealth
2 Are your average money holdings greater than, roughly equal to, or less than your income, or is this a meaningless question?
3 Explain why demand deposits are included in the definition of money.
4 Explain how a medium of exchange economizes on effort. Do so also for a standard of value.
5 What characteristics distinguish money from other stores of wealth?
6 Explain the meaning of the following terms and state how they differ:
   a. full-bodied commodity money
   b. representative commodity money
   c. credit money
7 Explain why credit money has value.
8 Discuss the meaning of the term near-monies. What items are included?
9 Discuss what is meant by liquidity. How would you describe the liquidity of the following:
   a. corporate stock
   b. an expected inheritance
   c. a house
   d. a deposit in a savings and loan association
10 Rather cynically one may describe the exchange of gifts at Christmas as barter. Why do we use barter at that time instead of giving each other money when money is a much better medium of exchange?

FURTHER READING

ALCHIAN, ARMEN. "Why Money?" *Journal of Money, Credit and Banking* 9 (February 1977), part 2:133–41. An excellent discussion of the medium of exchange role.

AVERY, ROBERT, et al. "The Uses of Cash and Transactions Accounts by American Families," *Federal Reserve Bulletin,* 72 (February 1986):87–108. The results of a comprehensive survey of family payment habits.

BRUNNER, KARL and ALLAN MELTZER. "The Uses of Money: Money in the Theory of an Exchange Economy," *American Economic Review,* 61 (December 1971):784–806. An excellent discussion of the medium of exchange function of money, but one that assumes some knowledge of economic theory.

FRANKEL, S. HERBERT. *Two Philosophies of Money.* London: St. Martin's Press, 1977. A short book that asks some basic questions about the government's right to manipulate money.

MELITZ, JACQUES. *Primitive Money.* Reading, Mass.: Addison-Wesley, 1974. An interesting discussion of the anthropology of money.

———. "The Polanyi School of Anthropology on Money: An Economist's View," *American Anthropologist,* 72 (October 1970):1020–1040. An interesting survey.

RADFORD, R. A. "The Economic Organization of a P.O.W. Camp," *Economica,* 12 (November 1945):189—201. A fascinating description of how "money" arose in a special situation.

CHAPTER 2

The Financial System: An Overview

The next four chapters discuss financial institutions in some detail. But first, it is useful to look at the big picture by considering a few salient characteristics of financial institutions and of the financial system in general. Hence, this chapter takes up three basic issues: (1) the nature of financial institutions and what they do, (2) how households decide what assets to hold and what claims on themselves to issue, and (3) why governments regulate financial institutions.

THE ROLE OF FINANCIAL INSTITUTIONS

Financial institutions do not produce goods as manufacturing firms do, nor do they transport and distribute goods. So why have them? Because they serve other important functions. Some clear payments for other participants in the economy and thus facilitate the division of labor. For example, a bank clears checks and provides its customers with important bookkeeping services when it sends out monthly statements. Others, such as realty firms and stockbrokers, bring potential buyers and sellers together.

An important segment of the financial industry are the **financial intermediaries,** for example, savings and loans, that, while they may clear payments, do something else too. They *intermediate by obtaining the funds of savers in exchange for their own liabilities* (such as entries in a passbook), *and then, in turn, make loans to others.* They do not merely bring savers and ultimate borrowers together, but instead sell to their depositors claims on *themselves* and then buy claims on borrowers. (For example, a depositor in a savings and loan holds a claim on the savings and loan and not a claim on the mortgage loans made by the savings and loan.) Other examples of such financial intermediaries are mutual savings banks and, to some extent, commercial banks.

Essentially, financial intermediaries buy and sell the right to future payments. For example, someone opening an account at a savings and loan association gives it a sum of money in exchange for the right to receive a larger sum back in the future. And the savings and loan then turns around and uses the deposit to make a loan, that is, to make a current payment to someone else, in return for that person's promise to make payments to it in the future.

This activity of trading in current payments and promises for future payments is extraordinarily important. To see this, consider first the extreme case of an economy with no borrowing and lending at all. In such an economy people would still want to save and invest. Many would want to defer income from the present to the future, either because they expect their income to dwindle as they get older, or their needs to rise, or else because they hope to earn some yield on their savings. But some people would not be able to earn anything on their savings at all because they lack the opportunity to buy a physical asset that produces income, and they would not be able to lend to anyone who has this opportunity. At the same time, those who have the opportunity to acquire highly productive physical assets could do so only to the extent that they cut back on their own consumption—and this hardly is the way to finance a steel mill! Obviously, such an economy would be very inefficient.

Now allow savers and potential investors in physical assets to get together and to "trade." Savers with no opportunity to invest directly are now able to earn interest on their savings by lending them to investors. Investors are no longer limited to their own savings in undertaking such projects. As a result the economy is much more productive. But such borrowing and lending generate certain costs. Savers and investors face costs in making contact, such as having to advertise. In addition, savers have to investigate the riskiness of each loan, and that takes specialized knowledge that few people have. As a result, some savers are unwilling to lend, some potential borrowers cannot finance projects that *look* risky even if they are really quite safe, and some savers suffer losses because they cannot differentiate between sound and unsound loans. Imagine, for example, how troublesome and difficult it would be for you to make a mortgage loan. You would have to undertake a credit investigation, draw up a loan document, etc.

Obviously, what is missing in such an economy is the division of labor that occurs when specialized institutions intermediate between the borrowers and lenders. This is why we have a system of financial intermediation.

Advantages of Using Financial Institutions

Under this system the lender and the ultimate borrower do not go to the trouble of seeking each other out, and since the lender does not take the borrower's IOU, she does not have to investigate the borrower's credit standing. Instead, she gives her funds to, say, a savings and loan association, which, in turn, makes a mortgage loan. Now obviously every financial intermediary levels a charge for services by paying the lender a lower rate on the deposit than the rate paid by the borrower. What makes it worthwhile for borrowers and lenders to pay this charge? Let us look at the benefits provided by financial intermediaries.

Minimize Cost. We have already mentioned one benefit of using a financial intermediary: it economizes on the information and transaction costs of borrowers and lenders. As a concrete example, consider a corporation that wants to borrow $10 million. Since not many households are able to make a $10 million loan, the corporation would have to scurry around and borrow, say, an average of $10,000 from a thousand households. Since these households would not know that this corporation wants to borrow from them, the corporation would have to seek them out by extensive advertising. And then it would have to convince them that it is a sound borrower. A financial intermediary, say, a savings and loan, on the other hand, is set up to collect the funds of many small depositors. It does not have to let households know that it wants their funds every time a borrower approaches it for a loan. The public already knows that it would like its funds. Moreover, since its deposits are insured, the public does not have to investigate its credit standing. To be sure, the financial intermediary itself has to investigate the credit standing of the borrower, but a single investigation by an expert is much less costly than a thousand separate investigations by amateurs.

Long-Term Loans. A second advantage of financial intermediaries is that they make it possible for borrowers to obtain long-term loans even though the ultimate lenders are making only short-term loans. Much borrowing is done to acquire long-lived assets, such as houses or factories. Someone who borrows to buy such assets does not want to finance them with a short-term loan. Few families, would want to finance the purchase of their homes by borrowing on a thirty-day promissory note, and each month face the problem of refinancing the loan. But now consider the same family in its role as lender. Would it want to make a twenty-year loan? Probably not, because it wants to have these funds available in case an emergency arises.

Here is where the financial intermediary comes in. Despite the fact that it has used depositors' funds to make long-term loans, a bank or a savings and loan association can promise its depositors that they can withdraw their deposits at any time. If it has many individually small depositors whose decisions whether or not to withdraw their deposits are independent of each other, then it can predict quite well the probability distribution of deposit withdrawals on any given day and hold small but sufficient reserves to meet such withdrawals. Under normal conditions, the decision whether or not to withdraw a deposit depends largely on the particular circumstances of each depositor, for example, his decision to make a large purchase. Hence, one can, under normal conditions, assume that the decisions of various depositors are independent of each other, so that the law of large numbers applies. However, this fortunate state of affairs does not *always* hold. Suppose, for example, that the public becomes afraid that banks or other financial institutions will fail. It will then try to withdraw deposits on a massive scale. The financial intermediaries will then not have sufficient liquid funds available to repay these deposits. Until 1934, when the federal government started to insure deposits, the United States suffered numerous financial panics in which many banks failed.

Liquidity. Since many claims on financial intermediaries are liquid they should be distinguished sharply from claims on other borrowers. Suppose you lend $1,000 to General Motors for ten years. In return you get a certificate called a bond that promises to pay you $90 per year, and to return your $1,000 after ten years. Suppose, three years after you have bought this bond, you suddenly need your $1,000 back. General Motors will not pay off the bond for another seven years, and the only way you can get your $1,000 back before then is to sell the bond on the open market to some other investor. The price you will get depends on supply and demand, and may be significantly less—or more— than your original $1,000. By contrast, if you have a deposit in a savings and loan association, you can get your $1,000 back at any time, though, on some kinds of deposits, you lose some of the interest you have previously earned on it.

Risk Pooling. Financial intermediaries also pool risks. Suppose there are 100 loans made, and that it is reasonable to expect that 99 of them will be repaid. Every lender is then afraid that he or she will be the unlucky one. But if the lenders pool their funds, then each lender will lose 1 percent of his or her loan and not more, thus avoiding the small risk of a large loss in exchange for accepting a more probable small loss. Thus, by pooling the funds of depositors, financial intermediaries reduce the riskiness of lending.

In summary then, indirect finance has three great advantages: it reduces the risk of lending; it makes loans more liquid than they otherwise would be; and it greatly reduces the information and transaction costs of lenders and borrowers.

Do these advantages mean that all finance takes place through financial intermediaries? Of course not. Since they charge a fee for their services, it is sometimes worthwhile for borrowers and lenders to deal directly with one another. Beyond this, people who want to invest sometimes do not borrow at all, but reduce their own consumption to avoid either the charges of a financial intermediary, or the costs of finding a willing lender. This is likely to occur if the investment project is very risky, so that the potential borrower would have to pay a high rate of interest to compensate the lender for the risk the lender sees in the project. The investor, say, the proverbial inventor of the better mousetrap, may well think that the risk is much less than lenders think it is, and hence does not want to pay the substantially higher interest rate the lenders require as compensation for assuming the risk.

PORTFOLIO BALANCE

In the previous section we pointed out that financial intermediaries bridge the gap between the types of loans that borrowers want to obtain and the ones that lenders want to make. We now take up this idea in more detail by looking at the different characteristics of loans that borrowers and lenders prefer.

Most lenders and borrowers are not specialists in finance and do not want to pay the costs of acquiring a great deal of information. At the same time they are usually averse to taking risks. Both of these factors suggest that they should try to play it safe.

Types of Risks

So far we have used the term "risk" rather loosely. One type of risk is **default risk,** that is, the risk that the *borrower will simply not repay the loan,* due to either dishonesty or plain inability to do so. Another type of risk, called **purchasing-power risk,** is the risk that, due to an unexpectedly high inflation rate, the *future interest payments, and the principal of the loan when finally repaid, will have less purchasing power* than the lender anticipated at the time the loan was made. A similar risk is faced by borrowers. A borrower may cheerfully agree to pay, say, 15 percent interest, expecting that a 12 percent inflation rate will reduce the real value of the loan. But inflation may be only 4 percent.

A third type of risk is called **"interest-rate risk"** or **"market risk,"** that is, the *risk that the market value of a security will fall because interest rates will rise.* We will discuss this further later; here we just present the intuitive idea. Suppose that five years ago you bought a ten-year $1,000 bond carrying a 6 percent interest rate, and that the interest rate now obtainable on similar bonds that also have five years to go until they mature is 8 percent. Would anyone pay $1,000 for your bond? Surely not, because they could earn $80 per year by buying a new bond, and only $60 per year by buying your bond. Hence, to sell your bond you would have to reduce its price. But suppose the bond, instead of having five years to maturity, would mature in, say, ninety days; what would its price be then? It would still be less than $1,000 since the buyer would get 6 percent instead of 8 percent interest for ninety days; but since getting a lower interest rate for only ninety days does not involve much of a loss, the bond would sell for something close to $1,000. Hence, while holding any security with a fixed interest rate involves *some* interest-rate risk, the closer to maturity a security is, the lower is this risk. On the other hand, if interest rates fall you gain because your bond is worth more; and the longer the time until the bond matures, the greater is your gain. But the fact that you may gain as well as lose does not mean that you are taking no risk.

Diversification

All three types of risks are relevant for deciding what assets to include in a portfolio, and what debts to have outstanding. (The term *portfolio* means the collection of assets one owns.) Anyone holding more than one type of asset has to consider not the risk of each asset taken by itself, but the totality of the risk on various assets and debts jointly. Suppose someone holds stock in a company that is likely to gain from inflation, and stock in another company that is likely to lose from inflation. The riskiness of a portfolio that combines both of these stocks may be less than the riskiness of each stock taken separately. *A portfolio consisting of assets that are affected in opposite directions by given future events is less risky than are the assets that compose it when taken individually.* Hence a low-risk portfolio need not contain only assets that individually have little risk; sometimes one reduces the riskiness of a portfolio by adding some high-risk assets that offset the risks of other assets in it.

Another way to reduce risk is to hedge your assets and debts by matching the maturity of your assets and liabilities. Suppose you buy an asset that you plan to sell at a profit five years from now. If you finance it by borrowing at a fixed interest rate for five years you avoid both interest-rate risk and purchasing-power risk. On the other hand, if you finance it by borrowing on a thirty-day promissory note, or at a variable interest rate, you assume both interest-rate risk and purchasing-power risk. Matching the maturities of one's assets and liabilities is a major way to reduce risk.

Buying assets with offsetting risks and matching the maturities of assets and fixed interest debt are two examples of portfolio diversification. But one can also diversify a portfolio in another way. Suppose, for example, that you have the choice between an asset lasting one year with an expected 40 percent yield, but with a 20 percent chance that it will become completely worthless, and another asset that yields 5 percent, but is virtually riskless. Which asset should you buy? Obviously, this will depend upon your willingness to take risks. Most people are not willing to risk all their livelihood even for an exceptionally high expected rate of return, but many are willing to take a risk with a small proportion of their assets. Hence, they hold some proportion—often only a small proportion—of their portfolio in risky assets. Most large portfolios are diversified, both by containing assets with offsetting risks and by containing some assets with small and some with large risks. One of the major functions of a financial adviser is to tell people how they can diversify their portfolio efficiently.

To decide what assets to hold in a portfolio, one has to know the characteristics of assets. Table 2.1 shows the typical yields, liquidity, and risks on the following assets: money, saving or time deposits at fixed interest rates in banks or savings and loan associations, government securities, corporate bonds and stocks, and capital held directly, such as houses or consumer durables. The first column ranks these assets by their monetary yields, starting with the lowest-yielding one. However, this ranking changes from time to time; sometimes deposits have a higher yield than short-term securities, and sometimes short-term securities have a higher yield than long-term securities. Similarly, the yield on stock (that is, the dividend plus capital gains and losses) fluctuates a great deal, and to the chagrin of stockholders it is sometimes negative. The next column shows the imputed yield (apart from liquidity) that an asset may have by providing free services, such as check clearing in the case of deposits, and shelter in the case of housing. The third column shows the asset's liquidity. The remaining three columns deal with the three types of risks. Interest-rate risk includes here not only the danger of actually selling an asset at a loss, but also the foregone opportunity cost if interest rates rise. For example, owners of bonds paying 6 percent may hold on to them when interest rates have risen to 9 percent, and thus avoid taking an explicit loss, but they still suffer a loss in the sense that, had they not previously bought the 6 percent securities, they could now buy the 9 percent ones.

From Table 2.1 one can see the role that various assets play in the portfolios of households. Money is held mainly for its yield in terms of convenience and for its liquidity. Although money is also safe—except for purchasing-power risk—it would be naïve to hold it primarily for this reason because in this respect it is dominated by time deposits. Savings and time deposits, as well

Table 2.1 Characteristics of Selected Assets *(ranked with lowest yield, liquidity, or risk denoted by zero)*

Asset	Typical monetary yield	Imputed yield from convenience	Imputed yield from liquidity	Default risk	Interest-rate risk	Purchasing-power risk
M-1	0–1[a]	1	4	0[b]	0	1
Insured fixed-rate savings and time deposits	1 or 3[c]	0	0–3[c]	0	1–2[c]	1
Short-term government securities	2	0	3	0	1	1
Long-term government securities	3	0	2	0	3	1
Corporate bonds[d]	4	0	1	1	3	1
Corporate stock	5	0	1	2	3	2[e]
Physical capital used by households	0	1	0	—[f]	0	0

a: Zero for currency, 1 for some checkable deposits.
b: Default risk exists only for deposits of over $100,000.
c: Depends on type of deposit.
d: Large-denomination bonds traded frequently on major exchanges.
e: Assumes, on basis of recent experience, that inflation depresses real stock prices.
f: No default risk per se, but risk that capital asset will be less useful than planned.

as short-term government securities, are held primarily because of their high liquidity and safety, though their yield provides an additional motive. Long-term government securities often have a higher yield, but involve more interest-rate risk than the previously discussed assets. Still they are often included in portfolios to provide safety in the sense of avoiding default risk. Corporate bonds are riskier since they have a default risk. Corporate stock typically has a higher risk than corporate bonds, but its yield has, over the long run, been higher than the yield on corporte bonds. Capital owned directly has usually a high *imputed* yield such as providing the family with shelter, transportation, and so on, but it is highly illiquid.

Another way to look at the seven types of assets listed in Table 2.1 is to consider the types of institutions that issue them. The government issues part of the money stock, currency, and, of course, government securities. Financial intermediaries issue the remainder of the money stock. Financial intermediaries also issue saving and time deposits, and corporations issue corporate bonds and stock. With respect to default risk the safest assets are the obligations of the government and of financial intermediaries. It is simple to explain why the government's obligations are safe; since the government has the power to tax, and the power to create money, it can always pay off its debts. But what ensures the safety of the obligations of financial intermediaries? The answer is that the government insures and supervises them. We will take up the insurance systems in later chapters.

GOVERNMENT SUPERVISION OF FINANCIAL INSTITUTIONS

Financial intermediaries are very heavily regulated by both the federal and state governments. For example, one cannot just start a bank the way one can start another business. Instead, a prospective bank organizer must obtain special permission, called a charter, from either the federal or state authorities. Moreover, various government agencies supervise banks and financial intermediaries by inspecting the assets they hold and requiring them to get rid of risky ones.

While in other industries the government prosecutes attempts to limit competition, in banking, as in some other regulated industries, it imposes regulations that reduce competition. Why is this? Essentially the answer is that an unregulated banking system would take too many risks. But this does not *necessarily* mean that government regulation is desirable, since it has its own disadvantages. As a general principle, the fact that the private market (or government regulation) suffers from some inefficiencies does not provide a sufficient case to replace it; the alternative might be worse.

What are the reasons for government supervision of banks? The first reason is *consumer ignorance.* For competition to work effectively the buyer must be able to evaluate the quality of the product with some degree of efficiency. Otherwise, various producers could succeed by offering a defective product at a low price. Consumers can evaluate most products in either, or both, of two ways. One is through experience. They buy, say, a quart of milk advertised by a new dairy. If they don't like it not much is lost. The other way is by evaluating the product before purchase; for example, they may not buy a car that looks flimsy.

Unfortunately, neither method works well for deciding whether to buy the deposit services of a financial intermediary. The foremost characteristic most households look for in a financial intermediary is that it be safe and not fail. But experience provides little help here. Once a bank has failed, depositors know that they should not have entrusted their funds to it, but by then it is too late.[1]

The other method of evaluating a product, inspecting whether it is flimsy or not, does not work for financial intermediaries either. Extensive effort and technical knowledge are required to evaluate the soundness of a bank or other financial intermediary. Just looking at the balance sheet won't do. Depositors

---

[1] Deposits are not the only example of large and infrequent expenditures on items whose technical soundness it is difficult to evaluate. This is so for houses, too. And here too we have government regulation (building codes) and inspection for safety and health defects that would not be obvious to the buyer. In the absence of such government regulations buyers would probably rely on private housing inspectors and on certificates by the builder. But the certificate of a failed bank would give a depositor little protection, and buildings are easier for a specialist to evaluate than are banks.

cannot tell whether the item listed as "loans" consists of loans to sound or risky borrowers.

Unfortunately the financial intermediary has an incentive to buy assets that are too risky from the point of view of the depositor and the economy as a whole. This is so not because it wants to fail, but because if it makes a risky loan all the additional interest the borrower pays because the loan is risky accrues to it. (The depositor, not knowing that the financial institution is taking these risks, does not ask for higher interest.) But the institution does not bear all the corresponding potential loss, since in the absence of deposit insurance, the depositor stands to lose too. Thus, since the depositor bears part of the risk, the cost of risk-taking to the financial institution and to the depositor combined exceeds the cost of risk-taking to the institution alone. But in deciding how much risk to take, the financial institution sets the marginal revenue from taking risk equal to the marginal cost that risk imposed on it alone, so that it takes more risk than is justified when one considers the combined cost of taking the risk.

Some mechanism is obviously needed to prevent financial intermediaries from taking too much risk. One possibility would be extensive consumer information. Thus, in principle, depositors could subscribe to reports, written by accountants and financial analysts, that evaluate banks and other financial intermediaries. However, such reports may not be reliable enough and may be expensive, both in terms of purchase price and in terms of the time it takes to read and evaluate their perhaps competing recommendations. But, even so, large business firms that have deposits greatly exceeding the insurance limit do try to evaluate the soundness of their banks.

Another way to protect the depositor is to insure deposits. One possibility would be to have banks or the other financial intermediaries insured by private insurance companies, but there would be the danger that if many large institutions fail, so would the insurance company. Bank failures cannot be predicted from actuarial tables the way deaths, or car accidents, can. However, the government is an institution that can always pay off its debts, and hence we have it insure deposits. But if the government insures deposits (up to $100,000), what protects the government against the danger of depository institutions (banks, savings and loans, and savings banks) taking excessive risks? The answer is that the government prohibits them from buying certain risky assets.

A second, even more important, reason for government supervision of depository institutions is that they *create the major part of our money supply.* Thus a wave of bank failures could wipe out a significant proportion of the money stock. Suppose that massive bank failures did reduce the supply of money. With the money supply now being smaller it would no longer suffice to buy all the goods and services offered on the market. Production would be curtailed and unemployment would rise, perhaps substantially so. During the Great Depression bank failures and the withdrawals of currency from banks reduced *M-1* by about one-quarter. This could explain the extraordinary severity of this depression.

Third, banks manage our payments mechanism. If paychecks bounce because the employer's bank has failed, some employees will not be able to make their mortgage payments. This in turn may make it impossible for the holders of these mortgages to meet *their* payment commitments, and so on. With the average dollars of demand deposits being spent more than four hundred times a year, even a short disruption in the payments system could cause great confusion and damage. The government has a responsibility to prevent this, similar to its responsibility to prevent disruptions in other essential services, like electricity or water.

A fourth reason for government supervision and insurance is that, without it, even sound, well-run banks would be in danger of failing when some other banks that took too much risk go under. The public cannot distinguish very well between sound and risky banks. The cost of being caught in a bank failure greatly exceeds the cost of withdrawing a deposit. Hence, in the absence of government supervision and insurance, when the public sees some banks fail it is likely to withdraw deposits from other banks too. Such runs may destroy well-run and safe banks.

These four reasons justify both deposit insurance and the accompanying regulations needed to ensure bank safety. Another set of regulations has been imposed for a variety of other reasons, such as constraining the growth of giant banks and protecting bank customers from discrimination.

A fifth explanation of government regulation is that the federal government has in the past tried to use regulation over depository institutions as *a way of subsidizing residential construction and the building industry*. One way it did this was to prohibit savings and loans from making most kinds of business and consumer loans so that they would make more mortgage loans instead. However, this regulation was not very effective, and in 1981 savings and loan associations were given the right to make a limited amount of consumer and business loans. Another way the government tried to subsidize residential construction was to set a ceiling on the interest rates that could be paid to depositors, in the (questionable) belief that depository institutions would then charge lower rates on the mortgages they make. This regulation turned out to be ineffective, and was eliminated.

Do these five reasons for government regulations mean that the current heavy regulation of banks and other financial intermediaries is justified and not excessive? Not necessarily. While the authors believe that the difficulty of evaluating the safety of financial institutions and the need to prevent sharp declines in the stock of money and of near-monies justify some government regulations, we are skeptical about the last reason, subsidizing residential construction.

SUMMARY

1 Financial institutions play an important role. Some (banks) clear payments. Others (such as real estate firms and stockbrokers) bring buyers and sellers together. Still others (financial intermediaries) interpose their own liabilities between savers and borrowers. This greatly facilitates saving and investment.

2 Portfolio risk can be reduced by diversifying the portfolio and by holding assets with maturities similar to one's liabilities. Assets are subject to default risk, purchasing-power risk, and interest-rate risk. These risks differ for various assets.

3 Financial intermediaries are heavily regulated, often in ways that inhibit competition. The reasons for heavy regulations are protection of the payments mechanism, the difficulty people have in deciding whether a financial intermediary is safe, and a fear of great aggregations of economic power. While some regulation is justified, it is not obvious that the present level of regulation is.

QUESTIONS AND EXERCISES

1 Explain why we have financial intermediaries.

2 Financial intermediaries hold relatively illiquid and somewhat risky assets and yet can issue very liquid and safe claims on themselves. Explain how they can do this magic. Can they do this without limit?

3 Which argument for government regulation of financial institutions do you find most convincing? Which least convincing? Give your reasons.

4 Suppose you had $100,000. How would you distribute your portfolio over various assets? Why? How about if you had $10,000?

5 Many households hold claims on financial intermediaries, and, at the same time, borrow from financial intermediaries. Why don't they "borrow" from themselves?

6 Suppose that you decide to set yourself up as a financial institution and take $1,000 deposits from each of four customers. Suppose further that the probability of any one depositor demanding repayment of his or her deposit within the relevant period is 20 percent (and that the probabilities of various depositors demanding repayment are independent of each other). How much would you want to keep in reserves to meet potential depositor demand? (Hint: the answer involves more than just a simple number.)

FURTHER READING

BENSTON, GEORGE. "A Transactions Cost Approach to the Theory of Financial Intermediation," *Journal of Finance*, 31 (May 1976):215–232. A thoughtful, elegant discussion, though a bit difficult at points.

GOLDSMITH, RAYMOND. *Financial Institutions.* New York: Random House, 1968. This is an excellent survey of the financial system.

GURLEY, JOHN, and EDWARD SHAW. *Money in a Theory of Finance.* Washington, D.C.: Brookings Institution, 1960. An advanced, seminal treatise.

MOORE, BASIL. *An Introduction to the Theory of Finance.* New York: Free Press, 1968. Chapter 2 provides a very useful and thorough, yet brief, discussion of portfolio management.

SHAW, EDWARD. *Financial Deepening in Economic Development.* New York: Oxford University Press, 1973. An important discussion of the role of finance in less-developed countries.

CHAPTER 3

The Banking Industry

The previous chapter presented a bird's-eye view of financial institutions and their functions. This and the following chapter deal with our most prominent financial institutions, commercial banks or just *banks*, as we will call them. Banks are our most important financial institutions; they create much of our money stock, and have such a wide range of activities. We take up banking in considerable detail, both because the behavior of banks is relevant for monetary policy and because, on a more personal level, readers are likely to deal with banks as depositors, and perhaps as borrowers. In dealing with a bank, it is obviously useful to be able to see things from the bank's point of view, and this requires some knowledge of how they operate.

This chapter deals with the banking industry as a whole, and takes up the way banks are regulated, and how they interact with each other. The following chapter then looks at the individual bank as a profit-maximizing institution and at its assets and liabilities. We postpone discussion of foreign banks in the United States and the foreign activities of U.S. banks until Chapter 28.

A SKETCH OF BANKING HISTORY

Banking is an old business. Banks existed in ancient Babylon and in the classical civilizations, particularly in Rome. But modern banking started in Renaissance Italy where bankers, apart from buying and selling foreign currencies, also took demand and time deposits. These demand deposits were usually transferred orally by the owner visiting the banker who sat behind his bench or table, though checks were not unknown. (Our term *bankruptcy* comes from the Italian custom of breaking the bench of a banker who could not pay off his creditors.) The most famous of these Italian bankers were the Medici family, who for a time ruled Florence and made loans to princes and merchants both in Italy and in the rest of Europe.

In England banking grew out of the custom of goldsmiths, who took in their customers' gold and silver for safekeeping. They then discovered that they could lend such coins out, keeping just a certain proportion as a reserve, since not all customers would come in for repayment at the same time. Moreover they gave their depositors receipts, which these depositors could pass on to other people. Eventually, to make such transfers more convenient, they issued receipts in round-number sums. These receipts thus became private bank notes; that is, currency notes issued by, and repayable on demand by, the banker.

In colonial America the first bank, in the modern sense of the term, was the Bank of North America, founded in 1782. Subsequently, banking spread rapidly as the states chartered more and more banks, some of them owned by the state itself. Between 1781 and 1861 over twenty-five hundred banks were organized, but many of them were unsound; almost two-fifths of them had to close within ten years after they had opened.[1]

In 1791, at the urging of Alexander Hamilton, Congress temporarily chartered a national bank, the First Bank of the United States, in part owned by the federal government. This bank, which was much larger than the state-chartered banks, held deposits of the federal government and transferred funds for it to various parts of the country. It also tried to discipline the state-chartered banks that had issued too many bank notes, either by refusing to accept their notes in payment or by collecting a lot of them and presenting them all at once to the unfortunate bank for redemption in gold.

Not surprisingly, in 1811 when the charter of the First Bank of the United States came up in Congress for renewal, the state-chartered banks tried to kill it. Among the arguments against it were that it was, in part, owned by foreigners, that it had dabbled in politics, the doubts of some that the Constitution permitted Congress to charter a bank, and a belief that the bank had too much monopoly power. These arguments were effective. Congress did not renew the First Bank's charter.

In 1816 the Second Bank of the United States was chartered with the federal government owning one-fifth of the stock and appointing one-fifth of the directors. Although it did a lot of good in curbing excessive expansion by state banks, its charter was allowed to expire in 1836. This occurred in good part because it was opposed by President Andrew Jackson, who was concerned about the concentration of economic power in the Northeast and was an opponent to the bank's president, Nicholas Biddle.

The 1830s also saw another important change in banking. Until then states could charter banks only by a special act of the legislature. This led to much corruption and favoritism. In 1837 Michigan led the way to a new system, called **free banking.** Under this system, anyone who met rather easy conditions could organize a bank and issue bank notes as well as take deposits, checks by this time having come into widespread usage. Although free banking avoided the scandals of the previous system, it developed its own problems. Many new banks were organized and issued their bank notes, and with so many different bank notes around, it was hard to differentiate between genuine and counterfeit notes, or notes issued on nonexistent banks. Moreover, notes of

[1] Benjamin Klebaner, *Commercial Banking in the United States: A History.* Hansdale, Ill.: Dryden Press, 1974, p. 48.

certain banks, considered unsafe or located far away, circulated at less than full face value. Merchants had to look up in registers of bank notes the value of notes presented to them as payment. In addition, a few—though not very many—banks, the so-called wildcat banks, made it hard to present their bank notes to them for redemption in coin by locating in out-of-the-way places. As a result, some bank notes circulated well below their face value. Bank failures, too, were common.

These problems, as well as the need to develop an additional market for government bonds to finance the Civil War, led Congress to establish the National Banking System starting with the National Currency Act of 1863 (later amended and renamed the National Banking Act). The bank notes, issued by each of the *national banks* chartered by the federal government, were made uniform, and they were safe because each national bank had to deposit $10 of federal government bonds with the Comptroller of the Currency for each $9 of bank notes it issued. (Thus it would put up $1 of capital, borrow $9 from depositors, and hold $10 of interest-earning government bonds.) If a bank failed, the holders of its national bank notes were repaid by the Comptroller of the Currency out of the bonds the bank had deposited with him. State-chartered banks were effectively prevented from issuing bank notes by the imposition of an annual 10 percent tax on their notes. There was now a uniform and sound currency that, unlike the previous bank notes, was accepted at **par** (that is, at full value) throughout the country. Funds could now be transferred all over the country at a cost that could not exceed the small cost of shipping bank notes, and was frequently less. But state banks, though they could no longer issue bank notes, did not disappear, as had been thought they would, because, with the rapidly growing use of checks, they could still provide a medium of exchange—demand deposits.

Although the national banking system solved the problem of there being too many types of bank notes and reduced the frequency of bank failures, it was far from perfect. Thus it did not provide an efficient system of check collection. A check passed from one bank to another in a long chain until it was finally presented to the bank on which it was drawn. Hence, if it bounced it would take much too long until this was discovered.

To reduce bank failures the federal government required national banks to keep reserves against their deposits. Some of these reserves had to be kept as currency in the banks' vaults, but (except for banks in the three largest financial centers) banks could keep part of their reserves as deposits with banks in larger cities. When these banks then withdrew these reserves the banks in the financial centers would find themselves short of reserves, and had to call in some of the short-term loans they had made to dealers in the money market and the stock market. As a result interest rates would rise sharply. Sometimes a financial panic—in which banks could not get at their reserves —would result.[2] Banks did, however, develop a device to ameliorate the impact of financial panics. They would jointly stop paying out currency to the public, and would pay instead in *clearinghouse certificates*, which were notes

---

[2] Besides, some banks would close their doors and fail rather than touch their reserves, so these reserves did little good.

that could be used to make deposits, and hence would be accepted as payments in many cases, albeit often at a discount. Moreover, payments could still be made by check.

There was no central bank that could adjust the money supply to meet the need for money, and the money supply could therefore not expand along with the demand for money. Hence, there were frequent complaints about a "shortage" of money in the fall when the harvesting season raised the demand for money, and interest rates would rise. (Whether these complaints were justified, in the sense that the supply of money *should* expand along with the demand for it, is another matter, which we will take up in Chapter 21.) A related complaint was that in a financial panic no additional currency was available to meet the increased demand as the public, afraid of bank failures, tried to shift out of deposits into currency. Bank failures were frequent, particularly among state banks, which, being less heavily regulated than national banks, had grown at a faster rate.

In 1907 the country suffered a severe recession, which, along with previous dissatisfaction with the banking system, resulted in the appointment of the National Monetary Commission. After exhaustive studies it recommended the establishment of a central banking system, what was to become the Federal Reserve. But there was a great deal of opposition to the creation of a central bank out of fear that it would be run by bankers and lead to a banking cartel. It was not until 1913 that this opposition was overcome and the Federal Reserve Act was signed by President Woodrow Wilson.

We will discuss the Federal Reserve System in considerable detail in Chapter 7, but we will note here the ways in which this new system was intended to solve the problems that beset the National Banking System. Checks could now be cleared through the Federal Reserve instead of routing them through a whole chain of banks. Required reserves had to be kept initially with the Federal Reserve rather than with other banks. (Subsequently banks were allowed to keep them also as currency in their vaults.) The money supply was made more responsive to the demand for money by enabling banks to borrow from the Federal Reserve. But the attempt to make banks safer failed miserably. There were many more bank failures in the period 1931–1933 than at any other time.

CHARTERING, EXAMINATION, AND FED MEMBERSHIP

Government control over banks comes in several layers. Initially, there is chartering. A prospective bank has to obtain a *charter, either from the federal government* (through the Comptroller of the Currency) as a **national bank,** *or from its state government* (through the state banking authorities) as a **state bank.**

The second layer of government control is the Federal Reserve. Although its main function is the conduct of monetary policy, it also regulates banks. All national banks must, and state banks may but need not, join the Federal Reserve System, becoming a **member bank**—this term *always refers to membership in the Federal Reserve System.* Third, there is the Federal Deposit Insurance Corporation (FDIC). All member banks *must* join the FDIC while

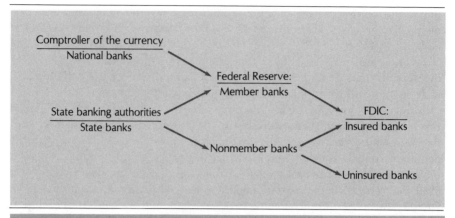

Figure 3.1 **The Structure of Bank Regulation.** The number of agencies regulating a bank depends on the type of bank. National banks are regulated by the Comptroller of the Currency, the Federal Reserve, and the FDIC. At the other extreme, uninsured banks are regulated only by the state banking agency.

nonmember banks *may* join if they meet the FDIC's admission criteria. The resultant structure of government contacts is shown in Figure 3.1.

No recent data on the number of uninsured banks are available, but in 1982 fewer than 4 percent of all banks were uninsured, and they held only .1 percent of all bank assets. Table 3.1 shows the distribution of banks by type. Fewer than half of all banks are member banks, but they hold over three-quarters of all assets. One-third of all banks are national banks, and they hold more than half of all bank assets.

After a national bank is in operation it has many contacts with the government. One form of this contact is the **examination.** With a frequency depending upon the perceived riskiness of the bank, employees of the Comptroller of the Currency, called bank examiners, make an unannounced visit to each national bank. Although preventing fraud is one of the purposes of bank examination, it is not the major one. The main emphasis is on seeing whether

TABLE 3.1 **Distribution of Commercial Banks by Type, December 1984**

	Percentage of all banks	Percentage of all bank assets
Member banks	41.1	77.9
National banks	33.8	59.7
State banks	7.3	18.2
Nonmember banks	58.9	22.1

Note: Includes trust companies, which are institutions that operate just like commercial banks, but have a somewhat different charter.

Source: FDIC *Statistics on Banking 1984*, pp. 32–33.

the bank is complying with various rules and regulations concerning its asset holdings, if it is carrying assets on its books at a conservative value, and whether any securities held, and loans made, involve excessive risks. If a security is deemed too speculative the examiner can order the bank to sell it. If repayment of a loan is doubtful the examiner can order the bank to "classify" it as "loss," "doubtful," or "substandard." Depending upon the particular classification the bank may have to stop treating the interest it receives on the loan as income, or it may have to put aside, out of its profits, a special reserve against losses on the loan, or it may have to write off the loan altogether as a loss. Since a bank is required to keep an acceptable minimum ratio of capital to deposits, the write-down of capital that results from writing off loan losses, or from selling low-quality securities at a loss, may force it to raise more capital or curb the growth of its deposits. And the fact that it has to write off loans can hurt a bank by reducing the price of its stock. Obviously, since the quality of loans and securities is a matter of opinion, disputes between banks and examiners do arise. However, in some cases bank officers welcome the advice of examiners who, as outsiders, can take a more objective view than do the bank's officers.[3]

The examiners classify banks into five categories depending on their capital adequacy, management, earnings, and liquidity. This rating, known by the acronym CAMEL, determines how often a bank is examined. If the news that it has been classified as a problem bank leaks out, as has happened occasionally, neither the bank's customers nor its stockholders are likely to react favorably.

However, it is easy to exaggerate the power of bank examiners, particularly in their dealings with a large bank. Such banks are complex institutions, and it is difficult for examiners to acquire enough knowledge to be able to dispute successfully with the bank's officers and lawyers. A senior official of the office of the Comptroller of the Currency was once quoted as saying, "How can I tell David Rockefeller how to run his bank? I've never made more than $40,000 in my life."[4] Small banks, however, offer an easier target. All in all, a recent study discussing bank capital concluded:

> The lack of objective standards creates difficulties. Except when a bank is asking for a privilege, regulators can only urge or attempt to convince a bank that more capital is required. Arguments as to what is or is not adequate are difficult if not impossible to resolve. . . . The list of enforcement proceedings shows long delays when a bank decides not cooperate. Examiners do find illegal and illogical actions, but they also miss many. In large banks they can be overwhelmed by details. . . .[5]

Apart from the chartering authorities, the Federal Reserve has the right to examine member banks, and the FDIC to examine insured banks. However,

---

[3] Since a bank examiner becomes familiar with the operating methods of many banks and thus obtains a thorough knowledge of banking, some banks like to hire former bank examiners.

[4] *New York Times*, 22 December 1977, p. 49.

[5] Sherman Maisel et al., *Measuring Risk and the Adequacy of Capital in Commercial Banks.* Chicago: University of Chicago Press/National Bureau of Economic Research, 1981, p.150.

to avoid duplication or even triplication, the Fed usually leaves examination of national banks to the Comptroller of the Currency, and examines only state member banks. Similarly, the FDIC usually examines only nonmember insured banks.

As Table 3.1 showed, more than one-third of all banks, but few state banks, are member banks. What kept many banks out of the Federal Reserve System in the past is that the Fed then imposed relatively high reserve requirements on member banks. By contrast, nonmember banks only had to meet the usually much less stringent reserve requirements set by their states. However, in 1980 the law was changed to phase in by 1988 the same reserve requirement for all banks, so that the reserve requirement is no longer a deterrent to Fed membership. However, member banks still have to meet some Fed regulations that are stricter than the corresponding state regulations. The advantage of membership for larger banks is that it facilitates their acting as city correspondent banks, an activity we discuss later in this chapter. Moreover, Fed membership confers prestige and status on a bank.

BANK CAPITAL

Banks have to meet a minimum capital requirement. **Bank equity capital** or **primary capital** is the *stockholders' equity in the bank.* It is represented on the balance sheet mainly by outstanding stock, surplus, and retained earnings. In addition to equity capital, banks can count as part of their capital long-term funds they have obtained by selling bonds and notes with an average maturity of at least seven years. Such **secondary capital** is used mainly by large banks.

The purpose of a capital requirement is to provide a cushion of safety both for the FDIC and for uninsured depositors. The reason that a large capital stock helps to make a bank safe is because capital represents those funds that the bank can lose without endangering its ability to repay its creditors. Suppose that a bank's capital is equal to 5 percent of its assets. Then, even if, as a result of making unsound loans, it loses 5 percent of its assets its creditors are still covered; only the stockholders lose. And protection of stockholders is not a legitimate reason for bank regulation—they are responsible for how they invest.

From the bank's point of view a certain cushion of equity capital is clearly desirable. Not only does it help to protect the bank's stockholders against the danger of the bank failing, but in addition business borrowers, as well as large depositors, are reassured by a high capital ratio. Developing a borrowing relationship with a bank is time consuming, and a firm prefers to borrow from a bank that is likely to be around next year. However, the marginal yield from adding capital declines after some point. Suppose, for example, that a bank already has a high stock of capital relative to its liabilities. The chance of its failing is already so low that adding even more capital does not influence its potential customers much.

At the same time, the more equity capital a bank has per dollar of assets, the greater is the number of dollars of capital over which the bank's earnings have to be spread. Assume, for example, that the bank earns a 1 percent profit on its total assets. If equity capital equals 10 percent of total assets, then this 1 percent yield on assets represents a 10 percent yield to the bank's stockholders; on the other hand, if the bank has the same earnings, but only a 5 percent ratio of equity capital to total assets, then the stockholders earn 20 percent on their capital. For each bank there exists therefore an optimal ratio of capital to assets at which the marginal advantage of additional capital is just offset by its disadvantage.

But what constitutes an optimal capital stock—and hence the optimal amount of risk—from the bank's point of view is insufficient capital, and hence excessive risk, from the social viewpoint. If a bank would be the only one to lose if it fails, the social and private costs of risk-taking would be the same. But this is not so. If a bank fails, the FDIC has to step in and rescue the insured depositors and in addition, depositors with accounts above the insurance ceiling may lose. More important, if a large bank fails, or many smaller banks fail almost simultaneously, the public may lose confidence in other banks, and try to withdraw deposits from them, thus causing them to fail.

When a bank decides how much risk it should accept it does not take these external costs of its potential failure into account. It selects a level of risk at which the marginal loss from risk-taking is just equal to the marginal yield from taking this risk. Hence, it takes more risk than is socially optimal. This is why the government is justified in stepping in and limiting the amount of risk a bank takes. It does this both by limiting the riskiness of the bank's loans and securities and by requiring the bank to hold more capital than it would in the absence of regulations.

The amount of capital a bank should have depends on its size; clearly a bank with $1 million in assets does not need as much capital as a bank with $1 billion. But a $10-billion bank does not have to have a thousand times as much capital as a $10-million bank. A large bank holds more diversified assets, and therefore its losses can be predicted better. Second, fraud is a frequent cause of bank failure. But a, say, $100-million fraud is extremely unlikely. Hence, a $10-billion bank with $300 million in capital is much less likely to be bankrupted by fraud than a $10-million bank with half a million dollars of capital. The amount of capital needed also depends on the diversification of assets. If loans are heavily concentrated in a few industries there is a greater danger that many will turn sour at the same time. Hence such a bank needs more capital.

Another factor that determines the capital required by a bank is the riskiness of its assets. For example, if a bank were to hold mainly government securities it would require a much smaller ratio of capital to assets than if it were to hold mainly loans to risky firms.

Current (1986) regulations require banks to have a total capital ratio of no less than 6 percent of adjusted assets, with banks that are taking special risks having to hold a higher ratio than that. At least 5.5 percent of this 6 percent must be primary capital. The reason banks are allowed to count long-term borrowings as part of their total capital ratio is that bondholders' claims are subordinated to depositors' claims and to the FDIC's contingent liability. Borrowed capital protects depositors and the FDIC in case the bank fails, the same way primary capital does. If so, why not allow banks to have only borrowed capital and no primary capital? The reason is that in one respect borrowed capital is inferior to primary capital: the bank has to continue to pay interest on its bonds even if it is making losses, while it can, if it absolutely has to, cut or eliminate the dividend on its primary capital. Hence, the greater the proportion that borrowed capital is of total capital, the greater is the danger that the bank will not be able to make all its required payments and therefore fail.

DEPOSIT INSURANCE

The Federal Deposit Insurance Corporation (FDIC) commenced operations in 1934 in response to massive bank failures that had occurred between 1930 and 1933. Almost all banks have joined the FDIC.[6] This is not surprising since membership in the FDIC gives a bank a great advantage over an uninsured bank in competing for deposits. Since competitive pressures, as well as the unwillingness of states to charter uninsured banks, make FDIC membership necessary for nearly every bank, the FDIC, in effect, has veto power over the formation of just about any new bank. In addition to insuring commercial banks the FDIC also insures mutual savings banks (institutions discussed in Chapter 5).

In return for an insurance premium paid by banks, the FDIC insures deposits up to $100,000. If a depositor has several accounts in his or her own name in one bank, the total that is insured is still $100,000. But if a person has several accounts under different names (for example, a personal account, a joint account with a business partner or a spouse), or if these accounts have different beneficiaries (as in the case of trust funds, for example), then each of these accounts is insured separately for $100,000. Similarly, if a person has accounts in several banks, all of these accounts are insured. Although nearly all accounts are fully insured, the very few that are not include some very large accounts, so that only about three-quarters of the dollar value of deposits is insured. However, large depositors are frequently protected by the fact that if they have a loan from a failed bank they can subtract the amount of their deposits from what they owe to the bank.

The existence of a $100,000 ceiling does not mean that in most bank failures depositors with larger accounts suffer losses. Such losses are extremely rare because of the way the FDIC handles bank failures. One way, called *deposit assumption,* is that the FDIC merges the failing bank into a sound bank. (As an inducement to the sound bank the FDIC frequently provides a subsidy.) Since the sound bank then takes over all the liabilities of the failing bank, including deposits over $100,000, large depositors do not lose anything.[7] This

---

[6] The fact that insured banks are *members* of the FDIC is legalistic (but generally used) terminology. Insured banks do not control the FDIC. Its directors are presidential appointees and the funds accumulated by the FDIC do not belong to its members.

[7] However, if you have an outstanding bank loan the FDIC will subtract the value of the loan from the size of your deposit, and pay out only the difference. This offset provision can reduce substantially the amount the FDIC has to pay out.

way of dealing with a failing bank has been by far the most common, particularly if it is a large bank, whose failure could result in the bankruptcy of many business depositors, and conceivably even start a run on other banks.

A second way of handling a failing bank, a way the FDIC has used occasionally with small banks and once with a medium-sized bank, is simply to let the bank fail and pay off deposits up to $100,000. But in 1986 the FDIC announced that for the time being it would normally avoid this method, and would instead use the merger route, thus protecting all deposits. This is intended to be a temporary measure, but it *might* turn out to become permanent. The FDIC also announced that it would ask Congress to give it permission to take over and operate temporarily a bank that is failing.[8]

Why is there a $100,000 ceiling at all? Why not bring the law into conformity with the predominant practice by insuring all deposits fully? This would prevent all bank runs. The establishment of the FDIC eliminated runs by small depositors. But with a $100,000 ceiling large depositors and other creditors of banks, such as those who sold it federal funds, still run a bank rumored to be failing.

The reason for not changing the law to insure all deposits fully is not the expense. It would cost the FDIC very little. Instead, the problem with covering all deposits is that this would remove an incentive that large depositors have to choose their banks carefully. As long as there is an insurance ceiling, large depositors, predominantly businesses, have an incentive to avoid banks that take too many risks. Hence, banks are under pressure to follow safe policies. Depositor surveillance thus supplements the FDIC's surveillance.

But it is far from obvious that depositor surveillance is effective.

THE FDIC AND BANK FAILURES

The FDIC's history can be divided into two parts. In the first, from 1934 until the mid-1960s, few failures occurred and they were small. This may have been due in part to older bankers still remembering the massive bank failures of the Great Depression. In addition, banks came out of World War II holding a great stock of government securities which they got rid of slowly. But as Figure 3.2 shows, since the mid-1960s bank failures have grown substantially. Not only have there been more failures, but failures are no longer confined to small banks. From 1946 to 1970 the average bank that failed had deposits of about $14 million, while the largest bank to fail had only $40 million in deposits.

The frequency and size of bank failures began to change dramatically in 1972, when a large Detroit Bank, Bank of the Commonwealth, experienced heavy losses. The FDIC had to provide it with funds to keep it alive. And 1973 saw the first insolvency of a billion-dollar bank, the U.S. National Bank of San Diego, a rare case in which a very large bank was destroyed by the self-dealing of its president.

---

[8] There are additional, though rarely used, ways in which the FDIC can treat a failing bank. For example, as will be discussed shortly, when Continental Illinois was failing the FDIC provided it with funds in exchange for stock in the bank.

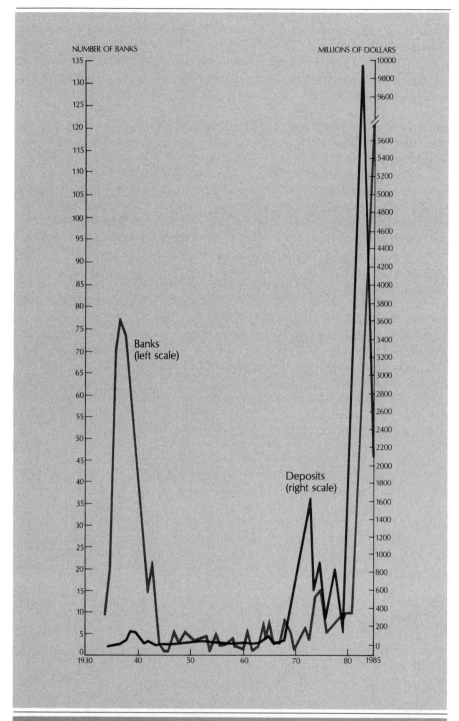

Figure 3.2   Frequency of Bank Failures. Bank failures rose dramatically in the 1930s, then fell and rose sharply in recent years. **Source:** FDIC *Annual Report,* 1982, p. 30.

The next shock involved Franklin National Bank, then the twentieth-largest bank, with close to $3 billion in deposits. This New York bank, which had expanded at an extremely rapid pace by making risky loans, announced in May 1974 that it would have to cut its dividend due to losses in foreign exchange speculation. A large bank does not ordinarily cut its dividend, so this step frightened large depositors, and other banks that had lent to it. As a result, funds drained out of Franklin National, and it had to borrow an unprecedented amount, $1.75 billion, from the Fed. In this way it was kept afloat until October 1974, when the FDIC was able to merge it into another bank after taking over many of its bad loans.

In 1980 a large Philadelphia bank, First Pennsylvania, that had taken too much interest-rate risk in its bond portfolio, and had also made too many risky loans (in effect), failed, and was bailed out by loans from other big banks and from the FDIC. In November 1981 it cost the FDIC close to half a billion dollars to merge the failing Greenwich Savings Bank—also a victim of interest-rate risk—into another savings bank.

By making highly risky loans a medium-sized Oklahoma bank, Penn Square, had grown rapidly: from $30 million to $500 million in five years. It failed in 1982 when falling oil prices showed up the extremely poor quality of its loans. Since there was uncertainty about the magnitude of its contingent liabilities the FDIC could not get another bank to merge with it on terms acceptable to the FDIC. Hence the FDIC paid off small depositors, and for the first time let the numerous large depositors take their losses.

Ordinarily the failure of a medium-sized bank like Penn Square would not have nationwide repercussions. But the Penn Square failure did because this bank had sold a large number of its loans to other banks.[9] Many of these banks had not sufficiently checked the quality of these loans when they bought them. They now found that many of these loans would probably not be repaid in full. Hence, some of these banks were now in trouble. One of them, Seafirst, was a large bank in the Pacific Northwest. In an unusual move, the FDIC had to merge it with a bank in another state, California's Bank of America. An even more significant victim of the Penn Square collapse was Continental Illinois, then the eighth-largest bank with over $40 billion in deposits. This bank had also made many unsound loans on its own. Moreover, it was in a vulnerable position because it had obtained an unusually large proportion of its funds from large depositors and from loans by other banks. Large creditors, not being insured, will withdraw their funds as soon as they hear that a bank *might* be in trouble. (As someone remarked at the time: money managers are people specially trained to panic at the slightest opportunity.)

Hence, in May 1984, Continental Illinois faced a massive outflow of funds. To meet this outflow it borrowed an extraordinary amount from the Fed, $4 billion. In addition, a consortium of large banks granted it a line of credit up to $5.3 billion. Moreover, the regulatory agencies and some large banks provided a capital infusion of $2 billion. But even these measures did not stop the run. So the FDIC took the unprecedented step of guaranteeing all deposits and other debts of the bank, no matter how large. But the run

---

[9] Banks can sell loans. Usually they continue to collect the interest and ultimately the principal, but pass these payments on to the buyer of the loan.

continued. Presumably creditors were afraid that in case of failure the FDIC might keep them waiting for their funds.

Something had to be done. Continental Illinois was a big bite to swallow, and no bank was willing to risk merging with it on terms acceptable to the FDIC. Hence, in July 1984 the FDIC took the drastic step of restructuring the bank. It provided $1 billion of additional capital and bought from the bank $4.5 billion of shakey loans at full face value. In return the FDIC got 80 percent ownership of the bank and the right to "buy" the remaining shares at one-thousandth of a cent per share if its losses exceeded the value of the 80 percent share it previously got. It appears that the FDIC will have to exercise this right, thus wiping out the stockholders' equity entirely. Currently (May 1986), the FDIC is planning to sell the stock it holds. The FDIC also fired the top management.

The Continental Illinois episode raised some big, as yet unanswered, questions regarding the FDIC's handling of bank failures. Did the FDIC do the right thing in nationalizing this bank de facto? Should it have protected the large depositors of this bank when it sometimes lets the large depositors of smaller banks suffer losses? Or should it have let Continental Illinois fail, and take the risk that this might start runs on other large banks?

What the Continental Illinois rescue did was to wreck, at least temporarily, the FDIC's previous policy of relying on independent pressure by large depositors to keep banks from taking excessive risk. Will the FDIC be able to control excessive risk-taking without such pressure?

This discussion of bank failures might convey the idea that bank failures are a calamity. Obviously all business failures are bad in the sense that they indicate wasted resources and human suffering. But failures are needed to keep business efficient and to withdraw resources from where they are less useful. Failures of banks, like failures of other firms, do serve a useful function. Even the failure of a large bank, or of several large banks, would not be a national disaster. Small depositors, being insured, would not run other banks. Large depositors would run banks they consider risky, but this would not reduce bank reserves and hence bank deposits, because they would have to redeposit their funds into another bank. A firm that withdraws $50 million from a risky bank will not hold it in currency.

CHECK CLEARING

We now turn from a serious but episodic problem to a minor but continual one. Suppose that a check drawn on one bank is deposited in another one. How is this check **cleared,** that is, presented for payment? Since a vast number of checks—about 65 million per day—have to be cleared, elaborate mechanisms for doing so have been developed. One mechanism is a **clearinghouse.** This is usually an organization of local banks that meets every working day for a few hours. Each bank appears at the clearinghouse, and presents the checks it has received that are drawn on the other banks belonging to the clearinghouse. The banks then offset their claims and liabilities against each other, and any bank with a favorable net balance receives payment.

Checks drawn on banks in other cities usually move through the Federal

Reserve's clearing system. If the check is deposited in a bank in the same Federal Reserve District (there are twelve of them) on which it is drawn, the Federal Reserve Bank directly debits the account that the bank on which it is drawn has with it. If it is drawn on a bank in another Federal Reserve District, the Federal Reserve Bank passes it on to the Federal Reserve Bank of that district, and this Federal Reserve Bank then debits that bank's account. The depositing bank gets credit from the Fed after one or two days, depending on the distance the check has been sent. However, banks normally will not permit the depositor to withdraw the funds for several days, sometimes for two weeks or more. This is to protect the bank in case the check bounces.

This system of check clearing may change substantially. In 1980 Congress ordered the Fed to charge banks for check clearing. Previously it had been free. This means that private firms can now compete with the Fed, and if they can clear checks cheaper and better they may succeed in taking away much of the Fed's business. They have already taken over a significant part of the market.

To save time and hence earn interest sooner, most large payments are made by wire transfers rather than by check. The amounts transferred by wire are immense. On some days the amounts transferred by the Fed and by CHIPS, a clearing system set up by the banks themselves, jointly exceed a trillion dollars.

CORRESPONDENT BANKING

A private network among banks called the **correspondent system** connects banks and eliminates many of the disadvantages that would otherwise follow from having so many small, isolated banks. Under this system country correspondent banks keep deposits, primarily demand deposits, with large city correspondent banks, frequently with several of them. These deposits are by no means small, currently amounting to about 1.5 percent of all deposits.

The city banks pay for these deposits, by providing their country correspondent banks with many services. One important service is the clearing of checks in a more convenient way than the Fed does. In addition, city banks provide direct loans to country banks, and also participate with a country bank in making loans that are too large for the country bank to make on its own. Or, conversely, a country bank experiencing too little loan demand can participate in a profitable loan made by a city bank. The numerous other services that city correspondent banks provide to country correspondent banks include the sale or purchase of securities, access to the federal funds market (which, crudely defined, is a market for reserves), investment advice and general business advice, and buying or selling of foreign exchange for its customers. Thus city correspondent banks provide many of the services that the head office of a large branch bank provides for its branches.

HOLDING COMPANIES

A **holding company** is a corporation whose assets consist of a controlling stock ownership in one or more corporations. This financial device is used in many industries. In banking it is sometimes used to get around restrictive banking laws. In many states in which a bank is not allowed to have branches it can nevertheless form a holding company that holds a controlling stock interest in several banks. In many cases a bank can use the holding company device to operate what are, in effect, branches in other states. But a more important use of holding companies in banking is to avoid the restrictions that prevent banks from entering other industries. Bank holding companies can get permission to have subsidiaries in those industries that are "closely related" to banking, such as finance companies, companies offering computer services, credit-card companies, discount stockbrokers, etc.[10]

The ability to enter these other lines of business is only one of the advantages of forming a holding company. Another important advantage for large banks is that holding companies can generate funds for the bank in ways the bank itself is not allowed to. For example, although a bank itself is not permitted to issue commercial paper (a type of short-term promissory note) and thus borrow short-term funds in this way, a bank holding company can do so in its own name, and then give these funds to its bank.

It is therefore not surprising that nearly all of the country's largest banks are owned by holding companies, and that more than three-quarters of all commercial bank assets are in banks affiliated with a holding company. While the holding company legally owns the bank, actually the holding company is an organization set up and dominated by the bank. The nonbank assets of the holding company are normally very small compared to the bank's assets.

CONCENTRATION IN BANKING

There are approximately fifteen thousand commercial banks in the United States. The ten largest banking organizations held only 17 percent of total domestic deposits in 1977, while the hundred largest held 45 percent. Very few industries have that many firms and so little concentration, and one might therefore think that there is no "monopoly problem" in banking. Indeed, one might wonder whether the problem is not rather that there are too many banks, too many, that is, to reap economies of scale, and to be able to provide a sufficient range of services to bank customers. However, the empirical evidence suggests that once a bank gets above a fairly moderate size economies of scale probably are modest.

The fact that banking is an unconcentrated industry does not mean that we do not have a problem of insufficient banking competition. While large firms can borrow from banks anywhere in the country, small firms, being known only in their locality, can borrow only from a local bank. It is not worthwhile for banks elsewhere to acquire the information needed to lend to them. And within a firm's area there may be only one bank. In 13 percent of all rural counties there was only a single bank in 1973.

---

[10] To be "closely related" to banking an activity must meet at least one of the following criteria: (1) a significant number of banks have undertaken it for a number of years; (2) it involves taking deposits or lending; (3) it is complementary to banking services, for example, selling life insurance that extinguishes the borrower's debt to the bank in case of death; and (4) it is something in which banks have considerable expertise, for example, data processing.

On a national level there is, of course, much less concentration. Table 3.2 shows the ten largest banks, and Table 3.3 the size distribution of banks.

As far as household depositors are concerned, they generally deal with banks in their own locality, and hence those living in some areas may have insufficient competitive alternatives. However, savings and loan associations and mutual savings banks do provide depositors with an important competitive alternative. Moreover, with the spread of automatic teller machines and other forms of electronic banking, depositors can more easily use banks outside their own locality if their local banks do not provide satisfactory service.

Table 3.2	The Ten Largest U.S. Banks, End of 1985		
Bank holding companies	Total assets (billions of dollars)	Foreign deposits as percentage of total deposits	Capital ratio[a](%)
1. Citicorp, N.Y.	173.6	52	3.9
2. BankAmerica, S.F.	118.5	32	3.5
3. Chase Manhattan, N.Y.	87.7	47	4.1
4. Manufacturers Hanover, N.Y.	76.5	44	3.7
5. Morgan (J.P.), N.Y.	69.4	65	5.7
6. Chemical, N.Y.	57.0	34	4.2
7. Security Pacific, L.A.	53.5	21	4.4
8. Bankers Trust, N.Y.	50.6	58	4.6
9. First Interstate Bancorp, L.A.	49.0	5	4.8
10. First Chicago, Chicago	38.9	47	4.2

a: Equity capital only.
Source: Business Week, 7 April 1986, p. 66.

Table 3.3	Size Distribution of Insured U.S. Commercial Banks, 31 December 1984	
Banks with total assets (millions of dollars) of:	Percentage of all banks	Percentage of all assets
Less than 25	38.3	3.2
25–50	26.0	5.4
50–100	18.9	7.6
100–300	11.7	10.8
300–500	1.8	4.0
500–1,000	1.4	5.7
1,000–5,000	1.2	12.1
5,000–10,000	0.5	16.9
10,000 and over	0.2	34.5

Source: FDIC, Statistics on Banking, 1984, p. 22.

BRANCHING

Until fairly recently branch banking was severely circumscribed. While some states, California, for example, permitted unlimited branching, other states, such as Illinois, prohibited all branch banking. Many other states allowed branch banking with severe restrictions. For example, banks might be permitted to have branches only in counties adjacent to the county in which their main office was located. Banks were forbidden from opening branches in other states, and bank holding companies could not acquire banks in another state unless that state specifically permitted it, which few did.[11]

Most of the prohibitions on branch banking have evaporated. Either the law has been changed, or banks have found ways around the law. States have liberalized their branching laws, and many now permit statewide branch banking. After much discussion, interstate banking, usually through a holding company, was permitted. One way interstate banking is achieved is through compacts between states in a certain region. These compacts permit bank holding companies in any one of these states to buy banks, or start new banks, in another one of these states. Some states have allowed large New York banks to enter their states in exchange for specified benefits, such as providing jobs or merging with failing banks or thrift institutions in that state.

Banks have also exploited a loophole in the federal law. The law that prevents a bank holding company from owning a bank in another state defines a bank as an institution that makes business loans and gathers deposits. Accordingly, some bank holding companies have bought banks in other states and immediately sold off their business loans, so that these institutions are no longer defined as banks. These so-called "limited service banks," or "nonbank banks," can then continue to gather deposits and make consumer and mortgage loans. The fact that they cannot make business loans matters little because banks are in any case permitted to have "loan production offices" in other states to generate business loans. Limited-service banks have also provided a convenient device for large commercial firms that want to enter the financial service industry. For example, Sears, Roebuck & Co. has used this device to distribute its "Discovery" credit card through a small limited-service bank that it owns.

For many years now, large banks have tried to persuade Congress to repeal the restrictions on branch banking. So far they have not succeeded. But unless Congress changes the law to curb limited-service banks, the federal prohibition of interstate banking will become little more than a nuisance to banks that want to operate in more than one state.

Are the limitations on branching—both intrastate and interstate—justified? It is true that they limit the growth of large banks and hence the aggregation of economic power. But, given the size of the country, it is unlikely that even with completely unlimited branch banking a handful of banks would

---

[11] When the law prohibiting holding companies from owning banks in other states was passed some bank holding companies already owned such banks. They were allowed to keep them.

succeed in dominating the industry as is true in Canada and Britain, for example. The economies of scale in banking are not that great. In California, where there is unlimited branch banking, small banks are able to coexist alongside very large branch systems. Similarly, when the New York City banks received permission to open branches in upstate New York, the local banks there were able to meet the competition from these much larger banks.

The limitations on branching, while serving to limit large aggregations of economic power, have also worked to preserve the monopoly or oligopoly positions of banks in small cities. In a number of localities the market is not large enough to support more than one independent bank, but in addition to this bank it could support a branch of another bank. In these situations branching would reduce monopoly power. Moreover, in other industries, when a firm has a local monopoly it has to worry that if it sets it prices too high it will induce other firms to come into its market. But, insofar as branching regulations prevent banks from entering another bank's market, a local banking monopoly is more secure in exploiting its monopoly position. Hence, in the view of many economists, the limitation on branching has in many cases worked to preserve small business at the cost of *reducing* competition.[12] However, this view has been challenged on the argument that the empirical evidence shows that the easing of bank-branching laws has not actually increased competition, since banks frequently enter new markets not by starting new branches, but by merging with existing banks in these markets.[13]

Banks have merged for many reasons. Sometimes it is a way to get around the prohibition against establishing branches. At other times it is a way in which capital can flow easily from low-growth areas to more rapidly growing areas where the yield on capital is higher. Moreover, many mergers have increased the efficiency of banking by allowing efficient banks to take over lethargic and badly managed ones. Such a device for eliminating mediocre management is badly needed because bank regulations have prevented efficient banks from entering and driving inefficient banks out of business. In addition, mergers have allowed management to satisfy its preference for growth while allowing managers to diversify their assets. And for many small banks, mergers have been a way in which the banker can sell out upon retirement and provide new management for the bank.

There has been much concern about the effect of mergers on competition. Clearly, if there are five banks in a city and they all merge, competition is eliminated. But it is much less clear that competition is reduced if banks in different cities merge. Competition would be reduced only if, for at least some of the customers, the merging banks are potential competitors, that is, if the market areas of these banks overlap.

[12] What is involved here is the distinction between the popular and the technical concerns about monopoly. On a popular level very large firms are often thought of as monopolists, while economists define monopoly in terms of the elasticity of the demand curve. More liberal branching regulations would result in larger banks, but would increase the elasticity of the demand curve for many banks.

[13] For a survey of the empirical evidence, see Stephen Rhoades, "Competitive Effects of Interstate Banking," *Federal Reserve Bulletin* 66 (January 1980): 1–8.

The law prohibits mergers that would "substantially" reduce competition, but this is a vague standard that has led to much litigation. Banks operate in many different markets—deposit markets, business loan markets, consumer loan markets, and so on—with some business customers being able to borrow anywhere in the nation and others not. It is therefore hard to define the "market" a bank serves, and hence to determine if a merger would actually reduce competition. The Department of Justice, which administers the antitrust laws, and the Federal Reserve have sometimes invoked the doctrine of potential competition by arguing that if a merger is prevented the frustrated acquirer will probably establish its own new branch, thus adding to competition. Obviously such an argument is hard to evaluate, and on the whole, the courts have not looked kindly upon it.

SOCIAL REGULATIONS OF BANK LOANS

A number of regulations try to protect bank customers from exploitation and discrimination. An obvious example is state **usury laws.** These set ceilings on the interest rates charged for consumer loans. Such laws are defended on the grounds that some people lack the financial sophistication needed to protect themselves from exploitation, or that there is insufficient competition among lenders. However, if state law sets an interest-rate ceiling below the equilibrium interest rate, lenders can simply avoid making loans in that state. Alternatively, they may make loans only to the most credit-worthy customers, so that the very people the usury law is intended to protect often cannot get loans.

The federal **Truth in Lending Law** requires that borrowers be given sufficient information to compare readily the interest rates charged by different lenders. Prior to the passage of this law such comparison was often hard to make. But whether the benefit of the additional information to the customer matches the bank's cost of compliance with the law is a controversial issue. Another law protects customers from having to continue to make payments on a loan when the item that they bought on credit is defective. Discrimination in lending on the basis of race, sex, age, or creed is prohibited by other laws. One of these laws specifically prohibits **redlining,** that is, refusing to make loans, or being reluctant to make loans, in certain areas, such as inner-city neighborhoods with large minority populations. The extent to which banks actually did redline certain areas is a much-debated issue.

The **Community Reinvestment Act** states that banks and other insured lenders have an obligation to meet the reasonable credit needs of the low-income neighborhoods in which they are located or have a branch. When they apply for permission to open a new branch or to merge with another institution, the regulatory agencies are supposed to take into account how well they have served their low-income neighborhoods. Whether such a law is needed, or whether the profit motive already gives banks enough of an incentive to meet the "reasonable credit needs" of low-income neighborhoods, is unknown.

SUMMARY

1 Banking has a long history. In the United States there were two national banks chartered by the federal government and their demise was followed by a period of free banking. This in turn was followed by the National Banking System that provided safer banks.

2 Banking is heavily regulated by the federal or state chartering authorities, by the FDIC, and, for members banks, by the Federal Reserve.

3 Banks are required to maintain a capital ratio to protect the FDIC and depositors. Since this ratio exceeds what banks would hold on their own, this is an area of continual conflict between banks and regulators. Nearly all deposits are now insured up to $100,000.

4 Checks are cleared through local clearinghouses, through the Federal Reserve, or by private firms.

5 Banks have extensive correspondence relationships that provide small banks with services from large banks.

6 A common form of bank organization is the holding company. This allows banks to enter certain other industries and to raise capital in ways they otherwise could not. Although banking is an industry with many firms and with a low concentration ratio on the national level, there is still a problem of banks having excessive market power on a local level. Restrictions on branch banking are disappearing due both to changes in the laws and to banks exploiting a loophole in the law.

7 In recent years various types of discrimination in granting credit, such as redlining, have been outlawed. Lenders are also required to provide extensive information to borrowers.

QUESTIONS AND EXERCISES

1 Sketch the history of banking in the United States.

2 Describe how banks are regulated.

3 Banking is much more heavily regulated than other industries. How can this be justified?

4 Discuss the following proposals to modify deposit insurance:
   a. Allow banks to obtain insurance from private insurance companies instead of the FDIC.
   b. Insure depositors instead of banks, and permit depositors, who would pay for the insurance premium, to decide whether they want to buy this insurance.
   c. Insure only the accounts of households, not those of businesses.

5 Describe the process by which checks are cleared.

6 Critically discuss:
   a. "Banks should be allowed to decide on their own how much capital they want; after all, they are the ones who lose if it turns out that they have insufficient capital."
   b. "Banks should be required to keep a capital to deposit ratio of at least 25 percent."

7 What do you think is the most serious *current* problem facing bank regulation? (Articles on current banking problems can be found frequently in *Business Week*.)

FURTHER READING

BENNETT, BARBARA. "Bank Regulation and Deposit Insurance: Controlling the FDIC's Losses," Federal Reserve Bank of San Francisco, *Economic Review*, Spring 1984, 16–30. A short but thorough discussion.

BENSTON, GEORGE. "Optimal Banking Structure," *Journal of Banking Research*, 3 (Winter 1973): 220–237. An excellent survey of a voluminous literature.

BENSTON, GEORGE. et al. *Safe and Sound Banking*, Cambridge, Mass.: MIT Press, 1986. A useful study sponsored by the American Bankers Association.

FEDERAL RESERVE BANK OF CHICAGO. *Bank Structure and Competition*. This annually published volume contains interesting papers from an annual conference on banking structure.

GILBERT, ALTON, COURTNEY STONE, AND MICHAEL TREBLING. "New Bank Capital Adequacy Standards," Federal Reserve Bank of St. Louis, *Review*, 67 (May 1985): 12–20. A useful discussion of the new capital standards.

GILBERT, MILTON. Bank Market Structure and Competition: A Survey," *Journal of Money, Credit and Banking*, 16 (November 1984): 617–644. See also the comments by Arnold Heggestad, Sam Peltzman, and Peter Schmidt in the same issue, pp. 645–660. An interesting discussion of the impact of bank concentration.

HAVRILESKY, THOMAS, and JOHN BOORMAN. *Current Perspectives in Banking*. Arlington Heights, Ill.: AHM Publishing Corp., 1976. An interesting collection of readings.

KLEBANER, BENJAMIN. *Commercial Banking in the United States: A History*. Hinsdale, Ill.: Dryden Press, 1974. A compact and useful source of information.

MAISEL, SHERMAN (ed.). *Risk and Capital Adequacy in Commercial Banks*. Chicago: University of Chicago Press, 1981. A highly sophisticated analysis of bank capital adequacy, the FDIC premium, and related issues.

SPONG, KENNETH. *Bank Regulation*. Kansas City: Federal Reserve Bank of Kansas City, 1985. A useful survey.

CHAPTER 4

The Banking Firm

We now look at the bank as an individual firm. Banks are a mixed lot, ranging from extremely small ones with deposits of less than $1 million that serve small towns to huge ones with deposits of over $100 billion that serve a worldwide market. Some large banks have an extensive network of branches—at one time the Bank of America had over a thousand branches. Other banks have no branches. Either they are too small, or their business does not warrant it. Some extremely large banks that deal primarily with large corporate customers, rather than with retail depositors, do not have to be located near their customers. When you go to borrow $100 million you do not mind if the bank is a mile away.

THE BANK'S BALANCE SHEET

There is one thing all banks have in common. They are financial intermediaries that issue their own debts, including deposits, and lend out the funds thus acquired. Both the direct debts they incur and the lending they undertake are listed on their balance sheets. Hence one can study the business of banking by looking at the items on banks' balance sheets. Table 4.1 shows such a balance sheet for all U.S. banks combined, and it is worth learning each of the items on it. We will start with the liabilities.

Transactions Accounts

A transactions account is simply a deposit against which you can write a check.[1] Such accounts are called "checkable deposits" and they come in several forms. First, there are **demand deposits** on which banks are not allowed to pay interest. However, as so often happens, the law is an imperfect barrier against economic pressures. Although banks cannot pay "explicit interest,"

---

[1] This is not strictly correct; legally some of these "checks" are not checks, but "negotiable orders of withdrawal." Since they function just like checks we can treat them as such.

Table 4.1 Assets and Liabilities of Commercial Banks, December 1985			
Assets	**%**	**Liabilities**	**%**
Total cash assets:	8.6	Deposits:	71.7
Cash in vault	.9	Transactions deposits	21.8
Reserves with Federal		Savings and time deposits	49.9
Reserve Banks	1.1	Borrowings	14.7
Demand deposits at U.S.			
depository institutions	1.5	Other liabilities	7.3
Cash items in the process		Capital (assets − liabilities)	6.4
of collection	3.2		
Other cash assets	1.9	TOTAL LIABILITIES AND	
Securities:	16.8	CAPITAL	100.0
U.S. government	10.2		
Other	6.6		
Loans:	65.6		
Interbank	6.1		
Commercial and			
industrial	20.2		
Real estate	17.2		
Loans to individuals	11.8		
All other loans	10.2		
Other assets	9.0		
TOTAL ASSETS	100.0		

Source: *Federal Reserve Bulletin*, April 1986, p. A18.

that is, interest in money terms, they can pay "implicit interest" by providing free services. Many banks figure this quite precisely; they apply a certain interest rate to the deposits of their business customers, and then provide them with free services, such as payroll preparation and purchases of foreign currencies, up to that amount. In addition, a bank often charges a lower rate of interest on loans to a firm that keeps a large demand deposit with it.

Second, there are **NOW accounts** and **Super-NOW accounts** that pay interest.[2] Third, we have **money-market deposit accounts** that pay a higher interest rate than NOW accounts, because, unlike NOW and Super-NOW accounts, banks do not have to keep reserves against them. However, there are restrictions on the number of checks that one can write each month against a money-market account. Corporations are not allowed to hold any of these accounts, but must hold their checkable deposits as demand deposits.

[2] The term "NOW" is an abbreviation of "negotiable order of withdrawal." This device was developed by Massachusetts savings banks to avoid the prohibition against paying interest on demand deposits. They could not permit their depositors to write "checks" against their interest-paying savings accounts, so they allowed them to write "negotiable orders of withdrawal" that work just like checks.

Savings and Other Time Deposits

One type of savings deposit is the passbook account, but savings accounts can also be set up by a written agreement between the depositor and the bank rather than by a passbook. Another type, certificates of deposits, usually abbreviated as CDs, is for a fixed sum. Although households can cash their CDs before the stated maturity date, Federal Reserve regulations impose an interest penalty for this for some accounts. This penalty also exists for fixed-maturity passbook accounts but not for other passbook accounts.

Large depositors can purchase negotiable CDs, which are issued only by relatively well known banks. They are negotiable, which means that the purchaser can reclaim the funds prior to the maturity date by selling the CD on the money market. Then, at maturity, the bank pays off the CD to whoever is holding it. Most such negotiable CDs are purchased by businesses and governments since the minimum denomination is $100,000 and the normal denomination is $1 million or more. They are highly liquid assets since there is an active market for them. The maturity of negotiable CDs is usually a year or less and is often set to suit the convenience of the particular purchaser.

Liabilities

In addition to their deposits, banks have other liabilities. One of these is purchased **federal funds.** Federal funds are *not* funds belonging to the federal government as the name might suggest. Instead, they are deposits usually held at the Federal Reserve and traded among banks and some other institutions, such as savings and loans, government security dealers, and government agencies. They have the characteristic that they are transferred immediately, with the Fed giving the receiving bank credit the same day. The lending bank wires the Fed and tells it to transfer some of its reserves to the borrowing bank's account. However, federal funds can also take other forms; for example, a city bank can borrow the correspondent balances a country bank keeps with it. But the major part of federal funds consists of the reserve accounts that depository institutions keep with the Fed.

The federal-funds market is a large one, and the big money-market banks use it at times, not just to obtain the funds to meet their reserve requirements, but also to obtain funds for additional lending. The total amount borrowed in recent years has been substantially more than the required reserves of these banks. Most loans are made on a one-day basis, and it is a way in which banks can quickly obtain more reserves, or lend excess funds. Many small banks enter this market—typically as lenders—through their city correspondent banks. For them, it is a convenient way to earn interest on what would otherwise be excess reserves. The great majority of banks are active in this market. Although it is actually a market for loans, the language of the money market calls such transactions "sales" on one end and "purchases" at the other. The interest rate that the selling bank charges is called the **federal-funds rate.**

Another liability on the bank's balance sheet is "securities sold under repurchase agreements." Repurchase agreements, also called "repos" or

RPs, work as follows: a bank "sells" a security to someone with an agreement to repurchase it at a certain date at an agreed-upon price. In essence the repo is just a loan the bank has received since it has to repurchase the security. It is therefore a liability of the bank. Such repurchase agreements can be used to pay interest on what is, in effect, a demand deposit. Banks have agreements with some corporations that toward the end of the day when all incoming checks have already been cleared they "sell" the corporation a security for some of the funds in its demand deposit, with an agreement to repurchase the security the next morning. The corporation then has the funds available to meet incoming checks. The corporation also receives one day's interest on the overnight loan of its funds. Banks would prefer not to have to offer such overnight repos, and thus not have to pay interest. But competition among banks forces them to pay this interest.

Another liability item is outstanding acceptances. Acceptances arise in a rather complicated way. A firm selling to another firm on credit may not know enough about the buyer to feel safe in accepting a promise to pay. This is particularly likely with a foreign customer, in part because it is more difficult to sue in a foreign court than in a court in one's own country. But while the seller does not want to take the customer's IOU, he is willing to take the IOU of the customer's bank. Hence, a financial instrument, called a banker's acceptance, was developed. To explain it, let us back up and look first at a transaction *not* involving a bank. The seller draws up an order to the buyer to pay a sum of money by a certain date and releases ownership of the merchandise when the buyer "accepts" the order to pay by writing "accepted" across it. It is now a **trade acceptance** and is legally binding. Alternatively, the buyer can make an arrangement with his or her bank allowing the seller to draw the order to pay not on the buyer, but on the buyer's bank. *When the bank writes "accepted" on this order to pay,* it becomes a **banker's acceptance.** Since the bank is liable to make the payment on it, it is listed on the bank's balance sheet as a liability. However, the buyer is supposed to make payment to the bank by the date the bank has to make its payment on the acceptance. The bank lends its reputation, not its funds, to the buyer, who usually has to pay a small fee for this service. The seller receiving the banker's acceptance need not hold it to maturity but can sell it (at a discount from face value) in the money market.

The final item on the liabilities side, called "residual," is the capital account. This is a liability only in an accounting sense, since it represents the value of the bank and not a debt that the bank has. We discussed capital already in the previous chapter.

THE BANK'S ASSETS

Primary Reserves

The first three assets listed on the left side of the balance sheet in Table 4.1 compose the bank's primary reserves. They are currency and coin in the bank called vault cash, reserves with the Fed, and demand deposits with other banks, that is, correspondent bank balances. These three items form the first line of defense against a deposit or currency outflow.

Table 4.2	1986 Reserve Requirements		
		Initial rate (%)	Range within which Fed can vary requirement[a] (%)
Normal reserves:			
Transaction accounts			
On deposits of			
Less than \$31.7 million[b]		3	—[c]
\$31.7 million and over[b]		12	8–14
Nonpersonal time deposits		3	0–9
Supplemental reserves[d]		0	0–4

Note: The first \$2.6 million reserveable liabilities are exempt from the reserve requirement. This figure will be raised each year by 80 percent of the increase in total reserveable liabilities.

a: In extraordinary circumstances the Fed may for 180 days set reserve requirements outside this range.

b: The \$31.7 million breaking point will be increased each year to reflect 80 percent of the increase in total transaction accounts in that year.

c: The Fed cannot vary this requirement except as indicated in Note a.

d: Imposition requires affirmative vote of five governors.

Virtually all institutions (the exception is the very smallest banks) that have **transactions accounts** have to keep reserves against these accounts. These reserve requirements, as of September 1986, are shown in Table 4.2. The reserve requirements are less for smaller institutions, in part to give them a competitive advantage over larger ones. The Fed is empowered to vary these reserve requirements within certain limits. While the Fed might do this to control the quantity of money, it would be most unusual. The reserve requirement is much lower for nonpersonal time deposits, that is, for time deposits owned by corporations, partnerships, and nonprofit institutions, than it is for transaction accounts.[3] For personal time deposits there is no reserve requirement at all.

Member banks have to keep their reserves as vault cash or as reserves with the Fed. Most are kept in the latter form. Other institutions can keep them also as deposits with member banks (or certain government agencies) that then, in turn, pass them on to the Fed. Reserve requirements do not have to be met on a continuous basis, but only as an average over a two-week period.[4] Thus a bank can keep low reserves for, say, ten days, and then make it

---

[3] There are no reserve requirements for nonpersonal time deposits with a maturity of eighteen months or more.

[4] Banks can make up a reserve deficiency of no more than 2 percent during the following period, and can meet up to 2 percent of their reserve requirement by excess reserves they held the previous period.

up by keeping high reserves for the next four days. There is also a two-day lag for reserves against transactions deposits because the two weeks over which deposits are measured end on a Monday, but the two weeks over which the corresponding reserves are figured end on the following Wednesday. (For reserves against other deposits the lag is two weeks.)

The Fed does not pay any interest on reserves. Hence, one can think of the reserve requirement as a requirement to make an interest-free loan to the government. In this respect it functions as a tax. For example, suppose the interest rate is 10 percent and a bank has to keep 12 percent reserves. If so, for each dollar of deposits it is foregoing 1.2 cents (12 cents $\times$ 10 percent) of interest income per year that it would have earned had it lent out the funds it keeps as reserves. But the main reason we have reserve requirements is not to boost tax revenue. Nor is it to ensure the safety of depositors' funds, which is the function of deposit insurance and of the examination process that tries to ensure the safety of all the bank's assets, not just of a small reserve ratio. Instead, as will be discussed in Chapter 20, the function of the reserve requirement is to allow the Fed to control the quantity of money in special cases.

Obviously, vault cash, reserves with the Fed, and interbank deposits are all extremely liquid. Cash items in the process of collection are another highly liquid item on the balance sheet. These consist of checks and similar instruments that have just been deposited in the bank and that the bank has sent on for clearing.

Securities and Loans

Beyond its primary reserves a bank holds mainly loans and securities. These two items are known as **earning assets** because they bring the bank income. One part of these earning assets composes its **secondary reserves**. These are *assets that are not quite as liquid and safe as primary reserves, but still are very liquid.* They therefore provide the bank with a second line of defense if its primary reserves are insufficient. Unlike primary reserves they earn a modest income, though their yield is usually less than that on less liquid and less safe assets.

It is not possible to identify secondary reserves on a bank's balance sheet, since the items constituting the secondary reserves are classified together with other items. One item included in secondary reserves is short-term government securities. Others are **banker's acceptances, commercial paper** (short-term promissory notes issued by large and very sound corporations), and **call loans** (loans mainly to brokers and security dealers on which the bank can demand repayment in a day).

Banks do not put all their available funds other than primary and secondary reserves into loans; they also hold fixed-income securities, mainly those issued by federal or state and local governments. Federal securities provide banks with assets that have no default risk and have a very wide market. State and local government securities provide income that is exempt from federal taxes, and buying the securities issued by local governments in its area helps a bank to obtain the deposit business of those governments. Although state and local government securities are usually safe with respect to default risk, if interest rates have risen a bank selling a bond with, say, 15 years to maturity can incur a substantial loss. And if it holds the bond to maturity it is still incurring a loss in terms of opportunity costs because it could have made more elsewhere.

Banks believe that they should place some of their funds into securities rather than into loans, that too high a ratio of loans to deposits is dangerous. Conventional ideas about the acceptable ratio of loans to deposits have varied over time, and they have increased along with the actual loan to deposit ratio —an example of rules conforming to behavior. In 1986 the ratio was 79 percent; in 1948 when it was 29 percent, a 79 percent ratio would have been considered an outrage.

Loans involve personal relationships between the banker and the borrower. Hence, they differ sharply from security purchases in which the bank buys securities usually from a dealer on the open market and does not know the borrower personally. Moreover, while a bank can sell a security again in the open market, there are fewer facilities for selling a loan, and the bank normally holds it until maturity. Bank loans fall under one of four broad categories: business loans, real estate loans, consumer loans, or foreign loans.

Business Loans. Banks have a strong comparative advantage in making commercial and industrial loans. Retail banks, though not the large wholesale banks, make most of their loans to fairly small, local borrowers. Such loan applications require evaluation by someone on the spot, such as the local banker. This gives banks a powerful advantage over large, distant lenders, such as insurance companies. Compare, for example, the position of a bank and an insurance company in making a loan to a local grocery store and in buying a corporate bond. The bank knows much more about the local grocery store than the distant insurance company does and, hence, is in a much better position to decide whether to make it a loan. By contrast, the insurance company with its large staff of security analysts can reach a much more sophisticated decision about buying a corporate bond than can the typical bank.

An important characteristic of bank lending to business is **credit rationing.** A bank, unlike other firms, does not stand ready to provide as much of its product, loans, as the customer is willing to pay for. A fruit store will normally be happy to provide the buyer with, say, ten times as much as he normally buys, but a bank will usually not be ready to make a borrower ten times the normal loan. Similarly, a bank will not make loans to just anyone who applies for one, even if she is willing to pay an interest rate high enough to offset the fact that this loan is risky. Banks ration loans among applicants, both by turning away some loan customers and by limiting the size of loans to others. A major reason that banks, unlike other sellers, limit the amount of the product (loans) they provide to each customer is surely that the bank takes a risk. It hands over its funds, and cannot be certain that it will be repaid.

Credit rationing has both its defenders and its critics. The defenders point out that a banker's evaluation of loan requests acts as a check on the overoptimism of the firm's management. By scrutinizing loan requests, granting some and denying others, the banker provides the economy with the services of a more or less objective outsider. The critics of credit rationing, on the other hand, point out that it allows banks to favor large depositors over other borrowers. Moreover, the critics argue, it gives bankers, particularly in small towns, a lot of arbitrary power, and it can be used as a weapon in forcing tie-in sales of bank services.

One factor that plays an important role in credit rationing is the existence of a customer relationship between the banker and the business borrower. Most of the business loans that banks make are to previous borrowers; it is a repeat business. Firms establish a customer relationship with a particular bank (or in the case of a large firm, with several banks) and, as long as the arrangement is mutually satisfactory, continue both to borrow from this bank and to keep deposits with it. This customer relationship comprises more than just a borrower-lender relation. The firm also uses other services of the bank, such as the provision of foreign exchange, the preparation of payrolls, etc. These services are often profitable and important for the bank. Large firms establish their customer relationships primarily with large and medium-sized banks, not only because such banks can provide these ancillary services, but also because national banks (and in many states, state banks) are allowed (with some exceptions) to lend to any one borrower an amount equal to no more than 15 percent of the bank's capital, except on fully secured loans where the maximum is 25 percent.

This customer relationship implies that the bank has an obligation to take care of the reasonable credit needs of its existing customers. A bank is therefore not a completely free agent in making loans; it has to accommodate the reasonable demands of its customers. To do this it might have to turn away other potential customers, even though these new customers would be willing to pay a higher interest rate than do existing customers. Similarly, it might have to ration loans among its existing customers rather than turn some of them down altogether. Or else it might have to sell some of its securities, or obtain the funds needed for extra loans by raising the interest rate it pays on large CDs. In the short run such actions may be costly for the bank, but are necessary to maximize long-run profits.

The existence of stable banking relations provides a major benefit: information. Over the years a bank learns much about its customers. If these customers were to change banks frequently, this information would become worthless to the firm's old bank, and its new bank would have to spend resources to acquire this information.

The maturity of bank loans varies widely. Banks make many **term loans,** that is, loans *usually having a maturity of from one to five years,* and some are even for longer periods. A borrower can use these term loans to finance fixed investment. They are often **amortized,** that is, repaid in installments just like a consumer loan. On term loans the bank can protect itself by imposing certain restrictions on the borrower, such as limiting the amount of other debt that can be incurred.

Another way banks sometimes take care of customers' needs for long-term capital is to purchase capital equipment and lease it to the customer. Thus banks own ships, airplanes, and even cows. Such equipment leasing gives the bank the tax benefit of accelerated depreciation, while, if certain conditions are met, the leasor gains from the fact that its balance sheet does not show a debt, as it would had it borrowed from the bank to buy the item directly.

Instead of a term loan, a borrower may prefer to get frequent short-term loans. One way to do this is under a **line of credit.** This is an *arrangement whereby the bank agrees to make loans to a firm almost upon demand up to a certain amount.* Lines of credit are usually established for a year. Under a firm line of credit the bank is more or less committed to make loans unless the firm's credit standing seriously deteriorates and frequently charges a fee on the amount of the line that is *not* used, in addition to the interest on the amount that *is* used. As an alternative, a firm may obtain a revolving credit arrangement whereby it can borrow up to a certain amount, and then repay the loan at will without penalty. Later it can then borrow again up to the designated amount. A firm can also obtain a formal commitment from a bank to make it a loan in the future. For this it frequently has to pay a small fee. As Table 4.3 shows, in early November 1985 about 71 percent of the dollar value of all business loans was made under some form of loan commitment such as a line of credit or revolving credit.

A bank frequently requires business borrowers who have a line of credit, and many who don't, to keep a **compensating or supporting balance** in the bank. This means that the firm has to keep as a demand deposit, say, 10 percent of its line of credit, or, under other arrangements, say, 15 percent of its outstanding loans. Compensating balances may be set as an average balance during the life of the line of credit or, more burdensomely, as a minimum balance. A compensating balance requirement is not legally binding, but if the borrower does not adhere to it the bank may refuse further loans, or may charge a higher interest rate on any subsequent loan. There is much variation in the compensating balance requirements of different banks. Some have rigid policies, while others merely consider the potential borrower's deposits as one factor in deciding on a loan request.

The compensating balance requirement raises the effective interest rate. Suppose the bank makes a $100,000 loan at an 8 percent interest rate with a 10 percent minimum compensating balance requirement. The borrower can then use only $90,000 of that, but still pays 8 percent on $100,000, or $8,000, which is equivalent to 8.9 percent on the $90,000 actually used. However, in many cases the borrower has a partially offsetting benefit: the compensating balance can be drawn on if things get really bad. In addition to compensating balances many firms (particularly small and medium-sized firms) keep interest-free "service balances" that compensate the bank for certain services, such as payroll preparation.

Another requirement frequently imposed on a borrower is to provide the bank with collateral for the loan so that, in case it is not repaid, the bank can sell the collateral to pay it off. The collateral, which may consist of securities, inventory, and so on, often, though not always exceeds the value of the loan. This protects the bank in case the collateral's market value declines.

The interest rate charged on bank loans varies of course, along with interest rates in general, though with a lag. Table 4.3 shows the interest rates

Table 4.3	Commercial and Industrial Loans Made, 3–7 February 1986[a]				
Size of loans (thousands of dollars)	Percentage of number of loans	Percentage of value of loans	Weighted average maturity	Percentage of loans made under commitment	Loan rate (weighted average)
			Short-Term Loans (days)		
All short term	84.7	89.7	45	76.9	9.3
		Made at Fixed Rates			
1–24	33.4	.9	107	27.7	13.1
25–49	2.5	.3	113	33.2	12.5
50–99	1.8	.5	102	42.2	11.9
770–499	1.2	1.0	63	47.5	10.9
500–999	.3	.7	51	71.1	9.8
1,000 and over	1.9	55.3	19	77.4	8.8
		Made at Floating Rates			
1–24	23.8	.9	155	57.8	11.7
25–49	6.2	.8	152	66.2	11.4
50–99	5.4	1.4	158	68.0	11.2
100–499	6.0	4.5	151	72.6	10.8
500–999	1.0	2.7	147	61.6	10.6
1,000 and over	1.2	20.7	90	85.4	9.3
			Long-Term Loans (Months)		
All long term	15.3	10.3	54	79.3	10.3
		Made at Fixed Rates			
1–99	7.2	.3	62	11.9	13.0
100–499	.6	.3	87	20.9	12.1
500–999	.1	.2	95	92.3	10.1
1,000 and over	.1	1.7	49	82.0	9.6
		Made at Floating Rates			
1–99	5.7	.6	46	32.5	11.8
100–499	1.1	.9	49	63.1	10.8
500–999	.2	.5	45	80.9	10.6
1,000 and over	.3	5.8	55	92.6	9.9

a: Excludes construction loans and development loans.
Source: *Federal Reserve Bulletin,* 72, May 1986, p. A70.

charged on loans in November 1986. It shows that the larger the loan the lower the interest rate. This is not surprising since the interest rate paid has to compensate the bank for the cost of making the loan, and the cost of making a $10 million loan is not a thousand times the cost of making a $10,000 loan.

This does not mean that the average borrower who obtains a small loan could lower the interest rate by taking out a large loan; instead, if the loan is made at all, the interest rate would be higher, because a large loan to a small firm is risky.

Many loans are made at the **prime rate.** This is a rate established by each bank for large loans to its better customers. The prime rates of various banks tend to move together. Typically a large bank changes its prime rate and other banks follow. Some banks set the prime rate by a formula based on the cost of funds to them, while others set prime rates equal to those of large banks.

Since only strong firms can borrow at the prime rate, getting the prime rate is prized as an important symbol. However, particularly in periods when banks are scrambling for loan business, many top firms can borrow at (unannounced) rates below the prime rate. Some large firms are offered the alternative of borrowing at a small fixed margin over the London Interbank Offered Rate (LIBOR), that is, the rate at which large international banks lend to each other on the international market.

Loans to firms that do not receive the prime rate are often scaled up from the prime rate. For example, the loan agreement may state that the interest rate will be half a percent above the prime rate.

As Table 4.3 shows, the interest rate charged is frequently a variable rate, rather than a fixed rate; as the prime rate on newly contracted loans changes, the rate on many previously made business loans changes along with it. Sometimes, however, the loan agreement contains a "cap" on how high the interest rate can rise. A survey of major corporations in 1984 found that three-quarters of them had taken out their most recent bank loan at a floating rate.

Real Estate Loans. These loans account for almost a third of all bank loans. Residential mortgages may be insured or guaranteed by the Federal Housing Administration (FHA) or the Veterans Administration (VA). Mortgage loans are long-term loans that can seriously reduce the bank's liquidity. But the actual maturity of mortgage loans is much less than their apparent maturity, since they are amortized (that is, repaid in installments) and, in addition, are frequently repaid when the house is sold. Moreover, a secondary market for mortgage loans, particularly FHA and VA loans, has developed on which banks can sell their mortgage loans. However, those mortgage loans that are made at fixed rates do create a serious interest-rate risk for banks.

Consumer Loans. Another major outlet for bank funds is lending to consumers, which accounts for about 20 percent of total bank loans. One substantial advantage of consumer loans for banks is that they are liquid. Since they are usually short term and amortized, their turnover is fairly rapid.

Most consumer loans are made for the purchase of durables, which then serve as collateral for the loan. Banks make consumer loans both directly to consumers and indirectly through durable-goods dealers (car dealers, for instance) by financing loans originated by the dealer. Banks also make general-purpose loans to consumers. Among these are credit-card loans on which the bank receives not only interest from the borrower, but also a commission from the vendor. Some banks have set up an arrangement by which credit-card holders can have their checking accounts credited and the card debited automatically if the balance in the checking account is insufficient to meet incoming checks. Other banks have set up similar arrangements for automatic loans to customers who do not have the bank's credit card. Another type of consumer loan is the federally subsidized student loan.

Banks also make loans for the purchase of securities. Such loans are made not only to households, but also to security dealers and brokers who use them to finance their customer's purchases, as well as their own security holdings. Loans to security dealers and brokers are often made on a (renewable) one-day basis (referred to as **call loans**) and are therefore extremely liquid for banks.[5]

Foreign Loans. Many large banks, as well as some medium-sized banks, have banded together into so-called syndicates to make large loans to foreign firms and foreign governments. Loans to foreign governments are safer than loans to foreign or domestic firms in one respect: a country—unlike a firm—is not likely to go out of business. However, they are riskier in another way since, if a foreign government refuses to repay, the bank cannot go to court, have the country declared bankrupt, and all its assets distributed among creditors. Instead, the sanctions against a country just walking away from its debts are twofold. First, its assets that are located elsewhere, for example, bank deposits in another country, or ships in foreign ports, can be seized. This makes it hard for a country to carry on normal foreign trade. Second, and more serious, a country that has defaulted on its debts cannot borrow abroad even for the short-term financing of imports.

While these sanctions are sufficient to prevent countries from defaulting in normal times, they can turn out to be insufficient to prevent default when a country is hit by a severe problem, such as a catastrophic drop in export earnings. Thus, in 1981 when the Polish economy was in crisis, Poland declared itself unable to repay outstanding loans. U.S. and European banks that had made large loans to Poland and to other East European countries on the assumption that, as a last resort, the Russians would bail out any of these countries now found that there was no Russian umbrella. There was talk about declaring Poland in default, both on these bank loans and on loans made by the governments of various countries. In part for political reasons default was avoided; Poland agreed to continue to pay interest on the loans and the banks agreed to reschedule, that is, extend them. Moreover, they made additional loans to Poland, thus in effect lending Poland part of the money it used to pay interest on the original loans.

In 1982 and 1983 there were more actual and threatened defaults. Argentina, Brazil (both of which have massive foreign debts), and Rumania

---

[5] The last two entries under loans in Table 4.1 are accounting adjustments. Banks have to set aside a reserve against potential loan losses. To obtain the net value of loans these reserves have to be subtracted, and the same is true for any unearned income that is included in the face value of some loans.

refused to make scheduled loan repayments. Mexico also asked its lenders to reschedule outstanding loans. In addition, these countries wanted to obtain additional credit. These defaults or near-defaults were due to several factors. One that is obvious—by hindsight—is that these countries had borrowed more than they should have. Since at the time they borrowed the real rate of interest was often negative, it is hardly surprising that they were eager to borrow. A second factor is the severity of the 1981–1982 recession, the most severe since the 1930s, which sharply reduced the prices of raw materials exported by many debtor countries. A third factor is that in early 1983 nominal interest rates declined much less than the inflation rate. Hence the real rate of interest that these countries had to pay rose sharply. And in 1986 when oil prices fell drastically Mexico suffered a devastating shock.

In asking banks to reschedule their loans and to make new loans these debtor countries are not powerless. They can threaten that unless they get what they ask for they will default. If so, then the banks will have to write off these loans on their books as losses, something they are most reluctant to do, since it would reduce their profits and their capital. By contrast, on a rescheduled loan the banks can, at the very least, postpone recognizing the loss for accounting purposes, and if things turn out well they will be repaid. Hence debtor countries have a big bargaining chip. Thus the *Wall Street Journal* (29 July 1982) reported a U.S. banker as saying, "I find it absolutely hilarious when I hear bankers talking about getting tough with the Poles . . . . In some ways it is the Poles who are in the driver's seat."

These near bankruptcies created a serious problem. In mid-1982 the loans that the ten largest banks had made to third world countries equaled 169 percent of their equity capital! There was fear that if several large debtor countries defaulted some banks might fail, or at least have their capital (and hence lending capacity) severely impaired. On the other hand, the alternative of having the federal government directly, or through the IMF, make loans to these countries to bail out the banks is not an appetizing choice either.

Rescheduling the loans of weak borrowers occurs also on domestic loans. It is a fairly common procedure when a large borrower is unable to repay. In such cases banks have an incentive to avoid forcing the borrower into bankruptcy because they would then have to write off the loan as a loss. By rescheduling the loan, at the very least, they postpone recognizing the loss for accounting purposes and, at best, they allow the borrower to recover and repay the loan in full. This gives the borrower some power.

Other Assets

Apart from the major assets discussed so far, a bank's balance sheet contains a number of minor assets listed in Table 4.1 as "Other Assets." Included in this category are items such as "customer's liabilities on account of acceptances," which is the counterpart of the acceptance item listed as a liability. When a bank accepts a draft for a customer the customer incurs a liability to the bank and this is an asset for the bank. Additional examples of "Other Assets" are federal funds sold and bank premises.

ASSET AND LIABILITY MANAGEMENT

A bank makes its living borrowing money at one price and lending it at a higher price. Historically bankers paid more attention to the lending side than to the borrowing side of their business. Obtaining funds was treated as a more or less mechanical operation with the interest rate paid on deposits set at one time by a cartel arrangement, and subsequently by government-imposed ceilings. By contrast, judging loan applicants called for much more skill and imagination.

This is no longer the case. Now neither government-imposed ceilings nor a cartel of banks set deposit rates. Moreover, banks are no longer dependent entirely on deposits. They can "buy" funds in an open market. Even small banks can join this game by buying federal funds from their city correspondent bank, by borrowing from the Fed, or by borrowing from a money broker. These are firms that split up large deposits into $100,000 units (to keep them within the insurance limit) and deposit them into whichever bank pays the highest interest rate. Medium-sized and large banks can also buy funds in many other ways. One way is to issue what are called "large CDs," that is, CDs for $100,000 or more. Such CDs have a national market, and, normally, if a bank offers a slightly higher rate in this market it can readily obtain additional funds.[6] In addition, banks can bid for funds on the national money market through repurchase agreements. Another way is for the bank's holding company to sell commercial paper (something the bank itself is not allowed to do) and to make the proceeds from this sale available to the bank. Still another way is to borrow so-called **Eurodollars,** that is, dollar-denominated deposits in European and Caribbean banks or in European branches of American banks.

The business of a large bank therefore extends beyond the traditional making of loans. For example, the treasurer of a large bank that is $100 million short of funds will call another bank and inquire at what rate that bank is buying and selling funds. If the bank quotes a buying rate that seems high, the treasurer, instead of buying, say, $50 million from it, may sell it $50 million, and hope to buy the now-required $150 million from other banks later in the day at a lower rate.

Reliance on purchased funds has both advantages and disadvantages for a bank. The advantage is that the bank can readily obtain funds that way. It does not, like the traditional bank, "lend out its deposits"; instead it will frequently make a loan, and then raise its CD rate enough to get the deposits that make the loan possible. It can therefore make profitable loans it would otherwise have to turn down. On the other hand, living off purchased funds has it dangers. First, the interest rate that has to be paid to attract purchased funds may rise sharply. The suppliers of such finds provide them only because the bank pays a competitive interest rate, not because of loyalty to the bank or because it has a conveniently located branch! Hence, such purchased funds are at times much more expensive than are the so-called "core deposits" of

---

[6] The interest rate a bank has to pay to sell large CDs depends both on its reputation and on its size because of a belief that the FDIC is not likely to allow a very big bank to fail.

households and firms that are the bank's regular customers. Second, suppose a rumor starts that the bank is unsound. Small depositors will stay with the bank, their deposits being insured, but the providers of purchased funds will cut and run, as banks such as Franklin National and Continental Illinois found out.

Matching the Maturities of Assets and Liabilities

A bank has to watch the relation between the maturities of its assets and those of its liabilities. Several factors tempt it to hold assets that have much longer maturities than its liabilities. One is that its loan customers frequently want term loans at fixed interest rates, so that they can predict their future interest cost. At the same time, its depositors and suppliers of purchased funds prefer short maturities for their claims on the bank. Moreover, since short-term interest rates are usually lower than long-term rates, a bank can often make a profit by lending long and borrowing short.

But such a maturity mismatch creates a serious risk. Suppose, for example, that a bank buys five-year bonds paying 10 percent, and initially finances this purchase by issuing ninety-day CDs at 9 percent. If interest rates then rise, so that the bank is now paying, say, 12 percent on the CDs it uses to finance its holdings of 10 percent bonds, it will not be a very happy bank. In the late 1970s First Pennsylvania, then the twentieth largest bank, got into trouble that way, and had to be rescued by the FDIC and a consortium of other banks. Hence, banks have been careful in recent years to limit the size of the maturity gap between their assets and liabilities, though they have not eliminated it entirely.

OTHER BANKING ACTIVITIES

Taking deposits, making loans, and holding securities are not the only activities of banks. In 1984 about 12 percent of the income of insured banks came from sources other than interest income. (Three percent of it came from service charges on deposits.) One way large banks earn this **fee income** is by putting together consortiums of banks to make loans to foreign governments or other large borrowers. (If these loans run into problems and have to be refinanced, then the banks earn another fee for arranging this.)

In addition, large banks receive fees for making loan commitments and assuming contingent liabilities that do not appear on their balance sheets, but do create additional risk for the bank. One example of a liability off the balance sheet is a **standby letter of credit,** which guarantees that a borrower will pay off a bond when it is due (if the borrower cannot pay, the bank pays). Commercial paper is usually provided with such a bank guarantee. Another example is when the bank sets up a **Note-Issuing Facility** and guarantees that a borrower can issue short-term promissory notes at a fixed spread over some other interest rate.

In such ways banks assume what may, in some future crisis, turn out to be substantial risks. The advantage for banks is that, since these contingent liabilities do not show up on their balance sheets, they do not have to keep capital against them, and thus are able to dilute the regulatory requirements for adequate capital.

Banks take other risks. They speculate in foreign exchange and on the money market. For example, a bank that expects interest rates to fall may buy federal funds early in the week and hope to sell them at a profit later in the week.

In a less risky way all banks, but particularly small banks, earn significant income from the charges they levy on depositors. Those banks that have credit cards also receive fees from card holders as well as commissions from merchants.

Some banks also earn fees from their trust departments, which control very large amounts of capital. Only about one-quarter of all banks have them, and a relatively small number of bank trust departments account for the bulk of trust department assets. They only administer funds for wealthy households, estates, pension funds, and so on. For some trust funds the bank provides only investment advice, but for much the greater part the bank has sole investment responsibility. Banks can, and do, invest these funds, unlike their own assets, in common stocks as well as in fixed-income securities.

There has been some concern about these trust activities of banks, and proposals have been made to take trust departments away from banks and turn them into separate institutions. The main arguments for this are, first, that trust departments allow banks to accumulate great economic power, and, second, that banks might not separate their trust and commercial banking activities as they are supposed to do. For example, if a bank in its capacity as a lender hears of unfavorable developments ahead of the firm's other stockholders it might have its trust department sell this stock to the detriment of other stockholders. But banks are not supposed to do this, and whether this actually occurs on a significant scale is a matter for debate.

Apart from personal trusts, the larger banks also handle trust matters for corporations. They administer corporate pension funds, send out interest and dividend payments on corporate bonds and stocks, and register bond transfers. These activities can be a profitable part of the customer relationship for the bank.

Finally, there are the nonbank subsidiaries of bank holding companies that were discussed in the previous chapter.

SUMMARY

1 Banks issue checkable deposits and savings and time deposits. Other bank liabilities include federal funds bought, bankers' acceptances, and capital.
2 All, except the smallest depository institutions with transactions accounts or nonpersonal time deposits must hold reserves set—within limits—by the Federal Reserve.
3 Bank loans are the biggest bank asset. Banks ration credit. Business firms have a customer relationship with banks, and are able to get long-term as well as short-term loans. They often have a line of credit, but have to keep compensat-

ing balances and frequently have to offer collateral. The best customers can sometimes borrow below the prime rate but many other customers have to pay more than the prime rate. On term loans the interest rate is often variable.

4   Mortgage loans are an important part of a bank's assets, though they are relatively illiquid. In addition, banks make consumer loans and security loans.

5   Banks now manage their liabilities by actively buying funds in the CD market and in the federal-funds market. Large banks rely heavily on such purchased funds.

6   Banks have to watch the maturity match between their assets and liabilities. They are tempted to hold assets that are much longer term than their liabilities, but this is risky.

7   Banks earn fee incomes from various activities. The biggest banks have very large trust departments.

QUESTIONS AND EXERCISES

1   Describe the way banks manage their liabilities.
2   Describe both negotiable and nonnegotiable CDs.
3   Describe:
   a. bankers' acceptances
   b. repo
   c. federal funds
   d. primary reserves
4   Describe credit rationing. Why do banks do this?
5   Describe the characteristics of the following business loans:
   a. lines of credit
   b. compensatory balances
   c. collateral
   d. the prime rate
6   Suppose a banker tells you that in his twenty-five years as a loan officer he has never made a loan that went into default. Should you congratulate him for sound business judgment?
7   Describe the functions of bank trust departments.
8   "Capital requirements on banks should be lowered. If they have a smaller proportion of their funds tied up in capital they can make more loans." Discuss.

FURTHER READING

HAVRILESKY, THOMAS, and JOHN BOORMAN. *Current Perspectives in Banking.* Arlington Heights, Ill.: AHM Publishing Co., 1976. An interesting collection of readings.

HAYES, DOUGLAS. *Bank Funds Management.* Ann Arbor, Mich.: University of Michigan, Graduate School of Business Administration, 1980. A compact discussion of how banks manage funds.

LINDOW, WESLEY. *Inside the Money Market.* New York: Random House, 1972. A fascinating discussion of liability management as seen by a banker.

MAYER, MARTIN. *The Money Bazaar,* Part 3. New York: E. P. Dutton, 1984. A fascinating description of how banks operate.

WEINTRAUB, ROBERT. *International Debt: Crisis and Challenge.* Fairfax, Va.: Department of Economics, George Mason University, 1983. A stimulating discussion.

CHAPTER 5

Other Financial Intermediaries

Most of us have a hard time saving, but when we do manage to save something we find it difficult, in an increasingly complex economy, to decide how to invest. A number of other institutions besides commercial banks serve to intermediate between savers and investors, and provide an alternative to direct investment by savers. Lumped together under the term **financial intermediaries,** these institutions include mutual savings banks, savings and loan associations, credit unions, life insurance companies, and pension funds.

Most Americans depend on these financial intermediaries to do their investing for them. Some sacrifice of investment income is required to pay the cost of operating financial intermediaries, but most people, especially those of modest means, are willing to pay that price for the safety and convenience offered by intermediaries. Wealthy individuals buy common stocks and may hold municipal bonds for tax-free income, but few American families hold common stocks, and even fewer hold tax-exempt bonds. Most families invest their savings in commercial banks and other intermediaries. Table 5.1 shows the distribution of household financial assets among the different kinds of directly held securities and financial intermediaries. Table 5.2 shows how the flow of household saving has been distributed among different kinds of securities and financial intermediaries. Note that less than 20 percent of household financial investment flows directly into security markets.

In Chapter 2 we discussed the rationale for the use of financial intermediaries. In this chapter we will review the development of several of the more important kinds of intermediaries. In addition to those mentioned above, we will consider the role of consumer finance companies and several important financial agencies.

Table 5.1 Household Balance Sheet, 31 December 1984	
Assets	Billions of dollars
Deposits and credit-market instruments[a]	$3,299.9
Deposits	2,471.0
Checkable deposits and currency	384.8
Small time and savings deposits	1,689.8
Money-market fund shares	209.7
Large time deposits	186.7
Credit-market instruments	823.8
U.S. government securities	405.3
Treasury issues	327.0
Savings bonds	74.5
Other treasury	252.5
Agency issues	78.3
State and local obligations	212.5
Corporate and foreign bonds	46.0
Mortgages	160.4
Open-market paper	−.4
Corporate equities	1,491.3
Mutual fund shares	161.2
Other corporate equities	1,330.2
Life insurance reserves	246.0
Pension fund reserves	1,436.6
Security credit	18.1
Miscellaneous assets	99.2
TOTAL, Financial Assets:	6,586.7
Liabilities	Billions of dollars
Credit mortgage instruments	$2,034.0
Home mortgages	1,308.5
Other mortgages	41.4
Installment consumer credit	460.5
Other consumer credit	116.6
Bank loans n.e.c.	36.5
Other loans	79.3
Security credit	34.6
Trade credit	25.6
Deferred and unpaid life insurance premiums	15.1
TOTAL, Liabilities:	2,169.5

a: Excludes corporate equities.

Table 5.2	Annual Change in Financial Assets of Households	*(billions of dollars)*

Year	Savings associa-tions[a]	Savings banks	Com-mercial banks	Credit unions	Life insurance reserves	Pension fund reserves	Credit and equity instru-ments	Money market fund shares	Total[b]
1960	$ 7.6	$ 1.4	$ 2.7	$ 0.5	$ 3.2	$ 8.3	$ 6.2		$ 31.6
1965	8.5	3.6	14.9	1.0	4.8	12.1	2.8		55.1
1970	11.0	4.4	27.0	1.2	5.5	18.4	−1.2		75.1
1971	28.0	9.9	28.1	1.7	6.3	21.1	−8.9		98.3
1972	32.7	10.2	29.0	2.5	6.9	22.6	6.0		122.2
1973	20.2	4.7	35.3	3.6	7.6	25.4	32.0		142.7
1974	16.1	3.1	34.1	2.6	6.7	29.6	36.6	$ 2.4	138.5
1975	42.8	11.2	24.6	5.4	8.7	34.9	27.0	1.3	162.8
1976	50.6	13.0	37.9	6.0	8.4	44.0	23.9	0.0	199.5
1977	51.0	11.1	37.8	7.7	11.5	54.6	27.8	0.2	223.0
1978	44.9	8.6	40.4	6.4	12.0	61.8	56.2	6.9	259.7
1979	39.3	3.4	27.3	4.4	10.7	84.3	52.9	34.4	278.0
1980	41.8	7.5	68.8	8.3	9.7	106.5	28.4	29.2	310.5
1981	20.0	3.0	40.5	3.1	9.2	107.9	12.6	107.5	339.3
1982	46.8	5.3	55.9	11.2	7.2	143.0	43.6	24.7	354.0
1983	101.4	15.8	66.4	14.9	8.0	146.0	83.9	−44.1	453.0
1984[c]	112.3	8.8	74.6	12.9	8.0	124.1	57.3	47.2	476.1

Note: No data are given for money-market funds prior to 1973.
a: Includes most federal savings banks insured by the FSLIC.
b: Includes checkable deposits and currency not classified elsewhere.
c: Preliminary.
Source: *Savings Institutions Sourcebook,* 1985 (U.S. League of Savings Institution).

THRIFT INSTITUTIONS: A PROFILE

The **thrift institutions**—mutual savings banks, savings and loan associations, and money-market funds—provide the best and most important example of the functions of financial intermediaries. As we indicated in Chapter 2, they reap economies of scale and the benefits of diversifications, and create liquidity by pooling the assets of many individual savers.

Our present financial arrangements reflect the origins and historical evolution of our financial institutions and markets. At one time there was a clear division of function between commercial banks and thrift institutions. Commercial banks specialized in demand liabilities (bank notes and checkable deposits) and provided short-term loans to businesses. Savings banks and savings and loan associations provided deposit services for households' savings and held long-term assets, especially home mortgages.

The dividing line between commercial banks and thrift institutions is now blurry, at best. Commercial banks have long been active in the savings account and mortgage markets. More recently thrift institutions have begun to provide checkable deposits (NOW and Super-NOW accounts) and have broader powers to provide consumer credit and to make loans to businesses. Clearly, the deposit institutions are becoming more alike. However, it will be some time before the differences among them disappear. A review of their history may help to explain some transitional problems.

Savings Banks

Mutual savings banks were organized early in the nineteenth century to encourage saving among the growing artisan class in cities like Boston, Philadelphia, and New York. Mutual savings banks are controlled by self-perpetuating boards of trustees. Earnings in excess of expenses either are paid out as interest to depositors or are added to surplus as a cushion against large losses.

The great majority of mutual savings banks have state rather than federal charters. Most of them are in New England and New York with a very small number in other states. Until the 1980s they were conservatively managed and had few failures. But then there were some dramatic failures in Ohio and Maryland. Depositors suffered losses because these savings banks were insured by private insurance systems and not by a federal agency.

Savings and Loan Associations

Savings and loan associations originated as self-help organizations. A group of people who wanted to finance their own houses agreed to pool their savings in order to build homes. Savings and loan associations now operate in much the same way as savings banks. They differ from savings banks, however, in several important respects.

First, many savings and loan associations are now organized as corporations rather than as mutual associations; there are only a few "stock" savings banks. Also, savings and loans were restricted to mortgage loans and government securities until the law was changed in 1980.

The two thousand federally chartered savings and loans hold about 60 percent of all deposits. The remainder is held by over twenty-five hundred state-chartered associations. Nearly all the deposits are insured up to $100,000 by the Federal Savings and Loan Insurance Company (FSLIC) which is similar to the FDIC. Most of the remaining deposits are insured by state-operated funds.

State-chartered associations are examined and supervised by state banking commissions and the FSLIC. Federally chartered associations are supervised by the twelve regional Home Loan Banks. The **Federal Home Loan Bank System** was founded in the 1930s after the failure of a large number of savings and loan associations. It consists of twelve regional Federal Home Loan Banks, nominally owned by the federally chartered associations in its area. But the activities of the regional banks are controlled by the Federal Home Loan Bank Board, appointed by the president. The Federal Home

Loan Bank Board sells securities on behalf of the twelve regional banks to finance loans to member associations. However, the lending capacity of the system is more limited than in the case of the Federal Reserve. Ordinarily the Home Loan Banks must charge borrowing associations a rate that covers the banks' own borrowing costs. In emergencies the Home Loan Bank Board may borrow directly from the U.S. Treasury. Savings and loans can also borrow from the Federal Reserve if they have exhausted other means of borrowing.

Money-Market Funds

Money-market funds first became important in 1974 when short-term interest rates rose to record levels, and had an explosive growth in 1979–1982 when rates again rose sharply. The funds, organized by brokerage firms and firms managing other types of mutual funds for stocks and bonds, invest in Treasury bills, commercial paper, and bank CDs. They arrange with banks to honor checks drawn by fund shareholders on the fund's account, though often only for checks of $500 and over. When the bank presents the check, the fund liquidates assets and, of course, reduces the number of shares credited to the person drawing the check.

Credit Unions

Credit unions have grown rapidly in recent years. They are cooperative organizations like savings banks but are often sponsored by employers, who provide free office space and arrange for payroll deduction savings plans. Credit unions usually provide consumer loans and mortgage loans to members.

INVESTMENT PORTFOLIOS OF THRIFT INSTITUTIONS

Through most of their long history thrift institutions had a fairly steady growth in deposits and rarely suffered deposit outflows. From a maturity matching standpoint, their total deposits could be treated like long-term liabilities even though individual deposits could be withdrawn on short notice. Accordingly, they always invested most of their funds in long-term assets.

The thrift institutions have always invested heavily in home mortgages. Their concentration on mortgages is partly due to legal restrictions but also reflects their comparative advantage over other long-term investors, such as insurance companies and pension funds, in mortgage investment.

The managers of local thrift institution offices can readily keep up with changes in real estate values, zoning laws, and taxes in the immediate area. Thrift institutions also hope to attract deposit business from mortgage borrowers.

Because of legal restrictions, savings and loan investment portfolios consist mainly of real estate loans, U.S. government securities, and cash. But since 1980, savings and loans have been taking advantage of legal changes permitting a wider range of investment choices. Nevertheless, as Table 5.3

shows, their portfolios are dominated by real estate loans. Savings and loans have specialized in mortgages on single-family homes, but they also lend to apartment developers and provide commercial mortgages for developers of shopping centers and other office and store buildings. Savings and loan associations make construction loans to builders. They advance funds as construction proceeds and are repaid when the building is sold. They also make mortgage "commitments" to builders, agreeing to make mortgage loans to the purchasers of homes in a tract development when the homes are completed and sold.

While the demand for mortgage credit is fairly steady, savings and loan associations have to adjust their policies to fluctuations in deposit inflows. When there is a temporary decline in deposit inflow they may borrow from a Federal Home Loan Bank. However, in very tight money periods, they have had to ration their lending more severely by limiting new commitments to deposit customers and builders with whom they have a continuing relationship. When their deposit inflow is large they repay the Federal Home Loan Bank and temporarily build up their holdings of government securities. In the longer run, of course, savings and loans adjust mortgage rates upward when they cannot meet demand for new commitments, and downward when they have surplus funds.

Table 5.3	Balance Sheet of Savings and Loan Associations, 31 December 1984					
	Assets			**Liabilities**		
	Billions of dollars	%		Billions of dollars	%	
Mortgages	606.8	61.3	Deposits	796.2	82.4	
U.S. government securities	163.6	16.5	Federal Home Loan Bank loans	74.8	7.7	
Consumer credit	41.3	4.2	Federal funds and repos	46.1	4.8	
Federal funds and repos	29.1	2.9	Bank loans	13.7	1.4	
Open-market paper	14.9	1.5	Corporate bonds	4.9	.5	
Demand deposits and currency	10.6	1.1	Miscellaneous liabilties	30.4	3.1	
Time deposits	9.6	1.0	TOTAL	966.0	100.0	
Tax-exempt obligations	.7	.1				
Miscellaneous assets	112.9	11.4				
TOTAL	989.6	100.0				

Source: Board of Governors, Federal Reserve System, Flow of Funds Accounts, Financial Assets and Liabilities, Year End, 1961–84, p.22.

The investment activities of mutual savings banks are somewhat more complex because they have different lending powers than the savings and loans. Mutual savings banks can buy corporate bonds and even some stocks and, like savings and loans, they have limited consumer-lending powers. Table 5.4 shows their balance sheet. Nonetheless, because they have a comparative advantage over insurance companies and pension funds in mortgage lending and because of the tax advantage they obtain if 72 percent of their assets are in mortgages, mutual savings banks as a whole have placed about half of their funds in mortgages. Commercial mortgages make up about one-third of their mortgage portfolio. Since the savings banks are concentrated in states with relatively slow population growth, mutual savings banks often lend on mortgages in areas outside their home state.

Because they have the option of buying corporate bonds, mutual savings banks have an investment choice and are willing to shift funds into the bond market whenever bond yields rise relative to mortgage yields. As we shall see in the next chapter, their exercise of this choice is one of the links between bond rates and mortgage rates.

Together the thrift institutions hold about $700 billion in mortgages, nearly half of the total from all sources. Since they play such an important role in the mortgage market, some people believe that any reduction in their lending activity affects the rate of residential construction. Because the home-

---

Table 5.4   Balance Sheet of Mutual Savings Banks, 31 December 1984

	Assets Billions of dollars	%		Liabilities Billions of dollars	%
Mortgages	103.0	50.3			
U.S. government securities	33.8	16.5	Deposits	180.6	93.4
Corporate and foreign bonds	20.4	10.0	Miscellaneous liabilities	12.7	6.6
Consumer credit	11.3	5.5	TOTAL	193.3	100.0
Commercial paper	7.7	3.8			
Federal funds and repos	6.0	2.9			
Demand deposits and currency	4.6	2.2			
Corporate equities	4.1	2.0			
Tax exempt obligations	2.1	1.0			
Time deposits	.4	.2			
Miscellaneous assets	11.3	5.5			
TOTAL	205.7	100.0			

Source: Board of Governors, Federal Reserve System, Flow of Funds Accounts, Financial Assets and Liabilities, Year End, 1961–84, p. 22.

building industry is large and politically powerful, the competitive problems of the thrift institutions have produced a good deal of political controversy and much legislation to assist the thrift institutions and to provide alternative sources of mortgage financing.

HOW THRIFT INSTITUTIONS COMPETE FOR THE CONSUMER'S DOLLAR

The thrift institutions face two kinds of competition. They must compete with commercial banks, which offer savings deposits and certificates like those offered by thrift institutions, and they must also compete with issuers of marketable securities—bonds, stocks, Treasury bills—and with money-market funds.

Households now hold over fifteen times as much in time and savings deposits, in nominal terms, as at the end of World War II. Thrift institutions increased their share of the "savings market" from about 45 percent in 1945 to 60 percent in 1960. Thereafter, the share of commercial banks has moved erratically with a small net gain.

On average, household investment in marketable securities has absorbed only a few percent of household savings. On a number of occasions, however, rapid increases in money-market rates have induced households to shift funds from thrift institutions directly into marketable securities or money-market funds.

COMPETITION FOR SAVINGS

Over the past three decades, financial institutions have been competing vigorously for savings deposits. Altogether more than fourteen thousand banks, six thousand savings and loans, six hundred mutual savings banks and credit unions have sought to attract savers' dollars. Also in the competition are the money-market funds sold through hundreds of brokerage offices.

In most urban areas there is vigorous competition among a number of institutions offering savings deposits. Customers are clearly responsive to interest-rate differentials as well as to locational and convenience factors. Changes in the rates paid by different institutions have a significant influence on their share of the local market for savings deposits. Consumers can choose among several banking offices located near their home, place of work, or shopping center. When the rates offered are the same, consumers often choose one institution over another on the basis of locational convenience, hours of business, or because they like the clerks. Some households keep their savings account with the bank that gave them a mortgage loan.

Regulation Q

The New Deal attempted to expand home ownership, and has succeeded: in 1930 about one-third of households were home-owners; now about two-thirds are. To accomplish this goal, the prevailing type of mortgage was changed.

The typical mortgages at that time were not the long-term amortized mortgages we now know, but mortgages due in lump sums about every five years. In practice, mortgages were often renewed for another five years, but, even so, this type of mortgage was better suited to the well-to-do than to the average person. To help more people buy houses, thrift institutions were encouraged to make what is now known as the "traditional" type of mortgage, that is, a long-term, fixed-rate mortgage repayable in installments. This policy was successful—families found long-term amortized mortgages manageable, and home ownership increased substantially after World War II.

But something was overlooked. The long-term, fixed-rate mortgage is feasible as long as interest rates are not rising fast and short-term rates are below long-term rates. The thrift institution borrows short and lends long, and with stable interest rates it has a predictable spread between what it receives on its loans and what it pays to its depositors.

Although interest rates did rise in the years between World War II and the Vietnam War, the rise was fairly modest. The rate on ten-year government bonds was 2.85 percent in 1953, and 4.00 percent in 1963, and short-term rates were below long-term rates in every year of this period. But after 1965 rates rose substantially; by 1982 the rate on ten-year government bonds was 13.9 percent, and the Treasury bill rate was 14.0 percent. When interest rates rise sharply thrifts are in trouble. In 1981, savings and loans were, on the average, paying 10.92 percent for their funds but earning only 10.11 percent on their assets. Such a negative spread of .81 percent is hardly a good way to pay the costs of operations!

What was to be done? Interest rates on outstanding mortgages obviously could not be raised. But interest rates paid on deposits could be kept from rising. The Banking Act of 1933 had ordered the Federal Reserve to set maximum rates on time deposits. The Fed had enforced this rule, **Regulation Q,** with an easy hand, raising the ceiling whenever interest rates on the open market rose high enough to make banks uncomfortable with it.[1] But in 1967 the thrifts were complaining bitterly that competition for deposits among themselves, as well as competition from banks, was forcing deposit rates to levels that would bankrupt many thrifts. So, instead of raising the Regulation Q ceiling, the Fed lowered it slightly to help the thrifts. Similar regulations were issued by the FDIC for nonmember banks and by the Federal Savings and Loan Insurance Corporation (FSLIC) for savings and loans.

Problems with Regulation Q

Regulation Q took care of the immediate emergency in 1967, but as a forward-looking policy it was defective. It took eighteen years of painful experience before Regulation Q was completely eliminated.

In the meantime Regulation Q did a great deal of damage. First, it was discriminatory. Wealthy households, for whom it is worthwhile to acquire financial sophistication, could earn a high rate of interest by buying securities,

---

[1] The term "Regulation Q" has no deep meaning. The Fed called its first regulation "Regulation A," and had reached Q by the time it regulated deposit rates.

while the government held down the interest rate that the less sophisticated lower- and middle-income households received on savings deposits. This discrimination became more blatant in 1970 when the Regulation Q ceiling was removed from deposits of $100,000 or more because it had made it difficult at times for banks to sell large CDs. But those with $100,000 to deposit were not the only ones who could buy securities. Hence Regulation Q was subsequently modified to provide higher ceilings for large deposits. The lowest ceiling applied only to passbook deposits, the type of deposit owned by the smallest depositors.

Second, when interest rates rose the Regulation Q ceiling resulted in **disintermediation.** This ugly word describes the shift of funds out of financial intermediaries into direct investment. With rising interest rates on securities it became worthwhile for depositors to withdraw their deposits and buy securities instead. Hence, whenever interest rates rose sufficiently, the net inflow of funds into thrift institutions fell drastically. As a result, these institutions had to cut back on their mortgage lending because of the tightening of the ceiling in 1967. This is hardly what Regulation Q was intended to do. It had been imposed not just out of concern for thrift institutions as such but so that they could continue to be a ready source of mortgage loans for the politically powerful building industry. Instead, disintermediation occurred. This reflects a basic principle of economics: if you set the price you lose control over the quantity, and vice versa.

Another basic principle of economics is that if you block one channel of competition you stimulate others. When Regulation Q prohibited depository institutions from competing by price (i.e., by altering the interest rate on deposits) they competed by offering "free gifts" to depositors instead. In addition, they competed by providing depositors with new branch offices to choose from. Such nonprice competition is wasteful.

Yet another basic principle of economics is that if you impose controls on one type of institution unregulated institutions offering similar products will flourish, or new ones will appear. Thus Regulation Q caused money-market funds to grow from a trivial segment of the financial system to a substantial one. The growth of such near-monies made it harder to define and measure "money," something that concerns economists. The greater concern to those who actually determine policy was that money-market funds had the potential to drain deposits rapidly from both banks and thrift institutions.

Still another problem with Regulation Q was that it did not address the basic issue that our whole system of thrift institutions is viable only under special conditions. As previously discussed, financing long-term, fixed-rate mortgages with short-term deposits works only if interest rates are not rising rapidly. And in the 1970s and early 1980s they *were* rising rapidly. As a result, in economic terms (though not in legal and accounting terms), most thrift institutions had negative net worth. What saved them was that accountants value mortgages at acquisition prices, not at market prices. One study calculated that by 1981 insured savings and loans had had implicit losses (i.e., the difference between the actual values and the book values of their portfolios) that were equivalent to what they would have lost had 35 percent of their mortgage loans been in default. For mutual savings banks the equivalent figure was 39 percent.[2] What kept thrift institutions alive was an asset that never appears on their books: the value of the deposit insurance guarantee. In the absence of insurance, sophisticated depositors would start a run on a thrift if they knew that the firm's liabilities exceeded its assets.

Phasing Out Regulation Q

Obviously, something had to be done, and many things were tried. One was price discrimination. Not all savers withdraw their deposits when market interest rates rise relative to the fixed Regulation Q rate. So, instead of raising all interest rates, with consequent losses to thrifts, why not raise the Regulation Q ceiling rate only for those types of deposits that are sensitive to interest rates —that is, large deposits and long-term deposits. This approach was tried. But when other depositors saw that rates on large deposits and long-term deposits were much higher than the rate they were getting, they too moved into long-term deposits, and sometimes also into large deposits by combining several of their small deposits. Hence, paying higher rates on long-term and large deposits became expensive for thrifts.

Another approach was to reduce the maturity gap between assets and liabilities. When variable-rate mortgages were introduced, some mortgages became the equivalent of short-term assets.[3] But not much was achieved this way because borrowers were reluctant to take out variable-rate mortgages, in part because it made them bear the risk of rising interest rates. Another way the mismatched maturity of assets and liabilities was reduced was by permitting thrift institutions to make consumer loans and business loans, which have much shorter maturities than mortgage loans. But this too did not help in the short run. Thrifts still had all those old mortgages on their books, and it would take a long time for consumer and business loans to become a substantial proportion of their portfolios.

It became more and more obvious that Regulation Q, while a successful patch in the sense that it had prevented most thrifts from failing, was not a viable long-term solution. Hence, in 1980 a new law was passed requiring a phase-out of Regulation Q by March 1986. In return, thrift institutions were given nationwide NOW accounts and other benefits.

Problems with Maturity Mismatch

The phase-out of Regulation Q took care of disintermediation and the competition from money-market funds. But it did nothing to eliminate the maturity mismatch that still troubled thrift institutions. Most of them retained

---

[2] Edward Kane, *The Gathering Crisis in Deposit Insurance*. Cambridge, Mass.: MIT Press, 1985.

[3] A variable-rate mortgage is a mortgage whose interest rate varies along with some other interest rate, such as the rate on five-year government securities, or the average cost of funds to savings and loans. Such variable-rate mortgages are similar to short-term mortgages because the lender avoids most of the interest-rate risk inherent in fixed-rate, long-term mortgages.

liabilities in excess of the true value of their assets. This problem was handled partly by merging weak institutions into stronger ones, and partly by a policy of "say it ain't so." As long as a thrift's deposits are insured and it can meet day-to-day cash outflows, it can stay afloat even with a negative net worth. Hence, the regulatory authorities allowed some institutions to remain open even if their net worth, as measured by standard accounting procedures, fell below the minimum set forth in the regulations. In addition, the FSLIC provided a few weak savings and loans with funds that they could apply toward their net worth requirements. They were obligated to pay interest on these funds only (if ever) they had income rather than losses. Another example of creative accounting was merging two institutions so that they ended up with more capital on their books than they had had as individual firms. These ways of ignoring reality were only short-term palliatives. But they helped. As interest rates fell in 1982 and 1983 many institutions that had survived only due to the "let's pretend" policy became truly viable again. Honesty is not *always* the best policy.

But creative accounting did not save all thrift institutions. Some had a maturity mismatch that was too severe. Others suffered from a policy that was intended to aid them: in 1980 and again in 1982 savings and loans were allowed a substantially wider choice of assets. The result for some was that they collapsed as a result of unsound loans rather than of a maturity mismatch. Between 1980 and 1983 the number of savings and loans fell by 24 percent, while the number of savings banks declined by almost one-quarter.

Deposit Insurance

Excessive risk-taking destroyed not only some savings and loans, but also part of the deposit insurance systems. In several states deposits in thrifts were insured mainly by private deposit insurance systems sponsored, but not guaranteed, by the state. One of these states was Ohio. In 1984 one Ohio thrift, Home State Savings Bank, had big losses due to alleged fraud by a government security dealer with whom it had made large repurchase agreements. When Home State failed, the private insurance fund was not big enough to cover its deposits. This provoked a run on other Ohio thrifts. To stop these runs the state temporarily closed down all thrift institutions insured by the state fund. After a few weeks the sound ones were reopened. The following year it was Maryland's turn, when one of its thrift institutions was found to have made unsound investments. To stop the resulting run on all privately insured institutions, a limit was placed on the amount depositors could withdraw.

As a result, all states now require federal insurance, though in Massachusetts the state system still operates to insure deposits of over $100,000. The demise of the state insurance systems demonstrates that to be fully effective, deposit insurance must be backed by the funds of the federal government. Since de facto the FDIC and FSLIC are backed by the full faith and credit of the federal government, there is no danger of their failure. But, of course, it would be embarassing to have to invoke this guarantee. Hence, in the early 1980s, in handling failing institutions, the FSLIC used accounting methods that avoided showing large losses on its books. Moreover, the FSLIC did not close down many institutions that were insolvent even under these relaxed standards. In early 1986 there were 461 of them with deposits of $114 billion. The FSLIC was afraid that the costs of merging them with other institutions or paying off their depositors would seriously weaken its insurance fund, which amounted to $6.8 billion at the time. But by staying in business these institutions continue to pile up losses. Unless interest rates decline and stay low, the longer they continue to operate, the more it will ultimately cost the FSLIC. Accordingly, the FSLIC is currently (May 1986) planning to obtain additional funds from the Federal Home Loan Banks (institutions that will be discussed subsequently) and the capital market, so that it can close down these institutions.

INSURANCE AND RETIREMENT SAVINGS

Household claims against life insurance companies and pension funds are comparable in size to their holdings of time and savings deposits at commercial banks and thrift institutions. These institutions play a dominant role in the market for corporate bonds and have become increasingly important holders of common stock. Both kinds of institutions have grown in the postwar years, but pension-fund growth has been especially rapid.

Life Insurance

Life insurance companies have been in operation for over two hundred years, but their growth and importance accelerated with urbanization and industrialization as people found themselves less able to rely on their children for support in their old age. Farmers and owners of small businesses have less need for life insurance because they can rely on their family farm or business to provide for dependents in case of the death of the principal earner. Moreover, they usually find it necessary to invest all their savings in the farm or business. Industrialization created a salaried middle class that could save and needed to provide for dependents. Life insurance is a way to provide for dependents but it usually also combines insurance with investment.

It is possible to buy life insurance without building up an asset. The holder of a **term-insurance policy** pays a premium just equal to the probability of death for his or her age group (plus sales and administrative costs). The insurance company, with a large number of similar policies, collects just enough in premiums to cover the death benefits to those who die in the current year as well as its costs (and profit, if any). The policyholders do not build up any claims, and the insurance company's assets are only a fraction of a year's premiums. However, term-insurance rates rise with age, and become painfully high just as the insured person begins to think seriously of the possibility of death.

Many people find a so-called **ordinary-life** or **level-premium policy** more attractive than term insurance. The holder of an ordinary-life policy pays a more expensive premium in early life than he or she would for term insurance. The insurance company invests the excess premiums and accumulates the earnings in a reserve account. The ordinary-life premium remains constant. It is calculated so that the total premiums paid plus earnings on reserves less expenses will always cover death benefits. In effect, holders of ordinary-life policies pay in advance for their insurance so that they will not have to face increasing term-insurance premiums. In the process they build up an investment in the life insurance reserve. If a policyholder cancels his or her policy he or she is entitled to get back most of the reserve against the policy. The amount that can be returned to the individual is called the **cash surrender value.** Policyholders may also borrow against the reserve at a rate specified in the policy.

With increasing population and rising income the amount of insurance in force has grown rapidly; life insurance reserves generally grow annually at a rate of about $6 billion.

Since life insurance contracts run for many years and promise a fixed minimum rate of interest on reserves, life insurance companies invest most of their insurance reserves in long-term assets. Their investment income is not taxed at the regular corporate rate, so they invest only limited amounts in the tax-exempt state and local securities. Their liabilities are fixed in dollar amounts, so life insurance reserves are not ordinarily invested in common stock (this is an example of the portfolio hedging we discussed in Chapter 2). That leaves mortgages and corporate bonds as the principal investment outlet for life insurance funds. At times, life insurance companies have invested substantial amounts in single-family home mortgages. In recent years, however, they have concentrated on commercial mortgages for relatively large offices, shopping centers, and apartment buildings leaving the retail mortgage business to local thrift institutions and banks.

Pension Funds

The same forces of industrialization and urbanization that influenced the inception and growth of life insurance also created the need for retirement saving. Longer life spans and the widespread practice of mandatory retirement have intensified the need for retirement funds. The Social Security System, developed in the 1930s, provides retirement income for nearly everyone, but many people wish additional retirement support. Anyone who wishes to can, of course, do his or her own saving and investment during working life and then retire on the income from the savings, gradually liquidate capital, or buy an annuity. However, there are tax advantages to saving through a pension fund. Many unions have negotiated for employer-funded pension plans and have been willing to take part of their wage increases in the form of pension contributions. Employer contributions to retirement funds approved by the Internal Revenue Service are treated as wage costs for tax purposes. Since employees pay no tax until the benefits are received, they defer taxes by saving through a pension fund.

Employer-sponsored pension funds are administered either by a bank trust department or by an insurance company. The contributions are invested by the fund manager mainly in corporate stock or bonds. Because the number of employees covered by pension funds has grown so rapidly, and because nominal wage rates have risen substantially, the contributions on behalf of current employees exceed the benefits paid to retired employees, and the assets of penson funds have increased greatly.

Other Forms of Insurance

Other insurance companies, principally marine, fire, and casualty companies, have much smaller financial assets than the life insurance companies. Still, the $60 billion they hold is not negligible. Their sources of funds and investment patterns are quite different from those of the life insurance companies. Marine, fire, and casualty companies offer fire, theft, and accident liability insurance to home owners, automobile owners, and businesses. There is much more variation in their payments for losses than there is in the death-benefit payments of life insurance companies. Their capital is invested in financial assets. In addition they collect premiums in advance and have the use of the policyholder's funds until losses are paid. (If premiums are collected at the start of the policy year and losses are evenly distributed, they have the use of half a year's premiums.)

Marine, fire, and casualty companies have to keep part of their assets in liquid form, for example, in Treasury bills, commercial paper, or bank CDs, but most of their funds are invested in long-term assets. Since they are fully taxed corporations, these companies, like banks, prefer municipal bonds to corporate bonds. They also hold substantial amounts of corporate stock. Like the pension funds they are prepared to switch from bonds to stock or vice versa in response to changes in yields. Marine, fire, and casualty companies are the only group whose portfolio choices provide a direct link between the yields on municipal bonds and anticipated yields on common stock.

MUTUAL FUNDS

A good many people enjoy following the stock market, studying brokers' research reports, and making their own investment choices. They boast about the winners and keep quiet about the losers. Others, who want to invest in common stocks because they hope for a better yield than they can get on fixed-income securities, find the task of investment management onerous. Wealthy people can afford to pay investment counsel and can buy a diversified portfolio of stocks without paying too much in brokerage charges. People with $10,000 or $20,000 to invest in stocks cannot afford to pay much for investment advice and find it difficult to obtain a diversified portfolio. Mutual funds solve their problem.

Common-stock mutual funds issue shares at, say, an initial price of $100 per share. They invest the proceeds, less a commission, in common stock. The value of the funds' shares fluctuates with the fortunes of the stocks held by the fund. The net asset value of a share is computed daily. After the initial offering the fund stands ready to sell new shares each day at the net asset value of existing shares or to redeem existing shares at the same price. When new sales exceed redemptions the fund buys additional stocks; when redemptions exceed new sales the fund must sell some of its holdings. The commission mentioned above is called a **loading** and usually runs about 4 percent. Most of the loading charge is used to pay commissions to brokers and other selling expenses. Many funds do not charge any loading. These no-load funds pay no sales commissions and spend little on advertising. Mutual funds are managed by professional money managers. The investment managers get an annual fee, usually ¼ to ½ percent of asset value. The remainder of dividends earned is paid to the holders of the fund's shares. If it pays out all dividends, the fund need not pay income taxes, but its shareholders must pay income tax on the dividends they receive. If the fund sells stock at a profit, it pays out a capital gains dividend, taxable to the fund's shareholders.

Mutual funds provide a good example of the functions of intermediaries. Since they operate on a relatively large scale, they can provide professional investment management at relatively low cost per dollar invested. They can also manage and monitor a diversified portfolio to reduce risk at relatively low cost in management and brokerage charges.

A number of stock market studies question the value of professional investment advice. There is no proof that any fund management can beat the market averages. However, few investors can buy all the stocks in Standard & Poor's five-hundred-stock index, or even the *much* smaller number needed to get sufficient diversification, much less the fifteen hundred in the New York Stock Exchange index. Whatever the merits of fund managements, they attract a continuing flow of funds from investors who want stocks but do not want to either throw darts or spend a lot of time and effort choosing investments.

There are many types of funds. Some announce that they will invest for growth and capital gains. They do not say that their shares involve a relatively high risk of loss as well as a chance of big gains. At the other end of the spectrum, balanced funds buy a variety of securities including bonds as well as stable dividend stocks and some growth stocks. A few **index funds** hold a portfolio of stocks to achieve a stratified sample of the whole market. Their performance comes close to that of the market average.

Though they have grown rapidly since World War II stock mutual funds still own only a small percent of all common stock. Nonetheless, they provide an opportunity for equity investment to a large number of people who would otherwise find it difficult to participate in the equity market.

FEDERAL CREDIT AGENCIES

The federal government sponsors a number of agencies that act as financial intermediaries. Altogether these federal credit agencies, along with credit agencies that are partially private but sponsored by the federal government have outstanding assets of about $300 billion.

There are two reasons for the federal agencies. First, some agencies provide an outright subsidy to an activity considered desirable by Congress. The Rural Electrification Administration provided 2 percent loans to rural cooperative electric utilities for many years. Second, many credit agencies were created because Congress was convinced that the private financial system was not working properly. The Farm Credit agencies (the twelve Banks for Cooperatives, the twelve Federal Intermediate Credit Banks, and the twelve Federal Land Banks) were created in the 1930s when the farmers complained that they could not obtain sufficient credit from the small banks that served them. The Farm Credit agencies sell securities guaranteed by the Treasury and lend the proceeds to farmers through a complex network of local institutions. The farm borrowers pay interest rates that cover the interest on the guaranteed securities plus administrative costs. No direct subsidy is involved, but the farmers get the benefit of the superior credit standing of securities guaranteed by the U.S. Treasury. There is an indirect subsidy in the sense that the government assumes the credit risk. The Farm Credit agencies have over $40 billion of securities outstanding. In 1986, as a result of the prolonged farm crises, the federal farm credit agencies faced serious losses. Schemes for bailing them out are currently (mid-1986) being considered.

The most important federal credit agencies are those providing home mortgage credit. The Federal Home Loan Bank Board sells its own securities in the open market and lends the proceeds to twelve regional Federal Home Loan banks, which lend in turn to savings and loan associations, which finally make mortgage loans.

The Federal National Mortgage Association (FNMA) also sells securities in the open market and buys federally insured mortgages from banks and other lenders. FNMA makes mortgage commitments from three to twelve months in advance, so that developers building a large number of houses can be assured that mortgage financing will be available when the houses are completed.

The FNMA and Federal Home Loan Bank Board serve as intermediaries in drawing funds from the general credit market into the mortgage market. They help to create a unified national mortgage market. They also provide a source of funds for mortgages that is independent of the growth of deposits at the thrift institutions. Their activities have greatly expanded since 1965 when the growth of deposits at thrift institutions began to fluctuate. The large increase in agency securities has provoked some controversy. Some security analysts argue that the increase in the volume of securities of federally sponsored agencies has an adverse effect on other security issuers. Others maintain that intermediation by government agencies serves to perfect the market and to provide low-cost pooling of risks.

The Federal Financing Bank began operations in 1974. It borrows from the Treasury and in turn buys loans previously made by a variety of federal credit agencies or makes direct loans to borrowers whose obligations have been guaranteed by a government agency. The FFB reduces the cost of federal credit programs since the Treasury can borrow at a lower cost than can federal credit agencies.

SUMMARY

1 Mutual savings banks and savings and loans are major channels for savings. Mortgages are their main assets.
2 When interest rates rose rapidly in the 1960s these mortgages provided an insufficient income for many thrifts. To protect them, Regulation Q, setting interest ceilings on deposits, was tightened. But this had many disadvantages. It discriminated against the poor, and it led to disintermediation, to greater nonprice competition, and to the rise of competing types of institutions that were not regulated.
3 By 1981 most thrift institutions had negative net worth. Among the techniques used to save the industry in the 1970s and 1980s were price discrimination, variable-rate mortgages, greater investment powers for the thrifts, and last, but not least, creative accounting. Deposit ceilings were finally eliminated in 1986.
4 Life insurance companies and pension funds are also important financial intermediaries that provide retirement income. Mutual funds provide investors with diversification and professional management. Federal credit agencies provide access to credit markets on favored terms to certain borrowers.

QUESTIONS AND EXERCISES

1 As net worth increases, the proportion of financial assets invested through financial intermediaries tends to decline. Explain.
2 Look at data on the growth of deposits in various institutions (the *Economic Report of the President* has such data). How would you explain recent changes?
3 Life insurance companies invest mainly in long-term assets. Why?
4 Discuss the following statement, "The traditional fixed-rate mortgage was a blessing until the mid-1960s and a disaster after that."
5 "Making the Regulation Q ceiling restrictive in 1967 was good policy. Keeping it that way was bad policy." Do you agree? Why?
6 What was done to keep the thrifts viable when interest rates rose?

FURTHER READING

CARGILL, THOMAS and GILLIAN GARCIA. *Financial Reform in the 1980s.* Stanford: Hoover Institution, 1985. An excellent analysis of the problems.
CARRON, ANDREW. *The Rescue of the Thrift Industry.* Washington, D.C.: Brookings Institution, 1983. An insightful discussion.
GURLEY, JOHN and EDWARD SHAW. *Money in a Theory of Finance.* Washington, D.C.: Brookings Institution, 1960. A pathbreaking analysis of the role of financial intermediaries.
MELTZER, ALLAN. "Credit Availability and Economic Decisions," *Journal of Finance* 29 (June 1974): 763–778. A sharp criticism of the thesis that credit rationing is important.

CHAPTER 6

Capital Markets

A growing, changing economy needs vast amounts of capital to take advantage of improved technology, and to provide plants and equipment for a growing labor force. Much of the savings that is the ultimate source of the needed capital is done by households who do not own businesses or farms. They want to put their savings to work. Businesses and governments want to invest in physical capital but do not have the needed savings. In a large, complex economy a very elaborate set of arrangements is needed to bring savers and investors together. We noted in Chapter 2 how financial intermediaries assist in that process, but they are only part of the system of capital markets. The function of the capital markets is to provide arrangements so that households, businesses, and governments that want to invest more than they save can bid for the funds of other spending units who have surplus funds.

There cannot, however, be a single pool of funds up for competitive bids. There have to be separate markets for long-term funds and short-term funds; some borrowers are well known, others have to establish their credit worthiness. Some loans involve collateral, some involve monthly payments or lots of bookkeeping. The markets for small loans are different from those involving large sums. The capital markets thus consist of a network of submarkets each dealing with a different type of loan or security. Nonetheless, these submarkets are closely linked so that interest-rate movements will draw funds from one market into another. Moreover, the pattern of financing demands is constantly changing. As the relative supplies of different kinds of securities change over the business cycle, interest rates must change in order to induce lenders to shift their pattern of security purchases and induce borrowers to change their methods of financing.

In this chapter we will examine the adaptation process in the markets for short-term assets and for long-term securities, and then look at the interaction between the two sets of markets. We will be concerned mainly with the way changes in interest differentials bring about an adjustment to changing supplies and demands for securities. In Chapter 13 our concern will be the level of interest rates.

SURPLUSES AND DEFICITS

Disputes over deficits in the federal government are familiar to almost everyone, especially in the last few years when deficits of close to $200 billion have been recorded. While we do not hear as much about deficits in other sectors of the economy, these deficits are often as large as those of the federal government. For purposes of financial analysis, a household or business has a **surplus** *when saving exceeds investment,* and a **deficit** *when investment exceeds saving.* While most households usually have a surplus, many will show deficits in years when they buy automobiles or houses. State and local governments seldom record deficits in their ordinary operations; however, they often borrow for construction of schools and other public buildings. Businesses usually run deficits during booms. Of course, they are making profits then; but they are spending even more for investment than they are saving, so they have to borrow. Federal deficits usually rise during recessions when tax revenues decline and expenditures continue to rise, or during wars, when expenditures also outrun taxes.

Since 1965 the federal government has reported a surplus in only one year. Businesses have shown deficits every single year, while households in the aggregate have had surpluses every single year. It is important to note, however, that there is a lot of variation within these groups. Some businesses have surpluses even when there is a deficit for business as a whole, while many households have deficits even when there is a substantial surplus for the whole household sector.

To bring total surpluses and deficits into balance, the financial markets have to match the supplies and demands for each separate kind of financial asset (from the point of view of a financial investor with a surplus) or liability (from the point of view of a borrower with a deficit). To understand the nature of that problem we must first make a quick examination of the methods used to finance particular kinds of expenditures. Figure 6.1 shows the distribution of amounts borrowed by major sectors of the economy.

The Federal Reserve System has developed a system of Flow of Funds accounts to keep track of the movement of funds from surplus sectors to deficit ones. The detailed accounts report the saving and investment of households, governments, and businesses as well as the sources of finance for deficit units and the uses of funds for the surplus units. The accounts also report the funds raised and supplied by financial institutions.

Financing Deficits

Spending units with deficits may be able to finance a deficit for a particular month or year by using cash or selling financial assets accumulated in earlier periods when they had a surplus. In fact, large amounts of short-term deficits are financed in that way. Firms may then borrow to replenish liquid assets. Thus, particular types of borrowing are not necessarily associated with particular expenditures, but special forms of financing are commonly used for purchases of durable goods and housing. A substantial proportion of automobiles

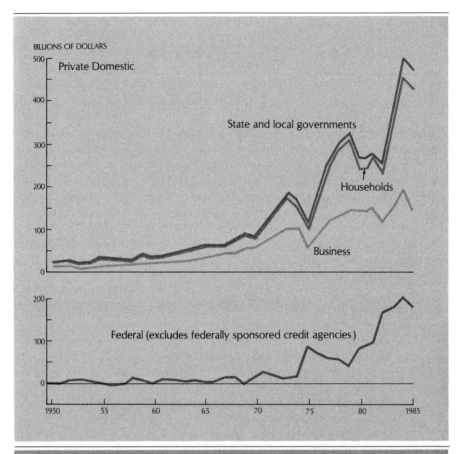

BILLIONS OF DOLLARS

Private Domestic

State and local governments

Households

Business

Federal (excludes federally sponsored credit agencies)

Figure 6.1   Major Nonfinancial Sectors: Net Funds Raised Annually.
Businesses, households, and in recent years the federal government have all been
large users of funds. **Source:** *Federal Reserve Chart Book,* 1986, p. 29.

and other purchases of durable goods are financed with installment credit,
provided either by banks or by consumer finance companies. Gross extensions
of consumer credit vary closely with sales of durable goods. However, households are always making payments on outstanding debts. Almost all home
purchases are at least partially financed with mortgages. The gross volume of
mortgage loans is much larger than the amount of residential construction
since new mortgages are often taken and old mortgages repaid when existing
homes are sold. In addition home owners make regular monthly payments,
thus reducing the total mortgage credit outstanding on their mortgages. For
both reasons the net flow of mortgage credit is much smaller than the gross
amount. The net increase in mortgage credit goes up and down with the
amount of residential construction but the two do not exactly match.

   Except for limited amounts of seasonal borrowing in anticipation of tax
receipts, state and local governments do not—or at least are not supposed to
—run deficits on their current operations. Most of their borrowing is directly

connected to particular construction projects. They issue bonds to build schools, college dormitories, or water and sewer systems. Because of increasing population and strong popular demand for all kinds of public facilities, state and local debt has been growing rapidly since World War II.

As might be expected, and as Figure 6.2 shows, business financing is more complex than government or household financing. Except in the case of office and store buildings, where mortgage financing is often used, business financing is not usually tied to particular expenditure projects. Businesses use a wide variety of sources of funds. Much of their investment is financed from their own retained earnings. But they may also sell new shares of stock, issue bonds, borrow from banks, or sell commercial paper. Moreover, corporations operate on both sides of the market, lending as well as borrowing. To provide for short-term fluctuations in receipts and expenditures they build up substantial holdings of demand deposits, bank CDs, and Treasury bills. One corporation may hold commercial paper issued by another. Moreover, corporations supply trade credit to smaller firms; that is, they ship their goods and allow the firm that is buying them, say, ninety days to make payment on them.

In choosing among alternative sources of finance, corporate treasurers have to balance a number of conflicting considerations. Other things being equal, they would like to borrow as cheaply as possible, but they also want to arrange their financing so as to limit the risk of bankruptcy. Short-term borrowing is often cheaper than long-term debt. However, the firm that relies too heavily on short-term debt might have trouble if market interest rates rise rapidly, if lenders short of funds decide to ration credit more stringently, or if the firm's credit rating declines. Therefore, most firms want to finance only a small fraction of total assets with short-term debt. They also want to limit their total debt so as to limit the risk of bankruptcy in a depression. Moreover, even when bankruptcy is not an important concern, it is necessary to consider the effect of debt financing on the value of the corporation's stock. An increase in fixed interest charges will increase the variability of the corporation's net earnings and that may reduce the price of the stock.

Instead of borrowing, the corporation can obtain equity capital by retaining part of its earnings or issuing new shares. The tax law favors retention of earnings. The stockholders must pay income taxes on dividend receipts. If, on the other hand, the corporation retains part of its earnings and reinvests them profitably, the corporation's earnings will increase. The increase in earnings will be reflected in the price of the stock. The stockholders will then obtain capital gains, but by holding the shares stockholders can postpone tax payments. Moreover, retained earnings have the advantage of providing equity funds without the cost of selling new shares. Also, stockholders who are not willing to buy new shares might be willing to hold more equity in the company in terms of higher values of their shares.

Treasurers like to have a substantial amount of liquid assets on hand. By holding liquid assets they obtain flexibility to choose an advantageous time to borrow and avoid the risk of needing funds at a time when banks are cautious about expanding their loans. But to hold liquid assets they have to borrow in advance or hold as liquid assets funds they would otherwise invest more profit-

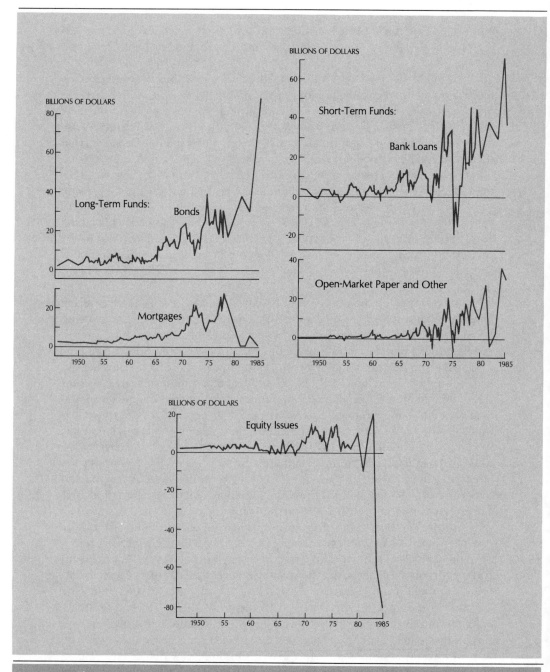

Figure 6.2   **Net Funds Raised by Nonfinancial Corporations—Annually 1952–1985, Seasonally Adjusted Annual Rates, Quarterly.** Business has relied on a number of sources for its funding. **Source:** *Federal Reserve Chart Book*, 1986, p. 45.

ably in longer term assets. It will usually cost more to borrow than the interest they receive on their liquid assets.

Most firms try to maintain a balance among sources of funds—equity from retained earnings and sale of shares, long-term debt, short-term debt. The mix they choose reflects the risks of the business and the relative costs of different kinds of financing. Firms with stable markets use more debt financing than cyclically sensitive businesses. Changes in the relative costs of different kinds of financing will cause shifts in the sources used and in the amount of liquid assets held.

In the short run, however, most firms adjust to the changing balance of receipts and expenditures by varying their holding of liquid assets and their short-term debt. When they feel their short-term debt is too high and their liquid assets too low, they will issue bonds or sell stock. Thus their long-term financing will reflect their average deficit, whereas liquid asset holdings and short-term debt respond to short-term changes in their position.

CAPITAL MARKETS: A PROFILE

The process of transferring funds from households, businesses, and governments with surpluses to those with deficits involves far more than the collection and disbursement of funds. For each loan or security issue, lenders must evaluate the credit standing of borrowers; interest rates and terms of payment must be arranged. Moreover, since individual lenders frequently shift from a surplus position to a deficit position, or change their view about the prospective value of securities, there must be facilities for trading in existing securities. These processes are carried out through a variety of arrangements that bring borrowers and lenders together.

You can take a tour of a stock exchange, but most other financial markets do not have a physical identity. They exist in the form of organizations that buy and sell securities and well-established arrangements for bringing buyers and sellers together. The market organization for each type of transaction reflects the characteristics of the loans or securities involved and the numbers of buyers and sellers involved in the market. Security markets are usually classified as **primary markets,** *for new securities,* and **secondary** markets, *for trading in old securities.* They are also divided between **open markets,** *where buyers and sellers compete in a kind of auction market,* and **negotiated markets,** *where borrowers negotiate terms with lenders directly.* Markets are also divided into short term, for bank loans, Treasury bills, and other short-term securities, and long-term, for bonds, stocks, and mortgages. In the next section we will consider the organization and functions of short-term markets giving particular attention to the close linkages among the markets for different types of short-term securities. Then we will consider the long-term markets.

SHORT-TERM SECURITY MARKETS

In considering the organization of short-term markets we have to discuss the markets for short-term Treasury securities, commercial paper, bank certifi-

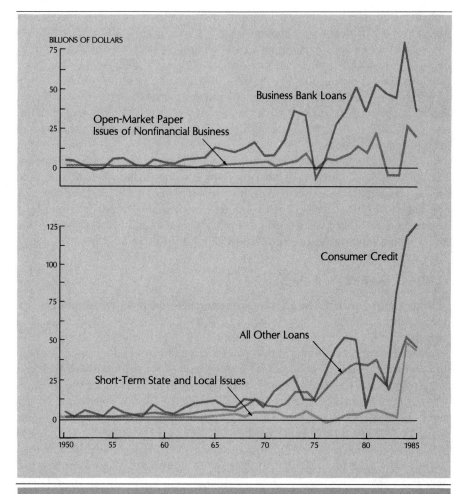

Figure 6.3   Short-Term Borrowing, Annually. Bank loans to business have provided a highly variable volume of funds. For households, consumer credit has fluctuated a great deal. **Source:** *Federal Reserve Chart Book,* 1986, p. 31.

cates of deposit, federal funds, and bank loans. Figure 6.3 shows the amounts of funds raised by the different kinds of short-term loans and security issues.

The secondary market for U.S. Treasury securities involves a volume of transactions far larger than the activity of the stock exchanges. The volume of transactions in Treasury bill and other short-term Treasury securities can reach $20 billion in a single day. Purchases and sales of existing government securities are usually made through government security dealers, some in banks, some affiliates with large brokerage houses. The dealers borrow from banks and buy an inventory of Treasury securities. At any time each dealer stands ready to offer to buy or sell government securities. Dealers make their profits from small spreads between their buying and selling prices. The dealer spread for transactions in Treasury bills is less than $500 for a $1-million trans-action. Usually they hold securities for only a brief time but because of the very large volume of activity their average inventory runs to above $5 billion.

Over the past twenty years the government bond dealers have done an increasing volume of business in repurchase agreements (repos). The dealer may sell a security to a corporate treasurer for a short period, perhaps one week, together with an agreement to buy the security back at a certain price. The difference in price is the equivalent of interest paid by the dealer for use of the corporation's funds. In effect, the dealer borrows from the corpora-tion, posting the securities as collateral. In 1985 some new small dealers went bankrupt when it was discovered that they had sold the same security to more than one buyer.

These cases caused serious losses to some banks. As a result, Congress began to consider legislation to regulate bond dealers.

Commercial Paper

Commercial paper is one of the oldest forms of business financing in the United States, dating back to the 1830s. The securities called commercial paper are *promissory notes of well-known corporations* that, unlike the promissory notes given for bank loans, may be bought and sold. Although it is an old form of financing, it has played a relatively small role in the credit markets until recent years. Much of the commercial paper is issued by finance companies.

Commercial paper is issued in two ways. Large issuers, particularly the "captive" finance companies of the automobile producers, such as the Gen-eral Motors Acceptance Corporation, have salesmen to sell commercial paper directly to banks and corporations. Smaller issuers sell their commercial paper to dealers, who in turn sell it to banks and corporations. A number of the gov-ernment bond dealers also act as dealers in commercial paper. There is also a resale or secondary market for commercial paper and the dealers who partici-pate in the issuance of new commercial paper buy "secondhand" commercial paper from banks and corporations and resell it to others.

Bank Certificates of Deposit

A third important component of the short-term securities markets is the mar-ket for **negotiable certificates of deposit** (CDs), the *transferable promissory notes issued by commercial banks*. These certificates are very similar to commercial paper except for the fact that they are issued by banks. Commercial banks generally sell their certificates of deposit directly without the assistance of dealers or brokers. A large proportion of the sales of certificates of deposits is made to their own customers, though large banks may also sell to investors. Each bank sets the rate on its own issues of certificates of deposits each day. Since the market is highly competitive, it must match the rates offered by competing banks. Corporations, state and local governments, or banks that wish to resell certificates of deposit before the maturity date do so using the network of dealers who also serve the Treasury bill and commercial-paper markets.

The market for federal funds is also an important component of the short-term securities markets. Since bank loans were discussed in Chapter 4, we need only note here that the market for bank loans is linked to the open short-term securities markets in three ways: banks obtain funds for loans from the open market by selling CDs and buying federal funds; they supply funds to the market by buying short-term assets; and they finance dealers in securities.

FUNCTIONS OF THE SHORT-TERM MARKET

The short-term markets perform three important functions. First, these markets make it possible for businesses and governments to finance their short-term deficits and invest their short-term surpluses quickly and cheaply. Second, the short-term markets serve to integrate the banking system so that the deposits of individual banks can in effect be pooled in a national credit market. Third, much of the adjustment to cyclical and seasonal changes in surpluses and deficits of businesses, governments, and households is made through the short-term market.

Each day thousands of businesses find that their receipts exceed their payments, while others find themselves in the reverse position. They can of course build up their bank deposits when they are running a temporary surplus and draw them down when the balance of receipts and payments swings the other way. But since demand deposits yield no explicit interest, corporate treasurers prefer to invest temporary surpluses in interest-bearing securities that can be sold when they need cash. To do that, they need securities that are safe and readily salable at low cost. Treasury bills, commercial paper, and negotiable certificates of deposit meet these requirements very satisfactorily. By trading in the secondary markets for these securities, corporations in effect pool their surpluses and deficits so that they cancel out, without recourse to the banking system or to the sale of securities to the general public. State and local governments also participate in this pooling of surpluses and deficits. Because of the timing of tax receipts many governmental units have surplus funds for a period after collection of taxes. They invest their surplus funds in Treasury bills and other short-term securities and sell them later on when their budget shows a seasonal deficit. Corporations and state and local governments also finance one another by buying securities issued by other corporations or state and local governments.

Corporations and state and local governments also finance one another indirectly using the commercial banking system as an intermediary. Businesses frequently borrow from banks to finance temporary deficits. The banks in turn obtain the funds by selling certificates of deposit to other corporations. The effect is the same as though one corporation had made a loan to another but the two corporations need never have any direct contact. The "lending corporation" obtains a lower rate of interest on the certificate of deposit that it buys than the bank obtains on the loan. The lending corporation, in effect, is paying the bank for its specialized services in evaluating the credit of the borrowing corporation and administering the loan.

The processes just outlined serve to cancel out many of the short-term surpluses and deficits of individual corporations and state and local governments. However, corporations usually run a net deficit and must borrow funds from the household sector. While a few wealthy households may buy commercial paper directly or buy short-term securities of local governments, most of the net short-term financing of both businesses and governments is obtained from the banking system, even though households may in some sense be the ultimate suppliers of the funds. Corporations usually borrow from banks with which they have a well-established relationship and state and local governments usually borrow their short-term funds from local banks.

Short-term credit markets serve to pool the funds of all banks so that banks whose deposit growth is large relative to their loan demands may supply funds to other banks in the reverse position. This adjustment takes place in several different ways. Banks faced with a particularly strong demand for loans may sell Treasury bills or commercial paper that was purchased at an earlier time when they had surplus funds. These securities may be bought by another bank that has greater deposit growth than loan demand. And if they are bought instead by a household or corporation, the buyer pays for them by writing a check on his or her bank, so that the funds are transferred between banks in an indirect way. Large banks, with strong loan demand, issue certificates of deposit and these may be bought by smaller banks with temporary surplus funds. To serve their large customers, banks may arrange for other banks to "participate" or share in large loans. Finally, banks with surplus funds may sell federal funds to banks who need funds. This interchange of short-term assets creates a national pool of funds so that customers of one bank can gain access to funds supplied by depositors in other banks that may be in different parts of the country. In the business-cycle upswing when businesses are borrowing heavily, large city banks will have the heaviest loan demand and will draw funds from suburban banks whose deposits are growing faster than loan demand.

Households obviously play an important role in the short-term market as suppliers of funds to commercial banks. They do not participate directly as borrowers in the open markets for short-term securities but they do obtain funds from the short-term market indirectly by borrowing funds from banks or finance companies. Households obtain large amounts of installment credit from banks and finance companies. Their demands for bank credit obviously compete with other demands for bank credit. In addition, finance companies obtain most of their funds either by borrowing from banks or by issuing their own commercial paper. Through banks and consumer finance companies, households are often important competitors for short-term funds. They supply funds through money-market funds as well as through banks.

The federal government is also an important participant in the short-term securities markets. The Treasury finances a large part of its deficits by sale of additional Treasury bills and other relatively short term securities. In addition, the federal financing agencies such as the Federal Home Loan Banks and Federal National Mortgage Association (FNMA) finance most of their operations by issuing short-term securities.

Balancing Cyclical Swings

As already noted, businesses finance cyclical variations in their deficits by increasing borrowing from banks and by reducing liquid asset accumulation when their expenditures rise above their receipts. They reduce their borrowing and acquire liquid assets in the opposite case. The federal government also adjusts to changes in the size of its deficit by varying the increase in its short-term debt. At times these changes are offsetting; the government deficit may increase while business deficits decrease. Businesses then buy Treasury bills and borrow little from banks while the Treasury sells its securities to businesses and banks. At other times businesses have heavy deficits while the Treasury deficit is small. There are times, however, when both businesses and governments have large deficits while households have unusually large surpluses. Much of the household surplus will be reflected in commercial bank deposits, which will be channeled into business loans or acquisition of Treasury securities.

    The swings in the deficits and surpluses of different sectors of the economy can be balanced off within the short-term securities markets a good part of the time. At times, however, there may be excess demand for short-term credit, which will have a significant effect on long-term mortgage and bond markets. We will discuss the interactions between long-term and short-term markets in the section on term structure. First, however, we need to discuss the operations of the short-term markets in more detail to see how the different submarkets are linked together.

Short-Term Interest-Rate Linkages

The markets for the different types of short-term credit are closely integrated. The interest rates in these markets move together because each class of market participants can choose to raise funds or supply funds in more than one way and can shift its asset portfolio or liability structure in response to changes in interest rates. A corporate treasurer needing funds to cover a short-term excess of payments over receipts can choose among selling the liquid assets (commercial paper, CDs, and Treasury bills) he holds, issuing new commercial paper, or borrowing from a bank.

    Differences in interest rates and other costs involved in raising funds from alternative sources will be considered in making the choice. Corporate treasurers faced with a short-term excess of receipts over payments may acquire commercial paper, bank CDs, or Treasury bills, or fail to renew bank loans or commercial paper already outstanding.

    If the interest rate on any one type of short-term credit tends to rise relative to other short-term rates, some treasurers will change their mode of adjustment to short-term cash-flow problems. A rise in Treasury-bill rates relative to commercial-paper rates will cause some treasurers to sell commercial paper rather than Treasury bills, while those with surplus funds will buy Treasury bills rather than commercial paper. Thus the amount of Treasury bills demanded will rise and the amount supplied will decrease while the reverse will be true for commercial paper. These adjustments will tend to hold the rates for different kinds of short-term credit together. Banks, of course, play a central role in these market adjustments since they deal in all forms of short-term credit and act as both borrowers and lenders. Small banks switch their liquid asset holdings between Treasury bills, commercial paper, CDs of large banks, and overnight federal-funds loans to large banks in response to rate changes. The large banks price their loans to business in relation to the cost of raising short-term funds and, of course, try to obtain funds in the cheapest market.

Since the different types of short-term credit are such close substitutes for both banks and corporations it is hardly surprising that the interest rates involved move together, as Figures 6.4 and 6.5 show.

Indeed it may seem surprising that the structure of short-term interest rates varies as much as it does. Treasury bills, commercial paper, and bank

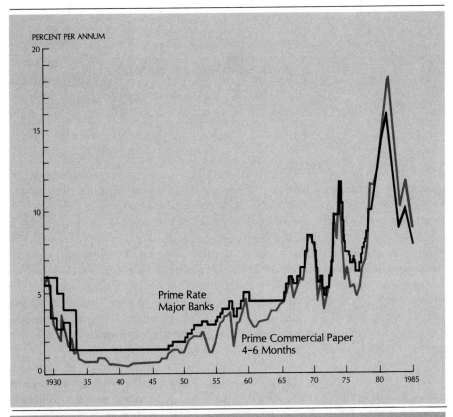

Figure 6.4   Short-Term Interest Rates: Business Borrowing. Short-term interest rates have moved closely together. **Source:** *Federal Reserve Chart Book, 1986, p. 72.*

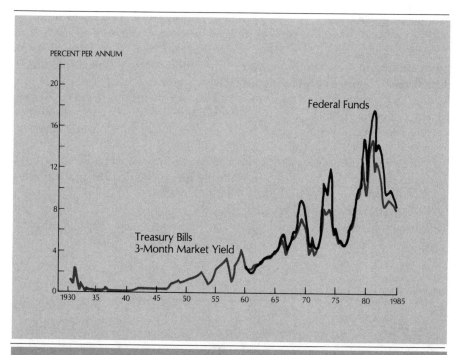

Figure 6.5   Short-Term Interest Rates: Money Market Discount Rate, Effective Date of Change; All Others, Quarterly Averages. The federal-funds rate is more volatile than the Treasury-bill rate. The discount rate is sluggish. **Source:** *Federal Reserve Chart Book,* 1986, p. 72.

CDs appear to be very similar instruments. They all run for short periods, can be sold before maturity, and are issued by borrowers with high credit ratings. From the standpoint of the buyers they differ in two respects: their risk, or more accurately the trouble of avoiding risk, and their marketability, the cost and speed with which they can be resold.

Treasury bills usually carry a slightly lower interest rate than other short-term securities because of their ready marketability and greater safety. Because the outstanding volume is so large and because they are so widely held there is an active and continuous market for Treasury bills. Dealers are prepared to buy or sell Treasury bills in amounts as large as $50 million on a moment's notice at a very low charge. Other short-term securities can be sold in the secondary market, but it may take longer and cost more.

Treasury bills, of course, are regarded as completely riskless while there is always at least a bit of risk of repayment problems for commercial paper, even that issued by the largest and best-known corporations, or for the CDs of even the largest banks. Some banks and corporations buy commercial paper or CDs to earn a very slight differential in interest rate over the Treasury bill rate. Others are more risk averse and will prefer Treasury bills unless the rate spread is much larger.

The differential between the yields on Treasury and other securities may vary for two reasons. First, concern over risk varies; for example, after Penn Central went bankrupt, many commercial-paper buyers became concerned over risk, and commercial-paper rates rose relative to Treasury bill rates. Second, the distribution of liquid asset holdings varies so that sometimes the more risk-averse asset buyers become relatively more important and the spread between bills and short-term securities widens. For example, at times foreign countries buy up a large amount of U.S. dollars to keep the dollar from falling relative to their own currencies. They tend to use these dollars to buy Treasury bills rather than CDs or commercial paper, and this has sometimes lowered—as in 1978 and 1979—the Treasury bill rate relative to other short-term rates. Thus, as a first approximation, all types of short-term credit can be regarded as nearly homogeneous substitutes with rates moving together in the major swings in credit conditions. But from day to day and week to week special factors affecting different short-term credit markets can cause significant differences in the spreads among rates.

LONG-TERM MARKETS

The long-term capital markets provide financing for home buyers and for commercial building through the mortgage market. They finance schools, hospitals, and other public facilities through the municipal bond market. Corporations seeking permanent financing turn to the markets for corporate stock and bonds. Foreign corporations and governments also sell substantial amounts of securities in the U.S. long-term capital markets. Finally, the U.S. Treasury and various federal credit agencies sell long-term bonds and their securities are widely held and actively traded. Figure 6.6 shows the amounts of long-term funds raised in the capital markets.

The securities issued and traded in the long-term markets are far less homogeneous than short-term securities, and the markets in which they are issued and traded reflect the differences among long-term securities.

Bond Markets

Investment banking firms specialize in issuing long-term corporate, municipal, and foreign bonds as well as common stock. A corporation proposing to sell securities arranges with an investment banking firm to underwrite the securities. The investment banking firm undertakes to buy the entire issue at an agreed-upon price. It then sells the issue piecemeal to life insurance companies and pension funds in the case of foreign and corporate bonds, or to banks, marine, fire, and casualty companies, or to wealthy individuals in the case of municipal bonds. If the issue is a large one, the investment banking firm may form an ad hoc group called a syndicate, joining with other investment banking firms and brokerage houses to share the risk. The syndicate tries to sell the bonds at a price a little above the buying price. If they have guessed the market correctly, they sell out the issue quickly and make money. When they misjudge the market they may have to sell part of the issue at a loss.

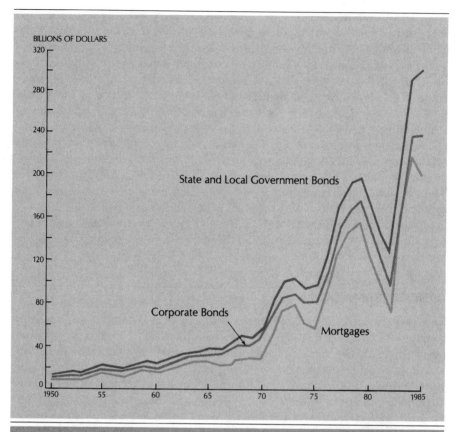

Figure 6.6 Long-Term Borrowing. Mortgage borrowing has dominated the market for long-term funds. **Source:** *Federal Reserve Chart Book,* 1986.

To protect investors, the Securities and Exchange Commission (SEC) requires that a corporation provide much information when it sells a large bond issue. Providing this information and meeting all the required government regulations are expensive. Some corporations sell a whole bond issue directly to insurance companies or pension funds at a negotiated price. These sales are called **private placements.** By using this method the seller avoids paying the underwriter's profit and the cost of SEC registration for a public issue.

Competitive bidding is usually required by law for the bond issues of state and local governments and public utilities. Competition among investment banking firms and brokerage houses for these issues is very sharp. Sometimes the interest rates offered differ only in the fourth decimal place. Competitive bidding is, of course, inconsistent with private placements.

The secondary markets for corporate and municipal bonds are limited. Most issues are held to maturity. There is some trading in old bonds on the New York Stock Exchange, and financial institutions sometimes trade bonds privately. Municipal bonds may be resold through brokers but the market is poorly organized because there are so many relatively small issues outstanding.

The Stock Market

In the bond markets the volume of new issues is large relative to the amount of secondary trading. The reverse is true of the markets for common stocks. Daily trading on the stock exchanges can exceed $5 billion, while new common-stock issues run to only a few billion dollars per year. Indeed, in some years, the value of stock retirements (when companies buy back their own stock) has exceeded the value of new issues. The importance of the stock market cannot be judged by the volume of funds raised through stock issues. Though most corporations obtain equity capital by the retention of earnings, the opportunity to raise equity capital may be vitally important to a limited number of rapidly growing firms. Without the opportunity to sell equities they would have to sell out to some larger firm. The survival of independent, growing firms strengthens the competitive process.

Moreover, the stock market values the performance of managements and exerts pressure for efficiency and innovation. When a firm's management does not appear to be exploiting the opportunities available to it, the company's stock will be priced at a level that encourages a takeover bid by another firm.

Finally, the stock market provides capital indirectly. Stockholders are willing to forgo dividends so that firms can retain earnings and reinvest. The stockholders hope that successful investment of retained earnings will produce higher earnings with increased dividends later on, and ultimately a higher price for the stock. They are prepared to forgo dividends in the hope of a capital gain. An active stock market makes it possible for investors to realize their capital gains at any time by selling some of their stock. If it were not for the fact that the stock markets permit investors to sell their stocks, many of them would not be so willing to hold as much stock as they now do.

New common-stock issues are usually sold through underwriters as in the case of bonds. Secondary trading in existing stocks is carried on through the New York Stock Exchange, the American Stock Exchange, and several regional exchanges. The shares of smaller unlisted corporations are traded through brokers in the so-called over-the-counter (OTC) market.

Residential Mortgage Markets

In many ways the residential mortgage market is the most complex of all the credit markets. It is by far the largest of the long-term credit markets. The annual net increase in mortgage debt exceeds $100 billion in most years and the gross flow of mortgage credit is still larger, sometimes reaching $200 billion. The market for mortgages on single-family homes is almost necessarily a retail market in which millions of families arrange for mortgages with several thousand commercial banks, mutual savings banks, savings and loan associations, and other lenders. Although mortgage contracts are fairly well standardized, lenders must evaluate each property separately to be sure that its value exceeds the amount of the mortgage. Since foreclosures are expensive, lenders also want to know about the financial position of the borrower to assure themselves that the required payments will be made.

Most of the mortgage financing for the purchasing of existing homes is provided by local financial institutions—commercial banks, mutual savings banks, and savings and loans. Those institutions also provide the financing for single homes built for the owner or by small building firms. Mortgage financing for large tract developments and for apartment buildings can be obtained from a wider range of sources. Insurance companies provide mortgage credit for some large apartment projects. In the West and South, mortgage "banks" act as intermediaries between distant financial institutions and local builders of tract developments and apartments. These firms—not really banks at all—arrange mortgages on properties meeting the specifications of the lender, collect payments, and do all the legal work for a fee. Their operation has helped to make a national mortgage market.

Savings and loans, mutual savings banks, commercial banks, and, to a lesser extent, insurance companies provide most of the funds for home financing. However, the Federal Home Loan Bank Board (FHLBB) and the Federal National Mortgage Association (FNMA) also play an important role in the mortgage market. FHLBB sells bonds in a national security market and lends to savings and loan associations, which in turn lend to local mortgage borrowers. FNMA, originally a federal agency and now a private corporation, also sells its securities in the national market and then buys mortgages from financial institutions.

Another federal agency, the Government National Mortgage Association (GNMA), guarantees securities backed by federally insured mortgages. These securities are issued by thrift institutions, which originate the underlying mortgages, and are sold to pension funds, insurance companies, and individual investors.

These institutions provide a source of mortgage funds not dependent on the flow of deposits to banks and thrift institutions. Thus, in spite of the local character of mortgage markets, funds may be drawn from any part of the country to any other area. After many years of evolution a unified national mortgage market has developed.

VALUATION IN LONG-TERM MARKETS

An important distinction between long-term and short-term capital markets is the types of risks involved. An investor who buys a short-term security has to worry only about the credit-worthiness of the borrower. If the borrower remains solvent the lender will receive a fixed payment in a few months. Long-term lenders too have to worry about credit risk. In fact, they have to worry more because there is more time for a change in the borrower's fortunes before repayment is due. But long-term lenders have an additional risk.

For one reason or another a long-term investor may want to sell the bonds before they mature. Even if the borrower's credit standing remains good, the price of bonds can fall before they mature if the interest rates have risen since they were issued.

Valuing Bonds

For example, a $1,000 Treasury bond due in 1998 with a 3½ percent annual interest payment sold for $851 in 1983. The fall in price was not due to a deterioration in the Treasury's credit standing but to the general rise in interest rates. In 1983 new long-term bonds with $1,000 maturity value could be bought at $1,000 with an annual interest payment of 10½ percent. No one will pay $1,000 for a bond promising $35 each year in interest payment plus repayment of principal in twenty years when he or she can get an annual interest payment of $105 and repayment of principal at the same date. Obviously, the old bonds with the low interest payment must sell for less than $1,000. To find out how much less, we use the present-value approach to valuing contracts for future payments.

Start from the proposition that the promise—even if guaranteed—of $1.00 in the future is always worth less than $1.00 in hand now. The reason is that money in hand now can be invested at interest. If I invest $1.00 now at 7 percent, I will have 1.07 dollars in a year. Conversely, if I want $1.00 a year from now, I can invest $1.00/1.07 or $.934 and get $1.00 in a year. If you promise $1.00 in one year I will give you only 93¢ now for your promise, even if I have absolute faith in your honesty and ability to pay. $1.00/1.07 = .934 is called the present value of $1.00 discounted at 7 percent for one year. What about the value of $1.00 to be paid in two years? One dollar invested for the first year produces $1.07; the whole $1.07 can be invested for the second year at 7 percent, and principal and interest at the end of the second year will be worth $1.07 × 1.07 or $1.145. To get $1.00 in two years, invest $1.00/1.145 or $.873. This is the present value of $1.00 discounted at 7 percent for two years.

Following the same procedure the present value of $1.00 discounted at 7 percent for twenty years is $1.00 divided by 1.07^{20} or $2.58. In general, the present value of $1.00 discounted at any interest for any number of years is $1.00/[(1 + r)^n]$, where r is the interest rate and n is the number of years. Notice how small the present value has become when discounted for a period as long as twenty years. That is because the denominator in the calculations reflects the compounding of interest and grows rapidly as the time period increases. The curve marked 7 percent in Figure 6.7 shows how present value declines with the increase in numbers of years of discounting. Of course, the rate of decline of present value also depends on the interest rate used. At 5 percent the numbers in the denominators of present-value calculations are always smaller (present value larger) than at 7 percent. The curve marked 5 percent in Figure 6.7 illustrates the difference.

To value a bond we have to calculate separately the present value of each of the interest payments and the present value of the final repayment of prin-

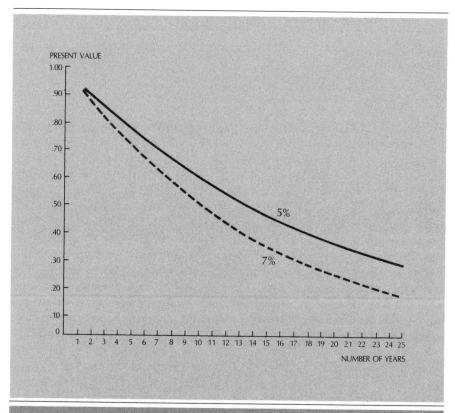

PRESENT VALUE

NUMBER OF YEARS

Figure 6.7   Present Value of One Dollar. Even at moderate interest rates, such as 5 or 7 percent, the present value of a dollar *n* years from now declines sharply as *n* increases.

cipal and then add them up. Because the present value of payments due in the distant future is more sensitive to interest-rate changes than payments due in the relatively near future, the prices of long-term bonds will fluctuate much more in response to interest-rate changes than will the prices of shorter-term bonds.

Valuing Common Stocks

Bond valuations are based on more or less secure promises of future payment of interest and principal. Equity investors, on the other hand, often appear to show little concern for dividends. They seem to be a lot more interested in the prospective change in the price of the stock than in the current dividend. The day-to-day gyrations of the market are hard to understand. Commentators can always explain what happened yesterday but are not very good at predicting tomorrow. The only really safe prediction of stock market behavior is the one made many years ago by J. P. Morgan. When asked what the market would do, he said, "It will fluctuate." Nonetheless, the underlying basis of stock prices is the same as that of bond prices. The value of a stock depends upon the present value of the payments that the actual or prospective stockholders expect to receive.

Lots of people buy stocks that have never paid a dividend. Small, growing companies may reinvest all their earnings. Investors expect that earnings will continue to grow and that eventually the company will start to pay dividends. Other companies have losses but are expected to "turn around" under new management or because they have a new product line. Some firms limp along barely surviving for years. The value placed on their stock may have the same explanation as Samuel Johnson's description of second marriages: "the triumph of hope over experience." But in most cases stocks are valuable because there are good reasons for believing that they will pay dividends in the future. When everyone becomes convinced that there will never be any dividend payments, a stock becomes worthless.

The so-called investment value of a stock is the present value of the expected future dividends. One may imagine a company that is expected to pay a fixed dividend for an indefinite period. In that case the stock will be valued in the same way as a perpetual bond. A perpetual bond promises interest payments "forever" with no principal payment. The value of a perpetuity of $1 discounted at 5 percent is $20. It takes a capital sum of $20 to generate interest of $1 per year. In the case of a stock we would expect discount rates to be relatively high because future dividend payments can never be certain.

A steady dividend is unusual in a growing economy. A typical company usually hopes to grow and increase its earnings over time by reinvesting part of its profits. Consider, for example, a company currently earning $2.00 per share after taxes and paying a $1.00 dividend. The company reinvests $1.00, and expects to earn 10 percent after taxes on its reinvested profits. Earnings will grow at 5 percent per year and, if the company always pays out half its earnings, dividends will also grow at 5 percent. We now have to value a growing stream of earnings. To do so, we apply the present-value method as in the case of bonds. The prospective stream of dividends is $1.05, $1.05^2, and so on, in successive years. Discounting this stream of dividends at r percent per year, we have:

$$\text{Present value} = \frac{1.05}{1+r} + \left(\frac{1.05}{1+r}\right)^2 + \ldots$$

This is equivalent to present value $= 1/(r - .05)$. If, for example, r is 10 percent, present value is $1/(.10 - .05)$, or 20 times dividends or 10 times earnings. The price-earnings ratio increases with the prospective growth rate and decreases with the discount rate applied to future earnings.

More complicated cases arise for companies expected to grow unusually rapidly for a time, and then settle down to a more ordinary rate of growth. There are tables that give present values for two-stage growth paths. They show that an expectation of unusually high earnings growth for a period of ten years or so will justify very high ratios of price to current earnings. That is the explanation of the high price-earnings ratio of "growth stocks."

The theory of investment value has a perfectly sensible logic, but its application rests on a number of assumptions about the future. To calculate investment value one must assume a future earning stream and apply a discount rate. Any student of the stock market knows that earnings for next year are hard to predict, let alone the growth paths for earnings years ahead. The price of a stock can suddenly rise or fall in response to information leading to a revaluation of earnings prospects. Moreover, discount factors can change. They will be influenced by competing long-term bond yields, but they can be influenced even more by changes in confidence or lack of it about the future of the economy or of the particular company.

On the whole the stock market reacts quickly to new information relevant to the values of stocks. Many investors are ill-informed or inactive, but studies of stock-price movements show that the active, well-informed investors cause prices to reflect any available information about the values of stocks. One might think that if a stock has been rising for some time it is likely to continue to rise and is therefore a good buy. But this is not so. Investors have bid up its price to a level so high that the stock is just as likely to fall as to rise from then on. It is impossible to "beat the market" unless one has information that others lack, or luck.

Inflation and Common-Stock Prices

It used to be thought that common stocks were a good hedge against inflation. An all-around rise in prices, wages, and other costs should raise dollar earnings in proportion to prices and leave the real value of earnings and stock prices unchanged. In fact, when inflation comes as a surprise, companies with substantial outstanding long-term debt should gain. Earnings before interest should rise in proportion to prices, and contract interest remains the same, so earnings after interest should increase relative to prices.

The response of stock prices to a fully anticipated, but not yet realized, inflation depends on the accompanying change in interest rates. Anticipated inflation will raise the projected growth of nominal earnings, but it will also raise interest rates. If the increase in interest rates exactly balances the anticipated increase in prices, the increase in the numerator in the present-value calculation is canceled out by the increase in the denominator. In general, we do expect interest rates to rise with anticipated inflation, but the change in interest rates need not be exactly the same as the change in the expected rate of price increase. In fact, as almost everyone knows by now, common stocks have been a poor hedge against inflation in the last decade. In the period 1966–1982, stock prices rose at an average annual rate of about 3.0 percent, while the consumer price index rose at a rate of 6.2 percent. After taxes, corporate earnings have not kept up with prices. The tax system has worked against them. In calculating profits, many firms value the cost of materials drawn from inventory at the prices they originally paid for them, rather than at the replacement costs. These corporations earn paper profits in the rise in the value of materials. The profits are not real since the materials drawn from inventory must be replaced at higher prices. Nonetheless, they have to pay taxes on those paper profits. In the same way depreciation on fixed capital is based on historical rather than replacement costs. Hence, the tax code does not allow firms to subtract from their taxable income a sufficient and realistic amount for depreciation. Their taxable income is therefore overstated, they have to pay more taxes, and this reduces the after-tax profits that are available for stockholders. In addition, during inflations, the stock market's evaluation of earnings is adversely affected by investor fears that efforts to fight inflation will lead to a recession or price control.

SPECIALIZATION AND COMPETITION IN LONG-TERM CAPITAL MARKETS

The markets for long-term debt are linked together but the different kinds of long-term debt are not such close substitutes as the short-term securities. Each type of long-term security has special features that make it more attractive to some groups of investors than others. The interest on most municipal bonds is exempt from federal income taxes. Individuals and fully taxed corporations including banks will buy them at substantially lower yields than taxable corporate bonds. The tax advantage is much less significant to insurance companies, mutual savings banks, and savings and loan associations, which do not pay the regular corporate income-tax rate.

Mortgages are less attractive to most investors than corporate bonds because there are significant costs associated with acquiring and servicing them. The costs of collecting payments and making sure that taxes and insurance payments are kept up is considerably higher per dollar invested than the cost of managing a corporate bond portfolio. In addition, the lenders cannot invest safely without acquiring considerable expertise in the local real-estate market involved. Those negative considerations are more important to some investors than others. Savings and loan associations have to invest in mortgages because of restrictions on their investments. Savings and loan associations, mutual savings banks, and commercial banks with suburban branches can acquire and maintain information on residential markets more cheaply than other investors. Moreover, depository institutions expect to gain deposits by making mortgage loans to local customers.

Institutional participation in the stock market is limited. Pension funds and marine, fire, and casualty companies together own about 15 percent of the common stocks. But most stocks are owned by individuals either directly or through mutual funds or bank trust departments. As noted earlier, corporate bonds are mainly held by life insurance companies and mutual savings banks.

Since each type of lender specializes in a limited range of securities, the long-term market appears to be partially segmented into a number of separate compartments. The supply of funds to the different kinds of lenders follows a pattern unrelated to shifts in the offerings of different kinds of securities. If the long-term markets were completely separate from one another, supply and demand for each type of security would have to be balanced separately in each segment of the market. It would then be possible for interest rates in the different markets to move independently of one another.

In fact, however, the compartments in the security markets are far from watertight. Most lenders participate in more than one market. Their choices among the different securities help to link markets together directly. Insurance companies, for example, operate in both the commercial mortgage market and the corporate bond market. A rise in the supply of corporate bonds will first push up corporate bond yields and then induce insurance companies to buy more corporate bonds and less commercial mortgages. Commercial mortgage rates will then be pulled up, so that they move with the corporate bond yield. There are several of these competing portfolio pairs: corporate bonds versus home mortgages for savings banks, mortgages versus municipal bonds for commercial banks, common stocks versus corporate bonds for pension and endowment funds, and common stocks versus municipals for wealthy individuals.

In addition, all the markets are linked to the market for long-term U.S. securities. Almost all institutional investors hold substantial amounts of longer-term U.S. securities. A rise in the yield of any one type of asset will cause lenders specializing in that asset to sell U.S. securities so as to buy the asset in question. The resulting rise in yields on U.S. securities will cause lenders specializing in other assets to try to sell them in order to buy U.S. securities. This shift will pull up the yields of those assets so that all the yields will move up together.

In spite of the specialization of financial institutions and the apparent segmentation of long-term security markets, the bond markets appear to function reasonably well. Yields on different types of securities do move together (see Figure 6.8). The differences in yields appear on the whole to reflect differences in taxes, risk, and costs of placement and servicing of different kinds of securities in a fairly rational way. This reflects the fact that various markets can be tied together so long as a sufficient number of participants on the margin move readily from one market to another in response to interest-rate changes. As usual in economics, the action is at the margin.

However, the linkages among the long-term markets are not nearly so tight as in the short-term markets. The spread between municipal and corporate bond yields varies considerably because of the wide variation in commercial bank demand for municipals. When demand for bank loans is growing more rapidly than deposits, commercial banks often sharply reduce their purchases of municipal bonds. More bonds must be sold to individuals. The yield of municipal bonds will have to rise sharply relative to the yields of other assets. When commercial banks have rapid deposit growth they return to the municipal market and yields of state and local bonds fall relative to others. The differential tax treatment of competing investors is ultimately responsible for the shifts in the relative yields of municipals.

You will notice that the two problem areas—the municipal and mortgage markets—are ones in which the long-term market is affected by activity in the short-term market. Variations in demand for short-term bank loans are responsible for variations in bank demand for municipal bonds. Variations in short-term interest rates are primarily responsible for variations in the flow of

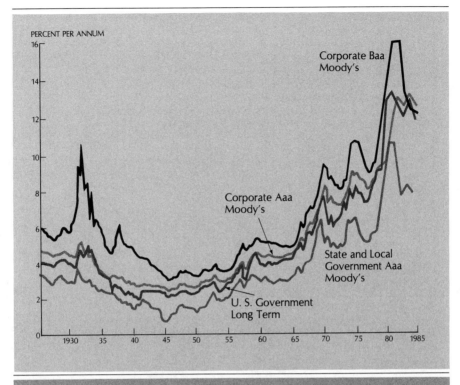

PERCENT PER ANNUM

Corporate Baa
Moody's

Corporate Aaa
Moody's

State and Local
Government Aaa
Moody's

U. S. Government
Long Term

Figure 6.8   Long-Term Bond Yields. Long-term bond yields have generally moved closely together. Their relative levels depend on riskiness and tax treatment. **Source:** *Federal Reserve Chart Book,*1982, p. 97.

funds to thrift institutions and thereby for shifts in demand for mortgages. These are obvious cases, but there are other more pervasive links between the movements of short-term interest rates and those of long-term rates. This rather tricky and controversial subject is considered in the next section.

TERM STRUCTURE

We have seen that the yields on different types of short-term securities all move together, though with some variations in the spreads among the rates on different short-term assets. We have also seen that rates on all the different kinds of long-term securities show similar patterns but with wider variations in the spreads among different rates. In both cases the rates are held together because security buyers are willing to substitute one kind of security for another in response to changes in the relative yields. Sellers will also change their methods of financing if one source of funds appears to be cheaper than another. The same thing applies to the relation between yields on short-term securities and yields on long-term securities. Figure 6.9 shows the rates on short-term commercial paper and the rates on long-term corporate bonds. If

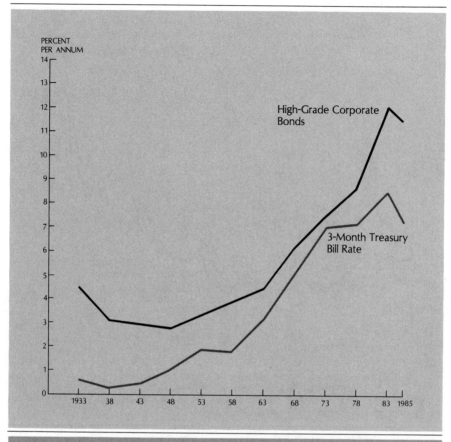

Figure 6.9 Long- and Short-Term Interest Rates. Short-term interest rates are much more volatile than long-term rates. Note: High-grade corporate bond rate is Moody's Aaa rate. **Source:** *Economic Report of the President,*1986, p. 332.

you examine it closely you will note that both rates usually move up and down at the same time; they show common trends, and the short rates move up and down much more than the long rates. The short rates in the period were usually below the long rates but occasionally short rates rose above the long rates.

Figure 6.9 shows rates for two kinds of securities: a Treasury bill maturing in three months and corporate bonds maturing in twenty years. At any one time there are securities available maturing at a variety of dates from one day to thirty years or more ahead. Figure 6.10 shows actual yields on Treasury securities. The yield is shown on the vertical axis. The horizontal axis shows the number of years to maturity. The rising yield curve is typical of recession periods, when investors think that short-term yields are abnormally low. As we'll see later, the yield curve will slope downward at times when investors

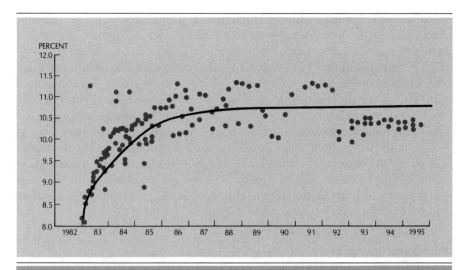

PERCENT

Figure 6.10 **Yields of Treasury Securities, 28 June 1985.** Source: *Federal Reserve Chart Book,*1986, p. 2.

think that yields are abnormally high. Changes in yield curves reflect the investment decisions of investors in the financial markets as well as the decisions of security issuers.

Though some investors, like insurance companies, tend to specialize in longer-term securities, they are not locked into any rigid investment pattern. An insurance company can put investment funds received from premiums and from repayments of maturing bonds into short-term securities, if their yields appear sufficiently attractive. A bank will shift toward longer-term securities if their yields look better than those on short-term assets. In this respect, long- and short-term securities are linked together in the same way as different kinds of securities of the same maturity.

The linkage is a good deal more complex than in the case of competing securities of the same maturity. It involves two kinds of elements. First, as in other cases in which investors specialize in certain kinds of securities, the relative yield of long- and short-term securities may be influenced by the relative amounts of those securities outstanding, and by the distribution of financial resources as between those institutions specializing in long-term securities and those specializing in short-term ones. There is some controversy over the importance of this consideration.

Second, yield curves are clearly influenced by expectations about the future of interest rates. A buyer choosing between Treasury bills and commercial paper is choosing between two investments running for the same length of time. A buyer choosing between a bond and a one-year Treasury bill is choosing between an investment running for a year and another running for twenty years. To compare them he or she has to guess what future interest rates will be when the Treasury bill matures. The comparison depends very heavily on the investor's expectations about the future. It follows that yield curves will be influenced by the way investors form their expectations about future movements of interest rates.

Some economists take the view that only expectational factors are important in determining yield curves. In the next section we will show how yield curves are determined when only "permanent investors," who want to hold bonds to maturity, are in the market. In the following section we will show how the same approach applies to investors who may wish to sell bonds before maturity. In both cases we assume that expectations about the future are given. We must then consider briefly how investors form expectations about future rate movements. Finally, we have to examine how the maturity distribution of outstanding bonds and the resources of different kinds of financial institutions influence yield curves.

Permanent Investors

The importance of expectations in determining the shape of the yield curve can be shown by a simple example. An investor with funds available for two years can purchase a one-year bond now and use the proceeds (including interest) to buy another one-year bond a year from now or he or she can purchase a two-year bond now.

To make a wise choice three things should be known: the yield on two-year bonds now; the yield on one-year bonds now; and the yield on the one-year bonds that will be available a year from now. The first two figures are found in the newspaper, but the third involves a guess, and this guess may be the crucial element in the decision. Suppose, for example, that one-year bonds now yield 4 percent, but our investor thinks that short-term interest rates are going to rise to 6 percent in the coming year. In that case $1.00 invested in two successive one-year investments will produce $1.04 \times $1.06 at the end of two years. (One dollar invested now produces $1.04 at 4 percent in one year, $1.04 invested for the second year at 6 percent produces 1.04 times 1.06 dollars.) What yield is required to make a single two-year investment equally attractive? If the yield on two-year bonds is r percent per year the investor will have $\$(1 + r)^2$ at the end of two years, so $(1 + r)^2$ must equal $\$(1.04)(1.06)$. It turns out that $r = 5$ percent will be close to right. Exactly the same argument holds if we consider a three-year bond versus three successive one-year investments, or for that matter a twenty-year bond versus twenty successive one-year investments.

The following example will show how yield curves are related to the pattern of expected future interest rates. The economy is in a recession. The current rate on one-year securities is 4 percent, but investors foresee a vigorous recovery with rising rates. They expect the rate on one-year securities to rise to 5 percent in a year with a continued rise to 6 percent a year later and to 7 percent in another year at the peak of the boom. Thereafter, their foresight runs out, but investors expect that the boom will peter out and that rates on one-year securities will then fluctuate between 5 percent and 7 percent with an average of 6 percent. Accordingly, the yield on a one-year security will be 4 percent, and on a two-year security it will be about 4.5 percent. Yields will gradually rise toward 6 percent as the maturity increases.

Holding-Period Yields

The expectations theory outlined above assumes that investors intend to commit themselves for some considerable length of time. If they buy long-term securities they plan to hold them to maturity. If they buy short-term securities they plan to keep reinvesting in short-term securities. Some investors, like insurance companies, *do* plan to hold the securities they buy, but others may consider buying long-term securities even though they only want to hold them for a year. Or they may consider buying long-term securities to hold for a year and then reconsider whether to sell them or to continue holding them. Those investors are not directly interested in average yields over a long period. They are concerned with comparing the yield on one-year securities with the yield on long-term securities over a holding period of, say, a year.

If security prices stayed the same, the holding-period yield on a one-year investment would simply be the annual interest payment divided by the price. A bond paying $6 per year and selling for $100 is said to have a "coupon" yield of 6 percent because a set of dated coupons each redeemable for $6 is attached to the bond.

The one-year holding-period yield will exceed or fall short of the coupon yield by the percentage change in price during the year; for example, if the bond with the 6 percent coupon were purchased for $95 at the start of the year and sold for $97 at the end, the holding-period yield would be 6.32 percent plus 2/95 or 8.42 percent. If it sold for $93, the holding-period yield would be 6.32 percent minus 2/95 or 4.22 percent.

Any investor who buys a bond maturing in more than one year wants to obtain a first-year holding-period yield at least equal to the yield on a one-year bond. That requirement is closely related to the requirement that the yield on a long-term bond should depend on the expected short yield in future years. Go back now to our first example of a choice between a two-year bond and two successive one-year investments. We assumed there that the initial one-year rate was 4 percent, and the expected one-year rate a year hence 6 percent. The equivalent average yield for a two-year bond is approximately 5 percent. Suppose a two-year bond is issued at $100 with a $5 annual coupon interest payment. What will its price be a year hence? In the second year it must yield 6 percent, but it pays only a $5 coupon. Its price at the end of the first year, and start of the second year, must be $99 to produce a 6 percent holding-period yield—5 percent coupon yield, 1 percent gain in price from 99 to the maturity price of 100. For the first year the holding-period yield will be 4 percent—a 5 percent coupon yield less a 1 percent capital loss. In each period the holding-period yield equals the one-year yield. This kind of calculation can be extended to any number of years in the future.

Thus for any given set of expectations about future short-term yields, investors will accept the same bond yield whether they plan to hold the bond for one year or until maturity.

Expectations and Timing

The holding-period yield on a security is clearly the yield that is relevant to the decisions of a speculator considering whether to hold bonds for a short period, but it is also important to other investors. Speculators play a relatively small role in bond markets. The bond markets are dominated by issuers who will sooner or later need long-term financing, and by institutional buyers who normally invest most of their assets in long-term securities. However, the holding-period yield is relevant to the timing of bond issues and bond purchases. An insurance company may plan to keep most of its assets in long-term investments, but it can hold short-term securities when its investment managers expect the holding-period yield on bonds to be lower than the current short-term yields. They can invest in short-term securities until the holding-period comparison becomes more favorable to bonds. In the same way, corporate treasurers may borrow short-term funds while planning to refinance by a bond issue. For example, a corporation buying a new factory has the option to finance it initially by issuing short-term security, and later on when those securities become due, to redeem them by issuing long-term bonds. The question is whether to bring out the issue now or wait until next year. If the holding-period yield on bonds is below the current short-term yield, now is the time to make the issue; otherwise it is better to wait.

The effect of these considerations is to move the holding-period yield for bonds toward equality with the current short-term yield. If everyone thinks the holding-period yield on bonds is below the current short-term yield, borrowers will tend to issue more bonds, investors will hold back on purchases, and bond prices will have to fall enough to raise the holding-period yield to equality with the short-term yield.

So far we have been concerned with the arithmetical relationship between yields and prices of long-term securities and expectations about future yields on short-term securities. In our examples we have supposed that we know what investors expect to happen. That provides only half a theory of yield curves. The other half of the explanation depends on the theory of how investors form their guesses about the future. Two kinds of considerations enter into the formation of expectations. First, investors may try to judge the future of interest rates from their past history. Second, investors try to understand the economy and use their information to deduce in a logical or "rational" way how interest rates will move in the future.

Many investors lack confidence in their ability to make a very accurate analysis of the future path of interest rates. Nonetheless, they have to make decisions and they may therefore be forced to assume that the future will be like the past. The simplest forecast of short-term interest rates is to assume that they will stay where they are. However, short-term interest rates jump around from day to day and week to week. Most investors will think that they can improve their forecast by using an average of rates for a few months back to iron out the random fluctuations. Moreover, they know that there are business fluctuations so that rates move up and down cyclically. They do not want to assume short-term rates will stay at the peak level or at the trough level. A more reasonable assumption is to suppose that future rates will tend to equal the average of past rates over three or four years. If current rates are above the average of the past few years, investors then expect them to fall back to normal; if current rates are below the average of the past few years, investors expect them to rise toward normal. If investors form their expectations in that way, long-term yields will show common cyclical fluctuations. But long rates will show cycles with a much smaller amplitude than short rates. Long and short rates will show similar trends since the "normal" rate is gradually adjusted upward in response to a rising trend in short rates.

Rational Expectations

Most investors try very hard to use all available sources of information. They make or buy forecasts of the economic outlook and try to anticipate changes in fiscal and monetary policy. Instead of basing their forecasts on mechanical or arithmetical projections based on the past history of rates they try to form rational expectations that take into account all the information available that might help them to forecast. The theory of rational expectations is still a matter of controversy and its implications have been fully worked out only for cases where investors are assumed to believe in a fairly simple model of the economic world.

However, it does have important implications that can help us to understand how security markets work. First, the rational-expectations theory implies that at any one time investors have already made full use of all the information available at the time. It is sometimes thought that information percolates through the market gradually. If something happens to increase the value of a security, the "smart money" finds out first and acts to drive up prices; other investors catch on a little later and push prices up some more until the new information is fully reflected in security prices. That does not seem to happen. There is enough "smart money" so that the entire price rise implied by any event occurs very quickly. In particular, if short rates rise, perhaps because the Federal Reserve has changed its monetary policy, or because business investment is picking up, and there is a reason for thinking that the new level of rates will persist, long-term yields will respond at once, not gradually as implied by the backward-looking approach outlined earlier. Second, the rational-expectations theory has important implications about the way security markets respond to policy actions. If the central bank follows any regular pattern in guiding short-term interest rates the market will take that pattern into account. Suppose, for example, that the Fed always pushes down short rates in a recession and gets them back up in a recovery. When a recovery occurs the market will act to bid up yields even before the Fed has done anything. But the extent of the rise in long-term yields will be limited by the expectations that short-term yields will be high for only a short time. The expected action of the Fed is built into the security prices. Some further implications of the rational-expectations approach are discussed in subsequent chapters.

Inflation and Term Structure

The theory of rational expectations can be applied directly to the relationship between expectations of inflation and the structure of interest rates. We have yet to discuss the determination of the absolute level of short-term interest rates, but we are giving away no secrets by asserting that experience shows that a high rate of inflation is generally accompanied by high interest rates. It follows that when investors anticipate an acceleration in the rate of inflation they expect that all interest rates will rise sooner or later. Investors may believe that inflation will accelerate for any of a variety of reasons—for example, an expansion of government expenditures or a rapid growth in the money supply. Whatever the reason, they will respond by holding back on bond purchases until rates have risen to a level consistent with their expectations about inflation. If they are right, short-term rates will eventually rise, but at the moment of the change in expectations, long-term rates will rise relative to short-term rates.

Supply and Demand Factors

Expectations about future interest rates must play an important role in determining the term structure of interest rates. However, the expectations approach does not provide a complete theory of term structure except under some rather special conditions. The expectations approach provides a complete explanation if all buyers and sellers of securities have exactly the same expectations about future interest rates and the market participants hold their expectations with certainty or are indifferent to risk. In the latter case they seek to maximize the *expected* short-term holding-period yield on their portfolio and act in the same way as they would if they were certain of the outcome.

Given those two conditions the prices of bonds of any maturity must move in such a way as to equate their holding-period yields with current short-term yields. Moreover, the structure of yields will be the same regardless of the quantities of securities in the market. An increase in the volume of bonds outstanding and a corresponding decrease in the volume of short-term securities outstanding will have no effect on the pattern of yields.

What happens if the participants in the market disagree about the future of interest rates? At times there will be investors who expect short-term yields to rise rapidly in the near future while others expect them to rise slowly or not at all. The latter group will be willing to buy bonds at yields only a little above the current short-term yield. The first group will want a big spread before they will buy bonds. Now the relative quantities of long-term and short-term bonds will matter. If the volume of bonds is small they can all be sold to the investors who think short-term rates will not rise much, and the bond yield will be only a little higher than the short yield. If there are more long-term bonds and fewer short-term securities, some of the long-term bonds will have to be sold to the group expecting more rapid short-term rate increases, and, to induce them to buy, bond yields must be higher relative to the short yield.

In practice there may be a continuous spectrum of opinion. Moderate changes in the distribution of outstanding securities will have some effect on yields but not a very large one.

A very similar argument applies to the willingness of investors to take risks and to the degree of certainty of their expectations.

Differences of opinion about expected future interest rates, differences in uncertainty about the future, and different degrees of concern about risk all tend to make the spread between long- and short-term rates depend on the relative volumes of securities of different maturities outstanding.

Attitudes toward the risk involved in long-term investment are not just a matter of personal taste; they also reflect the nature of the investor's liabilities. Insurance companies, for example, have long-term liabilities promising a fixed interest rate on insurance reserves. They need not worry much about capital losses on bonds because they will not have to sell them. On the other hand, if they hold short-term securities, rates might fall and they might not earn the contract interest. They will usually prefer to hold long-term securities when expected long-term yields equal short-term yields. Commercial banks, though, may have to liquidate securities if deposits decline or loan demand surges. They prefer shorts to longs at equal expected yields. Because of institutional differences in risk position the spreads between long- and short-term yields may depend on the distribution of assets among the different financial intermediaries as well as on the relative quantities of securities outstanding.

VALUING WEALTH

The bulk of the wealth of any market economy consists of claims made directly or indirectly against income-producing property: land, houses, offices, factories, and other equipment. The claims are stocks, corporate bonds, mortgages, and deeds to houses. Their aggregate value depends on the present value of the income they will produce as estimated by the securities markets. Thus the value of corporate securities depends in part on the judgments of security buyers about the future movements of corporate earnings. But the valuation of securities also depends on the interest rate used to discount future income. Thus a fall in interest rates, other things being equal, should increase the present value of any given future stream of income. That conclusion applies not only to corporate securities but to farmlands, houses, and unincorporated businesses. Thus, if interest rates fall while prospective property income remains the same, total wealth should increase.

Wealth and Government Debt

Most of the national wealth consists of claims against private property, but the holders of state, local, and federal securities certainly think of them as part of their wealth whether they hold them directly or indirectly through intermediaries. However, it is difficult to estimate the net increase in wealth resulting from increases in government debt.

When federal or state governments issue bonds, the bondholders have more assets. The public has an offsetting liability to pay more taxes of some sort but their tax liability is mixed up with all the other taxes and constitutes a relatively small part of the total tax burden. If the taxpayers are fully aware of their future tax liability and discount their future taxes at the same rate as the yield on the bonds, the implicit liability has the same value as the government bonds and there is no net increase in wealth from the bond issue per se. Prospective future income may be increased by the expenditures financed by government debt, but, in many cases (for example, in defense expenditure), government purchases financed by debt will not increase prospective future income.

However, many economists believe that taxpayers do not discount the future at the same yield as that paid on bonds. If the public discounts uncertain future tax liabilities at a rate higher than the yield on government bonds, then the issuance of debt causes a net increase of total nominal wealth. The controversy about government bonds being net wealth or not is a hotly debated one in economics.

Real versus Nominal Wealth

So far we have discussed wealth in nominal terms, but it is the real value of wealth that counts. The real value of private wealth should be independent of the price level. If all wages and prices double, the nominal value of property incomes from profits or rent should double and, given the interest rate, the nominal capital value of claims to profit and rent should also double. But since all other prices have doubled the purchasing power of those claims should remain unchanged. Individual debtors gain from a price level rise while creditors lose, but those gains and losses cancel out.

The wealth associated with government debt and money, however, is stated in nominal terms and its real value is affected by changes in the price level. When the price level rises, the real value of the money supply declines and the moneyholders as a group are poorer. To be sure, for that part of the money supply that consists of bank deposits there is an offset since the banks who are the debtors for these deposits are better off as a result. (As creditors banks lose too, but those who borrowed from them gain.) However, for that part of the money supply that consists of currency, everyone is poorer. Moreover, as prices rise the real value of government bond holdings is reduced, and so people feel poorer unless, as discussed before, they believe their tax burden will fall too. This change in real wealth resulting from this decline in the real value of currency and government debt is called the **real balance effect.**

We have now noted a number of different ways in which wealth can change. Wealth based on private property can change in real value if either the expected future value of property income increases or the capital value of a given stream of prospective property income receipts changes. In the short run prospective future property income will change with business-cycle fluctuations. In the long run the accumulation of physical capital tends to increase expected real property incomes. The valuation of property incomes can change if the uncertainty of the outcome changes or if the interest rate falls.

Total real wealth can also be increased by the accumulation of government debt and by the exchange of interest-bearing for non–interest-bearing government debt through open-market operations, while the price level remains unchanged. Finally, a given stock of interest-bearing and non–interest-bearing government debt will decline in value if the price level rises.

It is important to recognize that the price level factor and the other routes for changing wealth are not independent. The magic of wealth creation by increasing government debt or the money supply is limited by the fact that too much of it may raise prices, thereby causing a decline in the real value of wealth to offset the increase generated by deficits and open-market operations.

SUMMARY

1 The capital markets perform the task of transferring very large amounts of funds from surplus spending units to deficit ones.

2 On an annual basis over $200 billion of funds pass through the credit market.

3 If we counted the short-term shifts in surplus and deficit positions of individual households, businesses, and governments the amount transferred would be far larger. These transfers involve credit evaluation, collection of monthly payments for mortgage and installment credit, and a good deal of legal work, so they are far from a routine matter.

4 In order to perform the transfer function the markets have to operate in such a way as to match the kinds of liabilities borrowers wish to issue with the kinds of assets lenders wish to hold. They do this in two ways: (1) by intermediation: liabilities issued by borrowers are held by intermediaries who in turn issue a type of liability more attractive to the lenders; (2) by adjusting the relative yields of different kinds of assets in such a way as to induce borrowers to issue the kinds of liabilities lenders want, or to induce lenders to accept the kinds of liabilities borrowers want to issue, or both.

5 For this to happen interest rates must be flexible and markets for different kinds of securities must be linked together so that all types of securities are competing with one another directly or indirectly.

6 The test of performance is that intrinsically similar kinds of securities should pay similar, risk-adjusted interest rates regardless of their origin.

7 On the whole, U.S. capital markets seem to meet that test. Credit markets are geographically unified so that interest rates are similar throughout the country. Institutional specialization does not create segmented or compartmentalized markets. However, the market for municipal bonds is significantly affected by the differential tax treatment of financial institutions.

8 On the whole, the short-term markets are very well integrated, and so, with certain exceptions, are the long-term markets.

9 The two sets of markets are also closely linked but the relationship between long-term and short-term rates is heavily influenced by expectational considerations. There is also some evidence that the investment specialization of financial institutions does influence the relation between long- and short-term interest rates.

QUESTIONS AND EXERCISES

1 All short-term open-market interest rates tend to move up and down together. Why?
2 Treasury bill rates are almost always lower than commercial-paper rates. Explain.
3 Cite some reasons why spreads between Treasury bill and commercial-paper yields may vary from time to time.
4 Markets for short-term securities serve to link together all sectors of the capital market. Explain.
5 Since the volume of new equity issues is relatively small, the stock markets's role in the capital markets is really not very important in spite of the attention given to the stock market in the press. Comment.
6 Markets for bonds and mortgages are dominated by financial institutions. Each type of financial institution specializes in certain types of security; therefore, the long-term security markets operate in separate compartments that have little effect on one another. True or false? Explain your answer.
7 What is meant by a *yield curve*?
8 A falling yield curve usually indicates that investors expect bond yields to (a) rise or (b) fall. Choose one and explain.
9 The annual increase in the wealth held by Americans is equal to the annual net saving of businesses, households, and government during the year. True or false? Explain.
10 Does an increase in government debt increase wealth (a) always, (b) sometimes, or (c) never?
11 An open-market operation does not generate wealth. People just exchange bank deposits for government debt. Is this (a) always, (b) sometimes, or (c) never true?

FURTHER READING

BAUMOL, WILLIAM J. *The Stock Market and Economic Efficiency.* New York: Fordham University Press, 1965. This study reviews the theory and evidence of the efficiency of the stock market as a means of allocating capital among competing uses.

BOARD OF GOVERNORS OF THE FEDERAL RESERVE SYSTEM. *Joint Treasury–Federal Reserve Study of the U.S. Government Securities Market,* 1969. This is a summary of an exhaustive study of the operations of the market for U.S. government securities.

DOUGALL, HERBERT E., and JACK E. GAUMNITZ. *Capital Markets and Institutions,* 3rd ed. Englewood Cliffs, N.J.: Prentice-Hall, 1975. This short text describes each of the major capital markets and provides a wealth of detail on the volume of transactions and the decision-making process of the major participants.

FEDERAL RESERVE BANK OF BOSTON. *Financing State and Local Governments.* Conference Series No. 3, 1970. The papers in this volume discuss policy issues relating to the organization of the market for state and local securities and the role of tax-exemption in those markets.

FEDERAL RESERVE BANK OF BOSTON. *Issues in Federal Debt Management.* Conference Series No. 10, 1973. The papers in this volume discuss a number of policy issues relating to the organization of the market for U.S. Treasury securities and the possible effects of alternative policies.

FORTUNE, PETER. "Tax-Exemption of State and Local Interest Payments: An Economic Analysis of the Issues and an Alternative," *New England Economic Review,* Federal Reserve Bank of Boston, May/June 1973, pp. 3–20. This paper proposes an alternative to tax exemption of state and local security and analyzes its implications.

HURTLEY, EVELYN H. "The Commercial Paper Market," *Federal Reserve Bulletin* 63 (June 1977):523–536. This article explains the organization of the commercial-paper market, reviews the history, and outlines the factors accounting for differences in yields on commercial paper and other short-term instruments.

KUZNETS, SIMON. *Capital in the American Economy*. New York: National Bureau of Economic Research, 1961. Though out of date in some ways, this volume offers a broad perspective into the history of saving capital formation in the United States.

LIGHT, J.O., and WILLIAM L. WHITE. *The Financial System*. Homewood, Ill.: Richard D. Irwin, Inc., 1979. This volume discusses the organization of the capital markets in terms of the decision-making processes.

MELTON, WILLIAM C. "The Market for Large Negotiable CD's," *Quarterly Review,* Federal Reserve Bank of New York, Winter 1977–1978, pp. 22–34. This paper gives a detailed description of the market for commercial bank certificates of deposit. It outlines the organization of the market for each of the major short-term securities.

CHAPTER 7

Central Banking

With money, the banking firm, other financial intermediaries, and capital markets introduced in earlier chapters, the cast of characters in the financial system is almost complete. One player is missing: the central bank. In this chapter we will discuss our own central bank, the Federal Reserve System, in some detail. Before doing so, however, we have to look more generally at what central banks in developed non-Communist countries do.

THE CENTRAL BANK: A PROFILE

Despite their name, central banks are not "banks" in the same sense as commercial banks. They are governmental institutions that are not concerned with maximizing their profits, but with achieving certain goals for the entire economy such as the prevention of commercial bank failures, or of high unemployment, and so on. Central banks, even if in a formal sense owned by private stockholders, carry out governmental functions, and are therefore part of the government.

Origin of Central Banks

Central banks have developed in two ways. One is by way of a slow process of evolution, the prime example being the Bank of England, which started out as a commercial bank, but acquired over the years the added powers and responsibilities that slowly turned it into a central bank. In this process of evolution it is hard to say when it ceased to be a commercial bank and became a central bank. In contrast to the Bank of England, many central banks did not just grow into central banks, but, like the Fed, were central banks right from the start. Such a central bank is from the outset owned de facto by the government, although it may, like the Fed, have private stockholders. When a bank acts as a central bank, that is, determines its actions on the basis of the public interest rather than its stockholders' interest, it operates as a public institution even if the stockholders formally elect all of its chief officers.

PURPOSES AND FUNCTIONS OF CENTRAL BANKS

The two most important functions of central banks are to control the quantity of money and interest rates and to prevent massive bank failures. But they also have certain "chore functions."

Controlling the Money Supply

The reason we need a central bank was stated succinctly by the nineteenth-century British economist and financial journalist Walter Bagehot, when he wrote, "Money will not manage itself." Each commercial bank, as it obtains reserves, expands its deposits. With no central bank, the growth rate of deposits and hence of the money stock would depend upon what could be completely arbitrary factors that change bank reserves, and it could differ sharply from the appropriate rate.

Lender of Last Resort

One aspect of controlling the money supply is the need to guard against bank failures, particularly if there are many relatively small banks. This is not to say that central banks always did prevent widespread bank failures; the Fed certainly did not do so in the 1930s. But a central bank *should* act as a **lender of last resort,** that is, as an institution able and willing in a crisis to make loans to banks when other banks cannot, or will not, do so. The reason the central bank is able to make loans at such a time is that (as we will see in Chapter 10) it has the power to create reserves. In the United States, one defense against bank failures is, of course, the FDIC, but the Fed stands ready to support the FDIC by acting as a lender of last resort. If it were not for this, the threatened failure of a large bank with many deposits above the $100,000 insurance ceiling could easily set off a run by big depositors on other banks.

Being ready to act as a lender of last resort is an extremely important function of a central bank. It is easy to forget this because potential financial panics arise only rarely. Hence, when one looks at the day-to-day activities of a central bank, its lender of last resort function seems irrelevant and unimportant. But one can say a similar thing about a fire extinguisher! Don't forget, therefore, that, although a central bank does not *normally* act as a lender of last resort, it must always stand ready to do so, even if it means that it must temporarily abandon other goals such as fighting inflation.

Chore Functions

One set of chore functions consists of services the central bank provides for commercial banks. Thus it acts as a banker's bank, holding most of the reserves of commercial banks. These reserves have no physical existence; they are just entries on the liabilities side of a central bank's balance sheet. Since the central bank holds reserves for commercial banks it frequently also clears checks for banks.

In addition to its services for commercial banks, a central bank provides many services to the government. Thus it acts as the government's bank. The government keeps an account at the central bank, writes its checks on this account, and, in some countries, sells its securities through the central bank.

Another group of services to the government arises directly out of the central bank's close relation with commercial banks. Thus the central bank typically administers certain controls over commercial banks. For example, the Fed controls bank mergers and examines member banks. In a number of countries the government has imposed controls (so-called exchange controls) over the purchase of foreign assets by its residents, and these controls are often administered by the central bank.

In some countries, in particular the less-developed countries, the central bank also makes loans to the Treasury. And, in fact, a number of central banks—the Bank of England again is the prime example—originally started out as commercial banks that made loans to the government and got certain privileges in exchange. But having the central bank make loans to the Treasury can be highly inflationary since in many countries the central bank often has no choice about making these loans, but must make them even if they result in high inflation. To prevent this, in the United States the Fed is not allowed to lend to the Treasury directly. However, what cannot be done openly can be, and is, done indirectly by using the public as an intermediary; the Treasury sells securities to the public, while the Fed buys the same amount of government securities from the public.

Another function of a central bank is to issue currency. In many countries all the currency notes in circulation are issued, that is, placed into circulation, by the central bank, though sometimes the Treasury issues some currency notes as well.

The central bank acts as an adviser to the government. Particularly in the area of international finance, many governments rely strongly on the advice of their central banks.

Other Aspects of Central Banking

Before leaving the topic of central banks in general there are two items to be discussed: the relation of central banks to the rest of the government, and their ability to create reserves.

Relations between the central bank and the government are complex. Although central banks are part of the government, they maintain a certain detachment from the rest of it. They usually have much more independence from the administration than do such government agencies as the Treasury Department.

Central banks have the power to create reserves. Unless there is a law stating that the central bank must keep, say, 20 cents in gold for each dollar of its outstanding currency notes or deposits, it can create as many reserves for the commercial banks as it wants to. After all, these reserves consist, apart from currency, merely of entries on the central bank's books.

THE FORMAL STRUCTURE OF THE FEDERAL RESERVE SYSTEM

The United States started a central bank only in 1913 when President Wilson signed the Federal Reserve Act. In 1907 an unusually severe financial panic with many bank failures had finally convinced enough people that a central bank was needed. Even then there was much opposition to it because of a fear that Wall Street would be able to use it as a tool to dominate Main Street. The opposition was eventually overcome as it became increasingly clear that a lender of last resort was needed. But, given the great concern that a central bank could lead to a powerful cartel of banks, on the one hand, or to political control over banking, on the other, a careful and elaborate system of checks and balances was written into the Federal Reserve Act.

At its start, the Federal Reserve System was looked upon more as a cooperative enterprise of bankers, an institution that would pool the previously dispersed reserves of banks, than as a government agency concerned with the goals of high employment and price level stability. But although its structure has changed less than its functions, the Federal Reserve System we have today is not the system that was originally set up in 1913. It has been changed both by major pieces of legislation, particularly the banking acts of 1933 and 1935, and by the slow evolution in modes of functioning that is a matter of internal organization and practice rather than of statutory change. The Federal Reserve Act of 1913 envisioned a highly decentralized system. Some people even saw the Fed not as a single central bank but as twelve federated regional central banks. But over the years the Federal Reserve has become more centralized. The twelve regional Federal Reserve Banks, most of all the initially extremely powerful New York Bank, have lost power to the Board of Governors in Washington.

The major features of the Federal Reserve System, however, have not changed. It consists of twelve Federal Reserve Banks and the Board of Governors.

The Federal Reserve Banks

The locations of the twelve Federal Reserve Banks, and their branches, are shown in Figure 7.1. The assets of various Federal Reserve Banks are far from equal. More than half the assets are held by just three: New York, Chicago, and San Francisco. The New York Bank alone accounts for about 30 percent of all Federal Reserve assets. Apart from its size, the New York Bank is the "first among equals" because its location gives it direct contact with the country's main money market. Hence, it is this bank that carries out all the purchases and sales of securities on behalf of the whole Federal Reserve System. In addition, it is the Federal Reserve System's contact point in many, though not all of the Fed's dealings with foreign central banks and international institutions.

Each of these Federal Reserve Banks is controlled by a board of nine part-time directors. Three of these directors, called Class A directors, are

Figure 7.1   **Federal Reserve Banks and Their Branches By Location.** The country is divided into twelve Federal Reserve Districts. Alaska and Hawaii are in the 12th district.

elected by the member banks, and are bankers themselves. Member banks also elect three Class B directors. These directors may not be officers or employees of banks. To prevent domination by any particular size group of banks, member banks are divided into large, medium, and small banks, and each of these groups votes for one Class A and one Class B director. But actually, neither Class A nor Class B directors are "elected" in the proper sense of the term since there is usually only a single candidate for each election. Frequently the single candidate for the election as a Class B director, and often also the single candidate for the Class A directorship, is someone suggested to the banks by the president of the Federal Reserve Bank.

Finally, there are three Class C directors. These are not elected by the member banks. They are appointed by the Board of Governors to embody the broader public interest beyond that of banks and their borrowers. One of these Class C directors becomes the chairman of the board, and another the vice-chairman.

It is sometimes said that the member banks elect the majority of the Federal Reserve Banks' directors, but this is misleading. When one takes account of the fact that, in addition to the appointed Class C directors, the president of the bank often de facto nominates the Class B directors, and apparently in many cases even the Class A directors, it is more accurate to say that in actuality the Federal Reserve System selects the majority of the directors.

In describing the various classes of directors we were careful to avoid saying that any of the three classes "represents" a particular group, because all directors are supposed to represent the public interest rather than the narrow interests of bankers or borrowers. The public interest, however, is like the proverbial elephant described by the blind men. One's social background, associations, and experience affect one's perception of the public interest.

There have been many complaints that the directors are selected only from "establishment types" and that until recently women and minority groups, as well as labor and consumers, were virtually unrepresented even among the Class C directors. Part of this is due to the fact that the main function of the directors is not to make monetary policy, but rather to guide the bank's president in his administrative work of running the bank, a task in which those with business experience of their own have an obvious advantage. However, by participating in the selection of the bank's president, and also by informing him or her of their views on policy, which, however, he or she is free to ignore, the directors do have some influence on policy, so that the criticism that the directors are unrepresentative cannot be dismissed entirely.

The chief executive officer of each Federal Reserve Bank is its president. He or she is chosen by the directors with the approval of the Board of Governors. In recent years he or she has frequently been someone initially suggested to the directors by the Board of Governors. Most of the recently appointed presidents, unlike most of the directors, have been professional economists.

The Federal Reserve Banks examine member banks, approve or disapprove some bank-merger applications, clear checks, withdraw worn currency from circulation, and issue new currency. But, in addition to those chore functions, the Federal Reserve Banks have some policy functions too. Each "sets" a **discount rate,** that is, *the rate the Fed charges on its loans to banks and other depository institutions in its district.* But this rate has to be approved by the Board of Governors and, furthermore, the Board of Governors, by its power to approve or disapprove the existing discount rate, can force a Federal Reserve Bank to change its current rate. Hence, the only real power the Federal Reserve Banks have over the discount rate is the power to advise, and to delay a change in the discount rate for as long as two weeks. However, each Federal Reserve Bank administers its own discount window; that is, under general rules applicable to all Federal Reserve Banks, it makes the particular decision when a bank or other depository institution in its district applies for a loan. A more important policy role of the Federal Reserve Banks is, as will be described later, to participate in the Federal Open Market Committee.

Still another function of the Federal Reserve Banks is to provide the Federal Reserve System with local contacts. Despite the vast amount of information that flows into Washington, statistical data become available only with some delay. However, by talking to local businesses, the Fed is able to obtain some indication of economic developments right away. Another important function of the Federal Reserve Banks is to explain, and justify, Fed actions to the local business community, and thus to generate political support for the Fed. This is an important, though informal, part of the directors' jobs. Finally, each Federal Reserve Bank has a competent staff of economists who carry out research on monetary policy and related problems, as well as on local conditions.

The Board of Governors

At the apex of the Federal Reserve System is the **Board of Governors** (sometimes called the "Federal Reserve Board") located in Washington, D.C. The seven governors are appointed by the president of the United States with the advice and consent of the Senate. They can be removed only for "cause," something that, so far, has never happened. A full term of office is fourteen years, and governors cannot be reappointed after serving a full term. This is supposed to remove them from needing to seek the president's favor, or fearing his threats. In the ideal case all governors would serve out their full fourteen-year terms, which are staggered. If so, there would be only two vacancies on the Board every four years, so that within a single term a president could not dominate the Board. But the chairman's term, as chairman, though not as board member, is only four years so that each president can appoint his own chairman. These provisions are examples of the checks and balances built into the Federal Reserve System.

However, not all of them have worked well. Board members usually retire before their full fourteen-year terms are up, sometimes because of age and sometimes for financial reasons. In the period 1960–1982, of the twenty-two governors who were appointed, only six—little more than one-quarter—served for as long as seven years. Hence, usually more than two vacancies occur on the Board during any one presidential term. For example, there were four vacancies on the Board during President Carter's first three years in office. Moreover, when a governor resigns the president can, if he wants to, appoint someone to the remaining years of the former governor's term. This not only means that some governors have less than a fourteen-year term, but also that they are then eligible for reappointment to a full term of their own and might therefore be tempted to favor the president's view. The majority of the board members are professional economists.

The Board of Governors makes monetary policy; it controls the discount rate and, within limits, can change reserve requirements. Together with other members of the Federal Open Market Committee it controls the most important tool of monetary policy, open-market operations. In addition, its chairman is one of the main economic advisers to the president, as well as to Congress. And governors sometimes also act as U.S. representatives in negotiations with foreign central banks and governments. Beyond this, chairmen frequently press their views on fiscal policy and other economic issues in statements to Congress and to the general public. The Board has a large and competent staff of economists to aid it in this work.

Despite the fact that determining monetary policy is by far the Board's most important task, much of its time is spent on bank regulatory problems. For example, it passes on many bank-merger applications and decides the permissible lines of nonbank activity for bank holding companies. In addition, it administers the laws that prohibit discrimination and untruthful statements in lending. In these activities the Board of Governors' control extends beyond banking to credit in general. Closer to home, it exercises some rather loose supervision over the Federal Reserve Banks, which have to submit their budgets for Board approval.

The Federal Open Market Committee

The focal point for policy-making within the Federal Reserve system is the FOMC, the **Federal Open Market Committee.** This committee consists of the seven members of the Board of Governors, whose chairman is also chairman of the FOMC, and five presidents of the Federal Reserve Banks.[1] The Federal Reserve Banks rotate in these five slots on the FOMC except for the New York Bank, which has a permanent slot. However, those Federal Reserve Bank Presidents who are not currently members of the FOMC are usually present at its meeting and participate in its discussions, though, of course, they do not vote. But since the FOMC tries to reach a consensus rather than just rely on a majority, their presence, even in a nonvoting capacity, gives all Federal Reserve Bank presidents some influence over FOMC decisions. The FOMC meets about eight times a year, and sometimes holds telephone conferences between meetings.

The FOMC's function is to decide on **open-market operations,** that is, *Federal Reserve purchases and sales of securities.* The FOMC does not carry out security purchases or sales itself. Instead, it issues a directive telling the New York Federal Reserve Bank the open-market policy it should follow for the accounts of all the Federal Reserve Banks.

There are some other Federal Reserve components, but they are *much* less important than the FOMC. One is the Federal Advisory Council, which consists of one commercial banker (usually a president of a large commercial bank) from each district. As the name implies, this committee advises the Board of Governors, but that is all. Figure 7.2 summarizes the structure of the Federal Reserve System.

---

[1] Although the law permits the first vice-president of a Federal Reserve Bank to serve on the FOMC in place of its president, this is normally not done, except when a president is unable to attend a meeting.

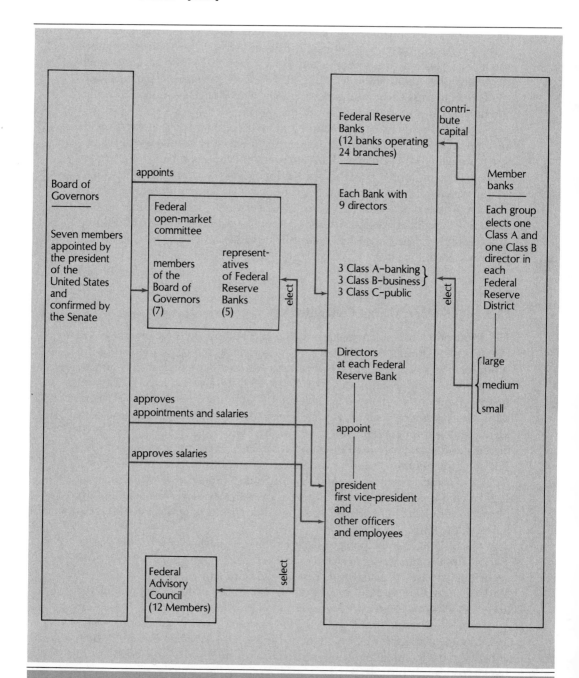

Figure 7.2   The Structure of the Federal Reserve System. A system of checks and balances disperses power in the Federal Reserve System. **Source:** Board of Governors, Federal Reserve System, *The Federal Reserve System, Purposes and Functions* (Washington, D.C., 1974), p.18.

THE INFORMAL STRUCTURE OF THE FEDERAL RESERVE SYSTEM

Merely to know the formal, legal aspects of an organization is rarely sufficient. The Fed, like any other organization, has developed certain traditions and other attributes that strongly affect its operations. These informal aspects are neither definite nor clear-cut. They involve the distribution of power within the Fed, the constituency of the Federal Reserve, and its behavior as a bureaucracy.

Distribution of Power within the Federal Reserve

Although the distribution of power over monetary policy within the Federal Reserve System and among "outsiders" is a matter of judgment, former Fed governor Sherman Maisel has given an estimate of the distribution of power, shown in Table 7.1. However, there are two qualifications to Table 7.1. First, the distribution of power cannot be quantified precisely; as Maisel states, "Other knowledgeable persons would certainly draw charts with different weights."[2] For example, one former senior Fed official believes that the chairman has more power than Table 7.1 suggests. Second, the distribution of power depends, in part, on the personalities involved. For example, a president who takes great interest in monetary policy exercises more influence than one whose main concern is foreign policy. It also depends on the particular issue. The FDIC, for example, has influence on matters like bank capital ratios, but not on monetary policy.

The chairman's power is based on five sources. First, as the head of the Board, his opinions and statements carry great weight with the public. Second, a number of decisions do not even come before the Board, but are taken by the chairman himself as the Board's representative. For example, it is the chairman, and not the whole Board, who meets with the president. Third, the

Table 7.1	An Estimate of the Distribution of Power Over Federal Reserve Policy		
Insiders	**Percent**	**Outsiders**	**Percent**
The chairman	45	The administration	35
Staff of the Board and FOMC	25	Congress	25
Other governors	20	The public directly[a]	20
Federal Reserve Banks	10	Financial interests	10
		Foreign interests	5
		Other regulatory agencies	5
TOTAL	100		100

a: Includes the press, economists, lobbyists, and general public.
Source: Sherman Maisel, *Managing the Dollar*. New York: W.W. Norton, 1973, p. 110.

---

[2] Sherman Maisel, *Managing the Dollar*. New York, W.W. Norton, 1973, pp. 109–111.

chairman arranges the agenda and exercises the leadership role at the Board's meetings. Fourth, the chairman maintains supervisory powers over the Board's staff members, who therefore have a greater incentive to please him than other Board members. Finally, the foregoing powers of the chairman give him an aura of authority, which tends to induce other board members to vote the way he does. But he does not always get his way. In 1986 Chairman Volcker was outvoted at a Board meeting by the four governors President Reagan had appointed. Even though a compromise was worked out a few days later, this was widely considered a blow to Chairman Volcker's stature.

The Federal Reserve's Constituency

To refer to the Fed's *constituency* is to use the term in a broader sense than when it is applied to the geographic constituency of a member of Congress. A government agency tends to view itself as speaking for a particular group, and tries to represent this group's interests within the government. In return, the agency receives political support from its constituency. As former secretary of the treasury and current secretary of state George Shultz put it: "Advocacy government is part of our unwritten constitution."[3] An example of this is the Department of Agriculture's acting as spokesman for farmers and receiving the support from congresspersons elected from rural districts. The Department of Labor has a similar relation to labor unions. This does not mean that these agencies necessarily disregard the public interest; rather the public interest is supposed to emerge as a consensus of the views of various groups as expressed by "their" government agencies. Admittedly, the view of the public interest that does emerge can too often be summarized as "more for me," and the power of various groups is not always appropriate.

It seems plausible that the Fed views itself as having two major, and perhaps two minor, partly overlapping constituencies. One major constituency consists of banks and the financial community. The other major constituency is composed of the fixed-income groups who stand to lose by inflation. Several government agencies (such as the Departments of Agriculture and Labor) represent producer groups. Hence someone should represent those who lose when producers raise their prices or the government adopts excessively expansionary policies. The Fed has assumed some of this task, at least in the sense of worrying more about inflation than most other government agencies do. Whether or not it has worried sufficiently about inflation, or has become an engine for inflation, is another issue.

Two other, though minor, constituencies that the Fed *may* have are the financial press and academic economists. With the Fed being in the news so much it obviously wants to get a favorable reception by the press and also by academic economists, who, at times, have been sharply critical of it, both in their writings and in their testimony before Congress. But it is hard to say to what extent, if any, the Fed's policy has been influenced by its concern about the opinions of these two groups.

---

[3] "Reflections on Political Economy," *Journal of Finance* 29 (May 1974):325.

The Federal Reserve as a Bureaucracy

Interest groups outside the Fed are not the only beneficiaries of its concern; to a considerable extent it probably also takes good care of its own institutional interests. The modern theory of bureaucracy argues that a government agency is not a Platonic philosopher-king, interested only in the public welfare. It is also concerned with its own survival and prestige, which it can easily rationalize as being indirectly a concern for the public welfare.

Assuming that the Fed is actually concerned with its own strength as an institution, how would one expect it to behave? First, it would, whenever possible, avoid conflicts with powerful people who could harm it. In practical terms this means that, for example, it would be tempted to follow expansionary policies that in the short run would meet Congress's and the administration's wish to keep interest rates down. Second, one would expect it to try to maintain its power and autonomy: to be unwilling, for example, to give up any of its policy tools, even those tools that are not very useful. Third, an organization that is trying to maintain its power and prestige is unlikely to admit that it made mistakes in the past, since to do so may suggest that it could conceivably be making mistakes currently too.

Fourth, a way for an organization to protect itself from criticism is to act myopically, that is, to pay a great deal of attention to the direct and immediate impact of its policies, and to pay too little attention to the longer run or less direct damage these policies may do. This is so because the organization is more likely to be blamed for those bad effects of its policies that are immediately visible and clearly its fault than for those bad effects that could be the result of many other causes. Finally, the Fed has an incentive to announce vague targets, so that if it misses its target this will not be obvious.[4] In any case, many central bankers tend to think of their task as an art that is practiced better by relying on the intuition of knowledgeable people than on rigorous analysis. For example, the preeminent central banker of the pre–World War II period, Sir Montague Norman, was once asked the reason for a decision he had made. He replied: "Reasons, Mr. Chairman? I don't have reasons. I have instincts."[5]

Do central banks in general, and the Fed specifically, really behave in this way? Some economists have argued that this is so, but the subject is still very much open to debate.

Some economists have criticized the Federal Reserve for trying to protect itself against criticism by not making enough information about its actions available to the public. While there may be much truth to this criticism, compared to foreign central banks the Fed is a veritable chatterbox. In addition to occasional studies, the Board publishes each month the *Federal Reserve Bulletin,* which contains articles on current developments, a record of previous

---

[4] A central bank is not the only one who faces this temptation. A student who announces to her parents that her goal this semester is to get all As is taking a bigger risk of disappointing them than another student who announces that his goal is the much more difficult task of transforming himself into a thoughtful and perceptive person.

[5] Quoted in Andrew Boyle, *Montague Norman.* London: Cassel, 1967, p. 327.

FOMC actions, detailed financial statistics, and so on. The Federal Reserve Banks issue without charge their own publications containing articles on banking, local economic conditions, and monetary policy.

FINANCES OF THE FEDERAL RESERVE SYSTEM

The outstanding stock of the Federal Reserve Banks is owned by its member banks, who receive a fixed 6 percent dividend on this stock. The fact that the member banks own all the stock of the Federal Reserve Banks is sometimes taken to mean that they own these Federal Reserve Banks. But this is completely misleading. Ownership means two things: the right to appropriate all the net earnings, and the right to control the property. Member banks have no claim on the residual earnings of the Federal Reserve Banks. They get their 6 percent dividend, regardless of the Fed's earnings. Similarly, they have *very* little control over the Federal Reserve Banks, and none over the Board of Governors. Hence, the do *not* control the Fed.

The net earnings of the Federal Reserve Banks come from the securities they hold, and to a much smaller extent from interest on the loans they make. They also charge financial institutions for the services they perform for the institutions, such as clearing checks. But where do the funds that the Fed invests in securities come from? The main source is the issuance of Federal Reserve notes. Suppose the Fed prints $1 million of Federal Reserve notes and ships them to a bank that asks for them. It then debits the bank's reserve account. If it wants to keep total bank reserves constant it then offsets this decline in bank reserves by buying $1 million of securities in the open market. Hence, in its books its liabilities for outstanding Federal Reserve notes are up by $1 million, but so are its government security holdings. Apart from this, the Fed can buy securities in a way akin to deposit creation by banks. It simply pays for the securities by giving banks credit on their reserve accounts. Similarly, when the Fed makes loans to member banks it just writes up their reserve account.[6]

Out of the earnings on this capital the Fed pays its dividends on member bank stock (which amounted to .6 percent of net earning in 1958). After taking care of this item it places a relatively small amount into its surplus account; the great bulk of net earning ($16.8 billion in 1985) is normally turned over to the U.S. Treasury. There is no law requiring the Fed to do this; though, if it did not, there would soon be one.

FEDERAL RESERVE INDEPENDENCE

The Fed has a great deal of independence, much more than other government agencies. While the president of the United States with the advice and consent

---

[6] It may seem that when a member bank deposits reserves with the Fed the Fed obtains funds, which it can invest and hence earn interest on. But the total amount of currency and reserves is fixed. Assuming that there is no change in currency held by the public, then the only way one bank can obtain more reserves is for another bank's reserve to decline. Hence, there is no change in the total reserves, and hence in the earning assets, held by the Federal Reserve.

of the Senate appoints new governors as vacancies occur, and chooses his own chairman, once he has made these selections, *officially* he does not have any more power over the Federal Reserve; in principle the Fed could ignore his wishes completely. To be sure, in a legalistic sense the Fed is a "creature of Congress," but Congress neither is set up to exercise day-to-day control over it nor, under present legislation, has the right to do so. Thus, while the Fed reports its targets for the growth rate of the money stock to Congress, *in principle* it could ignore any congressional reactions to these targets.

Actual Independence

But, as usual, the formal situation as set forth in legislation is only part of the story. Actually, the president and Congress have considerable influence over the Fed. One source of the president's influence is moral suasion; the governors are reluctant to oppose the views of the one person elected by the whole nation; they go along if they feel they can do so without dereliction of duty. Second, the Fed is continually active in Congress, trying to obtain certain legislation or to block other legislation. It wants the support of the president in these legislative struggles, and hence has an incentive to keep on good terms with him. Third, the chairman wants the president's goodwill, so that when the president appoints a new governor, it will be someone the chairman prefers. As John Woolley, a leading authority on the politics of the Fed, has put it: "Rather than conclude that the presidents generally get the monetary policy they want, it would be more accurate to say that only infrequently are presidents extremely unhappy with the monetary policy they get."[7]

In general, the Fed cannot take the continuation of its independence for granted. It is to some extent "a prisoner of its independence." It may have to give in on some issues to prevent Congress from taking away some of its independence.

But the influence of the president and Congress should not be overestimated; on some issues the Fed can mobilize an extraordinary powerful lobby of bankers in each congressional district to pressure Congress into preserving its independence. Congress, by and large, doubts its ability to challenge the Federal Reserve, in part because the Fed claims to possess esoteric knowledge about monetary policy, and in part because the Fed claims that it is our protector from explosive inflation. Moreover, there is usually little political benefit in challenging the Fed.

All in all, as Sherman Maisel has written:

> . . . independence is both ill-defined and circumscribed. . . . Although no legal method exists for the President to issue a directive to the System, its independence in fact is not so great that it can use monetary policy as a club or threat to veto Administration action. The System's latitude for action is rather circumscribed. . . . In any showdown, no nonrepresentative group such as the Fed can or should be allowed to pursue its own goals in opposition to those of the elected officials.[8]

[7] John Woolley, *Monetary Politics.* New York: Cambridge Press, 1984, p. 111.

[8] Sherman Maisel, *Managing the Dollar.* New York: W.W. Norton, 1973, pp. 24, 136.

INDEPENDENCE: PROS AND CONS

Does the Fed have too much or too little independence? From time to time this question becomes a political issue, and it *may* sooner or later become a major issue in a presidential election. Political debates about the Fed's independence do not result so much from fundamental disagreements about the proper role of the Fed in the government (an issue that evokes little public excitement) as from strong disagreement about the policy that the Fed is following. One way to change this policy is to bring the Fed under control of those in Congress or the administration who oppose this policy. Another way is to frighten the Fed enough so that it will change its policy. Thus, in 1982 several bills to reduce the Fed's independence gained powerful support in Congress. Shortly thereafter the Fed changed its policy, *perhaps* in part because of these threats.

We discuss the pros and cons of monetary policies in Part 4. Here we will discuss more general arguments about the Fed's independence. Although these arguments sound abstract and philosophical, they are relevant to what may soon become a major political issue.

The Case for Independence

There are several arguments on both sides of the independence issue. Supporters of independence argue that monetary policy, and hence the value of the dollar, is too important and too complex an issue to be left to the play of political forces. As a former chairman of the Board, William McChesney Martin, put it:

> An independent Federal Reserve System is the primary bulwark of the free enterprise system and when it succumbs to the pressures of political expediency or the dictates of private interest, the groundwork of sound money is undermined.[9]

In this view the political process is myopic: being overly concerned with the next election, it overplays the importance of short-term benefits, and hence is unwilling to make those hard and unpopular decisions—such as tolerating more unemployment in the short-run—that are needed to obtain the long-run benefits of a stable price level. Moreover, politicians, if they can, are likely to use the central bank to finance increased government expenditures without raising taxes. In addition, pressure groups impart an inflationary bias to government policy. Hence an independent central bank largely removed from political pressures is needed to ensure justice to those who lose from inflation. Anyone familiar with the case for a gold standard will probably see a similarity with the argument that the gold standard guards against unwise inflationary actions.

Another variant of this argument puts it in terms of a *political business*

---

[9] Quoted in A. Jerome Clifford, *The Independence of the Federal Reserve System.* Philadelphia: University of Pennsylvania Press, 1965, p. 18.

cycle. Before an election the government is tempted to adopt too expansionary a monetary policy, which results in lower interest rates and lower unemployment just before the election. The resulting inflation and rising nominal interest rates then occur only after the election. At that point the government adopts restrictive policies, which it hopes the public will have forgotten by the time of the next election. It is far from clear, however, that the Fed has actually behaved in this fashion. It does not have a strong incentive to do so. If it supports a president who, nevertheless, loses the election, the new president might punish it. Moreover, the Fed derives much of its prestige and power from being perceived as an expert objective agency that is nonpartisan. Why relinquish this? But a number of economists do believe that the empirical evidence does support the hypothesis of a political business cycle. This is disputed by others.

The Case against Independence

Critics of central bank independence reject these arguments. They believe that it is fundamentally undemocratic to say that elected officials should not be trusted to judge monetary policy. To be sure, monetary policy involves difficult decisions that need a long-run point of view, but the same thing is true of foreign policy or defense policy. Moreover, for better or worse, the public holds the president responsible for the economic conditions that result from *all* the policies followed during his administration. Hence, he should have control over monetary policy, one of the most important of these policies.

In addition, some economists maintain that the Fed has not used its independence well and therefore should be deprived of it. At times it has tolerated inflation, as in the late 1960s and 1970s, and in other years, the 1930s, for example, it has had a deflationary bias and allowed too much unemployment to develop. In addition, its independence has not really removed it from politics. Instead, it has had to become a political animal in order to defend both its actions and its independence. Moreover, its independence allows the Fed too much leeway to indulge in that characteristic weakness of a bureaucracy, continuous overemphasis of narrow, parochial interests.

Finally, monetary and fiscal policies should be integrated, and adequate integration cannot be achieved, the opponents of Fed independence claim, merely by a process of informal consultation. Rather it requires that the Fed be part of the administration. Giving the President control over the Fed need not necessarily weaken its influence, and might even strengthen it. If it were part of the administration, the Fed's counsel would then be better heeded by the administration.

Possible Compromises

These pro and con arguments may give the misleading impression that the choice is between two irreconcilable extremes. but this is not so. Even if the Fed were to lose its formal independence, and become part of the administration, there would still be at least an attempt to keep it out of partisan politics. Moreover, as just pointed out, the independence that the Fed currently has is far from complete.

On a more practical level, the relevant debate does not deal with such "fundamental" issues as the Fed's complete independence, but focuses on proposals for relatively minor reductions in its independence. For example, one proposal would make the chairman's term of office coincide better with the president's so that each president could appoint his own chairman a year after he took office. Other proposals would shorten the term of the governors or eliminate the FOMC and shift its work to the Board of Governors. A more radical proposal would put the secretary of the Treasury on the FOMC, and an even more radical one would make the Fed turn all its gross earnings over to the Treasury and finance its activities through congressional appropriations. This would give Congress much more control over it. Recently, some senators filed suit claiming that the Reserve Bank presidents should not be allowed to vote on the FOMC since they are not appointed by the president and confirmed by the Senate. If this suit succeeds in the Supreme Court, presidential appointment of Bank presidents might be required. This might lead to the appointment of Bank presidents who favor more expansionary policies than Bank presidents do now.

SUMMARY

1 Central banks are not "banks" in the conventional sense; they are institutions concerned with managing the money stock, preventing financial panic by acting as lenders of last resort, and other government tasks.
2 Central banks perform services, such as holding reserves and clearing checks for banks, and also act as the government's bank, doing such chores as issuing currency. Central banks can create reserves for the banking system.
3 The Federal Reserve System has become more centralized since its establishment in 1913. Its current organization is shown in Figure 7.2.
4 Each Federal Reserve Bank has nine directors chosen in a way that provides checks and balances. While formally the Federal Reserve Banks are "owned" by member banks, this does not give member banks ownership in any meaningful sense.
5 The Board of Governors consists of seven members appointed by the president. Together with five Reserve Bank presidents, they serve on the Federal Open Market Committee. This committee controls the Fed's most important tool, open-market operations.
6 Within the Federal Reserve, the chairman has a great deal of power; among outsiders, the administration and Congress have the most power over the Fed. The major constituencies of the Fed are the financial community and fixed-income groups. The Fed also has its own interests in preserving its power and independence.
7 The Fed's independence is circumscribed. Historically it has gone along with the president's overall views on monetary policy. There are numerous arguments for and against Fed independence.

QUESTIONS AND EXERCISES

1 The term *central bank* is a misnomer; it is nothing like a bank. Discuss the extent to which this statement is true for the Federal Reserve System.
2 Why do countries have central banks?
3 What does the term *lender of last resort* mean?
4 Discuss the chore functions of the Federal Reserve.
5 What monetary policy functions are carried out by:
   a. the Federal Reserve Banks
   b. the Board of Governors
   c. the FOMC
6 Critically discuss: "The Federal Reserve Banks have nothing at all to do with monetary policy; they only undertake the chore functions of the Federal Reserve System."
7 The Federal Reserve System is an example of a system of "checks and balances." Describe these checks and balances.
8 What does it mean to say that the Federal Reserve has constituencies? What are they?

FURTHER READING*

ACHESON, KEITH, and JOHN CHANT. "Bureaucratic Theory and the Choice of Central Bank Goals: The Case of Canada," *Journal of Money, Credit and Banking* 5 (May 1973):637–656. A pioneering application of bureaucratic theory to central bank behavior.

BECK, NATHANIEL. "Politics and Monetary Policy," in Thomas Willet (ed.), *The Political Economy of Stagflation.* San Francisco: Pacific Institute, forthcoming.

GALBRAITH, JOHN A. *The Economics of Banking Operations.* Montreal: McGill University Press, 1963. Chapter 7 gives a useful and compact discussion of central banking.

KANE, EDWARD. "External Pressures and the Operations of the Fed," in Raymond Lombra and Willard Witte (eds.), *The Political Economy of the Domestic and International Monetary Relations.* Iowa City, Iowa: University of Iowa Press, 1982. A superb discussion of the Fed as a political animal.

———. "The Re-Politicization of the Fed," *Journal of Financial and Quantitative Analysis* 9 (November 1974):743–752. An important contribution to the debate about the Fed's independence.

MAISEL, SHERMAN. *Managing the Dollar.* New York: W.W. Norton, 1973. Provides important insights into Fed behavior by a former member of the Board of Governors.

MAYER, THOMAS. "The Structure and Operation of the Federal Reserve System: Some Needed Reforms," in U.S. Congress House Committee on Banking, Currency, and Housing, *Compendium of Papers Prepared for the Fine Study,* 94th Congress, 2nd session, 1976, 2:669–726. A survey of the Fed's organization with proposals for changes.

WEINTRAUB, ROBERT. "Congressional Supervision of Monetary Policy," *Journal of Monetary Economics* 4 (April 1978):341–363. An important discussion of the extent to which the Fed is actually independent.

WOOLLEY, JOHN. *Monetary Politics.* New York: Cambridge University Press, 1985.

---

* The reviews published by all of the Federal Reserve Banks are available free of charge. Particularly useful for discussions of monetary policy and macroeconomics are the ones published by the Boston, Kansas City, Minneapolis, New York, St. Louis, Richmond, and San Francisco banks. The Chicago and Atlanta banks are better on banking problems.

CHAPTER 8

Current Issues in Financial Structure

The previous chapters described the way American financial institutions function. In this chapter we go beyond description and take up current and emerging problems—having looked the car over we now listen to the engine and worry about how it sounds. The financial system is not static. Problems arise, they are eventually resolved, but the solutions then create new problems. For example, in the 1930s the FDIC was an effective response to the problem of massive bank failures, but it led to excessive risk-taking by banks in the 1970s and 1980s. Eventually this problem too will be more or less resolved in some way, but that solution will, in turn, create other problems.

Not all the problems that arise are the result of fixing previous ones. Some are due to economic or technological change. In the 1970s, sharply rising interest rates provided an incentive to get around Regulation Q, which capped the interest rate on deposits. Anyone who could offer what are, in effect (though not under law), deposits could garner much business. There was now a potential niche for money-market funds, and the falling costs of electronic bookkeeping turned the potential niche into a profitable area. As money-market funds grew Regulation Q, which in 1967 had saved the thrifts, was no longer viable.

One must therefore take an evolutionary view of the financial structure. We do not solve problems once and for all, and then live happily ever after. Today's solutions generate tomorrow's problems. Or, even if harmless in themselves, today's solutions may be outdated by tomorrow. Mathematical problems have lasting solutions; problems of economic policy do not. Even in the short run, every solution has its problems. This is hardly surprising because we want the impossible: to have institutions that take some risk on the asset side of their balance sheets, and yet provide totally safe deposits.

We cannot discuss here all the problems of financial institutions, but three major issues merit study: the crisis in deposit insurance, the separation between banking and other lines of business, and problems with the regulatory structure.

DEPOSIT INSURANCE: YESTERDAY'S SUCCESS AND TODAY'S PROBLEM

In 1934 deposit insurance was the obvious answer to a crisis. Successive waves of bank failures had cut the number of banks by about one-third, and nobody knew how many more banks would fail. Deposit insurance was a major achievement. Perhaps even without it there would have been few additional bank failures after 1934, perhaps there would have been many, nobody knows. But obviously it would not have been a good idea to try to find out the hard way.

The Incentive to Take Too Much Risk

All the same, the principle of deposit insurance has a fundamental flaw. It provides an incentive for excessive risk-taking. Suppose a kind (or naive?) uncle lends you $10,000 to play the stock market, and tells you that you get to keep all the gains if your stocks rise, but he will take the loss if the stocks fall. You then have a strong incentive to buy risky stocks, where the chances of gains and losses are both high. In the game of heads I win, tails you lose, I might as well bet the family farm.

Suppose now that, instead of giving you the $10,000, your uncle gives it to your brother, but still lets you keep all the gains from the investment of this money without suffering any of the losses. You then have an incentive to make the following arrangement with your brother: "I will pay you something if you allow me to invest that money in extremely risky stocks." Since your brother does not stand to lose anything he would agree to this. If your gamble turns out badly, neither you nor your brother, but uncle, is the loser. This is the trouble with deposit insurance; a bank has an incentive to make risky loans and the insured depositors have no reason to object. The FDIC and the FSLIC, in effect, subsidize risk-taking.

Given this fundamental flaw, the interesting question is not why deposit insurance is in trouble now, but why it took so long for serious trouble to develop. The most obvious reason is that banks are not entirely free to decide how much risk to take. Bank examiners have something to say about it too, but not all that much. First, as discussed in Chapter 3, a large bank is a complicated institution that is better understood by its president than by the examiner. Second, there is safety in numbers. An examiner can mount a strong argument when any one bank steps out of line and does what others do not do, but when most banks do the same thing, the examiner's complaint is not nearly so persuasive. For example, in the 1970s, despite complaints by the regulatory agencies, capital ratios generally fell.

Third, suppose a bank wants to take a given amount of risk, and therefore tries to make a certain type of risky, high-yielding loan. If the examiners stop it from making these loans it will go ahead and make other risky loans instead. Eventually the examiners discover these risky loans and put a stop to them too. So the bank goes on to some other risky activity that does not show up on its balance sheet. We thus experience what Edward Kane of Ohio State University has called the "regulatory dialectic"—the closing of one loophole creates an incentive to develop others. As these new loopholes are closed, still others are developed. Regulation curbs excessive risk-taking to *some* extent, but to a considerable extent it merely changes the type rather than the amount of risk that banks take.

Apart from regulation, a factor that *may* perhaps limit risk-taking is that bank managers may be willing to forgo some earnings in favor of job security. Somewhat lower earnings are usually not a threat to management, but, if a bank fails, the FDIC throws out its top management. Whether or not the wish to protect their jobs actually does make bank managers less willing to take on risk is hard to say. But it might.

The memory of the Great Depression is another factor that may perhaps have inhibited risk-taking in the past. A banker who, when young, experienced the bank failures of the Great Depression may be somewhat leery of great risk-taking.

For whatever reason, in the early years of the FDIC its subsidy to risk-taking was not a serious problem. But now it is. There are several reasons for this change, quite apart from the obvious but perhaps irrelevant fact that today's bankers did not experience the depression of the 1930s.

Today's Incentives to Take Risk

Subsidized risk-taking has become a more serious problem because, with the elimination of Regulation Q, it is much easier for the banking *system* as a whole to assume excessive risk. Consider a banking system that consists of two banks, one conservative and the other a great risk-taker. As long as the risky bank cannot pay a higher rate on deposits, its high earnings from greater risk-taking will not allow it to grow much faster than the conservative bank. In 1970, however, it was allowed to attract large deposits by paying a higher rate on large CDs. Since then, the demise of Regulation Q has allowed it to attract small deposits by offering a higher interest rate. Hence, it can grow faster than the more conservative bank. As a result, the risky bank now accounts for a larger proportion of total deposits.[1]

This problem of deposits moving to risky banks is particularly serious if a bank is facing insolvency. Such a bank has nothing to lose by attracting a lot of additional funds and investing them in extremely risky, high-yielding assets. If the gamble pays off the bank prospers; if it does not, the bank is no worse off

---

[1] At first glance it may seem that the elimination of Regulation Q has made banks and thrift institutions take more risk in another way. Some people argue that, since depository institutions now have to pay a higher interest rate to depositors, they want to make higher yielding and hence riskier loans. But this is doubtful. A profit-maximizing bank or savings and loan has an incentive to make those loans that place it on its highest feasible indifference curve (drawn with income on one axis and safety on the other). Its optimal trade-off between safety and income is independent of how much of its income it then has to pay out to its depositors.

than before. It is no worse to go out with a bang than with a whimper. Money brokers facilitate such "go for broke" behavior. These firms take large deposits, break them into units of $100,000, and deposit these $100,000 units in the banks that pay the highest interest rate, regardless of risk. If the bank fails it is the FDIC, not the insured depositor, that loses. The FDIC (and the FSLIC) have been trying to stop this activity, but so far with little success.

The second reason excessive risk-taking is now a much more serious problem is that it has become harder for examiners to catch it. The types of risks have changed and the examiners have not yet adjusted fully to this change. Loans to risky companies are no longer the earmark of excessive risk. As interest rates have become more variable, long-term securities, even government bonds with no default risk, have become riskier for institutions whose liabilities run for a shorter term than their assets. When First Pennsylvania was almost destroyed in 1980 the major reason was not unsound loans, but losses on its bond portfolio.

Foreign lending has also grown, particularly to foreign governments in less developed countries. Loans to less developed countries are harder to evaluate than loans to domestic corporations. Countries do not issue balance sheets, and no one can say how great the political pressures to default will be. Moreover, banks have assumed new types of risks by using their holding companies to enter other lines of business and by off-balance-sheet financing. Much more volatile exchange rates have also raised the potential losses of banks. It is hard for examiners to evaluate such unfamiliar types of risk. Thrift institutions have used their new powers to make business loans, in some cases despite a lack of needed expertise.

What makes the situation worse is that the capital ratios of banks are lower now than they were in the 1960s, and those of thrifts are *much* lower. Hence, a small amount of overoptimism by a bank and by its examiners can cause the bank's losses to exceed its capital, so that the bank fails.

Solutions Proposed: Changes in the Deposit Insurance System

What can be done to stop depository institutions from exploiting the FDIC and FSLIC by taking on more risk?[2] Something that might help, albeit only to a limited extent, is to strengthen the supervisory process. For example, one could cut the lengthy procedures now required for the FDIC to terminate the insurance of a bank or thrift institution.

A more radical reform would be to replace the fixed insurance premium with a premium that varies with the riskiness of the institution. If bad drivers have to pay a higher insurance premium, why shouldn't a riskier bank pay a higher premium too? Selling the right to take more risk would introduce the

---

[2] Who is *ultimately* being exploited? Since the FDIC and the FSLIC raise the effective insurance premiums when they make losses, unsafe institutions are exploiting safe ones that have to pay the higher insurance premiums, rather than the taxpayer. Would this still be true if there were massive failures, so that the U.S. Treasury would have to bail out the FDIC or FSLIC? The bailout would probably consist of a loan that the surviving institutions would then have to pay through higher insurance premiums. If so, it is the surviving institutions that are being exploited by those that took more risk and failed.

price mechanism into the insurance system, something that appeals to many economists.

But there are problems. First, the risk that matters is not the risk of the institution failing, but the risk that the FDIC or FSLIC has to pay out a large sum of money. This risk depends on how quickly they find out that the institution is unsafe, and hence close it down. Suppose a bank uses 90 percent of its assets to play roulette in Las Vegas. If the FDIC closes it before its capital is gone there are no losses to the FDIC. But measuring the potential loss to the FDIC is even harder than measuring the riskiness of an institution's balance sheet. Moreover, the premium would have to be adjusted quickly as an institution takes more risk—by the time the examiners come around it may be too late. All the same, the FDIC and the FSLIC have asked Congress for permission to adjust insurance premiums for risk to a small extent.

Higher Capital Ratios

Another proposal is to require insured institutions to retain more capital—and in 1985 the regulators did raise the capital requirements of banks. The reasons for requiring more capital are simple: the more capital there is, the bigger is the cushion that protects the FDIC and the FSLIC. In addition, a higher capital ratio makes failure, and therefore excessive risk-taking, a more costly alternative for the insured institution.

But once again, there are problems. Banks complain that it is difficult for them to raise equity capital when bank stock is selling at a low price. A more serious problem arises from the nature of capital. Capital is not some asset that a bank holds in its vault. It is just an accounting entry, being the difference between the bank's assets and its liabilities to others. Suppose that a bank's assets consist of a $10-million loan that it has made, and its liabilities consist of $9 million in deposits. What is its capital? You cannot tell from this information alone. Supposing that the loan is a sound one, its capital is $1 million. But if the loan is unsound and has a value of 90 cents on the dollar, then its true capital is zero. Figure 8.1 shows the capital ratios of fifty-seven large banks that hold over half of all bank assets. One line measures capital by its book value, that is, by the capital recorded on the banks' balance sheets. The other line uses a more realistic estimate of the banks' capital, the stock market's valuation. These two estimates of the capital ratio show substantial differences.

A possible solution might be to force banks and thrifts to carry their assets on the books at the actual market value rather than at their cost of acquisition. But banks and thrift institutions would strongly oppose such a solution. Previously when interest rates were high most thrifts would have failed had they been required to carry their mortgage portfolios at true market prices. Moreover, for many assets it would be difficult to estimate the market price. Institutions that were declared insolvent could go to court and challenge the FDIC's estimates.

Another potential problem is that if banks and thrifts have more capital

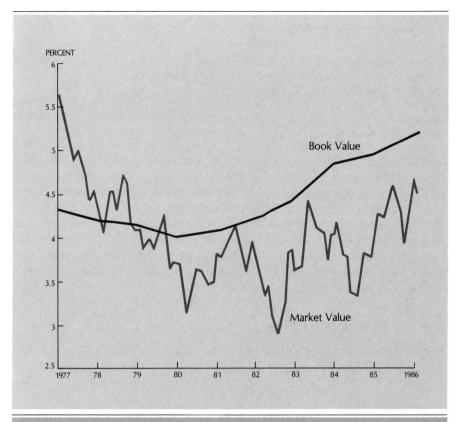

PERCENT

Book Value

Market Value

1977 78 79 80 81 82 83 84 85 1986

Figure 8.1 **Capital-Asset Ratios of 57 Large Banks.** The net worth of banks as measured by their book values does not coincide with what the stock market thinks it is. **Source:** Michael Keeley, "The Health of Banks and Thrifts," Federal Reserve Bank of San Francisco, *Weekly Letter*, 21 February 1986, p. 3.

the FDIC and FSLIC might use this as an excuse to delay closing down an unsafe institution. The financial cost of, as well as the political fallout from, the failure of a bank or a thrift would provide an incentive for holding off, and hoping for the best.

Given these problems—industry opposition, the difficulty of measuring capital, and the danger of regulatory lethargy—can a higher capital requirement really help to protect the FDIC and FSLIC? Probably it can, but the amount of protection is less than appears at first glance.

A related proposal is to require banks to have more secondary, that is, borrowed, capital. Such borrowed capital would protect the FDIC the same way primary capital does. It would also make it more costly for banks to assume too much risk, because the bondholders who provide the secondary capital would then require a higher interest rate on their bonds to compensate them for the greater risk. Presumably these bondholders would look behind the book values of a bank's assets, and if they thought that the true capital of a bank was zero, they would not buy its bonds. In addition, if the bonds that a bank has issued suddenly trade at a heavy discount this could be a signal to the FDIC that this bank has become riskier and should be watched closely. But, of course, there is a problem: small banks that are not known in the capital market would find it extremely difficult and expensive to sell bonds.

Greater Disclosure

Another proposal that has, to some extent, been put into effect by the FDIC is greater disclosure. If banks have to provide more information about the quality of their assets (for example, the countries to which they have made large loans), then they have a greater incentive not to put risky assets on their books. This solution has been attacked from two sides. Some people argue that greater disclosure could have too strong an effect—that it may cause depositors to run a bank. Others argue just the opposite—that even large depositors do not react to unfavorable news about their bank, mainly because they expect the FDIC to protect them.

Lowering the Insurance Ceiling

Still another possibility is to give depositors more of an incentive to monitor the riskiness of their banks. One way would be to lower the insurance ceiling, perhaps to $50,000 or even $10,000. Another way is to provide only partial protection in case of deposit assumption. (As described in Chapter 3, the FDIC and FSLIC could make large depositors bear some of the cost when a failing institution is merged into a sound one.)

Like increased disclosure, this proposal can be challenged from both sides. Some say that depositors would pay little attention to the danger of loss, in part because they cannot obtain reliable information on the bank's safety, and in part because business depositors (i.e., most large depositors) are concerned primarily with the loans and services they get from the bank. Others are worried that depositors would be too sensitive to the riskiness of their bank, and hence would be liable to run the bank at the slightest hint of trouble, thus causing many banks to fail. Ideally depositors would not run a bank, but simply force the bank to pay a higher interest rate on its deposits. However, this does not sound realistic. A treasurer who has a deposit in a bank that failed is not eager to explain to the company president that he knew the bank was risky but maintained his deposit in that bank because it paid 2 percent more interest.

In addition, lowering the insurance ceiling or making depositors bear some of the cost of bank failures is unfair to small banks. Most sophisticated depositors realize that, despite what it might say, the FDIC is not likely to let one of the largest banks fail. Hence, if deposit insurance is weakened they have an incentive to transfer their deposits from small banks to a handful of large banks.

Deposit Insurance in Perspective

At this point an optimist might say that there is no easy answer to the problem of protecting the FDIC and FSLIC from excessive risk-taking. A pessimist might say that there is no answer, easy or otherwise. Perhaps the truth lies in between: there are policies that would ease the problem but not solve it completely.

In any case, even if the problem of excessive risk-taking is not solved, it is much less serious than the problems we would have had in the absence of the FDIC and the FSLIC. Without deposit insurance there would surely have been massive runs on thrift institutions in the 1970s when rising interest rates made most of them de facto insolvent. Similarly, suppose that, in the absence of insurance, banks would have made the Latin American loans they actually did make. In the early 1980s many of our large banks would probably have been destroyed by bank runs. The collapse of Continental Illinois, and perhaps also the previous failure of Franklin National, could also have started runs causing other banks to fail.

Such runs need not, and should not, have caused a drastic reduction in the money stock because the Federal Reserve could, in ways we will describe in Chapter 20, have provided banks with the additional reserves needed to meet the deposit outflow. Most of the funds withdrawn from one bank would, in any case, have been redeposited into another bank. Thus the money stock would not have declined had there been no FDIC. All the same, the collapse of some major banks would have had highly disruptive effects. And the collapse of insolvent thrift institutions that would have occurred in the absence of the FSLIC would have substantially reduced depositors' wealth. This, in turn, could have caused a recession as households then reduced consumption.

THE SEPARATION OF BANKING FROM OTHER LINES OF BUSINESS

In Chapter 3 we described how banks use holding companies to enter other businesses closely related to banking. Not surprisingly, banks would like to extend the list of industries that they can enter. They argue that by offering various financial services (for example, selling life insurance) they would not only raise their profits, but also help consumers by increasing competition. The banks also say they should be allowed to enter other industries, because firms in other industries are allowed to compete with banks. Sears Roebuck operates a money-market fund through a subsidiary and, in effect, takes time deposits by paying interest to its credit-card holders if their accounts have a positive balance. The Ford Motor Company competes with banks, not only by making automobile loans, but also through a savings and loan that it owns.

Firms in the industries that banks want to enter object strongly. They claim that banks obtain special privileges from the government, specifically deposit insurance, and that they would therefore have an unfair advantage if allowed to compete in other industries. In addition, banks might be more willing to give loans to customers of their subsidiaries, and in this way compete unfairly. Why banks would prefer to give loans to customers of their other businesses is far from clear. They would be better off making their loans to those who pay the highest interest rate. Another charge is that, if banks enter other industries, they would be assuming too much risk. Whether or not this is so is hard to say. It depends not only on the riskiness of the business, but also on the correlation of that risk with the risk that banks already face. Recall the discussion of portfolio risk in Chapter 2. More serious is the argument that if a bank's subsidiary is in danger of failing the bank might make risky loans to it to prop it up. In addition, the failure of a subsidiary might cause a bank to fail. Although the law could be written to reduce this danger, it is not clear whether it could be eliminated entirely.

In this conflict much of the banks' efforts have been devoted to breaking down the barrier between banking and investment banking. Investment banks are institutions that help firms to raise capital by advising them on what stocks and bonds to issue. Sometimes they also act as middlemen by buying the newly issued securities of firms at wholesale and then retailing them to the public. At other times they distribute the securities for a commission. Until 1933 banks were allowed to act as investment bankers, but then the Glass-Steagall Act greatly limited underwriting activities of member banks.

PROBLEMS WITH THE REGULATORY STRUCTURE

The way we regulate banking is not so much a logically developed system as the outcome of historical accidents and political compromises. Hence there are frequent attempts to reform it.

"Competition in Laxity"

The regulatory system is not unified. Commercial banks and mutual thrift institutions can decide whether to operate under a federal or a state charter, and hence whether to be regulated by the state or entirely by the federal government. Thus, in 1979, when the New York State banking commissioner did not permit a large bank, Marine Midland, to merge into a foreign bank, the Hong Kong and Shanghai Banking Corp., Marine Midland simply handed in its state charter and took out a national charter instead. Not only can a bank choose its chartering agency, but a state bank can also choose whether or not to be a member bank. Giving banks the right to decide whether they want to abide by the stricter federal regulations or by the generally more relaxed state regulations may seem strange.

Banks can also play one supervising agency off against the other. Many economists believe that, since the regulatory agencies do not want to lose banks from their supervision, they compete among themselves for banks by limiting the severity of their regulations. This "competition in laxity" has drawn much criticism from those who are concerned that banks are permitted to take too many risks.

By no means do all economists agree that such alleged "competition in laxity" is bad. Many argue that it provides a useful balance to the inherent tendency of bank regulators to impose excessive regulation, and to discourage risk-taking too much. Bank regulators have an incentive to be too severe because they get blamed if they allow banks to do something that results in some bank failures. But they do *not* get blamed by the public if they prohibit something, say, a new type of loan, that would actually have been quite safe. If they prohibit it nobody ever finds out about its safety. Insofar as this bias in the regulators' own reward and punishment system outweighs the bias that results from the pressures brought to bear by the banking industry, and from the regulators' tendency to be "nice" to their industry, regulations tend to be too severe, and some competition among regulating agencies is desirable. For example, NOW accounts would probably not have developed if all depository institutions were regulated by a single government agency.

From time to time, bills are introduced in Congress to limit "competition in laxity" by abolishing one or more of the federal regulatory agencies. This would also have the advantage of reducing complexity and duplication of effort. One solution would be to centralize federal bank supervision in a single government agency. But which one? State banks would not like to be regulated by the parent of national banks, the Comptroller of the Currency, nor would nonmember banks like to be regulated by the Federal Reserve. In one way the FDIC would be the logical choice since it has to pay up in case of bank failure; but this very fact may make it too cautious. Hence, some economists have proposed creating a new agency that would do nothing except regulate banks, but others are afraid that such an agency could be captured by the industry it is regulating.

A related issue is the Federal Reserve's role in bank regulation. The Board of Governors now has to spend much of its time on this task. Hence, some economists believe that it should be relieved of these duties, so that it can spend more time on monetary policy and also so that it would be less likely to be influenced in its monetary policy by any special concern about banks. But the Fed believes that the information it gains from bank supervision is useful to it in making monetary policy.

The Role of Congress in Regulation

In a general sense Congress, too, is a regulator of banks and thrift institutions since it passes the laws under which they operate. Ideally, Congress would stay on top of developments and quickly modify laws as conditions change. But this is not the case. Congress is reluctant to change banking laws, and does so only under great pressure. Any change in the law, such as allowing banks to sell insurance, permitting interstate banking, or eliminating Regulation Q, hurts some people. They then complain bitterly and threaten to support at the next election the opponents of those who voted for the change. It might seem that the opposition of those who lose from a proposed change in the law is fully offset by the potential support a congressperson could receive from those who would gain from the change. Usually it does not work that way. We are angry with those who take something away from us, but feel that those who give us something are merely doing what is obviously reasonable and fair. It is not surprising that Congress does not like to consider banking legislation.

Hence, Congress prefers banking legislation that provides a net benefit to all the powerful groups. For example, when Congress phased out the Regulation Q ceiling cherished by savings and loans, it allowed them in return to offer NOW accounts. The legislator's task is to find some compromise that keeps everyone, if not happy, at least quiescent. The trouble is that in such trade-offs the interests of the larger public may be brushed aside. To most voters financial reform is an arcane issue, nothing to get exited about. Hence, a congressperson gains little by defending the public interest instead of the interests of the industries involved.

The difficulty of finding a compromise that is acceptable to various interest groups is not the only factor slowing down financial reform. The chairpersons of the Senate and House banking committees must be ready to compromise on any differences between them. Suppose that the chairperson of the Senate banking committee wants a law that does X and Y, while the chairperson of the House banking committee wants only X and not Y. Despite both of them wanting X, it may not be enacted because the Senate chairperson believes wrongly that by insisting on both X and Y he or she can force the House to go along with Y too. Moreover, there is still another hurdle—to become law the president's support is also needed, and may not be forthcoming.

SUMMARY

1 Deposit insurance gives depository institutions an incentive to take excessive risk. This has become a much more serious problem in recent years.
2 Among the proposed solutions to excessive risk-taking are making insurance premiums dependent upon risk, requiring more capital, requiring greater disclosure, and reducing the protection that large depositors now receive. All of these solutions have their problems.
3 Banks would like permission to have subsidiaries in other industries. Those already in those industries are opposed, arguing that such subsidiaries would pose excessive risks to banks, that due to deposit insurance, banks would have an unfair advantage, and that banks would require borrowers to become customers of their subsidiaries.
4 Bank regulation is decentralized among several agencies, thus reducing the power of the bank regulators. Pressures brought by interest groups, as well as internal problems, make Congress slow to react to emerging regulatory problems.

QUESTIONS AND EXERCISES

1 Why do depository institutions have an incentive to take too much risk? Do other firms have a similar incentive?
2 Among the proposed solutions to excessive risk-taking are making FDIC premiums dependent on risk and requiring banks to have more capital. What difficulties do these proposals face?
3 Why has the problem of excessive risk-taking become more serious in recent years?
4 Discuss the pros and cons of "competition in laxity."
5 What factors inhibit effective congressional action on banking legislation?

FURTHER READING

FEDERAL RESERVE BANK OF ATLANTA. *Economic Review,* March 1984. This issue has several good articles on the problems of deposit insurance.

FEDERAL RESERVE BANK OF SAN FRANCISCO. *The Search for Financial Stability,* 1985. A collection of excellent articles on excessive risk-taking.

KANE, EDWARD. *The Gathering Crisis in Deposit Insurance.* Cambridge, Mass.: MIT Press, 1985. An excellent discussion of current problems with deposit insurance, written in a spirited style.

KAREKEN, JOHN, et al. "Symposium on Bank Regulation," *Journal of Business,* 59 (January 1986):pp. 1–117. A collection of papers that raises many important points about deposit insurance.

PART TWO

THE
SUPPLY
OF
MONEY

CHAPTER 9

The Measurement of Money

Chapter 1 defined money in quite general terms. The time has now come to be more specific, and also to see how money is measured.

THE A PRIORI AND EMPIRICAL APPROACHES

There are two major approaches to defining money. One, called the **a priori approach,** is a rather philosophical one that focuses on the nature of money. It searches for the singular characteristic that distinguishes money from other things, and then defines money in terms of this characteristic. This is the way we usually define something.

To the question, what is *the* distinguishing characteristic of money, there is a simple answer: its medium of exchange function. This function is unique to money; nothing else is a general medium of exchange. By contrast, the store of wealth function is not unique to money; money shares this function with many other things. Hence, the a priori approach defines money as anything that is a generally accepted medium of exchange.[1]

The a priori definition of money has the advantage of providing, at least on an abstract level, a fairly clear-cut differentiation between those items that are money and those that are not. Items that can normally be used to make payments, such as demand deposits and travelers checks, are money, while time deposits are *not.* Hence, this approach defines money as *M-1.*

While the a priori definition of money focuses on what is distinctive about money, that is, on its essence, the rival **empirical definition** *focuses on what makes the money supply important.* Money is important for policy for two reasons. One is that changes in the money supply have a major, and numerous economists would say a dominating, impact on nominal income. The second

---

[1] The standard of value function is also unique to money. But one cannot use it to define money since it is an abstraction rather than a concrete unit. Thus, it is meaningless to ask, for example, whether the standard of value increased at a 5 percent rate last year, or whether time deposits are included in the standard of value.

Table 9.1	Measures of Money, March 1986	
	Billions of dollars (not seasonally adjusted)	%
M-1		
Currency	172.3	27.3
Travelers checks	5.8	.9
Demand deposits	267.2	42.3
Other checkable deposits	185.3	29.4
Total	630.6	100.0
M-2		
M-1	630.6	24.3
Small time deposits	891.8	34.4
Money-market deposit accounts	520.5	20.1
Savings deposits	306.5	11.8
Money-market mutual balances (general purpose and broker/dealers)	186.3	7.2
Overnight repurchase agreements	50.3	1.9
Overnight Eurodollars	16.2	.6
Consolidation adjustment[a]	−8.7	−.3
Total	2,593.5	100.0
M-3		
M-2	2,593.5	79.5
Large time deposits	450.7	13.8
Term Eurodollars	80.4	2.4
Term repurchase agreements	71.4	2.2
Money-market mutual funds (institutions only)	70.2	2.2
Consolidation adjustment[a]	−6.9	−.2
Total	3,259.3	100.0
Memorandum		
Transaction accounts:		
in commercial banks	413.3	15.6
in thrift institutions	60.0	2.2
Nontransaction accounts:		
in commercial banks	1,135.2	42.9
in thrift institutions	1,035.0	39.2
Total	2,643.5	100.0

Note: IRA and Keogh accounts are excluded. For other details of the items covered, see the source.

a: Adjustments to prevent double-counting. For example, the deposits in commercial banks that thrift institutions hold as reserves against their own deposits should not be counted in *M-2*.

Source: Board of Governors, Federal Reserve System, Release H.6, 15 May 1986.

reason is that the Fed can control the supply of money. Since economists are interested in policy, variables that the government can control are, obviously, more important to them than other variables, such as expectations, that may also have a powerful effect on nominal income, but cannot be controlled so easily.

The empirical definition of money therefore defines money, not by any inherent characteristics, but as that liquid asset, or collection of liquid assets, that (1) has the most predictable impact on nominal income and (2) can be controlled by the Fed.

Many—probably most—economists believe that the monetary measure that has the closest relation to income is M-1, but some believe that broader measures, such as M-2 or M-3 (shown in Table 9.1), are more closely related to income. With respect to the controllability criterion, M-1 is probably more accurately controlled, but the difference may perhaps not be very great.

Which is better, the empirical or the a priori definition? Those who adhere to the a priori definition argue that the empirical definition is inadequate because it misses the essence of money and is subject to erratic shifts. Thus, it may define money as M-1 at one time and as M-2 at another time depending on which of these shows the closest correlation with income. This seems arbitrary to supporters of the a priori definition. Besides, the advocates of the empirical definition do not agree among themselves about which measure of the money stock is the best "handle" in controlling income. Supporters of the empirical definition, on the other hand, see nothing wrong with the definition of money changing from time to time, and each of them believes that he or she has evidence that allows one to choose between M-1 and M-2.

Fortunately, this disagreement is unimportant. It is essentially a dispute about how to use the word "money," and is not a disagreement about how the economy operates. Thus, one could accept the a priori definition of money as M-1, and yet if it turns out that M-2 has the more predictable effect on income one could think and talk mainly about M-2, using some word other than *money*, say, *bread*, if one does not like to say M-2. On the other hand, one can go along with the empirical definition, and use the term *money* for, say, M-2, while being fully aware of the fact that the item that is the medium of exchange has a unique and interesting characteristic.

THE MEASURES OF MONEY

Table 9.1 shows the various measures of money as defined by the Federal Reserve. Of these, M-1 and M-2 are by far the most important. M-3 is used only occasionally.

M-1, sometimes called "narrow money," consists of items that can be spent immediately, that is, currency, travelers checks, and those deposits in commercial banks, mutual savings banks, and savings and loan associations against which unlimited checks can be written, as well as share drafts in credit unions.

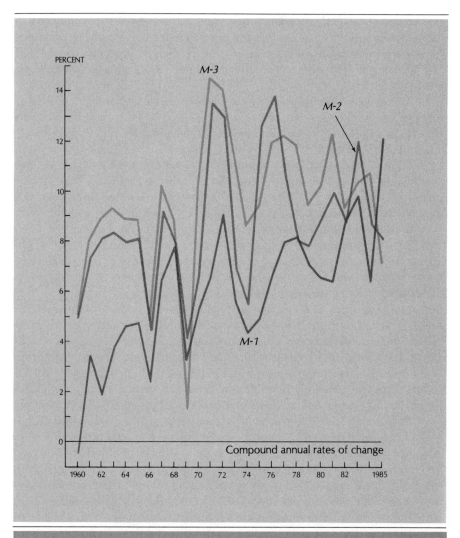

Figure 9.1 Rates of Growth, M-1, M-2, and M-3, 1960–1985. The growth rates of the various measures diverge at times. **Source:** Board of Governors, Federal Reserve System, *Money Stock Revisions*, 1986, Table 1.

M-2, also called "broad money," adds to *M-1* various items that are almost as liquid as checkable deposits. These are small time deposits, that is, time deposits of less than $10,000, which, at a small penalty, can usually be redeemed on demand, and money-market deposit accounts, which are time deposits against which a limited number of checks can be written. It also includes savings deposits, which can be cashed by presenting the passbook at the bank, and shares in money-market mutual funds, which often have a $500 minimum on checks that can be written on them, as well as overnight repurchase agreements and overnight Eurodollar deposits, redeemable overnight.

Large time deposits cannot be redeemed, though they are often negotiable and thus can be sold in the secondary market. Hence they are included in *M-3* and not in *M-2*. *M-3* also includes Eurodollars and repurchase agreements for longer than overnight and shares in those money-market funds that deal with institutions and not with the general public.

Figure 9.1 shows the behavior of *M-1*, *M-2*, and *M-3* in recent years, and illustrates the considerable divergence in their growth rates. Hence, it *does* make a difference how money is defined.

ALTERNATIVE DEFINITIONS AND MONEY SUBSTITUTES

The definitions currently used by the Fed are not etched in stone. As the financial system changes and new financial instruments are developed, the Fed is likely to change these definitions. Even now they are not beyond criticism. For example, some economists are uneasy about the Fed's treatment of money-market funds.

Whichever way one defines money there will be some near-monies that are similar to money and make the measurement of something called "money" rather arbitrary. The most obvious example is credit cards. One can think of a credit-card line of credit as a substitute for holding money—or else as money itself. Lines of credit, such as those provided by credit cards, are like money in the sense of providing a widely, though not quite generally, accepted medium of exchange. However they differ from money in one important way: money is part of a person's wealth, but a line of credit is not; for example, wouldn't everyone rather receive a $1,000 check as a gift than have the ceiling on their credit card raised by $1,000?

Similarly, many American banks have adopted a common practice of British banks, the extension of overdraft privileges. These allow certain customers to write checks in excess of their demand deposits, and these overdrafts are treated as automatic loans.

Another troublesome problem is created by Eurodollars. Since most Eurodollar deposits consist of large CDs, they should at most be included in *M-3* rather than in *M-1* or *M-2*, and should perhaps be treated as short-term securities rather than as "money." More generally, does it make sense to talk about the U.S. money stock in isolation? Some economists point out that large firms can hold foreign currencies to meet their needs for transactions balances by selling them on the foreign exchange market just before they make payments in dollars.

MEASURING MONEY AS A WEIGHTED AGGREGATE

Perhaps the solution is to measure money in a more sophisticated way. So far the discussion has been in terms of a simple dichotomy: an item either is—or is not—money, and there is nothing in between. But this is a crude procedure. Why not allow for the obvious fact that for the empirical definition of money the difference between those items included in money and other highly liquid assets is a matter of degree rather than of kind? This suggests that one should measure money as a *weighted average* of various components rather than as their simple sum. For example, currency might be given a weight of 1, and savings deposits a weight of, say, .3. The problem is then to find some way of assigning appropriate weights to various monetary components. One way, called the "monetary services index" method, is to use the interest rate paid by a monetary asset as an (inverse) measure of its moneyness. Financial assets provide two yields: liquidity (i.e., moneyness) and interest. In equilibrium the total perceived yields on assets must be equal; thus, the less explicit interest an asset pays, the greater must be its implicit yield in the form of moneyness. Hence, one can use the interest rates paid on an asset as an (inverse) weight of its moneyness. One can then combine various assets into a monetary total by weighting them in this way. This approach is still experimental.

REFINING THE MONEY MEASUREMENTS

So far we have discussed some broad issues in defining and measuring money. Now we get more specific. It is easy to say that demand deposits should be counted as part of the money stock, but do we really want to include all types of demand deposits? No, we do not. We are interested in the size of the money supply, not because this knowledge ennobles a person's otherwise drab life, but because changes in the money supply bring about changes in expenditures, and hence in nominal income. This suggests that we should include only those deposits that affect expenditures.

It follows that the deposits of the federal government should not be counted. Federal government expenditures are not influenced at all by the Treasury's money holdings. They are set by congressional authorization and, in some cases, by the behavior of the economy. The U.S. Treasury is never constrained in its expenditures by having insufficient money—it can always borrow. For this reason U.S. government deposits—but not state and local government deposits—are excluded from the money supply.

Another item that is excluded is currency held by banks in their vaults. We exclude this because it too does not affect the bank's expenditures. And for the same reason interbank deposits are also excluded. In addition, we exclude cash items in the process of collection, that is, checks, etc., currently in the process of clearing. This is done on the (perhaps somewhat doubtful) assumption that those who wrote the checks have already deducted them from their outstanding balances. And what affects expenditures are the deposits that people *think* they have.

HOW RELIABLE ARE THE DATA?

We now come to a painful topic. Early estimates of the growth rate of the money stock are very poor. The way we know this is that the initially published data are substantially revised later on. This is illustrated by Table 9.2, which gives the results of a revision made in February 1983. (And such revisions are made throughout a five-year period.) The mean absolute change in the money growth rate that resulted from this revision was 4 percent for *M-1* and 2 per-

Table 9.2	Growth Rates of Money: Old and Revised Series			
	M-1[a]		M-2[a]	
Period	Old	Revised	Old	Revised
December 1981–January 1982	23.1%	21.5%	13.0%	10.6%
January 1982–February 1982	− 3.4	.5	4.5	3.8
February 1982–March 1982	2.7	1.6	11.8	9.0
March 1982–April 1982	11.5	1.9	10.5	4.2
April 1982–May 1982	− 2.4	8.6	11.3	10.5
May 1982–June 1982	− .3	2.7	6.8	9.5
June 1982—July 1982	− .3	2.7	10.3	11.0
July 1982–August 1982	10.9	10.8	15.3	15.5
August 1982–September 1982	14.9	13.6	5.2	8.8
September 1982–October 1982	22.6	15.5	8.3	8.1
October 1982–November 1982	18.3	14.4	12.2	9.9
November 1982–December 1982	9.2	11.4	7.9	9.1

a: Compounded annual rates of change, seasonally adjusted.

Source: Federal Reserve Bank of St. Louis, *Monetary Trends*, 3 March 1983, p. 1.

cent for *M-2*. This is equivalent to the difference between an expansionary and a restrictive monetary policy! Hence, errors in estimating the money growth rate can give a misleading picture. For example, in March 1978 the data showed a sharp retardation of the money growth rate for several months that some economists thought would lead to a recession. But when the data were revised shortly afterward, a recession no longer seemed likely.

The unreliability of the data until several years afterward when they have been completely revised has two major implications. First, one should not get upset about data showing that money was growing at a highly undesirable rate for a short period of time. Over a period of, say, three or six months, errors tend to average out, but the weekly data on the growth of the money stock that are published in many newspapers are, in all probability, going to be revised substantially. When one adds to this the fact that the actual weekly growth rate of money fluctuates very erratically in any case, it follows that the publication of the weekly money stock figures could constitutionally be banned under the Supreme Court criterion of having no redeeming social value. Second, the Federal Reserve has to make its current policy on the basis of preliminary data. Since these data do not give a reliable indication of what the current monetary growth rate is, the Fed can hardly be expected to achieve the precise growth rate it desires.

The main source of errors is that the money data, like most economic statistics, are adjusted for seasonal variations. For example, the demand for money always increases at Christmas, and to reduce seasonal fluctuations in interest rates the Fed adjusts the supply of money for such seasonal variations in demand. To prevent these seasonal changes in supply from distorting the figures, the money stock for each month is divided by a seasonal adjustment factor that should cancel out these seasonal variations. If the seasonal pattern is constant, then this is a simple procedure that does not lead to significant errors. But the seasonal pattern is unstable; for example, in a year when the public feels prosperous its demand for money at Christmas may rise by more than it does in another year in which it feels pessimistic, and hence less generous. Obviously, such a variable seasonal pattern is hard to adjust for, and if the seasonal movements are large, the seasonal adjustment can lead to large errors.

If the errors in the levels of the money stock were constant—for example, the money stock always being overstated by, say, 5 percent—these errors would not matter because they would not affect money *growth rates,* which is what matters in predicting *changes* in income. But, unfortunately, this is not the case. If the error in the seasonal adjustment factor is positive for one month it must be negative for another month, since over the whole year the seasonal adjustment factors cancel out.

One reason why the money growth figures are so bad is that small percentage errors in estimating the money *stock* can, purely as a matter of arithmetic, result in very large percentage errors in the estimate of how fast money has grown over a short period of time. For example, suppose that the actual money stock stood at $1,000 billion at the start of the month, and at $1,004 billion at the end of the month. This is a growth rate in annual terms of approximately 4.8 percent (.4 percent times 12). But suppose that the money stock at the end of the month is estimated by mistake as $1,006 billion, an error of only .2 percent. The growth rate then appears to be about 7.2 percent instead of 4.8 percent. The shorter the period of time covered by the data, the greater is the error in the growth rate (expressed as an annual rate) that results from a small mistake in estimating the stock at either the beginning or the end of the period.

Someone trying to gauge the growth rate of money has to worry not only about errors in the data, but also about erratic, and hence essentially meaningless, factors that cause the money growth rate to vary from time to time. Many people who watch the money growth rate are not interested in such erratic changes that are likely to wash out soon, but would like to know what the underlying money growth rate is. Accordingly, one study asked the following question: suppose the *estimated* money growth rate is x percent, and one wants to set out a range so that the probability is two-thirds that the *true* growth rate falls within this range. How much would one have to add or subtract from x percent to get this range? This figure is given by a statistic called the "standard error." It is shown in Table 9.3. To illustrate its interpretation assume that the estimated *M-1* month-to-month growth rate is 6 percent. This 6 percent should be interpreted as a best guess with a two-thirds chance that the true underlying growth rate is between 1½ and 10½ percent. Since a 1½ percent growth rate is a highly restrictive policy, while a 10½ percent growth rate is a highly expansionary policy, this table illustrates that month-to-month growth rates have little meaning. But over a six-month period the range around the estimated 6 percent growth rate is only 5.2 to 6.8 percent, so that over a six-month period monetary growth rates are meaningful.

Table 9.3	Standard Errors of Money Growth Rates	
	M-1	*M-2*
Monthly	4.5%	3.5%
Quarterly	1.7	1.3
Half-yearly	.8	.6

Source: David Pierce, "Trend and Noise in Monetary Aggregates," in Board of Governors, Federal Reserve System, *New Monetary Control Procedures,* Vol. 1, Washington, D.C., 1981, p. ii.

SUMMARY

1 There are two general approaches to defining money. The a priori approach focuses on the essence of money. This leads to the *M-1* definition. The empirical approach focuses on that collection of monetary assets that has the closest correlation with nominal income and is readily controlled by the Fed.
2 *M-1* is defined as currency, checkable deposits, and travelers checks. *M-2* adds to *M-1* savings deposits, small time deposits, money-market fund shares, overnight repurchase agreements, and overnight Eurodollar deposits. *M-3* adds to this large time deposits and term repurchase agreements.
3 Eurodollars and credit cards create problems for measuring meaningful monetary totals. One approach to measuring money combines various components by giving them different weights.
4 Federal government deposits, vault cash, interbank deposits, and cash items in the process of collection are excluded from money.
5 The published data are subject to substantial revisions over time, largely due to faulty seasonal adjustment.

QUESTIONS AND EXERCISES

1 Write an essay defending:
   a. the a priori approach to the definition of money
   b. the empirical approach to the definition of money
2 Describe a change in Federal Reserve or FDIC regulations that would induce you to make a change in the definition of money.
3 Explain why federal government deposits, vault cash, interbank deposits, and cash items in the process of collection are excluded from the money supply.
4 Should food stamps be included in *M-1* or *M-2?*

FURTHER READING

ADVISORY COMMITTEE ON MONETARY STATISTICS. *Improving the Monetary Aggregates.* Washington, D.C.: Board of Governors, Federal Reserve System, 1976. A storehouse of technical details on how the money data are constructed and on how they could be improved.

BARNETT, WILLIAM, EDWARD OFFENBACHER, and PAUL SPINDT. "New Concepts of Aggregate Money," *Journal of Finance* 36 (May 1981):497–505. A good discussion of measuring money as a weighted aggregate.

BRYANT, WILLIAM. *Money and Monetary Policy in Interdependent Nations.* Washington, D.C.: Brookings Institution, 1980. An argument that one needs to look beyond a country's borders in defining money.

COOK, TIMOTHY. "The 1983 M1 Seasonal Revisions," *Economic Review,* Federal Reserve Bank of Richmond, 70 (March/April 1984): 22–33.

FRIEDMAN, MILTON, and ANNA SCHWARTZ. *Monetary Statistics of the United States.* New York: Columbia University Press, 1970. Chapter 3 gives a cogent and powerful defense of the empirical approach to the definition of money.

HART, ALBERT. "Regaining Control over an Open-ended Money Supply," in U.S. Congress Joint Economic Committee, *Special Study on Economic Change,* Vol. 4, Washington, D.C., 1980, pp. 85–143. An important discussion of the erosion of the concept of money.

SIMPSON, THOMAS. "The Redefinition of Monetary Aggregates," *Federal Reserve Bulletin* 66 (February 1980):97–114. This is the Fed's statement of how it defines money, and its reasons for adopting its definitions.

U.S. CONGRESS, HOUSE, SUBCOMMITTEE ON DOMESTIC MONETARY POLICY, COMMITTEE ON BANKING, FINANCE, AND URBAN AFFAIRS. *Measuring the Monetary Aggregates,* 96th Congress, 2nd session, February 1980. A useful compendium of economists' views.

YEAGER, LELAND B. "The Medium of Exchange," in Robert Clower (ed.), *Monetary Theory,* pp. 37–60. Baltimore: Penguin Books, 1969. A rousing and subtle defense of the a priori approach to defining money.

CHAPTER 10

The Creation of Money

Having looked at the definition of money we now turn to its creation. The central point here is that the most important form of money—checkable deposits—is created by depository institutions. Specifically, these institutions undertake *multiple deposit creation*. This means that when someone deposits $100 of currency, or a $100 check drawn on, say, the U.S. Treasury, total deposits will rise by more than $100. This is by no means obvious, so in reading this chapter try to understand the principles involved, without becoming mesmerized by the numerical examples or the algebra. Before going directly to how checkable deposits are created, let us look at the origin of the other type of money, currency.

CURRENCY CREATION

The first step in the creation of currency notes (dollar bills, etc.) is that the Bureau of Printing and Engraving, an agency of the U.S. Treasury Department, produces the currency notes. It then "sells" them to the Federal Reserve, which pays for them by crediting the account that the Treasury has with it. Then when a bank needs currency, the bank calls the Fed. The Fed ships it currency, and debits the bank's reserve account. The bank then puts this currency into circulation by paying it out to customers. At this point, when the currency gets into the hands of the nonbank public, it becomes part of the money supply. Coins, too, become money in this way.

The amount of currency in circulation therefore depends on how much currency the public wants to hold. People can always turn any checkable deposits they own into currency. Monetary policy does not operate by controlling the quantity of currency directly; instead it controls the supply of deposits by controlling the reserves of banks.[1]

---

[1] There are good reasons for this. Suppose that, to limit the money supply, the Fed provided no additional currency to banks. Banks would then not be able to meet their legal obligation to pay out demand deposits on demand and would be closed. Conversely, if the Fed tried to raise the money supply by increasing outstanding currency, it would have no way of getting this currency to the public, and, even if it did, the public could get rid of the currency by depositing it.

MULTIPLE DEPOSIT CREATION

When someone deposits a dollar of currency this results in several dollars of deposits. This may seem bizarre, since it suggests that something is created out of nothing. But this puzzle disappears once one sees what a deposit really is.

The Nature of Deposits

What actually is a **deposit**? It is not a physical object like currency, but merely *a property right evidenced by an entry in the bank's books.* You cannot see a deposit, or hold it in your hand, any more than you can hold in your hand the right to a jury trial or someone's promise. This is confusing because when we speak of someone drawing a deposit out and receiving currency in exchange for the deposit, there certainly is a tangible item, currency, being withdrawn. But when you "draw out your deposit" what you are actually doing is *exchanging* your right to receive payment from the bank in the future for currency *right now.* When banks create deposits, they no more create something out of nothing than the Supreme Court does when it creates a new legal right. In neither case does what is created have any physical existence. It is important to keep this in mind; otherwise, the subsequent discussion of deposit creation becomes incomprehensible.

Two Special Cases: 100 Percent Reserves and 100 Percent Currency Drain

As another preliminary to multiple deposit creation, here are two special cases in which multiple deposits are *not* created, and they provide a clue why multiple deposit creation does occur in more realistic situations.

100 Percent Reserves. The first special case is one in which the law in its awful majesty requires that the bank keep 100 percent reserves against its demand deposits. Consider what happens when someone deposits $10,000 of currency. We can see this best by looking at a **T account**, *a condensed version of the bank's balance sheet,* which leaves out all previous entries, and shows just the ones we are currently considering. Such a T account now shows:

(1)

Assets		Liabilities	
currency	$10,000	deposits	$10,000

This bank is now in equilibrium; it has exactly the reserves that the law says it must hold against its deposit. Has there been multiple deposit creation? Certainly not. A $10,000 deposit has been created against $10,000 of currency reserves. This is a one-to-one ratio; there is nothing multiple about it.

Loans in Currency Only. Consider another unrealistic case in which the required reserve ratio is only, say, 20 percent, but in which a borrower when granted a loan takes the proceeds entirely in the form of currency, and continues to hold this currency. In this case, since the required reserve ratio is less than 100 percent, the above T account does not represent an equilibrium for the bank. It can increase its profits by lending out $8,000 of the initial $10,000 deposit or by buying an $8,000 security, keeping the other $2,000 as a reserve against its deposits. Its T account now, after it has made a loan, looks as follows:

(2)

Assets		Liabilities	
currency	$2,000	deposits	$10,000
loan outstanding	$8,000		

This bank is now in equilibrium; it holds just the reserves (currency) it must hold against its deposit. But again, there has been no multiple deposit creation: the bank initially received $10,000 of currency, that is, reserves, and has $10,000 of deposits outstanding, so that deposits have increased in a one-to-one ratio to reserves.

How Multiple Deposit Creation Occurs

Now drop the peculiar assumption that a borrower, or seller of a security, holds the proceeds in the form of currency. This is most improbable because someone is not likely to borrow and pay interest unless he or she wants to use the money to make a purchase. And whomever he or she buys from is not likely to hold currency either, but will deposit the funds into a bank or other depository institution. One can assume, as a first approximation, that *all* the proceeds of a sale will be deposited. (Later on we will modify this assumption.) We will also assume that there is a 20 percent reserve requirement, and that the public does not increase its savings or time deposits, but puts all the funds it receives into transaction accounts. Finally, we assume that depository institutions use all their available reserves to make loans or to buy securities instead of holding some idle reserves.

Assume now that someone deposits a $10,000 check obtained from selling a security to the Fed into Bank A. When the check has cleared, this bank's T account looks as follows:

Bank A

(3)

Assets		Liabilities	
reserves with Federal Reserve	$10,000	deposits	$10,000

As before, since the bank has $8,000 more than the required 20 percent reserves, it increases its loans, and writes up the borrower's deposit account by the amount of the loan. Its T account is:

Bank A

(4)

Assets		Liabilities	
reserves with Federal Reserve	$10,000	deposits	$18,000
loans outstanding	$ 8,000		

The borrower does not keep the loan idle, but uses it to make a purchase. And the seller now deposits the $8,000 check received into, say, Savings and Loan B, which sends it to the Fed for clearing. After it clears, Bank A's T account is:

Bank A

(5)

Assets		Liabilities	
loans outstanding	$8,000	deposits	$10,000
reserves with			
Federal Reserve	$2,000		

Its reserves, $2,000, are now just sufficient to cover the $10,000 deposit it has outstanding, so it is in equilibrium. However, Savings and Loan B has now received $8,000 of deposits and reserves, which gives it the following T account:

Savings and Loan B

(6)

Assets		Liabilities	
reserves with			
Federal Reserve	$8,000	deposits	$8,000

But there is no reason why B should want to keep 100 percent reserves against the deposit. It needs to keep only $1,600 ($8,000 times 20 percent) reserves and can use the remainder, $6,400, to make a loan or buy a security. When the borrower, or seller of the security, spends the $6,400 the recipient deposits the check into Bank C, which sends it to the Federal Reserve for clearing. As a result, B's T account becomes:

Savings and Loan B

(7)

Assets		Liabilities	
reserves with			
Federal Reserve	$1,600	deposits	$8,000
loans outstanding	$6,400		

B is now in equilibrium, having just the $1,600 reserves it needs, and no more. But the story continues with C, which has received $6,400 of deposits and reserves. It, too, will keep only 20 percent, that is, $1,280, as a reserve against the $6,400 deposit, and use $5,120 to buy a security or make a loan, which, by the now familiar process, will become a deposit in D, so that D can now lend out 80 percent of it, $4,096, which, in turn, will become a deposit in E, and that depository institution will again lend out, or buy a security with, 80 percent of this.[2]

In this process, deposits are being created by every depository institution in the chain; there are deposits of $10,000 in A, $8,000 in B, $6,400 in C,

---

[2] As an exercise, write out the T accounts for C, D, and E.

$5,120 in D, $4,096 in E, and so on. In other words, there is **multiple deposit creation;** *the initial increase in reserves has called forth a series of subsequent deposits.* The two salient reasons this occurs are, first, that no institution keeps a 100 percent reserve against its deposit and, second, while each one loses an equivalent amount of reserves when it makes a loan or buys a security, *it loses these reserves not to thin air, but to another depository institution that then expands its loans or security holdings.*

The Deposit Multiplier

How much does the multiple deposit creation amount to? We have a series here that goes as follows: $10,000, $8,000, $6,400, $5,120, $4,096, and so on, each figure being 80 percent of the preceding one. (There is, of course, nothing special about the 20 percent reserve ratio. It is just a number picked arbitrarily. Had a 50 percent reserve ratio been used, the sequence of deposits would have been $10,000, $5,000, $2,500, $1,250, . . .) Such a sequence forms a geometric progression:

$$R[1 + (1 - rr) + (1 - rr)^2 + (1 - rr)^3 + \ldots],$$

and its sum is

$$D = \frac{1}{rr} R,$$

where D stands for deposits, rr is the reserve ratio, and R is the initial increase in reserves that occurred when Bank A obtained a $10,000 deposit. With a 20 percent reserve ratio the total of deposit creation amounts to $(1/.2)$ $10,000, that is, $50,000. Hence, we have here a deposit multiplier $(1/rr)$ of 5. The **deposit multiplier** is the *change in deposits per dollar change in reserves.* (Unlike the Keynesian multiplier that relates some autonomous expenditure item, such as investment, to income, this multiplier relates reserves to the deposits.)

Another way of explaining the creation of $50,000 of deposits is as follows. The process of a depository institution making a loan, losing reserves to another depository institution which then makes a loan, and so on, continues until all of the original $10,000 of extra reserves has become required reserves. (Strictly speaking, of course, the process never comes to a stop, but we can allow for this by rounding to the nearest dollar.) If the required reserve ratio is 20 percent, then, when all of the $10,000 has become reserves, deposits must be equal to five times required reserves, that is, to $50,000.

The story told so far may seem unrealistic in one way. Bank B received $8,000 of reserves and deposits and then lent out exactly $6,400. Obviously, it is not likely to make a loan of just that amount. In actuality, banks do not look at particular receipts of reserves and deposits, and then try to lend out 80 percent of these particular receipts. Instead, banks have a continual inflow and outflow from a large number of transactions. Each morning a bank looks at the total inflow and outflow of reserves during the previous day, estimates the major changes likely to occur during the current day, and then decides whether it should expand or contract its loans and investments. There is no reason to tie particular loans closely to particular reserve receipts. As a result, there can be a significant delay between the acquisition of reserves and the full expansion of deposits.

MULTIPLE DEPOSIT CONTRACTION

Now take the opposite case where reserves decrease. This time assume that the reserve ratio is 25 percent, so that we get some variation into our figures. Assume again that there are no excess reserves being held. When a customer of Mutual Savings Bank A buys a $10,000 security from the Fed, the Fed debits A's reserve account as the check is cleared. Its T account now looks as follows:

Mutual Savings Bank A

(8)

Assets		Liabilities	
reserves with Federal Reserve	−$10,000	deposits	−$10,000

But since A kept only $2,500 of reserves against the $10,000 deposit, it is short $7,500 of reserves and has to replenish them by selling a security or calling in a loan for $7,500. When it does so, and the check it receives is credited to its account, its T account—considering both the initial and the new transaction—becomes:

Mutual Savings Bank A

(9)

Assets		Liabilities	
reserves with Federal Reserve	−$10,000 +$ 7,500	deposits	−$10,000
loans and securities	−$ 7,500		

Mutual Savings Bank A is now in equilibrium. It has lost $10,000 of reserves and made this up both by reducing its required reserves and by obtaining new reserves. But it has merely shifted part of its reserve shortage to another depository institution since by selling a security or calling a loan it received a check drawn on Bank B.

As this check clears, Bank B's T account becomes:

Bank B

(10)

Assets		Liabilities	
reserves with Federal Reserve	−$7,500	deposits	+$7,500

Bank B kept $1,875 (= $7,500 × .25) against the $7,500 deposit, and it is now short $5,625 (= $7,500 − $1,875) of reserves. Hence, it too sells a security, or else calls in a loan, for $5,625. Its T account becomes:

Bank B

(11)

Assets		Liabilities	
reserves with		deposits	−$7,500
Federal Reserve	−$1,875		
(= −$7,500 + $5,625)			
loans and securities	−$5,625		

Bank B has therefore lost reserves equal to exactly 25 percent of its decline in deposits, and hence is not short of reserves anymore. But when it obtained $5,625 by selling a security it received a check drawn on a deposit in Bank C. As this check is cleared, Bank C is short of reserves, its T account looking like this:

Bank C

(12)

Assets		Liabilities	
reserves with		deposits	−$5,625
Federal Reserve	−$5,625		

Bank C does not have to worry about $1,406 (= $5,625 × .25) of this loss in its reserves because its deposits have fallen too. But it is still short $4,219 of reserves. So, suppose that it sells a security for $4,219 to a customer of Savings and Loan D. It now has sufficient reserves again, but D is short $3,164 ($4,219 × .75) of reserves. So *it* sells a security, thus passing the problem on to Bank E, and so on.

In this process, deposits are decreasing again in a geometrically declining sequence. They fell by $10,000 in A, by $7,500 in B, by $5,625 in C, and so on. Applying the equation for the sum of a declining geometric series again, we can see that deposits must fall by $40,000, or

$$\frac{1}{rr} R = \frac{1}{.25} \$10,000.$$

Thus, multiple deposit contraction is just as possible as multiple deposit creation, and not surprisingly, the two are symmetrical though the numbers differ here because we used different reserve ratios.

LEAKAGES FROM THE DEPOSIT CREATION PROCESS

The story told so far is that of a multiplier process in which required reserves are the only leakage that absorbs the reserves with which the story started out. But there are also other leakages, which we now take up: excess reserves, currency holdings by the public, and reserves held against nonpersonal time deposits. (It is convenient to think of the term "deposits," which we have used in a vague way so far, as deposits into transactions accounts.[3])

---

[3] More precisely, they are deposits against which unlimited checks can be written.

Excess Reserves

A bank or other depository institution will frequently hold excess reserves to avoid either borrowing from the Fed or buying deposits in the CD market, or else having to sell short-term securities. However, excess reserves are typically small. In the period 1984–1985 they averaged 1.9 percent, and in only one month did they get as high as 2.5 percent of total reserves.

How can we introduce excess reserves into the demand deposit creation process? The simplest way is to think of them as functioning just like required reserves. Suppose a bank gets a $10,000 deposit and lends out only, say, 85 percent of it, holding 15 percent as reserves against this deposit. It does not matter for the deposit creation process whether all of the 15 percent represent required reserves, or whether, say, 14 percent are legally required and 1 percent are excess reserves. In either case, as the bank lends out $8,500, the next bank receives an $8,500 deposit. Hence, now that banks hold some excess reserves the demand deposit multiplier is not $d = 1/rr$, but

$$d = \frac{1}{rr + e},$$

where e is the *percent of a dollar of deposit that banks hold voluntarily* as **excess reserves.** If the required reserve ratio is 14 percent and banks hold 1 percent excess reserves, the deposit multiplier is $1/.14 + .01$ or 6.67.

Deposits into Currency

As the volume of deposits expands and income rises along with it, people exchange some of their additional deposits for currency. Suppose that for each dollar of checkable deposits the public wants to hold, say, 30 cents more currency. The 30 cents of currency that depository institutions have to pay out to the public for every dollar of new deposits are lost to the deposit creation process just as much as are the 14 cents that, in this example, they have to keep as required reserves. A bank receiving a $10,000 deposit keeps $1,400 as a legal reserve, $100 as a legally excess reserve, and pays out to the public $3,000 as currency. Hence it can lend only $5,500, which then becomes a deposit in the next bank. So the demand deposit multiplier now becomes

$$d = \frac{1}{rr + e + k},$$

where k is the proportion of each dollar of checkable deposits, d, that the public withdraws as currency. In this example, we have

$$d = \frac{1}{.14 + .01 + .30} = 2.22.$$

Checkable Deposits into Time Deposits

As checkable deposits increase some of them will be transferred into time deposits. It may seem that a term for time deposits could simply be added to the denominator as was done for excess reserves and for currency. But this is not so. When a depository institution holds additional reserves or a person withdraws additional currency, this sum is completely lost to the deposit creation process; the next institution in the chain does not get any of it. But this is not the case for a dollar shifted into a time deposit. Here the dollar stays in the system. All that happens is that reserves have to be held against it, and only these reserves (not the time deposit itself) are lost to the deposit creation sequence. Thus, to adjust the checkable deposits multiplier for the shift into time deposits, one must add to the denominator the leakage into time deposits per dollar of demand deposits *times the reserve ratio against time deposits*, that is,

$$d = \frac{1}{rr + e + k + t(rr_t)},$$

where t is the proportion of checkable deposits that are shifted into time deposits and rr_t is the reserveable ratio (plus excess) held against these time deposits. (Since the required reserve ratio is 3 percent against shorter term nonpersonal time deposits and zero against other time deposits, rr_t must be measured as a weighted average of 3 and 0 percent.) Suppose that t is 20 percent and rr_t is 1 percent; the multiplier then is

$$d = \frac{1}{.14 + .01 + .30 + .2(.01)} = 2.21.$$

This multiplier, 2.21, is less than a third of the 7.14, which it would be if the required reserve ratio, 14 percent, were the only leakage.

FROM MULTIPLIER TO STOCK OF DEPOSITS: THE MULTIPLICAND

Previously, when there was only one leakage, required reserves, we showed that the stock of deposits, D, is $D = (1/rr)R$, where rr is the required reserve ratio and R the volume of reserves. What happens when we introduce the other leakages?

Suppose someone finds a $100 bill and deposits it. Some depository institution now has excess reserves of $(1 - rr)\$100$, and it goes ahead and expands its deposits in the same way as if it had received the $100 from someone depositing a check received from the Federal Reserve in payment for securities. Hence, an increase in currency that is deposited leads to multiple deposit creation just as much as an increase in reserves with the Fed.

But suppose the $100 bill is not deposited. Then it would serve to satisfy the public's demand for currency, kD, so that some other $100 is now deposited instead, since the total demand for currency is, in the first instance, unchanged. (Only as deposits go up will more currency be demanded.) Hence, once one introduces the currency leakage, the multiplicand is no longer R, but is $R + C$, which is called the **base**.

How about the other leakages? They do not change the multiplicand. Those reserves that leak into excess reserve holdings or into reserves against time deposits are already part of total reserves, R.

The Money Multiplier

The main reason for discussing the deposit multiplier is that it permits one to calculate the money multiplier. To go from checkable deposits to $M-1$ one must add currency.[4] Since the public is holding a proportion k of its checkable deposits as currency, each dollar of checkable deposits results in k dollars of currency being held. Total currency holdings are

$$kD = k \frac{1}{rr + e + k + t(rr_t)} (R + C) = \frac{k}{rr + e + k + t(rr_t)} (R + C).$$

Adding this to checkable deposits, which are

$$D = \frac{1}{rr + e + k + t(rr_t)} (R + C),$$

one gets

$$M\text{-}1 = \frac{1 + k}{rr + e + k + t(rr_t)} (R + C).$$

MONEY SUPPLY THEORY

We could end the story at this point and say that there is a fixed money multiplier determined by rr, e, k, t, and rr_t. One could take the average values of these coefficients and easily calculate the money multiplier. But why assume that the values of these leakage coefficients are fixed? While obviously the reserve requirements are set by the Fed, the others depend on how the public wants to hold its assets. Since these decisions of the public are susceptible to economic analysis we need not take these leakage coefficients as "given," but can see how they change with economic conditions.

The excess reserve ratio, e, that banks want to hold depends, on the one hand, on the interest rate that banks could earn by investing these excess reserves, and, on the other hand, on the benefits that banks expect to obtain from holding them. A profit-maximizing bank keeps excess reserves up to a point at which the marginal (opportunity) cost of idle reserves (the yield obtained from investing them minus the cost of investing) is equal to the marginal benefit to the bank (avoidance of the cost of obtaining additional reserves if the bank runs short of reserves, multiplied by the probability that the bank will actually run short).

The public's desired currency ratio, k, depends on the opportunity cost of holding currency, that is, on implicit and explicit yields on deposits, as well as on the interest rate paid on securities. If this latter interest rate rises the public will switch to securities. But people are *much* more likely to treat their

---

[4] We ignore the complication that the money stock includes travelers checks, but excludes interbank and federal government deposits.

additional security holdings as a substitute for deposit holdings than as a substitute for currency holdings. Hence, as they buy securities they reduce their deposits, so that the ratio of currency to deposits rises. The currency ratio also depends on income or wealth, because these variables measure the extent to which people can afford to forgo earning interest on deposits or securities to obtain the convenience of holding currency, and on retail sales, the variable that measures the work to be done by currency. Some economists believe that the currency ratio also varies with tax rates because in transactions where taxes are evaded it is safer to use currency than checks, which leave records. Another factor influencing the currency ratio is the rise in the drug trade and other illegal transactions in which payment is made by currency and not by check.

The time deposit ratio, t, depends on the interest rate on time deposits compared to the yields on checkable deposits and securities. Obviously, if banks raise the interest rate they pay on time deposits, and neither the yields on checkable deposits nor yields on securities rise, the public will want to hold more time deposits. The time deposit ratio also depends on total wealth, since time deposits are one way of holding wealth.

Thus, income, wealth, and interest rates are factors determining e, k, and t, and hence the money multiplier. As income rises and interest rates increase, one would expect e to decline somewhat. But since it is already small to start with, this does not make much difference. At the same time, with income and retail sales as well as interest rates on securities all rising, k rises too.

Hence, the deposit multiplier is partly endogenous, that is, affected by income, so that, even if the Fed keeps bank reserves constant, the stock of money tends to rise as income increases, and fall as income falls—in other words, to behave procyclically.

This analysis of money creation, which makes the *money multiplier partially endogenous by allowing* e, k, *and* t *to vary,* is called **money supply theory** to distinguish it from the mechanistic "textbook" approach that takes the money multiplier to be a constant.

THE "NEW VIEW" OF MONEY CREATION

Although money supply theory is a substantial advance over the simple mechanistic approach, it has been challenged in recent years by some economists who believe that it does not go far enough. Their approach is unfortunately called the "New View," though by now there is nothing new about it.

Adherents of the New View ask why banks and thrift institutions would necessarily want to supply more deposits merely because their reserves have increased. Don't they, like other firms, set their level of output at the point that maximizes profits rather than producing the maximum feasible output? Surely we would not accept an analysis of the volume of steel produced that tells us that it is determined only by the amount of iron ore, etc., that steel companies have available. A profit-maximizing bank will look at demand (marginal revenue) as well as at costs in determining its output. But the deposit creation story just told looks only at the supply side, the maximum quantity of deposits that banks can create. Does the public's demand for deposits not matter at all? Does the public meekly accept whatever volume of deposits the banks can supply? Couldn't one go to the opposite extreme, and assume instead that banks are always able to create all the deposits that the public is willing to hold, so that the volume of outstanding deposits is determined by the demand for deposits? Suppose, for example, that the public wants to hold more total deposits. Banks would then find that they can "sell" deposits to the public at a lower imputed yield, that is, at a lower cost, and would therefore expand their total deposits.

But how would banks obtain the required reserves? To start with, since the public wants to hold more deposits, it will presumably deposit some of its currency holdings into banks, and this raises bank reserves. Second, the increased demand for total deposits can also be met by banks raising the yield on time deposits, thus inducing some depositors to shift from checkable deposits to time deposits. Given the difference in reserve requirements, with personal time deposits having no reserve requirement at all, this reduces the reserves that have to be kept against the average dollar of deposits. Hence, the New View argues, the supply of reserves is not as critical to the creation of money, particularly of *M-2*, as the traditional approach suggests.

Fortunately, the conflict between the two approaches is not as serious as may appear at first. Consider what happens when reserves increase. We start out with an equilibrium situation in which banks are producing their optimal volume of deposits, so that their marginal revenue from holding the public's deposits just equals the marginal cost of servicing these deposits. Now suppose that the Fed makes more reserves available. One of the costs of servicing deposits is the forgone interest from holding reserves against these deposits. But with more reserves available, interest rates fall, and as a result the marginal cost of servicing deposits falls too. Marginal costs are now less than marginal revenue, so that banks expand their volume of deposits. Hence critics of the New View believe that, as the traditional view predicts, when banks obtain additional reserves bank deposits increase.

Moreover, these critics argue that although the traditional approach analyzes bank deposits in a way very different from that used for other goods, since it seems to ignore demand, this does not necessarily mean that it is wrong. Deposits differ radically from other goods: an increase in their supply, after some time, raises the demand for them. It does so because, as will be shown subsequently, an increase in the money supply raises nominal income. And the higher is nominal income, the greater is the demand for nominal money. Hence, when banks supply more deposits, after some time the demand for deposits increases too. With supply creating its own demand, one does not have to pay so much attention to demand.

In any case, money supply theory is much less vulnerable to the New View's criticism than is the crude "textbook" multiplier, since it allows the leakage coefficients to be determined by economic conditions. For example, suppose that income rises. This raises interest rates, and hence, changes *e, k,* and *t.* Money supply theory therefore makes some room for the demand factor stressed by the New View, but gives it much less emphasis than the New View does. In a sense, it is a simplified version of the New View that gambles on the assumption that the leakage coefficients are stable enough so that one can avoid the full complexity (and it is a very great complexity) of the New View. *If,* in actuality, most of the observed changes in the money stock are due to changes in the volume of bank reserves, rather than in the money multiplier, then the relatively limited analysis of fluctuations in the money multiplier that money supply theory gives us may be sufficient.

SUMMARY

1 Currency notes are created by the Bureau of Engraving and Printing. Banks buy them from the Fed and put them into circulation.
2 Multiple deposit creation is best understood by focusing on a set of rules that explains under what conditions banks can make certain book entries. What makes multiple deposit creation possible is that the funds one depository institution loses when it makes a loan or buys a security are received by another one.
3 Simple examples of multiple deposit creation show a decreasing series of deposits created by various depository institutions in a chain. Multiple deposit contraction operates by the same mechanism as deposit expansion.
4 There are various leakages in the deposit creation process: required reserves, excess reserves, and the flows into currency and time deposits.
5 The deposit (transactions accounts) multiplier can be used to derive the *M-1* multiplier $(1 + k)/[rr + e + k + t(rr_t)]$. The multiplicand is $R + C$.
6 Money supply theory shows why the various leakages in the money multiplier are not constant, and why the money multiplier rises in expansions.
7 The New View argues that the traditional money multiplier approach is too mechanistic, that one must look at the profit-maximizing behavior of banks and bring in the demand for deposits

QUESTIONS AND EXERCISES

1 Carry out the example set out on p. 164 through to Bank G. Assume that G just holds the reserves it receives and does not make additional loans. On this assumption, what is the deposit multiplier?
2 What happens in the example of deposit creation on p. 164 if the proceeds of the loan made by B are redeposited in B?
3 Set up an example of the deposit creation process using a 50 percent reserve ratio. Work it through for four banks.
4 Work out an example of deposit *contraction* using a 10 percent reserve ratio. Follow it through for six banks.
5 How would you answer a banker who claims that banks cannot create deposits, that they can lend out only the money deposited with them?
6 Carry the example of deposit contraction on pp. 166–167 forward and assume that F has excess reserves, and hence does not have to call a loan. What is the deposit multiplier now?
7 Suppose that we have an economy in which there is only a single bank, which has a reserve ratio of 20 percent. If someone deposits $1,000 of currency in this bank, how much can this bank lend out?

8 Why do changes in income and wealth affect *e, k,* and *t?*
9 Explain the New View in your own words. How can adherents of the traditional view try to answer it?

FURTHER READING

BRUNNER, KARL. "The Role of Money and Monetary Policy," *Review,* Federal Reserve Bank of St. Louis, 50 (July 1968):9–24. A strong criticism of the New View.

BURGER, ALBERT E. *Money Supply Process.* Belmont, Calif.: Wadsworth Publishing Co., 1971. Chapters 1–4 give an extremely thorough and detailed discussion of the deposit and money multipliers.

CACY, J. "Alternative Approaches to the Analysis of Financial Structure," *Monthly Review,* Federal Reserve Bank of Kansas City, 53 (March 1968). A good survey of the New View.

FEDERAL RESERVE BANK OF CHICAGO. *Modern Money Mechanism: Workbook.* Chicago: Federal Reserve Bank of Chicago, 1961, pp. 1–14. A very clear and lucid discussion of deposit creation.

PESEK, BORIS. "Monetary Theory in the Post-Robertsonian 'Alice in Wonderland' Era," *Journal of Economic Literature,* 14 (September 1976):867 ff. The latter part of this article is a forceful and stimulating criticism of the traditional view of deposit creation. For the traditionalist's response, see the debate in the *Journal of Economic Literature,* 15 (September 1977):909–927.

TOBIN, JAMES. "Commercial Banks as Creators of 'Money'," in Deane Carson (ed.), *Banking and Monetary Studies,* pp. 408–419. Homewood, Ill.: Richard D. Irwin, 1963. A sharp critique of the traditional explanation of deposit creation.

CHAPTER 11

Bank Reserves and Related Measures

In the previous chapter we discussed deposit creation. In this chapter we discuss how banks get the reserves that allow them to create deposits. Any individual bank can obtain reserves by competing for them with other banks, perhaps by selling a large CD to another bank's customer. But obviously the depository institutions system as a whole cannot gain reserves this way. It can obtain reserves only from some entity outside itself, that is, from either (1) the Fed, (2) the U.S. Treasury, (3) the domestic public, or (4) foreigners.

BANK RESERVES

The way in which bank reserves change is set out in a standardized accounting framework published by the Federal Reserve and carried every Friday in the *Wall Street Journal*. Table 11.1 shows a condensed example. It is arranged so that factors that increase bank reserves are listed first, followed by those that decrease bank reserves.

Factors that Increase Bank Reserves

The first of these items consists of the open-market operations that the Fed carries out precisely for the sake of changing bank reserves. Suppose the Fed buys these securities directly from a member bank. It pays for them by crediting the selling bank's reserve account, so that the bank's reserves go up automatically. The bank's and the Fed's T accounts look as follows:

Bank

(1)

Assets		Liabilities
reserves with Federal Reserve securities held	+ −	

Federal Reserve

Assets		Liabilities	
securities held	+	deposits	+

Suppose now that the Fed had bought these securities not from a bank, but from General Motors. General Motors gets a check, which it deposits in its bank, and the bank clears the check by sending it to the Fed for credit. The bank's T account becomes:

Bank

(2)

Assets		Liabilities	
reserves with Federal Reserve	+	deposits	+

In both of these cases the bank's reserve account goes up. The only difference is that in the second case demand deposits go up automatically, whereas in the first case, where the Fed bought the securities from a bank, deposits go up only when the bank uses the reserves to make a loan or to buy another security. (The Fed's balance sheet is the same in both cases.) Conversely, when the Fed sells a security to a nonbank, bank reserves fall, and the T account of the buyer's bank shows:

Bank

(3)

Assets		Liabilities	
reserves with Federal Reserve	−	deposits	−

The next item, borrowings, refers to the loans that depository institutions can obtain from their Federal Reserve Banks. The Fed makes these loans by crediting the borrowing institution's reserve account, so that we have the following T account entries:

(4)

Bank

Assets		Liabilities	
reserves with Federal Reserve	+	borrowings from Federal Reserve	+

Federal Reserve Bank

Assets		Liabilities	
loans to banks	+	deposits	+

Table 11.1	Changes in Member Bank Reserves, Week Ending 15 May 1986

	Change from week ending 9 May 1986 (millions of dollars)
Purchase of U.S. government securities, securities of U.S. government agencies, and acceptances	+ 13,776
Borrowings from Federal Reserve	− 587
Float	+ 199
Other Federal Reserve assets	+ 3,885
Gold stock	− 6
Special Drawing Right (SDR) certificates	+ 114
Treasury currency outstanding	+ 615
Currency in circulation	+ 13,492
Treasury cash holdings	+ 34
Treasury, foreign, and other deposits with Federal Reserve	− 2,519
Other Federal Reserve liabilities and capital	− 28
Service-related balances adjustment	+ 229

Source: *Wall Street Journal*, 16 May 1986.

When the bank repays the loan the Fed will take the amount of the loan out of the bank's reserve account, so that the T account will show negative entries for all of these items, and the reserves will therefore disappear.

Float, the next item, works like a loan from the Fed. If the Fed were to give credit for a check it is sent for clearing at exactly the same time that it debits the account of the institution on which the check is drawn, then there would be no float. But the Fed credits the account of the depositing institution after one or two days, despite the fact that, due to transportation delays and so on, it may take longer than this before the check is debited against the account of the institution on which it is drawn. As a result of one reserve account having been credited for the check, while the other has not yet been debited, total reserves increase for a time. Thus the T account of the institution that received the check and that of the one upon which the check was drawn looks as follows:

Receiving Bank

(5)

Assets		Liabilities	
reserves with Federal Reserve	+	demand deposits	+

Drawer Bank

Assets	Liabilities
reserves with Federal Reserve unchanged	demand deposits unchanged

For both banks together, reserves have temporarily increased. When the check finally is debited to the drawer bank, its reserve account is debited, and the increased reserves and deposits generated by float disappear.

Another factor raising bank reserves is an increase in "other Federal Reserve assets." Whether the Fed buys paper clips from a local store, or foreign currency from another central bank, it does so by drawing a check on itself. When the check is deposited and cleared the Fed credits the reserve account of the institution that received it. Here are the relevant T accounts when the seller has deposited the Federal Reserve check, and it has cleared:

Savings and Loan

(6)	Assets		Liabilities	
reserves with Federal Reserve		+	deposits	+

Federal Reserve Bank

Assets		Liabilities	
paper clips	+	deposits	+

Then there are various U.S. Treasury operations that change bank reserves. The first of these are changes in the U.S. gold stock. If the Treasury sells gold, the check it receives in payment is debited against the reserve account of the institution on which it is drawn.

The next item, Special Drawing Right (SDR) certificates, we defer until later (see Footnote 2) and turn now to Treasury currency in circulation. Since currency held by depository institutions is part of reserves, an increase in outstanding Treasury currency that ends up in depository institutions obviously increases their reserves. But how about Treasury currency that is held by the general public? We will make allowance for that part of Treasury currency by subsequently subtracting—as a factor of decrease—currency held by the public.[1]

Factors that Decrease Member Bank Reserves

Bank reserves *decrease* if certain items increase. One of these is currency in circulation, that is, currency held by the public. Clearly, if someone withdraws $1,000 from a depository institution, then vault cash and hence reserves decrease by $1,000. A similar story applies to the next item—Treasury cash holdings. If the Treasury holds more currency, and the public's currency holdings are constant, then the depository institutions must be holding less currency and hence fewer reserves. (If the increase in the Treasury's currency holding comes from a reduction in the public's currency holdings, then a rise in one factor that decreases reserves—Treasury cash holdings—is fully offset

---

[1] What about Federal Reserve currency in circulation? This is already taken care of indirectly by taking account of the factors that change the Fed's balance sheet, such as loans. The proceeds of these loans can be taken either as a credit to the bank's reserve account with the Fed or, if the bank wants to, by having the Fed ship Federal Reserve currency to it.

by a fall in another factor that decreases reserves—currency held by the public.)

The Treasury deposits tax payments and receipts from sales of its securities initially into depository institutions. But since it writes its own checks on its account with the Fed, from time to time it has to transfer funds from its accounts with depository institutions to its account with the Fed. When this happens the Fed credits the Treasury's account and debits the accounts of the depository institutions.[2]

The T accounts are:

Depository Institutions

(7)

Assets	Liabilities
reserves with Federal Reserve —	demand deposits of U.S. Treasury —

Federal Reserve Bank

Assets	Liabilities
	member banks deposits — U.S. Treasury deposits +

Some foreign governments also keep accounts with the Fed. When they transfer funds from their deposits with banks (or checks they have received drawn on U.S. banks) to the Fed, then bank reserves fall the same way as they do when the U.S. Treasury transfers deposits to the Fed. And the same is true when certain other institutions that hold deposits with the Fed, such as the United Nations or the FDIC, increase their deposits with the Fed.

The next item is "other Federal Reserve liabilities and capital." Suppose that a new member bank buys stock in the Fed, thus raising Fed capital. It pays for this stock by having the Fed debit its reserve account, so that total bank reserves fall. "Other Federal Reserve liabilities" are brought in to keep the books straight. Previously we treated all the increase in other Fed assets as though it meant an increase in bank reserves because the Fed pays for these assets. But insofar as these assets have not yet been paid for—so that Federal Reserve liabilities increase—bank reserves have actually not yet increased. Hence, we now compensate for this by subtracting the increase in Fed liabilities.

The final item, "service-related balances and adjustments," consists

---

[2] Now consider SDR certificates. These are Special Drawing Rights, a form of international reserves created by the International Monetary Fund (IMF). When the IMF distributes additional SDRs, as it does from time to time, the Treasury as a matter of government bookkeeping adds their dollar equivalent to its account at the Fed. Hence, occasionally there is an increase in Treasury deposits with the Fed that does not result in a decrease in bank reserves. To make up for the fact that we are treating *all* increases in the Treasury deposits at the Fed as though they were decreases in bank reserves, we have to add increases in SDRs back in by treating them as a factor that increases bank reserves.

mainly of clearing balances that nonmember depository institutions keep with the Fed. Although they are reserves they are subtracted here because the table shows the reserves only of member banks, and not total reserves.

THE FED'S CONTROL

All of these factors changing reserves can be classified into two groups: those that are controlled by the Fed and can therefore be used to change reserves, and those that are beyond the Fed's immediate control. One factor the Fed can obviously control is its purchase or sale of securities. To some extent it can also control borrowings from it by changing the discount rate. All the other factors, called "operating factors" or "market factors," are not normally controlled by the Fed. Hence, to control reserves the Fed has to forecast changes in these operating factors, and if need be offset them by open-market operations. Its forecasts are necessarily subject to some error and, in the short run, this limits the Fed's control over bank reserves, and hence the money stock. Of course, over a longer period of time such errors wash out.

THE RESERVE BASE AND OTHER MEASURES OF RESERVES

It is time to look at several important concepts that are widely used in discussions of monetary policy: base, adjusted base, unborrowed reserves, excess reserves, and free reserves.

Base. A frequently used measure of Fed policy is the behavior of the base, sometimes also called "monetary base" or "high-powered money." One can think of the base in terms of the accounting framework of "sources" and "uses." From the uses side, it consists of reserves and currency in circulation. From the sources side, it consists of the factors, described in this chapter, that increase or decrease reserves. Since currency in circulation is included in the base, an increase in it, although it decreases reserves, does not decrease the base.[3]

Adjusted Base. In gauging whether monetary policy has been expansionary or restrictive the base can sometimes give misleading results. Even if the base has not expanded at all, monetary policy could still be expansionary if the reserve requirement ratio was reduced, thus raising the money multiplier. And the *average* reserve requirements ratio may fall to some extent even if the Fed does not change the reserve requirement ratios, if deposits shift from depository institutions with a high reserve ratio to those with a lower reserve ratio. Hence, to gauge monetary policy one should make an adjustment to the base for the change in the average reserve requirement ratio. This is done in the following way. Suppose the average reserve requirement ratio has fallen, thus releasing, say, $100 million of required reserves. This $100 million is then added to the base to get the adjusted base.

Unborrowed Reserves. Depository institutions are, at least to some extent, reluctant to be in debt to the Fed. To the extent that this is so, when they

---

[3] An increase in currency in circulation does not change the base. It decreases one component of the base, reserves, but increases the other, currency in circulation, by a corresponding amount.

obtain additional reserves the first thing they do is to repay these loans rather than to use the reserves to make loans or buy securities. If this view is correct —and this is disputed—then deposit creation depends less on total reserves or the base than on *unborrowed reserves,* sometimes called *"owned reserves."* To obtain owned reserves all one has to do is to subtract from total reserves the amount that depository institutions have borrowed from the Fed.[4]

Excess Reserves. These are total reserves minus the reserves the depository institution are required to keep against their deposits.

Free Reserves. This measure subtracts from unborrowed reserves the reserves that have to be kept against existing deposits in an attempt to measure the reserves that are available to expand deposits.

Table 11.2 gives the various reserve and base measures. Which of these is the best measure in the sense of predicting how the money stock will change? This is an unsettled issue. The adjusted base is obviously better than the base since the money multiplier applicable to it has one less variable, changes in the required reserve ratio, and hence one thing less that cannot be estimated without error.

The base has an advantage over bank reserves because it takes account of currency holdings of the public, which are ignored by reserves. But, on the other hand, it gives currency holdings too much importance by counting a dollar of currency held by the public as equal to a dollar of reserves held by banks, despite the fact that a dollar of bank reserves, unlike a dollar of currency, results in several dollars of money.

Unborrowed reserves and the unborrowed base are better measures than total reserves or the total base if—*but only if*—depository institutions are

Table 11.2	Reserve Concepts
Measure	Definition
Base or monetary base or high-powered money	Reserves of depository institutions plus currency held by the public
Adjusted base or extended base	Base adjusted for changes in reserve requirements
Reserves	Reserves of depository institutions
Unborrowed reserves	Reserves minus borrowings from the Fed[a]
Excess reserves	Total reserves minus required reserves
Free reserves	Excess reserves minus borrowings from the Fed[a]

a: The borrowings that are subtracted do not include seasonal and extended borrowings.

[4]"Seasonal borrowings" as well as "extended borrowings" (both of which will be discussed in Chapter 20) are not subtracted since they do not generate such strong pressures to repay.

reluctant to expand deposits on the basis of the reserves they have borrowed from the Fed. Excess reserves and free reserves are measures with a potential problem. Suppose the data show that excess reserves have increased. This need not be a signal that deposits will increase; excess reserves may have increased just because the federal funds rate has fallen, while the discount rate has not, so that banks find it worthwhile to hold more excess reserves.

THE RESERVE BASE, THE MONEY MULTIPLIER, AND THE MONEY STOCK

The Fed can exercise good control over the monetary base through its open-market operations by offsetting changes in the market factors, such as float. Does this mean that it also has good control over the supply of money? This depends upon its ability to predict changes in the money multiplier. If the money multiplier is stable, or otherwise highly predictable, the Fed could attain its target for the money supply very easily. If it wants the money supply to increase by, say, $10 billion, and it knows that the money multiplier applica-

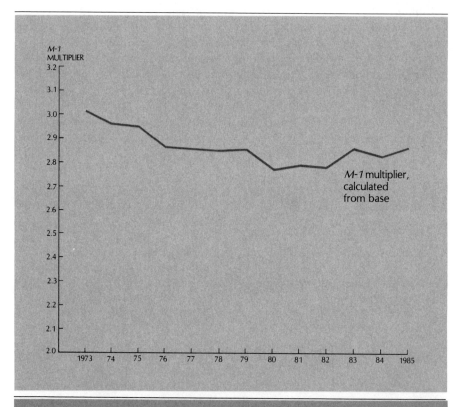

Figure 11.1   The Money Multiplier, 1973–1985. The multiplier, calculated from the base, fell in the 1970s and rose in the 1980s at fairly steady rates. **Source:** Board of Governors, Federal Reserve System, *Money Stock Revisions, 1986,* and *Reserves of Depository Institutions, Banking and Monetary Statistics, 1941–1975* and *Annual Statistical Digest.*

ble to the base is 2.5, it would simply raise the base by $4 billion. But is the money multiplier so highly predictable?

As Figure 11.1 shows, it fell in the 1970s and rose in the 1980s. If it rises (or falls) at a stable rate this does not matter because the Fed can then easily predict what the money multiplier will be. But in the 1980s it changed in a more erratic way, so that the Fed would have to use more complex methods to predict it than just projecting the trend.

The relation between changes in the adjusted base and changes in *M-1*, as shown in Figure 11.2, is a relatively close one. But is it close enough? What is involved here is a trick of arithmetic. Assume that the Fed predicts that the money multiplier for the month will be 2.500, and it actually turns out to be 2.525. Such an error of 1 percent looks like a very good forecast, but it may be large enough to get the Fed into trouble. It means that for a given size of the base the money supply is 1 percent greater than the Fed predicted. This is more serious than it seems. Suppose the Fed is aiming at an annual money growth rate of 6 percent, which is approximately .5 percent per month. Now

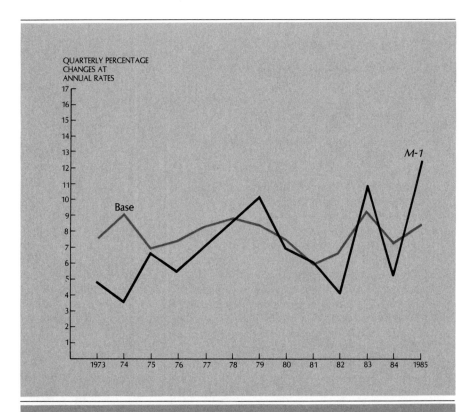

Figure 11.2   Changes in the Adjusted Base and in *M-1*. The base and *M-1* fluctuate together, but are far from perfectly correlated. **Source:** Board of Governors, Federal Reserve System, *Money Stock Revisions*, 1986, and *Reserves of Depository Institutions*, 1986.

due to its error in estimating the money multiplier, all of a sudden money is growing at a 1.5 percent rate this month, three times as fast as intended. It is growing at a more than 18 percent *annual* rate, which, if continued, would be highly inflationary. Hence, despite its "accurate" estimate of the money multiplier, the Fed may be subject to much criticism.

SUMMARY

1 Reserves are created or destroyed by Fed security purchases and loans, by increases in float and in Fed assets, by Treasury gold purchases or sales, and by changes in Treasury currency outstanding, currency in circulation, Treasury cash holdings, certain deposits with the Federal Reserve, and other Federal Reserve liabilities and capital.

2 Important measures of reserves are the base, adjusted base, unborrowed reserves, excess reserves, and free reserves.

3 The money multiplier has been declining in a fairly stable manner. But even a small error in predicting it can have large effects on the money growth rate when this is expressed as an annual rate of growth.

QUESTIONS AND EXERCISES

1 Given the following data, calculate the change in bank reserves:

	Change
1. Fed security purchases (including repurchase agreements)	10
2. Gold stock	−10
3. Currency in circulation	15
4. Acceptances bought by the Federal Reserve	− 3
5. Treasury currency	10
6. Float	− 3
7. Other Federal Reserve liabilities and capital	1
8. Other deposits with the Federal Reserve	− 1
9. Other Federal Reserve assets	5
10. Foreign deposits with the Federal Reserve	5
11. Federal Reserve loans	20
12. Treasury deposits with the Federal Reserve	− 5
13. Treasury cash holdings	− 5

2 Take the data given in the previous example and: (a) eliminate the figure shown for Fed security purchases; (b) add the following:

14. Member bank deposits at the Fed	− 3
15. Currency held by banks	− 2
16. Currency held by the nonbank public	5

Now calculate Fed purchases of securities.

3 Take each of the items in Question 1 and explain in your own words the effects of this item on bank reserves. Do not merely state whether it raises or lowers reserves, but explain why.

4 Evaluate the following statements:
   a. When the Treasury buys gold, the money stock increases because the country now has more gold.

    b. An increase in float increases the money stock because it means that there are more checks in transit, which in turn means that people are receiving more money. This increases the money stock.

    c. An increase in currency in circulation raises bank reserves because some of this currency will be deposited in banks.

    d. When Federal Reserve loans increase, bank reserves decline because by increasing the liabilities of banks to the Fed it reduces their *net* assets with the Fed.

5 Take each of the items in Table 11.1 and set up, wherever relevant, the T accounts for commercial banks, the Fed, the Treasury, or the nonbank public.

6 Look at the factors supplying and absorbing bank reserves in last Friday's *Wall Street Journal*. Write a paragraph explaining in your own words what has happened.

7 Define and discuss the relations between reserve base, extended base, high-powered money, free reserves, and unborrowed reserves.

8 "The money stock depends upon the actions of the Fed, the Treasury, the commercial banks, and the public." Explain this statement.

FURTHER READING

BERGER, ALBERT, *The Money Supply Process*. Belmont, Calif.: Wadsworth Publishing Co., 1971. A very thorough and comprehensive survey of the factors that determine the money stock.

MELTON, WILLIAM. *Inside the Fed*. Homewood, Ill.: Dow Jones–Irwin, 1985, Chapters 7 and 8. An excellent discussion of how the Fed operates in the money market.

NICHOLS, DOROTHY (Federal Reserve Bank of Chicago). *Modern Money Mechanics*. Chicago: Federal Reserve Bank of Chicago, 1971. A simple and clear discussion of the factors changing bank reserves and of deposit creation.

PART THREE

MONEY, NATIONAL INCOME, AND THE PRICE LEVEL

CHAPTER 12

The Determinants of Aggregate Demand

We now look at theories that explain the behavior of real income and the inflation rate. Two rival explanations, both widely accepted, merit our attention. One is the **Keynesian** approach, developed by the great English economist John Maynard Keynes and his followers. The other is the **monetarist** approach identified with the work of Nobel laureate Milton Friedman (formerly of the University of Chicago, and now of the Hoover Institution) and Karl Brunner (University of Rochester) and Allan Meltzer (Carnegie-Mellon University).

We will set out the basic frameworks of both the Keynesian and the monetarist theories. We then will look at some of the main variables in the Keynesian theory: consumption, investment, government expenditures, and net exports (i.e., exports minus imports).

The previous chapters have been mainly descriptive. Although there is much dispute about how our financial system should be managed, many facts about the financial system can be readily observed, so that there is little disagreement about them. When one says that banks offer NOW accounts nobody will disagree. But about macroeconomic theory there is disagreement. In Part 3, we will set out the broad areas of agreement while, at the same time, explaining how and why economists differ on other issues.

In explaining the behavior of real income and prices, we are actually explaining the behavior of nominal income, because total output (i.e., real income) times prices is equal to nominal income. Nominal income is usually measured by nominal gross national product (GNP), which is the dollar value of all final output before subtracting depreciation. As Figure 12.1 shows, both nominal GNP and real GNP have fluctuated substantially. Most economists attribute these fluctuations not to variations in the capacity to produce, but primarily to variations in the demand for goods and services, that is, variations in aggregate demand. What accounts for these changes in aggregate demand?

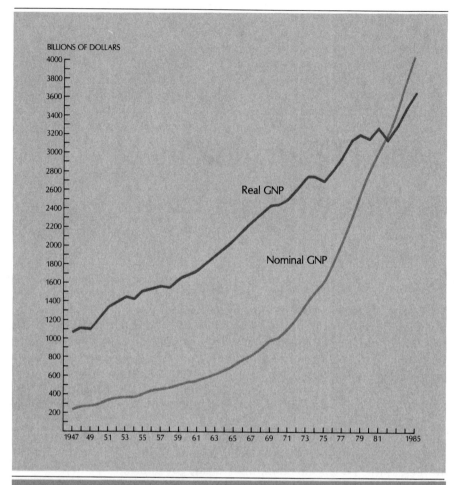

Figure 12.1   Nominal and Real GNP, 1947–1985. Both nominal and real GNP have grown at an unstable rate. **Source:** U.S. Department of Commerce, *Revised GNP Tables;* Board of Governors, Federal Reserve System, *Federal Reserve Bulletin,* April 1986 and May 1986, p. A51.

AGGREGATE DEMAND EXPLAINED FROM THE MONEY SIDE

Monetarists relate aggregate demand to the quantity of money that is used to effectuate this demand. Keynesians, on the other hand, link aggregate demand to the income that is used to purchase these goods and services. (Remember that income and money are not the same thing.) These two ways of looking at aggregate demand are not contradictory in the sense that if one is right the other must be wrong. Instead, it is a matter of which is the more useful approach to the question at hand—which provides a more manageable and convenient way of explaining and predicting aggregate demand.

THE QUANTITY THEORY EQUATIONS

The monetarist approach is based on the **quantity theory of money,** a theory that states that the quantity of nominal money determines the level of nominal income. Suppose you want to relate nominal income (YP, real income times prices) to the quantity of money (M). The simplest and crudest way would be to say that they are the same thing, and to write $M = YP$. This is simple—and wrong. Dollar bills, or deposits in a transactions account, do not just buy some good or service, and then give up the ghost. Instead, the recipient spends them again, so that they become income a second time, and so on. What occurs is illustrated by the story of two moonshiners (Jim and Tom) who were going to town to sell a $10 bottle of moonshine. The road was long and dusty and Jim told Tom: "I am thirsty and want a drink; here is a dollar for your share of it." After a few minutes, Tom felt thirsty too, took a drink, and gave the dollar back to Jim. Jim then took another drink and passed the dollar back to Tom. When they got to town the bottle was empty, but all they had between them was $1, not the $10 that the moonshine was worth.

What has to be done is to change the nonsensical $M = YP$ to $MV = YP$ by adding a term, V, for **velocity** (sometimes called "*income velocity*"). This term measures the number of times a dollar of money becomes income to someone during a given period, say, a year.[1] V measures not the number of times a dollar is spent, but the number of times it becomes income during the year. Suppose, for example, that someone spends $100 to buy a camera. The store's income is not the whole $100, but only its markup on the camera, say, $30. (The other $70 of receipts represents an exchange of assets, a camera for money.) Sooner or later two other things happen. One is that the owner of the store spends some of the $30 of income she received, so that someone else's income goes up by his markup. Second, the store orders a new camera from the manufacturer, whose income rises by her markup, and who then buys materials and hires workers to produce another camera. As a result, income rises again. Currently, a dollar of money (M-1) becomes income about $6\frac{1}{2}$ times a year. There is nothing set about this figure—in 1960 V was approximately 5.

The Cambridge Equation

An alternative formulation of this equation is called the **Cambridge equation,** after Cambridge University where it was developed by Alfred Marshall and A.C. Pigou. It is written as $M = kYP$ where k is the proportion of a year's (or other period's) nominal income that people keep as money. For example, if people hold, on the average, an amount of money equal to one month's income, then $k = \frac{1}{12}$.

Since $MV = YP$, and $M = kYP$, k must equal $1/V$. To illustrate, if people hold one month's income as money, so that $k = \frac{1}{12}$, then, on the average, a dollar of money enters someone's income twelve times a year.

[1] Velocity, having the dimension of number of times per year, is a flow variable that allows one to relate a stock variable, money, to a flow variable, income.

Although the two equations formally say the same thing, the Cambridge equation is more insightful. When one talks about velocity it is easy to think of velocity as a more or less mechanical thing; velocity just happens to be, say, 6, and that is all there is to it. By contrast, when talking about k, the proportion of their income that people want to hold as money, it is natural to think of this as the result of human choice. Hence, we treat it as governed by the same factors that govern our holdings of other durable goods, that is, as determined by income and by the cost of the good. However, discussions of monetary theory use both the velocity and the Cambridge k formulations, often interchangeably, so you must know both.

The Transactions Version

An earlier variant of the Cambridge equation is called the **Fisher equation,** after Irving Fisher (1867–1947), its leading proponent. It is $MV' = PT$, where M is again money, T all the transactions undertaken with money, and P the average price of all items included in T. The V' of this equation is called the **transactions velocity** and represents the number of times a dollar of money becomes *receipts* to someone even if it does not become income. Thus T encompasses not only the items included in GNP, but also intermediate products, purchases of secondhand goods (such as previously existing stocks and bonds), and factor services (such as wages, etc.). In particular, it includes financial transactions, for example, transfers of funds from a checking account to a money-market fund. Transactions velocity is much greater than income velocity.

This transactions V' is used much less frequently than income velocity for two reasons. First, while we are interested in predicting nominal GNP, we are less interested in predicting total transactions. For example, we would hardly say that economic growth is satisfactory if output falls by 10 percent, while stock market sales rise by a more than offsetting 2 percent.

Second, there is a statistical problem. We can readily measure income velocity by writing $V = YP/M$, and then using data on nominal GNP for YP and on *M-1* for M. To use the transactions equation is much messier. We do not have good data on total transactions. And while we do have good data on the turnover of deposits, we can only guess at the turnover of the other component of money, currency. Hence, from now on, when we say "velocity" we will always mean income velocity.

All of these "equations" are really "identities," or tautologies, that is, statements that are true by definition. Like other identities they cannot *by themselves* tell us anything about the real world. To obtain empirical statements, that is, statements about the real world, one has to add some assumptions to them. Thus, the income velocity equation is extremely useful *if* income velocity is stable, or otherwise predictable. The quantity theory of money asserts that this is the case—that if one knows the supply of money one can predict income. We will discuss this theory in Chapter 16. Now we turn to the alternative approach that tries to explain nominal income primarily by looking at the income-expenditure relationship.

THE INCOME-EXPENDITURE APPROACH: BASIC IDEAS

The Keynesian, or income-expenditure, approach received it greatest impetus from Keynes's *The General Theory of Employment, Interest and Money* (published in 1936), but many other economists, some of them sharp critics of Keynes, have also left their mark. Its basic equation is

$$Y = C + I + G + X,$$

where Y is nominal income, C is consumption, I is investment, G is government expenditures, and X is net exports. This too is an identity. It is true by definition because we define C, I, G, and X so that they encompass all expenditures. And since aggregate income is equal to total receipts from sales, that is, to aggregate expenditures, Y must equal $C + I + G + X$.

Another way of understanding this identity is to look at it from the side of output. All output must go to someone. One part, C, goes to consumers; another part, G, is used by the government. Some output, X, represents net exports and goes to foreigners. Business holds on to another part, I, for investment. This part has a special characteristic. The other sectors of the economy—consumers, government, and foreigners—decide how much they want to buy and go ahead and buy it. Business is in a different position because it is the seller of output. And sometimes it cannot sell all it thought it would. It then lands up with unsold output in its inventories. Such unintended increases in inventories, like intended increases in inventories, are counted as investment.

If firms find that their inventories have risen because they cannot sell as much as they thought they would, they respond by cutting back on production. Income now falls. Conversely, suppose that sales increase unexpectedly. When firms realize that they sold more of their inventories than they intended to, they restore their depleted inventories by raising production. Income now rises.

This critical role of inventories is shown in Figure 12.2, called the "45-degree diagram" or the "Keynesian cross." Income Y, that is, $C + I + G + X$, is measured along the horizontal axis. The vertical axis measures $C + I' + G + X$, where I' is not actual investment, but the amount that business wants to invest. It therefore excludes unintended changes in inventories. A 45-degree line allows one to "translate" from one axis to the other. At any point above this 45-degree line $C + I + G + X$ is less than $C + I' + G + X$. Hence I', the amount that firms want to invest, is greater than I, the amount they actually do invest. They therefore increase output to restore their depleted inventories. Similarly, at any point below the 45-degree line actual investment exceeds intended investment. Firms then try to reduce their inventories by cutting back production. Only at points along the 45-degree line are firms in equilibrium, meaning that they are adding to inventories exactly as much as they want to, and no more.

Now introduce aggregate demand into this diagram. It is shown by the $C + I + G + X$ line. It slopes upward because if income is higher households consume more. At the point where this aggregate demand line crosses the 45-

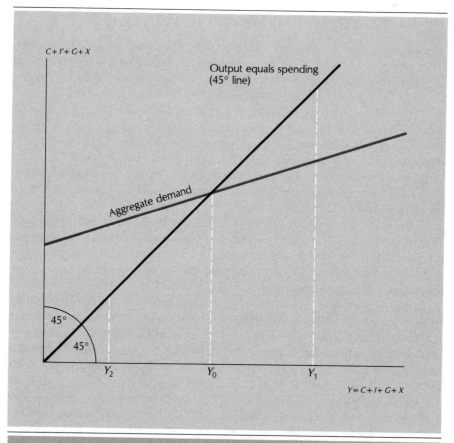

Figure 12.2   The Keynesian Cross. The horizontal axis shows aggregate demand. The vertical axis shows what firms plan to sell. The 45-degree lines enable one to "translate" from one axis to the other. Where the aggregate demand curve crosses the 45-degree line firms are selling as much as they intended.

degree line aggregate demand is just high enough for business to sell all it wants to. It neither accumulates unwanted inventories nor runs down its intended inventories. At Y_0 the economy is therefore in equilibrium. If business were to produce more, so that income would be, say, Y_1, total demand would not be sufficient. Firms would accumulate excess inventories, and hence cut production. Similarly, at Y_2 sales would exceed what firms expected, and they would be running down their intended inventories. Hence they would raise production again. Only Y_0 is an equilibrium.

Consumption

Households allocate their **disposable income,** which is income after personal taxes, either to current consumption or, through the act of saving, to future consumption. Thus, consumption depends on (1) the amount of disposable income and (2) the proportion of disposable income withheld from current consumption, that is, saved. What is not saved is consumed; hence, one can explain the proportion of income consumed by looking at the factors that determine the savings ratio. What are they?

In part they are broad sociological and historical ones. In some countries the urge for instant gratification is treated with tolerance, while in other countries (or in other historical periods) thrift and foresight are regarded as important virtues. Fortunately, such sociological factors change only slowly, so that, for most purposes, economists can disregard them.

Another factor is the age composition of the population. For most households income rises into middle age, and then drops sharply at retirement. At the same time, a household's needs are high in its early years when it equips itself and bears some of the costs of raising children. Hence, both young households and old households tend to save little, while middle-aged households save a great deal. Since the age composition of the population is not constant—think of the baby boom—the savings ratio and thus the propensity to consume are powerfully affected by the age composition of the population.

The **stock of wealth,** or total assets, is another important determinant of the savings ratio. Consider a household that does not intend to leave any bequests but saves only to finance its subsequent consumption during retirement. The more wealth it already possesses the less it needs to save to assure itself of a given standard of living in retirement. Similarly, someone who saves to leave a particular bequest obviously needs to save less if her wealth is already high. Since the only purpose of saving is to build up wealth, one would expect changes in wealth, due, for example, to a rise in stock prices, to have a strong effect on saving.

In its impact on consumption and saving not all wealth is alike. **Liquid wealth,** such as holdings of deposits and short-term securities, has a greater impact on consumption than do holdings of illiquid wealth, such as a house or a vested interest in a pension plan. This comes about because when we say savings we mean net savings, that is, the positive savings of some households minus the negative savings, or dissavings, of other households. Anything that makes it easier for some households to dissave (consume in excess of income) will reduce the overall savings ratio. And the possession of liquid wealth does make it easier to dissave. Someone without liquid wealth may not be able to obtain enough credit to dissave as much as he wants to, or may be discouraged from dissaving by the high cost of credit. By contrast, the possessor of liquid wealth can readily sell it and dissave.

The proportion of income saved is also affected by the reward for saving, the after-tax real rate of interest. The relation between saving and the interest rate is complex. But since money has much of its impact on consumption by changing interest rates, this relation cannot be passed over lightly.

Consumption and the Rate of Interest

Real interest rates affect consumption in several ways. First, they change the allocation of income between current consumption and saving. The direction of this effect is hard to determine. A fall in the real interest rate lowers the reward for saving which, taken by itself, should cause people to lower their savings ratio. At the same time, if interest rates fall then interest recipients are poorer and, hence, to restore some of their income losses, they increase their productive efforts, both by working more and by saving a larger proportion of their incomes. To take an extreme example, suppose someone insists on accumulating an estate of, say, $1 million in twenty years. Such a person must save substantially more if the interest rate falls from 10 percent to 5 percent.

A second way in which a change in interest rates affects consumption has to do with the way in which households want to hold their wealth. Households divide their wealth so that at the margin the imputed yield they obtain from consumer durables is just equal to the yield they obtain by holding financial assets, such as securities or bank deposits. When the interest rate on securities and bank deposits falls, households then have an incentive to hold fewer of these assets and to buy more consumer durables. Hence consumer expenditures increase. Third, as interest rates fall, credit rationing is relaxed. For example, sales finance companies find it easier and cheaper to borrow, and hence they are willing to grant loans to applicants whom they otherwise would have turned down.

Fourth, with interest rates falling the value of securities rise, so that households feel richer. And the higher their perceived wealth, the greater is their consumption. Fifth, a rise in the value of any of its assets raises a household's liquidity in the sense of raising its ratio of net worth to liabilities. And if households become more liquid they are more ready to trade some of their liquid assets for such illiquid assets as consumer durables.

The Consumption Function

In summary then, one can write the **consumption function** as

$$C = a + C(Y' - T) + bW + dL + er + fA,$$

where C is aggregate consumption, Y' is personal income, T is personal taxes (so that $Y' - T$ equals disposable personal income), W is wealth, L is a measure of the liquidity of wealth, r, is the real interest rate, and A is a measure of the age of the population, and a, b, c, d, e, and f are constants.[2] Or one can use a simpler, but less precise version that treats all the independent variables, other than income, as though they were constant. If so, the consumption function becomes just $C = a + cY$. The parameter a is called *autonomous consumption* because it is independent of income, while c is called the **marginal propensity to consume** since it measures the dollar change in consumption per dollar change in income.[3] The *average propensity to consume* is just C/Y.

---

[2] If the equation is written in natural logs, then b becomes the income elasticity of consumption.

[3] The factors discussed so far are not the only ones that can affect consumption. Other variables

Permanent Income, the Life Cycle, and Wealth

So far when discussing the relation between income and consumption we have not said whether consumption depends on the income of the same period, or on income over a longer period. At first economists took the seemingly obvious route of relating consumption and saving in one year to the income of that particular year. But this is questionable, and was challenged by the **permanent-income theory** developed by Milton Friedman and the **life-cycle hypothesis** developed by Nobel laureate Franco Modigliani. Both theories point out that we save to accumulate wealth, so that we, or our heirs, can consume in the future. An important motive, probably the most important motive, for saving is to even out consumption over time. This suggests that the relevant income is not the income of the current year, but income over the whole lifetime of the household. An alternative way of making this point is to say that consumption depends not upon current income, but upon the household's total wealth including its human wealth. (Human wealth is the present value of someone's earning power. Current income is no more important than the current discounted value of the income that will be received in some future year.)

But treating consumption as depending not at all on current income, and only on lifetime income or total wealth, may be going too far. Some people, most students for example, are capital rationed. Their lifetime income is high enough that they could afford to consume more now than they actually do. But they cannot increase their current consumption because they cannot borrow enough against their future income. Besides, future income is uncertain and some people may use their current income as a guide to how much they can afford to consume. Hence, it seems plausible that current and permanent income both belong in the consumption function.

INVESTMENT

Figure 12.3 shows the fluctuations of various types of investments. They are large, particularly the fluctuations of inventory investment.

Firms add to capital; that is, they invest, up to the point at which the expected yield on the investment is just equal to the **user cost** of the additional capital. The user cost has four components. One is *depreciation,* consisting of obsolescence as well as wear and tear. The second is the *interest rate* that the firm must pay to borrow the funds that it invests, or the imputed interest rate it charges itself when it invests some of its undistributed profits. The third is a *risk premium* that compensates the firm for venturing its funds. The final component is a *tax effect.* Under the current law, by investing, a firm can shelter some of its income from taxes.

---

that many empirical studies have found to be important include the rate of income growth and the relative levels of income.

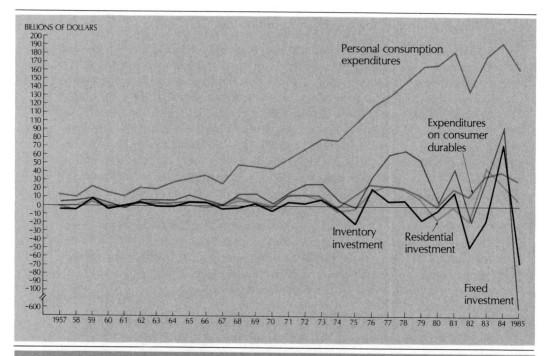

Figure 12.3   Percentage Change in Selected GNP Components, 1957–1985.
Shown is the actual growth pattern of consumption and investment expenditures
over the last twenty-nine years. **Source:** U.S. Department of Commerce, GNP
tables, 1986, unpublished.

The Marginal Productivity of Capital and the Pace of Investment

Figure 12.4 shows the yield on capital as a function of the existing stock of
capital. As additional capital is added, its yield or **marginal productivity of
capital,** declines. Given the declining marginal productivity of capital shown
in the figure, one might expect that, over time, as the capital stock rises, the
marginal productivity of capital falls. But Figure 12.4 shows the marginal productivity of capital on the assumption that the size of the labor force is constant, and that technology is unchanged. A growing labor force raises the
demand for capital, and new technology often does so too.[4] As a result, despite
the growing stock of capital, there is no reason to assume that the marginal
productivity of capital falls over time.

   If some factor, such as new technology, raises the marginal productivity
of capital, or if the user cost of capital falls, firms undertake new investment
until the marginal yield on capital once again equals the marginal user cost of
capital. A firm's capital is a stock, say, $10 million, while investment is a flow,

---

[4] By no means do all innovations raise the demand for capital; some save capital in the sense of
requiring less capital per dollar of output. The computing power that required the purchase of
a mainframe some years ago can now be obtained for a much smaller capital outlay from a PC.

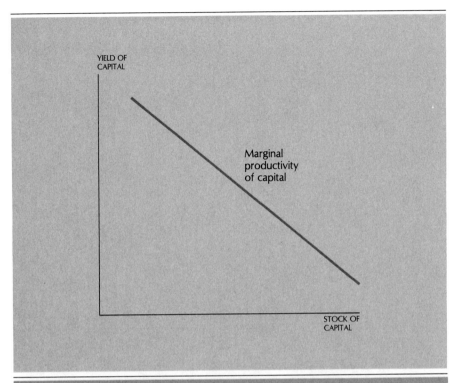

Figure 12.4   The Marginal Productivity of Capital. The marginal productivity curve slopes downward. With a given labor force and given technology, the larger the stock of capital, the lower is the yield per dollar of capital.

and thus has a time dimension, say, $2 million per year. Hence, even if one knows how much additional capital the firm wants, one does not know its rate of investment. A firm that increases its capital stock from, say, $20 million to $30 million can invest for one month at the rate of $10 million per month, or for five years at the rate of $2 million per year. How fast a firm attains its optimal stock of capital depends, on the one hand, on the relative costs of operating with insufficient capital and, on the other hand, on the greater costs that result from speeding up the pace of investment. One can draw a curve relating the yield from investment not to the capital stock, but to the amount that is invested each year. This curve, shown in Figure 12.5, measures the **marginal efficiency of investment.** It is this curve, and not the marginal productivity of capital curve, that directly determines investment.

The User Cost of Capital

One of the components of the user cost of capital, the depreciation rate, depends on technology, and hence will not be discussed here. Another component is the real rate of interest. The higher is the interest rate the lower is the *present* value of the stream of income that capital will yield in the future. As

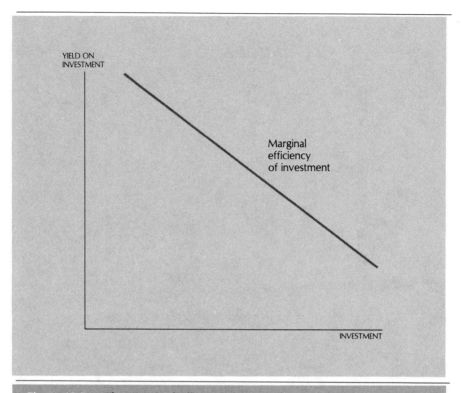

Figure 12.5   **The Marginal Efficiency of Investment.** The marginal efficiency of investment curve slopes downward. The more investment there is, the higher is the cost of investment, and hence the lower is the yield per dollar invested.

Chapter 6 showed, the present value of a future payments stream of $\$Y$ per year is $PV = Y(1 + r) + Y/(1 + r)^2 + Y/(1 + r)^3 \ldots + Y/(1 + r)^n$. Obviously, the higher r is the lower is the present value of such a sum. In particular, as Table 12.1 shows, the more distant payments lose value quite rapidly as the interest rate rises. Thus, at an interest rate of 10 percent, $\$100$ ten years from now has a present value of only $\$35.00$. At a 20 percent interest rate, its present value is only $\$16.00$! Hence, for some types of investments, such as building a railroad, which will begin to generate returns only, say, five years from now, and then do so for twenty years, the rate of interest is of overwhelming importance.

The interest rate that should be used to discount future receipts is often a complex mixture of various yields. One component is the imputed interest rate on the undistributed profits that a firm invests rather than paying them out to its stockholders. Since its stockholders would rather receive a dollar of dividends today than next year, the firm should charge itself an imputed interest rate on its own funds. Otherwise it would invest too much and pay too little in dividends.

Another cost of capital is the cost of borrowed funds. This is more than just the interest rate. Suppose a firm borrows $\$5$ million at 10 percent. The

Table 12.1	Present Value of $1 Received at Various Dates		
Number of years from now	Discounted at interest rate of		
	20%	10%	5%
1	83¢	91¢	95¢
2	69	83	91
3	58	68	86
4	48	62	82
5	40	56	78
6	33	52	75
7	28	46	71
8	23	42	68
9	19	39	65
10	16	35	61

true cost of this loan is greater than 10 percent, perhaps substantially greater. The more the firm borrows the higher is the ratio of its debts to its net worth. Hence it takes a smaller percentage drop in the value of its total assets to wipe out its equity and make it insolvent. Put another way, the more a firm borrows the greater is the chance that it will not be able to meet its required interest payments and be forced into bankruptcy. Hence when a firm borrows it not only has to pay interest, it also becomes more risky. If the firm has other loans outstanding, then when these loans come up for renewal the creditors will demand a higher interest rate to compensate them for the greater risk.

In addition, the firm's stockholders face greater risk, which reduces the value, and hence the price, of their stock. This fall in the price of the stock can be looked at as a rise in the risk premium. The expected yield on the firm's investments is the same as before, but it is less certain. Hence, holders of the firm's stock demand a greater reward for holding it.

The firm may respond to the increase in its riskiness by restructuring its balance sheet. It may issue more stock to prevent a rise in the ratio of its borrowed capital to its equity. Insofar as it does this, the user cost of its capital is a mixture of the interest rate it pays on the loan and the yield on its new stock. This yield on the new stock is reflected in a lower proportion of total earnings being available to the previous stockholders. Suppose a firm increases its outstanding stock by 10 percent. Each old share of stock is now entitled to 10 percent less of the earnings of the firm than it was before.

Output and Investment

Since the only reason for using capital is to produce output, the marginal productivity of capital and hence the rate of investment depend on the volume of output as well as on the user cost of capital. Assume that real wages, the user cost of capital, and technology are constant. Consider net investment, that is, investment beyond what is needed to take care of depreciation. How much will

Table 12.2	Output and Investment			
Value of output	Value of machines needed[a]	Replacement investment[b]	New investment	Gross investment[c]
$100	$500	$ 10	$ 0	$ 10
100	500	10	0	+10
120	600	10	100	+110

a: $5 of machines are required to produce $1 of output.
b: Depreciation is equal to 10 percent of last period's machines.
c: Replacement investment plus new investment.

a firm invest? If its output is constant its net investment will not just be constant; it will be zero. With constant output the firm's desired capital stock is constant too, so that it does not have to add capital by investing. If output falls, then the firm has more capital than it wants and will disinvest by not replacing depreciating capital. Such disinvestment is a slow process.

Only if output increases will the firm undertake net investment. How much it then invests depends, in part, on its optimal **capital coefficient,** that is, the optimal amount of capital per dollar of output. If output rises at an increasing rate (i.e., accelerates) then the rise in investment can be dramatic. Table 12.2 gives an example. As long as output is constant at $100 the only investment that occurs is $10 of replacement investment. But when output rises from $100 to $120 the firm adds $100 of new capital. As a result, gross investment (i.e., new investment plus replacement investment) rises to $110. Thus a 20 percent increase in output has raised investment not just by 10 percent, but to eleven times its previous rate.

The Stability of Investment

Since, from time to time, output does rise at an accelerating rate, the so-called **accelerator,** or **acceleration principle,** seems to imply that investment is highly erratic. This suggests that in the absence of government stabilization policy the economy would be highly unstable. But there is an ameliorating factor. Firms are likely to move slowly toward their optimal capital stock, so that investment *per year* is not all that variable. There are several reasons for this.

First, a firm does not react to a suboptimal capital stock like a badly programmed robot. Instead, it operates with the old capital stock if it expects the higher demand to be only temporary—toy makers do not raise their investment massively in December when demand rises. Second, a high rate of investment disrupts the firm's other activities, so that firms try to spread out investment over time. Third, as a firm borrows more, its cost of capital may rise. For example, if it wants to borrow more than its banks will lend it, it may have to raise capital by selling stock instead, or by **factoring,** that is, selling its accounts receivable. Both of these sources of funds might be much more expensive than bank loans. This could limit the firm's investment.

Fourth, when many firms try to invest at the same time the cost of capital goods may rise substantially, inducing some firms to postpone investment. Moreover, if many firms try to borrow more the interest rate rises. This discourages some firms from investing, while some other firms are rationed out of the loan market entirely. If the supply of funds available for investment is unresponsive to the demand for borrowing, then investment is not likely to increase much.[5]

But investment may also be unstable for reasons other than the acceleration principle. Some economists believe that the marginal productivity of capital curve, as it is perceived by firms is highly unstable. Thus Keynes wrote:

> Our knowledge of the factors that will govern the yield of an investment some years hence is usually very slight and often negligible. . . . We have to admit that our basis of knowledge for estimating the yield ten years hence of a railway, a copper mine, a textile factory . . . amounts to little and sometimes nothing.[6]

If we lack reliable knowledge then our opinions are not firmly anchored, and thus are subject to radical revisions. Hence, some economists have argued that irrational waves of optimism and pessimism cause violent swings in investment that destabilize the economy. Other economists doubt that firms behave so irrationally and emotionally in their investment decisions.

THE INTERACTION OF INVESTMENT AND CONSUMPTION: THE INVESTMENT MULTIPLIER

From the acceleration principle we know that changes in demand, and hence in output, bring about changes in investment. And the **investment multiplier,** which we now take up, shows how changes in investment generate changes in consumption. (Caution: do not confuse the investment multiplier with the money multiplier of Chapter 10.)

The basic idea of the investment multiplier is simple and obvious. When a firm undertakes investment its spending generates income. The recipients of this income then consume some of this income, and their consumption creates income for others, and so on.

At first glance it might seem that $1 of investment spending would generate a continuous $1 flow of income as it is spent by a chain of recipients. Not so. The recipients of the additional income, all along the chain, do not typically consume 100 percent of their increased income. They save some of it. Moreover, not all of the increased income represents disposable income. Some goes to pay personal taxes. Hence, at each link in the chain only one part

---

[5] Although the competition for capital goods and for financing suggests that investment for all firms jointly is more stable than for each firm individually, there is also a way in which the interaction of firms makes investment more unstable. When one firm purchases capital goods to undertake investment it generates demand, and hence an incentive to invest, for the firms producing the capital goods.

[6] John Maynard Keynes, *The General Theory of Employment, Interest and Money.* New York: Harcourt Brace, 1936, pp. 149–50.

of the increased receipts is consumed, so that the sequence of expenditures is decreasing. The chain of expenditures is

$$\$1c + \$1c^2 + \$1c^3 \ldots \$1c^n,$$

where c is the marginal propensity to consume.[7] Such a series approaches a sum of $1/(1 - c)$. Suppose, for example, that due to taxes and to the marginal propensity to save people consume only 50 percent of their before-tax income. Thus when someone receives an additional dollar of income he spends 50 cents, so that someone else's income rises by 50 cents, who then spends 25 cents, and so on. When one adds up this whole chain, income has risen not by $1, but by $2.

GOVERNMENT EXPENDITURES, TAXES, AND EXPORTS

Suppose the government buys more goods and services. Like the investment expenditures of firms such expenditures too become income to someone. These recipients consume it in the same way they consume income that results from private investment. Hence, the investment multiplier applies to government expenditures for goods and services just as much as it applies to private investment.[8] A rise in income taxes lowers aggregate demand by reducing the value of the multiplier. At each step in the chain the leakage into taxes is greater, so that the percentage of total income that is consumed at each step is less. This decreases the multiplier and lowers income.

Thus, both higher government expenditures and lower tax rates increase nominal income. Since the excess of government expenditures over government receipts is the **deficit**, this implies that a rise in the deficit raises nominal income. But, as we will see in the next chapter, a higher deficit also raises interest rates. The effect of higher interest rates then offsets part of the expansionary effect of the deficit, perhaps a large part of it.

Although the view that deficits raise nominal income is widely accepted by economists, not all economists accept it. It has been challenged by Robert Barro of the University of Rochester. His argument, called the **Ricardian equivalence theorem,** is that people look far ahead into the future. When the government runs a deficit they realize that either they or their descendants will have to pay off this debt, or else pay interest on it continually. Since they do not want to impose such a burden on their heirs, they raise their savings by an amount sufficient to leave their heirs as well off as before. To do this they cut their own consumption by an amount equal to the government's deficit. As

---

[7] To take account of the fact that expenditures on imports do not directly become income to residents in the United States, c can be defined as the marginal propensity to consume domestically produced goods and services.

[8] Suppose the government expenditures consist of transfer payments. These are not considered part of GNP. Hence GNP rises only when the recipients spend them. With the first term in the above sequence missing, the multiplier for government transfer payments is lower than it is for government purchases of newly produced goods and services.

a result, a deficit does not raise income. This argument is hotly disputed by many economists who doubt that people are that foresighted and that concerned about their heirs.

The final component of aggregate demand is **net exports,** or exports minus imports. Suppose U.S. exports increase. Those who produced these exports have increased income and consume some of it, so that there is again a multiplier sequence. The other—negative—component of net exports is imports. One can think of the payments made to foreigners as a subtraction from income payments made in the United States, and hence subtract imports from aggregate demand and nominal income in the United States. (This does not necessarily mean that higher imports reduce *real* income.)

THE STABILITY OF INCOME

The multiplier tells us that a dollar of investment raises income by more than a dollar. The accelerator tells us that a dollar of consumption, and hence output, can raise investment by much more than a dollar. This could lead to an explosive situation. Suppose that investment increases by $1 billion. With a multiplier of 2, this raises aggregate demand by $2 billion. The resulting demand for capital to produce this increased output could then raise investment by, say, $10 billion, which then raises income and consumption again. With high enough values for the marginal propensity to consume and the capital coefficient, the interaction of the multiplier and the accelerator could cause income to shoot up or down dramatically.

This could happen, but it need not. If people looked only at their current incomes in deciding how much to consume, then the marginal propensity to consume would be high. But suppose consumption depends on income over the long run or on wealth, as the permanent-income and life-cycle theories suggest. If so, consumption will not rise by much when income increases temporarily. As a result, the short-run marginal propensity to consume is low, so that the multiplier is less. Similarly, suppose that instead of responding immediately to a rise in demand firms adjust their capital stock only slowly for the reasons discussed previously, so that the short-run accelerator effect is smaller. This too reduces the probability of violent fluctuations. Moreover, as will be discussed in Chapter 15, when either consumption or investment rises interest rates rise, which then dampens the rise in income.

SUMMARY

1 Supply shocks could cause business fluctuations, but the majority of economists believe that most fluctuations are due to variations in aggregate demand. Aggregate demand is identical to nominal income.
2 Aggregate demand can be analyzed from the money side using the quantity theory equations, $MV = YP$ or $M = kYP$, or using transactions velocity, $MV' = PT$.
3 Consumption depends on disposable income, wealth, liquidity, interest rates, and the age of the population. The permanent-income theory asserts that the relevant income measure is long-term income, and the life-cycle hypothesis

uses the household's total, lifetime wealth instead of its current income to determine consumption.

4 Investment is the process of increasing the capital stock. It depends on the marginal efficiency of investment and the user cost of capital. The accelerator theorem relates the desired capital stock to output. Despite this, investment need not be highly volatile.

5 The investment multiplier relates consumption to investment, government expenditures, and net exports. The interaction of the multiplier and the accelerator could, in principle, cause dramatic movements in income. But this is less likely if there are lags in investment, and if consumption depends on long-run income or on wealth rather than on current income.

QUESTIONS AND EXERCISES

1 Explain the relation between aggregate demand and nominal income.
2 Explain the meaning of income velocity. Suppose you want to set up an equation relating money to the output and prices of consumer goods. How would you do it?
3 Discuss the effect on consumption of changes in current income, permanent income, wealth, and liquidity.
4 What is the user cost of capital?
5 Discuss the relation between output and investment.
6 What factors tend to stabilize income despite the operation of the multiplier and the accelerator?

FURTHER READING

Several excellent macroeconomics textbooks discuss in detail the material taken up in this chapter. Among them are RUDIGER DORNBUSCH AND STANLEY FISCHER, *Macroeconomics* (New York: McGraw-Hill, 1984); ROBERT HALL AND JOHN TAYLOR, *Macroeconomics* (New York: W. W. Norton, 1986); and ROBERT GORDON, *Macroeconomics* (Boston: Little, Brown, 1984). For the classic discussion of the quantity theory, see IRVING FISHER, *The Purchasing Power of Money* (New York: Macmillan, 1911).

CHAPTER 13

The Interest Rate

The previous chapter dealt with the variables determining aggregate demand. In a book on money and banking one of the variables, the rate of interest, deserves special attention. We discussed interest rates in Chapter 6, where we took as given a certain standard or generic interest rate and focused on the differences in interest rates on various types of securities. Now we look at what determines this generic interest rate.

IMPORTANCE OF THE INTEREST RATE

Changes in interest rates have an important impact on the economy. For example, the thrift institutions were devastated when interest rates rose unexpectedly in the 1970s and early 1980. Had they realized how variable interest rates could become they probably would not have taken on so much interest-rate risk. Similarly, the debts of the less developed countries would not have grown the way they did had either the borrowers or lenders known how high the real interest rate would be in the early 1980s. One of the most important causes of the farm crisis in the 1980s was that many farmers had borrowed too much in the belief that the real rate of interest would continue to be low.

The interest rate is important for two reasons. First, the interest rate is the price of obtaining goods, or resources, now instead of in the future. In other words, the interest rate measures the price of future goods and resources in terms of current ones. Even if there is no inflation a dollar next year is worth less to you now than a dollar this year. Exchanges of future goods against current goods pervade our economy. Households have to decide whether to consume more now, or save and consume more in the future, whether to work more this year or more next year. Firms have to make payments now to produce goods that will be finished in the future. Hence, the interest rate is one price that, usually implicitly, enters just about every nook and cranny of the economy.

Second, the more variable a price is, the more impact it has on the economy. And, as shown on the endpaper (located inside the front cover of this book), interest rates are highly variable. Our language hides the magnitude of changes in interest rates. Suppose that the price of butter rises from $1 to $2. We call this a 100 percent rise. But when the interest rate increases from, say, 6 to 12 percent, we usually call this a 6 percent rise instead of a 100 percent rise, just because interest rates are already quoted in percentage terms.

DETERMINANTS OF INTEREST RATES

As usual in economics we explain a price, such as the interest rate, by supply and demand. We will do so in two ways, first with the **loanable funds** theory, which looks at the market for loans, and then with the **liquidity preference** theory, which looks at the relative cost of holding money. Liquidity preference is just Keynes's term for demand for money. Both theories take the yield on other income-earning assets, such as corporate stock, and the quality of bonds (i.e., their riskiness and liquidity) as constant. They also use the term "bonds" to denote all types of promises to pay. Initially we will look at the private market and ignore the Fed.

The Loanable Funds Approach: Supply Side

In the market for loanable funds there are three sources of supply. One is the **real savings** of households, firms, and governments. In 1985 households accounted for 23 percent of gross savings, firms for 102 percent, and all types of governments jointly for −25 percent.

The second source is **real capital inflows,** that is, purchases of American securities by foreigners. Their demand for U.S. securities depends less on the amount they are currently saving than on the proportion of their total assets that they want to keep in American securities. This proportion, in turn, depends on the yield of U.S. securities relative to foreign securities, and on expected changes in the exchange rate. Suppose, for example, that the interest rate on American securities is 10 percent, while the rate on foreign securities is 8 percent. Unless the dollar depreciates by 2 percent or more, one can earn more by holding U.S. securities than by holding foreign securities. There is, however, some risk to holding one's assets in securities denominated in another country's currency. Hence, the expected yield (interest minus expected depreciation of the dollar) on U.S. securities can exceed the yield on foreign securities somewhat without generating large capital inflows.

The resulting inflows and outflows of foreign funds can be large. In 1985, admittedly an unusual year, net capital inflows equaled 20 percent of gross saving in the United States. From World War I to 1977 capital flows typically were negative; that is, Americans invested more in foreign countries than foreigners invested in the United States. We treat such capital outflows as a negative supply of funds.

The third source of loanable funds is the increase in the **real money supply.** (Later we discuss what happens if it is just the nominal money supply that increases.) Suppose that bank reserves rise. To earn income on these reserves banks now buy bonds or make more loans. In either case the supply of loanable funds increases, so that interest rates fall.

The Loanable Funds Approach: Demand Side

The demand for loanable funds has several components. One is the real demand for funds by investors who want to buy physical assets, ranging from a nuclear plant to a florist's inventory of roses. A second component consists of the real deficits that governments (federal, state, and local) have to finance by borrowing. Finally, some households and firms borrow, or reduce the amount they lend, so that they can increase their real money holdings. It is rational to reduce both transactions costs and risk by holding a certain amount of money, even though it costs interest.[1]

Supply and Demand in the Loanable Funds Market

Thus the following factors determine the interest rate: (1) the real supply of saving; (2) real net capital inflows or outflows; (3) increases in the real money supply; (4) real funds demanded for investment; (5) real government deficits; and (6) increases in the demand for real money to hold. As usual, we can put supply and demand together in a diagram, Figure 13.1, with a price—in this case the interest rate—on the vertical axis. The equilibrium interest rate is then that rate at which supply equals demand. In such a diagram we take income, wealth, and other prices as constant.

How do these curves slope? It is far from certain that people save more if the interest rate rises, but we will, rather arbitrarily, assume in Figure 13.1 that they do. Capital inflows are a positive function of the U.S. interest rate. With higher interest rates in the United States it is worthwhile for foreigners to hold more American securities, despite the risk that the exchange rate may vary, so that their dollar holdings may be worth less in their own currencies. (Capital inflows decrease, of course, if foreign interest rates rise.) The supply of money moves up as interest rates rise, provided that the Federal Reserve holds the monetary base constant, because the money multiplier increases as the interest rate does.

On the demand side, investment moves down as the interest rate rises. Similarly, the higher the interest rate, the less real money people want to hold because it costs more to hold money.[2] The federal government's deficit is insensitive, or else sensitive in a perverse way, to the interest rate. The government does not borrow less because borrowing is more expensive. On the contrary, it may well borrow more to meet the higher interest costs, while maintaining other expenditures.

---

[1] What about the demand for funds by those who want to consume? This is taken into account indirectly by treating saving, and not total income (i.e., saving plus consumption), as part of the supply of loanable funds. Hence we already subtract the funds demanded for consumption.

[2] But don't some types of money pay interest too, so that a rise in the interest rate provides little incentive to switch from money to bonds? Not quite. The rate of interest on money lags behind the interest rate paid on securities. Hence, when bond rates rise it is profitable to switch out of money into bonds.

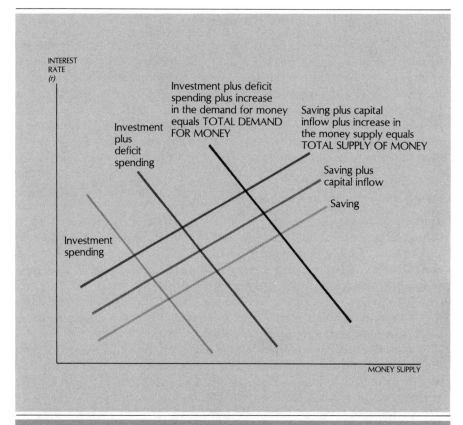

Figure 13.1   The Determinants of Interest Rates: Loanable Funds Approach. The supply curve of loanable funds consists of three components: saving, capital inflows, and increases in the money supply. The components of the demand curve are investment, the government deficit, and the increase in the demand for money to hold. The interest rate is set by the intersection of the supply and demand curves.

Where does the Fed fit into this? News reports often say that the Fed has raised or lowered interest rates. It does so by affecting supply and demand in three ways. The most important is to enter the market as a buyer or seller of securities, thereby changing bank reserves. The second way is by changing the discount rate, that is, the rate at which depository institutions can borrow from it. The third way is to change the public's expectations of future interest rates. Insofar as the expectations theory of the term structure is correct, the current long-term interest rate depends mainly on what interest rates are expected to be in the future. The Fed can influence these expectations.

Suppose now that the supply of loanable funds increases. As Figure 13.2 shows, the interest rate falls. Conversely, when the demand for loanable funds rises from D to D', while the supply is unchanged, the interest rate rises from r_0 to r_2.

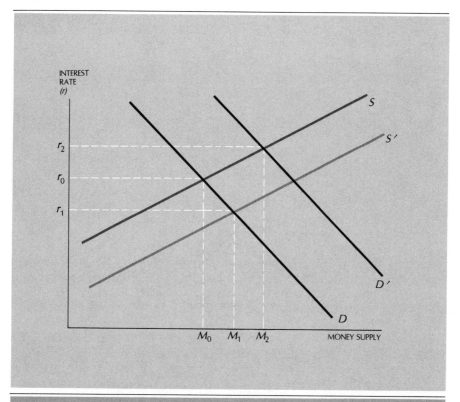

Figure 13.2 **Equilibrium in the Money Market.** The interest rate is in equilibrium at the point where the supply and demand for money are equal.

The Liquidity Preference Approach

An alternative way of looking at interest rates, the liquidity preference theory, focuses on the supply and demand for money. This theory runs in terms of *stocks* (as opposed to the loanable funds theory that talks about *flows* of saving, capital inflows, etc., per period). A supply of money, stated as a stock, confronts a demand for money, also stated as a stock. This is just a matter of exposition. Since a flow represents a change in stocks one can always reformulate a flow theory in terms of stocks.

The basic idea of the liquidity preference theory is that in equilibrium the interest rate must be such that the supply and demand for money are equal. For example, at the interest rate r_1 in Figure 13.3A, some people's money balances exceed what they want to hold at that interest rate, so that they have excess money to lend out. This lowers the interest rate. Similarly, at r_2 people want to hold more money than they have. As they borrow, or call in loans, the interest rate rises. The money market is at equilibrium only at r_3.

The liquidity preference theory is generally not in conflict with the loan-

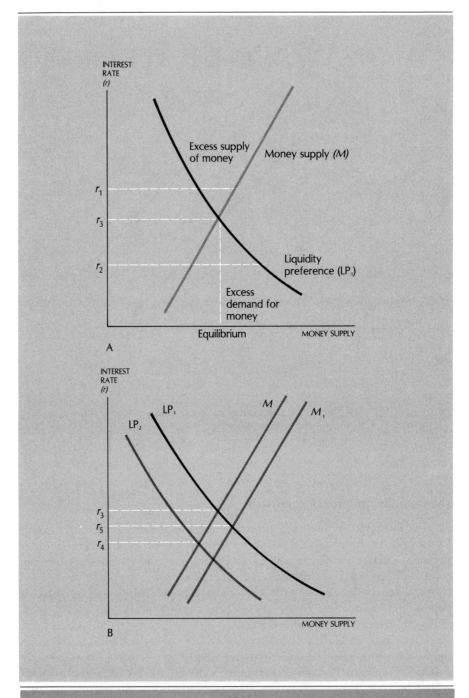

INTEREST
RATE
(r)

Excess supply
of money

Money supply *(M)*

r_1

r_3

r_2

Liquidity
preference (LP₁)

Excess
demand for
money

Equilibrium

MONEY SUPPLY

A

INTEREST
RATE
(r)

LP₂

LP₁

M

M₁

r_3
r_5

r_4

MONEY SUPPLY

B

Figure 13.3   The Movement to Equilibrium. At r_1 in Part A, there is an excess supply of money which drives the interest rate down. At r_2 there is an excess demand for money, so that the interest rate rises. In Part B, we see what happens as the liquidity preference (LP) and money supply (M) curves shift.

able funds theory. It is just an alternative way—at times a more convenient way—of looking at interest rates. This is so because the same six factors that determine the interest rate according to the loanable funds theory also determine it according to the liquidity preference theory.

To illustrate this, suppose that real saving increases. As people cut their consumption they also reduce the amount of money they hold to undertake consumption; their demand for money falls. Hence, according to the liquidity preference theory (as well as the loanable funds theory), as the liquidity preference curve shifts down from LP_1 to LP_2 (see Figure 13.3B), the interest rate falls from r_3 to r_4. Second, suppose that foreign capital flows into the United States. As will be explained in Chapter 22, U.S. exports then fall and imports rise; hence, U.S. income falls. With income falling, so does the demand for real money. The liquidity preference curve in Figure 13.3B again shifts down and the interest rate falls. Third, assume that the real money supply increases from M to M_1 in Figure 13.3B. Again, the interest rate falls, this time to r_5.

Fourth, suppose that investment increases. To undertake investment firms temporarily need to hold more real money. This shifts the liquidity preference curve upward, so that the interest rate rises. Fifth, if the government runs a deficit by buying more goods and services, the sellers of these goods and services now have higher incomes, and hence a greater demand for real money. Again, the liquidity preference curve shifts upward and the interest rate rises.[3] Finally, assume that people want to hold more real money. This is simply another way of saying that the liquidity preference curve has shifted upward.

Hence, all the variables that according to the loanable funds theory change interest rates also do so according to the liquidity preference theory. Conversely, the two variables of the liquidity preference theory, the supply of money and the demand for money, are part of the loanable funds theory.

The Effect of Selected Variables on the Interest Rate

The marginal propensity to consume, the riskiness of bonds, the yield on capital, and changes in income and wealth enter the two theories of interest rates only indirectly. How does the interest rate respond to changes in these variables?

A rise in the marginal propensity to consume lowers saving, and as both common sense and the loanable funds theory tells us, this raises the interest rate by reducing the supply of loaning funds. Now suppose that bonds become riskier, perhaps because interest rates have become more variable. To entice people to hold bonds despite this greater risk, bonds must now offer a higher rate of interest.

---

[3] In principle, a rise in government expenditures also has a direct effect on interest rates since, to spend more, the government must hold more money. But the amount of money the federal government holds per dollar of expenditures is trivial, and besides, the standard definition of money excludes balances held by the government.

An increase in the marginal productivity of capital raises investment and thus the demand for loanable funds, which, in turn, raises the interest rate. Moreover, with capital now having a higher yield, people want to sell some of their bonds so that they can buy more capital. But someone must hold the existing stock of bonds. Hence, the price of bonds must decline, so that the yield of bonds goes up enough to make people willing to hold the existing stock of bonds.

A rise in real income is more complex. On the one hand, the demand for real money increases when real income rises, and this raises the interest rate. On the other hand, with income being higher, saving is higher too, which should make the interest rate fall. Which effect dominates? To answer this question with the loanable funds theory would be quite difficult. However, it is easy using the liquidity preference theory. As real income rises the demand for real money increases, while the real supply of money is constant. Hence the interest rate must rise.

The impact of an increase in wealth is tricky. It depends on how wealth increases. Suppose wealth increases because the government issues more bonds.[4] It cuts taxes so that, instead of holding cancelled checks for taxes paid, people now hold government bonds. They will not want to hold all of this increase in their wealth in the form of bonds, but will try to diversify their asset holdings by selling some of these bonds to buy other assets, such as corporate stock, houses, time deposits, etc. As they sell bonds the price of bonds goes down, and the interest rate rises. In other words, when there are more bonds around, the yield on bonds has to rise to bribe people to hold more bonds.

But suppose wealth has increased for another reason. Perhaps stock prices have risen, so that the total value of stock portfolios is higher, or perhaps the money stock has increased. Now people diversify *into* bonds, bond prices rise, and the interest rate falls.

Predicting Interest Rates

Having learned what determines interest rates, can you predict what will happen to interest rates and bond prices? Yes and no. *If* you know what will happen to the productivity of capital, to wealth, etc., then you can predict interest rates. But this is a big *if*. Moreover, even if you know how interest rates will change you still cannot make money from this knowledge if others know it too. Suppose, for example, that you hear on TV that the federal deficit will decrease. You predict that interest rates will now go down, and bond prices up. Hence you want to buy bonds now to sell them subsequently. But it is too late. Other people do this too, so bond prices rise right away. To make money in this market you not only have to know what will happen, you have to know it ahead of others. This is an implication of **efficient markets theory,** a theory that states that markets set prices at a level that already takes all the available information into account. To make a killing in the market you have to know something that others don't. Old news is dead news.

---

[4] In Chapter 6 we discussed whether or not government bonds are net wealth. Here we just assume that they are.

NOMINAL MONEY SUPPLY AND THE INTEREST RATE

Both the loanable funds and the liquidity preference theories tell us that when the *real* quantity of money increases the interest rate falls. But what happens if the *nominal* quantity of money increases? This is complicated, so let's take it in stages. First assume that: (1) prices are constant; (2) there is no income tax; and (3) that a change in the inflation rate does not affect the marginal propensity to consume or the marginal productivity of capital.

Constant Prices

If prices are constant, then a rise in the nominal money supply is the same as a rise in the real money supply, and hence must lower the real interest rate. This is called the **liquidity effect**. The lower interest rate then stimulates investment and consumption, so that income rises. With income rising, the interest rate rises again—but not all the way back to its previous level.

To see why it cannot go all the way back, imagine that it were to do so. With the real interest rate then being back at its previous level, consumption and investment, and thus income, would also be back at their previous levels. After all, the only reason they had risen is that the interest rate had fallen. But with income and the interest rate now having returned to their previous levels, who would want to hold the increased supply of nominal money? Previously people wanted to hold more money because the interest rate was lower and income was higher. But in the hypothetical situation where the real interest rate goes all the way back to its previous level, these incentives to hold more money no longer exist. Hence, there would be an excess supply of money, and the interest rate would fall again.

Complete Price Flexibility

Now we drop the assumption that prices are constant and assume instead that they are completely flexible. With completely flexible prices equilibrium can exist only when there is no idle capacity or involuntary unemployment. If there were any idle capacity its owners would cut prices to get their resources working again.

Suppose that the nominal money stock rises in such a price-flexible economy. As before, at first the real interest rate falls and aggregate demand increases. But since output is already at the full employment level it cannot expand to meet the increased demand, so that it is prices, and only prices, that rise. They continue to rise as long as aggregate demand is above its previous level. And as long as the interest rate is below its previous level, aggregate demand will be above its previous level.

But as prices continue to rise the *real* money stock falls. Eventually it is back at its initial level. At that point the real interest rate too is what it was before the increase in the nominal money supply. This must be so because the only factor that caused the interest rate to fall was that the real money supply was larger, and now it no longer is larger.

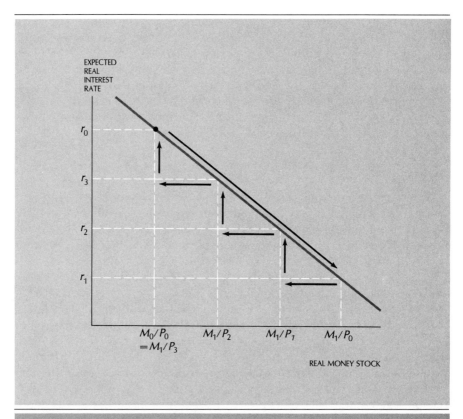

Figure 13.4   The Behavior of Interest Rates. An increase in the money supply at first lowers the interest rate. But as prices rise the real stock of money falls until it is back at its initial level. When it gets there the interest rate is then back at its initial level, too.

Figure 13.4 shows what occurs. Initially, the money supply increases from M_0/P_0 to M_1/P_0. (Right after the money supply has increased the price level is still P_0 because prices have not yet had time to adjust.) With the real money supply rising to M_1/P_0 the interest rate falls from r_0 to r_1. As a result, aggregate demand increases. Firms raise prices to P_1, so that the real money stock falls to M_1/P_1, and the interest rate rises to r_2. But since it is still below r_1 prices continue to rise, and the real money stock continues to fall. The same is true at r_3. This process ends only when the interest rate is back at r_0 and the real money supply has returned to M_0. The increase in nominal money has raised prices proportionately, and left the real interest rate unchanged.

What happens to the nominal interest rate depends on whether the price increases are expected or not. As people realize that prices have been rising they will probably expect them to rise further. Lenders will then add an **inflation premium** to the interest rate they demand to compensate them for the loss in the real value of their capital. For example, someone willing to lend at a 3 percent interest rate in the absence of inflation will want a 9 percent interest rate if she anticipates a 6 percent inflation rate. A borrower who expects a 6 percent inflation rate will agree to pay the extra 6 percent because he knows that for every $1 he borrows he will repay a real value of only 94 cents at the end of the year. This is called the **Fisher effect.**[5] Thus we have:

Nominal rate = Expected real rate − Expected inflation rate

or

Expected real rate = Nominal rate − Expected inflation rate.

Expressed in symbols this is:

$$r = r_r^e + dp^e \text{ or } r_r^e = r - dp^e,$$

where r denotes the nominal interest rate, r_r the real rate, dp the inflation rate, and the superscript e the expected values.

In these equations the real interest rate is the expected real rate, and not necessarily the actual real rate. When negotiating a loan neither borrower nor lender knows what the real rate will be since they can only guess at the inflation rate. The inflation premium they include in the nominal rate may be too high or too low to keep the real rate constant. The actual real rate is:

$$r_r = r - dp.$$

If dp^e differs from dp, then r_r^e will differ from r_r.

The Effect of Taxation

Taxes complicate the story because the tax system does not respond properly to inflation. Suppose that the real rate of interest is 3 percent, the inflation rate is 6 percent, and the nominal interest rate is 9 percent. Although the true earnings of the lender are only 3 cents for every dollar lent, the tax system ignores this fact. It taxes the lender not only on the 3 cents of genuine income, but on the whole 9 cents she received. At the same time it allows the borrower to deduct from his taxable income not only the 3 cents of genuine interest, but the whole 9 cents.[6] Hence the income tax, in effect, imposes a special tax on lenders while subsidizing borrowers.

To see what this does to the interest rate, imagine an analogous situation: suppose that every time a book is sold the government taxes the buyer $1, and gives this dollar to the seller. Since there is no reason for the equilibrium price of a book to change, the market would negate the government's action. The price of a book would simply decline by $1, so that the after-tax

---

[5] Irving Fisher developed the relation between the inflation rate and the nominal interest rate. But he did not believe that the nominal interest rate includes a full adjustment for the inflation rate, except perhaps in the very long run.

[6] Throughout this discussion we will assume that lenders and borrowers are in the same tax bracket, and will ignore the complication created by some types of income not being taxed.

cost to the buyer, and the after-subsidy receipts of the seller, would be the same as before.

Applying this principle to the interest rate yields:

$$r_{rat} = r(1 - T) - dp,$$

where r_{rat} is the real after-tax rate, T is the marginal tax rate on interest income, and, as before, r is the nominal interest rate and dp the inflation rate. This adjustment for taxes is called the **Darby effect** after its discoverer, Michael Darby of UCLA.

THE SEQUENCE OF INTEREST-RATE CHANGES: THE ERROR-LEARNING MODEL

We can now see how the interest rate responds to an increase in the money supply in an economy in which prices adjust only with a lag, and in which people form their expectations *adaptively*. Specifically they predict initially that the future will be similar to the past. If this turns out to be wrong they adjust their expectations part of the way to take account of the new experience. For example, suppose that initially they expect a 5 percent inflation. Prices then actually increase by 8 percent. They may then expect prices to rise at a, say, 6 percent rate in the next period.[7] Hence the inflation premium may lag behind the actual inflation rate for a considerable time.

What happens in such an economy when the nominal money supply rises? Initially the expected nominal and real interest rates have to fall. Eventually the expected real rate returns to its previous level. If, and it is a big if, expectations of inflation have not developed at this stage, so that p^e is zero, the nominal rate stays equal to the expected real rate. But this is implausible. As prices rise, people come to expect further price increases. Hence p^e is positive, lifting the after-tax nominal rate above the real rate. The before-tax nominal rate rises even more. At this stage both the expected before- and after-tax nominal rates could, but need not, be higher than they were before the money supply increased.

Eventually the real rate returns to its previous level. At that point the nominal rate is higher than it was prior to the money supply increase because borrowers and lenders expect that prices will continue to rise.

The story told so far assumes that price expectations adjust adaptively with some lag to the actual behavior of prices. This may, but need not, be the case. Instead of forming their expectations just by looking at what happened in the past, people may form their expectations *rationally* by taking account of all the information available at reasonable cost. If so, they are no more likely

---

[7] Why don't people adjust their expectations all the way to 8 percent? The reason is that they used quite a lot of information in deciding that prices will increase at a 5 percent rate. They don't discard all this information merely because they were wrong in one month.

to underestimate the inflation rate than to overestimate it. All this requires some explanation and hence a digression.

What Are Rational Expectations?

According to the rational-expectations approach, people forecast in a fully rational way, given all the information available to them. This is quite different from just projecting the past behavior of a series, such as interest rates, as is done in the error-learning model. In the error-learning model, when interest rates decline more than expected, people do not bother to ask why their previous forecast was wrong. Moreover, since they usually adjust their forecasts only part of the way each period, they tend to make systematic errors; for example, they overestimate for several periods. By contrast, in the rational-expectations approach people use all the information they can get to make their forecasts. To do this they must have in their minds some model of the economy that allows them to interpret the incoming information. For example, using what they have learned from economics courses, they predict that inflation will speed up substantially if Congress orders the Fed to lower interest rates. But, how about those who have never taken an economics course? They too will have some information that will allow them to make a judgment about how the inflation rate will be affected. Everyone has an explicit or implicit theory that is used to interpret incoming information.

Economics would be much further advanced if we knew these (largely inchoate) theories that people use. But we do not, so we have to make some assumptions. One possible assumption is that people's theories correspond fairly well to the economists' theories. This does not mean that everyone reasons the way economists do, but merely that their conclusions average out to what is shown by the economists' models. This is not as unrealistic as it sounds at first, because the most important decisions are made mainly by experienced managers who have reached their positions because they usually predict correctly. These managers can reach the same conclusions as economists without having the economists' theories in their toolbox. For example, someone may not know the theories that explain the term structure of interest rates, but many simply observe that long-term interest rates behave in a certain way when short-term rates change; birds can fly without having studied aerodynamics.

Moreover, assuming that expectations are rational is not the same thing as assuming that people have perfect foresight; economic models certainly do not. What it does mean is that, unlike in the error-learning model, people will not make *systematic* errors for any length of time. They will still make errors, but these errors will be random, and have a mean of zero. To illustrate, here is an example from everyday life. Suppose that without this being announced, trains are now running slower, so that the average trip takes ten minutes longer. On the first day almost everyone will arrive at work late. Someone using an error-learning model will leave the next day, say, six minutes earlier and be four minutes late. But someone operating according to rational expectations may remember that in previous years when the weather was like this trains were usually ten minutes late, or else may call the railroad to get a new timetable. Such a person will not always be exactly on time; some days the train is slower, and some days it is faster. But this person will be late (or early) no more frequently than before.

THE SEQUENCE OF INTEREST-RATE CHANGES: RATIONAL EXPECTATIONS

Suppose people behave as the rational-expectations theory states. Then, when the money growth rate rises firms realize that the equilibrium inflation rate is higher. Knowing that the increased demand for their products is not just a temporary fluke, they do not hesitate, but raise prices right away. Thus the *liquidity effect*, which in the adaptive-expectations story depressed the interest rate, does not occur. Moreover, inflationary expectations rise immediately, so that the Fisher effect takes hold right away. Hence the nominal rate increases immediately by enough to keep the after-tax real rate of interest constant.

The Plausibility of Rational Expectations

How plausible is the rational-expectations approach? This is a hotly debated issue. Economists like the idea that people behave rationally. Indeed, this assumption forms the basis of economics. Without more or less rational behavior, economic theory is not possible. More specifically, it seems implausible that people forecast the inflation rate merely by looking at past rates. Suppose the inflation rate is accelerating. They would underestimate it time after time. Wouldn't they eventually learn?

The critics of the rational-expectations approach do not deny that people behave more or less rationally, but emphasize the "more or less." Since it is costly to obtain and process information it may be *rational* to operate by a rule of thumb, such as projecting the past rate of inflation, perhaps with some adjustment for previous forecasting errors. The loss that results from such a rule of thumb may be so small that it is entirely rational to use such a crude rule.

In any case, the empirical evidence suggests that it is only in certain *auction markets,* mainly markets for homogeneous products, such as raw materials and financial instruments, that prices adjust rapidly. Prices of manufactured products and services usually adjust only when costs, such as labor costs, vary. Labor costs change only slowly because of the existence of formal and informal contracts. Hence, the argument runs, regardless of whether the expectations of firms are rational or not, they adjust their prices only slowly. If so, an increase in the nominal money supply can reduce both nominal and real interest rates for a significant time.

The Empirical Evidence

Figure 13.5 shows the monetary growth rate and the nominal Treasury-bill rate. It suggests that the Treasury-bill rate usually moved in the same direction as the money growth rate until the 1970s. (This does not deny the existence of

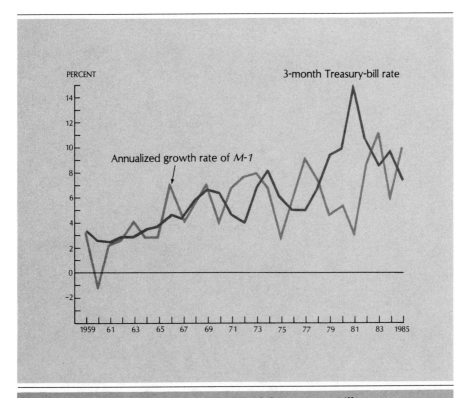

Figure 13.5   The Money Growth Rate and the Treasury-Bill Rate, 1959–1985. Over the past two and a half decades, the Treasury-bill rate has usually moved in the same direction as the money growth rate. The slight lag represents the liquidity effect. **Source:** U.S. Department of Commerce, *Handbook of Cyclical Indicators; Economic Report of the President,* 1986; Board of Governors, Federal Reserve System, *1986 Money Stock Revisions.*

a liquidity effect because it may be too short-lived to be picked up by the annual data of Figure 13.5.) Then in the early 1980s the money growth rate was very low while the T-bill rate was extremely high.

Figure 13.6 shows the real after-tax rate of interest on the assumption that the marginal tax rate on interest income was 30 percent.[8] It illustrates that in the 1970s when the money growth rate and the inflation rate were both high, the real after-tax Treasury-bill rate was often negative. This suggests that, at least at times, a high money growth rate may lower the real interest rate.[9] Why should this be?

---

[8] It is somewhat arbitrary to assume a 30 percent marginal tax rate; perhaps it is closer to 33 percent.

[9] See Dennis Hoffman and Don Schlagenhauf, "Real Interest Rates, Anticipated Inflation and Unanticipated Money: A Multi-Country Study," *Review of Economics and Statistics,* 67 (May 1985):284–296.

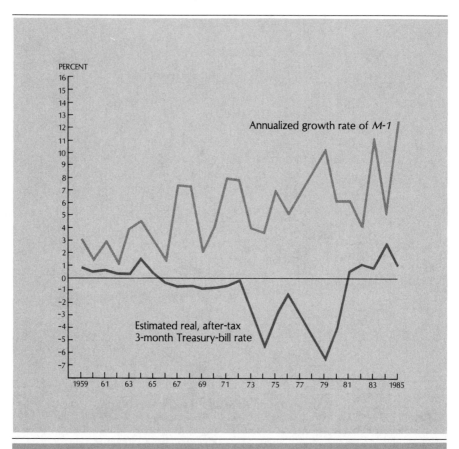

PERCENT

Annualized growth rate of *M-1*

Estimated real, after-tax
3-month Treasury-bill rate

1959 61 63 65 67 69 71 73 75 77 79 81 83 1985

Figure 13.6   The Real After-Tax Treasury-Bill Rate and the Money Growth Rate,1959–1985. Here, the Treasury-bill rate has been adjusted for both taxes and inflation. The prolonged lags in adjustment of interest rates to changes in the growth rate of money seem too great to be accounted for by lagging expectations or price adjustments. The data assume an after-tax interest rate of 30 percent and an inflation rate as measured by the CPI. **Source:** U.S. Department of Commerce, *Handbook of Cyclical Indicators* and *Business Conditions Digest;* Board of Governors, Federal Reserve System, *1985 Money Stock Revisions.*

More on the Real Interest Rate and Inflation

So far we have always assumed that the public wants to save and invest the same amount regardless of inflation. This is implausible. Inflation affects the savings rate in three ways. When prices rise the real value of the stocks of money and government bonds falls. In response people should save more to restore their wealth. Moreover, inflation creates uncertainty, and one reaction to uncertainty is to save more. On the other hand, in the absence of perfect inflation hedges, inflation also provides an incentive to save less because it lowers the real return on saving. It is far from certain which effect dominates, but, either way, there is no reason to assume that inflation leaves the savings rate unchanged.

Similarly, inflation affects investment in several ways. Firms face greater uncertainty. Will costs rise faster than prices? Will the government impose price controls, or will it adopt strong anti-inflationary policies that will cause markets to collapse? In addition, inflation raises the tax burden on some corporations.

Since the initial response to rising demand is to increase output, an increase in the money stock initially raises not just prices, but also real income. Hence, even if a rise in the nominal money stock would not change the marginal propensity to save, it would still change the total amount of real saving by changing real income. Similarly, through the accelerator, it could change investment.

With inflation affecting the real interest rate in so many ways, it is not surprising that the after-tax real rate of interest does not remain constant when the money growth rate and hence the inflation rate rise.

POLICY IMPLICATIONS

Many critics of the Fed believe that it can reduce interest rates by adopting a more expansionary policy. Are they right? With respect to the nominal interest rate they are probably correct only for a relatively short span of time. After that it is inflation, and not the nominal interest rate, that responds to an increase in the money growth rate.

However, the Fed's critics are probably right if they mean the after-tax real rate. But the reduction in this interest rate occurs only as a by-product of a higher inflation rate.

SUMMARY

1 The interest rate is an important variable because, usually implicitly, it enters most transactions and also because interest rates are highly volatile.
2 Interest rates are explained by the loanable funds theory and the liquidity preference theory. These theories are the same in the sense that the same variables determine the interest rate in both theories. These variables are saving, capital inflows, changes in the real money stock, the demand for funds to invest, government deficits, and changes in the real demand for money to hold. Yields on other assets, the marginal propensity to consume, and income and wealth enter the determination of interest rates indirectly.
3 An increase in the *nominal* money stock lowers both the nominal and the real interest rates initially. Subsequently they rise again. As inflation becomes expected the nominal rate rises further. This rise is exacerbated by the fact that nominal interest income and not real interest income is taxed.
4 If expectations are formed in an adaptive way, then it *may* take the real interest rate a long time to rise again after the nominal money supply has increased. This is not so if expectations are rational and prices adjust quickly. The rational-expectations approach is much debated.

QUESTIONS AND EXERCISES

1 The payment of net interest accounts for a smaller proportion of GNP than does payment for food. Why then do newspapers pay so much more attention to interest rates than to the price of food?

2 Take the various factors that in the loanable funds theory explain the interest rate. Show how they affect the interest rate in the liquidity preference theory.

3 Explain how the following affect the rate of interest:
a. a tax on purchases of corporate stock
b. a reduction in government expenditures with no change in tax rates

4 Discuss: "In an economy with flexible prices an increase in the growth rate of nominal money will raise nominal interest rates."

5 Discuss: "Our tax system ensures that the interest rate does not rise exactly in proportion to an increase in the inflation rate, but rises more than that."

6 What difference does it make for the behavior of interest rates whether expectations are rational or extrapolative?

7 State some arguments that might suggest that expectations are not rational. How convincing are these arguments?

FURTHER READING

CONARD, JOSEPH. *An Introduction to Theory of Interest.* Berkeley: University of California Press, 1959. A classic treatise on interest rates.

FRIEDMAN, MILTON. "Factors Affecting the Level of Interest Rates," in United States Savings and Loan League, *Proceedings of a Conference on Savings and Residential Financing,* pp. 11–27. Chicago: United States Savings and Loan League, 1969. An important analysis of how interest rates respond to changes in money growth.

MEHRA, YASH. "Inflationary Expectations, Money Growth and the Vanishing Liquidity Effect of Money on Interest: A Further Investigation," *Economic Review,* Federal Reserve Bank of Richmond, 71/2 (March/April 1985):23–35. A useful exposition, but it requires material which will be taken up only in Chapter 15.

CHAPTER 14

The Demand for Money

Two of the factors that determine interest rates, the supply of money and the demand for money, deserve particular attention. We discussed the supply of money in Chapters 10 and 11, and will discuss it again in Part 4. This chapter deals with the demand for money. The demand for money may seem a silly topic. Don't most people want as much money as they can get? Not in the way we are using the term "demand for money." As usual in economics the term "demand" here does not mean demand in the sense of how much one would like of a good if it were free, but demand for a good relative to the other goods one wants. We ask "How much money do you wish to hold, given that the more money you hold the less you can hold of other assets."

The demand for money is related to the velocity of money, and the Cambridge k. The Cambridge k can be defined as the amount of money demanded per dollar of income.

A SIMPLE-MINDED APPROACH

We begin with the simplest possible approach in which a person uses money only for anticipated transactions, and does so in a mechanical fashion. He receives an income of, say, $3,000 each month, and spends it at an even rate during the month. Until the last day of the month, he holds some money to cover expenditures during the remaining days. His money holdings are illustrated in Figure 14.1. On the first day of the month he holds $3,000, and at the end of the last day he holds no money. If he spends his $3,000 at an even rate during the month, his average money holdings are equal to $(3,000 + 0)/2 = \$1,500$.

Someone who conducts his business in this way can hardly be said to have a "demand" for money that is worth discussing. The amount of money he holds is determined purely mechanically by his income and by the number of days remaining in the month. His mechanical behavior may be inconsistent with utility maximization in two ways. First, he pays no attention to the benefits and costs he might obtain from investing some of his income for part of the month. Second, he has only a *transactions demand* for money; that is, he

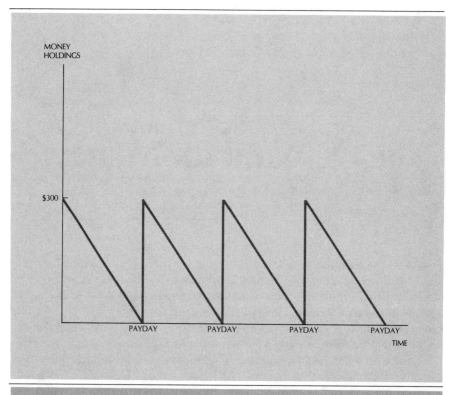

Figure 14.1   Time Pattern of Money Holdings: Simple Mechanistic Model.
Households receive a sum of money on payday and, in this example, run it down
at a smooth rate over the pay period, holding zero money at the end of the period.

holds money only for those transactions he anticipates, and ignores the fact
that he may have an unexpected need for money.

Undoubtedly some people decide on their money holdings in this crude
mechanistic way. But this is not typical. A large part of the money supply is
held in accounts large enough to make it worthwhile to manage them in a
sophisticated way.

Moreover, households keep much more money than can be explained by
the need to hold some money until the next payday. Per capita disposable
monthly income in 1985 was $977, while per capita money holdings were
$2,487, two and a half times as large. Obviously, the need to hold money until
the next payday does not explain money holdings adequately.[1] So, let's see
how those people who plan their money holdings carefully decide on them.

THE TRANSACTIONS APPROACH

There are many ways one can take care of one's transactions needs. At one
extreme one can, as already discussed, keep all one's receipts as money and
then spend this money in the period between receipts. This avoids the broker-

[1] Currency holdings too are surprisingly large, over $3,000 per family in 1985.

age cost and the trouble of investing in securities or in near-monies, such as a time deposit or a money-market account. But it has a disadvantage—foregoing the interest one could earn by investing some of the money. At the other extreme someone could invest all her income as soon as she receives it, and sell a security or, say, withdraw a time deposit every time she needs money to spend. This maximizes her interest earnings, but frequent buying and selling of securities generates large brokerage charges, and trips to the bank to withdraw money from a time deposit are a lot of trouble and bother.

How much, if any, of her income should she invest therefore depends on two factors. One is the cost of investing, that is, the expense and trouble involved in investing and later disinvesting in a security or near-money. The other is the *net* interest foregone by holding money, that is, the interest that could be earned on a security or a near-money minus the interest earned by holding money.

The trouble involved in acquiring and later liquidating securities or near-money does not rise in proportion to the amount involved. It is no more trouble to put $100,000 into one's time deposit than to put $1,000 in. The brokerage charge too is not 100 times as great for a $100,000 security as for a $1,000 security. Hence, holders of large money balances are much more likely to invest their transactions balances than are holders of small balances. At current interest rates it does not make sense for most people to put some of their pay into securities or near-monies for part of the pay period.

But this does not mean that the transactions demand for money is independent of the interest rate. First, for large holders of money, such as businesses, it is often worthwhile to invest excess money even if just for overnight. And they are more likely to do so the higher the net interest rate. Second, households maintain transactions balances for occasional large purchases they plan to make some time in the future. The higher the net interest rate the less likely are they to hold these funds in the form of money. Moreover, they also accumulate funds in their transactions accounts until it is worthwhile for them to buy securities or to move funds into a near-money. The higher the net interest rate, the smaller the amount of money required to make such a shift worth undertaking despite the cost and trouble involved in buying securities. Hence, the transactions demand for money depends on the net interest rate, even if no wage or salary earner would ever acquire securities or near-money on payday, with the intention of liquidating them again before the next payday.

Apart from the net interest rate the transactions demand for money also depends on the volume of intended transactions and hence on income. Obviously, the more money you plan to spend, the larger your transactions demand for money. The transactions demand for money is also a function of the cost and trouble of investing funds. This, in turn, varies with the available alternatives to holding money (e.g., the existence of money-market funds), the amount charged by brokers, and how much people value the time it takes to invest and later to disinvest.

In Chapter 4 we discussed the compensatory balances that firms have to hold in the bank as part of their customer relationship. They can be considered a transactions demand since they depend on the borrowing that firms do and on the services they demand from banks, and these in turn depend on their transactions. We do not know how large these balances are, but they *might* account for a substantial part of deposits by firms.

PRECAUTIONARY AND SPECULATIVE DEMAND

It usually makes sense to hold more money than you anticipate spending. As all of us have found out, frequently one spends more than one expects. Anything from car trouble to an unexpectedly high price for a purchase can force one to spend more than intended. Or a pleasant surprise may occur, because of an unexpected chance to snap up a bargain. Firms and some households also need to hold money because of the danger that they will not receive anticipated payments on time—that "the check is in the mail."

There are five ways to take care of such contingencies. One is to hold more money than one expects to spend, that is, to hold a **precautionary balance**. The second is to cut planned expenditures to make room for the unexpected ones as they arise. The third is to sell some asset, such as a CD, bond, or even physical capital, and the fourth is to borrow. A final possibility is to refrain from making a payment, a possibility that ranges all the way from just passing up a bargain to declaring bankruptcy.

All of these responses have their costs. Holding a precautionary balance means foregoing some net interest income. Cutting planned expenditures is usually painful, and sometimes may not suffice to meet the unexpected need. For some assets selling them quickly means selling them for substantially less than they would fetch in a more leisurely sale. Borrowing may be expensive. Passing up a bargain has an obvious cost. Reneging on a payment can involve embarrassment as well as a loss of reputation and legal penalties.

It will usually pay to hold a precautionary balance, but how large should it be? The benefit from holding such a balance is that this avoids the costs of the other four alternatives just discussed, while the cost is the foregone net interest, say, 3 percent. As usual in economics the answer to the question, "How big should it be?" is to set marginal cost equal to marginal revenue. Consider one of these costs, the cost of borrowing, say, at an 18 percent interest rate. The revenue you receive from holding a precautionary balance is then equal to the probability that you will actually use the precautionary balance times the 18 percent interest you avoid having to pay in this contingency. Since it is the essence of a precautionary balance that you hold it to guard against uncertain events, there will be times when you will not draw on it, and hence receive no benefit from it, while at other times it will save you a lot, 18 percent in this example.

Many unexpected events happen, but the probability that a household will have such bad luck that it has to make a large number of unexpected payments is much less than the probability that it will have to make just a few such payments. Similarly, a firm whose receipts from sales and whose required payments to other firms are not fully predictable will occasionally have the unpleasant experience that very few of its expected receipts are coming in, while very many of its bills are. But there is only a small chance that nearly all the bills it has to pay will arrive before any of its receipts do. Thus, both for firms and for households, the larger is your precautionary balance the less probability there is that you will actually use the last dollar in it. As a result, the marginal productivity of a dollar in a precautionary balance is less the greater the precautionary balance.

The marginal cost of holding a dollar in precautionary balances is constant, 3 percent forgone interest in this example, and with the marginal revenue of a dollar in a precautionary balance being less the larger the precautionary balance, there comes a point at which the marginal cost and the marginal revenue of the precautionary balance are just equal. At this point the precautionary balance is the right size. In our example, the marginal revenue (MR) of a dollar of precautionary balances is 18 percent times the probability of actually having to use that dollar. The marginal cost (MC) is 3 percent. To find the optimal balance, set MC equal to MR. This means that 3 percent equals 18 percent times the probability of actually using the dollar. Solving for the probability, we find that the precautionary balance in this example should be large enough so that the probability of using its last dollar is one-sixth.

The same principle applies to the other costs of running out of money. Suppose, for example, that you can sell an asset right away for almost the same amount as you would get if you took your time in selling it. In this case your response to running out of money would be to sell that asset rather than to borrow. The relevant marginal cost of having an insufficient precautionary balance is then the small amount you would lose by selling the asset quickly. Obviously, when faced with a shortage of money you should choose the cheapest solution, whether it be borrowing, selling an asset, cutting expenditures, or delaying payment, and it is the cost of this solution that, along with the probability of using the last dollar and the net interest rate, determines the optimal size of precautionary balances.

So far we have looked at precautionary balances only as a device for meeting unexpected needs to make payments or delays in getting paid. But there is an additional way in which the need to take precaution makes people hold money rather than bonds. Holding bonds involves the risk that interest rates may rise and the price of your bond may fall. Hence, you balance off the risk of holding bonds against the higher return you obtain from bonds. As a result you may want to hold some money (or near-money) rather than bonds.[2] The lower the interest rate on bonds the fewer bonds and the more money you will want to hold.

Thus, precautionary balances depend on numerous factors. Some of them—the probability of having to make unexpected payments, or the costs of cutting back on expenditures or of delaying payments—are usually constant. Hence we can assume that normally precautionary balances are not affected by variations in these factors.

---

[2] It might seem that if people decide it is too risky to hold bonds they will hold near-monies, say, Treasury bills, or time deposits rather than money, so that the demand for money is unaffected. But this is wrong. If people switch out of bonds into Treasury bills the price of Treasury bills rises and their yield falls. As a result, some other people decide to hold money rather than Treasury bills.

However, the cost of selling assets does vary from time to time, depending upon the public's security holdings. When households and firms are holding a large volume of liquid assets, such as Treasury bills and money-market accounts, they have less need for precautionary balances, since these assets can be turned into cash at little cost. Similarly, the demand for precautionary balances falls when the net interest rate rises, or when the rate at which firms and households can borrow decreases.

On the other hand, the demand for precautionary balances will increase if interest rates start to fluctuate more, so that the market values of securities, particularly long-term securities, become less stable. Moreover, in a sharp recession, the precautionary demand for money may increase. With unemployment widespread, households may decide to save more. Since for many wage earners it may not be worthwhile to hold near-monies, they may hold these savings as money instead.

Finally, some people may hold money rather than securities because they expect security prices to decline. But such people generally have ready access to money-market funds, and hence can hold these speculative balances in a near-money rather than as money. At a time when most large brokers provide their own money-market funds into which they shift their customers' idle funds, such speculative balances are surely not important.[3]

THE MONEY DEMAND FUNCTION

A more formal way of looking at the demand for money is to use the standard demand function of microeconomic theory. A rational household or firm will decide on its money holdings in the same way that it decides on its holdings of all other goods. Hence, the same factors that explain the demand for refrigerators, harpsicords, and bubble gum also explain the demand for money. Economists classify these factors by using a generalized demand function:

$$D_A = f(P_A, P_S, P_C, YP, Z),$$

where D_A is the demand for item A, P_A is its price, P_S represents the prices of substitute commodity, P_C represents the price of a complement (e.g., butter in a demand function for bread), YP is a nominal income, and Z is a catch-all variable called "tastes." Z includes not just what we normally think of as "tastes," but also technological factors. For example, if the demand for gasoline falls because cars become more fuel efficient, this is called a change in tastes. Anything that affects demand, and is not part of the other variables in the demand function, is dumped into "tastes."

Applying this demand function to money, the price of holding money is the yield on the assets that you would otherwise hold minus the yield on money. For example, if the alternative asset is a bond, the cost of holding money is the net interest rate on bonds. For some people, however, the alter-

---

[3] The speculative motive for holding money has received much attention because Keynes stressed it in his *General Theory of Employment, Interest and Money*. Since Keynes defined money broadly enough to include assets like money-market funds and time deposits, his stress on speculative money holdings was more justified than it is now, when we define money more narrowly.

native asset is not bonds, but common stock or physical capital. Then the net yields on these assets are the relevant cost of holding money.

The cost of money substitutes is more complex. One money substitute for firms is maintaining a line of credit with an unused balance. The cost of this is the bank's charge for the unused part of the credit line. For households a credit card is a money substitute, and its cost is the annual fee. Another money substitute is holding a liquid asset instead of a higher yielding, less liquid asset. The cost of this money substitute is the difference in the interest rates on the liquid and the less liquid asset. The category "money complements" is an empty box. It is hard to imagine what they could be.

Income and wealth affect the demand for money in two ways. One is via the work that money has to do. Obviously, the larger your expenditures the larger are the transactions balances and the precautionary balances you want. Second, the higher your income and wealth, the more you can afford of the good things of life, and one of these good things is not having to chase after every little bit of interest income. A poor person may balance his checkbook every day, and frequently transfer funds between a transactions account and a savings account to earn as much interest as possible. By contrast, a wealthy person can treat her time as more valuable, and forgo some interest income to avoid the bother of continually adjusting her money holdings.

The final variable, tastes, includes a whole set of factors, such as the payments technology that determines how fast payment can be made, payments habits that determine whether people are paid monthly or weekly, the availability of credit and money substitutes, attitudes toward delaying payments, etc.

Changes in the variables included in taste *might* cause sharp swings in the amount of money demanded. If this were the case the money demand function would not be so useful because we cannot predict, or even measure, many of the factors included in the tastes variable. One could still say that if the net interest rate falls, or if income rises, then, *other things being equal,* the demand for money will increase. This is far from useless, but it would not allow the Fed to predict what the demand for money would be in the future, because it could not predict how the demand for money would vary due to changes in tastes. The quantity theory of money would then be of little use. With the demand for money, and hence velocity, fluctuating a great deal, knowing the supply of money would not allow one to predict income.

By contrast, if the demand for money is stable and predictable, then the quantity theory can be used to forecast GNP. Using a simplified money demand function,

$$M = a + bYP + cr,$$

suppose that the coefficients *a*, *b*, and *c* are stable. Then, if one knows what *M* and *r* will be one can calculate *YP*.

STATISTICAL MONEY DEMAND FUNCTIONS

To see if the demand for money is predictable the generalized money demand function must be simplified. First, the empty box of money complements can be dropped. Most economists have also dropped the money substitutes variable. In principle, money substitutes belong in the money demand function, but if the demand for money is highly unresponsive to the price of money substitutes, or if the price of money substitutes shows little independent variation, then one can dispense with this variable. Moreover, the tastes variable is usually omitted because it is too difficult to measure.

This leaves the interest rate and income or wealth. Most statistical money demand functions, though not all, measure the interest rate by short-term rates, such as the Treasury-bill rate and an interest rate on time deposits. This is far from ideal. In principle the demand for money depends on many interest rates, as well as on the yields of other assets, such as common stock. But most economists believe that these other rates are correlated closely enough with the Treasury-bill rate so that this rate, together with the rate paid on time deposits, can serve as a proxy for interest rates in general. Income is often measured by current GNP. This is correct if the reason for including income in the money demand function is that one needs money to undertake transactions. But if income is included because the higher one's income is, the better one can afford the luxury of holding money rather than higher yielding near-monies, then one should not use current GNP. Either permanent income or wealth becomes a better measure. While some money demand functions use current GNP, others use permanent income.

The goodness of the fit of such money demand functions varies from time to time. It is excellent until the early 1970s, and then degenerates. Starting around 1973 the amount of money demanded fell greatly below what most money demand functions were predicting. The "case of the missing money" became a standard puzzle in economics. Then, in the early 1980s, the demand for money grew more rapidly than predicted.

What caused these large errors in the 1970s? It is by no means certain, but it seems that the major factor was the rapid pace of financial innovation. Interest rates paid on securities rose sharply. At the same time data-processing costs were falling rapidly. Hence, firms developed methods of economizing on money holdings. For example, they now make large payments by wire rather than by mail, so that they can keep their funds active until the very last moment. Many firms also use a "lock-box" system whereby customers are asked to send their payments to a centrally located post office box, which the firm's bank opens several times a day, depositing the checks right away to the firm's account. Another way firms reduce their money holdings is by using repos and deposit sweeps. (For households, there was also the growth of near-monies, such as money-market funds.) Some economists have included in their money demand functions a measure of cash management by business firms, such as the volume of wire transfers. This substantially reduced the error of the money demand function for the 1970s.

In the early 1980s several economists published more complex money demand functions that fit much better. One example, already mentioned, is a money demand function that includes a variable measuring cash management. Another money demand function uses a long-term interest rate, as well as the dividend/price ratio, a variable that measures stock market yields, and an adjustment for NOW accounts. It also forces the income elasticity of money demand to be unity. A different approach by economists at the San Francisco Fed adds the growth of bank loans, on the argument that a firm receiving a loan often holds part of it as a demand deposit for some time. Still another money demand function adds variables measuring the yield on non–transactions accounts, the riskiness of bonds, and the inflation rate. It also measures interest rates after income tax and not, as is usually done, before tax. It is too early to tell whether these attempts have been successful. In 1985 several of these money demand functions again predicted badly, and we will just have to wait and see how they perform in future years.[4]

THE BEHAVIOR OF VELOCITY

Some economists responded to the problem of the "missing money" by saying that it does not matter much. Velocity was growing at a stable rate of about 3.2 percent per year. Hence, they said, you do not need a money demand function to predict velocity. All you have to do is to assume that it will be 3.2 percent higher next year than it is this year. If you know the change in the supply of money you can predict income from the quantity theory without having to use a money demand function. This approach looked promising in the 1960s and 1970s when velocity was growing at a remarkably stable rate (see Figure 14.2). But what worked so well in the 1970s did not work in the early 1980s when velocity fell and became erratic. Table 14.1 shows the mean absolute errors for predictions of nominal GNP from simple money demand functions for M-1, M-2, and M-3, as well as for estimates of M-1 and M-2 that have been adjusted to eliminate the effects of deregulation, such as the nationwide spread of NOW accounts. It also shows the errors in GNP forecasts that result if, instead of fitting a money demand function, one just assumes that velocity will grow at a constant rate equal to its trend. In all cases the errors are much greater for the years 1981–1985 than for the years 1971–1980.

The cessation of velocity growth was unfortunate, not only for economists who had not predicted it, but also for many people who lost their jobs because the Fed had set monetary policy on the assumption that velocity would be growing.

The failure of velocity to grow can be attributed, at least in part, to falling nominal interest rates. It is not surprising that people want to hold more money per dollar of income when the cost of holding money declines. However, this is being wise only by hindsight; most economists who had projected the behavior of velocity had expected it to rise.

Figure 14.2 also shows velocity as more unstable in the early 1980s than in the 1970s. To some extent this is an illusion. Since it takes money some time to affect income, a rise in the money supply initially reduces velocity. (The denominator of the Y/M ratio rises right away while the numerator does not.) In the 1970s, when money was growing at a *relatively* stable rate, this did not matter much. But in the 1980s, when the money growth rate became much

---

[4] Moreover, some of these new money demand functions include independent variables, such as the dividend/price ratio, that are themselves hard to predict.

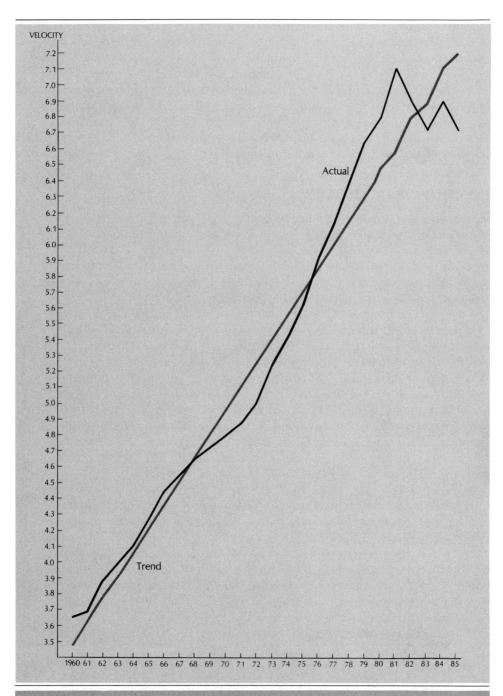

VELOCITY

7.2
7.1
7.0
6.9
6.8
6.7
6.6
6.5
6.4
6.3
6.2
6.1
6.0
5.9
5.8
5.7
5.6
5.5
5.4
5.3
5.2
5.1
5.0
4.9
4.8
4.7
4.6
4.5
4.4
4.3
4.2
4.1
4.0
3.9
3.8
3.7
3.6
3.5

Actual

Trend

1960 61 62 63 64 65 66 67 68 69 70 71 72 73 74 75 76 77 78 79 80 81 82 83 84 85

Figure 14.2   The Behavior of Velocity, 1960–1985. Using a stable figure of 3.2 percent annual growth in velocity, economists were able to predict income directly from changes in the supply of money in the 1960s and 1970s, but erratic velocity in the early 1980s put an end to this approach. **Source:** Board of Governors, Federal Reserve System, *Money Stock Revisions,* 1986, and *Federal Reserve Bulletin 1986;* U.S. Department of Commerce, revised GNP tables.

Table 14.1	Mean Absolute Error in GNP Predictions from the Money Supply				

	Standard measures of money			Measures of money adjusted for effects of deregulation	
	M-1	M-2	M-3	M-1	M-2
	Percentage Error				
Money demand functions					
1971–1980	1.6	.7	.8	1.6	.7
1981–1985	6.0	2.8	3.3	5.9	2.4
Velocity trend line					
1971–1980	1.9	1.8	2.0	1.9	1.8
1981–1985	7.6	4.3	4.5	6.2	2.4

Note: The mean absolute error is obtained by summing the individual errors regardless of sign and dividing by the number of cases.

Source: Richard Kopcke, "How Erratic Is Money Growth?" Federal Reserve Bank of Boston, *New England Economic Review* (May/June 1986):7.

more unstable, the lag of income behind money made velocity seem less stable. If one measures velocity as GNP divided by money two quarters earlier, this increased instability evaporates.[5]

SUMMARY

1 Transactions balances are held to avoid the cost and trouble of frequently acquiring and then liquidating a near-money or a security. The volume of transactions balances depends on the cost and trouble of investing and disinvesting, on the net interest rate on money, and on the planned volume of transactions.

2 People hold precautionary balances to meet unexpected needs. These balances provide an alternative to cutting planned expenditures, selling assets, borrowing, or not making payments. The amount held depends on a comparison of the lowest of these costs with the net interest rate, and the probability of having to make unexpected payments. Precautionary balances, too, are therefore a function of the net interest rate.

3 The demand for money can also be explained by use of a money demand function that includes the cost of holding money, the price of money substitutes, income or wealth, and tastes. Statistical money demand functions usually include the interest rate, and income or wealth.

4 Money demand functions give a good fit for the 1950s and 1960s, but overpredict money holdings for the 1970s. This is probably due to financial innovations. Velocity grew at a remarkably stable rate until the 1980s, when it ceased growing and seemed to become more volatile. This volatility could be due to a more erratic money growth rate.

[5] The instability of velocity in the 1980s is also reduced if one uses total domestic sales (i.e., GNP plus imports minus exports) in place of GNP. One can argue that the demand for money depends more on such sales than on output, which is what GNP measures. Prior to the large balance of trade deficits in the early 1980s there was little difference between these two measures.

QUESTIONS AND EXERCISES

1 Describe how you decide how much money to hold. How would your answer differ if your income were five times as large as it is now?
2 The demand for money depends on the interest rate for several reasons. What are they?
3 Discuss: "This chapter spends much unnecessary effort on showing that the demand for money depends on the interest rate. This elaborate discussion is not needed; elementary microeconomics makes it obvious that the demand for money depends on the interest rate."
4 How will you decide the size of your precautionary balances once you graduate and earn a high income?
5 Statistical money demand functions generally use either current GNP or a permanent income measure of GNP. Is GNP necessarily the correct variable to measure income? What are other plausible alternatives?
6 Explain the problem of the "missing money" of the 1970s.

FURTHER READING

DOTSEY, MICHAEL. "An Investigation of Cash Management Practices and Their Effects on the Demand for Money," *Economic Review*, Federal Reserve Bank of Richmond, 70 (September/October 1984):3–13. A useful description of cash-management practices and a statistical test of their ability to explain the "missing money."

FEDERAL RESERVE BANK OF SAN FRANCISCO. *Monetary Targeting and Velocity*. San Francisco: Federal Reserve Bank of San Francisco, 1984. This volume of conference proceedings contains several important papers on the great velocity decline.

JUDD, JOHN, and JOHN SCADDING. "The Search for a Stable Money Demand Function," *Journal of Economic Literature*, 20 (September 1982): 993–1023. An authoritative survey of the "missing money" problem.

LAIDLER, DAVID. *The Demand for Money*, 3rd ed. New York: Harper & Row, 1985. An excellent survey of the theoretical and econometric literature on money demand.

APPENDIX:
A MODEL OF TRANSACTIONS DEMAND

Many sophisticated models have been constructed telling firms how much money to hold for the transactions motive. We illustrate the principle involved by looking at a simple version devised by William Baumol of Princeton University.

Assume that you finance some expenditures by selling securities or near-monies that you own. Assume also that the brokerage cost and other costs of selling securities are a fixed amount per sale, independent of the number of securities you sell.

How frequently should you sell securities or near-monies? On the one hand, if you sell all your securities the very first time you need money you will have to pay the brokerage charge only once. But obtaining all the money you need right away has a high cost in another way: you forego some interest income you could earn by holding on to most of your securities for a longer time. To minimize the opportunity cost of losing interest you would want to sell them one at a time.

The best policy is to minimize the sum of both your costs, the brokerage cost and the opportunity cost of foregone interest. This total cost can be written as

$$Q = bT/C + rC/2,$$

where Q is the total cost, b the brokerage charge, T the amount of securities you will sell over the whole year, and C the amount of securities you sell at each sale, so that T/C represents the number of times per year that you will sell securities and pay a brokerage charge. The interest rate (or, more correctly, the interest rate on securities minus the interest rate on money) is r. The first term, bT/C, measures your brokerage cost. The second term, $rC/2$, measures the foregone interest. If you sell C dollars of securities at each sale, and spend these proceeds at even rate, you hold, on the average day, $C/2$ dollars. Hence your foregone interest is $rC/2$.

There is a mathematical technique (setting the first derivative to zero) that allows you to find the minimum value for Q. This minimum is reached at

$$C = \sqrt{2bT/r}.$$

Thus, the number of securities you should sell each time you sell is greater the higher is the fixed brokerage cost, and the lower is the interest rate. Correspondingly, you should sell securities less frequently, and in larger lots when you do sell, the higher is the fixed brokerage cost and the lower is the interest rate.

More specifically, the second equation tells you the interest elasticity of your cash holdings. Since C is a function of the square root of r, the interest elasticity is $-\frac{1}{2}$. Similarly, if one identifies the number of securities you will sell with your income, your income elasticity of demand for money is $\frac{1}{2}$.

These results should be interpreted with caution for two reasons. First, they apply only to the transactions demand for money. Firms actually hold much more money than that, probably in large part because they are required to hold compensating balances. Second, we started out the story with you holding securities and selling them during the year to meet expenses. But most of us meet expenses not by selling a portfolio of securities, but out of income that is paid in cash. Interest rates would have to be extraordinarily high to make it worthwhile for the average person to buy securities on payday, and then sell them during the pay period. However, for those corporations or wealthy persons who receive their incomes in lumpy form, it might be worth doing so. For example, for a manufacturer of Christmas tree ornaments who receives most of his income in November and December, it may be worthwhile to buy securities at that time, and then sell them off during the year in accordance with the second equation.

CHAPTER 15

A Complete Keynesian Model

Having taken up each of the variables that determine GNP we now combine them, and then see how monetary and fiscal policies affect GNP. For the time being, we assume that the inflation rate is fixed, an assumption discussed in the appendix to this chapter. Given this assumption, an increase in the money supply reduces the interest rate permanently since it does not affect the inflation rate, and hence the price level.

COMBINING THE ELEMENTS

Suppose the marginal efficiency of investment increases. Investment rises by, say, $10 billion per year. If the multiplier is, say, 2, shouldn't income rise by $20 billion annually? No, it shouldn't, because we have left something out. This is the response of the interest rate to the increase in investment and income, and the feedback effect on income of this change in the interest rate. With investment and income rising, the demand for money increases, and hence the interest rate rises. This then reduces income again. So, with income first rising, and then falling, how can one be sure that a rise in investment really increases income?

More generally, we seem to be caught in a trap. To know what income is one has to know what the interest rate is. But the interest rate depends, in part, on what income is. Fortunately, there is a way out. This is to solve for income and the interest rate simultaneously by looking, at the same time, at both the market for goods and services and at the market for money. This ensures that the interest rate that we are assuming in the process of determining income is the same interest rate that we get when we let income, along with other variables, determine the interest rate. This way of looking at income and the interest rate is illustrated by the IS-LM diagram, which shows equilibrium, at the same time, in both the market for goods and services and in the market for money.

In this discussion the term "interest rate" should be interpreted not just as, say, the Treasury-bill rate or the prime rate, but more broadly as a measure of the total cost and difficulty of borrowing. For example, if a firm can no longer borrow because money has become tight, we call this "a rise in the interest rate."

The Goods and Services Market

Figure 15.1 relates the interest rate to the level of income that is consistent with it. Part A shows the marginal efficiency of investment curve, and the investment that occurs at three interest rates, r_0, r_1, and r_2. Part B is Part A turned counterclockwise to lie on its side. Part C is the Keynesian cross diagram from Chapter 12. Each level of investment in Parts A and B leads, in Part C, to a particular level of income. As the interest rate falls from r_0 to r_1, investment rises to I_1, income rises to Y_1. Similarly, when the interest rate falls to r_2 income rises to Y_2. Thus, every interest rate implies a particular income. Figure 15.2 shows a curve, called the **IS curve**, that relates each interest rate to its corresponding level of income.[1] Put another way, the interest rate deter-

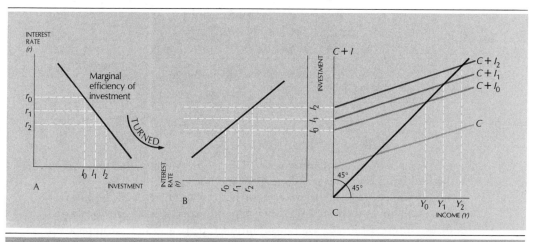

Figure 15.1   How Changes in the Interest Rate Influence Output. Part A shows the marginal efficiency of investment curve and the amount of investment at three interest rates. Part B shows Part A lying on its side to produce the different levels of investment for Part C, which shows the Keynesian cross diagram with these three levels.

---

[1] The name IS comes from the fact that when the market for goods and services is in equilibrium planned *investment* equals planned *saving*. At one time macroeconomics was formulated in a way that focused on this equality, hence an I(nvestment)-S(aving) curve. The term LM, to which we will come soon, is derived from "*money* and *liquidity* preference."

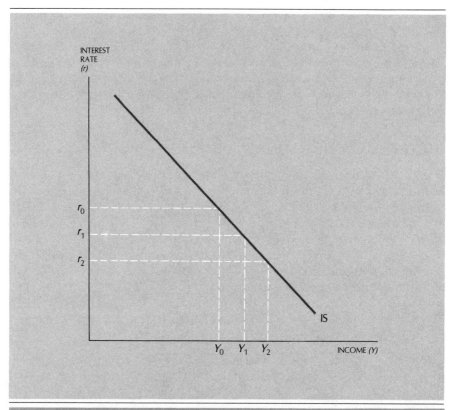

Figure 15.2   The IS Curve. The IS Curve relates the interest rate to the particular level of income that it generates.

mines the level of investment, and the level of investment then, in combination with the multiplier, determines the level of income.

So far we have assumed, quite incorrectly, that changes in the interest rate affect only investment and no other expenditures. But, as previously discussed, the interest rate affects consumption too. It also has an impact on imports and exports. If interest rates rise in the United States, foreigners want to buy more U.S. securities, and need dollars to do so. At the same time, Americans want to buy fewer foreign securities, so they demand less foreign currency. With the demand for dollars increasing and the demand for foreign currencies decreasing, the dollar rises on the foreign exchange market. U.S. goods now become more expensive to foreigners and foreign goods become cheaper in the United States. Exports fall and imports rise. The demand for U.S. output, and hence U.S. GNP, falls.

Even government expenditures on goods and services (the only government expenditures that are counted as part of GNP) *could* be influenced by the interest rate. The higher the interest rate, the more it costs the government to service the national debt. *If* there is some political or legal constraint on the size of the deficit, such as the 1986 Gramm-Rudman amendment, the more interest the government pays, the smaller are its expenditures on goods and services.[2] Hence, from now on we relate the IS curve to total expenditures on domestic goods and services and not just to investment.

The Money Market

In a textbook or in class, one can say: "Arbitrarily pick any interest rate and . . . ." But in the real world the interest rate is not an arbitrary rate. It is determined by the supply and demand for money. Many variables determine the interest rate. By holding all but one of them constant one can see how changes in this particular variable affect the interest rate. The variable we select is income.

Income and the interest rate are related by the **LM curve.** This curve is neither a supply curve nor a demand curve. Instead, it is a *"market equilibrium curve,"* that is, *a curve showing all those particular combinations of interest rates and incomes at which the supply and demand for money are equal.* It slopes upward because the higher income is, the greater is the demand for money. Hence it takes a higher interest rate to make the public want to hold no more than the existing supply of money. In other words, *the demand for money depends positively on income and negatively on the interest rate; hence there exists some combination of income and the interest rate that makes the demand for money just equal to any given supply of money.* Figure 15.3 shows the derivation of the LM curve. Part A shows the supply and demand for money. With income at $100 billion, supply and demand for money are equal at a 5 percent interest rate. But when income rises to $200 billion the demand for money exceeds the supply. The interest rate has to rise to 8 percent to make supply and demand equal again. Thus, as Part B of Figure 15.3 shows, in the money market every income level is associated with a particular interest rate.

Combining the IS and LM Curves

Since Figures 15.2 and 15.3 have the same variables on the axes they can be combined into a single diagram, Figure 15.4. The market for goods and services is in equilibrium anywhere along the IS curve. Similarly, at any point on the LM curve the money market is in equilibrium. Hence, only at the point at which the two curves intersect is there equilibrium in both the money market and the commodity market—and thus in the whole economy. *In other words, only at the point of intersection does the interest rate that was arbitrarily assumed in drawing the IS curve correspond to the interest rate actually set in the money market.* Put another way, there are two unknowns, income and the interest rate, and two equations, the IS equation ($Y = a + bi$) and the LM equation ($Y = c + di$).

---

[2] At the same time, however, the increased interest payments raise income, and hence consumption. But consumption does not rise dollar for dollar with income.

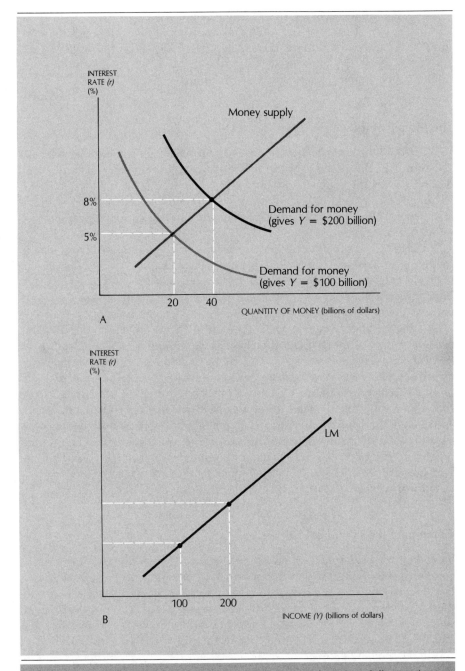

Figure 15.3 **The LM Curve.** In Part A, as income rises from $100 billion to $200 billion the demand for money rises from $20 billion to $40 billion. As a result, the interest rate rises from 5 percent to 8 percent. Part B shows this relation between income and the interest rate. As income rises the interest rate rises too.

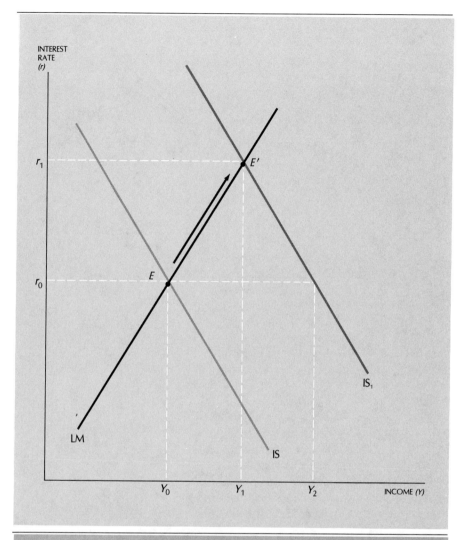

Figure 15.4   The IS-LM Diagram. When the IS and LM curves are combined, their point of intersection determines the interest rate and income. If the IS curve shifts upward, both income and the interest rate rise.

Taking the coefficients a, b, c, and d as known, these two equations can be solved simultaneously for both income and the interest rate.

The problem raised at the start of this chapter is now solved. Suppose the marginal efficiency of investment rises. At each interest rate firms now invest more, so that the income that corresponds to each interest rate rises. With the IS curve in Figure 15.4 shifting from IS to IS_1, income rises from Y_0 to Y_1. This raises the interest rate from r_0 to r_1. Nobody can argue that this rise in investment may *decrease* income because it increases the interest rate, which then lowers income. This feedback effect on income is already taken account of by the upward slope of the LM curve. If the increase in income had not raised the interest rate, perhaps because the Fed increased the supply of

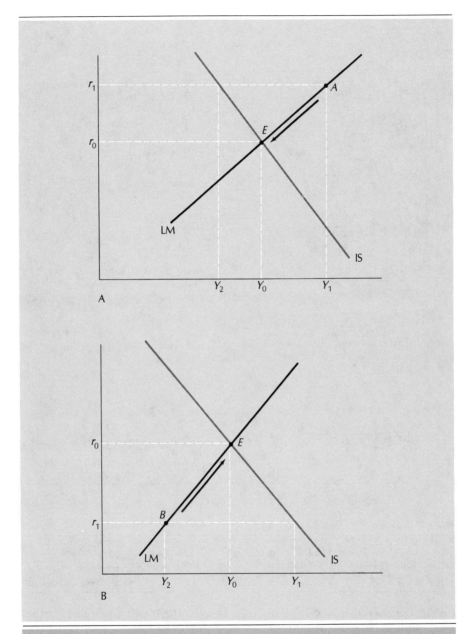

Figure 15.5   Disequilibrium Points in the IS-LM Diagram. Point A is a disequilibrium point. If the interest rate is r_1, then, as the LM curve tells us, income has to be Y_1. Given the high interest rate, r_1, it requires that high a level of income to make the public willing to hold all the supply of money. But such a high interest rate discourages expenditures. The IS curve tells us that at a rate of r_1, income is only Y_2. In Part B, at point B, at an interest rate of r_1, income is Y_2. But if income is Y_2 it takes an interest rate of r_2 to equate the supply and demand for money. Since the interest rate cannot be both r_1 and r_2 at the same time, the economy cannot be in equilibrium at point B.

money enough to keep the interest rate at r_0, then income would have risen to Y_2 instead of just to Y_1.

To see why only the point of intersection of IS and LM is an equilibrium, consider what happens at other points. In Part A of Figure 15.5, at point A the interest rate, r_1, is so high that it would require an income of Y_1 to make people willing to hold all the existing supply of money. But the IS curve tells us that with an interest rate of r_1 income would be only Y_2. Hence, if the interest rate were somehow to be at r_1, income would fall. With income declining the interest rate would also fall. Thus, both income and the interest rate would move toward their equilibrium values of Y_0 and r_0. Now consider point B in Part B of Figure 15.5. If the interest rate would somehow be at r_1, this would generate an income of Y_1 according to the IS curve. But the LM curve tells us that with an interest rate of r_1 it would take an income of Y_2 to make the supply and demand for money equal. Hence, point B cannot be an equilibrium.

The Slopes of the IS and LM Curves

The IS curve is constructed by taking the increase in expenditures that results from a fall in the interest rate and applying the multiplier to it. Hence, the slope of the IS curve depends on the responsiveness of expenditures to a change in the interest rate, which we will call the **expenditures slope,** and on the value of the multiplier. The greater the expenditures slope, or the larger the multiplier, the bigger the rise in income that occurs when the interest rate falls by a given amount, and hence the flatter the IS curve. At one extreme, the expenditures slope is zero. In this case the IS curve is a vertical line. A fall in the interest rate leaves income entirely unchanged. At the other extreme, the expenditures slope is infinite. If so, an infinitely small drop in the interest rate generates an infinitely great rise in income. The IS curve is then a horizontal line.

The slope of the LM curve is more complex. The LM curve shows those combinations of interest rates and income levels that make the public demand just the existing supply of money. Suppose that people increase their demand for money very much when income rises by a dollar. The interest rate then has to rise a lot to prevent the demand for money from exceeding the supply. With even a small movement along the x (income) axis thus being associated with a large movement along the y (interest-rate) axis, the LM curve is steep.

Now look at the response of the demand for money to the interest rate. If a small rise in the interest rate induces people to cut their money holdings substantially, then only a small increase in the interest rate is required to release the additional money that people want to hold as income rises. Hence, a given movement along the x axis then requires only a small movement along the y axis, so that the LM curve is relatively flat.

Thus, the more responsive the demand for money is to a change in income, the steeper the LM curve is. And the more responsive it is to a change in the interest rate, the flatter the LM curve is. In the limiting case where an infinitely small drop in the interest rate makes people demand an infinitely great amount of money, the LM curve is a horizontal line. Another limiting case is one in which a change in the interest rate has no effect at all on the demand for money. In this case the LM curve is a vertical line.

The slope of the LM curve also depends on the reaction of the money *supply* to changes in interest rates and in income. The LM curve is flatter if the money supply increases as the interest rate rises. In the limiting case where the money supply is infinitely elastic the LM curve is a horizontal line. The money supply is likely to increase as the interest rate rises for two reasons. First, the money multiplier is a positive function of the interest rate; second, to moderate this rise in the interest rate, the Federal Reserve is likely to increase reserves.

Shifts of the IS and LM Curves

The IS curve relates each interest rate to a particular income. Hence, anything that changes the income that corresponds to each interest rate shifts the IS curve. (This is analogous to the demand curve. Everything that changes the amount demanded at each price shifts the demand curve.) For example, the IS curve shifts outward if firms want to undertake more investment at each interest rate. Similarly, the IS curve shifts outward if an exogenous increase in consumption, exports, or government expenditures raises the level of income that corresponds to each interest rate.

The LM curve shifts outward if, for each combination of interest rate and income level, the public wants to hold less money than it did before. Some possible reasons for this are the development of new near-monies, lower borrowing costs, or a fall in the interest rate paid on checkable deposits. The LM curve also shifts outward if the supply of money increases exogenously because this curve shows all the combinations of interest rates and incomes that make the demand for money equal to the supply. The greater the supply of money the lower must be the interest rate, or else the higher must be income, to make the demand for money equal to the supply.

FISCAL AND MONETARY POLICIES IN THE IS-LM FRAMEWORK

The IS-LM framework can be used to sketch how monetary and fiscal policies affect GNP.

Fiscal Policy

Since government expenditures are part of aggregate demand, the obvious effect of these expenditures is to shift the IS curve outward. (We will deal with the less obvious effects later.) In Figure 15.6A, looking at the LM curve, as government expenditures shift the IS curve to IS_1 income rises from Y_0 to Y_1. It does *not* rise to Y_2 as it would according to the simple-minded multiplier formula, $Y = G/(1 - c)$, where G is government expenditures and c the marginal propensity to consume out of GNP. The reason is that, as income rises, so does the interest rate. Only if the LM curve were horizontal, like LM_1, would income rise as much as the simple multiplier formula predicts. Given the LM curve not being horizontal, the rise in the interest rate *crowds out* $Y_2 - Y_1$ of income. The steeper the LM curve, the greater is this crowding out.

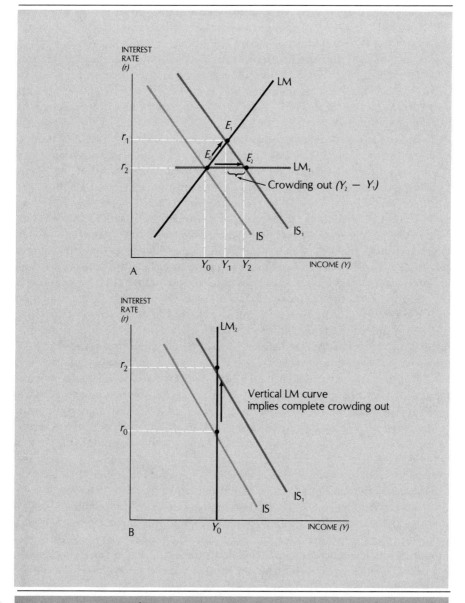

Figure 15.6   Crowding Out. We start with LM and IS (Part A). The government now raises expenditures or lowers taxes, shifting the IS curve to IS_1. Income rises from Y_0 to Y_1. In a simplified multiplier analysis in which the interest rate is taken as fixed, the LM curve would have been horizontal (LM_1) and the change in government expenditures would have been fully translated into a change in income. Income would have risen to Y_2. The difference between Y_2 and Y_1 is the "crowding out" of private investment that occurs as government finances its spending. Part B illustrates the extreme case of complete crowding out because the demand for money is completely unresponsive to the interest rate. Fiscal policy cannot increase income.

In the limiting case of a totally interest-inelastic LM curve, shown in Figure 15.6B as LM_2, higher government expenditures have no effect on income; they just raise the interest rate, from r_0 to r_2.

Tax cuts also shift the IS curve. If personal income taxes are cut, disposable personal income rises. Households respond by raising consumption. In Figure 15.7A, tax cuts raise income and the interest rate by shifting the IS curve to IS_1. Again, if the LM curve were completely vertical, income would not change.

But the LM curve is not completely vertical since the demand for money is not completely interest inelastic. If one wants to argue that fiscal policy has no effect on income one must rely on some indirect type of crowding out. One possibility is the Ricardian equivalence proposition discussed in Chapter 12. Another possibility is "portfolio crowding out." As the government spends more it must finance this increased expenditure either by selling securities or by creating new money to pay for it. Suppose it sells more securities. What does this do to the LM curve? One possibility is that as people hold more securities they also want to hold more money, either because they are wealthier or because money and securities are complements. If so, government expenditures, and the associated issues of government securities, do not just shift the IS curve to the right, they also shift the LM curve to the left. If the LM curve shifts far enough to the left, say to LM_1 in Figure 15.7A, income falls to Y_2, less than it was before government expenditures rose. This is crowding out with a vengeance.

But the opposite possibility exists too. Suppose that people treat government securities as a good substitute for money. Hence, when they hold more government securities their demand for money falls. The LM curve then shifts to the right. If it shifts far enough, say to LM_2 in Figure 15.7B, the interest rate falls to r_3. Instead of government expenditures crowding out private expenditures, there is "crowding in"; aggregate demand rises by an amount greater than the government expenditures times the multiplier. In addition, the increased demand might raise investment through the accelerator.

Both crowding out and crowding in are theoretical possibilities. Unfortunately it has proven extremely difficult to find convincing empirical evidence on whether government securities are complements or substitutes for money.[3] Hence, economists disagree about the existence of portfolio crowding in and (if it does exist) on whether it is strong enough to offset the movement *along* the LM curve that raises interest rates.

But there is much less dispute about a way in which *partial* crowding out occurs. As the government spends more and income rises, interest rates rise. This causes foreigners to buy more U.S. securities, and Americans to buy fewer foreign securities. The increased demand for dollars and the reduced supply of dollars on the foreign exchange market then cause the dollar to rise. U.S. exports fall while imports rise. With exports falling and imports rising, income falls in the United States.

---

[3] It seems plausible that Treasury bills are a money substitute since they are so liquid, while a thirty-year bond is more likely to be a money complement. However, the econometric evidence for this is far from compelling.

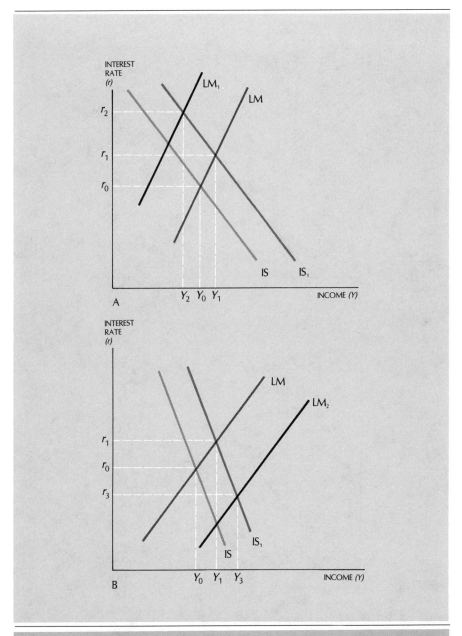

Figure 15.7   Extreme Assumptions about the LM Curve. The greater deficit that results from higher government expenditures or lower taxes could either raise or lower the demand for money. It is conceivable that an increase in government expenditures would shift the LM curve to LM_1, as in Part A, which implies a fall in income. Alternatively, the LM curve could shift to LM_2, as in Part B, so that income increases because of a shift in both the IS and LM curves.

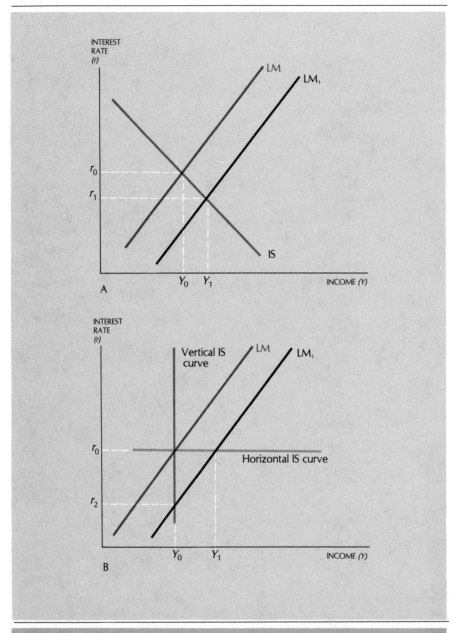

Figure 15.8 **The Completely Interest-Inelastic IS Curve.** Part A shows the normal case of an increase in the money supply: LM shifts to LM_1, and income increases. If expenditures are completely unresponsive to the interest rate, as in Part B, then shifts in the supply of money, and hence in the LM curve, have no effect on income.

Monetary Policy

If the Federal Reserve increases the money supply the LM curve shifts to the right, for example, from LM to LM_1 in Figure 15.8A. Income rises from Y_0 to Y_1, while the interest rate falls from r_0 to r_1. Figure 15.8B shows the limiting case of a completely interest-inelastic IS curve. With expenditures not increasing at all as the interest rate falls, the increase in the money supply has no effect on income. The other limiting case shown in Figure 15.8B is the horizontal IS curve. With expenditures being infinitely interest elastic, it takes only an infinitesimally small decline in the interest rate to increase expenditures enough to absorb all the increased money supply. The increased money supply now translates fully into increased income, from Y_0 to Y_1 in Figure 15.8B. Another limiting case is one in which the demand for money is infinitely elastic, so that the LM curve is horizontal.[4] We saw this in Figure 15.6A: monetary policy is then powerless.

SUMMARY

1 Given the mutual interaction between interest rates and income, to determine either one we have to look at both of them at the same time. This can be done in a diagram that has the interest rate on the y axis and income on the x axis.

2 The IS curve relates all mutually consistent interest rates and incomes, and thus connects all equilibrium points in the market for goods and services. A lower interest rate stimulates expenditures, and this, together with its multiplier effect, raises income. Hence, the IS curve slopes downward. Its slope depends on the response of expenditures to the interest rate and on the multiplier.

3 The LM curve relates all interest rates and income levels at which the supply and demand for money are equal. Its slopes depends on the responsiveness of money demand to changes in interest rates and in income, and on the response of the money supply to changes in interest rates.

4 The IS and LM curves show that, except in limiting cases, both monetary and fiscal policies affect income. Fiscal policy may crowd out, or crowd in, private expenditures. This depends on whether money and government securities are substitutes or complements, as well as on the slopes of the IS and LM curves, and on whether people cut their consumption as the national debt rises.

QUESTIONS AND EXERCISES

1 Explain in your own words why the IS curve slopes downward and the LM curve slopes upward.

2 Explain why the IS curve and the LM curve can intersect at only one point.

3 What factors shift the IS and LM curves?

4 Apart from an infinitely interest-elastic demand for money, what other assumptions would give you the limiting case of a horizontal LM curve?

5 Add a point E somewhere to Figure 15.4 and show why it is not an equilibrium. (If you pick a point that is off both the IS and LM curves you have to make some

---

[4] In principle this special case would arise only under the very special condition that people have become convinced that the interest rate has hit bottom. If so, they would not want to buy bonds at a lower interest rate because they would be convinced that the market value of bonds will fall as interest rates rise again.

assumption about the relative speed at which the money market and the commodity market equilibrate.)

6 Explain why government expenditures can crowd out or crowd in private expenditures.

FURTHER READING

FRIEDMAN, BENJAMIN. "Crowding Out or Crowding In? The Economic Consequences of Financing Government Debt," *Brookings Papers on Economic Activity,* 1978, 593–641. A classic discussion of crowding out.

Most intermediate macroeconomics texts have a chapter on the IS-LM model. See, for instance, the texts cited under Further Reading in Chapter 12.

APPENDIX:
FLEXIBLE PRICES AND THE IS-LM DIAGRAM

Although the IS-LM mechanism is widely used, it has been criticized by some economists, particularly Karl Brunner of the University of Rochester and Allan Meltzer of Carnegie-Mellon University. One reason is that the IS-LM diagram is valid only if the inflation rate is given exogenously. This is so because the x axis of the IS-LM diagram has to show both the real interest rate and the nominal interest rate. The real interest rate, or more precisely the expected real interest rate, is the appropriate rate to use when drawing the IS curve because investment depends on the expected real interest rate. But the demand for money, and hence the LM curve, depends mainly on the nominal interest rate.[5]

If the inflation rate is constant, then one can accommodate both the nominal and the real interest rates on the same axis. Suppose, for example, that the inflation rate is 5 percent. Then the point on the y axis that is marked as an 8 percent nominal rate also serves as a 3 percent real rate. But this does not work if the inflation rate is not constant, so that the two scales do not have a unique relationship. If, as is actually the case, the inflation rate is greater when income is higher, then the relation between the two interest-rate scales on the y axis depends on where you are on the x axis. This means that you cannot draw the IS and LM curves without already knowing what income is. This problem could be handled by adding a third dimension that has the inflation rate on the z axis.

But this graphical "solution" is only part of the story. If prices are flexible, and in the long run they are, then an increase in the nominal money supply (or a decrease in the demand for nominal money) does not reduce the interest rate. In the long run the interest rate is the same regardless of whether the LM curve shifts in or out.

A second problem is that the diagram does not allow for an increase in the stocks of assets.

Third, where does physical capital fit into the story? One need not choose just between holding money and buying an interest-yielding asset as the LM curve has it. Instead, one can buy physical capital, such as some common stock or a house. This would not matter if the return on physical capital always moves in step with the return on interest-yielding assets. The interest rate on these assets could then serve, in part, as a proxy for the yield on capital. But the two yields might diverge.

---

[5] If the utility of the last dollar in your cash balance is 5 percent, and the nominal interest rate on a security is 6 percent, then (assuming no transactions costs) you should buy the security regardless of the inflation rate. Inflation will hurt you just as much if you hold money as if you hold a security.

CHAPTER 16

The Monetarist Approach

The theory we have discussed so far is a Keynesian theory. It originated in Keynes's *General Theory* but has been revised substantially by Keynes's followers, in part in response to criticisms by monetarists. But since Keynesians have accepted only some of the monetarists' criticisms, Keynesians and monetarists are still quite far apart.

Two basic differences underlie the disputes between Keynesian and monetarist theories. One is a difference in research strategies. A theory (or more accurately a paradigm) is more than a set of assumptions and a logical chain connecting these assumptions to a conclusion. It is also a set of ideas about what questions are important, and what are the best ways to do research on them. In this respect an important difference between Keynesians and monetarists is that monetarists tend to focus on the long run, while Keynesians focus relatively more on the short run. This does not mean that Keynesians ignore the long run while monetarists ignore the short run. Far from it; it is just a matter of emphasis. Another difference in the research strategies is that monetarists emphasize equilibrium in the market for money, while Keynesians pay more attention to the market for commodities. Thus Keynesians talk about the marginal propensity to consume and the marginal efficiency of investment, as well as about the supply and demand for money. Monetarists focus on the supply and demand for money, with the marginal propensity to consume and the marginal efficiency of investment entering the story only indirectly by affecting the supply and demand for money. The center of monetarist theory is the **quantity theory of money.**[1]

Keynesians and monetarists disagree in their econometric estimates of some strategic variables. They do not differ on logical issues; if they would start with the same empirical assumptions they would end up with the same conclusions. This is as it should be, because purely logical disputes can be settled relatively easily. One major empirical dispute is that Keynesians believe

---

[1] The terms "monetarism" and "quantity theory" are sometimes used as synonyms. However, we mean by "monetarism" a broad set of propositions of which the quantity theory is just one, albeit a central one.

that a private enterprise economy would be unstable in the absence of government intervention, while monetarists believe that it would be stable, and blame government intervention for much of the instability that actually occurs in our mixed economy.

These differences should not be exaggerated. Economists are not split into diametrically opposed camps. Many economists accept part of both theories. Between moderate monetarists and moderate Keynesians there is no sharp line of division—it is sometimes difficult to tell them apart.

THE QUANTITY THEORY: BASIC PRINCIPLES

The basic idea—and research strategy—of the quantity theory is to look at equilibrium in only one market, the market for money. For example, suppose that the money market is not in equilibrium, that the demand for money exceeds the supply. People then try to build up their money holdings by cutting back on their net expenditures—either investment or consumption—so that aggregate demand falls. Conversely, if people have more money than they want to hold, they run down their money balances by spending more on consumption or investment. *Hence changes in aggregate demand can be explained as a result of people holding more or less money than they want to.*

To examine the quantity theory we temporarily introduce the simplification that only two assets exist, money and commodities—and no securities. Suppose now that as a result of, say, Fed open-market operations the public initially holds more (real and nominal) money than it wants to. It is easy to predict what will happen. People will try to exchange the excess money for commodities, and hence aggregate demand will increase. Conversely, if, perhaps due to Fed open-market sales, actual money balances are below desired levels, the public will try to accumulate more money by cutting back on its expenditures, and aggregate demand will fall.

Although each person can reduce his or her money stock easily by buying commodities, this is not true for the whole economy. As one person gets rid of money by making a purchase, the seller's money holdings go up. How then can the public as a whole bring its money balances into equilibrium? The answer is that, as people spend their excessive money balances, sellers face increased demand for their products, and hence raise their production and prices so that nominal incomes increase. And as nominal incomes increase, so does the nominal amount of money people want to hold. As this process continues, a point is reached at which nominal money balances are no longer excessive. The economy is now back in equilibrium.

If we take the special case where real income is fixed, and only prices respond to the increased aggregate demand, we get a nice and simple result: prices have to rise in strict proportion to the excessive money balances. For example, if 10 percent more money is created than the public wants to hold at the existing price level, prices will rise by 10 percent. This is then a new equilibrium because the public is holding the same *real* quantity of money (M / P) as before. Hence, in this simple case where real income is fixed, and there are no securities, we readily get the traditional quantity theory result that prices vary in strict proportion to the quantity of money.

In the more complex case where real income is not fixed, the story is different because there are now two factors that induce people to hold the previously excess money balances: the rise in prices and the rise in real income. Hence, in this case prices rise less than in proportion to the excessive money balances.

So far we have dealt only with an economy in which there are no securities. When one makes the analysis more realistic by introducing securities, people spend some of their excess money balances on securities rather than on goods. Excess money balances therefore raise security prices, and hence lower interest rates. This stimulates investment and consumption, so that aggregate demand increases. But *initially* (and we postpone discussing what happens subsequently) aggregate demand increases by less than it does in the case where there are no securities because, with the interest rate having fallen, the public wants to hold more money than before. For example, if the nominal money stock increases by 10 percent and real income is constant, prices may increase (in the first instance) by only, say, 7 percent (which increases the demand for nominal money by 7 percent), with the additional 3 percent of money being held because interest rates are lower.

This process can readily be expressed in terms of the previously discussed Cambridge equation, $M = kYP$, where M is the money stock and k is the proportion of nominal income, YP, that people want to hold as money. Suppose that initially M is 100 and k is $\frac{1}{5}$, so that YP is 500. If M now rises to 200 and k is unchanged, then YP rises to 1000. But if the fall in interest rates raises k from $\frac{1}{5}$ to $\frac{1}{4}$, then YP rises only to 800.

The process just described shows how income is determined by the interaction between actual and desired money balances. No mention was made of the marginal propensity to consume and the marginal efficiency of investment. This is so because once one knows by how much people want to change their money holdings, one can derive *as a residual* how much they will spend, since any part of income not spent on commodities or securities must have been added to money holdings. This illustrates the difference in the research strategies of Keynesian and quantity theories.

DEVELOPMENT OF THE QUANTITY THEORY

The quantity theory has a long history. For example, the Scottish philosopher David Hume advocated a sophisticated version of this theory in the 1750s. But it fell into disrepute in the 1930s, in part because it seemed at the time that this theory could not explain the Great Depression, and partly because of the publication in 1936 of Keynes's theory. Although some economists continued to advocate the quantity theory, most economists became Keynesians and treated the quantity theory as little more than ancient superstition.

Only in the mid- and late-1950s did the quantity theory become a serious rival to the Keynesian theory. There were several reasons for its revival. One was that, contrary to the prediction of many Keynesians, upon the conclusion of World War II the American economy did not revert to the depressed conditions of the 1930s, but instead underwent inflation. Second, one seemingly great benefit of the Keynesian revolution had been its demonstration that by manipulating expenditures and taxes the government could keep the economy close to full employment. But it turned out that there were serious political as well as economic difficulties in actually changing government expenditures and tax rates in these recommended ways, so that Keynesian theory appeared to be less useful than it had originally seemed. Third, the time was ripe for a change. Economists had expended much effort along Keynesian lines and were now ready for something new.[2] But the resurgence of the quantity theory should not be attributed merely to impersonal events. Its revival is also due to its being taken up by a group of extremely able economists. These economists developed several different versions of the quantity theory, or **monetarism**. Hence, we will have to take up several versions of this approach in this chapter and in Appendix A.

THE CHICAGO APPROACH

The best-known version of the monetarist approach is the work of Milton Friedman and of his former students at the University of Chicago, such as Phillip Cagan (Columbia University), David Laidler (University of Western Ontario), and David Meiselman (Virginia Polytechnic Institute and University). Friedman is known to a much wider audience as a leading free-market advocate. While his views on monetary theory are consistent with a general free-market position, they do not require it. One can accept his views on monetary theory and policy without having to accept his general political views, and vice versa. A major part of the work of Friedman and his students has centered on explaining the demand for money. Recall the Cambridge equation, $M = kYP$. If k is stable, then we can predict how nominal income has to change when the money supply changes. But is k some stable number like, say, $\frac{1}{5}$? Surely not. In Chapter 14, we saw that the real quantity of money demanded is a function of the interest rate and other variables.

Hence, Friedman's version of the quantity theory treats the quantity of money demanded (and thus k) not as a stable *number*, but as a stable *function* of other variables.[3] If the demand for money is, in fact, a stable function of a few measurable variables, then, if the values of these variables are known, one can predict how much money will be demanded. Suppose that, as we assumed in

---

[2] A major new theory opens up many exciting research opportunities because it raises questions that were previously ignored. After some time the more promising of these research opportunities have been exploited, and the profession is again in a receptive mood for a new theory.

[3] Another way in which Friedman has modified the traditional quantity theory is that he uses it primarily to determine nominal income rather than prices. The traditional quantity theory was a theory of the long run in which prices adapted to changes in the quantity of money while output was unaffected.

drawing the LM curve, the demand for nominal money is a function of nominal income (YP) and the nominal interest rate (r), that is:

(1) $M_D = f(YP, r)$.

Since the empirical evidence suggests that supply and demand for money are fairly soon equilibrated by the money market, we can write

(2) $M_S = M_D = f(YP, r)$,

or, more specifically,

(3) $M_S = M_D = a + bYP + cr$,

where a, b, and c are coefficients that can be estimated statistically. Now suppose that we also know r. In this case, *once we are told what will happen to the nominal money stock* M_S *we know how nominal income must change to make Equation 3 hold.* This is the approach of Friedman's refurbished quantity theory.

Keynesian theory tells us that income depends not only on the supply and demand for money (the LM curve), but also on IS curve variables such as the propensity to consume and the marginal efficiency of investment. What happens to these variables in the quantity theory? They enter indirectly. Suppose that the marginal propensity to consume or the marginal efficiency of investment increases. Nominal income rises. But Equation 3 tells us that if income rises, while the money supply is constant, then the interest rate must rise too. This, in turn, reduces the Cambridge K; that is, it raises velocity. Thus, since changes in the propensity to consume and in the marginal efficiency of investment enter Friedman's analysis indirectly, there is no substantive difference between the two theories on this formal, abstract level.

The real disagreement relates to two empirical issues. First, quantity theorists believe that the demand function for money is stable, while Keynesians think it varies more. In terms of Equation 3, Keynesians argue that the coefficients a, b, and c are unstable.

Second, Keynesians believe that when the money supply increases income does not rise proportionately. The interest rate falls, and at this lower rate of interest the public wants to hold more money per dollar of income, so that velocity falls. Hence income rises substantially less than in proportion to the rise in money supply. Quantity theorists reply that, as discussed in Chapter 13, when the money supply increases the nominal interest rate falls temporarily, but sooner or later rises again. They think that it is sooner rather than later. And once the nominal interest rate has risen back to its previous level, velocity is back at its previous level too. Besides, they believe that the interest elasticity of demand for money is not all that large, so that the LM curve is fairly steep. And the steeper is the LM curve, the greater is the rise in income that results from an exogenous rise in the money supply.

The crucial issue is therefore how fast the interest rate returns to its previous level. This is an empirical issue that is hard to resolve. What we observe in the data is the nominal interest rate. But what affects expenditures is the *expected* real rate of interest. To estimate this rate one has to subtract the *expected* inflation rate from the nominal interest rate. But there is no way of estimating this expected inflation rate that most economists find convincing.

The Transmission Process

What is the mechanism by which money affects income? Friedman's explanation of *how* money affects nominal income differs in several ways from the Keynesian explanations. First, he does not refer to the interest rate, but instead says that when people have excess money balances they raise their expenditures in an attempt to bring their money holdings into equilibrium. This difference between Friedman's approach and the Keynesian approach is not basic. In a formal sense, one can relate any point on a demand curve to either the price or the quantity axis, and no fundamental issue of theory is involved in whether one says that the quantity of money has increased or that the interest rate has fallen. The reason Friedman looks at the quantity of money rather than at the interest rate is that he believes (as will be discussed in Chapter 21) that the relevant interest rate is not measured properly by the available data. Hence, an analysis that focuses on interest rates is likely to give misleading advice when applied to practical problems.

A second difference is that Friedman believes that changes in the money stock affect expenditures in so many and such complicated ways that it is useless to try to discover them all. Any attempt to do so would surely fail to find some of them, and would therefore underestimate the total effect that money has on income. Hence, instead of setting up an ambitious econometric model, Friedman (who, in any case, has little faith in large econometric models) prefers to follow a different approach. This is to compare changes in the money supply and in nominal income over time without trying to trace through the particular channels by which money affects income. This has caused many economists to criticize him for relying on a sort of "black box" where changes in the money stock are seen going in at one end and changes in income emerging at the other end, without anyone knowing how the process works. This point is often put by saying that Friedman is relying on a mere correlation of changes in money and in income, and that there are numerous examples in economics of correlations that do not prove that one variable is causing the other. For example, there is a correlation between the number of school teachers in a city and per capita alcohol consumption. On the other hand, Friedman believes that the empirical evidence shows that the correlation between money and prices is causal rather than spurious. Moreover, economic theory tells us why, if the supply of a good increases, its price falls. This can be applied directly to explain why the purchasing power of money falls, that is, prices rise, when the supply of money increases. Do we really need much more than that?

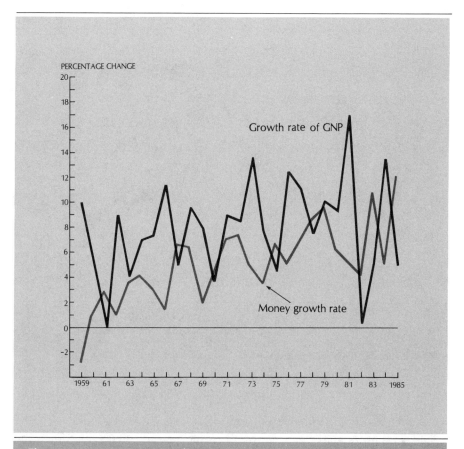

PERCENTAGE CHANGE

Growth rate of GNP

Money growth rate

Figure 16.1 **Money and the GNP, United States, 1959–1985.** Although in most years nominal income rises faster than money, the turning points of the two are closely correlated. To highlight the correlation, this diagram shows GNP lagged by two quarters. Growth rates are expressed as annualized rates. **Source:** Board of Governors, Federal Reserve System, *Money Stock Revisions,* 1986, and *Federal Reserve Bulletin 1986;* U.S. Department of Commerce, revised GNP tables.

Some Empirical Evidence on the Importance of Money

Figure 16.1 shows the close relationship between movements in money and nominal income in the United States. Such a relationship exists also for other countries—for example, for Japan (see Figure 16.2)—and Friedman and Anna Schwartz (of the National Bureau of Economic Research) have found a very high correlation between money and nominal income in Britain. Figure 16.3 shows the correlation of the growth rates of money and nominal income in various countries.

Does this high correlation between money and income mean that changes in the money growth rate cause changes in nominal income, or should the correlation be interpreted the other way round, as changes in income

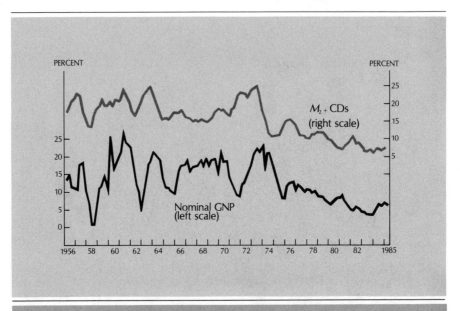

PERCENT   PERCENT

M_2 + CDs
(right scale)

Nominal GNP
(left scale)

1956 58 60 62 64 66 68 70 72 74 76 78 80 82 1985

Figure 16.2   Money Stock and the Nominal GNP in Japan. Money and the GNP in Japan show a close relationship. Money is defined here as *M-2* until 1971, *M-2* plus CDs thereafter. Source; Yoshio Suzuki, "Japan's Monetary Policy over the Past Ten Years," Bank of Japan, *Monetary and Economic Studies* (September 1985):2.

causing changes in the money growth rate? In the latter case the correlation would certainly not be evidence supporting the quantity theory. Friedman and Schwartz support the hypothesis that causation runs from money to income in several ways. One is that they, as well as Phillip Cagan of Columbia University, have undertaken extensive historical studies of what factors caused the money stock to change. They conclude that in severe recessions like 1920–21 or 1929–33 the money stock fell for some specific reason other than a fall in income, such as widespread bank failures or a restrictive Fed policy. Hence, they argue, in these cases causation *must* have run from money to income since we know that what caused the decline in the money stock was something other than the drop in income. Similarly, large increases in the money stock can be explained by factors such as the development of new techniques for refining gold. For the minor business recessions—which are by far the more common ones—Friedman and Schwartz concede that the historical evidence is not nearly so clear-cut.[4] This allows one to develop a compromise between the

---

[4] Friedman and Schwartz have also pointed to the fact that the peak in the growth rate of the money stock usually occurs prior to the peak in business cycles, but they consider this to be much less important evidence for their hypothesis that causation runs from money to income than the just discussed historical evidence. In any case, as James Tobin ("Money and Income: Post Hoc, Ergo Propter Hoc," *Quarterly Journal of Economics* 84 [May 1970]:301–17) has shown, this evidence is of doubtful value because one can develop a model in which income change is the cause and the change in the money growth rate the effect, and yet the money growth rate shows an earlier peak than does income.

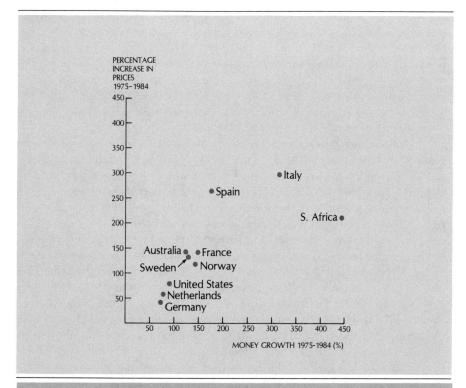

Figure 16.3 **Percentage Rise in the Money Stock and in Prices in Ten Countries, 1975–1984.** Over a decade there is a high correlation between the growth rates of money and prices in various countries. **Source:** *IMF International Financial Statistics,* 1984.

Keynesian and Friedmanian theories by saying that Keynesian theory can explain the usual minor recessions, but that major recessions are caused by a decline in the money growth rate.

Critics of the quantity theory, on the other hand, have argued that a rise in income can bring about a rise in the money stock. The money multiplier increases to some extent when interest rates and income do. Moreover, the Fed has tended to increase the growth rate of the base when the growth rate of income increases.

THE ST. LOUIS APPROACH

It may seem that the way to settle the Keynesian-monetarist debate is to undertake the following test. Let both Keynesians and monetarists select the variables that according to their theories explain income, and put them into a regression equation. We can then see which regression better explains past movements in income. Specifically, to have a test that is directly relevant to the question of what policy tools the government should use, let us see if income can be predicted better by looking at fiscal policy or at monetary policy. Since Keynesian theory asserts that changes both in the deficit and in the money stock bring about changes in nominal income, a finding that fiscal policy and monetary policy do so supports Keynesian theory. But if the data show there is little, if any, correlation between the deficit and changes in nominal income, while changes in the money stock have a powerful effect on income, then the quantity theory is vindicated and Keynesian theory is rejected.

This test was undertaken by two economists, then at the Federal Reserve Bank of St. Louis, Leonall Andersen and Jerry Jordan, who built on an earlier test by Milton Friedman and David Meiselman (of the Virginia Polytechnic Institute and University). The variables they used to explain income were the narrow money stock (*M-1*) and the monetary base as well as high-employment federal government receipts, expenditures, and deficits.[5]

The results that Andersen and Jordan obtained were dramatic. Changes in the nominal money stock, or in the monetary base, had powerful effects on nominal income, but the fiscal policy variables had no lasting effect. They raised income in the calendar quarter in which they increased, and in some equations in the next calendar quarter too, but in the subsequent quarters they lowered income. As a result, over a year, their *net* effect was close to zero. (A subsequent reworking of their analysis using more recent data showed fiscal policy having no effect in any calendar quarter.) These results suggest that fiscal policy is not a useful stabilization tool. Monetary policy—that is, changing the quantity of money—on the other hand, is a much more powerful tool. In addition, monetary policy affects income quicker and more predictably than fiscal policy does, and for these reasons, too, monetary policy appears to be the better policy tool. A subsequent study by Michael Keran (then also at the St. Louis Fed) found similar results for several other countries. These results surprised most economists. They led to an extensive debate of which we will discuss only a few highlights.

One set of criticisms relates to the monetary variables used by Andersen and Jordan, that is, the money stock (*M-1*) in some regressions and the monetary base in others. For their analysis to be valid, causation should run from these monetary variables to income, but not from income back to these monetary variables. Otherwise the observed correlation between changes in nominal income and in nominal money could hardly be used as an argument that changes in the money stock *cause* changes in income. But does the correlation run almost only from money to income, and not from income to money? The critics of Andersen and Jordan point out that as income rises so do interest rates, and when interest rates rise the Fed tends to increase the monetary base. Moreover, a rise in the interest rate tends to raise the money multiplier. Hence

---

[5] Andersen and Jordan used not the *actual* figures on the government's expenditures and deficits, but estimates of what government receipts and deficits would have been at a *given* level of income that corresponds to high employment.

these critics believe that the high correlation Andersen and Jordan found between changes in money and in nominal income does not confirm the quantity theory. Andersen and Jordan, however, believe that causation does run *primarily* from money to income.

It may seem that this criticism focuses on the wrong issue because what is surprising about the Andersen-Jordan study is not that the monetary variables are powerful, but that the fiscal variables are so weak. However, since the monetary and fiscal variables are correlated in their data, these two results are connected. In their regressions, reducing the role that monetary variables play raises the importance of the fiscal variables.

Another criticism focuses on Andersen and Jordan trying to explain nominal income by using a single equation rather than a large-scale econometric model. To investigate whether the single equation approach that Andersen and Jordan prefer is adequate, Franco Modigliani of MIT and Albert Ando of the University of Pennsylvania undertook a test to see whether this approach can yield a misleading answer.[6] They approached the problem indirectly. Suppose it can be shown that in a special situation, where we *know* that fiscal policy has a strong effect, the Andersen-Jordan technique shows fiscal policy as having no effect. If this is the case then one can argue that since the Andersen-Jordan technique gives a wrong result in one situation it should not be trusted in other situations. Accordingly, Modigliani and Ando used the Federal Reserve's large-scale econometric model to predict the change in income resulting from changes in monetary and fiscal policies. They then used the income data it predicted as though they were *actual* observations on income that should be explained by monetary and fiscal policy using Andersen and Jordan's technique. When they did this the answer they got was that fiscal policy has no lasting effect on income. But we *know* that this is wrong because the model that generated the income data is one in which fiscal policy does have a strong effect on income. Thus, the Andersen-Jordan technique can yield a misleading result, and hence their findings should be rejected. (But this test is not quite conclusive since Modigliani and Ando did not use exactly the same technique as Andersen and Jordan.)

SOME MONETARIST PROPOSITIONS

There is more to monetarism than just the quantity theory. We can isolate twelve major issues in the Keynesian-monetarist dispute.[7] Underlying the debate on these issues is a basic difference relating to the length of the horizon of one's analysis, and the speed with which the economy adapts. Keynesians accept many monetarist views as correct in the long run, but not in the shorter

---

[6] Franco Modigliani and Albert Ando, "Impacts of Fiscal Actions on Aggregate Income and the Monetarist Controversy: Theory and Evidence," in Jerome Stein (ed.), *Monetarism*, pp. 17–42. Amsterdam: North Holland Press, 1976.

[7] For a further discussion of these issues, see Thomas Mayer et al., *The Structure of Monetarism*. New York: W. W. Norton, 1978.

run that is relevant for economic policy.[8] Six of these differences relate to policy, and will be deferred until Chapter 25.

The first and most basic is the monetarist's belief in the quantity theory. The second is a hypothesis about the way in which changes in the money stock affect income, that is, the transmission process. We have already discussed Friedman's version of the transmission process, and in Appendix B at the end of this chapter we will look at the transmission process of two other prominent monetarists, Karl Brunner and Allan Meltzer.

Third, monetarists believe that the private sector of the economy is inherently stable. If the government would not destabilize the economy by ill-considered policies, there would still be *some* fluctuations in income but we would have tolerable levels of unemployment and little inflation. Keynesians, on the other hand, by and large, believe that the private economy is inherently unstable, and that fiscal and monetary policies are therefore needed to stabilize it.

Fourth, as already discussed, there is the monetarist research strategy of focusing on the supply and demand for money.

As a result, there is a fifth difference: while Keynesians generally use large-scale econometric models that describe various sectors of the economy in detail, monetarists prefer to use smaller, highly aggregated models that relate the money supply directly to GNP.

Finally, monetarists and Keynesians view the price level in a different way, with monetarists believing that prices are much more flexible—downward as well as upward—than Keynesians do. For example, suppose that the price of oil rises, say, by 20 percent. Keynesians tend to say that if oil accounts directly and indirectly as a raw material for, say, 10 percent of GNP, then this 20 percent rise in oil prices will raise the overall price level by 2 percent. Monetarists, on the other hand, say that, with the nominal money stock held constant, much of the rise in the price of oil and oil products will be offset by declines in other prices relative to what they would otherwise be. This is so because if, as oil prices rise, the price level were to rise by 2 percent, then the demand for nominal money would increase and exceed the supply, with the result that aggregate demand would fall, and hence prices would decline again.

These propositions are connected in many ways. Thus, one can readily see the quantity theory at work in the example of the rise in oil prices, and also in the monetarist proposition that one does not have to look at demands in particular sectors of the economy to determine aggregate demand.[9] Similarly, the hypothesis that the demand for money is stable fits in well with the view that the private sector is stable. And if the private economy is stable, then there is less reason to bother about demand in particular sectors. Moreover, if one thinks of the price level as a single unit, so that price increases in one sec-

---

[8] Keynes made his famous statement, "In the long run we are all dead," as a response to the quantity theory (*A Tract on Monetary Reform*, London: Macmillan, 1924, p. 80).

[9] But one has to look at much more than aggregate demand to determine what will be the change in prices as opposed to changes in output.

tor are offset by decreases (or a slowdown in the rate of increase) in other sectors as in the above example of oil prices, then the economy is much less subject to cost-push inflation, and hence is stable in this sense. Furthermore, if one does not have to bother with allocative detail in various sectors, then why use a large econometric model? These six monetarist propositions thus form an interconnected whole, though they are *not* so closely connected that to accept any one of them means that one *has* to accept the others as well.

THE STABILITY ISSUE

We now look further at one issue that divides monetarists and Keynesians: the stability of a private enterprise economy, that is, its ability to avoid—without the help of government stabilization policies—substantial periods of extensive unemployment and severe inflations.[10] The Keynesian approach developed as a response to the unstable behavior of the economy. For nearly two hundred years before World War II, the progress of capitalist countries was periodically interrupted by panics, recessions, and depressions. The Great Depression of the 1930s was the last straw. Although monetarists attribute this and other severe depressions to sharp declines in the growth rate of the money stock, the Great Depression was widely interpreted as a result not of poor monetary arrangements, but as an inherent fault in the capitalist system. Governments in all developed market economies became committed to interventionist policies aimed at preventing or limiting the erratic movements of production and employment that had caused so much waste and suffering in the past. Keynesian income-expenditure analysis provided a rationale for interventionist stabilization policy and a paradigm for the analysis of alternative stabilization policies.

Keynes's theory emphasized the instability of private investment and at the same time deprecated the notion that the private economy contained adjustment mechanisms that could offset the variations in income generated by variations in investment. Keynesians attributed the instability of investment to variations in the investment opportunities generated by new techniques and new products. They also supposed that those variations in investment were accentuated by speculation in security markets. Moreover, Keynes and his followers emphasized the tendency for swings in investment to feed on themselves. Increasing investment would increase consumption spending through the multiplier, and the resulting improvement in capacity utilization would cause further increases in investment in sectors not originally involved in the investment boom. When the original impetus weakens, the whole process could go into reverse.

In analyzing the sources of instability in an economic system, we have to make a distinction between primary causes of instability and the secondary responses of the system to those primary impulses. The oil shock of 1973–1974 stands as a classic example of a primary shock or cause of instability.

---

[10] For an example of the Keynesian view, see Hyman Minsky, *John Maynard Keynes*. New York: Columbia University Press, 1975.

Multiplier response to a change in investment is a simple example of a second-ary response.

Inventory cycles provide a more complex case. A rise in the rate of growth of income will tend to increase the rate of inventory investment, and that, in turn, will contribute to a further increase in the rate of growth of income. Exhaustion of the original impulse that set off the boom not only slows down the rate of growth of income directly but will cause inventory investment to decline and might even cause an absolute drop in output. In that case, producers will have excessive inventories, and will for a time attempt to reduce them so that inventory investment becomes negative. That, of course, will make the situation even worse, causing a further decline in income and accentuating inventory problems. Because inventory investment is only a small part of the total GNP, it will usually be possible to work off excess inventories. Nonetheless, the inventory mechanism can cause a fluctuation in output out of proportion to the original impulse that changed investment and the rate of growth of output.

Monetarists agree with Keynesians that all of these factors can, *in princi-ple,* create economic fluctuations. However, they argue that *as an empirical proposition* much the greater part of the income fluctuations we have actually experienced have been due to variations in the growth rate of the money sup-ply, and hence is the fault of the central bank. Second, monetarists put less emphasis than Keynesians on the *macroeconomic* effects of a given exogenous shock because they focus on the supply and demand for money, which works as an automatic stabilizer. Suppose, for example, that an innovation greatly raises investment in the airline industry. This tends to raise nominal income. But, since $M = kYP$, with the money stock constant and nominal income ris-ing, k must be falling. Ignoring changing interest rates for the moment, why should the public be willing to reduce its k? Since people are initially holding their desired ratio of money to nominal income, as nominal income rises they will try to increase their money holdings. And they do this by cutting expendi-tures (or selling assets), so that the increases in output and prices in the indus-tries producing the new capital goods for the airlines are offset by falling output or prices in other industries.

To be sure, the assumption that the public wants its k to remain constant despite the rise in the interest rate is extreme and implausible. But monetarists believe that the interest elasticity of the demand for money is not very great, so that an investment boom lowers k only moderately. With the money stock constant and k falling only moderately, income rises only moderately. In mon-etarist analyses shocks, such as innovations, have much more effect on *relative* outputs and *relative* prices than they do on total output and the overall price level.

Moreover, while monetarists agree that the economy is subject to *some* shocks, they do not believe that these shocks (apart from those resulting from government policy) are as frequent and as big as many Keynesians claim, since consumption may depend on long-run income and investment on long-run changes in demand.

The question whether a capitalist economy is stable or needs govern-ment intervention to avoid an unacceptable level of unemployment or inflation is obviously an extremely important one. Unfortunately, it is a question easier to pose than to answer. In our view there is no convincing empirical evidence that would allow one to decide who is right. The following illustrates some of the problems encountered in trying to answer this question. One possible approach is to take an econometric model and put into it a stable monetary and fiscal policy in place of the policy actually followed, to see if the model then shows less fluctuation in income than was actually experienced. But the answer depends on the model used. Moreover, monetarists doubt that these models are reliable enough to evaluate the effects of various policies. Another possible approach is to ask whether the economy has been more stable in the postwar years in which stabilization policy was used than before 1929 when it was not used. Even if it turns out that it is more stable now, an issue debated by economic historians, monetarists could reply that this is due to the more erratic fluctuations in the money stock before 1929. A third approach is to ask whether, in those countries in which the government does relatively little to stabilize income, income is actually more stable than it is in those countries that follow stronger stabilization policies. But the problem here is to determine the direction of causation. Certain countries may follow stronger stabilization policies precisely because they experience more income fluctuations. For the question whether a capitalist economy is inherently stable, every solution has its problems.

SUMMARY

1 The quantity theory focuses on equilibrium and disequilibrium in the money market. Changes in aggregate demand are interpreted as attempts to bring *real* money holdings into equilibrium. It treats the demand for money as a stable function of a limited set of other variables rather than as a stable number.
2 Dependence of the demand for money on the interest rate is consistent with the quantity theory if a change in the quantity of money changes the interest rate for only a short time. Once the expected real interest rate has returned to its previous level nominal income and money have changed proportionately.
3 The transmission mechanism of the Chicago approach is formulated in terms of changes in the quantity of money rather than in terms of interest rates, and it does not try to analyze the particular channels by which money affects income in detail, in part because there are too many of them.
4 There is much empirical evidence showing a close correlation between nominal money and nominal income or prices. A debated issue is direction of causation.
5 The St. Louis approach regresses changes in nominal GNP on changes in the money supply and fiscal variables. It finds that the money supply dominates, while fiscal policy has no effect on GNP.
6 Monetarism can be described as a conjunction of several related propositions. Leaving aside the ones relating to policy, they are the validity of the quantity theory, a particular transmission process, the stability of the private sector, a focus on aggregate demand as a whole rather than on demand in particular sectors, a focus on the price level as a unit, and a skeptical attitude toward large econometric models.
7 In the Keynesian view the economy is unstable, due both to external shocks and to internal factors, such as inventory cycles. Monetarists question the empirical significance of such destabilizing factors.

QUESTIONS AND EXERCISES

1 Describe, in your own words, the *basic* idea behind the quantity theory.

2 If both the interest rate and real income are constant, and there is no money illusion, then a 10 percent rise in the money stock results in a 10 percent rise in nominal income. Discuss.

3 Show why a rise in the money stock would lead to a proportional increase in prices if *(a)* the demand for money is completely interest inelastic and *(b)* prices are flexible and the economy is at full employment.

4 What are the main reasons why Friedman and the Keynesians come up with different answers?

5 Look up recent data on the money stock and on income. (They can be found in the appendix of the *Economic Report of the President,* for example.) See if these data support Friedman's theory. Also calculate the Cambridge *k.* How stable has it been?

6 Germany experienced a hyperinflation after World War I. In November 1923 wholesale prices were one *billion* times what they had been sixteen months earlier. But in this period, the stock of money (as measured by the currency circulation of the central bank) was only (!) about twenty-million times what it was sixteen months before. How can this be explained? Does it contradict the quantity theory?

7 Suppose income increases because of an increase in the marginal efficiency of investment. Describe the process in quantity theory terms.

FURTHER READING

ANDERSEN, LEONALL, and JERRY JORDAN. "Monetary and Fiscal Actions: A Test of Their Relative Importance in Economic Stabilization," *Review,* Federal Reserve Bank of St. Louis, 50 (November 1968):11–24. A classic.

FRIEDMAN, MILTON. "Money," in *International Encyclopedia of the Social Sciences.* An excellent survey of monetary theory from a quantity theory standpoint.

——. "The Role of Monetary Policy," *American Economic Review,* 58 (March 1968): 1–17. A powerful argument that changes in the money stock depress interest rates only temporarily.

——. *Studies in the Quantity Theory of Money.* Chicago: University of Chicago Press, 1956. A classic statement of Friedman's view together with essays by his students providing empirical evidence. Chapter 1 is particularly useful.

FRIEDMAN, MILTON, and ANNA SCHWARTZ. *Monetary Trends in the United States and the United Kingdom.* Chicago: University of Chicago Press, 1982. An outstanding piece of scholarship. (For review articles that survey its highlights see the December 1982 issue of the *Journal of Economic Literature.*)

——. "Money and Business Cycles," *Review of Economics and Statistics,* 45 (February 1963), supplement: 32–64. An important survey of the empirical evidence for the quantity theory.

GORDON, ROBERT J. (ed.), *Friedman's Monetary Theory.* Chicago: Aldine Publishing Co., 1974. This is the definitive statement of Friedman's monetary theory together with criticisms by eminent economists and Friedman's reply.

LAIDLER, DAVID. "Money and Money Income: An Essay on the Transmission Mechanism," *Journal of Monetary Economics* 4 (April 1978):151–92. An excellent survey of one of the major disputes about the quantity theory.

MAYER, THOMAS, et al. *The Structure of Monetarism.* New York: W. W. Norton, 1978. A survey of, and debate about, the broader aspects of monetarism by both monetarist and nonmonetarist economists.

MOORE, BASIL. "Monetary Trends in the United States and United Kingdom," *Financial Review,* 18 (September 1983):146–166. This is a good critical review.

SELDEN, RICHARD. "Monetarism," in Sidney Weintraub (ed.), *Modern Economic Thought,* pp. 253–74. Philadelphia: University of Pennsylvania Press, 1976. A very useful survey.

APPENDIX A:
THE REAL BALANCE EFFECT

A rigorous approach to the quantity theory, called the **real balance approach,** has been developed by Don Patinkin (of Hebrew University). This is concerned primarily with establishing two propositions. The first is that under certain specified conditions a change in the stock of money brings about a strictly proportional change in the price level, and the second is that Keynes was wrong when he claimed that there could be an equilibrium at less than full employment in an economy in which wages and prices are *completely* flexible. Patinkin does not deny that reestablishing full employment when, say, the marginal efficiency of investment falls may *perhaps* mean a much greater drop in wages that would be feasible; he is just concerned with showing that, in principle, falling wages and prices would bring about full employment.

Patinkin organized his analysis around the real balance effect. As a convenient, though hardly realistic, expository device, suppose that a helicopter flies over a country and drops currency. The lucky inhabitants now find that they hold more money than they desire to hold, given their incomes, wealth, and the interest rate. Hence, they use this excess money to buy securities and physical assets. This basic idea of the real balance effect is obvious, and we have already discussed it a various points. But to understand it fully, one must put it into a model that starts out with certain quite specific assumptions.

THE ASSUMPTIONS

The most dramatic assumption is that wages and prices are completely flexible so that, as long as the supply of labor exceeds the demand for labor, wages continue to fall. Patinkin is not saying that this is the way wages actually behave—he is merely trying to show what would happen if this assumption were to hold.

The second assumption is that people do not suffer from a "money illusion." This needs explaining. Suppose that prices double but that your income and wealth double also, so that you are as well off as before. Will you also double the *nominal* value of your expenditures, thus keeping your real expenditures constant? If you are fully aware of what has happened, and behave rationally, you will do so. Your propensity to consume depends on your real income, real wealth, and the real interest rate, and these variables are all unchanged. But it is certainly possible that you may not be fully aware that your real income and wealth are unchanged; for example, you may underestimate the rise in prices, and hence believe that your real income and wealth have risen. If so, you are said to suffer from a money illusion.

As prices rise or fall some redistribution of income takes place and if gainers and losers have different marginal propensities to consume or to invest, aggregate demand is affected. But to simplify the analysis Patinkin assumes such redistribution effects do not occur. In addition, he assumes that as prices change people do not hold back or accelerate purchases in the expectation of further price changes. For expository convenience, he also assumes that the government's budget is balanced. In addition to these assumptions, we will assume *temporarily* that there are no government bonds outstanding, and that all the money in existence is outside money, specifically, for example, currency. Later, when introducing government bonds, we will also assume that taxpayers are indifferent to the real value of the government's debt, and do not feel poorer, and hence cut their consumption, when the real value of the government's debt rises.

THE MODEL

Divide all the numerous markets in the economy into three. One is the commodity market in which a person's real expenditure on consumer goods and a firm's expenditure on capital goods are functions of real income, the interest rate, and real wealth.

The second market is the labor market in which both the supply and demand for labor depend upon the real wage; the higher the real wage the greater is the supply of labor willing to work, but the smaller is the demand for labor. Third, there is the money market in which the real interest rate depends on nominal income and upon the nominal money stock. The higher is nominal income, the greater is the demand for money and, hence, the higher is the interest rate. And the greater is the supply of money, the lower is the interest rate.

Another aspect of the model is that real expenditures (that is, consumption plus investment) are functions of real income and real wealth. This is not so much an assumption as something that follows directly from microeconomic theory. Real wealth consists of three types of assets: physical capital or claims thereon (e.g., stock), claims that the public has on the government (currency, government securities, and reserves that depository institutions hold with the Fed), and claims that one member of the public has on another, for example, corporate bonds or mortgages. For the public as a whole, these latter claims wash out, since each person's claim is balanced by some other person's debt. We first consider a model in which there are no government bonds and no reserves with the Fed, so that net wealth for the public as a whole consists only of capital and currency, and money is the same as currency.

WORKINGS OF THE MODEL

We now put this model through its paces by considering five cases: an expansion of the labor force, a rise in the nominal money stock, an increase in the demand for money, a rise in the average propensity to consume, and an exogenous rise in prices. To simplify we describe some processes that actually operate simultaneously as though they would operate sequentially.

An Expanded Labor Force. As more people seek work wages fall. And given our assumption of complete wage and price flexibility wages must fall until all those who want jobs have them. But with wages and, hence, prices falling won't aggregate demand fall too, so that real wages are constant and firms have no incentive to employ the additional workers? To see why this will *not* happen assume at first that it *does* happen and then see why this cannot be an equilibrium. Suppose that both wages and prices fall equally by, say, 10 percent. Real income is then constant. But real wealth has increased. With the money stock being constant in nominal terms, the real money stock has risen 10 percent, so that both the economy's wealth and liquidity have risen. This increased liquidity lowers the interest rate, which induces a rise in expenditures. The increase in wealth also raises consumption expenditures. These increases in expenditures in turn raise prices. Hence, in equilibrium prices fall less than wages. The resulting decline in real wages permits the additional workers to find jobs.

A Rise in the Nominal Money Stock. Suppose that, due to a benevolent helicopter, the money stock increases 10 percent. People now try to get rid of their excess money holdings by raising expenditures. As long as their real money balances are higher than before, their expenditures will also be greater than before. Only after prices have risen by 10 percent, too, will real money balances be back in equilibrium.

What happens to the real rate of interest? The factors that determine it are saving, the yield on capital (and hence the demand for capital), and any gap that exists between the real quantity of money demanded and supplied. In the Patinkin model a rise in the supply of money does not change the flow of saving or the yield on capital. And, as just discussed, the price level adjusts to eliminate the gap between the real quantities of money demanded and supplied. Hence, with none of the determinants of the interest rate being different, the real rate of interest must be the same as it was before the money stock increased.

An Increased Demand for Money. Suppose people want to hold 10 percent more real money. To do so they must reduce their demand for something else since their total assets are fixed. We assume that they reduce their demand for commodities and bonds proportionately. As they reduce their expenditures on commodities unemployment develops so that wages and prices fall. Once prices have fallen by 10 percent, the real quantity of money available has risen by 10 percent, thus matching the 10 percent increase in the demand for real money. The economy is back in full employment equilibrium and wages and prices no longer fall. In addition, as in the previous case of an increase in the supply of money, the interest rate must be back at its previous level too.

An Increase in the Average Propensity to Consume. Initially the rise in consumption raises prices. However, this reduces the real money stock, and with falling wealth and rising interest rates there is downward pressure on prices. But prices do not fall all the way back to their initial level. With the propensity to consume being higher, there is, of course, less saving. Hence, the interest rate rises, and at the higher interest rate the public wants to hold less real money. But the nominal stock of money is unchanged, and to make this unchanged nominal stock of money correspond to the desired smaller stock of real money, prices have to rise. So an increase in the propensity to consume raises prices.

An Exogenous Increase in Prices. Suppose that for some reason producers mistakenly believe that the equilibrium price level has risen and accordingly raise prices. This reduces real wealth, and also the real money stock, so that the interest rate rises. Both the rise in the interest rate and the decline in wealth reduce expenditures. As expenditures fall prices are forced down again. Equilibrium is restored only at the previous price level and interest rate.

Concluding Note. In two of these five cases (an increase in the money stock and an increase in the demand for money) there were no effects on the real economy. In this model purely monetary changes, such as these, have no *real* effects; money is just a veil. But in two cases, an increase in the labor force and a rise in the propensity to consume, the interest rate changed too. These were cases of changes in the real factors (the supply of labor and the supply of saving) so that one would expect a change in the relative price of labor and capital, and not just in the price level. In the final case, an autonomous price increase, neither the interest rate nor the equilibrium price level changed because all that had happened was that prices had been raised by mistake.

INSIDE MONEY, OUTSIDE MONEY, AND GOVERNMENT BONDS

The time has come to remove two assumptions—the absence of government bonds and that currency is the only type of money. If there are government bonds denominated, as they usually are, in nominal terms, than a 10 percent increase in the money stock must raise prices by *less* than 10 percent. Suppose prices rise by 10 percent. The real value of government bonds would then fall by 10 percent, so that the public would be poorer. It would therefore cut consumption. This, in turn, would force down prices. Hence, a new equilibrium can be reached only when prices have risen less than proportionately to the rise in the money stock.

Now assume that there exists inside money, that is, money which is a claim on someone within the private sector, such as deposits which are claims on banks. Assume that such inside money increases by 10 percent while currency and government bonds are constant. If prices were to rise by 10 percent too, then people would be poorer because the real value of their currency plus government bonds would then have fallen by 10 percent so that they would cut their consumption. Hence, when inside money increases by 10 percent prices must rise by less than 10 percent. (Prices will rise to some extent because, with the money stock having increased, the interest rate will fall so that people will want to hold more money.)

The upshot of all this is that, if there are government bonds or inside money, money and prices will generally not change proportionately as they do in the Chicago version of the quantity theory. But we must qualify this last statement by saying that some economists believe that inside money is also net wealth, and others believe that the taxpayers do treat an increase in the real value of the government debt as a corresponding reduction in their wealth. If they are right the above discussion has to be modified.

APPENDIX B:
THE BRUNNER-MELTZER MODEL

When discussing Friedman's monetary theory we mentioned that (rightly or wrongly) he is often criticized for not sufficiently explaining *how* money affects income, and for relying on "mere correlations." And the same criticism has been made of the work of Andersen and Jordan. But this criticism is certainly not applicable to the work of two other leading monetarists, Karl Brunner and Allan Meltzer. They have developed an extensive and very complex analysis of the transmission process. Brunner and Meltzer reject the standard Keynesian IS-LM transmission mechanism as oversimplified.

Hence, Brunner and Meltzer developed a different transmission mechanism, one that stresses changes in the stock of assets and in the relative prices of assets. In their model (built on some earlier work of Carl Christ of Johns Hopkins University), suppose that government expenditures increase. There is, as in the standard Keynesian model, a direct expansionary effect and also a multiplier effect. But in addition, Brunner and Meltzer point out, there is a stock effect. The government has to finance the deficit; it must pay for the increased expenditures by issuing either bonds or money.[11]

Consider first the case in which it issues money. Microeconomics tells us that if the supply of any one item increases its *relative* price must fall to clear the market. But

[11] Actually the Treasury does not, except to a trivial extent, pay for its expenditures by issuing money. What happens in this case is that the Treasury issues bonds, and that, at the same time, to keep the interest rate stable, the Fed buys government securities in the open market. But as a result of its security purchases bank reserves, and hence the money stock, increase.

an increase in the supply of money cannot lower the price of money in dollar terms; a dollar always sells for a dollar. However, it can lower the *relative* price of money by raising the prices of all other items, that is of consumer goods, capital goods, and bonds. As the prices of both consumer goods and capital goods rise, it becomes profitable to produce more of them, so that output now increases. And, similarly, the rise in bond prices makes it profitable for firms to issue more bonds and to buy capital goods with the proceeds of these bond sales. (Or, to express this in Keynesian terminology, the fall in the interest rate stimulates spending.) At first, all of this results in both output and prices rising. But output rises only as long as it is profitable to produce more because the price of output is high relative to the price of labor and other inputs needed to produce it. Once wages and other costs rise in proportion to the increase in output prices, the additional production is no longer profitable, so that output now falls back to its previous equilibrium level. Thus, an increase in the money stock raises real income only temporarily, but prices, and hence nominal income, rise permanently.

Consider now the opposite case in which the government finances its rising expenditures by selling bonds to the public, instead of increasing the money stock. The increased supply of bonds lowers bond prices relative to the prices of other assets. The critical question is now what this fall in bond price does to the demand for capital, and hence to investment. If one assumes, as the IS-LM model does, that bonds and capital are similar, and therefore good substitutes for each other, then as the public holds more bonds its demand for capital is reduced. Hence, stock prices and prices of capital goods such as houses fall, and firms cut their investment. But Brunner and Meltzer (as well as some Keynesians, such as James Tobin of Yale University) make the opposite assumption. In their view government bonds and capital are complements rather than substitutes. Hence, an increase in the supply of government bonds *raises* the demand for capital as the public tries to sell its excess government bonds to buy corporate stock and physical capital instead. As a result, stock prices rise, so that corporations now have an incentive to issue more stock and build more plant and equipment. Investment and income therefore increase. Thus, in the Brunner-Meltzer model, not only monetary policy, but also the size of the government deficit—fiscal policy—and the way it is financed can, at least in principle, have a powerful effect via an increased stock of government bonds.

Another important role that fiscal policy plays in the Brunner-Meltzer model arises from the fact that this model takes account of disequilibrium in the government sector. Most macroeconomic models look at the commodity and labor markets and at money or bond markets, and say that the economy is in equilibrium if all these markets are. But suppose the government is running a deficit. Can one still say that the economy is in equilibrium? Brunner and Meltzer say no because the government has to finance the deficit by issuing bonds or money, and hence—as long as there is a deficit —the public's stock of bonds or money must be growing. And with its wealth growing in this way the public's expenditures will be growing too. As long as the government runs a deficit the IS and LM curves are continually shifting upward so that the economy is not in equilibrium. And the same is true (though now with wealth and expenditures falling) if there is a surplus. Equilibrium requires a balanced budget.

How is it then that so many other economic models ignore the need for a balanced budget in equilibrium?[12] The answer is that they define equilibrium less comprehensively. They treat the rise in the public's stock of bonds and money due to the deficit in one period as an exogenous factor that disrupts equilibrium in the next period, and

---

[12] Not all other models ignore the effects of the deficit. Some Keynesian economists have built models incorporating these effects much along the lines of Brunner and Meltzer.

therefore they analyze the effects of the increase in these stocks separately. By contrast, Brunner and Meltzer look at the whole process as a single unit.

What makes equilibrium analysis so attractive to economists is that there usually exist forces that move the economy toward equilibrium. In the absence of new shocks, one can predict where the economy will end up. Does this work for the Brunner-Meltzer model? What mechanisms, if any, bring the economy to such a broader equilibrium in which the government's budget is just balanced?

Assume the government raises its expenditures, thus running a deficit. This has several effects. It increases aggregate demand both directly and also through multiplier effects as consumption increases. With income thus rising, tax receipts rise too. But they do not rise by enough to balance the budget. There are, however, additional effects. One is that the deficit, by raising the public's holdings of bonds and money and hence its wealth, raises the proportion of income consumed. Second, investment also increases as the rise in the stocks of money lowers interest rates. Both the rise in consumption and the rise in investment raise nominal income, and hence tax receipts. Moreover, rising prices lower the real value of the interest payments the government makes on its debts. For all of these reasons the increase in aggregate demand reduces the deficit. And since aggregate demand continues to increase as long as there is a deficit, eventually the deficit is eliminated entirely. At this point the economy is in equilibrium. A similar analysis applies if the government cuts its expenditures or raises taxes so that it runs a surplus; this too will be eliminated.

In this model where equilibrium requires that the government's budget be balanced, fiscal factors, such as the progressivity of the tax system, play a important role. The more progressive the tax system the smaller is the rise in income required to generate the revenue needed to eliminate a given deficit. Such a large role for fiscal policy has caused some economists to question whether the Brunner-Meltzer model is really monetarist and not Keynesian. *In principle,* their model could even produce the old-fashioned and rigid Keynesian conclusion that fiscal policy has a powerful effect on income, while monetary policy is almost powerless. But Brunner and Meltzer believe that this is as it should be: a theory sets out various possibilities, and empirical tests then determine which of these possibilities corresponds to the real world. Brunner and Meltzer have undertaken extensive empirical tests from which they conclude that the dominant impulse that drives nominal income is not fiscal policy, but changes in the nominal money stock. Since they have also shown that the Fed, if it wants to, can control the nominal money stock, they hold the Fed largely responsible for inflation and for fluctuations in real income.

CHAPTER 17

The Monetarist-Keynesian Debate in Perspective

It is sometimes difficult to get a clear view of the differences between monetarists and those who use the income-expenditure approach, because they appear to be using different languages to express their views. To compare their views, it is necessary to translate from one language to another, and there is always the danger that something will be lost in the translation.

In the income-expenditure approach, each component of the expenditure side of the national income accounts is "explained" in terms of other variables. Thus consumer expenditures are explained in terms of disposable income, wealth, and perhaps some other factors. Investment is supposed to vary with capacity utilization and interest rates. Price changes reflect changes in wages and in capacity utilization, but are also influenced by "exogenous" changes in food prices, taxes, and other factors. All of these linkages interact with one another in the complex system sketched out in Chapters 12 through 15. In that kind of system, prices, output, and unemployment are strongly influenced by both monetary and fiscal policy, but they can be influenced by many other variables as well. Moreover, the structure of the system itself is subject to change without notice. The relations between unemployment and wage change can be influenced by changes in the strength of trade unions, by import competition, and by changes in regulation as well as by expectations of future government policy. Investment expenditures can be influenced by "speculation" about the rapid growth of new industries, by threats of war, and by confidence or lack of confidence in government policy.

The income-expenditure approach is built up from a great many pieces. Economists who use this approach have disagreements about the relative importance of the many variables entering the system. For example, some think that changes in wealth have a powerful influence on consumer expenditures. Others are skeptical about the effect of wealth. Statistical studies do not yield sufficiently precise results to resolve the controversy. The result is that there can be considerable differences in judgments about the effects of any proposed policy. What links Keynesians is not their conclusions but their basic way of approaching the analysis of the economy.

Much the same thing can be said of monetarists. They too have their differences, but they share a belief in the critical importance of variations in the rate of growth of money in the explanation of changes in prices and output. They tend to emphasize the existence of direct links between money on the one hand, and expenditures, prices, and output on the other, thus bypassing the complex causal chains appearing in Keynesian models. Some of the direct linkages relate prices and outputs to actual and expected changes in asset markets, particularly money markets. They give great weight to the role of stocks of assets in determining flows of expenditures so that, for example, they emphasize the link between stocks of wealth and flows of consumer expenditures. In addition, as already discussed in Chapter 16, they consider that prices and wages are relatively flexible, that is, more flexible than Keynesians usually assume. And they also think of the private economy as relatively stable.

Finally, as mentioned in Chapter 16, monetarists tend to have a longer time horizon than Keynesians. They are often concerned, for example, with the consequences of an increased rate of growth of money supply persisting over a period of years. Keynesians are more often concerned with short-run changes. Some misunderstandings arise from this source, because the short-run effect of a policy change may be quite different from its long-run effect.

At a very general theoretical level, Keynesians and monetarists often agree about the nature of the factors influencing prices, expenditures, and output. In summary paragraphs they often sound very similar. Unfortunately, the apparent agreement often amounts only to what Robert Solow of MIT summarized as a student's progress in economics: in the elementary course he learns that everything depends on everything else; when he becomes a graduate student, he learns that everything depends on everything else in two ways.

For practical purposes, it is necessary to simplify things to some extent. Interactions considered to have minor effects must be neglected. The result is that Keynesians often neglect matters that monetarists consider important, and vice versa. In using different simplifications, they often appear to be talking different languages.

In many ways, however, the monetarist description of the qualitative linkages between money and expenditures, prices and output does not sound so very different from the Keynesian approach. Milton Friedman's analysis of the demand for money is not fundamentally different from the Keynesian analysis. Patinkin's model of real balance effects can certainly be given a Keynesian interpretation. The Brunner-Meltzer model overlaps the Keynesian one in many ways—though containing its own special features. Up to a point one can think of Keynesians and monetarists as using a common model and differing about numerical magnitudes such as the interest elasticity of demand for money or the flexibility of prices. At one time, until the mid-1960s, the debate centered on the relative slopes of IS and LM curves, to which we now turn.

INTEREST ELASTICITIES IN THE IS-LM MODEL

In any debate, it is helpful to define the question in your own way. In the early stages of the Keynesian-monetarist debate, Keynesians treated monetarism as a special case of the Keynesian model. They argued that the quantity theory of nominal income would be correct if the demand for money were inelastic to interest rates, or if investment demand were highly elastic to interest rates. They then proceeded to make empirical arguments to show that neither was true. Monetarists were never very enthusiastic about that formulation of the issue, but they did debate some of the questions involved. The result of a long statistical wrangle and the accumulation of experience was to bring both positions together. The result of convergence, however, was not to produce agreement, but to shift the argument to new grounds.

Demand for Money

Many early Keynesians believed that (especially at the low rates prevailing after World War II) the interest elasticity of demand for money was almost infinite. Consequently, velocity would adjust to any change in GNP with very little change in interest rates. That view, of course, reflected the experience of the late thirties, World War II, and the early postwar years.

However, statistical studies covering longer periods as well as the experience of monetary restraint indicated that the interest elasticity of demand for money was not as high as some Keynesians had thought. On the other hand, those estimates were not so low as to justify a simple fixed-velocity quantity theory in which "only money matters." A moderate interest elasticity of demand for money leaves room for fiscal and other influences on the IS curve as well as for monetary influence through the LM curve shifts. Milton Friedman's permanent-income approach offered an alternative explanation. He showed that a model in which demand for money is made to depend on the trend of income could explain much of the cyclical variation in velocity. Later studies showed that, even after taking the permanent-income effect into account, demand for money is generally still sensitive to interest rates. Nonetheless, Friedman's point was well taken, and many current formulations do use some average of past and current incomes as part of the explanation of demand for money.

Monetarists, including Friedman, as well as Keynesians agree that demand for money is responsive to interest rates. On the other hand, they also agree that the short-run interest elasticity of demand for money is fairly low so that changes in the growth rate of money can have substantial effects on aggregate demand. There is still disagreement in this area, but it is no longer the basis for fundamental differences between monetarists and Keynesians.

Interest Elasticity of Expenditure

A somewhat similar convergence of views about the interest elasticity of expenditures has taken place. Early Keynesian expositions linked money to expenditure through the effect of money on interest rates and the effect of interest rates on investment. While that linkage played an important role in Keynes's exposition, his followers tended to argue that investment demand is very inelastic to interest rates. That argument provided another justification for a "money-doesn't-matter" position.

Again, a long series of statistical studies and accumulating experience showed that interest-rate variations can have significant effects on business investment. However, the difficulty of measuring the expected *real* interest rates makes precise measurement difficult.

The effect of interest-rate variations on residential constructions is well established. In addition, the effects of interest rates extend to consumer expenditures through the influence of interest rates on wealth. Indeed, in a leading Keynesian econometric model, about half the total impact of monetary change results from the wealth effect.

As in the demand-for-money case, Keynesians have moved away from the "money-doesn't-matter" position. At the same time, interest elasticities are not so high as to provide any basis for an "only-money-matters" position. Again, there is room for disagreement about numbers, but the interest elasticity of expenditures is no longer a critical element in the division between Keynesians and monetarists.

RECENT MODELS

As discussed in the preceding chapter, the Keynesian-monetarist debate drifted away from the issue of the slopes of the IS and LM curves in the 1960s. Milton Friedman argued that the slopes matter only for a relatively short time, because if the money stock is increased the interest rate soon rises back to its previous level. On this issue of the behavior of the interest rate, there has so far been little convergence. Monetarists and Keynesians both can point to empirical studies that support their positions; regressions of the interest rate on changes in the money stock generally support the monetarist position, while econometric models tend to support the Keynesian position. And there is an extensive debate on the relative validity of simple regressions of one variable on another versus econometric models. This debate deals more with issues in econometrics than with issues of monetary theory.

Another important development in the debate has been the construction by Brunner and Meltzer of their model with its focus on changes in the relative prices of money, securities, and commodities (including capital), which was discussed in the previous chapter. While many Keynesians would dispute the practical relevance of this model, arguing that these relative price and wealth effects are unimportant in the short run, which is what they think matters for policy-making, there has been some convergence, since some Keynesian economists have built models that are more or less similar to the Brunner-Meltzer model. All in all, among economists this debate is by no means as dogmatic as some newspaper reports suggest. Many economists take an intermediate position, and agree with monetarists on some issues and with Keynesians on others.

POLICY DIFFERENCES

The monetarist-Keynesian debate has gone on for a long time, and it has not become any simpler. Indeed, as interest in monetarism has increased, the number of monetarists has grown and they now disagree among themselves as much as or more than the Keynesians do. However, monetarists tend to unite with one another in their disagreements with Keynesians about economic policy. In this section we will outline some basic differences between the Keynesian and monetarist approaches to the art of policy making, leaving a more detailed discussion until Part 5.

We can start with something everybody agrees about. At any one time there is a fairly well marked, practical limit to real GNP and a corresponding lower limit to unemployment. Unemployment cannot be reduced below that level for long.

Does the opposite proposition hold? Can unemployment remain above this minimum level for a long time? Keynesians generally think so. What drives Keynesians is a belief that unemployment is often much higher than it need be. Monetarists certainly recognize that disturbances from various sources (especially from rapid changes in the money growth rate) can cause unemployment to rise above the natural rate. However, they tend to believe that, in the absence of new disturbances, price and wage adjustments will soon bring the system back to equilibrium.

It follows immediately that fiscal and monetary policies have only short-run effects on real output. Moreover, an activist policy is likely to do more harm than good. Managing monetary and fiscal policies to counter short-run shocks could help in principle, they say, but in practice forecasting errors and politically motivated decisions will worsen rather than improve the economy's performance.

Keynesians, of course, are not nearly so sanguine about the self-adjusting capacity of the system. In their view, the balance between full-employment saving and investment is often disturbed. It needs to be corrected by shifts in monetary and fiscal policy. Moreover, they believe that the batting average of forecasters is good enough to permit policy actions to make the economy more rather than less stable and that policymakers can use these forecasts efficiently. Hence the dispute about policy involves much more than differing views about economic theory. It also involves differing views about the efficiency of the political process. A typical example of this difference is that Keynesians often point to sophisticated mathematical procedures by which the Fed could stabilize the economy, while monetarists point to blunders that the Fed has made in the past.

There is still a big dispute about inflation control. How can we keep the inflation rate from accelerating? Can we make it decelerate? Monetarists argue that we can prevent acceleration by keeping the growth of the money supply at a level equal to the existing rate of inflation, plus the growth of potential output, less the trend of velocity. If oil prices rise or if food prices are driven up by poor crops, there will be a temporary acceleration of inflation and a temporary rise of unemployment, but we will soon get back on the track.

Those who think that fiscal policy has some power would also want to avoid any strong fiscal stimulus. A widespread monetarist prescription for deceleration of inflation is a gradual deceleration in money growth. Again some extra unemployment would occur, but it would be temporary.

Keynesians on the other hand find themselves in a dilemma. They think it will take a lot of unemployment for a long time to bring the inflation rate down. Moreover, price pressures from oil, food, and increased tax rates would have to be offset by even more unemployment. Many Keynesians think that we must live with a continuing inflation, or use guidelines or other interference in the wage- and price-making process. These problems are discussed in Chapter 18.

Inflation and Unemployment

Having looked at what determines aggregate demand and hence nominal income, we now ask how changes in nominal income are divided between prices and output. This matters: a 5 percent increase in nominal income is good if it is a rise in real income, but not if it is a rise in prices. The extent to which an increase in aggregate demand results in rising output rather than in rising prices depends on the aggregate supply curve. Before we look at this curve, though, a description of inflation and unemployment is in order.

INFLATION: DEFINITION AND TYPES

Inflation is a significant and persistent increase in the price level. Unless prices are rising at a significant rate, say, more than 1 percent per year, it makes no more sense to talk about inflation than it does to call someone over-weight because he exceeds the appropriate weight by three ounces. Besides, our price indexes are not all that accurate. Since they make insufficient allowance for quality improvements and for the benefits obtained from new goods, it is far from certain that there really is inflation if the **consumer price index** (CPI) rises by, say, .5 percent per year. Although most people call any significant increase in prices "inflation," in economic theory that word is used only for *persistent* increases in the price level. For how long prices have to rise before one calls it inflation is somewhat arbitrary; some economists would say at least three years, while others would draw the line at perhaps one year. The reason for drawing this distinction between sustained and episodic increases in prices is that the theory required to explain them differs. Many factors that can produce episodic price increases cannot account for sustained increases.

Inflations are classified by their magnitudes. At one extreme is **creeping inflation.** As the name implies, this is a moderate inflation, perhaps 1 to 3 percent per year—exactly where to draw the line is arbitrary. Such a moderate

Table 18.1	Inflation Rates in Selected Countries[a]						
	Britain	Canada	France	Germany	Italy	Japan	United States
1961–65	3.5	1.6	4.0	2.8	4.9	6.1	1.3
1966–70	4.6	3.8	4.3	2.4	3.0	5.4	4.2
1971–75	13.2	7.3	8.9	6.1	11.5	11.7	6.8
1976–80	14.4	8.8	10.5	4.0	16.4	6.6	8.9
1981–84	7.5	8.4	10.6	4.3	15.1	2.9	6.0

a: Average annualized inflation rates measured by the consumer price index, year-to-year change.

Source: Based on *Economic Report of the President,* 1986, pp. 319, 376.

inflation may seem inconsequential, but it isn't. At a 3 percent inflation rate a dollar has lost half its value after twenty-four years. Even after only three years of 4 percent inflation the purchasing power of a dollar has fallen to 85 cents.

At the other extreme is **hyperinflation**—as this name implies, an extremely large inflation. Again, there is no sharp line of demarcation, but one study of hyperinflation dealt with inflations of more than 50 percent per month. It is hard to visualize the severity of some hyperinflations. For example, the German wholesale price index, which had been 100 in July 1922, was 1,261 trillion in December 1923. In such a situation someone going shopping has to carry his money in a suitcase. At the height of the German hyperinflation workers were paid twice a day because by the end of the working day their morning's earnings would have lost too much value. Although during hyperinflations money is still used as a medium of exchange it is no longer used as a standard of value. Instead, people figure in terms of a stable foreign currency which becomes worth more of the inflated domestic currency every day.

Typically inflations are neither creeping inflations nor hyperinflations. Table 18.1 shows the inflation rates of a sample of countries. For most industrialized countries the inflation rates of recent years were too high to be called creeping inflations, but were at most in the low double digits. Many less developed countries, on the other hand, experienced more substantial inflations.

Inflations in the United States

As late as 1955 one could say that the United States was free from peacetime inflation. All our inflations had been war connected, occurring either during a war or right after a war. America's only hyperinflation took place during the Revolution. The currency unit, called a "Continental," depreciated so much

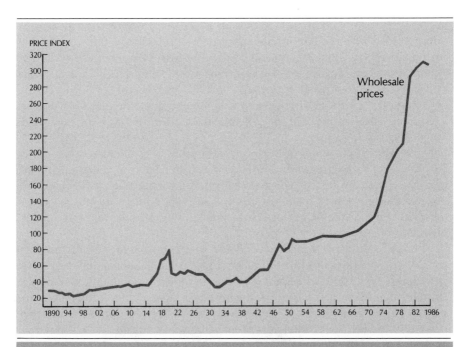

PRICE INDEX

Wholesale prices

Figure 18.1   Wholesale Prices, 1890–1985. Since 1890 there have been long periods of both rising and falling prices. Generally prices rose during wars, and fell afterward. However, they continued to rise after World War II. After 1965, war was no longer a requirement for inflation to be generated. Source; U.S. Bureau of the Census, *Historical Statistics of the United States;* U.S. Department of Commerce, *Handbook of Cyclical Indicators* and *Business Conditions Digest,* April 1986.

that the phrase "not worth a Continental" was born. During the Civil War wholesale prices more than doubled. There was also a major inflation during World War I. These inflations were followed by periods of falling prices. In 1890 wholesale prices were lower than they had been in 1860, and as Figure 18.1 shows, in 1929 they were approximately what they had been forty years earlier.

But after World War II the story was different. Prices did not fall after this war. Then, in 1965–1979, a major inflation occurred. The GNP deflator, our most comprehensive price index, rose on the average at an annual rate of 5.9 percent. And it rose in all years, not just during the Vietnam War. This proved unacceptable. Monetary policy was tightened, and the inflation rate, as measured by the GNP deflator, fell to 4.1 percent in 1985. The cost was high unemployment.

UNEMPLOYMENT

At first glance it might seem that unemployment is an obvious condition that is easy to define. But not at a second glance. For example, should workers who are laid off, but will be recalled to their jobs within a month, be counted as unemployed? How about someone who has turned down a job because it offers too low a wage? (And what is too low a wage?) How about workers who are employed part-time but would prefer full-time jobs, or those no longer looking for work because they do not think they can find it? Our data, which are obtained from household surveys, count among the unemployed anyone on temporary layoffs, and those who have turned down or quit a job and are looking for another one. But they exclude those who have given up and are no longer looking for a job.

Zero unemployment is not a meaningful target. There is some unemployment, called **frictional unemployment,** even when the demand for labor greatly exceeds the supply. Some workers may have quit their jobs to look for new ones, while others have just entered the labor force but not yet found jobs. (In 1944, at the height of World War II, the officially measured unemployment rate was still 1.9 percent.)

Some unemployment is needed for an efficient economy. By analogy, consider the rental market. If the vacancy rate for apartments were zero, then newcomers, and those who want to move to another apartment, would be in trouble. The *apparent* "waste" of having some apartments stand idle is not really a waste. Similarly, firms keep inventories of finished goods to meet their customers' needs. Such "idle" inventories may seem a waste, but without them an economy could not function efficiently. Microeconomic efficiency requires some unemployment to provide flexibility as well as labor discipline. But this does not mean that unemployment is not a serious problem. First, unemployment is probably much higher than is required for efficiency. Second, the fact that some unemployment increases the economy's productivity does not reduce the suffering of those who are unemployed. Why should they have to bear the cost?

Microeconomic efficiency is not the only criterion for the unemployment rate. Another criterion is to prevent accelerating inflation. This is related to the Phillips curve, to which we now turn, starting with a situation in which prices are expected to be constant.

THE PHILLIPS CURVE WITH EXPECTATIONS OF CONSTANT PRICES

How fast wages rise depends on the unemployment rate. Either firms that seek more workers can spend time and effort to search for additional employees at the prevailing wage, or else they can get more applicants by offering a higher wage. When unemployment is high a little recruiting effort suffices to obtain additional employees, but when the pool of unemployed workers is low, then it is more efficient for firms to offer a higher wage. Hence, if unemployment falls low enough employers raise wages faster than productivity is growing.

Moreover, in unionized industries, as unemployment falls wages rise because the bargaining power of unions increases. With fewer unemployed workers around, unions are less afraid that an excessive wage increase will cost them jobs by creating opportunities for nonunionized firms to expand. Moreover, with many jobs available, unemployment is not so terrible a threat. In

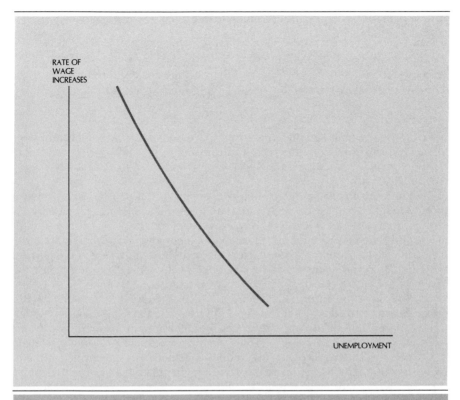

Figure 18.2 **The Short-Run Phillips Curve.** As can be seen here, the lower the unemployment rate, the faster wages rise.

addition, employers are more reluctant to endure strikes at a time of high employment when demand for their output is high too, and hence are then more willing to settle on the union's terms.

As a result one can find a relation, shown in Figure 18.2, called a **short-run Phillips curve,** after the late Professor A. W. Phillips. It shows that the lower the unemployment rate, the faster wages increase. Such Phillips curves, though perhaps not stable ones, have been found for several countries. The equation for this Phillips curve, in which prices are expected to be stable, is

$$dw = a - bu + cq,$$

where dw is the rate of wage increases, u the unemployment rate, q the rate of productivity increase, and c a parameter that measures the extent to which increases in labor productivity are passed on as higher wages. Since most firms set their prices primarily as a markup on their longer run labor costs, there is also a Phillips equation for prices:

$$dp = g - bu - hq,$$

where h measures the proportion of the increase in productivity that is passed on through lower prices.

The Expectations-augmented Phillips Curve

In the much more realistic case in which prices are expected to increase, the Phillips curve needs an additional term. Surely wages rise faster if prices are expected to rise at a 20 percent rate than if they are expected to rise at a 2 percent rate. Hence, we now write the Phillips curve as

$$dw = a - bu + cq + fdp^e,$$

where f is a coefficient that measures the extent to which expected price increases, dp^e, are taken into account in setting wages. Since what matters to both workers and employers is the real wage rather than the money wage, f should equal unity.

This adjustment for inflationary expectations has an important implication. When the Phillips curve was first discovered it seemed to provide a convenient menu of policy choices. The government could read off the Phillips curve the various combinations of unemployment and inflation that are feasible, and pick its preferred choice, say, 5 percent unemployment and 4 percent inflation. It could then use monetary and fiscal policies to keep aggregate demand just high enough to reach this combination.

But the **expectations-augmented Phillips curve** does not allow this game. Starting from a position of zero inflation, assume that the government raises aggregate demand enough to get 5 percent unemployment and 4 percent inflation. As prices rise by 4 percent people expect prices to rise again next year, say, by 2 percent. Hence, with the fdp^e term now equal to 2 percent, at 5 percent unemployment prices rise not by the planned 4 percent but by 6 percent. As a result of this 6 percent price increase the public then raises its estimate of next year's inflation rate, say, to 4 percent. That year prices rise by 8 percent, and people once again raise their inflationary expectations. Their expectations *may* lag behind inflation for several years, but, as rational-expectations theory reminds us, people are not so stupid that they underestimate the inflation rate every year. The closer expectations get to reality, the higher is the inflation rate needed to maintain a 5 percent unemployment rate. There is an ever-accelerating inflation until the government finally gives up its goal of a 5 percent unemployment rate. This problem would not have arisen had the government chosen an unemployment target equal to, or greater than, that required to keep inflation from accelerating.

This process can be described as the Phillips curve becoming steeper the longer the government stays with its target of a 5 percent unemployment rate. Ultimately, it becomes a vertical line. And it need not necessarily take so long to do so. As rational-expectations theory tells us, people could anticipate the inflation rate correctly, rather than just adjusting their inflationary expectations part of the way each year.

The fact that inflationary expectations are malleable is not entirely bad. If the government can convince the public that it will persevere with an anti-inflationary policy it can bring the inflation rate down with less unemployment than would be required if people do not change their expectations. But usually the government cannot make its policy credible. Throughout the inflation it has promised to do something about it, so how can it now convince anyone that this time it really means it?

The classic example of terminating an inflation through a credible policy was the end, in 1924, of the German hyperinflation. When the German government, which previously had not claimed to be fighting inflation, adopted a

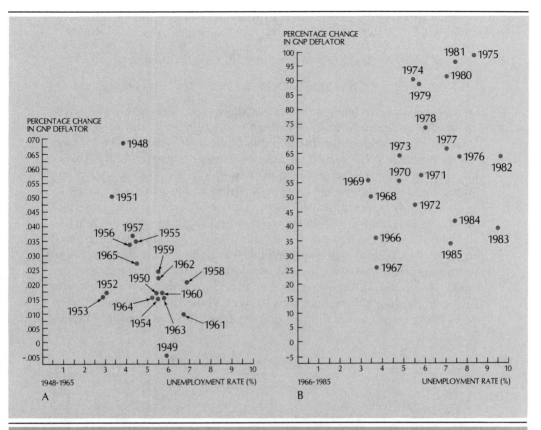

Figure 18.3   Unemployment and the Inflation Rate. When one charts unemployment and the inflation rate for the whole postwar period there is no sign of the Phillips curve: expectations of inflation are omitted, and they matter. **Source:** *Economic Report of the President,* 1986.

credible anti-inflation policy, the public believed it, and the hyperinflation quickly ended. What helped was that the inflation had become so extraordinarily severe. This made the government's announcement more plausible, since the inflation was causing so much damage. Moreover, during a hyperinflation, contracts and wage arrangements are, in effect, indexed. There were no three-year labor agreements setting a certain increase in the money wage each January. In an economy suffering from a lesser inflation such contracts can delay the adjustment to a lower inflation rate. Unless they are renegotiated, the scheduled rise in money wages results in real wages rising faster than planned, and hence in unemployment. Pneumonia can be cured, but a cold cannot!

Figure 18.3 demonstrates a simple Phillips curve without an adjustment for price expectations. In A, which covers the years 1948–1965 when inflation and hence expected inflation were fairly low, this Phillips curve gives a fairly good fit. But when, as in B, the observations for 1966–1985 are added, this simple Phillips curve falls apart. Not all of its collapse should be attributed to its failure to allow for expectations of inflation. Some of it, though only a minor part, is due to the rising "natural rate of unemployment," to which we now turn.

THE NONACCELERATING INFLATION RATE OF UNEMPLOYMENT

If unemployment falls below a certain rate there is ever-accelerating inflation. The unemployment rate that is just high enough to avoid this is called the **NAIRU** (for nonaccelerating inflation rate of unemployment) or the *"natural unemployment rate."* The term "natural rate" does not mean that this particular unemployment rate is ordained by nature. Various policies, such as the elimination of minimum wage laws, more stringent job-search requirements for those receiving unemployment compensation, a decline in racial discrimination, and programs to retrain the unemployed might all lower the NAIRU.

In the 1970s, the NAIRU rose substantially, as the baby boom expanded the number of teenagers seeking employment and as, with changing social attitudes, more women sought paid employment. These new entrants frequently lacked the skills required by employers, and hence had a high unemployment rate. In addition, since those who enter the labor force usually start out by being unemployed, the fact that the labor force was growing rapidly

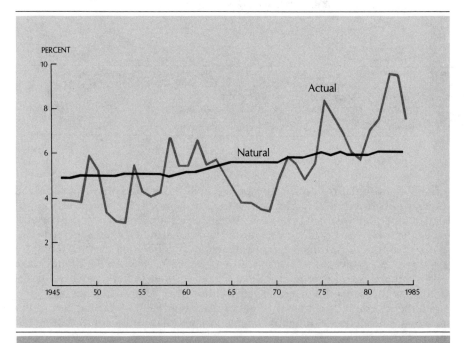

Figure 18.4   Unemployment Rates: Actual and Natural, 1945–1985. The unemployment rate has frequently exceeded the NAIRU. But in some years it was below it. **Source:** Stuart Weiner, *The Natural Rate of Unemployment: Concepts and Issues;* Federal Reserve Bank of Kansas City, *Economic Review,* January 1986.

raised the unemployment rate. So did the tendency of teenagers to change jobs frequently.

Economists in the mid-1980s measure the NAIRU at somewhere between 5 and 7 percent. Figure 18.4 shows the actual unemployment rate along with high and low estimates of the NAIRU. That we lack reliable and precise knowledge of the NAIRU has an important implication for policy. If we set macro policy to aim at "full employment," defined as the NAIRU, we may well end up either tolerating too much unemployment or setting off an accelerating inflation. It seems likely that in the 1970s a major reason for inflation was that the government had underestimated the NAIRU.

In the long run the actual rate of unemployment gravitates toward the NAIRU. It cannot stay any lower because that would set off an ever-accelerating inflation sure to bring with it a restrictive monetary policy that would raise unemployment again. Conversely, when the unemployment rate is above the NAIRU, the search for jobs by unemployed workers puts downward pressure on wages and prices and, as will be explained shortly, lower wages and prices lead to lower unemployment.

As Figure 18.4 shows, high unemployment—unemployment obviously in excess of the NAIRU—is not a new phenomenon. Going back earlier, prior to the Great Depression unemployment rose sharply in years of severe recession. Economic historians disagree about whether, on the average, the unemployment rate was much lower before 1929 than it was after World War II. Clearly, the Great Depression was an extreme, quite atypical case. We will consider the causes of massive unemployment later; for now we will look at what causes inflation.

THE CAUSES OF INFLATION

Aggregate supply and demand curves are useful tools in explaining inflations. The aggregate demand curves that we use now differ sharply from the aggregate demand curve in the so-called "45-degree diagram" used in Chapter 12. That diagram is drawn with income on the x axis, and with aggregate demand on the y axis. Since demand increases with income, the resulting aggregate demand curve slopes upward. By contrast, in the diagram we use now it is the price level, and not demand, that is on the y axis. The x axis shows real income.

The Aggregate Demand Curve

Figure 18.5 shows the aggregate demand curve. It slopes downward because as the price level rises the real value of the money stock falls. The public now finds that it holds an insufficient amount of real money. In addition, its wealth has fallen due to the decline in the real value of its money and government bonds. In response, people reduce the amount of goods and services they buy and output falls. With the price level and output thus being negatively related, the aggregate demand curve slopes downward.

Since the aggregate demand curve relates output, that is, real expenditures, to the price level, anything that changes real expenditures, other than a

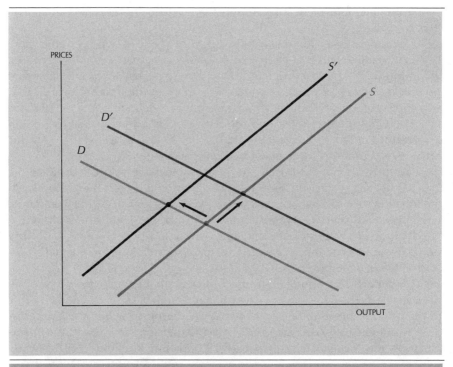

Figure 18.5   Aggregate Supply and Demand Curves. Outward shifts of the aggregate supply curve raise prices and lower real income. Upward shifts of the aggregate demand curve raise both prices and output.

change in the price level, shifts the aggregate demand curve. Some examples are changes in the real money supply, in the marginal efficiency of investment, and in taxes.

The Aggregate Supply Curve

The aggregate supply curve, also given in Figure 18.5, shows how much is produced at different prices. It associates a higher output with a higher price level for two reasons. First, some prices, primarily prices of raw materials, are set in auction markets, where they fluctuate freely in response to supply and demand. Higher output implies a greater demand for raw materials, and hence higher prices. Firms then pass these price increases on to their customers. Second, in the manufacturing and service sectors, prices are set primarily as a markup on labor costs. As firms increase output unemployment falls and, hence, as the Phillips curve tells us, labor costs rise. Firms then respond to these rising costs by raising prices. For both of these reasons the short-run aggregate supply curve is not horizontal, but slopes upward.

The long-run aggregate supply curve, however, is vertical because the Phillips curve is vertical in the long run. How long it takes for the short-run supply curve to evolve into the long-run curve depends on how fast expectations adjust to changes in the inflation rate.

PRICE INCREASES AND INFLATION: SUPPLY-SIDE SHOCKS

An upward shift of the supply curve, such as the shift from S to S' in Figure 18.5, raises prices. Many factors can generate such a shift. One is a foreign cartel raising import prices, as OPEC (the Organization of Petroleum-Exporting Countries) did in its stronger days. In 1973–1974 it quadrupled oil prices. Import prices also rise if the dollar falls on the foreign exchange market. Other examples of possible supply shocks are rising labor costs due to increased union power, increased markups of prices resulting from a decline in competition, and pervasive crop failures.

Nobody denies that such supply shocks can temporarily raise the price level. Can they also cause inflation, that is, a *continual* increase in the price level? In principle they could, but for two reasons this is not likely. First, supply shocks are often events that occur quickly and are not repeated in the following year. Prices rise, and can stay at the higher level for a very long time, but they do not continue to rise. Second, as the aggregate demand curve tells us, when the price level rises real income falls. The resulting unemployment then creates downward pressure on wages and prices.

If one wants to blame supply shocks for inflation one has to take a more subtle approach. One possibility is that, to prevent real balances from falling and unemployment from increasing, the Federal Reserve accommodates the supply shock by increasing the money supply. But, if so, one might want to blame the inflation on the Fed rather than on the supply shock.

Another possibility is that employees offer strong resistance to a reduction in real wages. Hence, if, say, oil prices rise, they demand wage increases to offset the higher prices. Firms then pass these higher labor costs on by raising prices, and this generates further wage demands. Such a "price-wage-price" spiral cannot be ruled out entirely. Had OPEC not raised oil prices in 1973–1974 and 1979–1980, money wages would have risen less than they did in subsequent years. All the same, as a general description of inflation, the price-wage-price spiral explanation of inflation is not entirely persuasive. Unions account for less than a quarter of the labor force. Moreover, the higher unemployment that results from rising wages and prices curbs wage increases. Hence, without denying that a supply shock can, in principle, cause some inflation, one might doubt that supply shocks, unless accommodated by expansionary monetary policy, can be an important cause of inflation in the United States. In Europe, where unions are more powerful and resistance to real wage cuts seems stronger, supply shocks may play more of a role.

Relative Prices and the Price Level

Suppose that OPEC doubles oil prices. Obviously, the *relative* price of oil has now risen, but how about the price level? Assume that the Fed does not increase the money supply to accommodate this supply shock. The price level starts to rise as the prices of oil and oil-related products go up. Real balances fall, and so does aggregate demand. Initially, most of this reduction in aggregate demand results in falling output and employment. But, eventually, this rise in unemployment reduces the growth rate of money wage enough so that the price level is no higher than it would have been had oil prices not risen. This scenario is highly improbable because the Fed is likely to respond to a rise in unemployment by increasing the money growth rate at least to some extent. But it does demonstrate the distinction between a rise in a relative price and a rise in the price *level*.

PRICE INCREASES AND INFLATION: THE DEMAND SIDE

If the aggregate demand curve in Figure 18.5 shifts upward, say, from D to D', prices rise. Such a shift could be due to increases in any of the following: the average propensity to consume, the marginal efficiency of investment, government expenditures, exports, and the money supply. The aggregate demand curve also shifts upward if taxes, imports, or the demand for money decrease.

To account for inflation rather than just for a one-time increase in the price level, these factors would have to continue to change for some time. For example, suppose government expenditures increase and stay at their higher level. Aggregate demand rises, and so do prices, but once having risen prices do not rise any further. To see this in the Keynesian framework, imagine an IS-LM diagram drawn for an economy at full employment that has the price level on the x axis. As the increase in government expenditures shifts the IS curve upward prices rise, but they then stay at this higher level. Or, expressed in monetarist terms, as government expenditures increase, the interest rate rises, which in turn raises velocity. Aggregate demand and prices go up. But since there is only a one-time rise in the interest rate, prices increase only once and not continuously. Of course, this rise in prices would be spread out over time. Even so, a prolonged inflation would occur only if government expenditures rise for a long time and at a high rate. This is possible, but not very likely. It is also possible, but again not very likely, that increases in government expenditures would set off a longer lasting price-wage-price spiral.

Similarly, a substantial inflation is not likely to result from changes in the propensity to consume, the demand for money, imports, or exports. Changes in the marginal efficiency of investment are a more controversial issue. Many Keynesians believe that the marginal efficiency of investment is highly unstable, that occasionally there occur prolonged and substantial investment booms that are inflationary. All in all, by far the most likely suspect in inflation is the supply of money. First, increases in the money supply have a powerful effect on income; in the long run a 10 percent rise in the money supply leads to a 10 percent higher price level. Second, the money growth rate does vary substantially, with the variations sometimes persisting for fairly long periods, so that changes in the money supply seem large enough to be responsible for inflation. Third, the empirical evidence demonstrates a close correlation between movements in money and in prices. It is therefore not surprising that

Milton Friedman has said that "inflation is always and everywhere a monetary phenomenon." By no means are all economists willing to go that far, but just about all would agree that a *major* inflation requires an increase in the money supply.

Is Money *the* Cause?

Although agreeing that major inflations cannot occur without a substantial increase in the money supply, some people are reluctant to say that money is *the* cause of inflation. They argue that attributing inflation to a rise in the money supply is superficial. Suppose, for example, that oil prices double and that the Fed increases the money supply to avoid the unemployment that would otherwise occur as prices rise. Shouldn't one blame the resulting inflation on OPEC rather than on the faster growth of the money supply? Similarly, suppose that those who are relatively more concerned about unemployment than about inflation obtain greater political power. The Fed then becomes more expansionary, and inflation results. It is hard to imagine that the great inflation of the 1970s could have been nearly as severe had the public, and hence the politicians, been much more strongly opposed to inflation. Isn't it therefore superficial to say that the inflation is caused by a rise in the money growth rate?

Not really. All causes, except the "First Cause," have other causes that underlie them. When someone explains why he got wet, he says that it is raining, not that there is a high pressure area to the south or that gravitational forces cause clouds to shed moisture. *If* inflation occurs whenever the money growth rate is high, why not say that the high money growth rate is the cause? This has the advantage of pointing to a single cause that underlies all, or most, inflations. By contrast, at various times different factors explain why the money growth was so high. A theory that points to the same cause in a wide variety of cases is (if correct) preferable to one that explains each case by a different factor. Moreover, the money growth rate is a useful variable to focus on because the Fed can control it.

POLICIES TO FIGHT INFLATION

One way to fight inflation is to reduce aggregate demand. The trouble is that the initial effect of a reduction in demand is to decrease output and employment more than prices, unless this anti-inflation policy is highly credible, or wages are flexible. In October 1979 the Fed changed to a more restrictive policy that, together with the cessation of unfavorable supply shocks, brought the inflation rate (as measured by the GNP deflator) down from 9.7 percent in 1981 to 3.8 percent in 1983. But the unemployment rate rose from 5.8 percent in 1979 to 9.5 percent in 1982 and 1983, a terrible cost in lost output and human misery.

An alternative type of policy, **income policy,** tries to avoid this cost. Recall the Phillips curve, equation $dw = a - bu + fdp^e + cq$. Instead of operating on the unemployment term, incomes policy focuses on the price-expectations term. Much of inflation is defensive because those involved—employees raising their wage demands and firms raising their prices—expect others to do so, and don't want to be left behind. It is like everyone at a parade standing up to see better. It seems obvious that a prohibition of excessive wage and price increases could stop inflation at relatively little cost.

One form of incomes policy is therefore outright wage and price controls. This was last tried by President Richard Nixon in 1971, and had previously been used during the Korean War and both world wars. Wage and price controls are the most rigid form of incomes policy. At the other extreme is "jawboning," that is, the president urging wage and price settlers to behave "responsibly" and to keep the public interest in mind. Inbetween are such policies as taking government contracts away from firms that raise prices excessively and offering tax cuts to firms that stay within certain wage and price guidelines. Incomes policy is sometimes formulated as a "social contract" whereby unions agree to settle for lower wage increases in exchange for price restraints by firms, or for a full-employment policy, etc. Such social contracts are more applicable in many European countries that have a higher degree of unionization than in the United States.

Incomes policies suffer from three major defects. First, a mild incomes policy, such as jawboning, may have little impact. There is much dispute about whether it worked when Presidents John F. Kennedy and Lyndon B. Johnson tried it. Second, a much stronger policy, such as wage and price controls, interferes with resource allocation. We rely on relative prices to guide production. Resources flow to where they are needed mainly because prices rise in those sectors. By prohibiting price increases, price controls eliminate this incentive to shift resources.

Third, suppose that the inflation resulted from money growing too rapidly. If money continues to grow at a high rate, real balances become more and more excessive, and tend to drive up prices in those sectors in which prices are not controlled. Worse than that, eventually, when the controls are taken off, these large balances cause a price explosion. The obvious answer is that controls should be accompanied by a monetary policy that is restrictive enough to eliminate the inflationary fuel. But this probably won't happen. Once controls are in place it is tempting to continue with expansionary macro policies so that unemployment will fall.[1]

INDEXING: GOOD OR BAD?

Many union contracts contain a so-called "COLA" clause that automatically adjusts wages at least part of the way for changes in the cost of living. Some

---

[1] A seemingly technical detail makes it particularly hard to combine an incomes policy with a restrictive monetary policy. If wages are held down it is only fair that interest rates should be held down too. But how can this be done? One possibility is to limit the demand for loanable funds by a system of credit allocation; but, as will be discussed in Chapter 22, credit allocation is cumbersome and has many disadvantages. A tempting alternative is to depress interest rates temporarily by increasing the money growth rate. In this way incomes policy ultimately increased the inflation rate during the 1970s.

economists have advocated indexing all wages. This would have two major advantages. First, it would make it much easier to curb inflation. Little unemployment would be generated by an anti-inflation policy, because a rate of inflation lower than was anticipated when labor contracts were signed would not result in higher real wages, and hence in lower employment. Second, indexing would eliminate the unwarranted gains and losses that result from errors in anticipating the inflation rate.

But indexing also has its problems. Suppose that a decline in productivity growth, or some other supply shock, reduces output. This requires a cut in someone's real income. But with indexation protecting the real wages of most employees, those whose income are not indexed would have to bear all the loss. Moreover, when an inflation gets started indexation makes it worse, because it makes wages respond much more readily to the inflation.

THE CAUSES OF UNEMPLOYMENT

The obvious explanation of a rise in unemployment is that aggregate demand has fallen. Any of the variables that determine aggregate demand, such as the marginal efficiency of investment or the propensity to consume, may be responsible. Unemployment, unlike inflation, does not require a continuous change in these variables. For example, if government expenditures fall and stay at the lower level, unemployment rises and remains high for some time.[2]

Supply shocks can also result in unemployment. If productivity falls firms demand less labor at the old real wage. Prolonged absolute declines in productivity are rare. But if productivity rises at a slower rate than was assumed when wage contracts were signed, then real wages will rise too fast, and employment will fall. A rise in import prices can have a similar effect. To protect their real wages as prices rise, workers demand a higher money wage. But since there has been no offsetting increase in their productivity, employers hire fewer workers at that wage. In the United States these supply-side factors probably do not result in much unemployment, in part because unions are weak and in part because unions tend to focus on money wages rather than on real wages. But in Europe workers stress real wages more and unions are stronger. There, excessive real wage demands are a more plausible, though still disputed, cause of substantial unemployment.

In one sense nearly all unemployment can be blamed on excessive *money* wage demands. Imagine that money wages are completely flexible, with unemployed workers willing to work for whatever wage they can get. Suppose that in such an economy the money stock drops by 10 percent. With aggregate demand falling, unemployment develops, but after wages and prices have fallen by 10 percent this unemployment disappears. In one sense it can be said that nearly all unemployment is voluntary since most of the unemployed could get jobs at *some* wage. This does not mean that those who say that they are

---

[2] Unemployment and inflation differ in this respect because unemployment refers to the level of a variable, whereas inflation refers to the change in a variable, the price level.

unemployed are lying—it is just that they are leaving out part of the story. They should not say that they cannot find work, but that they cannot find work at a wage they consider to be reasonable.

Most economists, and probably most other people, treat this as a semantic quibble. They talk of unemployment when someone cannot find work at a wage reasonably related to her previous wage, her experience, and her training. Moreover, they point out, minimum-wage legislation limits the ability of workers to accept lower wages.

New Classical Theory and Real Business Cycles

All the same, some economists, called "new classical," believe that the possibility of obtaining employment at a lower wage forces one to look at unemployment in a new way. They maintain that since people are rational utility maximizers they will enter into all contracts that are mutually beneficial. Since unemployment could be eliminated by an agreement to cut wages, those who say they are unemployed are simply people who have decided, perhaps rightly, that their time is better spent searching for a job at a higher wage than working for a lower wage. Their so-called "search employment" is just a particular form of unpaid self-employment.

How do the new classical economists account for the observed fluctuations in output and employment? They explain such fluctuations as being primarily due to a temporary confusion of relative and absolute prices. When demand rises a firm notices that its sales are up, but does not know whether this is due to a rise in aggregate demand or to a shift of demand toward it at the expense of other firms. Suppose that it assumes that it is a shift in demand when it is really a rise in aggregate demand. To take advantage of the fact that it can now sell its product for more, it raises output. But since what has really happened is that aggregate demand has increased, other firms also raise their prices. After some time each firm notices that it is no better off than before; all that has occurred is that the price level has risen. Hence, firms cut their outputs and employment back again. Similarly, if aggregate demand falls firms initially reduce their outputs until they realize that it is aggregate demand, and not the relative demand for their products, that has fallen, so that their relative prices are unchanged.

Some economists attribute business cycles primarily to changes in supply conditions. Suppose that productivity falls or import prices rise. Workers do not realize that real wages have to fall to maintain employment, and do not lower their real-wage demands. Unemployment occurs.

Most economists do not accept the new classical theory. They argue that wages and prices are much less flexible than the "new classicals" believe. Even when they can get enough labor at a lower wage, firms may be unwilling to cut wages because their employees would resent this. Morale and productivity would fall.

SUMMARY

1 Inflation is a persistent and significant rise in the price level. Inflations range from creeping inflations to hyperinflations. Until the 1950s it seemed that the U.S. economy was immune from peacetime inflations. This is no longer so.
2 Some unemployment is needed for efficiency, and if unemployment falls below the NAIRU, accelerating inflation results. Eventually the Phillips curve becomes vertical, and hence it does not provide a menu of trade-offs.
3 The aggregate demand curve, drawn in the price–real output plane, is downward sloping. The aggregate supply curve slopes upward.
4 Prices rise if either the aggregate demand curve or the aggregate supply curve shifts upward. But unless these shifts persist they do not cause inflation. The most likely culprit in inflation is the money supply. Supply shocks are more likely to account for high prices than for inflation.
5 Inflation can be fought either by reducing aggregate demand or by incomes policy. Reducing aggregate demand causes unemployment. There are reasons to question whether incomes policies would work.
6 Declines in aggregate demand create unemployment, but would not do so if wages were flexible downward. Supply shocks too can create unemployment.

QUESTIONS AND EXERCISES

1 Look at data on the unemployment rate and on inflation (shown in the *Economic Report of the President*) for the last ten years. Do they describe a stable Phillips curve?
2 Discuss: "The Phillips curve allows the government to select its preferred menu of inflation and unemployment."
3 The United States used to be immune to peacetime inflation. This is no longer true. Why do you think this is?
4 Explain why the aggregate demand curve drawn in the price–real income plane slopes downward while the aggregate supply curve slopes upward.
5 Discuss whether supply shocks can cause inflation. Are they likely to?

FURTHER READING

FRISCH, HELMUT. "Inflation Theory 1963–1975: A 'Second Generation' Survey," *Journal of Economic Literature*, 15 (December 1977):1289–1317. A useful survey of an extensive literature.

LAIDLER, DAVID, AND JOHN PARKIN. "Inflation—A survey," *Economic Journal*, 85 (December 1975):810–23. A thorough discussion.

MCCULLOCH, HUGH. *Money and Inflation.* New York: Academic Press, 1975. A well-written and simple account.

WEINER, STUART. "The Natural Rate of Unemployment: Concepts and Issues," *Economic Review*, Federal Reserve Bank of Kansas City, 71.

PART FOUR

MONETARY POLICY

CHAPTER 19

The Goals of Monetary Policy

Monetary policy shares the goals of general macroeconomic policy: high employment, price stability, exchange-rate stability, and a high rate of economic growth. But although monetary policy therefore has the same overall goals as fiscal policy it also has some specialized goals. These are interest-rate stability, an acceptable distribution of the burdens of restrictive monetary policy, and the prevention of large-scale bank failures and financial panics.

THE GOALS

We will first discuss these goals individually, and then take up the question of whether they are consistent in the sense that it is possible to meet all of them at the same time, or whether we have to sacrifice one to obtain another.

High Employment

High employment is an obvious goal. Regardless of whether one focuses on the loss of output or on the human misery involved, practically everyone prefers high employment to large-scale unemployment. But an employment goal does raise serious issues. One is its definition. Obviously, it does not mean zero percent unemployment. There is always some *frictional unemployment* that results from workers leaving one job to look for a better one, from new entrants to the labor force starting out as unemployed, and from a geographical or occupational mismatch of workers and jobs. A certain level of unemployment is optimal for economic efficiency.

Moreover, even if we did know the appropriate level of unemployment, we do not have a good statistical measure of actual unemployment. The unemployment data, which are gathered by monthly household surveys, are polluted in several ways. On the one hand, they understate the true extent of unemployment because they count only those looking for work, thus leaving out those who have ceased to hunt for a job because they believe that there is little chance of finding one. Second, part-time workers, who would prefer to work full time, are not counted as partially unemployed. One the other hand, if a worker loses a job, the spouse might then look for work too, so that the data count two people as unemployed, although the family is really looking for only one job. In addition, in some states people on welfare have to look for work, though presumably a number of them are not employable. Moreover, some people who work surreptitiously because they evade taxes, or are engaged in illegal activities, might classify themselves as unemployed in the household surveys. Beyond these statistical problems, the number of people actually unemployed also depends on the level and duration of unemployment-compensation payments. If these payments are high and obtainable for a long time, then workers have an incentive to look for good jobs rather than taking the first one that comes along. This is not necessarily bad. For example, if a skilled tool and die maker takes a job as a janitor when, with a few days' more search he could have located a job in his trade, there is a clear loss in national income. But in other cases unemployment compensation extends the period of unemployment unduly.

Thus, not only do we not know what the proper level of unemployment is, we also cannot measure current unemployment accurately. This means that it is sometimes difficult to decide whether unemployment is too high or too low. Obviously, this is not always the case. In the 1930s, when at times over a quarter of the nonfarm labor force was unemployed, there was little doubt the unemployment rate exceeded its desirable level, but this is much less clear if the unemployment rate is, say, 5 or 6 percent. However, even a 5 percent level of unemployment may well be undesirable in the sense that with some better manpower programs, such as job training and broader and better information on job vacancies, the appropriate level of frictional unemployment could be reduced.

So far we have talked about the optimal unemployment rate in terms of that level of unemployment that balances, at the margin, the social loss from having idle labor with the loss from not being able to find the workers needed to increase production. But probably a more relevant consideration is that a reduction in unemployment below the NAIRU raises the inflation rate. Hence, many economists define the optimal unemployment rate as the NAIRU. Unfortunately, it is hard to determine whether this rate is, say, 5 percent, 5½ percent, or even 6 percent.

Price Stability

The next goal, price stability, may *seem* an obvious one, but it is far from obvious. Consider an economy in which prices have been rising at a rate of, say, 100 percent per year for the last fifty years, and everyone knows with certainty that the inflation rate will continue to be 100 percent. What damage does this inflation do? It does not redistribute income because all wages and all contracts, as well as tax laws and accounting procedures, are adjusted for it. For example, if productivity is growing at a 2 percent rate, wages rise at a 102 percent rate each year, and the interest rate is, say, 103 percent instead of 3 percent. Such a fully anticipated inflation imposes only three types of losses. First, there is the bother and inconvenience of having to change price tags and catalogue prices frequently, and, furthermore, the buyer's knowledge about what is an appropriate price of a certain good is quickly outdated. Second, since prices cannot be changed continually, they will be out of equilibrium for the presumably short periods between price changes. Third, inflation creates an incentive to hold too little currency because currency holdings lose their real value without having the compensation of the higher nominal interest rate that other assets have. Hence, people are put to the inconvenience of continual trips to get currency. Yet this seems a rather minor problem.

But the inflations we actually experience are not fully anticipated, and our economy is not fully indexed. Thus, nominal rather than real interest income is taxed. For example, if the interest rate is 12 percent and the inflation rate is 10 percent, a taxpayer in the one-third marginal tax bracket receives an after-tax real rate of return of -2 percent ($12 \times \frac{2}{3} - 10$). At the same time, borrowers are allowed to deduct too much as interest payments from taxable income. In addition, depreciation that firms are allowed to deduct against taxable income is too low because it is based on original cost rather than on replacement cost. This raises their tax liability. Perhaps largely for this reason, perhaps for others, inflation lowers stock prices.

Since inflation affects the tax burdens faced by corporations to varying degrees it also leads to a socially inefficient allocation of investment funds, because after-tax profits become a less reliable guide to the true productivity of capital in various industries.

Another effect of unanticipated inflation is its impact on the distribution of income and wealth. Obviously, it hurts creditors, and hence the retired, and benefits debtors. In addition, it may help or hurt wage earners depending upon whether or not wages lag behind prices. All in all, the evidence suggests that in recent years inflation has helped the poor, thus making the distribution of income less unequal. But, this may not hold true for all inflations.

Regardless of what inflation does to the distribution of income among different income classes, it generates a substantial income redistribution *within* each income class, since some households are net borrowers and others net lenders. This type of redistribution is surely deplorable. It is no more equitable than would be a tax on everyone who was born on an even-numbered day. To anyone genuinely concerned with equity, this redistribution must be a major loss from inflation.

Another loss from inflation is that it creates uncertainty and insecurity. Households can no longer plan confidently for the distant future since they do not know what their fixed dollar assets will then be worth in real terms. More generally, people have been taught the virtue of saving for a rainy day. But such prudent behavior is punished rather than rewarded by unanticipated inflation. This is likely to cause people to lose faith in the government and in the equity and reasonableness of social conditions in general. While this effect of inflation cannot be quantified, it may well be a major, perhaps even *the* major, disadvantage of inflation. Thus in the 1979 *Economic Report of the President* President Carter wrote:

The corrosive effects of inflation eat away at the ties that bind us together as a people. One of the major tasks of a democratic government is to maintain conditions in which its citizens have a sense of command over their own destiny. During an inflation individuals watch in frustration as the value of last week's pay increase or last month's larger social security check is steadily eroded over the remainder of the year by a process that is beyond their individual control. All of us have to plan for the future. . . . The future is uncertain enough in any event, and the outcome of our plans is never fully within our own control. When the value of the measuring rod with which we do our planning—the purchasing power of the dollar—is subject to large and unpredictable shrinkage, one more element of command over our own future slips away. It is small wonder that trust in government and in social institutions is simultaneously eroded.[1]

Economic Growth

We defer the foreign exchange rate goal until Part 5 and turn now to the growth rate of potential output. There is now much concern that our current rate of growth is low relative to its trend in the postwar period, and relative to that in other countries. This lower growth rate is due to many factors, most of which are beyond the Federal Reserve's control, but the Fed can influence one important determinant of the economic growth rate: investment. A higher rate of investment not only means more capital per worker, but is also an important way in which technological progress comes about, since innovations are often embodied in new equipment. For example, the invention of a new machine does not increase productivity until firms invest by installing it.

One way of raising investment is to keep the real interest rate fairly low. But this is inherently expansionary, and to prevent inflation such a policy would have to be accompanied by a restrictive fiscal policy, that is, by a large government surplus or, more realistically, by keeping the deficit small. This depends, of course, on Congress and the administration, and is beyond the Fed's control. Another way the Fed can raise the rate of investment is by controlling the rate of inflation since the uncertainty created by an unpredictable rate of inflation lowers investment.

Prevention of Widespread Bank Failures and Financial Panics

The prevention of bank failures and panics is in a way not a separate goal, since the main loss resulting from large-scale bank failures is likely to be a depression with massive unemployment. We list it here among the goals just as a reminder of the importance of the Fed's lender of last resort function. American economic history prior to 1934 shows a number of examples of bank failures that resulted in financial panics and depressions. This certainly does not mean that the Fed has to be concerned about every single bank failure, or even about the failure of several banks at the same time. These cases can be safely left to the FDIC. But if somehow banks holding, say, 5 or 10 percent of total bank deposits were in danger of not being able to meet depositors' withdrawals, then it would be the Federal Reserve's job to step in and,

---

[1] Executive Office of the President, *Economic Report of the President.* Washington, D.C.: 1979, p. 7.

through massive open-market operations, provide the banking system with enough reserves (and hence access to currency) to meet depositors' demands. Less dramatically, in the summer of 1982, when there was much concern about large potential bankruptcies and the fragility of the banking system, it was widely believed on Wall Street that the Fed eased policy for that reason. This, of course, cannot be verified.

Interest-Rate Stability

Although the Fed allowed greater fluctuation of interest rates since October 1979, interest rate stability has traditionally been one of its goals. A reason for this is that fluctuating interest rates hurt those who, when interest rates rise, have to sell securities at a loss. Such losses are perceived as inequitable. Moreover, with sharply fluctuating interest rates firms that plan to borrow have to spend time and effort trying to predict the best time to do so, and financial institutions that borrow short and lend long, such as savings and loans, are in trouble. In addition, as will be explained in Chapter 27, interest-rate fluctuations generate fluctuations in exchange rates and thus are disruptive to foreign trade and investment. In general, the Fed is subjected to bitter criticism when interest rates rise sharply.

Sharing the Burden of a Restrictive Policy

This is certainly not a major goal of the Fed, but it does have to be concerned if the main impact of a restrictive policy is felt primarily by a few industries, particularly if these industries have many friends in Congress.

CONFLICT AMONG GOALS

Thus the Fed has many different goals, and its task is greatly complicated by the fact that there are numerous conflicts among them. Hence, it has to estimate the trade-offs and to decide the extent to which it will sacrifice one goal to attain the other.

The conflict between price stability and high employment in the short run has already been discussed in the previous chapter; the conflict between exchange rate stability and the other goals will be discussed in Part 5. Hence, we turn now to the relation of economic growth to price stability and high-employment goals. Since inflation that is not fully anticipated reduces economic growth there is no conflict between high economic growth and the price-stability goal in the long run. But in the short run there may be a conflict. To eliminate or reduce an existing inflation generally requires that unemployment and excess capacity increase. And the more excess capacity firms have, the less is the incentive to invest.

The prevention of widespread bank failures does not clash with the employment goal, but it can, at times, conflict with the price-stability goal, and hence in this way also with the economic growth goal. For example, in 1982 the Federal Reserve called a halt to the severely restrictive policy it had adopted to fight inflation because it was afraid that a financial panic might occur. Admittedly, this situation arises only rarely. Beyond this, bank regulation, by inhibiting financial innovations, also has some, though presumably small, deleterious effects on economic growth.

The relation between price stability and interest-rate stability is very different in the long run and the short run. In the long run there is no conflict between the two: the lower the rate of inflation, the lower is the nominal interest rate, and, similarly, the more erratic the inflation rate the more erratic is the nominal interest rate. But the short run presents a very different picture. Suppose that aggregate demand increases because investment has become more profitable. As firms try to invest more the rate of interest rises. The only way the Fed can postpone this rise (it cannot prevent it permanently) is to allow the quantity of money to increase at a faster rate. But this is obviously inflationary. A similar short-run conflict arises if an inflation is already under way. To stop the inflation the Fed has to cut the money growth rate, which results in temporarily higher interest rates.

Interest-rate stability has some, but probably only a small, effect on the rate of economic growth. But insofar as it changes the inflation rate and the capacity utilization rate it does affect economic growth indirectly in the ways just discussed. Interest-rate stability is helpful in preventing bank failures since a bank can be seriously hurt by the fall in the market value of its security holdings when interest rates rise.

The final goal is minimizing the special burden that monetary policy imposes on particular sectors of the economy. Here, too, one must distinguish between the long run and the short run. In the long run it is an expansionary policy that, by generating inflation, creates special problems for particular sectors of the economy because the health of many of our institutions is predicated more or less on price stability. The problem that thrift institutions face is mainly due to the inflation-induced rise in nominal interest rates. Thus, in the long run, the moderately restrictive monetary policy that is needed to curb inflation is consistent with minimizing distortions. But in the short run such a restrictive policy raises interest rates, and thus hurts sectors like residential construction.

WHAT SHOULD THE FED DO?

This whole problem of conflicts among goals would not arise if the Fed had as many independent tools as it has targets and constraints. But this is not the case. All its major tools operate by changing bank reserves and interest rates, so that in this sense it has but a single tool. Hence it frequently faces a dilemma: some of its goals suggest that it should increase bank reserves, and others that it should reduce them.

One possible solution would be to give the Fed only a single goal, or at least a predominant goal. *If* this is to be done, this should *perhaps* be price stability rather than full employment since a policy that focuses on unemployment could easily be too ambitious, and attempt to reduce the unemployment rate so low that accelerating inflation would result.

But during a substantial inflation, a policy to stabilize prices would probably result in much unemployment for some time. Besides, an overriding price-stability goal would prevent the Fed from taking expansionary action at those times when unemployment is very high, but a supply shock, such as a rising cost of oil, is raising prices. Most economists therefore believe that the Fed should deal with the conflict among its goals in an ad hoc manner, flexibly balancing the gain with respect to one goal against the loss with respect to another goal. In any case, political pressures on the Fed are likely to cause it to undertake such a balancing act. As discussed in Chapter 7, the Fed is not autonomous in its choice of goals.

This raises the next question—what does the Fed actually do? How much importance does it attach to each of the above goals? Unfortunately, this is difficult to determine. The Fed does not issue statements revealing its trade-offs between various goals, nor does it tell us which one it considers the most important.[2] Instead, it tends to deemphasize the conflict between its goals, and sometimes suggests that the achievement of any goal is necessary to attain another. Such an unwillingness to reveal its hard choices is not surprising. If the Fed were to say that it is relinquishing one goal for the sake of the others, the proponents of this goal would react angrily and might join a coalition that would trim its independence. But the reluctance to face conflict among goals is probably more than just a matter of political expedience. A governor who votes to adopt a restrictive policy knowing that it will create substantial unemployment, and hence much misery, would probably feel very uncomfortable about this, particularly since it is not certain that this restrictive policy is really needed. It is much easier for the governor to say to himself or herself that the restrictive policy is needed, both to curb inflation and to prevent greater unemployment subsequently.

The Fed's reluctance to spell out its goals has another great advantage for it. It makes it hard to evaluate its actions since, when accused of failing with respect to one goal, the Fed can frequently point to another goal that, perhaps for reasons having little to do with monetary policy, has been attained. The exasperating task involved in evaluating monetary policy is well exemplified by the following comment of Senator William Proxmire to former Federal Reserve chairman William McChesney Martin:

> I have the greatest respect for your ability, and I think that you are an outstanding and competent person, and everybody agrees with that, but the fact is, that when you try to come down and discuss this in meaningful specific terms, it is like nailing a custard pie to the wall. . . . And frankly, Mr. Martin, without specific goals, criteria, guidelines, it is impossible to exercise any Congressional oversight over you, and I think you know it.[3]

---

[2] Some economists have tried to explain the Fed's behavior by a regression equation in which the dependent variable is some measure of the Fed's actions, such as the growth rate of the base, and the independent variables are factors like the unemployment rate, the inflation rate, and the balance of payments. They have often found that unemployment and the balance of payments variables explain Fed behavior.

[3] Cited in John Culbertson, *Full Employment or Stagnation?* New York: McGraw-Hill, 1964, pp. 154–155.

The problem of determining the Fed's trade-offs between its goals is complicated not only by its reluctance to reveal them, but also by the fact that its
trade-offs probably vary from time to time. Given the great power and influence of the chairman of the Board of Governors, goals may change when a
new chairman takes over. In addition, as pointed out in Chapter 7 the Fed
tends to accept the president's goals, and in general it is influenced by changing political attitudes. In the late 1970s, for instance, the occurrence of double-digit inflation generated a strong constituency for curbing inflation. This
caused—or permitted—the Fed to take a more restrictive stance. On the
whole it *seems* that in the 1950s the Fed was relatively more concerned with
price stability, and that in the early and mid-1970s it placed more emphasis on
employment. In the late 1970s and early 1980s it then focused again on curbing inflation.

Coordination of Monetary and Fiscal Policies

The goals of monetary and fiscal policies overlap since both are macroeconomic stabilization tools. This raises the question whether one can use fiscal policy to ameliorate the problem that the Fed has too many and conflicting goals.
Or, on the contrary, does fiscal policy interfere with monetary policy?

An obvious way in which fiscal policy can support monetary policy is by
taking over part of the general stabilization task, so that monetary policy can
be used in a more moderate manner. If taxes are raised or expenditures are
cut when aggregate demand is excessive, then this reduces the severity of the
restrictive monetary policy that is required to prevent unacceptable inflation.
But fiscal policy cannot help monetary policy in one important way. It cannot
remove the conflict that exists in the short run between price stability and high
employment. Both fiscal and monetary policies operate by changing aggregate
demand, while the price stability–unemployment conflict is inherent in the
way product markets and labor markets react.

Can monetary and fiscal policies be made to share the burden in a way
that uses the comparative advantages of each? One idea might be to make use
of a possible difference in their timing. Unless there is widespread agreement
in Congress, changing taxes and government expenditures takes a long time.
On the other hand, the Fed can change monetary policy fairly rapidly. However, what matters is not just how long it takes to change policy, but also the
lag until the change in policy has its impact on income. When one takes
account of this lag it is not obvious that monetary policy is necessarily faster
acting than fiscal policy.

Another possibility is to use fiscal policy to moderate the loss that a
restrictive monetary policy imposes on some particular sectors. Thus, during
periods of sharply rising interest rates, one tool of fiscal policy—lending by
government credit agencies—has been used to provide additional funds to
thrift institutions. But, on the whole, the idea of employing fiscal and monetary policies together founders on the fact that government tax and expenditure policies usually are not employed as countercyclical tools. Rather,
government expenditures go up when there is a perceived need for additional

government services. Tax rates are raised primarily because government expenditures are going up, or are cut because the public is fed up with high taxes. Countercyclical considerations play only a quite limited role in actual fiscal policy.

The Government Budget Constraint

Fiscal and monetary policies are inevitably related in one way. This is that the government, like everyone else, has a budget constraint. The Treasury must finance its expenditures either from its revenues or by borrowing from someone. But the government, unlike other sectors of the economy, has an apparent "out." It can borrow from itself, that is, from the Fed. As the Treasury sells securities to the public, the Fed can at the same time buy securities from the public, so that the public's holdings of government securities do not increase. In effect, the Fed "lends" to the Treasury. But this "out" has a nasty side to it. As the Fed buys government securities it provides banks with additional reserves, so that the money stock increases. This process is called **monetizing the debt,** and is, of course, inflationary.

Does the Fed monetize increases in the Federal debt? One way it did so —and *perhaps* still does—is by trying to stabilize interest rates. As the Treasury sells more securities interest rates tend to rise, and if the Fed tries to stabilize interest rates it undertakes open-market purchases of government securities to increase the money stock. Some economists believe that, apart from this indirect way via interest-rate stabilization, the Fed, at least in the past, has also monetized part of the Treasury's security sales by increasing its open-market purchases when the Treasury has run a larger deficit.

But, regardless of whether the Fed does monetize deficits, it is obvious that at least at those times when inflation is a serious problem, large deficits complicate the Fed's task. It is therefore not surprising that Federal Reserve chairmen like to lecture both Congress and the administration on the need for fiscal prudence. These lectures also have the advantage of giving the impression that the Fed is a staunch foe of inflation, even if it should, at the same time, be allowing the money stock to grow too fast.

SUMMARY

1 The Fed has several goals—high employment, price stability, economic growth, exchange rate stability, prevention of bank failures, interest-rate stability, and an acceptable distribution of the burden of restrictive policy.
2 Unemployment creates an obvious loss. Inflation creates relatively few problems *if* it is fully anticipated. But if not fully anticipated then it distorts investment, has arbitrary effects on the distribution of income, and creates uncertainty and a feeling of loss of control.
3 There is a potential conflict among goals, but the Fed tends to downplay this conflict and does not spell out its priorities.
4 Fiscal policy and monetary policy share the same goals, but there are serious problems in coordinating them. Government deficits can be monetized. The avoidance of large deficits would make the Fed's task easier.

QUESTIONS AND EXERCISES

1 What are the goals of Federal Reserve policy? Either argue that one of them should not be treated as a serious goal, or argue that there is an additional goal that should be included.
2 Why does the Fed have an interest-rate stabilization goal? Do you think it is important?
3 Describe the problems an inadequate fiscal policy can create for the Fed. Do you think fiscal policy is currently helping or hindering monetary policy?
4 Read through the current *Economic Report of the President* and prepare a statement of the trade-offs between various goals that are either explicit or implicit in it. Do you agree with these trade-offs?

FURTHER READING

BACH, G. L. *Making Monetary and Fiscal Policy.* Washington, D.C.: Brookings Institution, 1971, pp. 3–25. A good discussion of the Fed's goals with emphasis on their evolution.

BLACK, ROBERT. "The Fed's Mandate: Help or Hindrance?" *Economic Review,* Federal Reserve Bank of Richmond, 70 (July/August 1984):3–7. A thoughtful discussion of the multiple-goals problem by a Fed Bank president.

BLINDER, ALAN. "Issues in the Coordination of Monetary and Fiscal Policies," in Federal Reserve Bank of Kansas City, *Monetary Policy Issues in the 1980s.* Kansas City, Mo.: 1983, pp. 3–34. An excellent response to much idle rhetoric.

BURNS, ARTHUR. *The Anguish of Central Banking.* Washington, D.C.: American Enterprise Institute, 1980. An excellent short discussion by a former Fed chairman.

FISHER, STANLEY. "The Benefits of Price Stability," in Federal Reserve Bank of Kansas City, *Price Stability and Public Policy.* Kansas City, Mo.: 1984, pp. 33–50. A good brief survey.

LEVY, MICKEY. "Factors Affecting Monetary Policy in an Era of Inflation." *Journal of Monetary Economics,* 8 (1981):351–373. A statistical analysis of the Fed's goals that brings out the Fed's monetization of government debt.

MAISEL, SHERMAN. *Managing the Dollar.* New York: W. W. Norton, 1973. Provides an excellent "feel" for the pressures under which the Fed operates.

CHAPTER 20

Tools of Monetary Policy

In this chapter we take up the Fed's tools. They can be divided into two groups: the much more important **general controls** that *affect the whole economy,* and some **selective controls** that are *designed to reinforce, or ameliorate, the impact of general monetary policy in specific areas of the economy,* such as the stock market. This distinction between general and selective controls is, however, not watertight; selective controls also have some effects on the rest of the economy.

OPEN-MARKET OPERATIONS

Open-market operations are by far the most important tools of monetary policy. The organization for open-market operations has already been discussed in Chapter 7. The FOMC sends a directive to the account manager (or "Desk") at the New York Federal Reserve Bank who undertakes the actual purchases and sales of securities. He deals not with the general public, but with a small number of security dealers, some of them banks and others specialized wholesalers of government securities. The Desk is in continual contact with them, asking them for bids or offers on securities. It therefore knows the price and the interest rate on these securities at all times, and has good information on money-market conditions, on what the Fed calls "the feel of the market." The Fed does not force anyone to buy or sell securities; it buys or sells at the prices the dealers quote to it.

Paul Meek gives the following description of the operations of the Trade Desk[1]:

> The time is just before noon on the Tuesday before Thanksgiving Day. The place is the eighth floor trading room of the Federal Reserve Bank of New York. The manager of the Federal Reserve System's Open Market Account has made his decision. He tells his second in command to buy about $500 million in United States Treasury bills for immediate delivery.

[1] Paul Meek, *Open Market Operations.* New York: Federal Reserve Bank of New York, 1978, pp. 1–2.

The decision made, the officer-in-charge turns to the ten officers and securities traders who sit before telephone consoles linking them to more than 30 primary dealers in U.S. Government securities. "We're going in to ask for offerings of all bills for cash," he says. Each person is quickly assigned two to four dealers to call.

Joan, a New York Federal Reserve trader, presses a button on her telephone console, sounding a buzzer at the corresponding console of a Government securities dealer.

"Jack," Joan says, "we are looking for offerings of all bills for cash delivery."

Jack replies, "I'll be back in a minute." The salesmen of his firm quickly contact customers to see if they wish to make offerings. Jack consults the partner in charge about how aggressive he should be in offering the firm's own holdings.

Ten minutes later Jack calls back. "Joan, I can offer you for cash $5 million of January 5 bills to yield 5.85 percent—$10 million of January 26 bills at 5.90—$20 million of March 23 bills at 6.05—and $30 million of May 30 bills at 6.14."

Joan says, "Can I have those offerings firm for a few minutes?"

"Sure."

Within minutes the "go-around" is completed. The traders have recorded the offerings obtained from their calls on special preprinted strips. The officer-in-charge arrays the individual dealer offerings on an inclined board atop a stand-up counter. A tally shows that dealers have offered $1.8 billion of bills for cash sale—that is, with delivery and payment that very day.

The officer then begins circling with a red pencil the offerings that provide the best—that is, the highest—rate of return for each issue. The large quotation board facing the open end of the U-shaped trading desk tells him the yields on Treasury bills as they were in the market just before the "go-around" began. An associate keeps a running total of the amounts being bought. When the desired amount has been circled, the individual strips are returned to the traders, who quickly telephone the dealer firms.

"Jack, we'll take the $5 million of January 5 bills at 5.85 and the $30 million of May 30 bills at 6.14 both for cash; no, thanks, on the others," Joan says.

Forty-five minutes after the initial decision, the calls have been completed, and $523 million in Treasury bills purchased. Only the paper work remains. The traders write up tickets, which provide the basic authority for the Bank's government bond department to receive and pay for the specific Treasury bills bought. The banks that handle the dealers' deliveries—the clearing banks—will authorize deductions of the securities from the book entry list of their holdings at the Federal Reserve. In return, they will receive credit to the reserve accounts the banks maintain at the New York Reserve Bank.

The Federal Reserve credits to the dealers' banks immediately adds over $500 million to the reserves of the U.S. banking system.

The Fed is authorized to deal in its open-market operations in U.S. Treasury securities, securities of government agencies such as GNMA (Ginnie May), certain state and local government securities, bankers' acceptances, and so on. But in practice the great bulk of open-market operations is in Treasury securities. Furthermore, most of the transactions are in Treasury bills. This is so because the Fed wants to minimize the extent to which it changes security prices in its open-market operations. Since the market for Treasury bills is extremely large, it can buy or sell a substantial volume without changing their price much. By contrast, if the Fed were to sell an equal volume of, say, twenty-year government bonds, their price could drop more. This would create unwarranted capital losses. Specifically, government security dealers, who hold a large volume of securities relative to their capital, could be seriously hurt. And the Fed is afraid that as a result they might cease to "make a market" in such securities, that is, that they would cease to hold an inventory of them, but would act merely as brokers who bring buyers and sellers together. This would reduce the efficiency of the capital market. Hence, while the Fed from time to time *does* deal in longer term securities, it conducts most of its operations in Treasury bills.

Actually, most open-market operations are not really sales or purchases in the usual sense of the words. The great bulk of "purchases" are done under repurchase agreements, often called **repos,** that is, under an agreement with the "seller" that he will buy the securities back again at a fixed price at a certain date. Similarly, most of the Fed's security sales are done under so-called **reverse repos,** more formally known as matched sale-purchase transactions, with the Fed pledging itself to buy these securities back at a fixed price at a particular time. The reason the Fed uses such repos and reverse repos is that most open-market purchases or sales are intended to affect reverses for only a very short time. By using repos and reverse repos the Fed lets the market know that these transactions will soon be reversed.

Such reversal results from the fact that most open-market operations are "defensive" rather than "dynamic." Dynamic operations are those in which the Fed wants to change the volume of reserves. By contrast, the Fed undertakes defensive operations when it wants to keep reserves constant. To do this it has to undertake open-market operations to offset the impact on reserves of "market factors," discussed in Chapter 11, such as changes in float or currency holdings.

Fluctuations in these market factors generate very large—but temporary—changes in reserves. To stabilize the money market and the supply of money, the Fed tries to offset these changes, except insofar as they happen to go in the direction the Fed wants. To do this the Fed expends considerable effort in predicting the probable behavior of various market factors. In addition, the Fed tries to gauge the overall impact of market factors by obtaining the "feel" of the money market in its contacts with government security dealers. Hence, something that frequently triggers open-market operations is changes in the federal-funds rate as market factors supply or withdraw reserves. Such defensive operations account for the great bulk of open-market operations.

The effect of open-market operations on bank reserves has already been demonstrated in Chapter 11 by means of T accounts.

Advantages of Open-Market Operations

Open-market operations are the prime tool of monetary policy for several reasons. First, the Fed can buy or sell government securities to set the size of reserves as it pleases. This tool is always strong enough to do the job. Second, open-market operations occur at the initiative of the Fed, unlike bank borrowing where the Fed can only encourage or discourage borrowing but has no precise control over the volume involved. Third, open-market operations can be carried out in small steps, very small ones if need be. This allows the Fed to make exact adjustments in reserves. Fourth, open-market operations enable the Fed to adjust reserves on a continuous basis as the federal-funds rate changes, and as it receives new information about the impact of market factors on reserves. Finally, open-market operations are easily reversed.

THE DISCOUNT MECHANISM

The discount mechanism is a device by which institutions that are required to keep reserves with the Fed can borrow from it.[2] It serves several functions. One is to fulfill the Federal Reserve's lender of last resort function. If many depository institutions are short of liquidity, then the discount mechanism has to be supplemented by extensive open-market purchases, but even then the discount mechanism is useful in channeling funds to those institutions that are particularly vulnerable. Second, the discount mechanism provides a way for the Fed to provide temporary liquidity to a particular institution that is in difficulty, such as the Continental Illinois bank discussed in Chapter 3. Third, by changing the discount rate the Fed can encourage or discourage borrowing, and this is one way it can change the volume of reserves.

Borrowing can take the form of "adjustment credit" or "extended credit." The former, which accounts for the bulk of the borrowing, can be done fairly automatically, often over the telephone. It is intended to tide depository institutions over until they can get other funds when they face a sudden liquidity drain, due, for example, to a large deposit loss or a rapid upsurge in loan demand. It is short-term credit only, in fact the largest banks are supposed to repay the next business day. However, banks that have a substantial seasonal pattern in their deposits or lending activities, such as banks in ski areas, can borrow longer term for these seasonal needs.

Extended credit is available under two circumstances. One is if a depository institution faces special difficulties, for example, an extended deposit drain. A second situation is when a large group of depository institutions experiences liquidity strains. Institutions obtaining extended credit have to explain the need in some detail and submit an acceptable plan for restoring their liquidity.

Since, as Figure 20.1 shows, depository institutions can frequently borrow from the Fed at less than prevailing market rates, it is necessary to limit

[2] Discounting is a process for deducting the interest due from the face value of the borrower's promissory note. For example, someone who borrows by discounting receives in exchange for a promise to pay, say, $10,000 next week, not the full $10,000, but only $9,990, the $10 interest being subtracted in advance. Banks normally borrow from the Fed by discounting their own promissory notes (using government securities as collateral), but they can, under certain conditions, instead discount a second time certain promissory notes they have discounted for their customers. Hence the term *rediscounting* is sometimes used.

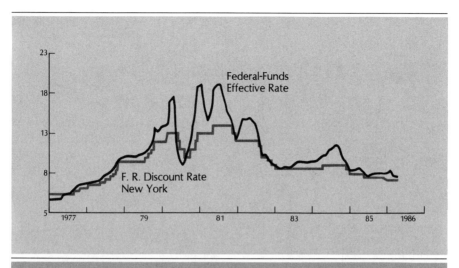

Figure 20.1   The Discount Rate and the Federal-Funds Rate, 1977–1985.
The discount rate is frequently, but by no means always, below the funds rate.
Source: *Federal Reserve Chart Book*, November 1985.

such borrowing. They are not supposed to borrow for the sake of reinvesting the funds at a profit, but only in case of need. The Fed tries to enforce this provision by scrutinizing the activities of borrowing institutions. But the prohibition against borrowing for profit is vague, and hence hard to enforce. For example, suppose a bank buys securities to increase its interest earnings, even though it knows that it may soon experience a deposit outflow. Then, when this deposit outflow does occur, and the bank is short of reserves, it borrows from the Fed. Is it borrowing for "need" or for "profit"? What the Fed *can* enforce is checks over how frequently and for how long a bank borrows. Hence the Fed has set out specific limitations on the quantity and frequency of borrowing by individual banks. All the same, it is hardly surprising that, as Figure 20.2 shows, borrowing increases when the discount rate is low relative to the federal-funds rate.

This does not mean, however, that all banks try to take advantage of any federal-funds rate–discount rate gap. Some may hold off borrowing because they know that if they borrow now the Fed may make it more difficult for them to borrow at a later time, a time when their need to borrow may be greater or the federal-funds rate higher than it is now. Others, as a way of demonstrating their conservative management, are reluctant to borrow from the Fed.

When banks do borrow they are under pressure to repay. The Fed believes that when a borrowing bank obtains additional funds its first priority should be to repay these loans, and not to buy securities or make loans. Whether banks actually behave this way is a disputed issue. It may depend on how much—and for how long—they have borrowed.

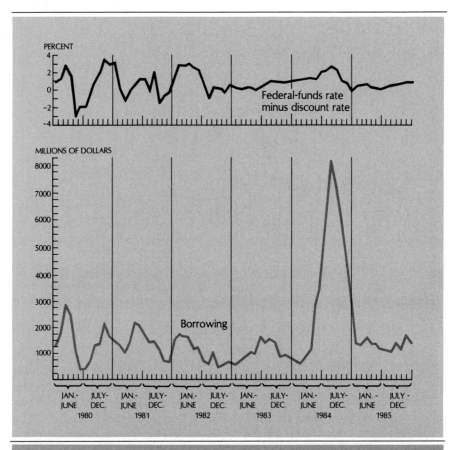

Figure 20.2   Relation of the Discount Rate to the Federal-Funds Rate and Borrowing. The more the federal-funds rate exceeds the discount rate, the more banks borrow. The 1984 spike in borrowings was due to the Continental Illinois crisis. **Source:** *Federal Reserve Bulletin,* February 1986; *Economic Report of the President,* 1985, Table B63, 1986, Tables B66 and B68.

Moreover, one should distinguish between the behavior of individual banks and of the whole banking system. Banks that have made extensive use of the discount privilege in the past may be under strong pressure to repay. But as they do so, and borrow on the federal-funds market instead, the funds rate rises, which then sends other banks that have not borrowed much in the past to the Fed's discount window. Hence, even if the Fed effectively controls borrowing by individual banks, it may exercise less effective control over the total volume of borrowing.

Whether or not a bank treats repayment of Fed loans as its first priority when it obtains additional funds has a bearing on the proper measure of bank reserves. If banks do feel under strong pressure to repay Fed loans, then unborrowed reserves and the unborrowed base are better predictors of how bank deposits will change than are total reserves or the total base.

THE DISCOUNT RATE

The Fed can vary the interest rate it charges borrowing institutions.[3] Thus it can induce banks and thrift institutions to increase or to reduce their borrowing, and can change reserves in this way. But the volume of reserves involved is usually small compared to the change that results from open-market operations.

The inducement to borrow can, and does, vary even if the Fed keeps the discount rate unchanged. If the federal-funds rate rises, say, from 8 percent to $8\frac{1}{2}$ percent, and the discount rate stays put at 8 percent, then banks and thrift institutions have a greater incentive to borrow. Thus discount rate policy becomes more expansionary without the discount rate itself changing. To keep its discount policy constant the Fed would therefore have to change the discount rate frequently. But this creates a problem. Many people interpret a rise in the discount rate as a restrictive policy, even if it is merely a response to rising interest rates on the open market. They argue that by increasing the discount rate the Fed has validated the rise in interest rates by showing that it thinks interest rates will stay high. And a restrictive monetary policy has many critics. Hence, the Fed is sometimes under considerable political pressure not to raise the discount rate. There have been occasions when a president has criticized the Fed for raising the discount rate and Congress has held hearings on the matter.

Reductions in the discount rate have less political fallout, though foreign central bankers and others might interpret a cut in the discount rate as a policy that will cause the dollar to decline in the foreign exchange market. Beyond this, the Fed is reluctant to lower the discount rate because it knows the criticism that will follow if it has to raise it again later on. Thus, the Fed has in actuality only limited freedom to change the discount rate.

If the discount rate is too low relative to the federal-funds rate so that borrowing increases, the Fed can offset the resulting increase in reserves by additional open-market sales. Hence, the main effect of a discount rate that is too low relative to open-market interest rates is that banks make a profit at the Fed's expense by borrowing from it and lending at a higher rate.

The Announcement Effect

In addition to its effect on borrowing, and hence on reserves, the money stock, and on interest rates, a change in the discount rate also affects peoples' expectations to some, albeit to a limited, extent. Not only the financial community, but also the general public read about it in the newspapers. Thus, in November 1978, when President Carter wanted to stop the fall of the dollar on the foreign exchange market by indicating to the world that the United

---

[3] Although we always speak of "the" discount rate there are actually several rates depending on the collateral and the maturity and size of the loan offered. In addition, the Fed charges a higher rate for unusually long term loans, or for unusually large loans due to special circumstances, such as a computer breakdown.

States was ready to adopt a firm anti-inflation policy, he announced that he had asked the Fed to raise the discount rate.

When the Fed raises the discount rate the public *may* interpret this as a sign that the Fed is acting to curb excessive expansion and feel that there is now less reason to fear inflation. It may therefore reduce such inflationary activities as buying ahead to beat price increases or demanding higher wages to offset expected inflation. By contrast, when the Fed cuts the discount rate this may be interpreted as a sign that the Fed is now taking action to moderate a downturn. However, the public *may* also react in just the opposite way, and treat a rise in the discount rate as a sign that the Fed shares its prediction that inflation is becoming a more serious problem.

Unfortunately, the public may also take the change in the discount rate as an indication of the Fed's predictions and policy stance even in those cases where the Fed changes the discount rate only because market rates have changed. All in all, it is far from clear that, on the whole, the announcement effect of a change in the discount rate is helpful. For reasons we will take up in the next chapter, some economists believe that the Fed should tie the discount rate to some open-market rate, making it, say, $1/4$ of 1 percent more than last week's federal-funds rate. This would eliminate the announcement effect of discount rate changes entirely.

The change in the discount rate is not the only tool of monetary policy that has an announcement effect. Changes in reserve requirements are also reported in newspapers. Moreover, the financial and business specialists whose decisions have the important effects are sophisticated enough to know how to interpret open-market operations and changes in the federal-funds rate. Large financial institutions employ economists—many of them former Fed employees—to predict what the Fed will do before the Fed either does it or announces it. "Fed watching" has become an important industry.

RESERVE-REQUIREMENT CHANGES

Congress has given the Fed the power to vary reserve requirements within broad limits (see Table 4.2, p. 51). Raising the reserve requirement affects the money stock in two ways. First, previously excess reserves of banks are now transformed into required reserves. Second, the reserve ratio is one of the components of the denominator in the money multiplier. Hence, a rise in the reserve ratio lowers the money multiplier, and thus lowers the deposit expansion that banks can undertake on the basis of their remaining excess reserves. Given the wide range within which the Fed can change reserve requirements it has a *potentially* powerful tool here. But, despite its strength, the Fed uses the reserve-requirement tool infrequently. For example, the reserve requirements against demand deposits that were in effect in May 1986 were set in December 1976.

SELECTIVE CONTROLS

The tools discussed so far operate on aggregate demand by changing reserves and interest rates, and thus affect the whole economy. By contrast, "selective controls" have their initial impact on specific markets that some economists think are relatively insulated from the effects of overall monetary policy. These controls are also designed to focus on trouble spots where demand may be excessive. One of them, Regulation Q, was discussed in Chapter 5.

Stock Market Credit

The Fed controls the use of credit to purchase stocks listed on stock markets plus certain unlisted stocks. It has set down payments, or *margin,* for stock purchases, limiting the percentage of the purchase price that may be borrowed. The Fed can raise the margin requirement to 100 percent to control a speculative stock market boom. The reason the Fed was given this power in 1934 can be seen by looking back at the situation in the years 1927 through 1929. Then prices were stable or gently falling, but there was a speculative boom in the stock market. The Fed was in a quandary. It had no power to affect the stock market directly. By raising the discount rate or by open-market operations it could have made credit generally less available and, hence, could have limited the purchase of stocks on credit. But with stock prices rising rapidly, it would probably have taken a *very* substantial boost in interest rates to have a significant effect on stock market borrowing. This would have been too restrictive for the rest of the economy. If the Fed had had margin regulations available at that time it could have limited stock market credit without such a restrictive effect on the rest of the economy.

In recent years there has been no great need for margin controls and the Fed has asked Congress to abolish its power over, and responsibility for, stock market credit.

Consumer Credit

During World War II, as well as during the Korean War and briefly in 1948–1949, the Fed set minimum down payments and maximum maturities on loans for consumer durable purchases. During World War II the Fed also controlled mortgage credit in a similar way. Then, in 1980, in part as a way to create confidence in the government's determination to fight inflation, President Carter had the Fed impose a 15 percent reserve requirement on unsecured consumer credit. Whether in response to this, or to the accompanying exhortations to cut spending, consumer credit fell—by much more than the administration intended. Since this came shortly before the onset of a recession it was hardly very helpful. The law permitting the Fed to impose direct controls over consumer credit has since expired.

MORAL SUASION

Another tool is **moral suasion.** This simply means that the Fed *uses its power of persuasion to get banks, or the financial community in general, to behave differently.* Since the interests of the Fed frequently coincide with the long-run self-interest of financial institutions, this form of control may *in certain cases* be more effective than appears at first. For example, during an inflationary expansion, the Fed may urge lenders to be more cautious in their loan policies, and lenders *may* treat this as sound business advice from someone who can forecast business conditions better than they can. To be sure, sometimes banks and other institutions may feel that the stress is more on the "suasion" than on the "moral." For example, in 1965 when the Fed laid down guidelines to limit foreign lending, some banks, at least according to some reports, were afraid that if they ignored the guidelines they might find it more difficult to borrow from the Fed. Admittedly, these fears may have been groundless; for an outsider it is hard to say. But in 1966 the Fed openly informed banks that discounting would be easier for banks that curbed their business loans and made more mortgage loans. The Fed's control over bank holding company activities, and its power to prohibit proposed mergers, has given it another potential threat over recalcitrant banks.[4] Some people think that this gives the Fed a powerful weapon, despite its questionable legal status.

PUBLICITY AND ADVICE

The Fed has many ways of making its opinions known to the general public. The chairman of the Board of Governors frequently testifies before congressional committees, and journalists pay attention to press releases by the Fed, and to the chairman's speeches. In addition, the Board of Governors publishes each month the *Federal Reserve Bulletin,* and the individual Federal Reserve banks publish *Reviews.* Given the high regard in which the business community and its journalists hold the Fed, it has no difficulty in getting its views across to the general public. In these ways it can affect business expectations, and hence actions. In addition, as discussed in Chapter 7, the Fed also acts as an informal economic adviser to the administration.

SUMMARY

1 Open-market operations are the dominant tool of monetary policy. This is a strong tool that can, however, be used in very small steps, and can be used frequently and with predictable effects on reserves. The great bulk of open-market operations are defensive rather than dynamic.

2 Depository institutions that are required to keep reserves with the Fed can borrow from it. Borrowing is supposed to be for need rather than profit. But this rule is difficult to enforce.

3 The Fed can vary the discount rate to influence the volume of borrowing. Borrowing responds to the gap between the federal-funds rate and the discount rate, which means that, to keep borrowing stable, the Fed would have to change the discount rate frequently. But this creates political problems. Discount rate changes, as well as the use of other tools of monetary policy, have an announcement effect.

4 The ability to change reserve requirements gives the Fed a potentially powerful tool. However, the Fed does not use this tool frequently.

5 The Fed also has selective controls over stock market credit and at one time had controls over consumer credit.

6 Moral suasion and publicity and advice round out the tools the Fed has available.

[4] See Edward Kane, "The Central Bank as Big Brother," *Journal of Money, Credit and Banking,* 5 (November 1973): 979–981.

QUESTIONS AND EXERCISES

1 Write an essay describing the use the Federal Reserve has made of its various tools in the last three years. (Information on this is available in the Federal Reserve's Annual Reports.)
2 Why are open-market operations the most important tool of Fed policy?
3 Borrowing from the Fed is supposed to be for need rather than for profit. How is it then that the volume of borrowing is correlated with the gap between the federal-funds rate and the discount rate?
4 Describe the Fed's selective controls.

FURTHER READING

FEDERAL RESERVE BANK OF NEW YORK (Paul Meek). *Open Market Operations.* New York: Federal Reserve Bank of New York, 1969. A lively and authoritative description.

FRIEDMAN, MILTON. *A Program for Monetary Stability.* New York: Fordham University Press, 1960. Chapter 2 is a stimulating discussion of reforms.

MEEK, PAUL. *U.S. Monetary Policy and Financial Markets.* New York: Federal Reserve Bank of New York, 1982. A highly informative and authoritative statement by a senior Fed official.

MELTON, WILLIAM. *Inside the Fed,* Chapters 7 and 8. Homewood, Ill.: Dow Jones–Irwin, 1985. An excellent detailed discussion of open-market operations.

ROTH, HOWARD, and DIANE SEIBERT. "The Effects of Alternative Discount Rate Mechanisms on Monetary Control," *Economic Review* (Federal Reserve Bank of Kansas City), March 1983:16–29. An excellent discussion of the floating discount rate.

CHAPTER 21

The Fed's Targets and Instruments

In the two previous chapters we have discussed the Federal Reserve's ultimate goals and its tools. But these tools do not operate directly on the goals. Primarily, they change bank reserves and the short-term interest rate, and it is a long way from there to high employment and price stability. It takes time until changes in bank reserves and short-term interest rates affect nominal income, and hence employment and prices. Thus, if the Fed changes bank reserves in the wrong direction, or by the wrong amount, by the time it notices that income is moving inappropriately and hence reverses its policy, it is too late; the damage has been done.

Hence, the Fed interposes between its tools and its ultimate goals two sets of intermediate variables. The first set, called **targets**, *consists of variables that have a direct effect on nominal income*, such as the money stock or long-term interest rates. But the Fed cannot reach even these targets directly with its tools. It determines directly and immediately not the money stock, but only the bank reserves and short-term interest rates. It therefore has another set of lower level targets called **instruments** or **proximate targets** that *stand between its tools and its targets*. These are variables like the federal-funds rate and bank reserves that it can affect directly. Figure 21.1 shows the relation between the Fed's goals, targets, instruments, and tools.

To illustrate, suppose that the Fed wants nominal income to grow by, say, 7 percent. What open-market operations should it undertake? Assume it believes that a 7 percent increase in nominal income requires a 6 percent increase in the money stock, which in turn requires a 6¼ percent increase in unborrowed reserves. The Fed now undertakes open-market operations that raise unborrowed reserves by 6¼ percent. But it turns out that the money stock is growing not at the predicted 6 percent rate, but at an 8 percent rate. Something has gone wrong. With money growing too fast income will probably rise too much, and the Fed should now reverse its open-market operations until money growth is back at the 6 percent rate that its model says is consis-

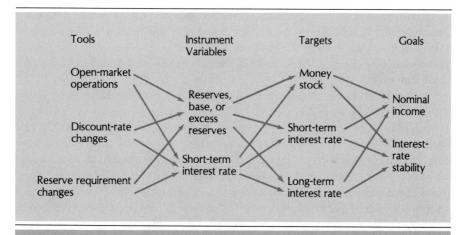

Figure 21.1 Relation between Federal Reserve Tools and Goals. The Fed's tools are related to its goals through instrument variables and target variables. The short-term rate appears as a long-run target as well as an instrument because it affects certain types of investment. It is also a goal variable if the Fed is concerned about interest-rate stability.

tent with the desired 7 percent growth rate of nominal income. After all, it is not open-market operations per se, but the resulting changes in the money stock and the interest rate that affect income. In reversing its open-market operations the Fed is using the money stock as its *target* and is setting its tools with a view to this target rather than focusing directly on its ultimate goal.

By using such targets and instruments it can make midcourse corrections if the incoming data tell it that the economy is departing from the path charted out for it. By contrast, if the Fed were to aim directly at its nominal income target it would not be able to make these midcourse corrections because data on the way its policy is affecting income are available only with a much longer lag than are the money-stock data. This does not *necessarily* mean that the use of targets and instruments is beyond criticism. Later on in this chapter we will discuss some alternatives, in particular focusing directly on income.

TARGET VARIABLES

The choice of a target, or intermediate target as it is sometimes called, is a crucial step in formulating monetary policy, since different target variables frequently tell the Fed to do very different things. For example, the interest-rate target may tell it to adopt an expansionary policy, while the money-stock target tells it to follow a restrictive policy. The selection of the proper targets is a major issue in monetary policy.

Criteria for Target Variables

To be a good target for monetary policy a variable, such as the interest rate, or the money stock, must meet four criteria: measurability, controllability, relatedness to the goal variables, and administrative and political feasibility.

The measurability criterion implies two things. First, accurate data must be available quickly. Unless the Fed can tell where it is relative to the target, it does not know what it has to do to attain this target. Second, the Fed should know which measure of the variable it should use. Should it look at *M-1* or *M-2*, at short-term or at long-term interest rates?

The second criterion for a target variable is controllability. Unless the Fed has a reasonable chance of achieving, or at least approximating, its target, having the target does not do much good. For example, suppose that the Fed would use as its target changing business expectations. This target is certainly related to its nominal income goal, but there is not enough that the Fed can do to affect expectations. Hence, changing expectations is not a useful target. Unrealistic targets are not just unhelpful, but also make for sloppy policy; if a target is not achievable there seems to be little purpose in even trying very hard to reach it. (The use of unattainable targets does, however, provide a bureaucracy—or for that matter, all of us—with a wonderful excuse for failure.)

The third criterion, relatedness, is what using a target variable is all about. The only reason why the Fed uses a target is precisely because it believes that achieving the proper value for this target variable will result in it attaining, or at least coming close to, its ultimate goals. For example, suppose that the money stock had no effect on nominal income; why then should the Fed care whether it is growing at a 2 percent or a 20 percent rate? The final criterion, administrative and political feasibility, relates to the extent to which the Fed can carry out its policy.

Potential Targets

There are three leading contenders for the role of intermediate target. They are the money stock, interest rates, and a credit or debit variable. The Fed has to make a choice. If it wants to aim precisely at one of these targets it must usually relinquish control over the other two. Suppose, for example, that the Fed brings about a particular money supply. To make the public willing to hold exactly this amount of money requires a particular interest rate. And if the Fed prefers a different interest rate this is unfortunate; there is nothing it can do about it. If it wants a different interest rate it can reach that interest-rate target only by relinquishing its money-stock target, and giving the public the money stock it wants to hold at *that* interest rate. In the short run (until income and hence the demand-for-money curve have changed) the public's existing demand curve for money tells us the interest rate that corresponds to each particular quantity of money demanded, and the Fed must settle for a combination of money stocks and interest rates that lies on this demand curve. A similar thing applies to bank credit. If the Fed selects a particular interest rate the quantity of bank credit outstanding at that interest rate depends upon the public's demand for bank credit, and not on the Federal Reserve's wishes. And a credit target also implies a specific money stock, and vice versa.

Hence, the Fed must choose to concentrate on only a single target variable, or else it must straddle by using a broad enough range for its targets, so that within this range two or more targets are consistent. This is illustrated in

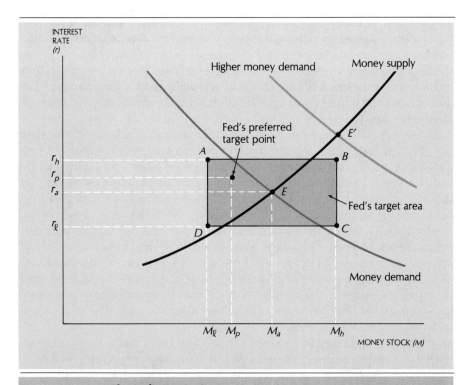

Figure 21.2   The Fed's Target Range. Point D is the lowest combination of the money stock (M_ℓ) and the interest rate (r_ℓ) acceptable to the Fed. Point B is the highest combination (M_h, r_h) acceptable to the Fed. The actual money stock is M_a, and the actual interest rate is r_a, producing an equilibrium point E. The Fed prefers a money stock of M_p and an interest rate of r_p, not quite the true equilibrium but still in the target area. If money demand were higher, equilibrium would be E', meaning that the Fed would have to either abandon its preferred money stock and interest rate or else widen the target area.

Figure 21.2, where the ranges set for the interest-rate target and the money-stock target (shown by the rectangle $ABCD$) are broad enough so that, given the money demand curve, r_p and M_p are consistent. And at times, as illustrated by the higher money demand curve, even a broad range around the target points may not suffice to make two target ranges consistent. In such cases the Fed has to make a choice, or else broaden the range.

With this background, let us now see how well the potential target variables meet the criteria. We will first discuss the choice between the money stock and the interest rate.

Measurability. In Chapter 9 we discussed the inaccuracies in the early estimates of the money stock, and it is these early estimates that the Fed has to work with. In addition, there is the problem of whether to use *M-1* or *M-2*. This depends on which of these measures is more closely related to income, and how well the Fed can control them. Unfortunately, the empirical evidence does not give unequivocal answers to these questions.

But however severe the measurement and conceptual problems are for the money stock, many—though certainly not all—economists believe that they are just as bad, if not worse, for the interest rate. First, the term "the interest rate" as used in economic theory is a theoretical term referring to the weighted average of all the interest rates at which borrowing takes place. But the interest rates recorded by our data do not cover all of these rates. They include mainly the interest rates charged on public markets. For example, they do not cover the imputed interest rates that firms charge themselves on internally generated funds.

Second, some of the recorded rates are not measured in the appropriate way. For instance, while the rate on government securities is measured precisely, this is not true of interest rates charged on bank loans. The data on bank interest rates fail to take into account certain costs of borrowing, such as the need to keep compensating balances, or the various restrictions that a bank imposes on the borrowing firm. More generally, the cost of borrowing —which is what affects investment decisions—contains much more than just the interest rate. The more a firm borrows now the smaller is the additional amount it can borrow in the future if it suddenly needs funds. Moreover, the more it borrows the greater is the proportion of its earnings that it is required to pay to its lenders. A relatively small drop in its revenues may therefore cause a firm that has borrowed a great deal to go bankrupt. The data do not pick up these costs of borrowing.

Third, as discussed in Chapter 4, banks and other lenders ration credit, so that for many borrowers the interest rate is of only limited relevance. Suppose, for example, that the interest rate is constant, but that credit becomes tighter, so that a firm that was previously a marginal borrower is now rationed out of the market. In one sense the interest rate for this firm has now become infinite, but this has no effect on the published interest-rate data.

Fourth, even if we had accurate data on interest rates charged on all borrowing, and if there were no capital rationing, there would still be the problem of how to combine the observed plethora of interest rates into a single weighted average that represents *the* interest rate. What weights are to be given, for example, to the Treasury-bill rate, to the rate on twenty-year bonds, and to the five-year rate? The actually observed volume of borrowing at each rate does not provide a meaningful set of weights, because in deciding how much importance to attach to the rise in any particular interest rate, one should look at the amount of borrowing that is choked off by this increase in the interest rate, and not at the amount of borrowing that occurs.

Fifth, what motivates investment decisions are *after-tax* yields and costs. If the corporate tax rate is 30 percent, a 15 percent interest rate represents an after-tax cost of only 10 percent. Unfortunately, it is not easy to determine what the applicable tax rate is. For firms with no income against which to write off costs, the relevant tax rate is zero, and a 20 percent before-tax rate is also a 20 percent after-tax rate.

But the most serious difficulty results from the distinction between the nominal and the real interest rate. Obviously, our data recorded only the nominal rate. But what is relevant for most expenditure decisions is the *expected* real rate of interest. Hence, unless we know the price expectations of borrowers we do not know how to interpret a given nominal rate. For example, if the nominal rate is 9 percent, this is an expected real rate of 4 percent if people think prices will rise at a 5 percent rate, but is only an expected real rate of 2 percent if they think prices will rise at a 7 percent rate. Thus an error in estimating the public's price expectations leads in this example to an error in estimating the expected real interest rate that is equal to 100 percent of the lower of the two rates.

The significance of having to estimate the expected real interest rate from data on the nominal interest rate varies from time to time. In a period when prices are stable, and have been stable for a long time, it is not significant because then one can assume that the public expects prices to be stable, so that the nominal rate and the expected real rate coincide. But in a period of high and variable inflation rates this is not so.

Controllability. The second criterion for a monetary target is controllability. There is no question that in the long run, say, over a period of a year or two, the Fed can reach or come close to its money-stock target. But the critical question is whether the Fed can do so in the short run. In a business-cycle context a year is a long time. The median contraction in postwar cycles has lasted only eleven months.

If changes in reserves had a rapid effect on the rate at which the money-stock is growing, then the Fed's task would be much simpler. If money is growing too slowly it could simply inject more reserves, and adjust the amount of reserves to get precisely the money growth rate it wants. But, unfortunately, there is a significant lag between changes in reserves and money growth. This creates two problems for the Fed. First, it obviously slows the impact of the Fed's policy on income. Second, suppose that the Fed injects additional reserves to raise *M-1* by, say, $1 billion with the expectation that in the first month *M-1* would grow by $200 million. It now observes that *M-1* grew by only $100 million in the first month. Should it then conclude that the money multiplier is lower than it believed and inject additional reserves, or should it assume that it merely underestimated the lag in the response of money to reserves, and hence not inject additional reserves?

Moreover, the existence of a substantial lag in the money creation process means that if the Fed wants to attain its money target right away it will have to allow reserves to overshoot at first. For example, suppose that the Fed wants to raise the money stock by $1 billion within the first month, but that in this time only 10 percent of the effect of an open-market operation on the money stock takes place. If so, the Fed will have to buy a volume of securities that would raise the money stock ultimately by $10 billion. Subsequently it will have to reverse itself sharply and adopt the opposite policy to offset the major part of the first policy when this first policy begins to have its main effects. Since major changes in bank reserves tend to bring about large changes in the federal-funds rate, the Fed does not like such erratic policies.

This brings us to a major issue in money-stock control. Many critics of the Fed, particularly monetarists, argue that the Fed could control the money stock much better *if* it were willing to let interest rates fluctuate more.

Turning from the general to the specific, it is obvious that the Fed cannot control the money growth rate with any degree of accuracy on a week-to-week basis. Quite apart from the just-discussed lag in response of money to changes in the base, the measurement problems described in Chapter 9 imply that the Fed's error in estimating the money stock is large, probably much larger than the change the Fed is trying to bring about in that week. Suppose, for example, that the Fed thinks that the money stock is $200 million too low. Even if it succeeds in raising it by exactly $200 million, due to measurement errors the money stock may be $300 million above (or below) what the Fed wants. Fortunately, neither week-to-week nor month-to-month changes in the money supply have much impact on income.

Year-to-year changes in the money stock—which certainly do matter for the behavior of income—can be controlled much better. Within a year most of the response of the money stock to changes in the base has taken place, erratic fluctuations have had a chance to wash out, and measurement errors are small when compared to the, say, $25 billion by which the Fed wants to change the money stock over the year rather than to the corresponding $500 million change it is trying to bring about during a week. Hence, as Table 9.3 showed on a year-to-year basis, the standard error of the money growth rate is fairly small (.8 percent for *M-1*). Some monetarist critics of the Fed believe that it could, if it really wanted, hit its money targets more accurately than Table 9.3 suggests.[1]

Can the Fed attain any specific interest-rate target? At one time this was questioned on the argument that at a low enough interest rate the liquidity-preference curve is infinitely elastic. Few economists worry about this anymore. But, there is another limitation on the Fed's ability to lower interest rates. As discussed in Chapter 13, a fall in the rate of interest generates a rise in income and prices that raises the interest rate again. Is this a serious limitation on the Federal Reserve's power? To the extent that it is an increase in real income that raises the interest rate back toward its previous level the Fed has nothing to worry about, because presumably it initially lowered the interest rate precisely to obtain this increase in real income. However, if the Phillips curve is vertical, and all the increase in nominal income stimulated by the lower interest rate is a rise in prices, then the Fed is obviously not achieving its goal of raising real income. But the problem then is not that the Fed has no power over the interest rate, but rather that the Fed's target, a rise in output, is unattainable, at least by conventional macro policies.

Even if the Phillips curve is not vertical, there is another limitation on the Fed's ability to lower interest rates. This is that, besides its income-stabilization goal, it also has another goal, exchange-rate stability. As we will explain in Part 5, if interest rates fall this reduces the value of the dollar on the foreign exchange market.

So far, we have talked about the interest rate without specifying what interest rate it is. Since the Fed conducts its open-market operations primarily in short-term securities, its initial impact is on the short-term interest rate. The effects on the long-term or intermediate-term interest rates may be much attenuated and late to arrive. Many, though by no means all, economists

---

[1] Thus James Johannes and Robert Rasche believe that the Fed could hit its *M-1* target with a monthly error of 1.5 percent and a year-to-year error of .5 percent: "Can the Reserves Approach to Monetary Control Really Work?" *Journal of Money, Credit and Banking*, 13 (August 1981):298–313.

believe that it is the long-term rather than the short-term interest rate that has the most effect on investment.[2] They therefore view the fact that monetary policy affects the long-term rate primarily via the short-term rate as a serious limitation on monetary policy.

Relatedness. The third criterion for a target is its relatedness to the Fed's higher level goals. What is important here is *not* by how *much* a given change in the target variable changes nominal income; if it has only a small effect on income, the Fed can simply change the target variable by a large amount. What is important is how *accurately* the Fed can predict by how much income changes when it changes its target setting.

Does the money stock or the interest rate have a more predictable relation to income? This is a tough question. To see why, consider a situation where the interest rate is initially at the Fed's desired level but then suddenly rises. The Fed does not know why. But it must make a decision. Should it take the interest rate as its target, and keep it stable temporarily by increasing the money stock at a faster rate, or should it treat the money stock as its target, and keep *it* growing at the previously decided upon rate, even though this means a higher interest rate?

The answer depends on why the interest rate is rising. With the supply of money growing at a constant rate, the unexpected rise in the interest rate must be due to a rise in the demand for money. In terms of the Cambridge equation, $M = kYP$, this rise in the demand for money must in turn be due either to a rise in k (the proportion of its nominal income the public wants to hold in the form of money) or to a rise in YP.

Suppose first that a rise in k is responsible. In this case the Fed should use the interest rate as its target, and since the desired level of income has not changed, it should keep the interest rate constant. With the demand for money per dollar of income having increased, to prevent a decline in income the Fed must meet the increased demand for money by increasing the supply of money by the same amount. Otherwise the interest rate rises and causes income to fall. *Thus in this case where the increase in the interest rate is due to a rise in the Cambridge* k *the Fed should use the interest rate as its target.*

But in the alternative case where the unexpected rise in the interest rate is due to a rise in YP rather than in k, the Fed should use a money-stock target. Since it does not want the rise in nominal income (for if it did it would already have adopted a policy to change income), it should keep the growth rate of money constant, and allow the interest rate to rise. This rise in the interest rate is desirable because it inhibits expenditures. In other words, when expenditure incentives (such as the profitability of investment) rise and income increases, the resulting rise in the interest rate acts as an automatic stabilizer that moderates the increase in income. *Hence, if the Fed uses an interest-rate target in this case, where the rise in the interest rate is due to an increase in income, the*

---

[2] However, Robert Hall of Stanford University has argued that it is the short-term interest rate that is relevant for investment decisions. In any one year a firm has to decide whether to invest this year or postpone the project until next year. Hence it compares the yield from investing this year with the cost of investing this year instead of next year, which is the one-year interest rate. See Robert Hall, "Investment, Interest Rates and Stabilization Policy," *Brookings Papers on Economic Activity,* 1 (1977):61–103.

Fed acts in a destabilizing manner. By preventing the rise in the interest rate it removes an important automatic stabilizer. In other words, with an interest-rate target the Fed generates the money to finance an increase in nominal income that it does not want.

This principle can be illustrated with IS-LM diagrams.[3] In Figure 21.3A, the IS curve shifts around anywhere between IS_1 and IS_2. If the Fed uses a money-stock target, it generates a fixed supply of money and lets the interest rate increase as a rise in income raises the demand for money. Hence, the LM curve slopes upward in the usual way. As a rise, say, in the profitability of investment, or in government expenditures, shifts the IS curve from IS_1 to IS_2, income increases from Y_0 to Y_1. By contrast, assume that the Fed uses an interest-rate target. It then keeps the interest rate fixed at the desired level by meeting changes in the demand for money with corresponding changes in the supply, so that the LM curve becomes a horizontal line, LM_2. As the IS curve shifts from IS_1 to IS_2, income now rises from Y_2 to Y_3, that is, by more than it would have risen had the Fed used a money-stock target.

In Figure 21.3B the IS curve is stable, but the demand for money fluctuates instead, so that the LM curve varies between LM_1 and LM_2. Suppose the Fed has a money-stock target that keeps the money stock constant (since it does not want income to change) and lets the interest rate fluctuate. Income then varies between Y_0 and Y_1. Now suppose instead that the Fed uses an interest-rate fixed all the time at r_2. This changes the LM curve to LM_3, so that income stays at Y_2.

Thus we have the following rule: *If the change in the interest rate is due to a change in the Cambridge k the Fed should follow an interest-rate target, but if the change in the interest rate is the result of a change in income as expenditure incentives change, in other words, a shift of the IS curve, then the Fed should use a money-stock target instead.*

Here now is the problem. *When the interest rate changes, the Fed cannot be certain whether this is due to changes in the Cambridge k or in expenditure incentives.* All it observes is that the interest rate is, say, rising and it has to decide whether or not to prevent this rise by increasing the money stock. Whatever decision it makes, under *one* set of circumstances it will be the wrong decision, and will destabilize the economy. By how much it will destabilize depends upon the slopes of the IS and LM curves.

This is a horrible situation. It would not be so bad if the Fed could know whether unexpected changes in the interest rate are *usually* due to a change in the Cambridge k or to a change in expenditure incentives. It could then do

---

[3] The previous discussion in terms of income and the Cambridge k can be translated into IS-LM language as follows. An increase in expenditure incentives shifts the IS curve. (This curve tells what income will be, given the interest rate, while an increase in expenditure incentives means that at each interest rate firms or consumers want to spend more.) The LM curve is drawn to equilibrate the money market by selecting those combinations of interest rates and incomes that equate the supply and demand for money. If people now want to hold more money, the curve shifts outward since it now takes a higher interest rate, or lower income, to make them demand no more money than is available. A problem with using a simple IS-LM diagram is that this assumes that prices are stable. Fortunately, the results illustrated here with the IS-LM diagram can be reached also in algebraic ways that do not require price stability.

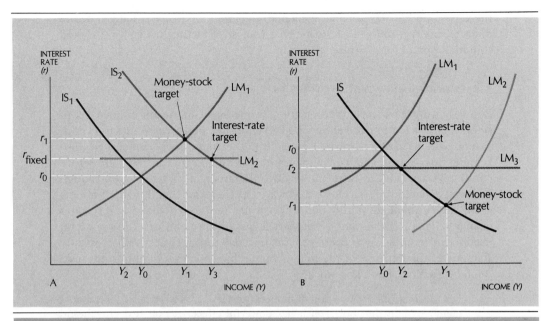

Figure 21.3   Money-Stock Target versus Interest-Rate Target. Whether a money-stock target or an interest-rate target contributes more to income stability depends on whether the shock to income is a shift in the IS curve, as in Part A, or a shift in the LM curve, as in Part B.

that which would *usually* yield the right result. But the Fed does not really know which is the usual case and which is the unusual one. Monetarists believe that the Cambridge k is stabler and more predictable then expenditure incentives, and hence support a money-stock target, but Keynesian theory can be interpreted to favor either a money-stock or interest-rate target. But it can be shown that if unexpected shifts in the IS and the LM curves are equally likely, then the money stock is a better target than is the interest rate.[4] Hence, unless

[4] The argument is complex, but comes down to the following. First, assume that the Fed wants to minimize the square of the deviations of actual income from the desired income level. Second, assume that when the interest rate changes the Fed does not know at all whether the IS or LM curve has shifted. In this situation, the Fed should adopt a policy that is intermediate between what it would do if it knew with certainty which curve had shifted. But, it turns out that the money-stock target is just such an intermediate policy. To see this, assume that the Fed is certain that the IS curve has shifted outward. Should it then adopt a policy of keeping the money stock constant? No, it shouldn't. While this policy would be better than keeping the interest rate constant, the Fed could do better still. It could *reduce* the money stock, thus offsetting the rise in income produced by the shift in the IS curve. Keeping the money stock constant is therefore already an in-between policy, and hence is the appropriate policy if shifts in the two curves are equally likely. See Steven LeRoy and David Lindsey, "Determining the Monetary Instrument: A Diagramatic Exposition," *American Economic Review,* 68 (December 1978): 929–934. Since the extent to which wrong policy destabilizes income depends on the slopes in the IS and LM curves, in principle, the slopes of these curves should be taken into account in deciding whether to use an interest rate or money-stock target. But little is known about the relative size of these slopes.

there is some halfway reliable evidence that the unexpected changes in the interest rate are more likely to be due to a shift in the LM curve, the Fed should adopt a money-stock target.[5]

Administrative and Political Problems

Before leaving the issues of targets there is one more important, practical consideration. We have talked about the Fed choosing an interest-rate target consistent with its desired income level. But the Fed is also concerned with keeping interest rates stable. With an interest-rate target the Fed is therefore continually tempted to keep the level of its target unchanged, even though income is changing in an undesired way. On the other hand, with a money-stock target the Fed would quite clearly be required to let interest rates change. Hence, a money-stock target is less subject to abuse; it does not lend itself to the temptation of overemphasizing a day-to-day concern (interest-rate stability) at the expense of the longer range, but much more important task. As the New York Bank has put it:

> For the long run the function of monetary policy . . . is to stabilize the value of money. . . . In the short run it has powerful effects . . . on real growth and employment. Monetary policy neither can . . . nor should entirely ignore these important short-run concerns. But it does remain true that pressure to focus on short-run concerns at the expense of long-run goals tends to be a constant problem in monetary policymaking. *A basic function of the monetary targeting approach . . . has been to keep the attention of the policymakers focused on the essential long-run price stability role of monetary policy—to put a little distance between monetary policy and the constant pressures to tinker for the sake of short-run objectives.*[6]

Moreover, the public opposes rising interest rates, but generally favors the accompanying lower money growth rate. Hence the Fed can "sell" a restrictive policy much easier to the public if it formulates it in terms of a certain money growth rate rather than a certain interest rate. To those who believe that a restrictive policy is needed this appears as a substantial advantage of a money-stock policy, though some may object on principle to such an attempt to manipulate the public.

All in all, the selection of a target variable involves controversies on three levels. First, there are narrow technical disagreements about the measurability of the variables, and the extent to which they can be controlled. Second, there are disputes about basic macroeconomic theory. Are fluctuations in income due more to fluctuations in expenditure incentives, so that by using a stable money growth rate as its target the Fed could stabilize income, or are income fluctuations due more to variations in the Cambridge k that the Fed should offset? More specifically, does economic analysis tell us that there is a particular monetary variable, such as *M-1* or *M-2*, that has a stable relation to income?

---

[5] Although we have discussed only the problem of choosing between a money-stock target and an interest-rate target, a similar analysis can be developed for the bank-credit vs. interest-rate targets choice.

[6] Federal Reserve Bank of New York, *1983 Annual Report*, p. 11.

Third, there is a dispute about what might almost be called the sociology of central banking. If the Fed uses an interest rate target will it be able to resist the temptation to keep the interest rate stable rather than move it to the proper level?

In Conclusion

To summarize, on the first criterion, measurability, both the money stock and the interest rate perform very badly. Similarly, both target variables have some though lesser problems on the second criterion, controllability. Their relative performance on the third criterion, the relationship to the income goal, is much disputed.

CREDIT OR DEBT VARIABLES

In recent years another potential target, outstanding credit or debt, has appeared on the scene, primarily due to the work of Benjamin Friedman of Harvard University. He has argued that the total outstanding debt of all nonfinancial borrowers (that is, all borrowers other than financial institutions) is as good or better a target variable than is money.

While the deregulation of the financial system and the resulting growth of new types of accounts have made the meaning of *M-1* and *M-2* uncertain, the outstanding debt of nonfinancial borrowers has retained its meaning. Moreover, it bears as stable a relationship to nominal income as does money. The Fed can control it to some extent because its open-market operations provide banks with the wherewithal to extend credit.

Friedman does not suggest that the Fed cease looking at money. Instead the Fed should set target ranges for the growth rate of both money and the total debt of nonfinancial borrowers. What if these two targets conflict; what if, say, bringing the money growth rate within its target range would mean allowing debt to grow above its growth rate range? This, says Friedman, should serve as a signal to the Fed to reconsider its ranges for both variables, and to decide which to readjust. Being guided by the behavior of two variables is better than looking at just one variable since it avoids putting all ones eggs into one basket. This idea has not yet received much professional discussion. However, some economists have questioned whether the Fed can control the debt variable as accurately as it can control money.

INSTRUMENTS

The problems that the Fed faces in controlling nominal income apply also to its control over its target variables. It therefore uses instrument variables to help it attain the desired levels of its target variables. The criteria for these are similar to those for the targets: measurability, controllability, and relatedness (now to the targets themselves rather than to the income goal). Since administrative and political feasibility do not create a problem with respect to instruments this is not a criterion for selecting an instrument.

The Instrument Variables

The Fed can use as its instrument variable any of the several measures of bank reserves and the base discussed in Chapter 11. These measures, together with measures of money, are often referred to as *"the aggregates"* to distinguish them from a very different instrument, the federal-funds rate. (The funds rate can also be a target variable because it affects certain types of investment directly. Insofar as the Fed tries to stabilize the funds rate it is also a goal variable.) The Fed has used the federal-funds rate as its instrumental variable by operating on the demand for money. Thus, if it wanted the money stock to grow it would lower the federal-funds rate so that the public would want to hold more money, and presumably the banks would create this additional money by running down their excess reserves or by borrowing from the Fed.

Evaluation of Instruments

Now let us see how good each of these instruments is at controlling one of the target variables, the money stock. Total reserves and unborrowed reserves pass the measurability test with flying colors. The Fed can at any time read off its own books the reserves that depository institutions keep with it and the amount of their borrowings. And it can easily estimate the other part of reserves, vault cash, from the reports filed with it. Similarly, the Fed can readily estimate the reserve base and the extended base by estimating the currency holdings of the public. All of these variables also meet the attainability criterion very well since the Fed can use open-market operations to change reserves by any desired amount.

   The relatedness criterion creates more of a problem. While monetarists generally believe that total reserves provides the best "handle" on the money stock, the Fed has been skeptical. From October 1979 until late summer 1982 the Fed used unborrowed reserves as its instrument. It set as its proximate target a certain level of unborrowed reserves. As illustrated in Figure 21.4 this instrument works as follows. Suppose that the demand for money increases and banks therefore want more reserves. They have to obtain these additional reserves from the discount window since the Fed, to keep borrowed reserves constant, is not providing them through open-market operations. But banks are reluctant to borrow, and this reluctance is greater the greater is the volume of outstanding borrowings. Hence, as borrowings go up each bank tries to avoid further borrowing from the Fed, and seeks to borrow on the federal-funds market instead. This raises the federal-funds rate. But as the funds rate rises the public wants to hold less money, so that an automatic stabilizer comes into play that partially offsets the initial increase in the demand for money. Hence the money stock rises less than it would have had the Fed supplied the additional reserves via open-market purchases. (The story is similar if the demand for money falls.)

   A problem with this complex procedure is that for the Fed to achieve a particular level of total reserves (and hence a money growth target) by providing a certain volume of unborrowed reserves, requires that the Fed estimate

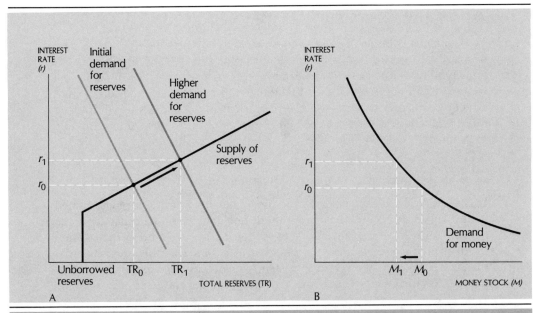

INTEREST RATE (r)

Initial demand for reserves

Higher demand for reserves

Supply of reserves

r_1

r_0

Unborrowed reserves TR_0 TR_1

TOTAL RESERVES (TR)

A

INTEREST RATE (r)

r_1

r_0

Demand for money

M_1 M_0

MONEY STOCK (M)

B

Figure 21.4   The Demand for Reserves and the Interest Rate. Part A shows the relation between borrowing and the federal-funds rate. The supply curve of total reserves is vertical up to the amount of unborrowed reserves that the Fed supplies. Part B shows the effect of the higher interest rate on the demand for money. A rise in the demand for reserves results in a fall in the money supply.

fairly accurately (1) the effect of the volume of unborrowed reserves it supplies on the volume of borrowings, (2) the effect of borrowings on the federal-funds rate, and (3) the effect of the federal-funds rate on the demand for money. Some economists object that the Fed cannot estimate all these relationships accurately enough to control the money stock.

In late summer 1982 the Fed changed its procedures, but in a direction that gives it *less* control over the money stock. (The Fed's move was connected with its temporary deemphasis of its *M-1* target, which will be discussed in Chapter 24.) Under the new procedure the Fed uses borrowed reserves as its instrument; that is, it sets as its target a certain level of borrowed reserves. If the demand for money and hence for reserves increases, so that banks start to borrow more, the Fed simply provides them through open-market operations with the additional reserves they need. Hence, borrowings stay at the Fed's target level and do not rise, the federal-funds rate is not pushed up, and there is no automatic stabilizer that limits the growth of the money supply. Thus, with a borrowed reserves target the Fed has less automatic control over the money stock than it does with an unborrowed reserves target.[7] Why then does the Fed use such a target? To understand this one has to step outside the framework we have used till now.

---

[7] However, the Fed could, if it wants to, compensate for this lack of automatic control by frequently changing its target setting for unborrowed reserves.

ALTERNATIVE APPROACHES

The instruments-targets-goals framework we have discussed so far is preferred by many economists, but not by all. Some argue that the Fed should *not* continually adjust its instrument variable in accordance with what the income goal seems to require. Others suggest that the Fed should focus directly on its GNP target rather than on intermediate targets, such as the money stock or interest rates. Still others would have the Fed go directly from an instrument variable to its income goal. We now take up each of these positions.

Accommodating versus Nonaccommodating Policy

Instead of trying to keep reserves and the money stock at their predetermined levels the Fed could, and in fact frequently does, accommodate changes in the demand for reserves and money. That is, the Fed supplies more reserves when the demand for reserves and for money is greater, and less when the demand is smaller. This seems entirely inconsistent with stabilization policy because it exacerbates the change in income when the IS curve shifts. So why does the Fed do this?

One reason is that *sometimes* accommodating changes in the demand for reserves and money is not inconsistent with keeping income on target—indeed it is required to keep income stable. Suppose, for example, that market factors are draining reserves out of banks. The Fed does not know this right away, but it does observe that banks are short of reserves. By accommodating the banks' demands for additional reserves it keeps total reserves, and hence the money supply, on target. Second, suppose that the money multiplier declines. Again, the Fed does not observe this right away, but it does see that banks are short of reserves. By accommodating this demand for reserves it keeps the money supply on target. Third, suppose that the Cambridge k rises, so that the public's demand for money increases. If the Fed accommodates this increased demand for money it keeps income stable. Only if the increased demand for reserves and money is due to a shift in the IS curve does accommodation destabilize income. In the three other cases it stabilizes.

Does the fact that there are three cases that call for accommodation and only one case that calls for an unaccommodative policy mean that the Fed should usually accommodate? Of course not.

First, the one case *may* be more frequent than the other two cases combined. Second, the damage done by accommodating in the case where this should not be done *may* greatly exceed the damage done by not accommodating when accommodation is the right policy. Suppose that the unexpected fluctuations in the Cambridge k or in the money multiplier are randomly distributed over time so that, except in the very short run, they largely cancel out. Since changes in nominal income depend on changes in the money stock only over a longer period of time, and not on week-to-week or month-to-month changes, not accommodating such short-run changes in k or in the money multiplier has little effect on income. But if, as seems plausible, unexpected shifts of the IS curve persist for longer periods of time, then changing the volume of reserves to accommodate these shifts can seriously destabilize income.

As an aside, we can now take up a topic postponed in the previous chapter: the desirability of hooking the discount rate to the federal-funds rate. Under the current system discounting works in a way that accommodates changes in the demand for reserves. As the demand for reserves increases, the federal-funds rate rises, and thus there is a greater incentive to borrow from the Fed at the fixed discount rate. Hence, those who believe that accommodation is undesirable tend to advocate making the discount rate vary automatically with the federal-funds rate, while those who favor accommodation prefer the present system.

Another reason why the Fed may accommodate changes in the demand for reserves and money is that this prevents or moderates changes in interest rates. Sharp changes in interest rates are disruptive to financial markets. Hence some economists, and many members of the financial community, believe that the Fed should not pursue its income goal in a single-minded fashion without regard to the behavior of interest rates. To prevent excessive interest-rate fluctuations it should, at times, change reserves by less than it would if interest-rate fluctuations did not matter.

Although academic economists may well argue that attaining the income goal is nearly always much more important than avoiding interest-rate fluctuations, it is likely that the Fed does not think so. The Fed has some responsibility for the smooth functioning of financial markets. Besides, remember it is the Fed, and not academic economists, who has to bear the brunt of criticisms from the financial community and from Congress.

Regardless of whether the Fed should or should not accommodate changes in the demand for money, it has usually done so. *In the postwar period the* M-1 *growth rate has generally been higher in business cycle expansions than in recessions.* This cannot be justified by saying that the Fed was offsetting changes in velocity because velocity too grows faster in expansions than in recessions. The procyclical behavior of the money growth rate *suggests* that the Fed may well have been destabilizing rather than stabilizing.[8] At the very least it calls into question the Fed's claim that it has, in its own classic phrase, been "leaning against the wind."

Why has the Fed been so accommodative? The main reason is probably

---

[8] In the period July 1953 to November 1982 the money growth rate was higher in every expansion than in the following recession. Going the other way round and starting with recessions, there is only one exception to the procyclical behavior of the money growth rate. This is not *necessarily* bad. It is *not* true that to stabilize the economy one should raise income in the recession and lower it in the expansion. During the first part of the recession income is still above its normal level, and during the first part of the expansion it is still below its normal level. Hence, to stabilize income around its trend, monetary policy *should* lower income during the early stages of the recession. Thus, instead of seeing whether the money growth rate behaves pro- or anticyclically, one should compare it to some indicator, such as the unemployment rate, that tells us whether aggregate demand is insufficient or excessive. And if one compares changes in the growth rate of either *M-1* or *M-2* to cyclical changes in unemployment, then the money growth rate is seen to respond fairly well to unemployment. Does this mean that the Federal Reserve is actually stabilizing the economy? Not necessarily, because changes in the money growth rate affect aggregate demand with a lag, so that monetary policy could easily be destabilizing after all. But whether or not it is destabilizing cannot be determined unless one knows the lag in the effect of money policy. In addition, there is a problem with how one reads the data. While monetary growth rates were procyclical in 1950s, for the 1960s it depends on whether one starts with recessions or expansions.

that it has tried to moderate changes in interest rates. The way the choice of accommodating or not accommodating arises in practice biases the Fed toward giving priority to interest-rate stability. The damage from sharply fluctuating interest rates, such as losses to thrift institutions as interest rates rise, is immediate and obvious. By contrast, the Fed can never be sure that the income level it is aiming at is really the right one; perhaps it will result in more inflation than the Fed expects. In addition, the Fed can never be certain that its target level of reserves or the federal-funds rate will generate the desired level of income. For example, it may increase reserves because it thinks that the money stock is too low, and next month the revised data might tell it that the money stock was not too low after all. When the losses from a policy are certain and immediate, while the gains are uncertain and remote in time, it is always tempting to procrastinate in adopting this policy even if its expected payoff exceeds the expected losses in an objective calculation.

Control Theory

We began this chapter by discussing the case where the Fed observes that the money stock differs from what it had predicted, and therefore adjusts the money stock to keep it on target. But, why does the money stock differ from the predicted one? Obviously something has gone wrong in one of the equations of the Fed's model. This is useful information since it is likely to affect also the model's prediction of the relation between the money stock and income. This information should not be discarded as it is by saying, oh, well, we will just bring the money stock to the level we originally planned for it. Moreover, the money stock and the interest rate are not the only variables that affect income. Hence the Fed should not use the money stock or the interest rate as its only target, but should instead use all the available information to predict how income is changing, and use this information in deciding on open-market operations.

Along similar lines, a number of economists have tried to extend the traditional analysis by focusing on the fact that when the Fed observes an unexpected rise in the interest rate or in the money stock this may well be due to shifts in *both* the IS and LM curves rather than in just one of them, so that the simple rule we developed in Figure 21.3 is not applicable. Hence, there is no easy way the Fed can respond. But the Fed is not the only one who faces this problem of being off target. Electrical engineers experience it too and have designed optimal mechanisms for bringing a variable back to its target. (The familiar furnace thermostat is one example.) They have developed a branch of mathematics called "control theory" that can be used to decide how a mechanism should respond to information that it is off target. This control theory has been applied to the problem of selecting a monetary policy target by having the Fed look at many variables. Unfortunately, it requires some quite complex mathematics, and therefore having looked the problem firmly in the eye we will pass on.

But having the Fed look at numerous variables, as control theory suggests, also has some problems. Even firm monetarists certainly concede that money is not the *only* variable that affects nominal income, so that *in principle* the Fed should look at many other variables as well. But, they argue, looking at many variables and giving each its due importance is too difficult a task. This argument may seem unconvincing, but it becomes more convincing if one reads the FOMC's minutes.[9] The FOMC's staff surveys the behavior of many variables, some of which are going up and others down, so that it is often very difficult to see what is actually happening. The behavior of the money stock may easily get buried in this plethora of variables, so that—if money is as important as monetarists think—the FOMC may be better off looking just at money. Too much information can be as bad as too little information. More-over, the Fed is subject to political pressures, and is frequently tempted to do the wrong thing. If it focuses its attention on a single variable, such as money, this variable can signal when the Fed is following the wrong, but politically advantageous, policy. Such a clear-cut signal is not likely to emerge if the Fed is looking at many variables. Hence the Fed is better able to resist the temptation to follow a popular, but short-sighted, policy if it pays attention to only a single variable, rather than to many.

The Nominal Income Target

Another approach that has received much attention in recent years is to aim directly at nominal income. This approach is closely connected with the control theory approach just discussed. Since other variables besides money and interest rates affect nominal income, why not look at nominal income directly? Targeting the money stock would result in the desired level of GNP only if velocity were constant, which it is not.

But targeting nominal GNP directly also has its problems. First, it is easy to say that the Fed should focus its attention on GNP. But which GNP—current GNP or future GNP? Since the monetary policy made today has its impact some time in the future, the obvious answer is future GNP. But future GNP is unknown. Hence, the Fed is tempted to focus on the GNP it knows, current GNP, and GNP of the immediate past. Moreover, political pressures direct the Fed toward looking at current GNP. If the Fed adopts a restrictive policy at a time when unemployment is still high, or an expansionary policy when inflation is high, it will be strongly criticized by those who do not realize that conditions may well be quite different by the time the policy becomes effective. Hence, the Fed is tempted to use current rather than future GNP as its GNP target. If the lag between the adoption of a monetary policy and its impact on GNP is short this would not matter much, but, as will be discussed in Chapter 23, if the lag is long this could make the policy destabilizing.

Another problem is that a GNP target makes it difficult, if not impossible, to monitor the Fed. Suppose the Fed has a money-stock target and misses it. It can then be criticized. But suppose that GNP departs from the Fed's target. The Fed can hardly be called to account since so many other factors besides monetary policy have an impact on nominal GNP.

A central aspect of GNP targeting is revealed when one asks how it relates to the instruments-targets-goals framework. At first glance there

---

[9] The minutes, officially called "Memoranda of Discussion," are publicly available up to March 1976. Since then no minutes have been kept.

appears to be a sharp conflict between the two. If monetary policy aims directly at GNP, a goal variable, it seems that the target and instrument variables are dispensed with. But this is not really the case. Suppose that the FOMC uses a GNP target. It cannot tell the New York Fed to undertake open-market purchases to make GNP reach this target because that would be too vague a directive. Instead, it must say to itself something like the following: GNP should grow at a 7 percent rate and this requires a 6 percent *M-1* growth rate. This, in turn, requires a certain level of borrowed reserves. Hence, use of a GNP target does not free the Fed from having to have other targets and instruments too.

Conversely, if the Fed follows the previously discussed procedure and sets a growth rate for reserves and money, it also has a GNP target in mind. It does not pick a particular money growth rate out of thin air. It selects one that it thinks will generate the desired level of GNP.

So what is all the fuss about? If a GNP target requires also having a money (or interest-rate or credit) target, while these other targets also require having a nominal GNP target, does it matter whether the Fed announces its target as a certain GNP growth rate or as a certain money growth rate or interest rate? Yes it does. Suppose the Fed announces a certain nominal GNP target, and subsequently changes its estimate of the growth rate of velocity. It can then change its implicit and unannounced money growth target without any trouble. But suppose that the Fed had had—and announced—a money growth target instead. Then, changing the money growth rate would involve a cost to the Fed since it would be accused of inconsistency or of missing its target. Hence, it is less likely to change the money growth rate if that is its announced target variable than if its announced target is a certain growth rate for nominal income. Thus a nominal income target provides the Fed with more flexibility than a money-stock target. Whether or not the Fed should have such greater flexibility depends on how stable velocity is, and on the extent to which the Fed is likely to misuse its flexibility due to political and administrative problems, which will be discussed in Chapter 23.

Another reason why it matters whether the Fed announces its money target or its GNP target is that, by stating its target as a money growth rate rather than as a growth rate for nominal GNP, the Fed can hide the fact that it is aiming at an income level that seems too low to many people. Is this good or bad?

A Real GNP Target

Instead of having a nominal GNP target the Fed can use a real GNP target, selecting a level of real GNP that it thinks is consistent with its unemployment and inflation goals. Suppose the Fed is correct in estimating the inflation rate that accompanies its real GNP target. Then it does not matter whether it sets its GNP target in nominal or real terms, since obviously the nominal GNP target is just the real GNP target adjusted for the inflation rate. But suppose the Fed's inflation forecast is wrong. Perhaps a supply shock occurs, or the Phillips curve is steeper than the Fed thought. Prices now rise more than the Fed anticipated. If the Fed has a real GNP target, and stays with it, it will do noth-

ing to offset the higher inflation rate. By contrast, if it has a nominal GNP target its policy will lower both the inflation rate and real GNP. With some
exaggeration one might say that with a nominal GNP target the Fed is, in
effect, telling the public, "If you raise prices you will also get a rise in unemployment," whereas with a real GNP target it is saying, "I will ensure a certain
level of employment regardless of what happens to prices." Admittedly, this is
something of an exaggeration because the Fed is likely to change both a nominal or a real GNP target as the inflation rate changes.

Currently (May 1986) real GNP may well be the target that the Fed pays
most attention to.

The Base

A money-stock target makes it easier to monitor the Fed than does a GNP target. But even with a money-stock target the Fed cannot be monitored precisely
because it cannot be held fully responsible for short-run variations in the
money growth rate. This is one reason some economists advocate using the
base as a target. This is a variable over which the Fed has great control. In
addition, they believe that the Fed could control nominal GNP more accurately by setting a base target rather than a money target.

The usual procedure of going from the base to the money stock, and
then from the money stock to income, introduces two errors: an error in the
equation estimating the money stock from the base, and a second error in the
equation linking the money stock to income. Some economists believe that the
error in the single equation linking the base directly to income is as small or
smaller than the error in the equation linking the money stock to income.
Hence, the total error in estimating income is greater if the money stock is
interposed as a target since we then have the additional error involved in going
from the base to the money stock. However, other economists believe that
using separate equations to go from the base to money, and then from money
to income, gives smaller errors. Unfortunately the data do not give an
unequivocal answer as to which is the better procedure. One reason some
economists object to relating the base directly to income is that approximately
70 percent of the base is currency. And although we can predict the demand
for currency quite well, we do not really *understand* why people are holding so
much currency. Reliance on badly understood statistical regularities can be
dangerous.

SUMMARY

1 It takes a long time for the effect of the Fed's actions to show up. Hence, the Fed
  measures the impact of its actions on a set of intermediate target variables.
2 The selection of a target variable is a crucial step; the relevant criteria are measurability, controllability, and relatedness to the higher level goals. The two
  main rival targets are the money growth rate and interest rates, but total debt of
  nonfinancial borrowers has also been suggested as a target. Controllability is
  also a serious problem. On the relatedness issue the rule is that if the IS curve is
  unstable while the LM curve is stable the Fed should use a money-stock target,
  while in the opposite case it should use an interest-rate target.

3 Since the Fed does not *directly* control any of the target variables, it uses instrument variables to attain its targets. The two main candidates here are reserves (or the base) and the short-term interest rate.

4 Some economists have advocated the use of nominal GNP as a target. This would give the Fed more flexibility. Other economists would reduce the Fed's flexibility by having it target the base.

QUESTIONS AND EXERCISES

1 To what extent is the money stock a good target? To what extent is the interest rate?

2 What are the criteria for targets and instruments? Explain in your own words.

3 Explain in your own words why the Fed should use an interest-rate target if the observed change in the interest rate is due to a change in the amount of money demanded per dollar of income, and a money-stock target if it is due to a rise in income.

4 Discuss the cases for and against targeting nominal income.

5 Write an essay either defending or criticizing accommodating changes in the demand for money.

FURTHER READING

BOARD OF GOVERNORS, FEDERAL RESERVE SYSTEM. *New Monetary Control Procedures.* Washington, D.C.: 1981. The first essay by Stephen Axilrod provides a useful summary of this massive and highly technical Fed study of targets and instruments.

FEDERAL RESERVE BANK OF ST. LOUIS. *Review.* Early each year this *Review* has an article on the previous year's FOMC decisions and discusses changes in Fed procedures.

FEDERAL RESERVE BANK OF SAN FRANCISCO. *Interest Rate Deregulation and Monetary Policy.* San Francisco, Federal Reserve Bank, n.d. A set of interesting papers from a 1982 conference on monetary targeting.

FRIEDMAN, BENJAMIN. "Values of Intermediate Targets in Implementing Monetary Policy," in Federal Reserve Bank of Kansas City, *Price Stability and Public Policy,* pp. 169–191. Kansas City: Federal Reserve Bank of Kansas City, 1984. A stimulating critique of the targets and instruments approach.

GAMS, CARL. "Federal Reserve Intermediate Targets: Money or the Monetary Base," *Review* (Federal Reserve Bank of Kansas City) 65 (January 1980):3–15. A provocative discussion of the issue of the base vs. money as a target.

MEEK, PAUL (ed.). *Central Bank Views on Monetary Targeting.* New York: Federal Reserve Bank of New York, n.d. A collection of useful papers on monetary targeting procedures in various countries.

MELTZER, ALLAN, ROBERT RASCHE, STEPHEN AXILROD, and PETER STERNLIGHT. "Is the Federal Reserve's Monetary Control Policy Misdirected?" *Journal of Money, Credit and Banking,* 14 (February 1982):119–147. The record of a very interesting debate.

MORRIS, FRANK. "Do the Monetary Aggregates Have a Future as Targets of Federal Reserve Policy?" Federal Reserve Bank of Boston, *New England Economic Review* (March/April 1982):5–14. A powerful critique of the use of monetary targets.

CHAPTER 22

The Impact of Monetary Policy

Having seen how the Fed changes the money stock and interest rates we now look at how, and to what extent, these variables affect nominal GNP and various sectors of the economy.

STRENGTH OF MONETARY POLICY

From the 1930s until the late 1950s or early 1960s the predominant view among economists was that monetary policy has little effect on GNP; changes in the money stock would be largely offset by changes of velocity in the opposite direction. But nowadays few (if any) doubt that a sharply restrictive monetary policy can bring about a recession or prevent a recovery. Any remaining doubts about this were stilled by the experience of the early 1980s. The evidence is less clear about whether an expansionary monetary policy could terminate a really severe recession within a reasonable time. Some—though by no means all—Keynesians argue that massive open-market purchases during a severe recession would be ineffective, because lower interest rates would do little to stimulate investment in a slump: "You can't push on a piece of string." But this is probably a minority view.

THE TRANSMISSION PROCESS

As pointed out in Chapter 16 a major difference between the monetarist and Keynesian analyses of *how* money affects the economy is that monetarists do not spell out this transmission process in detail, while Keynesians do. Hence, before turning to the detailed Keynesian story we present just a brief discussion of a portfolio process that summarizes the monetarist version of the transmission process, but is also entirely acceptable to Keynesians.

Portfolio Equilibrium

Everyone has a portfolio of assets and liabilities and tries to keep the (monetary plus imputed) yields of all the assets equal at the margin. Now suppose that the quantity of money increases, so that at least some portfolios now include more money. Given, for the usual reasons, declining marginal utility, the imputed yield on money is now less than before. Hence, portfolio holders now exchange money for other assets. What assets they buy depends upon the cross-elasticities of demand, which, in turn, depend on the similarity between assets. For example, money and Treasury bills, being similar, are close substitutes (have a high cross-elasticity of demand). Not only are they both very safe assets, but the types of risks to which they are subject are alike. They are both subject to inflation risk, but not to default risk. Similarly, there is no significant fall in their values if interest rates rise. Hence, those who initially hold excess money balances use them to buy mainly securities, like Treasury bills, and interest rates fall. But the sellers of Treasury bills now receive these excess money balances and they buy mainly assets that are not too dissimilar to Treasury bills, for example, commercial paper and three-year government securities. The sellers of these items, in turn, then buy other assets, and eventually the increased demand for assets spreads (in principle) to all assets in the economy, until in the new equilibrium the (monetary plus imputed) yields on all assets are again equal. Among the assets whose prices are raised in this way are common stocks, and thus the value of corporations. With the value of existing corporations exceeding the cost of creating new ones, investment takes place. For example, suppose that it costs $100 million to construct a new plant and that the public is willing to pay $110 million for the stock of a corporation that owns just this plant. It is now profitable to start a new corporation that owns such a plant, or to add such a plant to an existing corporation. Moreover, as the yield on various assets such as money and bonds declines, the imputed yield on consumer durables starts to exceed these other yields, so that households buy more durables. Similarly, nondurable consumption may rise.

The Keynesian Approach

The Keynesian version of the transmission process accepts the foregoing, but spells it out in greater detail and formulates it in terms of interest rates rather than in terms of the stock of money relative to other assets. In this analysis two relations are central in determining by how much a given increase in the money growth rate raises income. One is the slope of the liquidity preference (demand for money) curve. This slope determines how much the interest rate will decline as the money stock increases. The second is the slope of the marginal efficiency of investment curve, which determines how much investment increases in response to the fall in the interest rate. The third is the multiplier relating investment to income.

Impact of Money-Market Imperfections

In Chapter 12 we showed why a decline in interest rates induces firms to invest more. This discussion assumed a perfect capital market in which firms can borrow as much as they want to invest. We now extend this analysis by dropping the assumption of a perfect capital market and consider how a change in the interest rate affects investment by changing the availability of funds.

Chapter 4 discussed capital rationing, and how some firms are unable to obtain bank loans. If the Fed's open-market purchases now provide banks with additional reserves they are willing to make loans to some of these potential customers. These previously unsatisfied borrowers have a number of investment projects that they thought worth undertaking even at the previous higher interest rate, and they are even more eager to undertake these projects now that the interest rate has fallen.

In the past, market imperfections also played a role in the impact of monetary policy on residential construction. As interest rates rose disintermediation reduced the volume of mortgage loans that thrift institutions could make. But now with the demise of Regulation Q, this is no longer a problem.

Finally, some economists have pointed to an institutional factor that they believe substantially reduces the impact of monetary policy. This is the existence of trade credit. (Trade credit is the credit that a firm, say, a wholesaler, extends to another firm, say, a retailer, by shipping goods with payments to be made only in the future, perhaps in thirty or ninety days.) They have argued that if firms extend more credit to their customer firms this can, at least partially, offset the effect of a restrictive monetary policy. However, the empirical evidence suggests that, at least as far as manufacturing firms are concerned, trade credit does *not* expand when the Fed reduces the growth rate of the money stock, so that trade credit does not inhibit the impact of monetary policy.

Monetary Policy and Stock Prices

To see how changes in monetary policy affect stock prices we deal first with a situation in which there is no fear of greater inflation. Assume that the Fed adopts an expansionary policy and the growth rate of money rises. The way stock prices are affected can be explained in three ways. The first is to say that the public now holds more money in its portfolio, and since its money holdings were previously in equilibrium it now holds excessive money and tries to exchange some of it for other assets, including corporate stock. Another way of putting this is to look at relative yields and notice that as people get more money the yield on money falls at the margin, so that it is now less than the expected yield (adjusted for risk) on stock. As they buy stock they bid stock prices up until at the new price the expected (risk-adjusted) yield on a dollar invested in stock is no greater than the marginal yield on a dollar held as money. A third way is to say that the present value of a stock, and hence its price, is equal to an expected stream of future yields discounted at the interest rate. An increase in the quantity of money temporarily lowers the interest rate, and hence increases the present value of the expected future earnings on the stock, and thus its price.

Knowing this, can you go out and make money on the stock market? Unfortunately not. The trouble is that other people have this information too.

So when you rush down to your broker you find that there are already other people there who want to buy stock too, and potential sellers are demanding a higher price. Information that everyone else has is of no use to you in the stock market.[1] Only if you know something (something right, that is) that others don't can you cash in on it. Suppose, for example, you discover that the Fed raises the money growth rate in every month in which there is a full moon on a Thursday. Then, until others discover this too, you can predict stock prices in time to buy stocks before they go up.

Just to complicate things, there is the problem of inflation. If people believe correctly that the higher money growth rate is inflationary, then *real* stock prices will probably not rise. In fact, it used to be widely believed that they would then fall, though this view has now been challenged. If stock prices fall this stimulates investment since firms can finance a given investment project more cheaply. Suppose that a company is worth $10 million and has outstanding 1 million shares, each worth $10. To expand, the company sells an additional million shares at $10 each. Assuming that the former stock-holders do not buy any of the new stock, they now own only one-half of the larger company. But suppose the stock price had risen from $10 to $20 before the new stock was sold. The old stockholders would then have had to give up only one-third rather than one-half of the larger company to obtain the $10 million.

As explained in Chapter 12, monetary policy affects consumption as well as investment. This is important because, while gross private domestic invest-ment accounts for only about 15 percent of GNP, consumer purchases account for almost two-thirds of GNP. Hence, even if the interest elasticity of investment is much higher than the interest elasticity of consumption, much of the impact of monetary policy *could* still come from consumption.

The MPS Model

The time has come to put these various effects together. One way to do so is in an econometric model. Although there are many such models that could be used, we will employ the Federal Reserve's MPS model. (The acronym MPS stands for MIT, the University of Pennsylvania, and the Social Science Research Council—the latter contributed to its financing.) This large model, while essentially Keynesian, has a much more detailed monetary sector than most other models since it was built for the Fed, which uses it to forecast, combining its predictions with judgmental forecasts, that is, forecasts made in an informal manner by experts familiar with developments in various sectors of the economy. The Fed also uses the MPS model to simulate how its policies affect the economy. For example, it may use the model to predict how income would change if unborrowed reserves rose by $1 billion.

---

[1] This is an implication of the "random walk" theory of stock prices. For very clear discussions of this theory, see Burton Malkiel, *A Random Walk Down Wall Street,* New York, W. W. Norton, 1975, and Neil Berkman, "A Primer on Random Walks in the Stock Market," *New England Eco-nomic Review* (Federal Reserve Bank of Boston) (September/October 1978), pp. 32–50. The latter contains a formal model of how money affects stock prices.

Do not treat this model as though it were *the* model of the economy. Some other models, which predict approximately as well, have different monetary sectors, and hence describe the impact of monetary policies differently. Moreover, the MPS model is constantly being revised. The latest versions are not publicly available and the version described here is somewhat outdated. Hence, treat it more as an illustration than as the last word.

In this model, monetary policy affects income in three ways. One channel is the wealth effect; as interest rates rise, bond and stock prices fall, households feel poorer, and they respond by cutting consumption. This wealth effect is very important in the model, and at some times accounts for roughly half the *direct* impact (that is, the impact excluding the indirect multiplier and accelerator effects) of monetary policy as measured by the model. The second channel is the effect of changes in interest rates on the demand for capital, that is, a cost of capital channel. This applies not only to industrial plant and equipment, but also to consumer durables and to residential and nonresidential construction both by the private sector and by state and local governments. The third effect, called the *credit availability channel,* operates through credit rationing; as policy becomes more restrictive, more potential borrowers are unable to obtain mortgage loans.

Figure 22.1 shows the flow chart of the MPS model for the first-round effects of monetary policy. Since it deals only with the first round it excludes the various feedbacks, such as the effects of a change in income induced by the monetary policy on interest rates, consumption, and investment. To include these would make the figure much too complex. We start out by assuming a rise in the Aaa bond rate; that is, the interest rate paid on the highest-quality corporate bonds. Part A shows the wealth-consumption channel. This has already been discussed in Chapter 12, and the only thing that may need mentioning is that the model does not stop with the change in consumption, but breaks it down into its major components. The flow chart also shows the effect of the rise in the interest rate on the distribution of consumption between durables and nondurables. Part B shows the effects of higher interest rates on the availability of residential mortgage funds, and hence on residential construction. Such disintermediation is much less important now than it was at the time when this version of the MPS model was prepared.

Part C shows the direct cost effect of the rise in the Aaa bond rate. Since bonds and mortgages are substitutes in the portfolios of lenders, a rise in the bond rate raises the mortgage rate. This increase in the cost of borrowing lowers the profitability of investment in houses, so that housing starts and residential construction fall.

Part D shows the effects on industrial plant and equipment and on private nonresidential construction. A rise in the yields on bonds and mortgages raises the yield that firms must expect to obtain on investment in industrial plants to make them willing to undertake such investment. As this rate—called the *equilibrium quasi-rent*—rises the desired stock of capital is reduced. Hence new orders for equipment fall, and investment declines. Finally, as Part E shows, the rise in the corporate bond rate raises the interest rate on state and local securities, and this discourages state and local construction.

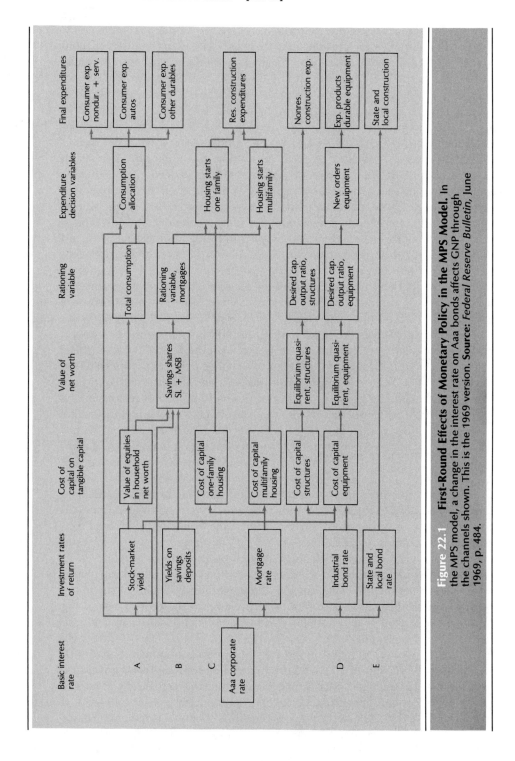

Figure 22.1 **First-Round Effects of Monetary Policy in the MPS Model.** In the MPS model, a change in the interest rate on Aaa bonds affects GNP through the channels shown. This is the 1969 version. **Source:** *Federal Reserve Bulletin,* June 1969, p. 484.

The version of the model shown in Figure 22.1 does not include an effect on inventory investment. A later version of the model has such an effect as well as a liquidity effect on consumption, and a Phillips curve that becomes vertical in the long run. Hence, the MPS model shows monetary policy as affecting many components of aggregate demand.

Figure 22.2 shows the impact of a rise in the federal-funds rate on various components of GNP and on the GNP deflator as estimated by the Chase econometric model. Figure 22.3 compares the impact of a change in unborrowed reserves on GNP shown by various models. The difference is quite substantial. (But *some* of the difference reflects the fact that in some models the unborrowed reserves injections are larger than in other models, that they occur at different stages of the business cycle, and that the models make different assumptions about the behavior of some exogenous variables.)

INTERNATIONAL TRADE EFFECTS

So far we have dealt only with a closed economy. But if exchange rates are flexible, monetary policy affects income also through its impact on foreign exchange rates. Suppose that the United States adopts a restrictive monetary policy so that interest rates in the U.S. rise temporarily. Since, in the first instance, interest rates in the rest of the world are constant, foreigners now have an incentive to buy U.S. securities. But to do so they must demand dollars on the foreign exchange market. At the same time, with higher interest rates in the United States, Americans have less of an incentive to buy foreign securities, so that their demand for foreign currency (which is needed to buy foreign securities) is reduced. Hence, on the foreign exchange market, with more dollars and less foreign currency being demanded, the value of the dollar rises. Foreigners therefore find that U.S. goods cost more in terms of their own currency, and so they buy fewer. Similarly, with foreign goods being cheaper in terms of dollars (since the dollar buys more British pounds, German marks, and so on) U.S. imports increase. For both of these reasons the demand for goods produced in the United States falls. This reinforces the domestic effects that a tight money policy has in constraining demand.

What has been presented so far is the traditional explanation. But in recent years another approach (called monetarist balance of payment theory), which emphasizes the supply and demand for money, has been developed. Suppose that the Fed adopts a restrictive policy. The decline in the growth rate of money results in the supply of money being less than the demand for money. Hence, Americans *try* to increase their money holdings by selling more goods and securities to foreigners, and by buying less from them.[2] But this succeeds in raising the dollar holdings of Americans only to the extent that foreigners relinquish dollars they hold, and this is rather minor. However, there is a more important—albeit indirect—effect. As Americans sell more

---

[2] Of course, Americans do not consciously decide to sell more to foreigners. Instead, Americans simply try to sell more regardless of whether it is to domestic residents or to foreigners. But since other Americans also try to sell rather than to buy, they end up, on the whole, selling more only to foreigners.

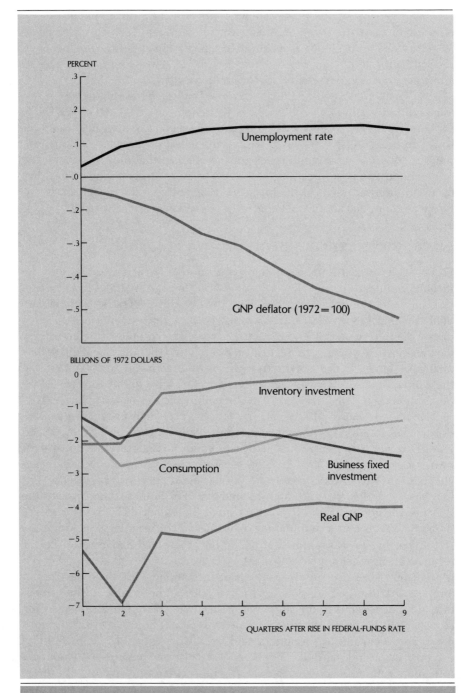

Figure 22.2   Effect of a 1 Percent Increase in the Federal-Funds Rate—Chase Econometric Model. An increase in the federal-funds rate changes unemployment, prices, and real GNP. **Source:** David Cross, *Model Notes—Part I,* Chase Econometrics.

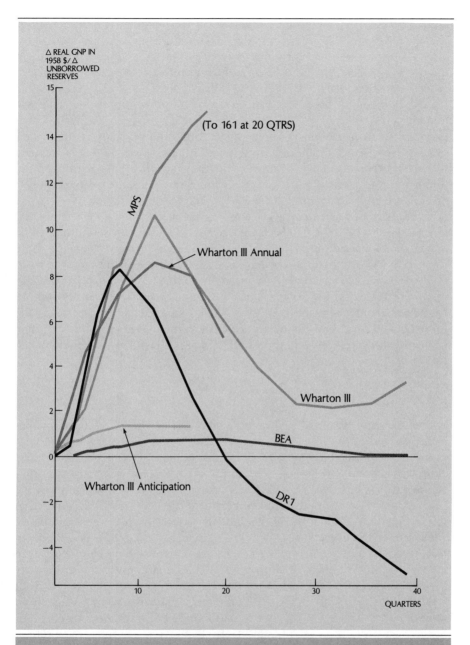

Figure 22.3   Impact of a Maintained $1 Billion Increase in Unborrowed Reserves upon Real GNP. Econometric models show considerable disagreement about the impact of monetary policy. MPS denotes the MIT–University of Pennsylvania–Social Science Research Council model; Wharton means the models used by Wharton Econometric Forecasts Associates. BEA denotes the model of the Bureau of Economic Analysis in the U.S. Department of Commerce. DRI refers to the Data Resources Inc. model. **Source:** Carl Christ, "Judging the Performance of Econometric Models of the U.S. Economy," *International Economic Review,* 16 (February 1975):71.

goods and securities to foreigners, and buy less from them, the supply of foreign currency on the foreign exchange market increases, and the demand for it falls. Hence, the price of foreign currency in terms of dollars falls; that is, the dollar rises. As the dollar rises relative to other currencies, the price of internationally traded goods *in terms of* dollars falls. This reduces prices in the United States both directly and indirectly as those producers who compete directly with imported goods have to reduce their prices. This in turn puts pressure on other producers who compete with those who have reduced their prices to compete with imports. And in an ultimate sense, all goods compete with each other. Moreover, with the inflation rate thus falling, workers are willing to settle for smaller nominal wage increases. Thus, the rise of the dollar on the foreign exchange market helps the Fed to curb inflation.

There is, however, another international finance effect of monetary policy that tends to weaken it. This is that, as the interest rate rises in the United States, the increased purchases of U.S. securities by foreigners (and by those Americans who would otherwise have bought foreign securities) work to moderate the rise in the interest rate. This, in turn, reduces the impact of the Fed's restrictive policy on investment and consumption. However, in a system of flexible exchange rates this offset is limited. Since exchange rates fluctuate, foreigners take a risk in buying securities denominated in dollars rather than in their own currencies, and this limits capital inflows. This will be discussed further in Part 5.

RATIONAL EXPECTATIONS

So far, the description of the way monetary policy affects the economy has been too mechanistic. It is high time to allow for the fact that people do not just react to events that have already occurred, but also respond to what they expect to happen. If one leaves room for expectations, there is yet another way in which monetary policy can affect prices, and hence nominal income.

Assume that at a time of full employment the Fed substantially increases the reserve base. Not only will this initially reduce interest rates, and hence stimulate expenditures, but people, particularly well-informed decision makers, will realize what is going on. They will expect aggregate demand to increase. More specifically, with the economy already operating at capacity they will expect wages and prices to rise. But if prices are expected to rise isn't it rational for people to try to protect themselves against this by buying ahead now, by withholding goods from the market to sell them in the future, and by raising wages and prices right away? Hence, an increase in the growth rate of the base can lead to an immediate increase in prices. This is, of course, much more likely to happen at a time when high and variable inflation rates have conditioned people to watch the growth rate of the base than at a time when people have had little or no experience with inflation.

At the cost of being somewhat unrealistic one can carry this example to an interesting conclusion. Assume that everyone knows that the increase in the base is inflationary, and, also, that all contracts have escalator clauses, and that laws and regulations do not inhibit a rapid adaption to inflation (for example, tax laws are fully indexed, and all outside money somehow is indexed too). If so, an increase in the growth rate of the base will result immediately in a rise in nominal interest rates as the higher rate of inflation is embodied in the inflation premium that is included in the nominal interest rate. Hence neither investment nor output rises, but the inflation rate responds instantly and fully to the higher growth rate of the base.

Admittedly the assumptions that people can predict accurately the impact of the higher growth rate of the base on prices and that long-term contracts, tax laws, and so on are fully indexed are extreme. But this example does warn us to watch for the way in which monetary policy affects expectations. Suppose, for example, that Congress would suddenly direct the Fed to aim at keeping unemployment to 3 percent, or to bring the Treasury-bill rate down to 3 percent. This would bring about an immediate and very substantial increase in the inflation rate. Conversely, if Congress were to order the Fed to make price stability its only goal, the inflation rate would start to decline even before the Fed takes any action.

A POTENTIAL PROBLEM: A FLEXIBLE INTEREST RATE ON MONEY

In recent years financial deregulation and financial innovation have allowed depositors to receive on their transactions accounts an explicit interest rate that varies along with open-market rates. This *may* have an important effect on the impact on the economy of monetary policy and of changes in expenditure incentives.

Suppose the Fed reduces the growth rate of money. As before, interest rates rise temporarily, but now the interest rate paid on money rises too. Hence there is now less of an incentive to switch out of money into securities. The liquidity preference curve (the demand curve for money) therefore becomes steeper, as does the LM curve. As the extreme case suppose that the interest rate paid on money moves precisely with the open-market interest rate. If so, an increase in the interest rates provides no reason at all to hold any less money than before, and the LM curve is completely vertical. However, since banks hold reserves on which they earn no interest, deposit rates cannot rise by the same amount as interest rates on securities do. Hence, as interest rates rise, depositors still have an incentive to switch out of money into securities, so that the LM curve is not vertical. Moreover, at least so far, the rate that banks pay on deposits has responded only sluggishly to interest rates paid on securities. Thus the extreme case is only a theoretical possibility.

With a steeper LM curve, a shift in the IS curve brings about a smaller change in income. Suppose that government expenditures increase. As the government borrows more the interest rate rises, and as a result private expenditures are cut back. The steeper the LM curve is, the greater is the rise in the interest rate that is required to equilibrate the money market, and hence the greater is the cutback in private expenditures. In the extreme case with a completely vertical LM curve, an increase in government expenditures lowers private expenditures dollar for dollar and nominal income is unchanged. Hence, the payment of a flexible interest rate on money makes income more stable with respect to a shift in the IS curve. But it becomes less stable with respect to a shift in the LM curve. Suppose that the Cambridge k rises. The resulting rise in the interest rate then provides an incentive to hold less money, partially offsetting the initial rise in the Cambridge k. But to the extent that the interest rate on money rises too, this offsetting effect is weakened.

The payment of a flexible interest rate on money also creates a transitional problem that *may* be serious. There is now an incentive to hold as checkable deposits some funds that would otherwise have been invested in other assets. The interest elasticity and the income elasticity of these checkable deposits may well differ from the elasticities of previous deposits. Hence the average interest elasticity and income elasticity of money have changed. It may take the Fed some time to discover what these new elasticities are, and in the meantime, its forecasts will be less accurate.

ALLOCATION EFFECTS

All in all, there is little doubt that monetary policy—or at least a restrictive policy—can be strong enough to do the job if it is carried far enough. But this alone does not suffice to recommend its use as the main stabilization tool. One should look also at its efficiency and its side effects. If monetary policy turns out to be extremely inequitable, or to discourage certain types of socially desirable investment too much, then one *may* want to adopt a policy mix that gives a smaller role to monetary policy and a greater one to fiscal policy or credit allocation (a system described below). Or else, one might decide to do without stabilization policy.

The Criteria

Obviously, the first step in deciding whether the impact of monetary policy is appropriately distributed is to select a criterion for an appropriate distribution. Here are two rival criteria.

One is a competitive free market allocation. According to this, the price of credit (i.e., the interest rate) should be set to clear the market. There should be no credit rationing or use of market power. Everyone uses credit until the point at which its marginal cost (the interest rate) equals the perceived marginal benefit. Hence, when the Fed reduces money growth, and the interest rate rises, borrowers cut back until the marginal utility of funds for each of them rises enough to equal the higher interest rate. There is no reason why all activities should be cut back equally. By analogy, when a family decides to cut back on its expenditures it does not cut its outlays for vacation trips and for bread equally! *If* one takes the distribution of income (after interest rates have risen) as beyond question, and assumes that there is adequate competition, and that there are no uncompensated externalities, then this free market criterion is applicable and there is no reason to be concerned about the allocation effects of monetary policy.

A popular alternative criterion is proportionality: a restrictive monetary policy should cut back borrowing and expenditures in each sector more or less in the same proportion. This criterion has no economic justification; it seems to represent an underlying ethical judgment that sacrifices should be shared equally. This ethical judgment, however, is not clearly formulated. It is usually employed only in an implicit way in arguments that a restrictive monetary policy is imposing too high a cost on some worthy sector or group.

Whichever criterion is used, complaints about monetary policy generally refer to a restrictive rather than an expansionary policy, because it is the former that takes something away from people.

Impacted Sectors

In the 1960s and 1970s there were massive complaints about the unduly harsh impact of restrictive monetary policy on several sectors. One of these sectors is investment in general. Some economists argued that a restrictive monetary policy cuts back investment substantially, but has little, if any, effect on consumption. Hence, by using a restrictive monetary policy and an easy fiscal policy, growth of the capital stock and hence the growth of productivity are reduced. It would be better to have a restrictive fiscal policy that curbs consumption and an expansionary monetary policy that stimulates investment. However, to the extent that rising interest rates reduce consumption as well as investment, the impact of this argument is weakened.

Residential Construction. Most criticism of the allocation effects of monetary policy concentrates on its effect on residential construction, a sector generally agreed to be highly sensitive to rising interest rates.

A sharp impact of a restrictive monetary policy on residential construction is not hard to explain. First, residential construction represents unusually long term investment, and hence is more sensitive than most other types of investment to the cost of borrowing. Second, in the past, several market imperfections made residential construction particularly sensitive to rising interest rates. One imperfection was the disintermediation that resulted from the Regulation Q ceiling. Others were state-imposed usury ceilings that made mortgage lending unprofitable and a sluggish interest rate ceiling on VA and FHA loans.

To the extent that the cutback in residential construction was due to it being long-lived investment, it was justified under the free market criterion, but, to the extent that the other factors just discussed played a significant role, the plight of the construction industry could be justified on neither criterion.

The problem is exacerbated by the fact that many people implicitly reject the free market criterion, and look upon residential construction as a particularly meritorious type of investment. They believe that housing investment should be carried beyond the point that the free market would select on its own. Hence, having it cut back by a restrictive monetary policy is reprehensible.

Moreover, it is not only builders or purchasers of new houses that are hurt when interest rates rise; those who want to buy or sell old houses are hurt too. This is so because in many cases the seller of a house cannot pass on to the buyer the implicit capital gain obtained from having an old low cost mortgage. The potential buyer would have to take out a new mortgage at the new, higher interest rate. Hence, the sale of old houses is reduced. This is an interference with efficient resource allocation that does little to help curb inflation.

It is not surprising that the government has tried to ameliorate the impact of rising interest rates on residential construction by providing massive infusions of mortgage funds from federal and federally sponsored agencies such as the Federal National Mortgage Association ("Fanny Mae").[3] Whether this really helps the mortgage market is another question. The government-sponsored agencies borrow on the open market to obtain the funds they provide to the mortgage market. But as they borrow on the open market they drive up interest rates. Some studies have therefore argued that these government rescue operations are useless.

Small Business. Another sector said to be hurt too severely by a restrictive monetary policy is small business, and particularly new firms. At first glance, this may seem implausible since profit-maximizing banks have an incentive to lend to those firms, regardless of size, that promise to pay the highest rate of return. However, large firms that are turned down by one bank can go to another bank or sell securities on the open market. Small firms often do not have these alternatives. The *extent* to which there is discrimination against small firms, is, of course, a matter of empirical judgment, and one that has generated much dispute.

Income Distribution. Finally, there is the distribution of income. It may seem obvious that a restrictive monetary policy, by temporarily raising the real rate of interest, helps the rich and hurts the poor. This is not necessarily so. With aggregate demand being excessive one has to be specific about what is the alternative to a restrictive monetary policy. Is it to raise taxes on the top quarter of the income distribution, or to cut government welfare programs? Or is it to let inflation accelerate by doing nothing? Moreover, the poor tend to hold a larger proportion of their assets (though not necessarily of their incomes) in fixed-rate assets, such as bank deposits, than do the rich.

Another distributional effect of a rising interest rate is the impact on buyers and sellers of assets. Someone who sells a long-term bond when interest rates have risen suffers a capital loss. This *seems* inequitable since he or she may not have had any choice about when to sell. One might reply that, in terms of opportunity costs, those who hold on to their assets rather than selling them suffer an equal loss. Nonetheless, people seem to feel worse about taking actual losses than book losses, and, in this respect, those who have to sell assets when interest rates rise do suffer.

---

[3] One reason for this solicitude about housing is a wish to improve living conditions in the slums, though it is not obvious that support for housing across the board is the best way to achieve this. Also, it seems to be widely believed that home ownership makes people into better citizens, or that there are important aesthetic benefits received by the public from good housing beyond those received by its owners.

SUMMARY

1 One can describe the transmission process in terms of portfolio balance. As firms and households receive more money they bring their portfolios back into equilibrium by acquiring other goods and assets instead.

2 In the Keynesian transmission story an increase in the money stock lowers interest rates, which raises investment via a lower cost of borrowing. In addition, interest rates also affect consumption.

3 The Fed has sponsored an elaborate econometric model, whose flow chart is shown in Figure 22.1.

4 Changes in interest rates affect the exchange rate of the dollar, so that, as interest rates fall, exports increase and imports decline, thus reinforcing the expansionary domestic effects.

5 Monetary policy also works through expectations; wages and prices could rise before the increase in the money stock actually takes places.

6 In deciding whether to use monetary policy as a stabilization tool its allocational effects should be considered. One criterion for evaluating these effects, the free market criterion, takes as optimal the allocation that would occur in a competitive economy. The proportionality criterion, on the other hand, takes as optimal that each sector suffers a roughly proportional cutback from a restrictive policy.

QUESTIONS AND EXERCISES

1 Do you think monetary policy has had much influence on the behavior of income over the last ten years? To answer this question look at data presented in the *Economic Report of the President*. Document your conclusion by references to these, or other, data.

2 Compare and contrast the monetarist and the Keynesian approaches to the impact of monetary policy on income. Explain why this impact seems stronger in the monetarist than in the Keynesian approach.

3 Describe the ways in which an expansionary monetary policy increases consumption.

4 Describe the impact of monetary policy on the MPS model.

5 "With exchange rates being flexible, the Fed's power to combat a recession is increased." Discuss.

6 Suppose you are an executive of a trade association in the construction industry. Write a "letter to the editor" of a newspaper objecting to a restrictive monetary policy because of its impact on your industry.

7 Write another "letter to the editor" answering the letter from the previous question.

FURTHER READING

DE LEEUW, F., and E. GRAMLICH. "The Channels of Monetary Policy," *Journal of Finance*, 24 (May 1969):265–290. This is an exposition of how monetary policy works in the MPS model.

JUDD, J., and J. SCADDING. "Financial Change and Monetary Targeting in the United States," Federal Reserve Bank of San Francisco, *Interest Rate Deregulation and Mon-*

etary Policy. San Francisco: Federal Reserve Bank of San Francisco, 1983. An interesting discussion of the impact of deregulation on monetary policy.

LAIDLER, DAVID. "Money and Money Income: An Essay on the Transmission Mechanism." *Journal of Monetary Economics,* 4(April 1978):151–193. An excellent survey, particularly strong on the expectational aspects.

MISHKIN, FREDERICK. "Monetary Policy and Liquidity: Simulation Results," *Economic Inquiry,* 16 (January 1978):16—36. An interesting analysis of the importance of changes in household liquidity.

WOJNILOWER, ALBERT. "The Central Role of Credit Crunches in Recent Financial History," *Brookings Papers on Economic Activity,* 2 (1980):277–326. A fascinating piece of "analytic description" arguing that monetary policy can curb a boom only by plunging the economy into a recession. It is brilliantly written—a pleasure to read.

APPENDIX: CREDIT ALLOCATION

In a system of credit allocation the government limits the amount of credit made available to certain sectors of the economy. This increases the availability of credit to all others sectors and lowers interest rates. Such a system has been used occasionally in the United States (World War II, 1948–1949, 1950–1952, and 1980) as well as in several European countries, particularly in France.[4] Credit allocation might be used only on special occasions, for example, at a time when a restrictive monetary policy has temporarily raised interest rates, or it might be used permanently.

The mechanics of credit allocation can take several forms. One is to prohibit certain types of loans. For example, the Fed's Regulation W in the 1940s set minimum down payments and maximum maturities for installment sales of consumer durables. A different approach imposes a ceiling on certain types of loans. This could take the form of a maximum growth rate of all loans of certain lenders or ceilings on specific types of loans. For example, banks might be told that they could not increase their business loans by more than 5 percent per year. Instead of such ceilings, floors could be used, for example, banks being required to increase their mortgage loans by at least 10 percent per year. Alternatively, instead of setting rigid floors or ceilings, banks and other lenders could be given an incentive to make—or to cut back upon—certain types of loans. For instance, banks could be given credit against their reserve requirements for a certain proportion of their additional mortgage loans, or special reserve requirements could be imposed on other loans. Thus, in March 1980 the Fed temporarily imposed a 15 percent reserve requirement against increases in the outstanding volume of certain consumer loans by all significant types of consumer lenders. Since then, the law has changed, so that the Fed no longer has the authority to allocate credit in these ways.

The case for credit allocation takes two forms. One is to argue that certain types of investment have large external benefits and hence deserve a government subsidy. By requiring banks and other lenders to make more loans to these sectors, the cost of credit to them is reduced, and their investment is stimulated without an expenditure of government funds. The second form the argument can take is to say that the discriminatory effects of tight money are so severe that they have to be offset by another policy, credit allocation. Admittedly, while credit allocation would, in part, abrogate the market mechanism of letting the credit go to the highest bidder, credit rationing by banks

---

[4] To a small extent credit allocation has been used in the United States at other times too. For example, in making certain types of loans, but not others, eligible for discounting, the Fed tried to influence the characteristics of loans made by banks. At other times it has indicated that member banks that extended certain types of loans could borrow more readily from it.

and other lenders already does so. And if we are to have credit allocation it should be done by the government, which takes social usefulness into account, rather than by bankers just concerned with profits.

But there exists a cogent case against credit allocation. It is not at all clear that governmental decisions about where credit should flow would be superior to the decisions of the private market. In principle, they should be, since the government can take into account any externalities that the private market ignores (though it is far from clear that the externalities that could be taken into account by credit allocation are all that large). But, in practice, various pressure groups may succeed in obtaining undeserved preference for their credit demands. In effect, with credit allocation, the distribution of political power may well determine access to credit.

Furthermore, while a system of credit allocation could work in the short run, eventually, it would become ineffective. If banks or other financial intermediaries were forced to make less profitable loans, they would reduce the interest rate they pay on deposits. Depositors would then switch to other intermediaries. If necessary, new types of uncontrolled intermediaries would spring up. Moreover, borrowers can also confound a system of credit allocation. For example, a family buying a house can take out a larger mortgage, and use its own funds thus freed to buy securities. *In the long run* one cannot control the allocation of credit by controlling the portfolio choices of financial intermediaries. Britain, which made heavy use of controls over bank lending as a tool of monetary policy in the 1950s and 1960s, found that this device became less and less effective with the passage of time and with the growth of nonbank financial intermediaries.

Moreover, credit allocation reduces the efficiency of the financial system. New institutions spring up that are viable merely because they can avoid this regulation, though they are otherwise less efficient than existing institutions. Efficiency is also reduced by a decline in intermediation below its optimal level. If financial intermediaries cannot invest savers' funds in the most profitable way, savers and ultimate borrowers both have an incentive not to use financial intermediaries, so that some of the benefits of financial intermediation are lost. All in all, our experience with Regulation Q does not make tampering with the financial system look particularly appetizing.

CHAPTER *23*

Can Countercyclical Monetary Policy Succeed?

The old-fashioned, traditional functions of monetary policy were to maintain the gold (or silver) standard and to prevent financial panics. In the early 1920s Keynes advocated using monetary policy to stabilize the domestic economy on a continuous basis. What was a radical proposal at that time became conventional wisdom after 1929. But this conventional wisdom has now been challenged by a number of economists who have argued that it is a vain hope; that in attempting to stabilize the economy, monetary policy is likely to generate further instability and inflation. In this chapter we take up the reasons why they think so, and in Chapter 25 we examine their preferred alternative of keeping the growth rate of money constant regardless of the stage of the business cycle.

The belief that a monetary policy that tries to be countercyclical will actually worsen economic fluctuations and inflation is based on any or all of five grounds. First, there is the problem of choosing the correct target, which was discussed in Chapter 21. As explained there, if the Fed uses an interest-rate target when the IS curve is shifting, then the Fed will cause income to fluctuate more. The second reason why countercyclical, or discretionary, monetary policy could enhance fluctuations is that it takes time for monetary policy to affect income. Thus, the Fed may adopt an expansionary policy in a recession, and this policy may raise income only after a long time when the recession is already over, and aggregate demand is excessive. Third, the public's reactions to the Fed's policy may cause it to be destabilizing. Fourth, due to political pressures, the Fed may follow a policy that is inflationary and destabilizing. Finally, the Fed may lack the administrative competence required for stabilization policy. We will now take up each of these potential problems in turn, except for the already discussed targets problem. Although the discussion will deal only with monetary policy, similar problems also confound fiscal policy.

THE PROBLEM OF LAGS

This problem arises only with a policy that tries to reduce the fluctuations of nominal income around its trend rather than with a policy that tries to raise, or lower, the trend of nominal income. But before discussing the problem that lags create let us see what this term means. Do not think of the lag as the time that elapses from the date the policy changes to a specific date at which income changes. Not all the change in income occurs at one particular time. Some of the change in income occurs quickly, but it takes a much longer time until the full effect is reached. We are dealing here not with a point-input-point-output situation, but with a "distributed lag," so that, instead of saying that it takes monetary policy, say, fifteen months to change income, we should say for example that 30 percent of the effect is reached after four months, 60 percent after twelve months, and 100 percent after twenty-four months.

If monetary policy had all of its effect on income immediately, the Fed's task would be greatly simplified. Once it becomes aware that the economy is in a recession it would simply adopt an expansionary policy, and, conversely, if demand is too high it would adopt a restrictive policy. By looking at the current level of income it could make sure that its policy is just strong enough to keep nominal income close to the right level. Admittedly, the fact that accurate data on current income are not available right away would create a problem, but this would be relatively minor.

Unfortunately, this is not the way it works; once the Fed changes policy it takes time for its main effects on income to show up. When they do, economic conditions *may* have changed so that an expansionary policy initiated in the recession raises income when income is already too high, or a restrictive policy adopted during the previous boom lowers income during the subsequent recession. When the Fed then reverses itself and adopts a new policy, the effects of this new policy may again come at the wrong time. We may therefore get the stabilizer's nightmare shown in Figure 23.1 in which monetary policy *increases* the amplitude of the business cycle. This possibility has to be taken seriously because in the postwar period business cycles have been short. In the years 1945–1982, the median length of a recession was only eleven months, and the median length of an expansion was thirty-four months.

A Formal Model

Milton Friedman has developed a model that highlights the importance of the proper timing of countercyclical monetary and fiscal policy. Assume that the trend of aggregate demand is just right, and that we want to minimize fluctuations around this trend. A convenient way of measuring fluctuations is a statistical measure called the **variance.** (To obtain the variance take the difference between each observation and the mean and square it. Then take the average of these squared differences.) Since the variance involves the *squared* deviations from the mean, treating the minimization of the variance as the goal of stabilization policy implies trying to minimize not the differences of aggregate demand from the desired level, but the *squares* of these differences. In turn, this implies that we are more than proportionally concerned about a

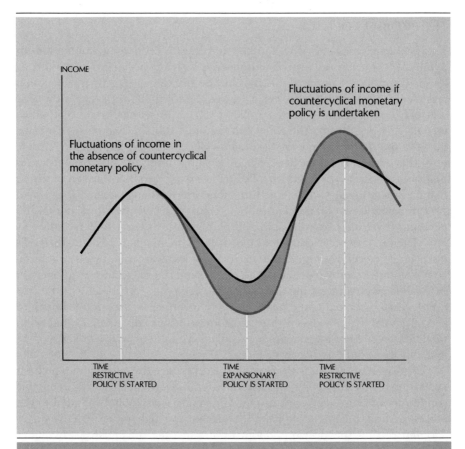

INCOME

Fluctuations of income if
countercyclical monetary
policy is undertaken

Fluctuations of income in
the absence of countercyclical
monetary policy

TIME	TIME	TIME
RESTRICTIVE	EXPANSIONARY	RESTRICTIVE
POLICY IS STARTED	POLICY IS STARTED	POLICY IS STARTED

Figure 23.1　Effects of Badly Timed Stabilization Policy. A badly timed
stabililization policy can be destabilizing.

few large differences than about more frequent small ones.[1] Another implicit
value judgment is involved in the treatment of a dollar of excessive income as
being exactly as undesirable as a dollar of shortfall in income.

All the same, let us assume that we *do* want to minimize the variance of
nominal income. Changes in the marginal efficiency of investment, etc., cause
income to vary. We designate the variance of income that is due to these "private sector" fluctuations and is independent of policy by σ_x^2. Stabilization then
consists of generating changes in income that offset these independent fluctuations. Since the average level of aggregate demand is just right, these policy-

[1] For example, compare two policies. Policy A generates the following series of deviations from
the mean: 0, 4, 0; Policy B results in deviations 2, 2, 1. If the criterion is to minimize the absolute
deviations, Policy A is superior. But if we are trying to minimize the square of the deviations,
Policy B (with a sum of 9) is better. Specifically, we are using what is called a quadratic utility
function, such as $U = f(P^2, U^2)$ where P is the excess of the actual inflation rate over the desired
inflation rate, and U the excess of the actual unemployment rate over the full-employment rate.
(Since both inflation and unemployment lower utility, f denotes a negative function.) This use of
a quadratic utility function involves a value judgment, which not everyone may wish to accept.

induced changes are sometimes positive and sometimes negative, and have a mean of zero. Their variance around this mean of zero we will call σ_y^2. The total variance of income, designated by σ_z^2, will be the result both of the original fluctuations in income and of the policy-induced fluctuations. A theorem in statistics tells us that this is

$$\sigma_z^2 = \sigma_x^2 + \sigma_y^2 + 2R\sigma_x\sigma_y,$$

where R is the coefficient of correlation between the original variance of income, σ_x^2, and the variance induced by the stabilization policy, σ_y^2.[2]

Applying this equation for the sum of two variances to the problem at hand one can see the great importance of the correlation between the original variations in income and the variations induced by policy—that is, the timing of policy. If a policy is badly timed—R being positive—so that it raises nominal income when nominal income is already above its mean, and lowers it when it is below its mean, then we have the case of the stabilizer's nightmare.

If this obvious point were all that the above equation shows we would not have bothered to introduce it. But it also shows two other, not so obvious things. One is that it does not suffice for the policy to be "neutral" in its timing, that is, to be right half the time. If it is, and $R = 0$, the last term in the equation drops out, and the variance of income is equal to $\sigma_x^2 + \sigma_y^2$, which is, of course, greater than σ_x^2. Hence, if the Fed's timing is half-right it is *destabilizing* income. This suggests that there is a genuine danger that stabilization policy may actually be destabilizing. Second, by algebraic manipulation one can obtain the maximum effective size of the stabilization policy's impact on income for each R. This is $\hat{\sigma}_y^2 = R\sigma_x^2$. Any policy that *tries* to do more than this will actually do less. For example, assume that the Fed adopts a policy powerful enough to offset all the fluctuation in income; that is, it sets $\sigma_y = \sigma_x$. If the correlation coefficient is $-.5$ such a policy will not succeed in reducing the net fluctuation of income at all.[3] And if the correlation coefficient were, say, $-.4$ it would actually *increase* income fluctuations.[4] Too much can be even worse than nothing at all.

This way of looking at policy therefore has much to teach. It shows the great importance of the timing of the impact of the policy since this deter-

---

[2] The correlation coefficient can best be explained by considering the regression equation $y = a + bx + u$ in which a is a constant, b measures the effect of x on y, and u is a randomly distributed variable. The computer is then kindly requested to select those values of a and b that allow x to explain most of the squared variation in y, that is, to minimize the square of u. If u is zero, then x and y are perfectly correlated; that is, since we know the constants, $a + b$, once given x we know what y has to be. In this case the correlation coefficient is unity (or minus unity if b is negative). Now suppose that there is no relation at all between x and y: assume, for example, that x is your age and y the last digit of your driver's license. In this case knowledge of x would not allow you to predict y at all. In this case the correlation coefficient is zero. The square of the correlation coefficient tells you the proportion of y "explained" by x.

[3] If $\sigma_x^2 = \sigma_y^2$ and $R = \frac{1}{2}$, then the expression $\sigma_x^2 + \sigma_y^2 + 2R\sigma_x\sigma_y$ reduces to σ_x^2, which is the original fluctuation of income in the absence of stabilization policy. If the correlation coefficient is $-.5$, the maximum by which policy could reduce the variation of income is 25 percent; any policy more powerful than that would be less effective.

[4] In this case the variance of income would be $2\sigma_x^2 - .8\sigma_x^2 = 1.2\sigma_x^2$ compared to σ_x^2 in the absence of policy.

mines R. It warns us (1) that it does not take great errors in timing to be destabilizing and (2) that one must beware of adopting a policy that is too strong. Hence, to reduce fluctuations in nominal income the Fed must be greatly concerned with forecasting accurately future nominal income, as well as the impact of its policy on nominal income. Remember, however, that all of this applies only to what is strictly a *stabilization* policy, that is, to a policy that tries to even out fluctuations in nominal income. Policy may be more concerned with changing the average level of income. For example, a policy that causes the unemployment rate to fluctuate between, say, 5 and 7 percent is surely better than one that causes the unemployment rate to be absolutely stable at 12 percent.

Problems Created by the Lag

If monetary policy would have most of its effect on income almost immediately, the prediction of "future" income would not create a problem for the Fed. Since income changes very little over a short span of time, such as a calendar quarter, the Fed could use the current level of income as its estimate of income at the time with perhaps a small adjustment for the growth trend. But, obviously, this does not work if monetary policy takes a long time to affect income. Assume that most of the effect occurs only after two years. In two years the economy may well be in a different business-cycle stage. Hence, if the Fed selects its policy on the basis of what income is currently, the correlation between the original income fluctuations (σ_x^2) and the income fluctuations caused by policy (σ_y^2) is likely to be close to zero, and monetary policy will destabilize the economy. If monetary policy has a long lag—as much of the empirical evidence suggests—then the Fed has to use a forecast of income. Since obviously the Fed's forecasts are not without errors, this provides a limitation of the effectiveness of stabilization policy.

A second way in which the length of the lag is important is the leeway the Fed has to offset errors it has made. Suppose that it expected income to decline and adopted an expansionary policy; income now turns out to be much higher than expected. If the lag is short, the Fed can quickly reverse itself, and offset the effect of its previous action, but it cannot do so if the lag is long.[5]

There is still a third problem. To use stabilization policy effectively, the Fed must know R, the correlation between fluctuations in income and its policy. But to know this it must also know not only future income, but also the

---

[5] In principle, the Fed could avoid this problem by adopting a corrective policy that is much stronger than the initial policy it is trying to offset. For example, assume that only 20 percent of the impact on income occurs in the first quarter, and that after one year monetary policy has 80 percent of its full effect. The Fed could then fully offset within a quarter a policy action that it took a year ago, *if* it were willing to adopt an offsetting policy that is four times as strong as the original policy. But such large policy changes have costs; in particular, they lead to violent swings in interest rates. There is also the *possibility* that a continual policy of quick offsets via stronger offsetting policies would cause an explosive increase in the magnitude of policy moves. However, this does not appear likely.

impact of its policy in each period, say, each quarter—that is, the distributed lag of the impact of its policy. This would be a difficult econometric problem even if the lag were fairly constant. But the problem is much worse if the lag is highly variable. Thus, suppose that the Fed's staff were to tell the FOMC that the lag is, *on the average,* one year, but that, in one-third of the cases, it is only three months, and in another third it is two years. In deciding whether to adopt an expansionary or a restrictive policy the FOMC would then not know whether to orient its policy toward the income level it expects to prevail in three months, in a year, or in two years. What the FOMC must consider is not the average lag, but the lag for the particular action it is contemplating. Hence, knowledge of the average lag is sufficient only if the lags cluster closely around this average. Thus, if the Fed uses the average lag from its econometric model, this *could* make its policy destabilizing in the majority of cases, even if the model estimates the average lag correctly. However, this is not so if the Fed avoids all explicit forecasting and simply bases its actions on the current level of income.[6]

The existence of a significant lag in the effect of monetary policy creates three problems for the Fed. It must forecast income, even if only by saying that income will not change; it cannot offset past errors easily and quickly; and it must estimate the effect of its policies in each period.

Hence, to evaluate whether the Fed has information reliable enough to be an effective stabilizer we would have to know how accurate its forecast of income is, and how well it predicts the effect of its policy in each period. Neither can be known precisely since the Fed does not make available its forecasts for the most recent years. However, data for an earlier period suggest that the Fed forecasts about as well as good private forecasters do.[7] Hence, the forecast record of a sample of private forecasters, shown in Table 23.1, provides some indication of how well the Fed can predict economic conditions.

Empirical Estimates of the Lag

It is convenient to divide the lag into two parts. There is first the *inside lag,* that is, *the lag from the time the need for action arises until the Fed takes action.* This is a distributed lag since the Fed is unlikely to undertake all its actions at one time. Usually it will undertake its new open-market policy in a series of steps spread out over several months because it is uncertain whether the new policy is really the appropriate one, and hence wants to move slowly.

This inside lag can, but need not, be very short; it depends on the extent to which the Fed is willing to take action on a forecast as opposed to waiting until conditions have actually changed. It also depends on whether the Fed changes policy in large steps or in many small steps spread out over time. Thus

---

[6] If the Fed bases its policy entirely on current income, then, surprisingly, the variability of the lag does no harm. In fact, the more variable it is, the greater is the probability that policy is stabilizing. We know of no intuitive explanation of this strange result that emerges from a mathematical analysis. See Haskell Benishay, "A Framework for the Evaluation of Short-Term Fiscal and Monetary Policy," *Journal of Money, Credit and Banking,* 4 (November 1972):779–810.

[7] Raymond Lombra and Michael Moran, "Policy Advice and Policymaking at the Federal Reserve," *Carnegie-Rochester Conference Series on Public Policy,* 13 (Autumn 1980): 9–68.

Table 23.1	Mean Absolute Error of a Sample of GNP Forecasts, One Year Ahead, 2nd Quarter 1971 to 1st Quarter 1985	
	Mean absolute error (%)	Mean absolute error as percentage of mean annual change
Nominal GNP	2.1	23
Real GNP	1.6	60
GNP deflator	1.4	21

Note: The mean absolute error is obtained by summing the individual errors regardless of sign and dividing by the number of cases.

Source: Based on Stephen McNees, "Which Forecast Should You Use?" Federal Reserve Bank of Boston, *New England Economic Review* (July/August 1985): 37, and unpublished U.S. Department of Commerce data.

if it is willing to undertake much of its open-market purchases before a business downturn actually occurs, the inside lag will be negative. The inside lag therefore depends upon the Fed itself, and hence depends on who the chairman of the Board of Governors is.

Then there is the *outside lag.* This is *the distributed lag from the time of the Fed's action until income changes.* Obviously, an increase in the money stock and a decrease in interest rates do not raise income immediately. For investment, firms have to make a decision to invest, they have to draw up plans, place orders, and so on. For consumption, it takes some time until interest rates on consumer credit decline and until households respond to the rise in their money holdings or the increase in security prices that results from lower interest rates.

The outside lag is more objective and less subject to Fed control than the inside lag. Many economists have tried to estimate it. Some have used econometric models, and we showed some of their results in Figure 22.3, while others have regressed income on money, or have measured the lag between turning points in the money growth rate and business-cycle turning points. Several economists have measured how long it takes firms to invest, while still others have (following the analysis described in Chapter 13) looked at the length of time it takes interest rates to return to their previous levels after changes in the money growth rate. Unfortunately, little agreement has been reached, though most, but not all, of these studies show that it takes *at least* two quarters for monetary policy to reach half of its ultimate effect.[8] Beyond this, the range of estimates is large with the big econometric models usually showing long lags. A major reason for the long lags shown by these models is that most of them use a term-structure equation that shows a very slow adaptation of long-term interest rates to the changes that the Fed brings about in short-term rates. All of these methods are subject to some criticisms, and the

---

[8] A complication here is that it is quite possible that the effect of monetary policy does not build up smoothly to a peak, but rises to a certain level and then declines again to a lower level, or cycles around some level.

substantial disagreement among their results suggests that we should not be confident about our knowledge of the lag in the impact of monetary policy. Moreover, although little empirical work has been done on the extent to which the lag of monetary policy varies from case to case, the limited amount of information that is available suggests that the lag is highly variable. If correct, this is most disturbing.

Policy Tools: A Further Consideration

We are now in a position to return to the discussion of the tools of monetary policy, and to take up a sophisticated problem that we could not discuss before. Suppose several tool are available, such as open-market operations, discount-rate changes, and reserve-requirement changes or, alternatively, fiscal policy and monetary policy, all of which are strong enough to change income by the required amount. Which one should be used? One possible answer is the strongest. But a moment's reflection will show that, unless there is a cost from using a tool too much or too often, there is no reason for choosing the strongest. Instead of looking at the strength one should use the tool that has the most predictable impact. Moreover, it is general better to use several tools at the same time. This is so because if their variances are not perfectly correlated, then an averaging-out process ensures that the variance of the impact is less for several tools jointly than it is for any single tool. The exact mixture in which the tools should be used depends on their relative variances and on the correlation of their variances.

RATIONAL EXPECTATIONS AND MARKET CLEARING

Some economists, led by Robert Lucas of the University of Chicago and Thomas Sargent and Neil Wallace of the University of Minnesota, offer a devastating critique of stabilization policy. They accept the rational-expectations approach discussed in Chapter 13, and they believe that firms adjust wages and prices fully and quickly to all the available information. Given these two assumptions, they assert that stabilization poicy is ineffective and unnecessary. Suppose, they argue, that aggregate demand falls. If everyone knows this, then firms reduce their wages and prices. The real quantity of money now rises, and hence interest rates fall until output returns to its previous level. Hence there is no need for the Keynesian remedy of using monetary or fiscal policy to offset any known fall in aggregate demand. Now suppose that aggregate demand falls without anyone knowing that this has happened. Firms then do not reduce wages and prices right away, and hence output and employment fall for some time. But this scenario leaves no room for stabilization policy; if nobody knows that aggregate demand has fallen, the government cannot know that it should now adopt an expansionary policy. Finally, suppose that the government knows that aggregate demand has fallen, while the public does not know this. Then, instead of undertaking an expansionary policy the government could simply share its knowledge with the public.

Most economists reject the assumption that wages and prices are flexible enough to support this extreme rational-expectations view. They point out, for instance, that even in severe recessions wages and prices are reduced only a little. Unemployment, therefore, occurs for a long time.

The Impact of Stabilization Policy

If the rational-expectation theorists are correct, *and* if wages and prices adjust quickly, countercyclical policy not only does no good, it does harm because it is inflationary. To see why, consider first an economy with rational expectations and high employment. The government now undertakes a long-run expansionary policy. The traditional story is that firms react to the increase in aggregate demand for their products initially by raising their output, and raise their prices only with a lag. This is so primarily because firms do not know whether this increase in demand is permanent or just temporary, and they want to avoid frequent price changes. But, say the rational-expectations theorists, this story is wrong. Entrepreneurs read newspapers, and, hence, *in this case*, when demand increases, they realize that it is because of an expansionary policy, and that the higher demand will persist. Hence, they raise prices right away instead of raising output.

This example has the government raising aggregate demand during a period of high employment, which is hardly an example of a good stabilization policy; so now assume instead that it raises aggregate demand only during a recession, but does so consistently. If so, whenever a recession occurs firms know that the government will raise aggregate demand, and hence they raise their prices. Or, more realistically, they refrain from doing what they otherwise would have done during the recession, cut prices.

Suppose, for example, that the government were to announce that every time unemployment exceeds, say, 6 percent, it will raise the money growth rate by 3 percentage points. Both firms and unions would then take an unemployment rate of over 6 percent as an indication that they should raise their wages and prices. Carrying this approach a bit further, rational-expectations theorists have argued that an *expected* increase in the money growth rate raises only prices and does not raise output even temporarily. Output rises temporarily only in response to an *unexpected* increase in the money growth rate. Hence, the only way the Fed could raise output and employment would be if it could adopt expansionary policies that are unexpected. But sooner or later the public will figure out any consistent Federal Reserve policy; and even if the Fed could somehow fool the public in the long run, it is far from clear that it should do so since this would cause people to make wrong decisions.

This theory is highly controversial. While the empirical evidence was initially favorable to it, in recent empirical tests its performance has, on the whole, not been good.

Although rational-expectations theories, if correct, eliminate the argument for most stabilization policy, they do enhance the efficacy of one stabilization policy. This is a policy to end inflation by cutting total demand. The usual story is that if a restrictive monetary or fiscal policy cuts aggregate demand, the initial result is a much greater fall in output than in the inflation rate. Firms and unions do not realize that the government is serious about ending inflation. They continue to expect inflation, and therefore raise their wages and prices. Only after a long time of great unemployment will the inflation rate decline substantially. Rational-expectations theory suggests such a period of high unemployment is not necessary; the government should let the public know by some dramatic gesture that it really will cut aggregate demand sufficiently to bring the inflation rate down. If this is done, then prices and wages will adjust relatively quickly.

Whether or not one accepts it in its extreme form, however, rational-expectations theory still has an important lesson: the public should be told if the Fed adopts a restrictive policy and intends to stick with it. In general, one does not have to accept rational-expectations theory completely to conclude that expectations do matter, and that monetary policies will have different effects depending on what expectations they generate. For example, some of the variation in the lag with which changes in the money stock affect income *may* be due to differences in the extent to which the public realizes what is happening.

Predicting the Effects of Policies

The rational-expectations approach has another important implication for policy. This is that policy may unintentionally change the way the public reacts to events. For example, take a new policy to cut personal income taxes during a recession and raise them again during the following expansion. To find out how big a tax cut is needed economists may calculate the marginal propensity to consume from past data on consumption and disposable income, or they may look at how consumption changed every time taxes were cut previously. But they may be in for a disappointment. When income taxes are now cut as a countercyclical policy, the public *may* raise its consumption very little. It knows that, unlike in the past, from now on income taxes will be raised again when the economy expands. And since it sets its consumption on the basis of its long-run disposable income, it now reacts very differently to a tax cut than it did before.

Thus, the adoption of a new policy has outdated and made inapplicable the information obtained from past experience. This implies that it is danger-ous to use the information generated by econometric models, regression equations, or economic history in general to predict the effects of any policy that may change people's expectations. Hence, rational-expectations theorists argue, we know very little about the effects that economic policies have, and this too makes it questionable that stabilization policy can succeed.

POLITICAL AND ADMINISTRATIVE PROBLEMS

The technical problems created by long and variable lags and by rational expectations are not the only difficulties that confront discretionary policy. Political difficulties, too, may prevent effective policy. The political assump-tion underlying economic policy is that the electorate knows what is best for it and that the technicians who operate the government carry out policies that will achieve these ends. Now obviously this is an idealization, and the question is not whether it mirrors reality exactly, but whether it is close enough to real-ity so that stabilization policy does more good than harm. Although econo-mists generally assume that this is the case, some economists, particularly monetarists, are challenging it. Unfortunately, this discussion is still in its very early stages, so that we can only give a rather impressionistic sketch of the problem.

Several things can go wrong in a process that has the public decide on its desired goal, which the technicians in government then carry out. One is that the public may not know what is best for it. A second is that special-interest groups may be able to substitute their wishes for those of the majority, and a third problem is that the majority may override the legitimate interests of a minority. And finally, the bureaucracy may be more responsive to its own interests than to the public interest.

The public may at times mistake its own interests in the goals it indirectly sets for monetary policy through its elected representatives. This does not imply that the public is unintelligent, but merely that any one person has so little influence on monetary policy that it is not worth his or her while to devote even a trivial amount of time to it. Consequently, the public may sometimes support policies that are clearly wrong. More specifically, the public *may* have a short memory about recent economic policy. This creates a danger of the political business cycle discussed in Chapter 7. Whether this has actually occurred in the United States is a debated issue.

Special-interest groups may exercise too much influence over monetary policy. Populists have long argued that banks pressure the Fed to adopt restrictive policies that raise interest rates. But the Fed is also subject to pressure from those who want highly expansionary policies, particularly the politically powerful residential construction industry and the thrift industry.[9] These industries can be expected to pressure the Fed, both directly and through Congress, or by arousing public opinion, into adopting an expansionary policy to postpone any substantial rise in nominal interest rates. The costs of adopting a policy that is too expansionary are diffused over the general economy, while the short-run benefits from such a policy are much more concentrated. Hence, those who gain from such a policy organize to pressure the Fed, while those who lose from it do not.

In addition, there is the **time-inconsistency problem.** The Fed would like output to be higher than it is. This is so even when unemployment is low because certain government policies, such as income taxes, reduce work incentives. Hence people work less than is optimal from the social viewpoint. Suppose that the Fed has convinced people that it will curb inflation. It can then do the following. It raises the money growth rate, and at first output rises. Once people realize that the Fed has broken its pledge and that inflation is higher than before, inflationary expectations rise and output falls again. There is now a permanently higher inflation rate for each level of unemployment, unless the Fed can somehow persuade people that it will not permit the higher inflation rate to continue. In this way, at each moment in time, the Fed has an incentive to make a commitment to the public which it will then break.

---

[9] The residential construction industry is so powerful because there are contractors and construction workers in every congressional district, and because of the industry's alliance with the influential thrift industry. Part of its power probably comes from the public's susceptibility to the emotional arguments for fostering housing.

Moreover, as discussed in Chapter 7, the Fed has its own bureaucratic interests. Rightly or wrongly, some economists believe that at times it puts these interests ahead of the public interest. Karl Brunner has written that we should not expect a central bank to

> naturally pursue the optimal social benefit achievable with cleverly designed sta-
> bilization policies. ... An activist conception of policy ... offers excellent
> opportunities for actions ... in the interests of the monetary authorities and
> their bureaucracies, or of the political coalitions formed with other agencies or
> the existing central executive.[10]

Robert Hetzel, of the Richmond Reserve Bank, has suggested some ways in which the interaction of political pressures and the Fed's incentive to maintain its autonomy may degrade the quality of monetary policy. His analysis is based on Kane's previously discussed conclusion that Congress uses the Fed as a whipping boy. It obtains political benefit from loudly complaining when the Fed undertakes unpopular—yet necessary—policies. But since it lets the Fed continue with these policies, it avoids having to adopt such unpopular policies itself. Hetzel argues that Congress is willing to play this game only up to a point. If the Fed's policies become too unpopular Congress would reduce the Fed's autonomy. Since the Fed treasures its autonomy it does all sorts of things to protect it. One is that it does not use a consistent analytic framework because such a framework might indicate policies that are too risky politically. Hence it makes policy in an inchoate way that pays little attention to economic analysis.

> Policy evolves under the assumption that an optimal long-run policy will result
> from a concatenation of policy actions each of which appears optimal within the
> context of a short time horizon. No systematic procedure is imposed whereby
> long-run objectives constrain these policy actions.[11]

Moreover, the Fed has to avoid clear-cut goals. The more it sets out its priori-ties the more difficult it becomes to convince various powerful groups that their interests are given sufficient importance. Furthermore, Hetzel points out, the Fed obtains support by adopting policies that seem to address current conditions, that is, by focusing on current GNP, not on future GNP.

Another set of problems that may inhibit efficient monetary policy is that, given the great uncertainty it faces, the FOMC might be reluctant to move quickly enough. Suppose that it seems as though a more restrictive pol-icy is needed. The FOMC knows that such a policy will create unemployment and hence much suffering. It may therefore tend to put off adopting a restric-tive policy until the need for it is clear-cut. Imagine how you would feel know-ing that you have adopted a policy that created much unemployment and then

---

[10] Karl Brunner, "The Case against Monetary Activism," *Lloyds Bank Review*, 139 (January 1981):19.

[11] Robert Hetzel, "The Formulation of Monetary Policy," unpublished manuscript, June 1983, p. 15.

turned out to be unnecessary. However, by the time it becomes obvious that a restrictive policy is needed it may be too late.[12]

SUMMARY

1 Monetary policy affects income with a distributed lag. Hence, it might be badly timed and therefore destabilizing. This depends upon the correlation between the policy and the original fluctuation in income, and on the strength of the policy.

2 The existence of the lag creates several problems. The Fed must forecast income, and it must predict the strength of its policy and its distributed lag. Moreover, the lag prevents the Fed from quickly offsetting any errors it made.

3 The Fed should use not necessarily the strongest tools, but those with the most predictable effects. Usually it is best to employ several.

4 Rational expectations creates another potential problem for the Fed. Under rational expectations, stabilization policy can be effective only if the government has better information than the public, or if its policy affects the economy before the public can act. This raises the question of whether wages are sticky or merely respond slowly due to limited information.

5 Rational-expectations theory also argues that if the Fed reacts to a recession by a predictable expansionary policy this policy will have its effects only on prices and not on output. However, this is much disputed. Rational-expectations theory also implies that, if the government changes its policy, then the economy will change too, so that the policy—which is based on past data—may no longer be valid.

6 The Fed does not make policy in a vacuum; political pressures impinge on it and may deflect it from the correct policy. Administrative problems, such as concern with its own interests and autonomy, lack of a clear framework, and overemphasis on current conditions may also inhibit effective policy. Very little is known about this.

QUESTIONS AND EXERCISES

1 "The problem with monetary policy is not, as was once thought, that it is too weak, but that it is too strong." Explain.

2 Explain why monetary policy is destabilizing if the correlation coefficient between σ_x^2 and σ_y^2 is zero or positive.

3 Discuss the problem that the lag in the effect of monetary policy creates for the Federal Reserve.

4 Why does a variable lag create a more serious problem than a stable one? What factors could account for it being variable?

5 Read one of the empirical studies that try to measure the lag. (The items by Hamburger and Uselton under Further Reading have references to these studies.) Write a critique of it.

---

[12] Another possibility is that tardiness in changing policy results from the way policy is made. Since FOMC votes are published, the FOMC wants to protect itself by presenting a united, or almost united, front to the public. But by the time doubters are convinced that a policy change is needed, too much time may have passed. See Robert Shapiro, "Politics and the Federal Reserve," *The Public Interest*, 66 (Winter 1982): 119–139.

6 Explain in your own words the rational-expectations criticism of stabilization policy.

7 "If expectations are rational, an expansionary monetary policy will raise only prices and not output." Discuss.

8 Is it sometimes more reasonable to use an error-learning model than rational expectations? If so, under what conditions? How do you form your own expectations?

9 What are the political problems that may hinder effective stabilization policy? Do they apply to fiscal policy as well as to monetary policy?

FURTHER READING

BRAINARD, WILLIAM. "Uncertainty and the Effectiveness of Monetary Policy," *American Economic Review*, 57 (May 1967):411–425. An excellent discussion of how to use various policy tools that have different degrees of predictability.

FRIEDMAN, MILTON. "The Effects of a Full Employment Policy on Economic Stability: A Formal Analysis." In his *Essays in Positive Economics*. Chicago: University of Chicago Press, 1953. This is a classic.

HAMBURGER, MICHAEL. "The Lag in the Effect of Monetary Policy: A Survey of Recent Literature," *Monthly Review* (Federal Reserve Bank of New York), 53 (December 1971):289–298. An excellent survey of several empirical studies.

HAVRILESKY, THOMAS. "A Theory of Monetary Instability," in M. Dooley, H. Kaufman, and R. Lombra, *The Political Economy of Policymaking: Essays in Honor of Will E. Mason*. Beverly Hills: Sage Publications, 1978, pp. 59–88. An interesting attempt to explain Fed actions.

HOLLAND, STEVEN. "Rational Expectations and the Effects of Monetary Policy: A Guide for the Uninitiated," *Review* (Federal Reserve Bank of St. Louis), 67 (May 1985):5–11. An excellent brief survey.

KANE, EDWARD. "Politics and Fed Policy-Making: The More Things Change the More They Remain the Same," *Journal of Monetary Economics*, 6 (April 1980):199–211.

SHEFFRIN, STEVEN. *Rational Expectations*. New York: Cambridge University Press, 1983. An excellent survey.

TAYLOR, HERB. "Time Inconsistency," Federal Reserve Bank of Philadelphia, *Business Review* (March/April 1985):3–12. A clear and simple discussion of the time-inconsistency problem.

TOBIN, JAMES. "How Dead Is Keynes?" *Economic Inquiry*, 15 (October 1977):459–468. A very good defense of Keynesian economics against the rational-expectations criticism.

USELTON, GENE. *Lags in the Effects of Monetary Policy*. New York: Marcel Dekker, 1974. Chapter 2 is a useful survey. Both this and the article by Hamburger above contain references to the numerous empirical studies the reader may wish to consult.

WILLETT, THOMAS. *The Political Business Cycle*. San Francisco: the Pacific Institute, 1986. Contains interesting papers on the political aspects of stabilization policies.

CHAPTER *24*

The Record of Monetary Policy

Having looked at the principles governing monetary policy, the time has come to see how the Fed has actually conducted monetary policy. Instead of discussing monetary policy in a seemingly "balanced" way by giving equal emphasis to all periods, we focus on particular episodes to see how the Fed has dealt with certain major problems. The focus is on evaluating the efficacy of monetary policy and on seeing what the Fed has learned from its experience, rather than on isolated facts.

THE EARLY YEARS

When the Federal Reserve System was inaugurated in 1913 one of its major goals, perhaps *the* major goal, was the maintenance of the gold standard, which at the time was generally considered the foundation of sound money. We will discuss the gold standard in Part 5. Here it suffices to note that under the gold standard "rules of the game" the Fed should let the quantity of money be determined by the country's gold stock. A gold inflow is supposed to increase the quantity of money, and a gold outflow to decrease it.

Although it also had some belief in the quantity theory, a second guiding idea of the Fed was the real-bills doctrine. According to this now-discarded theory, what matters is the *quality* rather than the *quantity* of money; as long as deposits are created as a result of short-term self-liquidating loans that finance real (as opposed to financial) activities, deposit creation cannot be inflationary.[1] Member banks could borrow from the Fed only by rediscounting **eligible paper,** that is, those *promissory notes they had discounted for their customers that*

---

[1] The argument was that a loan to finance short-term productive activity would increase the value of output by as much as it increased demand. And with supply and demand increasing equally, prices would be constant. This argument is invalid because part of the increase in the *value* of output may be due to higher prices. Under the real-bills doctrine the Fed could be financing ever-increasing inflation.

met the requirements of the real-bills doctrine, or by discounting their own promissory notes backed by government securities. The theory was that this would provide an "elastic" currency that would allow the money supply to expand when the demand for money for real transactions increased. At that time banks would discount more eligible promissory notes for their customers, and could then rediscount this eligible paper with the Fed. This is an extreme example of the accommodative policy the Fed has followed so frequently.

Another guiding idea was the need to avoid financial panics. It was widely believed that recessions were often the result of financial panics that were, in turn, caused by excessive speculation. Hence, one of the tasks of the Fed was to limit speculation. In addition, the provision of an elastic currency would also help to prevent financial panics since it would prevent banks from running out of currency. Bank failures, and the resulting panics, would also be reduced by the Fed's supervision of member banks, and the centralization of member bank reserves in the Federal Reserve Banks. The law of large numbers makes centralized reserves a more effective barrier against failure than are reserves kept individually by each bank.

A further goal of the Fed was to eliminate, or at least reduce, the pronounced seasonal swings in interest rates that occurred before 1914, and to avoid the sharp interest-rate increases that would accompany periods of financial stringency and panics.

All in all, the initial goals of the Fed were those that seemed reasonable to a small-town merchant in 1913, rather than those that an economist would now set for a central bank. Full employment had not yet been "invented"— there were not even unemployment statistics. Although in the 1920s there were attempts in Congress to add a price-stabilization goal to the Federal Reserve Act, these attempts failed. While we now set other goals for the Fed, these 1913 goals have not completely disappeared. We no longer have the gold standard, but the Fed has as one of its goals an appropriate exchange rate of the dollar. The Fed is still opposed to excessive speculation—a dislike of speculation being one of the few Puritan ideas not challenged in the turmoil of the 1960s. The Fed is still concerned about interest-rate fluctuations, and even the real-bills doctrine lives on in occasional admonitions to banks to avoid "unproductive" loans.

In its early years the Fed had little chance to aim at these goals. Shortly after it was organized, World War I broke out. Belligerents increased their purchases in the United States, resulting in a large gold inflow. The Fed could not offset the impact of this on bank reserves since it did not yet have enough securities to sell and open-market operations had not yet been invented.

In April 1917 the United States entered the war. It has been said that in every war truth is the first casualty. One might add that sound ideas on finance are the second. During the war the Fed became subservient to the Treasury Department. Its policy was dominated by the Treasury's goal of raising funds. Two-thirds of the government's wartime expenditures were financed by borrowing. The Treasury wanted to borrow at below-market interest rates and to rely on patriotic appeals to sell its securities. But to provide a material incentive, individuals could borrow from banks to buy government securities at an interest rate equal to the rate they received on these securities, that is, at no net interest cost. Banks could borrow from the Fed on their promissory notes secured by Treasury certificates at an interest rate below what the banks earned on these Treasury certificates. Hence, they had an incentive to borrow. All this was highly inflationary. And with this policy continuing after the war, so did the inflation. In the postwar expansion, March 1919 through January 1920, the wholesale price index rose by about 50 percent, and the GNP deflator by about 10 percent.

Although the Fed was concerned about the inflation, it was more or less willing to go along with the Treasury's inflationary policy until late 1919. Then in January 1920 it raised the discount rate applicable to commercial-paper borrowing from $4\frac{1}{2}$ percent to 6 percent, the sharpest jump in the discount rate that has ever occurred. In June 1920 this discount rate was raised to 7 percent, where it stayed, despite the recession, until May 1921.

The month, January 1920, in which the Fed shifted to such a highly restrictive policy was also the month of the upper turning point of the business cycle. The ensuing recession started mildly, but then turned into one of the deepest recessions in American history, though fortunately it was short-lived. Real GNP declined by 12 percent and, due to a sharp price decline, nominal GNP fell by 31 percent. Clearly the Fed is not to blame for *initiating* this recession since it started before the restrictive policy could have become effective. However, one can blame the Fed for making a bad situation worse. And the continuation of the restrictive policy despite a major recession was hardly a proud moment for monetary policy.

What were the reasons for this blunder? One was the Fed's concern about inflation. Another was the decline in the Fed's ratio of gold holdings to the currency and deposits it had issued. (At the time, the law specified minimum ratios.) But this was probably more a public justification for the policy than its main reason since the Fed had the legal power to suspend this reserve requirement. Instead, the main reason was probably the inadequacy of the Fed's underlying monetary theory. Thus, it did not understand that once high interest rates have succeeded in breaking the boom they should be lowered again to ameliorate the ensuing recession, and not be kept at a high level that would continue to exert deflationary pressures. This is so, particularly when sharply falling prices raise very substantially the expected real interest rate corresponding to a given nominal rate.

Moreover, the Fed held to the pernicious real-bills doctrine. It therefore wished, in accordance with the theory, to eliminate the money creation that had resulted during the war from the discounting of notes secured by government securities. It also wanted to reduce the excessive liquidity of banks that was due to their holding large amounts of government securities. In addition, the Fed believed that a deflation was desirable to offset the previous inflation, and it feared that an easy money policy would lead to excessive speculation. In general, the Fed did not think that it should manage the money stock with a view to cyclical factors and to secular growth in the demand for money. Rather, it saw its function as increasing reserves only temporarily to stabilize interest rates on a seasonal basis and during potential panics.

OTHER EVENTS IN THE 1920s

In the 1920s Fed policy was influenced by several considerations. One was the gold standard, though there is still considerable dispute about how important this really was in determining Fed policy. European countries, particularly Britain, were trying to return to the gold standard. To ensure that Britain had enough gold for this, the Fed wanted low interest rates in New York, so that gold would not flow from London to New York. Later on, the Fed was concerned with the opposite problem, preventing a gold outflow that could drive the United States off the gold standard. However, at the same time, the Fed was also paying attention to domestic conditions and, in particular, there was now some emphasis on the quantity of credit rather than just on its quality. There was some attempt at countercyclical monetary policy, and the Fed began to pay attention to the level of output as well as to prices.

The great stock market boom of 1928–1929 placed the Fed (which, at that time, did not have the power to set margin requirements) in a difficult position. It wanted to raise the discount rate to stop the boom, but this would have raised interest rates to business when business conditions did not call for this. Moreover, it would have stimulated a gold flow from London to New York, thus hurting British stabilization policy. Hence, the Fed decided to try indirect pressures, that is, moral suasion and the denial of discounts to banks making excessive loans for security purchases. Finally, in August 1929 the discount rate *was* raised. But by then the stock market boom was so strong that the relatively small increase in the price of credit did little to curb it, while it did hurt ordinary business borrowing. Had the Fed raised the discount rate earlier, it might have succeeded in stopping the stock market boom before it gathered steam.

THE GREAT DEPRESSION

Understanding the Great Depression is important, not only for evaluating the Fed's record, but also for understanding how the economy reacts to monetary policy. Since then, many economists have argued that the 1930s demonstrated that, at least during a major depression, monetary policy is ineffective. It was the experience of the Great Depression, as well as the publication of Keynes's masterpiece in 1936, that swung economists away from the quantity theory toward the income-expenditure approach. On the other hand, monetarists point to the Great Depression as showing exactly the opposite: the immense damage a perverse monetary policy can do, and hence the great importance of money.

Before turning to the rival explanations, here are some facts about the depression. The upper turning point was reached in August 1929, that is, a few months prior to the stock market crash. The recession continued until March 1933 when an upswing started. This upswing reached a submerged peak, a peak that still had very substantial unemployment, in May 1937. The following recession reached its trough in June 1938. The ensuing expansion carried into and through World War II. In the period 1929–1933, net

Table 24.1	Unemployment, Prices, and Money	1929–1941	
Year	Unemployment as percentage of nonfarm employees	GNP deflator (1958 = 100)	Per capita nominal money stock as percentage of 1929[a]
1929	5.3%	50.6	100.0%
1930	14.2	49.3	95.6
1931	25.2	44.8	89.5
1932	36.3	40.2	76.2
1933	37.6	39.3	71.2
1934	32.6	42.2	77.5
1935	30.2	42.6	92.1
1936	25.4	42.7	107.5
1937	21.3	44.5	110.4
1938	27.9	43.9	104.5
1939	25.2	43.2	115.8
1940	21.3	43.9	136.4
1941	14.4	47.2	158.1

a: Money stock data are for June of each year.

Source: Stanley Lebergott, *Manpower in Economic Growth* (New York: McGraw-Hill, 1964), p. 512 (used with permission of McGraw-Hill Book Co.); U.S. Bureau of the Census, *Historical Statistics of the United States* (1976 ed.), p. 224; Milton Friedman and Anna Schwartz, *A Monetary History of the United States* (Princeton: Princeton University Press, 1963), pp. 712–716.

national product fell by more than one-half when measured in current prices; real net national product fell by more than one-third, as did the wholesale price index. Table 24.1 shows the appalling unemployment rates as well as the GNP deflator. Note, incidentally, that despite very high unemployment prices rose after 1933.

Turning to the monetary data, from August 1929 to March 1933 nominal *M-1* fell by one-quarter. This decline in the stock of money was the accompaniment of widespread bank failures, which occurred in three waves: October 1930; October 1931; and the final one in March 1933, which led to the bank holiday when all banks were closed for a time and only the sound ones were allowed to reopen.

Figure 24.1 shows that the decline in the money stock was not due to a decline in the reserve base (high-powered money) but resulted from a fall in the deposit-reserve ratio and in the deposit-currency ratio. Not surprisingly, as many banks failed, the surviving banks tried to ensure their own safety by holding more reserves, while the public tried to avoid losses by withdrawing deposits.

The discount rate fell radically in this period: from 5 to 6 percent at various Federal Reserve Banks in the fall of 1929 to 1½ to 3 percent in September 1931. Figure 24.2 shows that other short-term rates declined sharply, too. However, in this period the rate on long-term government securities did

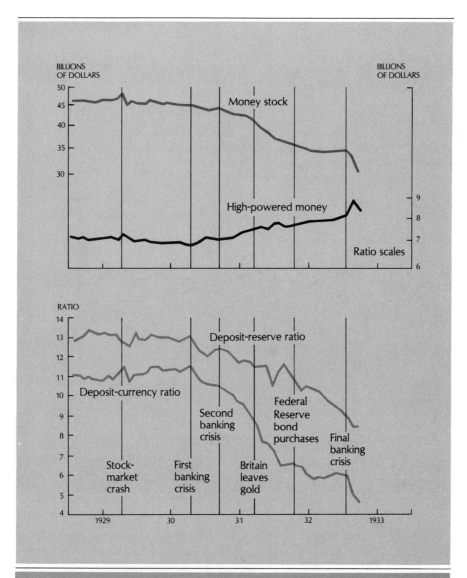

BILLIONS
OF DOLLARS

BILLIONS
OF DOLLARS

Money stock

High-powered money

Ratio scales

RATIO

Deposit-reserve ratio

Deposit-currency ratio

Second
banking
crisis

Federal
Reserve
bond
purchases

Final
banking
crisis

Stock-
market
crash

First
banking
crisis

Britain
leaves
gold

1929   30   31   32   1933

Figure 24.1   The Stock of Money and Its Proximate Determinants, Monthly, February 1929–March 1933. Declines in the currency-deposit ratio and deposit-reserves ratio were responsible for the decline in the money supply during the Great Depression. **Source:** Milton Friedman and Anna Schwartz, *A Monetary History of the United States* (Princeton: Princeton University Press, 1963), p. 333.

not decline as much, and the rate on Baa corporate bonds, that is, bonds of "lower medium grade" quality, actually rose substantially in the early part of the period, then fell, and in 1939 was not far from its 1928 level. Moreover, the price declines that occurred in the early 1930s meant that for these years the real rate of interest was substantially greater than the nominal rate shown

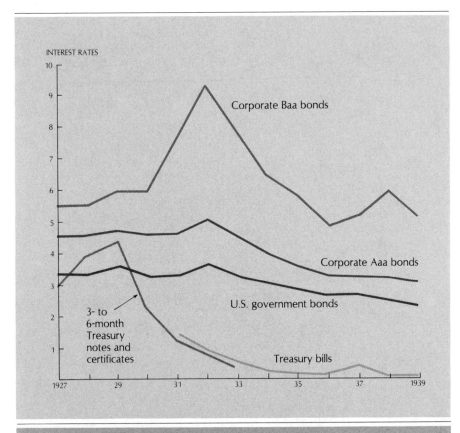

INTEREST RATES

Corporate Baa bonds

Corporate Aaa bonds

U.S. government bonds

3- to
6-month
Treasury
notes and
certificates

Treasury bills

Figure 24.2   Selected Interest Rates, 1927–1939. The Treasury-bill rate fell sharply in the Great Depression, but the corporate Baa rate did not fall. It rose in the early 1930s. **Source:** Thomas Mayer, *Monetary Policy in the United States* (New York: Random House, 1968), p. 219.

in Figure 24.2. For subsequent years the real rate of interest was less than the nominal rate. But since the price level was lower in 1939 than in 1929, for the decade as a whole the real rate exceeded the nominal rate of interest.

FEDERAL RESERVE POLICY

Where was the Fed while all of this was going on? For many years it was widely believed that, on the whole, it behaved well. Those who take this position argue that right after the stock market crash it cut the discount rate, and kept it low except in late 1931 when there was a gold outflow as fears developed that the United States would follow Britain off the gold standard. The Fed did make a serious mistake in raising reserve requirements in 1936 and 1937, but it certainly cannot be blamed for the depression. This resulted from a massive collapse in the marginal efficiency of investment, and, according to this view, monetary policy is almost powerless in such a situation. The Fed kept the discount rate and other short-term rates low, but business had little incentive to borrow. The Fed made reserves available, but banks simply held them as excess reserves because of an absence of sound borrowers, and an interest-rate level so low that banks had little incentive to buy securities. You cannot push on a piece of string.

Although some economists had challenged this view of monetary policy earlier, it was the prevailing orthodoxy until the 1960s, when it was powerfully challenged by Friedman and Schwartz and by Elmus Wicker (of Indiana University). Many economists who are not monetarists now accept the Friedman-Schwartz interpretation of the depression, at least in broad outline.

Given their monetarist outlook, Friedman and Schwartz placed much more emphasis on what was happening to the reserve base and the quantity of money than on interest rates. But they do point out that, while the discount rate and the commercial-paper rate were low during most of the depression, this was not true for the interest rates that are more important for business borrowers, for instance, the Baa bond rate. The public, fearing further financial crises, bid up the prices of highly liquid securities such as commercial paper, thus creating an unusually large gap between interest rates on extremely liquid securities and on less liquid and safe ones. Moreover, in the first part of the depression, with prices falling, the expected real rate of interest was presumably much higher than the nominal rate. Also, the discount rate, while low by historical standards, was not low relative to open-market rates, thus providing little incentive to discount. In addition, the low discount rate may not have had much significance because, as Clark Warburton had pointed out earlier, it was accompanied by a very restrictive policy of discount administration that generally prevented banks from borrowing.

However, Friedman and Schwartz focus not on interest rates but on the Fed's open-market operations, or lack thereof. The Fed did not undertake large-scale open-market purchases until 1932. In fact, until then it was offsetting the expansionary impact on the base that would have occurred naturally from large gold inflows. Friedman and Schwartz therefore describe the Fed's policy as restrictive. In 1932 the Fed finally undertook open-market purchases for a short period, a fact that Friedman and Schwartz attribute to a wish to mollify Congress, which was then considering a fiscal policy the Fed thought too expansionary.

Why was the Fed so restrictive? One reason Friedman and Schwartz suggest is that it did not realize how restrictive it actually was. Instead of looking at the decline in the quantity of money the Fed looked at the discount rate and excess reserves. Friedman and Schwartz argue that the Fed misinterpreted what was happening to excess reserves. It did not realize that the great increase in the excess reserve ratio (from .2 percent in 1929–1931 to 6.8 percent in 1935, and to 12.0 percent in 1940) was due to banks wanting excess reserves to protect themselves from potential runs. Instead it believed that the high excess reserves signaled a lack of demand for bank loans.

However, Gerald Epstein of the New School for Social Research and Thomas Ferguson of the University of Texas, who studied the Fed's records in great detail, concluded that other factors were responsible for the Fed's unwillingness to be more expansionary. One was a concern about gold out-flows, and about the fact that some Federal Reserve Banks were running short of the gold needed to back their notes and deposits. Another was a concern that if interest rates fell many banks would have insufficient earnings to stay alive. The last was a belief that a depression was needed to eliminate inefficient firms.[2]

But whatever the reason for the Fed's actions, or lack of actions, the Fed does not deserve any plaudits. As Wicker put it, by 1932 "it was becoming increasingly clear that [Fed] officials did not recognize any strong obligation to maintain the solvency of the banking system."[3]

Perhaps two things should be said in defense of this dismal record. First, the advice the Fed obtained from the writings of academic economists was not good either, and, second, by no means did all Fed officials agree with the prevailing policy. The New York Federal Reserve Bank generally advocated much more expansionary policies, but it did not prevail.

Effects of Federal Reserve Policy

How much difference would it have made had the Fed aggressively under-taken substantial open-market operations and been able to prevent bank failures in this way? There already was an unusually severe depression in 1930 before there were any large-scale bank failures. This part of the depression is not really explained well by the Friedman-Schwartz analysis. But the economy had suffered such depressions in 1908, 1914–1915, and 1921, and each time had recovered within a reasonable time. What was unique about the Great Depression was not only its depth, but also the tardiness of the recovery. Can these characteristics be attributed to the waves of bank failures, and could the Federal Reserve have prevented these failures?

The answer to the first of these questions depends in large part on the importance of the quantity of money. It also depends on whether there were other factors at work that caused this depression to be so severe and pro-longed. The answer to the second question, whether the Fed could have prevented the bank failures, depends on whether banks were basically sound or whether they held too many bad assets.

On the first issue, the importance of money, we have little to add to our previous discussion. But one does not have to be an out-and-out monetarist to accept a monetary interpretation of the 1930s given the great drop in the money stock. Modern Keynesians too consider such a decline to be a disaster.

---

[2] Gerald Epstein and Thomas Ferguson, "Monetary Policy, Loan Liquidation and Industrial Conflict: The Federal Reserve and Open Market Operations in 1932," *Journal of Economic History*, 44 (December 1984):957–984. Concern about Federal Reserve Banks running short of gold sounds strange now, but, at the time, the Federal Reserve Banks were required to back their currency notes and deposits with gold. Not just the whole Federal Reserve System, but each Bank individually had to meet this requirement. The argument that a depression purges the economic system of inefficiency also sounds strange now, but was popular prior to and dur-ing the early years of the Great Depression.

[3] Elmus Wicker, *Federal Reserve Monetary Policy, 1917–1933.* New York: Random House, 1966, p. 173.

To be sure, the fall in the money supply was not the only thing that happened, velocity also fell, but Friedman and Schwartz argue that this decline was not an independent factor causing the depression, but was induced by the fall in income. Hence, they say that the fall in velocity was ultimately the result of permitting banks to fail. Keynesians, on the other hand, usually do not accept Friedman's theory of velocity that underlies the calculation that velocity dropped just because of the decline in income; they stress instead the effect of low interest rates on velocity. But even if it turns out that there were many other factors at work that could have caused a depression, it seems plausible to attribute much of its persistence and severity to the great fall in the money stock.

Critics of the monetary explanation frequently argue that the drop in the money stock was only an intermediate cause and not the real or interesting cause. In their view, bank failures resulted from banks holding too many unsound assets, and hence these failures could not have been prevented by expansionary Fed policy. Friedman and Schwartz, on the other hand, argue that the massive bank failures would not have occurred if the Fed had under-taken large scale open-market purchases. In their view, any deterioration in the quality of bank assets that occurred in the 1920s was minor. They not only blame the Federal Reserve for dereliction of duty, but also suggest that most of the bank failures would not have occurred had the Fed not existed. Prior to 1913, when massive bank failures threatened, banks would all agree to suspend currency payments for a time, while still clearing checks among themselves. The public could then still use its deposits to make payments from one account to another. Banks that were temporarily short of currency and other liquid assets did not fail. But the existence of the Fed with its discount mechanism reduced the interest of strong banks in initiating, as they had previously done, a suspension of currency payments.

Challenges to the Friedman-Schwartz Interpretation

In the years since Friedman and Schwartz first presented their revisionist interpretation of the Great Depression it appears to have gained much support. But in recent years it has been challenged by a number of economists. The most systematic of these challenges was made by Peter Temin of MIT, who raised many important issues.[4] One of these is whether the observed decline in the money stock was the result of a shift in the supply curve of money, as Friedman and Schwartz claim, or the result of a shift in the demand curve for money. Suppose that the depression was actually caused by a collapse of the marginal efficiency of investment or an exogenous drop in consumption. As income declined the demand for money declined too, and hence interest rates fell. This fall then reduced the money supply by inducing banks to hold more excess reserves, and to borrow less from the Fed, and perhaps also by raising the currency-deposit ratio. Someone might then observe the reduction in the money supply along with the fall in income, and

[4] Peter Temin, *Did Monetary Forces Cause the Great Depression?* New York: W. W. Norton, 1976.

conclude that the decline in the money supply caused income to fall, whereas actually the story is just the other way around. Temin argued that Friedman and Schwartz failed to show that the decline in the money stock was the cause rather than the effect.

In Temin's view there is no evidence that money was tight, at least in the earlier part of the depression. The *real* money stock was slightly higher in 1931 than in 1929, though it did fall after that. Hence he argues that, since into 1931 prices fell enough to offset the decline in the nominal money stock, it was the decline in velocity, rather than a decline in the nominal money stock, that was responsible for falling output. What is going on here is the following: money, velocity, prices, and output all fell. Temin rather arbitrarily allocates the fall in prices to the fall in the money stock, and thus attributes the drop in output to the decline in velocity. Friedman and Schwartz might well reply that this is totally arbitrary; that in response to joint changes in money and velocity (that is, in aggregate demand) prices and output change jointly, with the aggregate supply curve determining by how much each of them changes.

In addition, Temin argues, interest rates on liquid securities were low, which again suggests that there was no shortage of money. (We already discussed Friedman and Schwartz's response to this argument.) Moreover, Temin criticizes Friedman and Schwartz for not explaining the causes of bank failures sufficiently. Temin argues that part of the decline in the stock of money should be attributed to falling prices of farm products and to the agricultural distress that caused rural banks to fail. Many bank failures, Temin argues, were ultimately due to a real factor, the relative decline of agricultural prices, rather than to a monetary factor, such as Federal Reserve policy.

In addition to the rural banks, a large New York bank, the Bank of United States, failed. Temin argues that, contrary to the Friedman-Schwartz view, this failure was due to fraud and illegal activities by the bank's management, so that the Fed could not have prevented this failure. All of these bank failures then frightened depositors into runs on other banks. When these banks tried to meet deposit withdrawals by selling bonds, bond prices fell. This then forced other banks to write down the prices at which they carried these bonds on their books, which in turn impaired the capital position of many of these banks, and forced them to close. Some other economists who have analyzed in detail the failures of certain large banks have supported Temin by pointing out that these failures were due to fraud and bad banking practices rather than to the Fed's policy.

Beyond the question of what caused bank failures, Temin accuses Friedman and Schwartz of overemphasizing the responsibility of the Fed, and underplaying the responsibility of the private sector for the Great Depression. In his view the changes in the money stock that occurred were not *caused* by the Fed merely because the Fed could have prevented them.

An important issue arises here. Friedman and Schwartz blame the Fed for the depression because it was passive, and did not move aggressively through open-market operations to provide banks with the reserves they needed. They take some bank failures as a given and focus on the behavior of the Fed that allowed these failures to spread to other banks. By contrast,

Temin takes the inaction of the Fed as his given and treats as the cause of the decline in the money stock those factors that initially caused some banks to fail. Hence, to a considerable extent, the protagonists are talking past each other since they are discussing different questions. Temin's work does not really vindicate the Federal Reserve.

WAR FINANCE AND INTEREST-RATE PEGGING

During World War II, as in World War I, the Fed's overriding goal was to ensure that the government could borrow all it wanted at a low interest rate. The traditional concerns of stabilization policy were shelved. But, in contrast to its restrictive policy after World War I, after World War II the Fed continued its expansionary policy.

Pegged Rates

The policy adopted during World War II was to "peg" interest rates by having the Fed stand ready to buy all government securities offered to it at least at par, that is, at 100 percent of face value. The level at which interest rates were pegged was the then-prevailing low level of the Great Depression, ranging from ⅜ths of 1 percent on Treasury bills to 2½ percent on long-term Treasury bonds, though after the war the bill rate was allowed to rise to over 1 percent. The decision to maintain the currently prevailing level of interest rates was an obvious one at the time. It would allow the deficit to be financed cheaply. Moreover, it would, most economists believed, be appropriate for the postwar period when, according to the generally prevailing view, the economy would again be depressed. It should have been obvious, but it was not, that a policy of pegging short-term interest rates much lower than long-term rates would generate trouble. If the Fed stands ready to buy long-term bonds at par, long-term bonds are in effect as liquid as short-term securities, so that everyone has an incentive to sell ⅜ths of 1 percent Treasury bills to the Fed and hold 2½ percent bonds instead. And, eventually, the Fed did end up holding nearly all the Treasury bills in existence.

During the war there was little dispute about monetary policy, and even in the early postwar years the Fed accepted interest-rate pegging with few complaints. This was so despite the fact that this policy had an obvious inflationary potential, since it eliminated the Federal Reserve's control over the stock of money. The Fed had to provide reserves to any bank that offered it government securities in exchange. Monetary policy was therefore completely passive in the sense of being unable to curb an expansion of the money stock.

Why was such a policy more or less acceptable to the Fed? One reason was the tardiness with which the persistence of the postwar inflation was recognized. Almost everyone expected a depression after the war, and it took some time for people to realize that the problem was excessive, rather than insufficient, aggregate demand. Another reason was the low repute of monetary policy, that is, the widespread belief that the Great Depression had demonstrated the unimportance of the quantity of money, and that the government should therefore rely on fiscal policy rather than on monetary policy.

This belief was, of course, connected with the victory of Keynesian theory and the eclipse of the quantity theory. Still another reason for the widespread acceptance of pegging was that this policy seemed harmless. Pegging interest rates provided the potential for an explosive rise in the money stock since the Fed had relinquished control over it, but the explosion did not occur. Just the opposite: in 1949 the money stock was slightly lower than in 1947. It seems that for much of the period the equilibrium interest rate was below the pegged 2½ percent bond rate, so that the Fed was not called upon to protect the peg by increasing bank reserves and the money stock. With velocity rising rapidly, the demand for money did not grow.

The Debate

All the same, as time went by, the Fed became more and more uneasy about its lack of control. With the outbreak of the Korean War in 1950, the Federal Reserve's restiveness turned into open opposition. As long as pegging was taking place it was the Treasury, and not the Fed, that was, in effect, conducting monetary policy since the Fed was bound to support the Treasury's decisions about interest rates paid on government securities. Now with renewed war, accompanied by inflation (the consumer price index rose by 11 percent between June 1950 and December 1951), the Fed wanted to reclaim monetary policy. A great debate occurred. The Treasury argued that a small rise in interest rates would be insufficient to restrain aggregate demand significantly, while a large increase could throw the economy into a recession. The Fed replied that somewhere between too little and too large there must be "just right," which was open to the rejoinder that nobody knows where this "just right" level of interest rates is.

The Treasury pointed out that a rise in interest rates would, given the large size of the public debt, raise government expenditures significantly, but the Fed's supporters replied that the Treasury got back in higher taxes approximately half of its interest payments. Apart from technical issues there were also some broader ones. President Truman had populist suspicions of high finance, and wanted interest rates to remain low in the belief that this would help the average citizen. Moreover, the Treasury held the bizarre notion that if government bond prices fell below par this would reduce confidence in the United States government and have terrible effects. Besides, there was the danger that the Korean War would turn into World War III, with massive financing needs that the Treasury did not want to meet at high interest rates. This does not mean that the Treasury and administration were oblivious to inflation; rather, instead of monetary policy, they wanted to rely on fiscal policy and price controls which were then in effect. The Fed had less faith in price controls.

In its dispute with the Treasury the Fed had substantial support among academic economists and, what is much more important, also in Congress. It therefore felt powerful enough to challenge the Treasury. In August 1950 it allowed some short-term securities to fall slightly below par. A major row occurred, but was resolved in March 1951 by an agreement known as the

"Accord" under which short-term interest rates were allowed to rise moderately and long-term rates to rise very slightly. The Fed was relieved of the burden of complete pegging, but, de facto, agreed to prevent government securities from falling much below par. This Accord lasted only until after the 1952 election, when the incoming Eisenhower administration restored the Fed's full freedom.

1952 TO 1969

After receiving its freedom the Fed mantained a low money growth rate. From 1952 through 1960, *M–1* grew at only a 1.9 percent rate per annum and *M–2* at a 3.2 percent rate. But since velocity was rising, GNP grew at a faster rate, and the price level rose at an average rate of 1.4 percent during this whole period. But during June 1957 to June 1958 it rose at a 2.9 percent rate, which at the time was considered a quite unacceptable rate of inflation.

The Fed was much criticized at the time for following a too restrictive policy, and many economists thought that the administration's fiscal policy was also too restrictive. By hindsight one possible interpretation is that the Fed was "drying out" the economy and eliminating the inflationary expectations that had developed during the post–World War II and Korean War inflations. One *possible* explanation for why, during the subsequent long expansion from February 1961 to December 1969, there was so little inflation until 1965 is that the Fed set the stage in the 1950s by creating the expectation that prices would be stable.

One important development in the 1960s was an increasingly severe balance of payments problem. The dollar was overvalued and large balance of payments deficits were the norm. It should have been clear, but for a long time was not, that unless the United States was willing to curb the growth rate of the money stock—and accept the accompanying unemployment—the dollar would *have* to be devalued. But instead of taking such a drastic step, various palliatives were tried.

Exchange control was tried in a modest way; a special tax was levied on interest earnings on foreign securities to eliminate the gains from buying foreign securities with a higher yield than domestic ones. There were restraints on large-scale capital exports by banks and other firms. Moreover, it is likely that, had it not been for the balance of payments problem, the Fed would have followed at least a somewhat more expansionary policy. But it is hard to know whether balance of payments considerations really were important in making monetary policy.

Another very important development was that, as the endpaper figure (inside front cover) shows, the growth rate of the money stock increased substantially in the second half of the decade, particularly in 1967 and 1968. A reason for this was the large deficits that resulted from the Vietnam War and the Great Society programs. In principle, this deficit could have been allowed to raise interest rates and crowd out private expenditures. But it was decided to hold interest rates down and monetize the deficit. The resulting rapid growth of the money stock in the late 1960s proved to be inflationary. The basis for long-run inflation was laid.

The Fed's response to the gathering inflationary pressure was strong, even brutal. The growth rate of *M–1* had been 4.6 percent in both 1964 and 1965; in the second half of 1966 it was cut to zero. As the endpaper shows, interest rates rose sharply. In addition, banks gave preference to their steady business customers and cut back on their mortgage loans. Moreover, the net flow of funds into savings and loans fell to one-quarter of the previous year's level. A sharp drop in residential construction occurred that was widely blamed on tight money. Signs of financial strain appeared. There was a danger of widespread failures of savings and loans. Moreover, the restrictive Regulation Q ceiling prevented banks from "buying" deposits as they had been able to do previously. The Council of Economic Advisers concluded that in August 1966 "monetary policy was probably as tight as it could get without risking financial disorder."[5]

Policy Formulation in the 1950s and 1960s

In making policy the FOMC did not consider the quantity of money to be central, and instead emphasized short-term nominal interest rates, credit conditions, and bank credit. It did not see its task as determining long-term interest rates, but rather as generating sufficient credit to finance "sound" expansions, while curbing unsustainable and inflationary overexpansions. It did not think of target variables in a quantifiable way, but would, for example, formulate a change in its policy as a shift from a policy of "ease" to one of "active ease."

Without distinguishing between targets and instruments the FOMC used short-term interest rates, free reserves (i.e., excess reserves minus borrowings), and "money-market conditions." The latter is an amalgam of a set of variables, dominated by free reserves, that sought to gauge in an impressionistic way the ease or restrictiveness of conditions in the money market. A major goal and target of the FOMC was to keep interest rates stable.

The use of such targets and instruments tends to make monetary policy procyclical rather than countercyclical if the shocks to the economy consist of shifts in the IS curve rather than the LM curve. Why an interest-rate target does so was discussed in Chapter 21.

To illustrate how the problem arises, consider a free-reserves target. Suppose the IS curve shifts outward so that interest rates rise. With interest rates rising while the discount rate is constant, banks borrow more, and also run down their excess reserves, so that free reserves fall, say, from $500 million to $200 million. The Fed now undertakes open-market purchases of $300 million to restore free reserves to their previous level. But since banks do not want to hold more than $200 million of free reserves at the prevailing interest rate, they reduce their free reserves again by making additional loans or buying securities. As free reserves fall again to $200 million the Fed pumps in $300 million more of reserves. As this process continues the increase in deposits that occurs as banks use their reserves reduces interest rates. Eventually, they fall by enough to make banks willing to hold all the $500 million of

---

[5] *Economic Report of the President*, 1967, Washington, D.C., p. 60.

reserves that are the Fed's free-reserves target. But in attaining this free-reserves target the Fed has lost control over the money stock and interest rates.

Similarly, during a recession, as the IS curve shifts downward, interest rates fall, banks therefore decide to hold more free reserves, and the Fed undertakes open-market sales to bring free reserves down to their previous level. Hence, such a policy *reduces* the growth rate of the money stock during a recession.

Many academic economists, led by Brunner and Meltzer, criticized the Fed for following a procyclical policy. And as the 1960s progressed the Fed slowly shifted its focus away from interest rates, free reserves, and money-market conditions and started to pay more attention to the growth rate of money.

1969 TO 1980

The quite modest inflation rate of the mid-1960s was followed by an accelerating inflation rate in the late 1960s. In 1969 the Fed then tried to break this inflation, even at the cost of risking a recession. In December 1969 there was a downturn with a trough in November 1970. This cycle too was accompanied by severe financial strains, and if the Fed had not acted promptly as a lender of last resort there could well have been a financial panic. The money market was extraordinarily tight, which is hardly surprising, given the Fed's restrictive policy and the fact that the United States' incursion into Cambodia had created great political tensions. By June 1970 stock prices had declined by more than 20 percent below their 1969 average.

In that month the Penn Central Transportation Company, one of the country's major corporations, filed for bankruptcy. Shock waves spread throughout the financial market. Penn Central's credit rating had been high enough for it to have issued commercial paper. Lenders were now asking themselves who would be next. There were rumors that Chrysler Corporation would not be able to sell new issues of commercial paper to replace the maturing ones, that is, to "roll over" its commercial paper. This would have made lenders afraid to buy the commercial paper of some other firms. Corporations issuing commercial paper frequently arrange bank lines of credit as a backup measure. There was now a danger that if firms were unable to roll over their commercial paper banks would suddenly have to find the wherewithal to increase their business loans substantially, and they might not be able to honor all their lines of credit.

Fortunately, the Fed stepped in promptly, and did what a central bank is supposed to do. It calmed the money market by announcing that the discount window was wide open for those banks that had to make loans to firms unable to roll over their commercial paper. In addition, it suspended the Regulation Q ceiling for certain large CDs, so that banks would be able to buy funds readily. In August 1970 it also lowered reserve requirements. All in all, the Fed emerged as the hero of this episode; however, one might suggest that had it not been for its sharply restrictive policy in 1969 (itself the consequence of its previous too expansionary policy) the market could have handled the Penn

Central failure. There would then have been no emergency that required heroic action.

In the early 1970s another event occurred that was just as dramatic as the incipient panic of 1970, and was to have a much longer lasting effect. This was the collapse of the fixed exchange-rate system, to be discussed in Chapter 28. In 1971 President Nixon imposed wage and price controls. These controls reduced inflation temporarily. After the removal of controls in April 1974, prices rose rapidly; the consumer price index rose by over 12 percent that year. The removal of price controls was not the only cause: oil prices had been raised by OPEC, and other raw material prices had risen due to poor harvests in much of the world and due to the coincidence of booms in many major industrial countries.

In 1973–1975 the economy suffered what until 1981–1982 was the most severe postwar recession. The inflation rate rose as the economy was hit by the effects of the oil shock and other supply shocks, as well as by the effects of the previous acceleration of the money growth rate. The term **stagflation** entered the public's vocabulary.

Due to the high inflation rate the Fed adopted a restrictive policy in the second half of 1974. This policy was much criticized. The inflation rate had risen in 1973–1974 in part because of supply shocks, and the Fed seemed intent to offset these shocks partially by putting downward pressure on other prices. Keynesians objected that while monetary policy should perhaps be used to fight demand-pull inflation, it should not be used to fight that part of the inflation that resulted from such obvious cost-push factors as bad harvests and the rise in oil prices. Specifically, they opposed adopting a sharply restrictive policy in the midst of a recession. Monetarists also objected to changing the money growth rate as abruptly as the Fed had done. The Fed caught it from both sides.

Policy Procedures in the 1970s

During the 1970s the Fed came to place more and more emphasis on the growth rate of money, so that by the late 1970s it may have *seemed* that the Fed had two targets—the money growth rate and the federal-funds rate. In part, but only in part, this greater emphasis on money was in response to congressional pressure. In 1975 a congressional resolution was passed that required the Fed chairman to appear before House and Senate committees to reveal and justify his targets for money growth. This put *some* pressure on the Fed to keep money growth within its targeted range. However, this pressure was greatly diluted by three factors. First, the growth rate target encompassed a broad range, say, 4–7 percent, even though a 4 percent growth rate may be consistent with a, say, 3 percent inflation rate, and a 7 percent growth rate with a, say, 6 percent inflation rate. Second, there was "base drift"; that is, the Fed could use as the base from which the growth rate is measured the money stock at the start of that period, even if this was outside the previously set range. Hence, if the money stock was too high, the old percentage growth rate would yield a larger money stock. (Under current rules, the Fed can let the

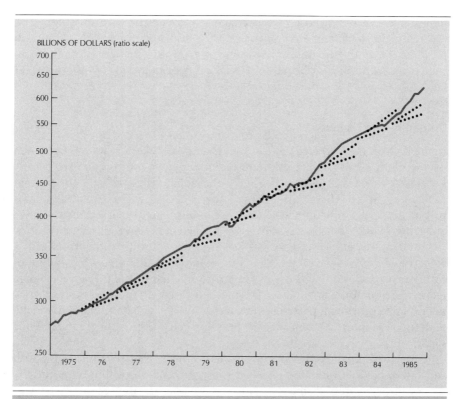

BILLIONS OF DOLLARS (ratio scale)

Figure 24.3 *M-1* and the *M-1* Target Range. The growth rate of *M-1* has frequently deviated from its target range. **Source:** William T. Gavin, "The M-1 Target and Disinflationary Policy," Federal Reserve Bank of Cleveland, *Economic Commentary* (1 October 1985):3.

base drift like this only once a year, not every quarter as before.) Third, the Fed set target ranges not just for *M-1*, but also for the broader money measures. Hence, when the Fed missed its target for one of its three money measures it might claim that it had to miss that target to attain one of the other two. With three fairly broad target ranges, the Fed could frequently hit one of them, even if only by accident. As Figure 24.3 shows, *M-1* was frequently outside its target range.

The fact that the Fed again and again missed its money targets is not surprising. Although in a formal sense the Fed was targeting money, it actually did not give this target priority. In addition to the money targets the FOMC also set a range for the federal-funds rate. Since the range for the federal-funds rate was fairly narrow, the Fed could not, for reasons discussed in Chapter 21, both meet its money target and stay within its range for the federal-funds rate. A choice had to be made, and generally the Fed chose to sacrifice its money target.

One should not interpret this procedure as the Fed choosing a Keynesian interest-rate target over a monetarist money-stock target. A Keynesian policy requires that the interest rate be changed as the IS curve shifts. But the Fed was reluctant to change the interest rate and adjusted it only lethargically, in part because of the disruption that rapid interest-rate changes cause in financial markets and in part because of political pressures to keep interest rates low.

Defending the Dollar

In the recovery from the 1973–1975 recession the inflation rate was both high and accelerating as the Fed allowed the money stock to grow at a steep rate. Largely as a result of this, in late 1979 the dollar fell rapidly on the foreign exchange market. There was a danger that foreign central banks, as well as private holders, would dump their dollar holdings on the market, thus accelerating the dollar's fall. In response, on 1 November 1978, President Carter followed up his earlier call for "voluntary" wage and price controls with a series of emergency measures. The United States would borrow $30 billion of foreign currencies it could use to support the dollar in the foreign exchange market. More fundamentally, Carter asked the Fed to adopt a restrictive policy. For a president, particularly a Democratic president, publicly to ask the Fed to raise interest rates was an extraordinary step with great symbolic significance.

But what matters are not dramatic gestures, but the consistency with which they are followed up. The initial follow-up was strong, but transient; the money growth rate fell sharply—but not for long. In the second quarter of 1979 it rose again and stayed high for the rest of the year. It seemed as though the Fed had lost control over it. This by itself might not have caused a radical change in policy but two other obviously connected events occurred: the inflation rate accelerated sharply and the dollar fell steeply on the foreign exchange market as foreigners lost confidence in it. The seemingly strong policy changes of the previous November had bought less than a year's respite.

One can make a reasonable case that the Fed faced disaster. It seemed unable to control the money stock. A rapid rise in the prices of gold (by $100 an ounce between late August and early October) and of certain raw materials suggested that the high inflation rate was generating a belief that the safe thing to do was to dump dollars and buy commodities. Obviously, if such a belief spreads, it results in much more inflation. In addition, there was a danger that the dollar would plummet on the foreign exchange market as foreigners saw that the Fed's action of November 1978 had failed. Foreign central banks held a large volume of dollars they could dump on the market to cut their losses.

On 6 October 1979, in an unusual and dramatic Saturday meeting, the Board of Governors adopted a new policy, which became known as the "Saturday night special." Despite the fact that it was widely (though wrongly) believed that the economy had already entered a recession, the Fed adopted a highly restrictive policy. It raised the discount rate by another percentage point to 12 percent, and it imposed an 8 percent reserve requirement on increases in certain managed liabilities of banks. In a more important step it announced that it would try to get a better grip on the money stock by allowing the federal-funds rate to fluctuate much more.

The October 1979 policy initiative succeeded in stopping the threatened collapse of the dollar on the foreign exchange market. In addition, the Fed succeeded in bringing the money growth rate down, though subsequently it was still high relative to the midpoint of the Fed's target ranges. Nominal interest rates rose sharply.

Although successful in the foreign exchange market, domestically the October 1979 program failed. Financial markets did not believe that the Fed would control inflation. Had they anticipated that the Fed would succeed, long-term bond prices would have risen, and long-term interest rates would have fallen along with the anticipated inflation premium that is contained in interest rates. But, instead, bond prices fell!

The market was right. In three months, from December 1979 to February 1980, the consumers price index spurted at an annual rate of 17 percent. Credit markets became demoralized by the fear that the inflation rate, and hence interest rates, would zoom. How could market participants determine what interest rates to set on new bonds? They couldn't. As a result the long-term bond market as well as the mortgage market in large part suspended operations for a time, and even short-term markets, such as the commercial-paper market, ceased to function properly. Some major banks were reported to have difficulties in selling large CDs.

By March 1980 the October 1979 policy was in shambles. Strange as it may seem, many people were actually hoping for a recession that would reduce both the inflation rate and interest rates. It is reported that when Federal Reserve chairman Volcker was asked whether monetary and fiscal tightening would result in a recession he replied, "Yes, and the sooner the better."[6]

It was clear that something had to be done, and in March 1980 President Carter announced a multifaceted program to break inflationary expectations. As part of this he revised the budget he had just sent to Congress to eliminate the projected deficit (though, as it turned out, not the actual deficit). The Fed's role was twofold. One part was to tighten conventional monetary policy by raising reserve requirements on certain managed liabilities and to impose a special three percentage points surcharge on the discount rate paid by large banks that borrow frequently. The second part was to impose credit allocation.

Banks were told to let their loans expand by no more than 9 percent, with banks that were growing slowly in any case, or had low capital and liquidity ratios, staying well below this ceiling. This part of the program was voluntary, but there is an old saying, "You don't have to, but you'll be sorry if you don't." Since large and medium banks frequently come to the Fed for permission to undertake mergers or to start holding-company affiliates, the Fed is not exactly powerless.

To cut consumer spending, which was growing rapidly, the Fed also imposed a 15 percent reserve requirement on unsecured consumer loans,

[6] Clyde Farnsworth, "Washington Watch," *New York Times,* 17 March 1980, p. D2.

such as credit-card and charge-account borrowing. This reserve requirement applied not only to banks, but also to other financial institutions, as well as to retailers. Finally, a 15 percent reserve requirement was also imposed on increases in the assets of money-market funds.

This credit control program was effective—much more effective than had been intended. The public seemed to respond to the president's wish that consumer credit be cut from a mixture of patriotism and fear of worsening economic conditions. Outstanding consumer credit stopped growing and fell. This response would have been most gratifying had it not been for one little fact—just two months earlier the economy had entered a recession!

Policy Procedures from October 1979 to August 1982

As part of the "Saturday night special" the Fed adopted new policy procedures that placed more emphasis on controlling the money growth rate. This was done because the previously used procedures had failed to control the money growth rate sufficiently, and also to give the domestic and foreign public a signal (a somewhat misleading signal as it turned out) that the Fed would now be willing to do whatever would be necessary to control the money growth rate and thus inflation. Hence the previous tight constraints were taken off the federal-funds rate. To attain the money-stock target the federal-funds rate would be allowed to vary within a broad band of 5 percent or so (compared to a band of about 1¼ percent before), and even this 5 percent range was not always binding. As its instrumental variable the Fed used unborrowed reserves, which functioned, as described in Chapter 21, indirectly by influencing bank borrowings, and thus the federal-funds rate, and finally the demand for money.

THE 1981–1982 RECESSION AND THE SUBSEQUENT RECOVERY

The 1980 recession was shortlived, but so was the ensuing expansion. In mid-1981, before the recovery was complete, another recession occurred, carrying unemployment to 10.8 percent, the highest level since the 1930s. Helped by favorable supply-side developments the inflation rate responded strongly to the recession, the GNP deflator rising by only 3.9 percent in 1982 compared to 12.4 percent in 1980. But this sharp contrast is deceptive since the high inflation rate of 1980 was in part due to the second OPEC oil shock.

A recovery started in November 1982 and is now (May 1986) still going on. Although the expansion is robust and unusually long-lasting, the unemployment rate is still high because the recovery started from such a low level. Unlike in most expansions, the inflation rate has not risen, in part because of the severity of the previous recession, and in part because of the decline in oil prices. Two other unusual characteristics of this recovery are the high federal deficit and the large import surplus.

During the recession there was worry about a financial collapse. The failure of some government security dealers, as well as of a medium-sized bank, Penn Square, combined with the threatened failures of some large firms and the inability of some countries (e.g., Mexico) to repay their loans all generated such fears. Many thrift institutions failed, or had to be merged into other ones. Interest rates declined, but not by as much as the inflation rate did, so that, at least on short-term loans, real rates were unusually high. While some blamed this on the large current and prospective federal deficits, others blamed the Fed for not raising the money growth rate sufficiently.

The Fed was in a quandary. On the one hand it wanted to continue with its disinflationary policy, but on the other hand it wanted to ameliorate the recession. Five factors complicated its task. First, raising the money growth rate could generate fears that the inflation rate would rise again. This would result not only in more inflationary wage and price setting but would also raise the inflation premium that is included in the nominal interest rate. Second, there was much pressure on the Fed to lower interest rates, and bills to curb the Fed's independence gathered extraordinarily strong support in Congress.

Third, with deregulation fostering new types of accounts the problem of measuring money became much more severe. For instance, NOW accounts were growing rapidly. Should the Fed interpret this just like an ordinary increase in *M-1* and take offsetting action, or did it merely represent a shift of long-term savings out of other accounts and securities into these NOW accounts, and hence not call for reducing the *M-1* growth rate?

Fourth, as Figure 24.4 shows, expected nominal interest rates did not decline as much as the inflation rate, so that the real interest rate rose substantially. This was hardly a desirable development during a deep recession.

Finally, there was a sharp fall in velocity. After rising at a trend rate of about 3 percent per year during the 1960s and 1970s velocity suddenly *fell* by 4 percent between 1981 and 1982, the first significant drop in about 30 years. *M-2* velocity also fell. In setting its money growth targets the Fed had expected velocity to continue to rise. Hence, the fall in velocity meant that monetary conditions were much tighter than the Fed had intended.

The Fed responded by easing policy. The *M-1* growth rate accelerated rapidly in the second half of 1982. Some economists feared, groundlessly as it turned out, that this would result in a sharp rise in the inflation rate sometime in 1983–1985. Others complained that the easing was not sufficient and left interest rates still much too high.

Lessons from the Monetarist (?) Experiment

The policy adopted on 6 October 1979 was widely, but not necessarily correctly, interpreted as a radical shift toward monetarism. It was certainly monetarist in one important way: the Fed now put control over inflation ahead of maintaining high employment. In addition, the Fed tried harder than before to attain its monetary growth targets, and hence allowed interest rates to fluctuate much more.

What were the results? As already mentioned, the inflation rate fell substantially, though with a lag, while unemployment rose sharply. As Figure 24.4 shows, interest rates became much more variable. Much, but not all, of this increased variability of interest rates was only temporary, being due to the

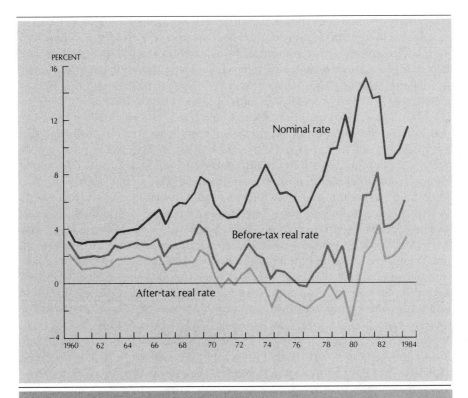

Figure 24.4   Nominal and Real Interest Rates. The expected real interest rate was low in the 1970s and high in the early 1980s. Real interest rates are calculated by subtracting an estimate of the expected inflation rate. Such an estimate for ten years ahead is available only since 1978, so the long-term rate is shown only after that date. **Source:** Steven Holland, "Real Interest Rates: What Accounts for Their Rise?" *Review* (Federal Reserve Bank of St. Louis), 66 (December 1984):19.

imposition, and subsequent elimination, of credit controls. That interest rates became much more variable once the Fed took its narrow bands off the federal-funds rate is hardly surprising. What is much harder to explain is that, as Figure 24.4 shows, the money growth rate also became much more variable. With the Fed no longer being constrained by a narrow range for the federal-funds rate, one would expect that it could control the money growth rate much more accurately and keep it much stabler. Prior to October 1979 monetarists had argued that the Fed should allow more interest-rate variability to reduce the variability of the money growth rate. Instead we got the worst of both worlds.

Was the new policy a failure, and, if so, should this be treated as a practical refutation of monetarism? This is a much-debated question that obviously cannot be resolved here. All we can do is to outline the major issues.

One issue relates to the sharp drop in the inflation rate that started in 1981. Was it worth the accompanying rise in the unemployment rate? Suppose the Fed had been less adamant in fighting inflation, and had tried to bring the inflation rate down more slowly. Could it have done so at a much smaller cost in unemployment, or was it necessary to adopt a drastic policy to break inflationary expectations? Many monetarists had hoped that a pronounced shift in Fed policy would by itself reduce inflationary expectations substantially, so that it would not take such a great increase in unemployment to bring down the inflation rate. But whether such a favorable expectations effect did operate is a matter for debate—it depends on which econometric estimate of the Phillips curve one uses.

Second, there is the sharp decline in velocity. Had the Fed been using an interest-rate target rather than a money-stock target it would have—as it should have done—accommodated this shift in the LM curve. Ironically, while a money-stock target would, we believe, have been preferable in the 1970s when the Fed was using mainly an interest-rate target, in the October 1979 through 1982 period, when the Fed was making more use of a money-stock target, an interest-rate target would have been preferable. Was this just a matter of bad luck, or is it a reflection of Goodhart's law (named after Charles Goodhart, then of the Bank of England) that a variable that has previously been stable will become unstable as soon as one uses it as a policy instrument or target?

Third, how much damage did the greater variability of interest rates inflict on the economy? Fourth, to what extent was this greater variability the *inevitable* result of a policy that eliminated the previously tight constraints on movements in the federal-funds rate? Much of it may have been due to the greater variability of the money growth rate, which, in turn, *may* have been the result of faulty Fed procedures (discussed below). If the money supply is less stable one would expect short-term interest rates, which measure the cost of holding money for a short period, to fluctuate more, too.

This brings us to a central issue. Does the high variability of the money growth rate indicate that monetarist policy must fail because the Fed simply cannot control the growth rate of money? At least on the surface this appears plausible. The Fed tried harder to control the money growth rate after October 1979, yet the money stock grew at a less stable rate.

But monetarists can respond that this appearance is deceptive. First, it is by no means clear that the Fed really tried to control the growth rate of money all that much harder than before. Someone looking at the money growth rate relative to its targets in Figure 24.3 might have difficulty locating a "monetarist experiment." In a detailed analysis of FOMC announcements during this period, Robert Hetzel of the Richmond Fed has argued that the Fed was looking mainly at current GNP, and tried to attain its money growth target only when it happened to point to the same policy as the GNP target.[7]

Second, the Fed tried to control the money growth rate by using borrowed reserves as its instrument. Monetarists consider this a complex Rube Goldberg procedure, much inferior to their recommended total

---

[7] Robert Hetzel, "Monetary Policy in the Early 1980s," Federal Reserve Bank of Richmond, *Economic Review,* 70 (March/April 1986). This fits in with a statement of Nancy Teeters, who was a Fed governor at the time, that the Fed's adoption of monetarism "was a camouflage for raising the interest rate."

reserves instrument. Moreover, at that time the Fed operated with a system of lagged reserve requirements. Under this system banks had to keep reserves not against their *current* deposits, but against their deposits two weeks earlier. This meant that in any one week the reserves that banks had to keep were predetermined by their deposits. Thus, if the banks had fewer reserves than the amount required the Fed had to provide them with the needed reserves either through open-market operations or through the discount window. Hence, monetarists argue, the Fed's control over reserves, and thus over the money stock, was severely limited by an unwise reserve requirements regulation, and by the use of an inefficient instrument. Monetarists therefore say that what was wrong with the post–October 1979 policy was not that monetarism failed, but that it was not tried.

The End of the Monetarist (?) Episode

In the second half of 1982 the Fed changed policy procedures again in what is often called the end of the monetarist experiment. This *may* be an over-statement. The Fed certainly moved away from the October 1979 policy, but it probably did not move all the way back to the previous policy. The federal-funds rate is now allowed to vary more than it did in, say, 1977, and it is likely that the money growth rate does get more attention now than it did then, if only because the financial community pays more attention to it.

Several reasons for the shift away from monetarism have already been mentioned. Given the dangers of widespread bankruptcies and possible financial collapse if interest rates rose further, the burden of high interest rates on debtor countries, and the resulting danger of defaults, as well as the threat of congressional retribution, the Fed had a strong incentive to bring down interest rates, even though this conflicted with its *M-1* growth target. Moreover, the large unexpected decline in velocity undermined the basic argument for adhering to a monetary target. If the linkage between money and nominal income is unpredictable, does it really matter if the Fed misses the money target? Given the rapid pace of financial innovation, is it possible to measure "money" sufficiently well to set a target for it?

Accordingly, for a time the Fed demoted *M-1* from the role of a target to the role of a "monitoring range." Since then it has restored *M-1* as a target, but, even so, it does not seem to pay much attention to it. Even if it wanted to, as long as the Fed uses borrowed reserves as its instrument it would be difficult to conrol *M-1*. Difficult, but not impossible. The borrowed reserves instrument, like the old free-reserves instrument, provides no automatic control over the money stock, but lets the money stock adjust to the demand for money. If the Fed would change its reserves target sufficiently frequently and by the right amount, it could control money with the borrowed reserves instrument. But it would be difficult to do. A sufficiently skilled climber could climb the Matterhorn in ballet slippers, and a sufficiently skilled ballerina could dance in climbing boots. But when one sees someone wearing climbing boots one can assume that he is going climbing and not dancing.

CURRENT GOALS AND TARGETS

Since the Fed does not clearly announce its goals and targets and their relative priorities, a description of the Fed's goals and targets requires some guess-work. Among the goals, keeping the inflation rate low *seems* to have a high priority. As a result of the great inflation of the late 1960s and 1970s the Fed is now more concerned about inflation than it was in, say, 1965. Michael Keran, a former Fed economist, has suggested that previously the Fed would wait for inflation to develop before taking action, but now takes action as soon as GNP rises to a level high enough to foretell an eventual serious rise in the inflation rate.

With respect to targets, the Fed is eclectic and uses several targets. Probably the most important one is real GNP, with the Fed looking more at current GNP than at future GNP. Nominal GNP is probably also a target. Interest rates, both long term and short term, appear to be another target. The Fed also looks at a credit or debt variable.

How about the money growth rate? The Fed still announces targets for money growth, but, as Figure 24.3 suggests, these targets do not greatly constrain the actual growth rate of money. As Gary Stern, the president of the Minneapolis Federal Reserve Bank, has put it:

> What the money ranges are meant to be are indicators to the public of the general course of monetary policy *if the economy performs as expected* [italics added]. . . . The Fed does what economic theory says is best. . . . It uses all the information available . . . to move as closely as possible to its broad goals. This means not targeting anything except these goals. . . . In this strategy the Fed's money measures are not targeted. They are instead among the many variables the Fed uses to determine how next to aim at its goals by adjusting its instruments. . . . The Fed does not, in a strict sense, target these [money supply] measures.[8]

SUMMARY

1 The Fed's original ideas were the great importance of maintaining the gold standard, the need to avoid financial panics, a wish to stabilize interest rates, and adherence to the real-bills doctrine.
2 In 1920 the Fed adopted a highly restrictive policy just when the economy went into a very severe recession. Later during the 1920s the Fed tried to facilitate the restoration of the gold standard in Europe, and in the late 1920s it faced the dilemma of a runaway stock market boom.
3 In the Great Depression the money stock fell substantially. Friedman and Schwartz blame the Fed for not undertaking massive open-market purchases. But Temin argues that the fall in the money stock was due to a decline in the demand for money.

---

[8] Gary Stern, "The Fed's Money Supply Ranges: Still Useful After All These Years," Federal Reserve Bank of Minneapolis, *1985 Annual Report*, pp. 3–5.

4 During World War II the Fed pegged interest rates at the depression level. After the war the continuation of this policy led to a great debate. The policy was modified by the "Accord" and was finally dropped in 1953.

5 The balance of payments deficit became an important consideration in the 1960s. The Fed became more professionalized and somewhat more monetarist, but the money growth rate rose substantially. The Fed then became sharply restrictive in 1966 and 1969, to the point that there was a danger of financial panic. In the early 1970s the fixed exchange rate system collapsed and price controls were imposed. Following the oil shock the Fed subsequently adopted another, more highly restrictive policy for which it was much criticized.

6 In late 1978 the dollar fell sharply on the foreign exchange market and a flight from the dollar was a real danger. The Fed responded with a temporarily restrictive policy which was insufficient, and in October 1979 the Fed had to adopt a stronger policy and to change its operating procedures by letting interest rates fluctuate much more. By early 1980 it was clear even this policy was insufficient. In March, policy was tightened again and credit controls were imposed. 1981–1982 saw the most severe postwar recession with fears about financial collapse.

QUESTIONS AND EXERCISES

1 Use the descriptions of monetary policy in recent issues of the *Economic Report of the President* and the Federal Reserve *Annual Report* to bring the discussion of this chapter up to date.
2 "In the Great Depression the Federal Reserve did all it could reasonably have been expected to do." Discuss.
3 "Prior to World War II the Federal Reserve usually did the wrong thing." Discuss.
4 "There has been little real improvement in the conduct of monetary policy. What looks like improvement is merely that the Fed, instead of being too soft on inflation, as it used to be, is now too soft on unemployment." Discuss.
5 What do you think has been the Fed's biggest mistake in the postwar period?
6 For what action does the Fed deserve the most credit in the postwar period?
7 What were the ideas with which the Fed started out? To what extent, if any, were they responsible for the Fed's actions in 1920?
8 Take one issue in the dispute between the rival interpretations of the Great Depression given by Friedman and Schwartz and by Temin and write an essay on it.
9 What do you think is the most effective argument used by (1) Friedman and Schwartz and (2) Temin in their discussions of the Great Depression?

FURTHER READING

BERNANKE, BEN. "Nonmonetary Effects of Financial Crisis in the Propagation of the Great Depression," *American Economic Review,* 73 (June 1983):257–276. An interesting hypothesis that bank failures had their main impact by disrupting financial channels.

BRUNNER, KARL (ed.). *Contemporary Views of the Great Depression.* Amsterdam: Martinus Nejhoff, 1981. A series of important articles on the Great Depression.

FRIEDMAN, MILTON, and ANNA SCHWARTZ. *A Monetary History of the United States.* Princeton: Princeton University Press, 1963. A classic. The chapter on the Great Depression has been published separately as *The Great Contraction.*

MAISEL, SHERMAN. *Managing the Dollar*. New York: W. W. Norton, 1973. An important source for the history of the Fed in the 1960s.

MELTON, WILLIAM. *Inside the Fed*, Chapters 4 and 10. Homewood, Ill.: Dow Jones–Irwin, 1985. An excellent discussion of Fed policy since 1979.

PIERCE, JAMES. "The Political Economy of Arthur Burns," *Journal of Finance*, 24 (May 1979):485–496. A very good survey of monetary policy in the 1970s.

POOLE, WILLIAM. "Burnsian Monetary Policy: Eight Years of Progress?" *Journal of Finance*, 24 (May 1979):473–484. Another very good survey of monetary policy in the 1970s.

TEMIN, PETER. *Did Monetary Forces Cause the Great Depression?* New York:W.W. Norton, 1976. A major response to Friedman and Schwartz by a leading economic historian.

TOBIN, JAMES. "The Monetary Interpretation of History," *American Economic Review*, 55 (June 1965):464–485. A response to Friedman and Schwartz by a leading monetary theorist.

U.S., EXECUTIVE OFFICE OF THE PRESIDENT. *Economic Report of the President*. Washington, D.C. Each issue carries a history of monetary policy in the previous year.

WALLICH, HENRY and PETER KIER. "The Role of Operating Guidelines in U.S. Monetary Policy," *Federal Reserve Bulletin*, 65 (September 1979):679–691. A first-rate survey of the Fed's targets and instruments.

WICKER, ELMUS. *Federal Reserve Monetary Policy 1917–1933*. New York: Random House, 1966. A very thorough piece of historical research.

CHAPTER 25

Alternative Monetary Standards

In modern usage the term *monetary standard* denotes a system of rules, traditions, and attitudes that govern the supply of money. So far we have dealt almost exclusively with our current monetary standard, a mixture of accommodative policies and countercyclical policies. This standard has been criticized frequently, both for permitting inflation and for not really having a countercyclical impact. In this chapter we consider some of the alternative standards that have been suggested. We pay most attention to the monetarists' proposal for a stable money growth rate rule, because this proposal has received considerable (though far from majority) support among economists, and also because it provides a useful perspective for evaluating our current standard.[1] We also take up the gold standard, and a proposal that has the private sector create its own money, as well as a full-employment standard.

A STABLE MONEY GROWTH RATE RULE AND OTHER MONETARIST RECOMMENDATIONS

A number of economists, of whom Milton Friedman is the most prominent, have advocated that, instead of trying to counteract the business cycle, the Fed should ensure that money grows at a constant rate. To the supporters of this stable growth rate rule, keeping money growing at *some* stable rate is much more important than the particular rate that is chosen. They believe that a stable growth rate rule would result in a relatively stable rate of change of the price level. Whether this rate is positive, zero, or negative is not as important

---

[1] In the most recent (1978) applicable survey of economists' opinions, 39 percent agreed with, or "agreed with provisions," and 51 percent disagreed with the proposition that the Fed should "be instructed to increase the money supply at a fixed rate." J. R. Kearl et al. "A Confusion of Economists," *American Economic Review,* 69 (May 1979):30.

as that it be stable—and hence predictable. The unfavorable results of inflation are largely due to the growth rate being unanticipated.

Before looking at the specific arguments for, and against, a stable money
growth rule, there are several characteristics of this rule that should be kept
firmly in mind. First, it is a second-best policy. Its supporters admit that even
with their rule there would still be some fluctuations in output and prices. But,
they argue, these fluctuations would be less severe than the ones now experienced, since currently the net destabilizing effects of monetary policy are
added to the fluctuations that are inherent in the economy. They therefore
advocate the use of a monetary growth rate rule as the best that can be done
under present conditions.

Second, since the main argument for a stable growth rate is that at the
present stage of our knowledge about monetary policy we can do no better, it
follows that one might advocate the rule as a temporary device until more is
learned about monetary policy. And Friedman has suggested that eventually
we may want to return to discretionary monetary policy. Third, the adoption
of the rule is not necessarily a matter of all or nothing. One might adopt the
rule in a partial form by, for example, telling the Fed to keep the money
growth rate within certain bounds.

The Case for a Monetary Rule

This case consists of two parts. One is that we lack the technical knowledge
required to stabilize the economy. The Fed makes substantial errors in forecasting nominal GNP, and in estimating both the magnitude and timing of the
impact of its policy on GNP. As a result, the correlation coefficient between
the initial fluctuation in income and the fluctuation induced by the policy may
well be positive, so that policy is destabilizing. And even if this coefficient is
negative, the policy will be destabilizing if it is too strong, as could easily
happen.

The second part is that, while the Fed claims that its policy is devoted to
stabilizing income, it actually gives priority to other goals that conflict with
stabilizing GNP, goals such as stabilizing interest rates and keeping them low,
stabilizing exchange rates, etc. As a result of political pressures and administrative problems (discussed in Chapter 23), the Fed would act in a destabilizing
and inflationary way even if it had the technical knowledge required to stabilize GNP. As Milton Friedman put it in a debate with Franco Modigliani, a
leading supporter of discretionary policy:

> My major difference of opinion with Franco is in two respects: First, with his
> assumption that he knows how to accommodate [changes in the demand for
> money] (or that I do, for that matter, or that anybody does); and second with the
> assumption that if in fact you adopt a policy of accommodation, Franco
> Modigliani will be twisting the dials. . . . Once you adopt a policy of accommo-
> dating to changes, there will be all sorts of changes that he and I know should not
> be accommodated, with respect to which there will be enormous pressure to
> accommodate. And he and I will not be able to control that. . . . The real argu-
> ment for a steady rate of monetary growth is at least as much political as it is eco-

nomic; that it is a way of having a constitutional provision to set monetary policy which is not open to this kind of political objection.[2]

While monetarists object to countercyclical policy on the grounds that the Fed lacks both the knowledge and the good intentions that such a policy requires, those economists who accept the twin hypotheses of rational expectations and rapid market clearing object that stabilization policy is not needed. Assuming that the private sector has as much information as does the Fed, it will readily lower prices when aggregate demand falls, so that output does not fall. If the problem is that the private sector does not possess all the information that the Fed has, well, then, the Fed should simply provide this information instead of undertaking countercyclical policy.

The Case against a Monetary Rule

The majority of economists reject these arguments. First, many economists doubt that the lag of monetary policy is really so long and variable that countercyclical policy is likely to be destabilizing. It is generally agreed that the lag makes countercyclical policy less effective, but does it reduce its effectiveness to zero? This is a tough, technical question. Second, many economists, while disappointed with the Fed's past policies, are not disillusioned, and believe that in the future it will conduct a more successful stabilization policy. Third, the rational-expectations case against countercyclical policy is accepted by only a distinct minority of economists because of its assumption that wages and prices are highly flexible. The monetary growth rate rule is also open to the objection that it ignores supply shocks. For example, in 1973, when OPEC and poor harvests raised oil and food prices the Fed could decide whether or not to raise the money supply to accommodate these price increases. Under a monetary growth rate rule it would not have had this choice, but would have had to let rising food and oil prices exert downward pressure on output and on prices in other sectors.[3]

Probably the most serious problem with the money growth rate rule is its assumption that velocity is stable, or, rather, growing at a stable rate. This assumption was plausible in the 1960s and 1970s when velocity was indeed growing at a stable rate. But in the early 1980s, when velocity reversed course, and fell at a substantial rate, the case for a stable money growth rate rule became much less compelling. It *may* turn out that in the future velocity will again rise (or fall) at a stable rate. If so, this will greatly strengthen the case for

---

[2] Milton Friedman and Franco Modigliani, "The Monetarist Controversy: A Seminar Discussion," *Economic Review* (Federal Reserve Bank of San Francisco) supplement (Spring 1977):17–18.

[3] Supporters of the growth rate rule could reply that the Fed responded to the rise in food and oil prices by adopting a restrictive policy in the second half of 1974. This suggests that it did not use its freedom from a confining monetary growth rate rule very effectively. However, one study found that the results of this policy were better than those that would have followed from adherence to a monetary rule. But it could not take into account that the adoption of a rule would have changed the public's expectations, and hence its behavior. See Roger Crane, Arthur Havenner, and James Barry, "Fixed Rules vs. Activism in the Conduct of Monetary Policy," *American Economic Review,* 68 (December 1978):769–783.

the money growth rate rule. But, even then, the experience of the early 1980s will leave some lingering doubt that the stable trend in velocity will continue. What is a particular danger is a fall, rather than a rise, in the growth rate of velocity below the level that was assumed in setting the monetary growth rate. If velocity, instead of growing at a 3 percent rate, falls, say, at a 2 percent rate, then a rule that previously would have been consistent with price stability now requires prices to fall by 5 percent each year if employment is to be maintained. But it may take a long time until business and labor become reconciled to cutting wages and prices every year.

Another problem with the rule is the danger of evasion. After the Civil War, when a tax was imposed on the state bank notes, banks turned to checks. If the growth rate of money is limited, near-monies may take over more and more of the work of money, so that the monetary growth rate rule would become irrelevant. But with respect to the deposit component of the money stock this would not be much of a problem if banks would be able to pay interest on demand deposits, and if the Fed pays the market rate of interest on required reserves. Deposits would then pay a market-determined rate of interest, so that there would be no temptation to develop substitutes for them. There would still be a temptation to find substitutes for currency since it does not pay interest, but if the inflation is low, so that the interest rate is also low, this would not be an insuperable problem.

A more serious problem *might* be that the Fed could evade a monetary growth rate rule if it wanted to. Whichever way "money" is defined for the rule, there are some excluded items that are not much less liquid than some items that are included. By adopting regulations that increase the liquidity of some of these excluded items, the Fed could make them into de facto money. Similarly, through its regulatory powers the Fed could increase the quantity of near-monies in general.

More generally, at a time of rapid financial innovation one might well doubt one's ability to select a particular measure of money, and to define the correct monetary policy as having this measure grow at the appropriate rate for the next, say, thirty years. It might be necessary to redefine money from time to time and that would create an opening for discretion. For example, if money is growing faster than the rule specifies the Fed could redefine money to exclude a component of money that is growing particularly fast.

A related problem is that the "money" that should be growing at a fixed rate is not, in the view of some economists, any particular country's money. Given the ease with which foreign currencies can be traded, if British interest rates are higher, American firms hold some of their money in the form of British pounds rather than as dollars, while if U.S. interest rates are higher more dollars will be held by Britons. Hence, to be effective, a monetary growth rate rule should be applied not just to any one country, but to, say, four major currencies jointly. But it would be hard to get these countries to collaborate on a monetary rule. Insofar as they do not, the Fed might have to reduce its money growth rate because, say, the German central bank is expanding its money at too fast a rate. The American public might not sit still for this. But other economists think that the international money market is not all that integrated, that people are reluctant to hold foreign currencies, so that you can still control domestic prices by controlling domestic money.

In addition, there is the fact that a monetary rule would require the Fed to ignore all targets other than the money stock. For example, it could not act to moderate swings in the exchange rate and in interest rates. While many economists would welcome this, others believe that the goals the Fed would have to relinquish are desirable goals.

Then there is the question of the political feasibility of adherence to a rule. If the rule is adopted, wouldn't it be abandoned as soon as interest rates fluctuate sharply, or unemployment rises substantially? The late Jacob Viner has argued as follows:

> In the economic field important rules affecting important social issues have in fact been extremely scarce, and to the extent that they have had a substantial degree of durability this has been largely explicable either by the fact that they evolved into taboos, or ends in themselves, and were thus removed from the area of open discussion and rational appraisal, or by the tolerance of widespread evasion. The most conspicuous instances of economic rules with a substantial degree of durability were the prohibition of lending at interest and the maintenance of fixed monetary standards in terms of precious metals. The most enthusiastic advocate of rules can derive little comfort from the availability of these historical precedents.[4]

Some Possible Compromises

Given these arguments for and against the monetary growth rate rule, it is not surprising that some economists have looked for a compromise position. One compromise already mentioned would give the Fed not a single-valued target, but a range, say, 4–6 percent for *M-1,* and perhaps allow it to move outside this range under special circumstances.

Another possible compromise is to adjust the monetary growth rate each quarter to offset the changes in velocity in the most recent quarter, or quarters. This would prevent the drift in the price level that would result if the long-term trend in velocity differs from what was assumed in setting up the rule.

Still another compromise is known by the inelegant name of "semi-rules." These are rules for a constant reaction to changes in income, not for a constant monetary growth rate. For example, the Fed could announce as its policy an equation that relates the growth rate of the money stock to the rate of change in income in the recent past. Some studies using both an earlier version of the MPS model and the St. Louis model have shown that, *if* either of these models is a correct description of the economy, there exists such a semi-rule that would have performed better than a constant monetary growth rate. But these studies have two great weaknesses. First, by assuming that the lag of

---

[4] Jacob Viner, "The Necessity and Desirable Range of Discretion to Be Allowed to a Monetary Authority," in Leland Yeager (ed.), *In Search of a Monetary Constitution,* p. 248. Cambridge: Harvard University Press, 1962.

monetary policy in each individual case is equal to the average lag, they assume away part of the case for the monetary rule. Second, as discussed in Chapter 23, the adoption of a rule would change the public's expectations, and thus the way it acts. Hence, even if the MPS model or the St. Louis model were absolutely true descriptions of how the economy functioned before the rule was adopted, this need no longer be so once a semi-rule is adopted.

All in all, the issue of whether the Fed should continue using discretionary monetary policy, a growth rate rule, or some compromise is far from settled.

OTHER MONETARIST POLICY POSITIONS

Support of a monetary growth rate rule is a major characteristic of monetarism. Thus Franco Modigliani has stated that this is *the* basic issue dividing monetarists and Keynesians, since nowadays Keynesians agree that money is a highly important variable.[5] However, this may go a bit too far; Keynesians generally still attribute less importance to changes in the money stock than do monetarists.

Moreover, there is much more to monetarism than just a preference for a stable money growth rate. In Chapter 15 we discussed briefly six attributes that characterize monetarist theory: the money supply as the dominant factor driving money income, a particular view of the transmission process, the stability of the private sector, the irrelevance for the determination of nominal income of the allocation of demand among various sectors, focus on the price level as a whole rather than on individual prices, and a preference for small models.

In discussing monetary policy we have looked at three other monetarist propositions: use of the money stock rather than the interest rate, or GNP, as the target (together with the belief that the Fed can control the money stock), the use of total reserves or the base as the instrument, and support of a monetary growth rate rule. Three remaining policy propositions serve to round out a set of twelve propositions that constitute a description of monetarism. One is that there is no useful trade-off between unemployment and inflation since the Phillips curve is in real terms. Most Keynesians agree that *ultimately* there exists little or no trade-off between unemployment and inflation, but believe that there is such a trade-off for a long enough time to be usable for stabilization policy. Second, monetarists are more strongly opposed to unanticipated inflation than are Keynesians, and are *relatively* less concerned with unemployment. Finally, monetarists usually favor free-market processes and oppose government intervention more than Keynesians do.

These characteristics of monetarism are interconnected and related to the monetarist's tendency to take a long-run point of view. If most of the historically observed fluctuations in nominal income are due to changes in the money growth rate rather than to variations in velocity, then a stable money

---

[5] Franco Modigliani, "The Monetarist Controversy; or, Should We Forsake Stabilization Policy?" *American Economic Review* 67 (March 1977):1–19.

growth rate seems desirable. Moreover, if, in the absence of fluctuations in the money growth rate, the private sector is stable, then countercyclical monetary policy is not needed. Similarly, someone who wants a stable monetary growth rate obviously wants the Fed to use a money-stock target rather than an interest-rate target. In addition, if one looks at the price level as a whole, then cost-push inflation seems less of a danger, and hence there is less need for the Fed to adopt the policy of increasing the money stock to maintain high employment despite rising prices. Besides, if there is no usable trade-off between unemployment and inflation, then there is one less thing that stabilization policy could potentially do. A monetary growth rate rule also eliminates the danger that the Fed will shift to an inflationary policy, and it gets rid of one type of discretionary, and hence to some people arbitrary, government action.

But this does not mean that one can accept the monetary growth rate rule only if one accepts all the other monetarist propositions too. Suppose, for example, that there are long and unpredictable lags in the effects of monetary policy, or that there is irresistible political pressure on the Fed, or that the rational-expectations criticism of discretionary policy is correct. If any of these conditions prevails, then the monetary growth rate rule would be preferable to discretionary policy in most cases.

The Gold Standard

A stable money growth rate rule is one way—but not the only way—of depriving the government of discretionary control over the money supply. Another way is a return to the gold standard. We will discuss the gold standard in some detail in the next chapter. Here we just discuss how it would limit the government's control over the money supply. For this it is not necessary that money actually consist of gold coins. All that is required is (1) that various types of money are convertible into gold; (2) that the government buys and sells gold at a fixed price; (3) that the government does not inhibit the free import or export of gold; and (4) that the government does not offset the automatic effect of a gold inflow or outflow on the money supply by, for example, open-market operations.

Suppose that these conditions are met, and that the Fed increases the base. The money supply expands and, as discussed in Chapter 22, the dollar now falls on the foreign exchange market. With the dollar worth fewer British pounds and French francs, etc., someone will go to the U.S. Treasury, buy gold at its fixed dollar price, and sell this gold abroad for foreign currency. This will be profitable since the foreign currency is now worth more dollars. As the U.S. Treasury receives dollars for the gold that it sells, the public's money stock falls. Moreover, as people take advantage of this opportunity the U.S. gold stock declines, which may induce the Fed to adopt a restrictive policy in any case. Thus, any attempt by the Fed to increase the money supply unduly does not succeed.

Conversely, suppose the Fed is restrictive. As interest rates rise and output and prices fall, the dollar rises on the foreign exchange market. This provides an incentive to buy gold abroad at its fixed price in foreign currency (i.e., at its lower dollar price) and sell it to the U.S. Treasury. With the Treasury paying out dollars for this gold, the U.S. money supply expands again, thus counteracting the Fed's restrictive policy.

Does this mean that the gold standard is desirable because it limits the Fed's powers? Not in the opinion of most economists. Obviously, those who believe that the Fed's actions have, on the average, a favorable impact on the economy oppose the gold standard. Those who want to eliminate the Fed's discretionary control over the money supply often reject the gold standard in favor of a stable money growth rate rule. The gold standard does not prevent the Fed from increasing the money stock at an inflationary rate—*if other countries do the same*. In this case the dollar does not fall on the foreign exchange market, so that the U.S. money stock is not reduced by gold exports. The gold standard does not prevent a country from inflating, just from inflating more than other countries. For the world as a whole, the supply of gold is a determinant of the worldwide inflation rate.

Another problem with the gold standard is that it fixes the value of the dollar relative to gold, but not necessarily in terms of other goods. Suppose that there are large-scale gold discoveries. With an increased supply of gold the price of gold must fall relative to the prices of goods and services. If the value of money is fixed in terms of gold, the value of money in terms of goods and services must fall; that is, we have inflation.

Moreover, one may question whether those who support the gold standard in principle would really allow it to operate in practice. Suppose a gold outflow would require a substantial deflation in the United States, or a gold inflow a substantial inflation. Would the supporters of the gold standard still be there? Given the recent great swings in foreign exchange rates and in gold prices, which under the gold standard would induce large swings in U.S. prices, this is a question worth asking. In addition, the gold standard requires countries to hold an asset, gold, that does not earn interest.

Private Money

Some economists, led by Friederich von Hayek of Freiburg University, West Germany, want to introduce competition into the monetary system as a way of exercising discipline over the central bank. They would allow banks to issue their own money, money that would be distinct for each bank. People could then write contracts denominated either in government monies, such as the dollar or the pound, or in privately issued monies. Both types of money would circulate. The public would tend to hold that money whose value is least eroded by inflation. This would give each bank—*and the government*—an incentive to preserve the value of its money by limiting its quantity.

This is an ingenious scheme, but it too has some problems. First, given the public's conservatism on monetary matters, private money issuers might find it impossible to compete against the well-established government money. Second, there is the danger that a money issuer would initially pursue a conservative policy, build up a good reputation so that many people will be willing to acquire this money, and then, all of a sudden, flood the market with this money, go out of business, and live happily every after.

A more radical approach would abolish government money altogether. It would also cut the link between the medium of exchange and the standard of value. The standard of value would consist of a commodity bundle containing a fixed amount of many different commodities. Since the price of such a bundle would move more or less in line with the general price level, anyone who makes a contract to pay a certain number of such monetary units would neither gain nor lose significantly from inflation. Hence, it would be an excellent standard of value. The medium of exchange would be a check or currency note from a money-market fund denominated in commodity bundles. In such a system inflation would be no problem because the standard of value, the commodity bundle, would have a stable value in terms of all goods and services. Decreases in aggregate demand would also not create a problem. If people decide to buy fewer goods and to hold more money instead, they would simply increase their accounts with the money-market funds which would then buy more of these commodity bundles. In such an economy that has no serious macroeconomic disturbances, the Fed could be abolished. Whether such a system would actually work needs much more investigation. But, in any case, it is too radical to have a serious chance of adoption in the foreseeable future.

The Full-Employment Approach

All the standards discussed so far would greatly reduce or eliminate the Fed's role. Another standard would give the Fed a very active role in maintaining full employment. It would have one predominant goal, full employment, and a secondary goal, keeping interest rates low and stable. Hence, it would accommodate just about all increases in the demand for money whether caused by shifts in the IS curve or the LM curve.

How about the longer run vertical Phillips curve and the danger that such an expansionary policy would generate accelerating inflation? Supporters of this standard reject the Phillips curve approach to policy. They consider it immoral to use unemployment to curb inflation. Instead, they would rely mainly on incomes policy. Moreover, they maintain that if we had a more equal income distribution then unions would push less hard for wage increases, and the slope of the Phillips curve would be less steep. A social compact, embodied in a widely accepted incomes policy rather than unemployment, is the appropriate way to curb inflation. Monetary restriction, and the resulting higher interest rates, only make inflation worse, rather than better, because rising interest rates induce firms to raise prices. This position is accepted by only a minority of economists. Most American economists are skeptical about the efficacy of social contracts and incomes policies.

SUMMARY

1 A number of economists have advocated a stable money growth rate rule as the best that can be done given our limited knowledge. They point to long and vari-

able lags, as well as to political pressures that are likely to interfere with discretionary monetary policy.

2 Supporters of discretionary policy doubt that the lag is really all that variable, and point to the occurrence of supply shocks, to the variability of velocity, and to the development of near-monies as vitiating the case for a fixed money growth rate rule.

3 Some economists advocate a compromise position, such as setting a band for money growth or the use of semi-rules.

4 One can identify a monetarist position on policy that consists of the use of the money stock as the target, a fixed money growth rate rule, use of total reserves or the base as the instrument, rejection of a Phillips curve trade-off, relatively greater concern about inflation than about unemployment, and a relatively greater preference for free-market processes.

5 Another proposal for curbing the Fed's discretion is a return to the gold standard. However, this would not prevent inflation if other countries inflate too, or if the world's gold supply increases.

6 Some economists advocate the institution of private money either alongside government money or as a replacement for it.

7 Other economists advocate a consistently expansionary monetary policy accompanied by an incomes policy.

QUESTIONS AND EXERCISES

1 Write an essay either defending or criticizing a monetary growth rate rule.
2 Now write an essay replying to your previous essay.
3 Describe the arguments for and against a gold standard.
4 Develop your own idea of a good monetary standard.

FURTHER READING

BRONFENBRENNER, MARTIN. "Monetary Rules: A New Look," *Journal of Law & Economics*, 8 (October 1965):173–194. An excellent discussion of the rules debate.

BRUNNER, KARL. "The Case Against Monetary Activism," *Lloyds Bank Review*, 139 (January 1981):20–30. A sweeping attack on discretionary policy.

FRIEDMAN, MILTON. *A Program for Monetary Stability*. New York: Fordham University Press, 1959. A classic statement of the rules position.

———. "Monetary Policy: Theory and Practice," *Journal of Monetary Economics*, 14 (February 1982):98–118. A powerful indictment of the Fed's procedures.

GREENFIELD, ROBERT, and LELAND YEAGER. "A Laissez-Faire Approach to Monetary Stability," *Journal of Money, Credit and Banking*, 15 (August 1983):302–315. A fascinating discussion of private money.

LAIDLER, DAVID. "Monetarism: An Interpretation and an Assessment," *Economic Journal*, 91 (March 1981):1–28. An excellent survey.

LERNER, ABBA. "Review of Milton Friedman's *A Program for Monetary Stability*," *Journal of the American Statistical Association*, 57 (March 1962):211–220. An outstanding criticism of the monetary growth rate rule.

MODIGLIANI, FRANCO. "The Monetarist Controversy; or, Should We Forsake Stabilization Policy?" *American Economic Review*, 67 (March 1977):1–19. An excellent criticism of monetarist policy prescriptions.

MODIGLIANI, FRANCO, and MILTON FRIEDMAN. "The Monetarist Controversy," *Eco-

nomic Review (Federal Reserve Bank of San Francisco) supplement (Spring 1977). An extremely stimulating debate.

TOBIN, JAMES. "The Monetarist Counter-Revolution Today—An Appraisal," *Economic Journal*, 91 (March 1981):29–42. A powerful criticism of monetarism.

———. "Monetary Policy: Rules, Targets and Shocks," *Journal of Money, Credit and Banking*, 15 (November 1983):506–518. A strong defense of discretionary policy.

PART FIVE

INTERNATIONAL MONEY AND FINANCE

CHAPTER 26

The Evolution of the International Monetary System

The international monetary system provides a framework that enables residents of one country to make payments to residents of other countries. Such payments are necessary because importers in one country must pay exporters in other countries; either the importers must first acquire the currencies of the countries in which the exporters live, or the exporters must, after being paid in the importer's currency, exchange it for their own.

The business and financial needs of industry and trade are served by arrangements that minimize the additional costs and inconvenience and risks of international transactions relative to domestic transactions. These costs, while generally small, have varied with changes in the international monetary arrangements. Over the last century, the international monetary system has evolved from reliance on gold to primary reliance on national monies—and especially the U.S. dollar—to meet the demand for international reserve assets, monies which provide the basis for international payments. The changes in international payments arrangements are not random, but instead are responses to both monetary and structural economic disturbances, and to changes in political relationships among the major countries.

An international monetary system can be identified by three key features—the organization of the foreign exchange market, the types of assets used for financing or settling payments imbalances, and the mechanisms of adjustment to payments imbalances.

As the institutional basis for organizing the foreign exchange market and for producing international reserve assets has changed, so has the name given to the international monetary system. Before World War I, the term **gold standard** was applied to international financial arrangements; after World War I the **gold-exchange standard** described the mechanism.

The term *standard,* when used in reference to the gold standard or a bimetallic standard, suggests a measure or unit of account, like a yard or a liter. National monies at that time had values that were stated in terms of gold; thus the U.S. dollar was equal to 1.672 grams of gold of .900 fineness.

A treaty-based system known as the Bretton Woods System was established during World War II and functioned until the early 1970s. With the breakdown of the Bretton Woods arrangement in the 1971–1973 period, arrangements for payments among countries have become more varied and eclectic, and no comprehensive term now adequately describes the payments arrangements. The term *system* has been applied since World War II to the arrangements for organizing the foreign exchange market and for producing international reserve assets.

This chapter first describes the three international monetary systems that prevailed for nearly a hundred years. Then attention is given to the economic and political factors that explain the evolution of the international financial arrangements, especially the rise of the United States as a dominant economic power.

THE GOLD STANDARD

The nineteenth century is frequently described as the gold-standard era, although more detailed analysis suggests that for most countries the term is more appropriately applied to the period 1880–1913. A country "joined" the gold standard when its national legislation required that its major banks and financial institutions redeem or repurchase their monetary liabilities at a fixed price, the mint parity, that stated the value of the national currency unit in terms of a specified amount of gold. Thus at the beginning of January 1879, the United States went back on the gold standard, having abandoned it in 1863; U.S. commercial banks were once again obliged to convert their monetary liabilities into gold. The mint parities of major countries are shown in Table 26.1, together with the prices of major foreign currencies in terms of the U.S. dollar. Thus the Act of Parliament of 1816 obliged the Bank of England to buy gold at 3 pounds, 17 shillings, 9 pence per ounce and to sell gold at the price of 3 pounds, 17 shillings, 10 ½ pence per ounce: the gold was .916⅔ fine or pure. Some countries pegged their currencies to silver as well as to gold, and so they were on a bimetallic standard; the monetary institutions in these countries were obliged to buy and sell gold and silver on demand at the respective parities. Managing a bimetallic system proved difficult because of the need to maintain the fixed-price relationship between the mint parity for gold and the mint parity for silver. From time to time, when there were large new discoveries of silver or gold, changes in one of the mint parities were necessary.

A major by-product of the commitments of individual countries to peg their currencies to gold was a system of pegged exchange rates. Thus, given the willingness of the Bank of England to buy and sell one ounce of gold at 77 shillings and 10½ pence and the willingness of the U.S. Treasury to buy and sell one ounce of gold at the parity of $20.67, the dollar price of 1 pound

				Value of one	U.S. dollar
Country	Unit	Weight[a]	Fineness[b]	ounce of gold	parity
United States (1879)[c]	1 dollar	1.672	.900	US 20.67	—
Great Britain (1816)	1 pound	7.988	.917	BP 3/17/10½	$4.865
France (1878)	1 franc	.322	.900	FF 107.1	.193
Germany (1871)	1 mark	.398	.900	DM 86.8	.238
Italy (1878)	1 lira	.3226	.900	IL 107.1	.193
Netherlands (1875)	1 florin	.672	.900	DF 51.4	.402

Table 26.1 Parities of Major Currencies under the Gold Standard

a: Weight of standard coin in grams.
b: Fineness of standard coin = proportion of pure gold.
c: The dates in parentheses indicate when the currency was pegged to gold.

Source: M. L. Muhleman, *Monetary Systems of the World.* New York: Charles H. Nicoll, 1894.

sterling could be calculated at $4.865 (once an adjustment was made for the somewhat greater purity of the British gold coin).[1]

Some central banks bought and sold gold at their mint parities. Most central banks, however, bought gold at prices fractionally below their mint parities and sold gold at prices fractionally above their mint parities. These small differences between the mint parities and the gold buying and selling prices were called handling charges, and were intended to compensate the national central banks for their transaction costs. In addition, some central banks varied their gold-selling prices modestly, increasing these prices when the demand for gold was strong so the amount demanded would decline; these countries were said to be on the "limping gold standard."

Gold and International Reserves

A key aspect of the gold standard was that central banks held a large part of their international reserves in the form of gold. The Bank of England held virtually all its assets in the form of gold; other central banks held a large proportion of their assets in gold and the rest in assets such as government securities denominated in the British pound, the French franc, and their own currencies. Differences among central banks in the proportion of gold in their international reserves reflected differences in their business needs. One reason that these banks outside Great Britain held such a large proportion of their assets in sterling was that they sold sterling-denominated debt in London; London was then the world's principal financial center. Similarly, borrowers resident outside France received French francs after selling debt in Paris. Moreover, these borrowers were obliged to acquire the British pound and the French franc to repay debts denominated in these currencies.

[1] Thus if an ounce of gold equals both 77 shillings, 10½ pence times .917/.900 (the adjustment for differences in the proportion of pure gold in the several coins) and $20.67, then 20 shillings, or 1 pound, equals $4.865.

Gold and Payments Imbalances

A second feature of the gold standard was that gold might flow from the countries with payments deficits—broadly, those whose imports of goods, services, and securities exceeded their exports of goods, services, and securities—to countries with payments surpluses. Gold flows were supposed to settle payments imbalances. One of the paradoxes of the gold standard period was that relatively little gold was actually transferred from deficit countries to surplus countries. Shipments of gold between New York and London incurred costs of freight and insurance as well as the forgone interest on the wealth invested in gold between the date the payer acquired the gold in one country and the date the payee received gold in the second country. Consequently, traders and investors sought less costly methods to make international payments.

As an alternative to the gold transactions, a market developed in bills of exchange, which were a type of postdated check. These bills were issued by importers or buyers, and were IOUs indicating that payment for the purchase would be made in thirty or ninety days. Thus, a U.S. exporter of wheat to Great Britain may have received a sterling-denominated bill of exchange due in thirty or ninety days; the market price of this bill of exchange would be below the face value on the maturity date, since the bill would have been sold at a discount to reflect the interest rate. The U.S. wheat exporter wanted dollars, not sterling; he could sell the sterling bill in London, and buy gold in London to ship to the United States, or he would sell the bill of exchange in New York to a U.S. importer with a payment to make in London and avoid the costs and inconvenience of the gold shipment. The U.S. importer would pay for the sterling bill in dollars, and the U.S. wheat exporter would receive dollars and both avoid the costs of shipping gold from London to New York and earn interest on the bill of exchange as it traveled from London to New York.

Because the costs of shipping the bill of exchange to London were below the costs of shipping gold to London, the U.S. importer would pay a higher price for the bill of exchange than for the amount of gold that would generate the same value of sterling payment. The ability to make the London payment by shipping gold set an upper limit to the dollar price of the sterling bills. Similarly, the ability to make a payment from London to New York by shipping gold set a lower limit to the dollar price that the U.S. exporter would accept for his sterling bill; if the U.S. exporter anticipated that the dollar price would be lower, he would instead ship gold.

"Rules of the Game"

The third feature of the gold standard was the concept of "rules of the game" —the idea that countries with balance of payments surpluses would follow expansive monetary policies because the gold inflows would lead to an increase in the monetary liabilities of their central banks. Conversely, the countries with balance of payments deficits and gold outflows would follow contractive monetary policies: the monetary liabilities of their central banks would decline. Commodity price levels would rise in the countries with the payments surpluses and fall in the countries with the payments deficits. As the international competitiveness of the two groups of countries changed, the imports of the first group would rise, and their exports would fall; in contrast, the imports of the second group would fall and their exports would rise. The change in the relationship among national price levels would continue until balance of payments equilibrium was achieved. Hence international payments imbalances would be automatically self-correcting without the need for the various national central banks to adopt discretionary measures.

The adjustment process appeared to be automatic, guided by an invisible hand. The evidence that countries followed the rules of the game is mixed. Yet countries, once they accepted gold parities, were able to maintain their parities, and so some mechanism in the system facilitated restoring payments equilibrium once disturbances occurred that led to payments imbalances.

One important aspect of the operation of the "rules of the game" should be noted—in order to maintain the fixity of one price, their gold parities, countries accepted variations in their national price levels. Increases in the national price levels occurred when countries had payments surpluses, and decreases in these price levels occurred when countries had payments deficits. These variations in national price levels made it possible for countries to maintain their gold parities.

Gold and the Commodity Price Level

The fourth feature of the gold standard was the promise of commodity price level stability in the long run. If on a worldwide basis monetary gold stocks were increasing rapidly, either because of new gold discoveries or because of new and lower cost techniques for gold ore refining, then central banks in many countries might experience gold inflows simultaneously, and their money supplies would rise at the same time. At the new and higher commodity price levels, gold mining would be more costly, the level of gold production would decline, and a damper or brake would be placed on further increases in the commodity price levels. Conversely, if the demand for gold increased relative to the supply, the commodity price levels would fall because less gold would be available for monetary purposes. At the lower commodity price levels, more gold would be mined, and eventually the decline in the commodity price levels would be checked. So just as national price levels changed to restore balance of payments equilibrium, so changes in the world price level would prove self-limiting. Thus, price level stability would be achieved over a period of several decades if not on a year-to-year basis.

The U.S. and British commodity price levels for 1800–1950 are shown in Figure 26.1. The commodity price levels at the outbreak of World War I are not very different from the price levels a century earlier. The average annual change in the price levels was small, much less than 1 percent. And there are very few years, except those at the times of major wars, in which the annual change in the price level exceeded 3 percent.

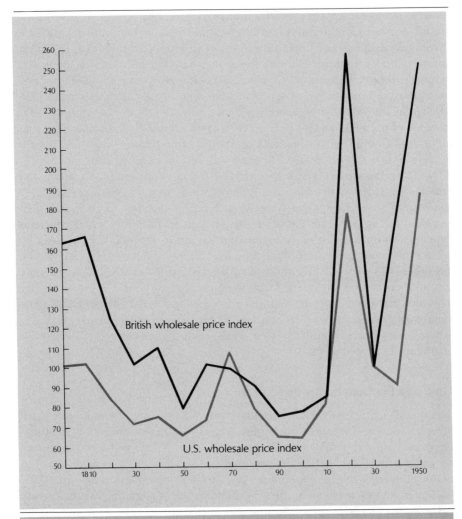

Figure 26.1   The U.S. and British Wholesale Price Indexes, 1800–1950.
Under the gold standard, price levels in the two countries moved together quite closely.

The attractions of the gold standard were in its anonymous, automatic, self-correcting properties and its promise of long-run price level stability. Balance of payments adjustments could be made easily. Finally, the tremendous economic growth in the international economy during the half-century before World War I contributed to the view that the gold standard was the ideal monetary arrangement.

During World War I most countries ceased pegging their currencies to gold. Moreover, their price levels increased sharply because of a surge in military expenditures. After the war some countries, primarily countries that had been neutral in the war, returned to their prewar parities. Great Britain returned to its prewar parity in 1925. High levels of unemployment resulted, since the needed changes in commodity price levels required deflationary monetary policies. Other countries eventually increased the price of gold in terms of their currencies. In retrospect, it appears that it would have been easier and less costly to reestablish the gold standard if countries had been willing to increase the price of gold in terms of their currencies to match the increase in their price levels that had occurred during World War I.

THE GOLD-EXCHANGE STANDARD

The gold-exchange standard developed in the early 1920s in response to an anticipated gold shortage due both to a reduction in the supply of gold and to an increase in the demand. The anticipated reduction in the supply would result from the combination of the increase in national price levels and the concomitant increase in costs of gold production together with the fixed selling price for gold. The increase in demand would result both from an increase in the number of central banks due to the breakup of the Austro-Hungarian Empire and from an increase in the demand for gold for monetary uses because of the increases in national price levels during and after World War I. Because of the higher commodity price levels, gold was cheaper in terms of silver and other precious metals—as long as gold parities remained unchanged.

The adequacy of gold was extensively discussed at two conferences sponsored by the League of Nations, one in Brussels in 1920 and one in Genoa in 1922. Because central banks were reluctant to raise the price of gold in terms of their currencies, the participants at these conferences recommended ways to economize on the use of gold. The use of gold coins for private payments was discouraged; monetary gold holdings would be concentrated in central banks. Moreover, a practice that had been evident before World War I received formal recognition and approval: some central banks would hold their reserves in the form of foreign exchange, such as bank deposits, Treasury bills, and bankers' acceptances, denominated in the British pound, the U.S. dollar, or some other currency.

The gold-exchange standard was supposed to modify only the composition of international reserves. Central banks were still supposed to follow the "rules of the game" for balance of payment adjustment. Countries would still maintain parities for their currencies in terms of gold. Yet there was a change: if the United States or Great Britain incurred payments deficits and the countries with the payments surpluses acquired assets denominated in the U.S. dollar or the British pound, the United States and Great Britain would not follow the rules of the game and reduce the outstanding liabilities of their central banks. The countries with the payments surpluses would increase their monetary reserves, the automatic adjustment tendencies of the gold standard were maintained, but in a somewhat more asymmetric way than before World War I.

The rationale for the development of the gold-exchange standard was that it would provide a stable framework in which national currencies would again exchange at their mint parities. Yet exchange rates were not pegged during most of the period between World War I and World War II. In May 1925, Great Britain pegged sterling to gold at its 1913 parity. In September 1931, Great Britain decided that maintaining the gold parity was too costly in terms of domestic employment, so sterling was allowed to float; however, the British authorities intervened extensively in the foreign exchange market. The 1930s were a decade of sharp changes in parities, which followed a domino-like pattern: the U.S. dollar was devalued in 1933–1934, and the French franc and the Dutch guilder in 1936. The alignment of the exchange rates at the end of the 1930s was not very different from that at the end of the 1920s. After the sequence of devaluations, the monetary price of gold was 75 percent higher.

The growth of international reserves denominated in sterling, the dollar, and other major currencies during the 1930s was modest. At the end of the 1920s, holdings of foreign exchange accounted for 20 percent of international reserves. At the end of the 1930s this ratio was lower because of the effective worldwide increase in the price of gold and the sharp increase in the value of monetary gold holdings. In the 1940s, in contrast, the foreign exchange component amounted to 30 percent of international reserves; most of the reserves involved U.S. dollar assets or British pound assets.

The monetary instability in the interwar period was reflected in the combination of sharp movements in exchange rates, high levels of unemployment, and especially in the growth of ad hoc restrictions on international payments. This instability is sometimes associated with the tension between Great Britain, whose economic power was declining, and the United States, whose economic position was getting stronger. One aspect of this tension was that the interest rates the United States felt appropriate for its domestic economy attracted funds from London, and the Bank of England had to counter by raising sterling interest rates to levels deemed too high given its unemployment. In the early 1930s, there was a conflict about the appropriate value for the U.S. dollar–British pound exchange rate. The value preferred by the U.S. authorities would have increased the competitiveness of U.S. goods more than the British authorities found acceptable.

This shift in economic power from Great Britain to the United States was almost inevitable given the increase in the size of the U.S. economy relative to the size of the British economy. Whether this shift could have been accommodated without the instability that actually occurred is conjectural. Major policy errors contributed both to the variability of exchange rates and to the high levels of unemployment. One error was the unwillingness to adjust exchange parities to reflect the increase in the post–World War I price levels. A second error was the unwillingness of many countries to raise the monetary gold price to correspond with the increase in the national price levels.

THE BRETTON WOODS SYSTEM

Early in World War II, the United States and Great Britain took the initiative in developing economic institutions to deal with the anticipated problems of the postwar period—and to avoid a repetition of the monetary and trade disturbances of the previous twenty years. Plans for an International Trade Organization (ITO) were developed to provide a framework for reducing tariffs, for establishing commodity arrangements to limit variations in prices of raw materials, and for coordinating national antitrust policies. Although the ITO never came into existence, the first article in its charter led to the General Agreement on Tariffs and Trade (GATT), which has been the dominant institution promoting a reduction of tariffs and other trade barriers. Thus, the International Bank for Reconstruction and Development (the IBRD, or World Bank) was established to facilitate the postwar recovery in Western Europe; once this task was completed at the end of the 1940s, the bank focused on extending financial assistance to the developing countries. The third institution, the International Monetary Fund (IMF), was established to enhance stability in international payments in several ways: by providing rules for changes in exchange parities and for exchange controls on international payments, and by managing a pool of national currencies that individual countries might borrow from to help finance their payments deficits. The World Bank and the IMF are known as the Bretton Woods institutions, for the treaties establishing both institutions were signed at a resort in Bretton Woods, New Hampshire. And *the exchange rate arrangements incorporated in the IMF Treaty* are known as the **Bretton Woods System.**

The International Monetary Fund

The IMF is the institutional embodiment of the Bretton Wood System. Hence, this system differs sharply from both the gold standard and the gold-exchange standard in its legal aspects, as the earlier systems had no international legal basis. Moreover, the Bretton Woods System was managed by international civil servants, responsible to the Board of Governors selected by the member countries (usually their secretaries of the treasury or ministers of finance), and a full-time board of Executive Directors, essentially ambassadors from its members.

Each member country of the IMF was required to state a parity for its currency in terms of gold or in terms of the U.S. dollar. Subsequent changes of the exchange parities required consultation with or approval by the Fund.

When the Fund was established, its capital was projected to be the equivalent of $10 billion. Countries joining the IMF were obliged to subscribe to its capital; the amount of each country's capital subscription or quota was based on a formula that included the country's share of world imports and its gold holdings. One-quarter of each country's capital subscription was payable in gold and the remaining three-quarters in its own currency in the form of a non–interest-bearing demand note.

Whenever a member country had a payments deficit, it could borrow one of these currencies from the pool held by the Fund, with the amount it might borrow geared to the size of its quota. About one-quarter of its quota was automatically available, and the rest was available on a discretionary basis. To finance these loans, the Fund would cash part of the non–interest-bearing demand notes. For example, in 1956, at the time of the Suez crisis in the Middle East, Great Britain borrowed nearly $2 billion from the Fund. In the Fund's terminology Great Britain "drew" or bought U.S. dollars from the Fund with British pounds, with the consequence that the Fund's holdings of U.S. dollars declined while its holdings of British pounds increased. The Fund obtained the dollars by cashing part of the dollar-denominated demand note received as part of the U.S. capital subscription at the U.S. Treasury. Great Britain paid interest to the Fund, with the interest rate based on the size of the borrowing in relation to its quota and the length of the period that the loan was outstanding. When Great Britain repaid the loan, it purchased British pounds with U.S. dollars or some other currency acceptable to the Fund.

One feature of the Bretton Woods System that merits attention is that the Fund rules sought to eliminate the use of exchange controls on payments for goods and services like shipping and tourism, although members were to be allowed to retain such restrictions during the postwar reconstruction period. Members could maintain restrictions on transactions in securities, such as stocks and bonds, for an indefinite period.

The Activities of the International Monetary Fund

The Fund's Articles of Agreement provided that the ability of a member to borrow would not be conditional on the Fund's approval of the member's economic and social policies. Over the years, however, the Fund management has taken the view that credit should be extended if there is a reasonable prospect that the member country could resolve its balance of payments problems. By 1980 the capital of the Fund was the equivalent of $50 billion, which resulted from an increase in the number of member countries and several increases in the size of each member's quota. Two important institutional innovations, one in the early 1960s and the second in the late 1960s, complemented periodic increases in IMF quotas as a way to increase the funds available to the IMF and the supply of international reserves. To alleviate a possible shortage of currencies in the Fund, the General Arrangements to Borrow, which formalized the terms on which the Fund could borrow the currencies of member countries, was attached to the Fund structure in 1963.

A major modification involved the establishment of special drawing rights (SDRs), a new international reserve asset. The rationale for introducing the SDR was the belief that there would be a shortage of gold and of international reserve assets, and that most countries could not satisfy their demands for reserves without forcing the United States to incur payments deficits. Initially, the value of the SDR was equal to $1 U.S. (the IMF determines the value of the SDR each day). Ten billion dollars of SDRs were produced in the 1968–1971 period, through a form of international open-market operation; each member country received newly produced SDRs in proportion to its share of total IMF quotas. Each member country could use SDRs to buy foreign currencies from other members or from the Fund. For example, if Great Britain had a payments deficit, it might sell some SDRs to the Fund to get U.S. dollars or some other national currency that it might use to support its currency in the foreign exchange market. In addition, SDRs began to develop some characteristics of a unit of account, and some countries began to state the parities for their currencies in terms of SDR, just as, at earlier dates, they had stated their parities in terms of gold and then the U.S. dollar.

During the 1950s and 1960s, international trade and payments grew rapidly, and exchange controls on international payments that had been adopted by countries in Western Europe in the 1940s were reduced. For the major industrial countries, the increase in national incomes was very large, so that the contrast between the post–World War I and post–World War II eras was sharp.

One interpretation was that this boom in national incomes and international trade was attributable to the Fund and especially to the orderly arrangements for changes in exchange rates and the reduction in exchange controls. Indeed, one of the surprising features of the 1950–1970 period was the infrequency of changes in exchange parities of major currencies. The British pound was devalued once and the French franc was devalued twice, while the German mark was revalued twice and the Dutch guilder once. Parities for the Japanese yen, the Swiss franc, the Italian lira, and the Belgian franc were not changed. An alternative explanation for the remarkable growth in the world economy was that the United States provided a stable framework for the growth of national incomes abroad by maintaining a relatively stable price level.

The irony of the IMF system was that, although the IMF rules were established to avoid frequent changes in parities, changes in parities proved to be infrequent. Payments imbalances were extended because there were no longer any "rules of the game" for the balance of payments adjustment. Countries were committed to their domestic full-employment policies, and were reluctant to adopt measures to reduce payments deficits when one consequence might be an increase in unemployment. There was no agreement or understanding about whether the countries with the payments deficits or those with the payments surpluses should take the initiative to reduce extended payments imbalances. The reluctance to change parities reflected that the countries with deficits believed that devaluations would be viewed as evidence of the failure of their economic policies, while the surplus countries believed that the persistent imbalances reflected the inflationary policies of the deficit countries.

The Fund's successes and failures are closely linked to the successes and failures of U.S. economic policy. When the U.S. inflation rate was low, the Bretton Woods System worked. As U.S. economic policies became less successful—as the U.S. inflation rate increased in the late 1960s—the U.S. payments deficit became larger than could be readily explained by the demand of other countries for payments surpluses and international reserve assets. The Fund was virtually powerless to effect a change in the alignment of exchange rates of the major countries. The United States could finance a large payments deficit as long as the surplus countries were willing to add to their holdings of dollar assets. As long as international payments imbalances were those of smaller industrial countries, the Fund had been useful in inducing the return to payments equilibrium. But when the imbalances involved the largest industrial countries, the Fund mechanism proved ineffective.

With the increase in the inflation rates in the 1970s, a move to floating exchange rates became inevitable because countries could no longer success-fully maintain their parities. The Fund rules on exchange parities became obsolete. And with the explosion in the growth of international reserves in the 1970s, the Fund mechanism seemed irrelevant in meeting the need for inter-national reserves.

THE MOVE TO FLOATING EXCHANGE RATES

When the Bretton Woods System was established, the U.S. international eco-nomic position seemed supreme. There was a strong belief that there would be a perpetual dollar shortage—that Europe's desire to spend dollars would persistently exceed its ability to earn dollars at any exchange rate. Even though the 1949 devaluations immediately led to a deficit in the U.S. pay-ments balances, the concern about a dollar shortage remained for a decade.

The story of the U.S. payments balance after 1950 can be segmented into three stages. In the first, which runs from 1950 to the mid-1960s, the annual U.S. payments deficits were small, and largely reflected the desire of other countries to add to their holdings of gold and U.S. dollar assets. Their demand for these assets was the cause of the U.S. payments deficit. In the late 1960s, the U.S. payments deficits began to increase above the levels that could be readily explained by the foreign demand for gold and dollar assets. In a three-year period, 1969–1971, the cumulative U.S. payments deficit reached $40 billion, partly as a consequence of a decline in U.S. competitiveness in an array of manufactured products and increasingly in response to speculation about a devaluation of the dollar. In the fall of 1969, the German mark was revalued; in the spring of 1970, the Canadian authorities ceased pegging their currency, and the Canadian dollar immediately appreciated by nearly 10 per-cent. For the next fifteen months, the pressures for a revaluation of the cur-rencies of other countries or a devaluation of the U.S. dollar became more intense.

The Breakdown of Bretton Woods

In August 1971 the U.S. Treasury formally suspended gold sales to foreign official institutions. The U.S. government also adopted a tariff surcharge of 10 percent to induce other industrial countries to revalue their currencies; the premise was that the surcharge would be dropped after they revalued. Negoti-ations with the Europeans and the Japanese formalized this bargain; at the end of 1971, in the context of the Smithsonian Agreement of 1972, the U.S. dollar price of gold was increased to $38, the U.S. dollar was effectively deva-lued by about 12 percent, and the tariff surcharge was withdrawn. The new system of pegged exchange rates lasted little more than a year. The U.S. pay-ments deficits renewed speculation against the dollar. Because of the inability of national monetary authorities to adopt policies that would have made the new system of pegged exchange rates viable, floating rates again became inevi-table, as in the years immediately after World War I.

The move to floating rates in the early 1970s occurred because there was no viable alternative mechanism to accommodate the changes in the international economy. One change was the more rapid inflation in the United States than in some of its major trading partners. Whereas the greater U.S. success in achieving price stability had increased the foreign demand for dollar assets in the 1950s and early 1960s, the failure to maintain a low inflation rate in the United States in the 1970s led to a reduction in this demand. Moreover, the foreign demand for dollar assets might have fallen because the United States seemed to have lost its dominant lead in the world market for manufactured goods. Finally, the sharp increase in the world price of petroleum and the large payments surpluses of OPEC nations led to sharp changes in money flows; movements in exchange rates were necessary to accommodate the sharp changes in payment surpluses and deficits.

The depreciation of the U.S. dollar in the foreign exchange market in the early 1970s was larger than would have been predicted from the change in relationship between the increase in the U.S. price level and the increase in foreign price levels. Until the 1980s, investors—both central banks and private institutions—had tried to develop alternatives to the dollar as international reserve assets. The problem was partly circular. Investors moved out of dollar assets because the dollar was weak in the foreign exchange market; however, the weakness of the dollar in the exchange market reflected that the foreign demand for dollar assets had declined as foreign official institutions were diversifying the currency denomination of their reserve assets.

Analogies were developed between the decline of U.S. economic power in the 1970s, the breakup of Bretton Woods, the weakness of the dollar, and the decline of British economic power in the 1920s, the breakdown of the gold standard, and the weakness of sterling. One factor common to both experiences was the reluctance to increase the monetary price of gold to compensate for the worldwide inflation during and after both world wars. One shortcoming to this analogy is that the dominant U.S. economic position in the 1940s and 1950s was bound to be temporary, and last only as long as Germany and Japan were still recovering from the economic decline associated with World War II. Hence, part of the decline in the U.S. international economic position was inevitable. In this sense, the ability of the United States to provide a framework for global monetary stability diminished.

In the early 1970s, the Fund charter was modified to accommodate the adoption of floating exchange rates by the major industrial countries—these practices were, in fact, in violation of treaty commitments. The purpose of the modification was to develop a set of rules to reduce the likelihood of competitive exchange market intervention practices that would be costly to the interests of their trading partners.

With the move to a system of floating exchange rates, the value of the SDR was based on a market basket of five currencies (the U.S. dollar, the British pound, the Japanese yen, the German mark, and the French franc).

The historical evidence suggests that there will again be a move back to pegged exchange rates, for such a system has been maintained for nearly ninety years of the last one hundred. Yet such a move seems unlikely until inflation rates among the major countries are similar and at a very low level.

SUMMARY

1 An international monetary system is identified by three key features—the organization of the foreign exchange market, the assets used to finance payments imbalances, and the mechanism for adjustment to payments imbalances.

2 The gold standard involved a set of mint parities for each national currency in terms of gold, transactions in gold to finance payments imbalances, and changes in national money supplies as a means to facilitate balance of payments adjustments induced by gold inflows and outflows.

3 Stability in U.S. and British price levels was greater during 1800–1920 than in the subsequent decades.

4 The gold-exchange standard was developed in the 1920s to provide a new source of international reserve assets in the form of assets denominated in the British pound, the U.S. dollar, and other national currencies.

5 The International Monetary Fund was established in the 1940s to ensure that changes in exchange rates would be orderly. The Fund was endowed with a pool of national currencies that might be lent to countries with balance of payments deficits.

6 Special drawing rights (SDRs) were a new reserve asset established in the late 1960s within the framework of the IMF.

7 The move from pegged exchange rates to floating exchange rates in the early 1970s occurred at a time of significant differences among the major industrial countries in their rates of inflation.

QUESTIONS AND EXERCISES

1 Describe the major differences between the key features of the gold standard and those of the Bretton Woods System of adjustable parities.

2 List the major alternative ways a country might achieve equilibrium in its payments balance when a disturbance has led to a payments deficit or a payments surplus.

3 Why did the gold standard break down at the beginning of World War I? Why did the Bretton Woods System of adjustable parities break down in the early 1970s?

FURTHER READING

ALIBER, ROBERT Z. *The International Money Game,* 4th ed. New York: Basic Books, 1983. A romp through the major issues in international finance.

COOMBS, CHARLES. *The Arena of International Finance.* New York: John Wiley and Sons, 1976. A central banker's brief for pegged exchange rates.

MAYER, MARTIN. *The Fate of the Dollar.* New York: Times Books, 1980. A journalist's view of international monetary developments.

SOLOMON, ROBERT. *The International Monetary System, 1945–1976.* New York: Harper & Row, 1977. A comprehensive blow-by-blow account of negotiations.

TEW, BRIAN. *The Evolution of the International Monetary System, 1947–77.* London: Hutchison, 1977. A succinct analysis of the Bretton Woods System and its breakdown.

TRIFFIN, ROBERT. *Gold and the Dollar Crisis.* New Haven: Yale University Press, 1961. A classic on the U.S. international financial dilemma.

YEAGER, LELAND B. *International Monetary Relations.* New York: Harper & Row, 1966. An excellent text with comprehensive historical treatment.

CHAPTER 27

The Organization of the Foreign Exchange Market

Trade and payments across national borders require that one of the parties to the transaction pay or receive funds in a foreign currency. If an American wishes to buy a Japanese car, then at some stage in the chain of payments between the purchaser and the producer, U.S. dollars must be used to buy Japanese yen. Moreover, knowledgeable investors based in each country are aware of the opportunities to buy assets denominated in foreign currencies because the anticipated returns are higher on debt denominated in foreign currencies, since interest costs are lower; these investors also must use the foreign exchange market whenever they invest or borrow abroad.

One feature of any international system is the exchange rate; a second is the payments balance. The **exchange rate,** which is the *price of foreign money in terms of domestic money,* is determined in the foreign exchange market. The **payments balance,** which is frequently viewed as a measure of "how well" a country is doing, is one entry in the **balance of payments,** which is the *accounting record of all international transactions.* The payments balance is the value of the transactions of the central bank or monetary authority in liquid assets, such as gold, U.S. Treasury bills, bank deposits, and claims on the International Monetary Fund.

At any moment, comparisons of prices of domestic goods, services, and securities with comparable goods, services, and securities available in other countries require use of the exchange rate. Merchants in each country seek to take advantage of any significant difference between the prices of domestic goods and comparable foreign goods; the exchange rates permit them to compare the prices of Chevrolets with the prices of Toyotas and of Fiats. Similarly, producers in each country seek to determine whether they may have a competitive advantage in foreign markets because their production costs are below those of firms producing abroad. Few individuals or investors use the foreign exchange market because they want to hold foreign monies; rather, they buy foreign exchange as a necessary intermediate step before they can buy a foreign good or security or sell a debt denominated in a foreign currency.

If imports of goods, services, and securities exceed exports of goods, services, and securities during any time period, the country has a deficit in its payments balance that must be financed by selling assets or borrowing abroad. Under a floating exchange-rate regime, the exchange rate would change to restore equilibrium; under a fixed (or pegged) rate regime, the equilibrium is restored by changes in national price and income levels.

The terms on which national currencies trade with each other determine the significance of the segmentation of the world into separate national currency areas. If exchange rates were fixed and known with certainty, then the differences among national monies would be a trivial matter (except for differences in political risk, which involves the application of exchange controls to international payments), of little more significance than the difference between $50 bills and $100 bills, or between the notes issued by the Federal Reserve Bank of San Francisco and the Federal Reserve Bank of New York. Individuals and investors would be indifferent about the currency denomination of their assets and liabilities. Changes in the consumer price level in one country would correspond to the changes in similar price levels in other countries, at least to the extent the goods in each national market basket are similar. National money supplies would be readily summed into a world money supply.

If exchange rates moved freely, and, at the same time, the exchange rates for all future dates were known with certainty, individuals and investors would still be indifferent about the currency denomination of their assets and liabilities. In this world, the differences in interest rates on similar assets denominated in different currencies would fully reflect anticipated changes in exchange rates. These differences in interest rates would compensate investors for losses incurred from holding assets denominated in a currency that would depreciate.

The assumption of the perfect substitutability between assets denominated in different currencies is extreme. Substantial uncertainty about future exchange rates characterizes the foreign exchange market. Even if countries pledge to maintain fixed or pegged exchange rates (for instance, when £1 was equal to $2.80 in the 1950s and 1960s), investors recognize that the parities could still be altered. Because of the uncertainty about future exchange rates, traders and investors are selective about the currencies in which they denominate their assets and liabilities. (The ease with which traders and investors can alter their holdings of assets and liabilities denominated in different currencies complicates the management of national monetary policies, and has an impact on both the supply of domestic money and the demand for domestic money.) Hence, the critical question is the significance of the factors that segment the U.S. dollar currency area from the currency areas for the German mark, the Japanese yen, and other national currencies.

THE MARKET FOR FOREIGN EXCHANGE

Although each of the financial centers in the major countries is sometimes said to have its own foreign exchange market, the markets for foreign exchange in London, New York, Frankfurt, and Tokyo are geographic components of one worldwide market. The banks in each financial center are linked by telephone and telex to each other and to the major banks in other centers. The units traded are demand deposits; the basic unit in U.S. dollar–British pound trades is a sterling deposit of £100,000, while the basic unit in U.S. dollar–German mark trades is DM200,000. At any moment, the prices or exchange rates for one currency in terms of another are virtually the same in every center, with the differences in prices quoted for comparable large transactions significantly smaller than $\frac{1}{10}$th of 1 percent, and frequently no more than several hundredths of 1 percent.

The foreign exchange market is the largest market in the world in terms of the volume of transactions; one some days, the volume of trading may reach $250 billion. The volume of foreign exchange trading is many times larger than the volume of international trade and investment; indeed, individuals and firms involved in international trade and investment participate in less than 10 percent of the foreign exchange transactions. Most foreign exchange transactions involve banks as both buyers and sellers.

The foreign exchange market is extremely competitive; there are many participants, none of whom is large relative to the market. Prices—exchange rates—change continuously, and the change can be as small as $\frac{1}{100}$th of 1 percent. The major international commercial banks act both as dealers for their own account and as brokers for the accounts of importers and exporters and international investors. In their dealer role, banks maintain a net long or short position in a currency, and seek to profit from changes in the exchange rate. (A long position means their holdings of assets denominated in one currency exceed their liabilities denominated in this same currency.) In their broker function, banks obtain buy-and-sell orders from commercial customers, such as the multinational oil companies, both to profit from the spread between the rates at which they buy foreign exchange from some customers and the rates at which they sell foreign exchange to other customers, and to sell other banking services to these customers. If a U.S. firm wishes to buy $150 million of German marks to make a payment in Frankfurt, the bank that offers German marks at the lowest price is most likely to get the business; almost immediately, the bank will seek to buy an equivalent amount of marks to minimize its risk of loss from any subsequent appreciation of the mark.

In their transactions with their customers, banks quote both the price at which they will buy and the price at which they will sell, usually in the form of 1.8380–1.8390 marks per dollar, for a standard volume; the small price difference reimburses the banks for the costs incurred in their foreign exchange transactions. If an investor or trader wants to buy U.S. dollars, the bank will buy German marks at the rate of 1.8390. If the investor or trader wants to buy

German marks, the bank will buy U.S. dollars at the rate of 1.8380. The bid-ask spread is 100 marks on a purchase of DM200,000, or about $60, which is ⁶⁄₁₀₀ths of 1 percent of the dollar value of the transaction. The size of the bid-ask spread differs by currency and by the bank providing the quotation. The major international banks quote a smaller bid-ask spread than banks in provincial centers, where the competition may be less extensive. The rates quoted also indicate whether the bank wants to increase or reduce its position in a currency; if a bank owns more German marks than it thinks optimal, it will set its quotes low enough to discourage sellers of marks and encourage buyers of marks.

Foreign exchange brokers are used in some financial centers to bring buyers and sellers together in an anonymous fashion; the brokers relay the exchange rates quoted by particular banks to various customers. Most commercial customers do not use brokers; instead they may "shop" the banks for the most attractive rate quotations. Commercial banks frequently deal with each other through brokers, and central banks deal with commercial banks through brokers.

ORGANIZATION OF THE FOREIGN EXCHANGE MARKET

The pattern of the organization of the foreign exchange market follows the pattern of trade financing. More international trade transactions are denominated or invoiced in the U.S. dollar than in any other currency. Thus, in U.S.-Canadian trade, Canadian exporters to the United States quote a price in U.S. dollars and receive payment in U.S. dollars. Similarly, Canadian importers agree to pay U.S. dollars for their purchases of U.S. goods. The Canadian importers and exporters prefer to undertake their foreign exchange transactions close to home—in Canada rather than in the United States—so a larger share of U.S.-Canadian dollar transactions occurs in Toronto than in New York. Importers and exporters with the need to undertake foreign exchange transactions prefer to deal with banks close to their home offices rather than with banks in distant foreign centers both because of inconvenience and because this reduces indirect transactions costs. Because the volume of foreign exchange transactions in each currency pair is so much larger in the centers outside the United States, the markets may be modestly more competitive and the rates quoted by banks to commercial customers somewhat more favorable than the rates quoted in the United States. Hence, the paradox is that, because such a large volume of international trade and financial transactions is denominated in the U.S. dollar, most foreign exchange transactions involving the U.S. dollar occur outside the United States.[1]

The principal center of German mark–U.S. dollar transactions is Frankfurt; New York is the secondary center. Similarly, Tokyo is the principal center for Japanese yen–U.S. dollar transactions and London for British pound–U.S. dollar transactions. Banks in each center specialize in trading the

---

[1]Prior to World War I much more of U.S. trade was denominated in foreign currencies, so relatively more of the foreign exchange transactions associated with U.S. trade occurred in New York.

Table 27.1	Distribution of Banks and Traders in Foreign Exchange	
	Number of banks with foreign exchange department	Number of traders
North America		
New York	108	793
Toronto	18	120
Chicago	14	81
San Francisco	7	43
Los Angeles	11	46
Western Europe		
London	258	1603
Luxembourg	74	353
Paris	75	459
Zurich	35	245
Frankfurt	48	334
Milan	37	191
Brussels	33	201
Asia and Middle East		
Tokyo	30	169
Singapore	69	293
Hong King	52	306
Bahrain	38	173

Source: *Foreign Exchange and Bullion Dealers Directory,* 1985, Hambros Bank, London.

domestic currency against the U.S. dollar. New York is a secondary center for all foreign currencies. Table 27.1 shows the distribution of banks and foreign exchange traders among centers. Paris is a tertiary center for trading in the U.S. dollar relative to all currencies other than the French franc, while Zurich is a tertiary center for trading in the U.S. dollar relative to the German mark, the British pound, and the French franc.

Within most major financial centers—London, Frankfurt, New York—a large number of banks participate actively in the foreign exchange market. A few banks are dealers in the currencies in which they specialize; these banks hold large inventories of foreign exchange. When banks are not dealers, they participate as brokers, buying and selling foreign currencies on the basis of exchange-rate quotations from dealers.

Once the rates for two currencies, such as the German mark and the Japanese yen, are known in terms of the U.S. dollar, the price of the German mark in terms of the Japanese yen, or the cross-rate, can be inferred. For example, on 31 December 1985 the yen-dollar rate was 200.15 yen per dollar, and the mark-dollar rate was 2.4450 marks per dollar, so the cross-rate was 81.86 yen per German mark.

One consequence of the organization of the market along the lines of a series of currency pairs, each involving the U.S. dollar, is that the financial counterpart of many international trade transactions involves two foreign exchange transactions. Assume, for example, that a German distributor of automobile parts buys Japanese-produced components. The banks in Frankfurt quote a Japanese yen–German mark rate based on their rates for the U.S. dollar in terms of both the German mark and the Japanese yen. The banks in Frankfurt are not likely to hold a significant amount of yen, so the bank supplying the yen to the Frankfurt importer undertakes two transactions: German marks are used to buy U.S. dollars and U.S. dollars are then used to buy Japanese yen. Since the Japanese yen–U.S. dollar market is primarily in Tokyo, the bank may act as a dealer in the first transaction and as a broker in the second.

Trading in foreign exchange occurs on almost a continuous basis, since the markets in various cities are located in different time zones. The Tokyo market closes for the day before the market in London opens.

THE RELATION BETWEEN THE SPOT EXCHANGE RATE AND THE FORWARD EXCHANGE RATE

Traders and investors who desire to alter the currency mix of their assets or liabilities can readily do so by **leading and lagging;** they increase their loans denominated in the dollar and reduce their loans denominated in another currency. Alternatively, they can increase their holdings of assets denominated in the German mark and reduce their holdings of assets denominated in the U.S. dollar.

Foreign exchange transactions are either **spot transactions,** which *involve an exchange of deposits two business days after the date of the contract,* or **forward transactions,** which *involve the exchange of deposits at specified future dates.* Most foreign exchange transactions are forward transactions, or swaps —an exchange of deposits thirty, sixty, or ninety days in the future. Traders and investors frequently prefer forward exchange contracts because they do not "tie up" scarce working capital.

Forward contracts are generally available on maturities of up to a year or longer in the major currencies. That some maturities are standardized—three months, six months, and one year—reflects the standardization of terms of payment on commercial-trade transactions. Banks also offer maturities to match traders' needs; the banks can readily supply a 39-day forward contract or a 78-day forward contract. (Forward contracts in foreign exchange which are bought and sold by the major banks should be distinguished from currency futures contracts, which are traded on financial exchanges in Chicago and London; these futures contracts have standardized maturities and amounts.) Transactions costs associated with forward exchange contracts are modestly higher than those on spot exchange contracts. Moreover, these costs are higher on the more volatile currencies than on the less volatile currencies. The spot exchange rates and the forward exchange rates for major currencies relative to the dollar are shown in Table 27.2.

If a currency is less expensive in the forward market than in the spot

Table 27.2	Foreign Exchange Rates			
	Closing market rates on 31 December 1985 (foreign currency units per U.S. dollar)			
		Forward rates		
	Spot rate	1 month	3 months	6 months
Canadian dollar	1.3980	1.3993	1.4020	1.4060
British pound	.6917	.6937	.6979	.7042
French franc	7.5025	7.5300	7.6025	7.6975
German mark	2.4450	2.4379	2.4257	2.4066
Swiss franc	2.0580	2.0501	2.0370	2.0180
Japanese yen	200.15	199.96	199.52	198.78

Source: *The Wall Street Journal*, 2 January 1986, p. 25.

market, the currency is at a forward discount. And if the currency is more expensive in the forward market, then the currency is at a forward premium.

The banks act as intermediaries between buyers and sellers in the forward exchange market, just as they do in the spot exchange market. A bank may combine a long spot position with a short forward position in a particular currency to limit its exposure in the currency; if the currency appreciates, the value of the long spot position increases and so, however, does the value of the short forward position. Or the bank may have a long position in some forward maturities and a short position in others.

One of the basic propositions in international finance is that the difference between forward and spot exchange rates, when expressed in percentage terms, equals the difference between domestic and foreign interest rates for assets with the same maturity as that on the forward contract. This relationship, known as the *interest-rate parity theorem*, results from the profit-maximizing behavior of individual investors. Those same investors who seek to profit from anticipated changes in exchange rates continually compare whether it will be more profitable to alter their position in foreign exchange by spot transactions or by forward transactions. They prefer the forward market if the currency is cheaper there than in the spot exchange market. Other investors take advantage of profit opportunities by buying a currency in the financial center in which it is cheap and selling the same currency in the center in which it is expensive, after adjustment for any difference between the spot and forward exchange rates and the interest-rate differential. The first group are called **speculators;** by definition *they seek to profit from anticipated changes in exchange rates.* The second group are known as **arbitragers;** *they seek to profit from deviations between the interest-rate differential and the interest equivalent of the spread between the forward and spot exchange rates.* Arbitragers avoid exchange risk, while speculators seek to profit from carrying this risk.

Assume a U.S. firm has agreed to pay 10 million marks to buy some machinery in Germany. The actual payment will be made three months after the date the parties sign the sales contract. The U.S. firm might buy German marks in the spot market and invest the mark funds in Frankfurt either in the money market or in a bank deposit, at the prevailing interest rate. At the maturity of the investment the importer will pay the German seller of the machinery. If the importer can invest funds in Frankfurt at 8 percent, the importer would buy 9,804,000 German marks to be invested at 8 percent for ninety days to yield 10 million German marks. If the spot exchange rate is 2 German marks per U.S. dollar the investor would need $4,902,000 to acquire the 9,804,000 marks. The cost of this transaction is the interest rate of 10 percent that the importer might earn on a comparable dollar investment for ninety days.

Alternatively, the importer might buy the German mark forward; he would then pay for marks in ninety days. If the mark is at a forward premium of 2 percent, the importer would pay $5,025,000 for 10 million marks. In this case, the U.S. importer would be able to continue to own a U.S. dollar money-market investment for ninety days, and earn an interest rate of 10 percent on these funds. An investment of $4,902,000 in the U.S. money market for ninety days at a 10 percent annual rate would yield $5,025,000. So the cost to the U.S. importer of buying the German mark in the spot market and buying the German mark in the forward market are the same, if the forward premium on the mark is equal to the difference between the interest rate on U.S. dollar assets and the interest rate on German mark assets.

Some U.S. importers may decide to acquire German marks immediately prior to the date when payment is due; in the interval between the date when they enter into the commitments to pay German marks and the date when they buy the German marks they have a foreign exchange exposure.

For both groups of importers, the choice of the financing pattern depends on the relationship between the spot and forward exchange rates, the interest rate on German mark assets, and the interest rate on comparable U.S. dollar assets. The formal expression of the **interest-rate parity theorem** is

$$a \, \frac{(F-S)}{S} = \frac{1+r_d}{1+r_f},$$

where a is the factor to convert the percentage difference in the two exchange rates into an annualized rate of return (a is 4 if the forward-rate quotation is on a three-month contract), F is the forward exchange rate, S is the spot exchange rate, r_d is the domestic interest rate, and r_f is the foreign interest rate.

Empirical studies indicate that the differences between the forward exchange rates inferred from the interest-rate differential and the observed forward rates are almost always less than 1 percent, and frequently only several tenths of 1 percent. That there is any measurable deviation from interest-rate parity reflects either that investors encounter costs and incur risks in undertaking transactions to take advantage of the "apparent" riskless arbitrage profit opportunity, or that the assets in the domestic and foreign money markets are not perfect substitutes for each other.

Traders and investors prefer forward transactions to leading and lagging as a way to alter their exposure because of the greater convenience. But traders and investors lead and lag if the costs of acquiring the foreign exchange in the forward market exceed the costs in the spot market—if the forward discount is significantly larger than the discount "predicted" by the interest-rate differential.

FORWARD EXCHANGE RATES AS FORECASTS OF FUTURE SPOT EXCHANGE RATES

Whether U.S. importers with payments to make in Germany in ninety days will hedge their foreign exchange exposure by buying the German marks in the forward exchange market or instead wait until the payment must be made and then buy the German marks in the spot exchange market partly depends on their views about how closely the spot exchange rate at the maturity of the forward exchange contract approximates the forward exchange rate. The empirical question involves the relationship between the values of the forward exchange rates and the values for the spot exchange rates on the dates when these forward contracts mature. If investors who buy and sell forward exchange contracts demand a risk premium, there may be a systematic difference between forward exchange rates and the spot exchange rates on the maturity of forward contracts. Then the question that arises is whether this risk premium is excessively large relative to the risk.

Each forward contract is not likely to "predict" accurately the spot exchange rate on the dates when the forward contracts mature, because of the large number of unforeseen disturbances or shocks between the dates when traders and investors buy forward contracts and the dates when these contracts mature. Those who suggest that the forward exchange rates are likely to be biased predictors of future spot exchange rates—that is, that investors demand a risk premium for buying foreign exchange in the forward market —rely on the analogy of payment for risk-bearing in other markets. They assert that if investors are risk averse, then the *average* of the exchange rates on a set of forward mark contracts would be below the *average* of the spot exchange rates on the dates when these forward contracts mature, so that the sellers of forward marks would incur—on average—a loss. Moreover, investors cannot avoid this loss by leading and lagging, for the difference between the interest rates on mark assets and the interest rates on dollar assets of comparable maturities would incorporate a comparable risk premium.

The response to this argument is that, while some traders and investors are sellers of forward marks, others are necessarily buyers of forward marks. If the first group pays a risk premium, then the second group, who are also hedging their foreign exchange positions, would receive a profit, which is the mirror of the cost incurred by the sellers.

Several empirical studies support the idea that there is a significant risk premium, but most do not; either the marginal investors are not risk averse or the willingness of each group of importers to pay a risk premium has proven to be more or less offsetting. However, forward exchange rates appear to be somewhat biased forecasts of future spot exchange rates. These two statements can be reconciled if the average forecast error between the forward rate and the spot rate at the maturity of the forward contracts is modest in size relative to the premium deemed appropriate for carrying the foreign exchange risk.

THE LEVEL OF THE EXCHANGE RATE

The foreign exchange market is one component in the international money market, which also includes the various national markets in bank deposits and money-market assets, such as Treasury bills, bankers' acceptances, and commercial paper. The unique aspect of the foreign exchange market is that neither of the assets traded in a particular transaction, domestic demand deposits and foreign demand deposits, is unique to that market, in the sense that gold is unique to the gold market and wheat to the wheat market. Instead, the demand deposits denominated in different currencies are acquired to facilitate payments in a foreign currency. Thus, U.S. traders and investors buy German marks so they can then acquire commodities and securities available in Germany.

Since all foreign exchange transactions are intermediate to some other economic transaction, the question is how the exchange rate is determined and why exchange rates vary so very extensively within a year or a few months, as evident in Figure 27.1. One response is that the exchange rate is the price of national monies that moves to the level at which prices of similar goods available in the several countries are more or less equal, or at least to the level at which prices differ by no more than transaction and transportation costs. If the prices of similar goods available in the several countries differ significantly at the prevailing exchange rate, traders would buy the goods in the countries in which they are cheap and ship them to the countries in which they are dear, and profit from the price differential. The prices of these goods would rise in the first country and fall in the second; at the same time, the foreign exchange value of the first country's currency would increase. Arbitrage in commodities would continue until the difference in the prices of the similar goods at the new exchange rate would no longer exceed transaction and transportation costs. In this case, then, the exchange rates move to reduce differences in the prices of comparable goods available in different countries.

This relationship between the prices of tradable goods and the exchange rate is the **purchasing-power parity theory.** At times the prices of similar goods available in the several countries are compared at the exchange rate in the *absolute version* of this relationship; usually, however, *changes* in the commodity price levels in the several countries are compared with changes in the exchange rate in the relative version of purchasing-power parity (PPP). This expression is

$$\dot{F}/\$ = \dot{P}_F - \dot{P}_{US},$$

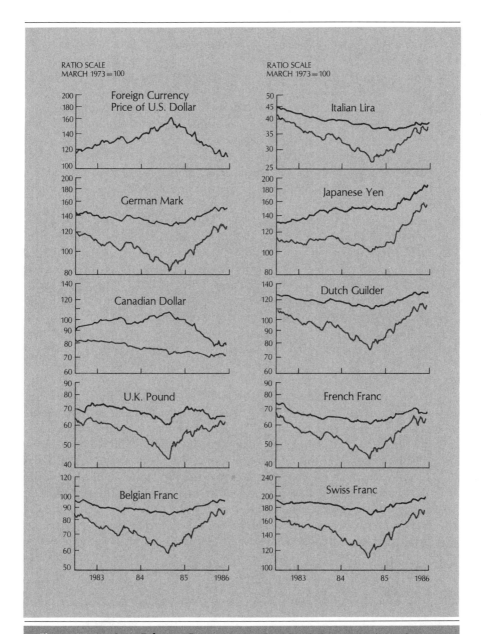

RATIO SCALE
MARCH 1973 = 100

RATIO SCALE
MARCH 1973 = 100

Foreign Currency
Price of U.S. Dollar

Italian Lira

German Mark

Japanese Yen

Canadian Dollar

Dutch Guilder

U.K. Pound

French Franc

Belgian Franc

Swiss Franc

Figure 27.1   Spot Exhange Rates. Here we see the dollar prices of nine foreign currencies (lower lines) and weighted average values (upper lines), averaged by week ending Wednesday. With the exception of Canada, the variation is dramatic. **Source:** Board of Governors, Federal Reserve System, *Selected Interest & Exchange Rates: Weekly Series of Charts* (Washington, D.C., 16 June 1986).

where $\dot{F}/\$$ is the rate of change of the U.S. dollar in terms of foreign currency, $\dot{P}_F$ is the rate of change of the foreign price level, and $\dot{P}_{US}$ is the rate of change of the U.S. price level.

During the 1970s, as in the 1920s, changes in the exchange rates in a month or a quarter or a year have been 15 to 25 percent larger than the contemporary change in relative national price levels. Thus, during the summer of 1976, the British pound became greatly undervalued when it appeared that the British government would not be able to limit increases in wage rates and price levels. In six months, the British pound price of the U.S. dollar increased by nearly 25 percent (or at an annual rate of 50 percent). British goods became greatly undervalued; Parisians flew to London for Saturday shopping. Then the British pound subsequently appreciated, so that by the end of 1977 exchange rates were back to the early 1976 levels. Similarly, in 1977 and the first ten months of 1978, the U.S. dollar became substantially undervalued; after a dramatic change in the Fed's monetary policy in October 1979, as was discussed in Chapter 24, the dollar appreciated. Yet, for an extended period, U.S. goods remained undervalued. Then with the sharp increase in U.S. interest rates following the change in the operating procedures of the Federal Reserve in late 1979, interest rates on U.S. dollar assets rose to peak values, and the U.S. dollar appreciated sharply in the foreign exchange market. The statement, then, that the exchange rate moves to reflect changes in national price levels is not consistent with much recent data, at least not on a month-to-month or year-to-year basis.

Transactions in commodities are only one of the reasons firms and investors participate in the foreign exchange market. The demand and supply of foreign exchange also are affected by investment or security transactions, as funds are moved between currencies to profit from the differences in interest rates on comparable assets denominated in different currencies, or from anticipated changes in exchange rates. From the investor's point of view, the level of the spot exchange rate is "just right" when, given the interest rates on domestic securities and the anticipated rate of change of the exchange rate, the interest rates on comparable foreign securities are at levels such that no significant profit can be made from shifting funds between these two securities.

Thus,

$$r_d = r_w + (\dot{E}/E)^*,$$

where r_d is the interest rate on domestic securities, r_w is the interest rate on comparable foreign financial assets of the same maturity, and $(\dot{E}/E)^*$ is the anticipated rate of change of the exchange rate during the interval until the maturity of the two securities. This statement is the **Fisher proposition.**[2]

As new information about the trade accounts, inflation rates, national

---

[2] The relationship between the money-market interest differential and the anticipated spot exchange rates is identified as the Fisher proposition, or Fisher Open, after Irving Fisher. Analysts frequently confuse the interest-rate parity theorem with the Fisher Open: the former

monetary policies, or election campaigns leads investors to conclude that the mark-denominated assets will prove a less attractive investment than dollar-denominated investments, they will sell German mark securities and buy U.S. dollar securities and the German mark will depreciate. The German mark will continue to depreciate until the return on the German mark securities adjusted for the anticipated change in the exchange rate equals the return on U.S. dollar securities.

The anticipated rate of change of the exchange rate, $(\dot{E}/E)^*$, depends both on investors' estimates of where the spot exchange rate will be at various future dates and on the level of the current spot exchange rate. In equilibrium, the anticipated rate of change of the exchange rate must equal the money-market interest differential. If investors believe there is a disequilibrium—that $r_d \neq r_w + (\dot{E}/E)^*$—then in the move to equilibrium the adjustment may occur in the current spot exchange rate, the anticipated spot exchange rate, and in either of the two money-market interest rates. But the adjustment is not likely to occur in the anticipated spot exchange rate, since this rate is set to be consistent with the projections for the domestic and foreign price levels. Some adjustments may occur in the two interest rates as investors shift funds from one money market to another; however, the volume of funds shifted may be small relative to the size of the two money markets. Consequently, much of the adjustment must occur in the current spot exchange rate, so that the changes in the current spot exchange rate may be much larger than the changes that would be inferred from the contemporary changes in the several national price levels.

ANALYZING EXCHANGE RATE DISTURBANCES

Two different types of disturbances that affect the foreign exchange market should be distinguished: nonmonetary and monetary. Assume investors become bearish on German mark-denominated securities at a time when interest rates on these securities and on comparable dollar securities are identical. Increased "bearishness" will be reflected in both an increase in interest rates on mark securities and a depreciation of the mark in the spot exchange market. If interest rates on mark securities do not increase, then the spot exchange rate will move to the level of the anticipated spot exchange rate, perhaps abruptly.

Alternatively, assume that the German Bundesbank follows a more contractive monetary policy, and interest rates on mark securities increase. At the same time, the anticipated spot exchange rate is unchanged, perhaps because investors believe that the move to a more contractive monetary policy eventually will be reversed. Then investors would acquire mark-denominated securities because of the higher interest rate, and the German mark would appreciate. As long as interest rates on German mark securities are higher

---

involves the efficiency of arbitrage in circumstances in which all values are known, while the latter involves investment decisions in an uncertain environment.

than those on U.S. dollar securities, the only factor that will equalize the return to investors from holding U.S. dollar securities and German mark securities is the subsequent depreciation of the mark. The paradox is that, in response to the increase in interest rates on mark securities, there is a sudden unanticipated appreciation of the mark, so the mark may then subsequently depreciate slowly, with the anticipated annual rate of depreciation equal to the excess of interest rates on mark assets over those on dollar assets.

Price movements in other financial markets, in the stock and bond market and in the wheat, soybean, and gold markets, are also large, and comparable to those in the foreign exchange market. At any moment, the spot prices in these markets in equilibrium are the anticipated spot prices discounted to the present by the interest rate. In the foreign exchange market, the discount factor is the difference between the money-market interest rates on similar securities denominated in different currencies. For example, if interest rates on U.S. dollar Treasury bills are 10 percent and interest rates on German mark Treasury bills are 8 percent, the discount rate is 2 percent a year. If the anticipated values are unchanged, then during each week and each month the German mark price of the U.S. dollar should increase at the rate of 2 percent a year (or .166 percent a month, .038 percent a week, or .0055 percent a day). Even a weak currency—one that might depreciate at a rate of 20 percent a year—would depreciate at an average daily rate of .0624 percent or by much less than the observed daily changes in foreign exchange rates. That the changes in exchange rates on a daily and weekly basis are many times larger than these values means that they reflect sharp movements in anticipated exchange rates.

Many factors affect anticipations of exchange rates in the future, including investor estimates of inflation rates or money-supply growth rates. Thus traders and investors may extrapolate recent changes in domestic and foreign price levels to obtain estimates of future national price levels, which serve as a basis for their anticipations of exchange rates. Moreover, changes in money-supply growth rates may be used to generate estimates of the national price levels, which in turn lead to estimates of the future exchange rates.

Some analysts believe that the German mark appreciates when U.S. monetary policy becomes more expansive or German monetary policy becomes more contractive. When the interest-rate differential changes, the exchange rate may change sharply. If investors focus on spot exchange rates anticipated in several years, then the change in exchange rates may be substantially larger, in percentage terms, than the change in the interest-rate differential. For example, assume U.S. monetary policy becomes more expansive and interest rates on U.S. dollar assets fall by 1 percentage point. If investors expect U.S. interest rates to remain at this level for two years, then the German mark might appreciate by 2 percent in the spot exchange market to equalize the anticipated returns on short-term German mark and U.S. securities.

CENTRAL BANK INTERVENTION IN THE FOREIGN EXCHANGE MARKET

For most of the last 100 years the currencies of the major countries have been pegged to each other, initially because each currency had a mint parity in terms of gold. After World War II, many foreign countries expressed the parities for their currencies in terms of the U.S. dollar. Under the Bretton Woods System of pegged exchange rates, each central bank committed itself to limit the range of movement in the price of its currency around its parity. These limits were narrow under the gold standard, usually set by the costs of gold shipments. In the post–World War II period, these limits were set in the IMF treaty, initially at $\frac{1}{4}$ of 1 percent either side of parity, and subsequently 1 percent either side of parity. Within these limits, currencies were free to float, although many monetary authorities intervened within these limits to smooth the hour-to-hour, day-to-day exchange-rate movement.

Intervention involved purchases or sales of demand deposits denominated in the national money against a foreign money, most frequently the U.S. dollar. A central bank was obliged to prevent its currency from depreciating below its lower support limit and appreciating above its upper support limit. The central bank would buy its own currency from commercial banks operating in the exchange market and sell them U.S. dollars. These transactions were effectively an open-market sale using U.S. dollar demand deposits rather than domestic bonds. Such transactions reduced the central bank's domestic liabilities in the hands of the public.

The ability of the central bank to prevent its currency from depreciating depended upon its holdings of U.S. dollars, together with the U.S. dollars that might be obtained by borrowing. Even if a national monetary authority had the foreign exchange necessary for intervention, its need to support its currency in the exchange market might be inconsistent with its efforts to undertake a more expansive monetary policy to achieve its domestic economic objectives.

If a country's currency was strong, its central bank was obliged to sell more of its currency to limit its appreciation in the exchange market. In effect, this central bank undertook an open-market purchase of dollars, with the purchase of dollars financed by the expansion of its own monetary liabilities. Such open-market purchases might confound its desire to limit the expansion of its monetary liabilities, perhaps because of its concern about the domestic inflationary implications. Thus Germany, with a strong currency in the 1960s and early 1970s, faced the decision either to maintain the established exchange parity for the German mark with the consequence of a more rapid than desired increase in the German money supply or to limit the growth in the reserves of the banking system in Germany at the cost of either revaluing the mark periodically or permitting the mark to float. While the Bundesbank might have undertaken open-market sales of mark-denominated securities to counter or neutralize its open-market purchases of dollar securities, such transactions were not without cost, for they raised interest rates on German

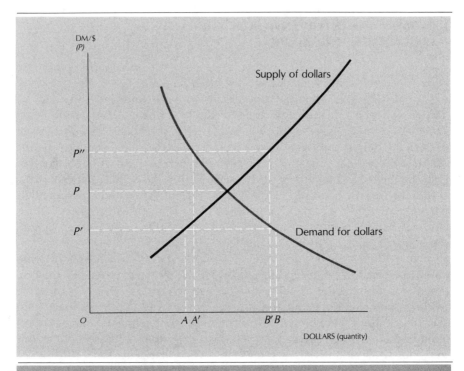

Figure 27.2   The Market for Foreign Exchange. In our example, the Bundesbank faces the market for dollars as shown. If it pegs the mark at P'', Germany would have a payments surplus; at P', Germany would have a payments deficit. At P, the market clears without official intervention.

securities more than was deemed desirable for domestic objectives. Moreover, as interest rates on German mark securities increased, investors would have shifted out of U.S. dollar-denominated securities into German mark-denominated securities, intensifying the problem for the Bundesbank.

The Bundesbank's transactions in the foreign exchange market are shown in Figure 27.2. The price of the U.S. dollar in terms of the German mark is measured on the vertical axis, and the volume of U.S. dollars demanded and supplied is measured on the horizontal axis. The demand for dollars by traders and investors is shown; as the German mark price of the U.S. dollar increases, the amount of dollars demanded declines. The supply of dollars by traders and investors is shown; as the mark price of the dollar increases, the amount of dollars supplied increases. At OP the demand and supply of dollars are equal; OP is the price or exchange rate that clears the exchange market without official intervention. If the Bundesbank had pegged the mark at OP', the demand for dollars would have exceeded the supply, and the Bundesbank would have sold dollars equal to AB during each period; Germany would have had a payments deficit. If, instead, the Bundesbank had pegged the mark at OP', the Bundesbank would have bought dollars equal to $A'B'$, and Germany would have had a payments surplus.

In the late 1960s and the early 1970s, the maintenance of the parity for the German mark appeared to conflict with the achievement of Germany's domestic economic objectives. No such conflict was supposed to occur with floating exchange-rate systems, since the exchange rates would change to neutralize any tendency to a payments surplus or deficit. Hence monetary policy could be directed solely to the attainment of domestic objectives; changes in the foreign exchange value for the German mark would continuously ensure that Germany's receipts would be equal to its payments. Hence the Bundesbank would not have to undertake open-market operations in foreign exchange that might offset either partially or fully its open-market operations in domestic securities. However, in practice, under the floating exchange-rate system market forces sometimes caused the exchange rate to deviate from the level deemed appropriate for domestic objectives and so central banks again felt the need to intervene in the exchange market, even at the cost of complicating attainment of their domestic objectives.

The paradox is that central bank intervention in the foreign exchange market has been much more extensive in the floating exchange-rate period, at least as judged by changes in their holdings of international reserve assets. Some central banks have intervened to limit or smooth the day-to-day and week-to-week movements in the foreign exchange values of their currencies. Some have intervened because they wanted to add to their holding of international reserve assets; in some of these countries the growth in the holdings of international reserve assets provides the basis for the growth in their domestic money supplies. Some have intervened because changes in the exchange rates complicated the attainment of their domestic economic objectives.

THE SEGMENTATION OF NATIONAL MONEY MARKETS

One of the key policy issues in international finance, known as the optimum currency-area issue, involves whether there are any economic gains from maintaining independent national central banks, each with its own currency. Does the Bank of Canada have the capacity to cause interest rates in Canada to change and deviate significantly from interest rates in the United States? If the Bank of Canada attempts to follow a more expansive monetary policy, and buys bonds denominated in the Canadian dollar, is it possible that the sellers of Canadian bonds then will buy U.S. bonds, so that the interest rates on Canadian bonds would remain virtually unchanged? If the Canadian dollar is pegged, is it possible for interest rates on Canadian dollar securities to differ significantly from interest rates on U.S. dollar securities? And if the Canadian dollar is not pegged, can changes in Canadian monetary policy affect any real variables, such as the level of employment, or will the impacts of these changes be limited to altering nominal values, such as the Canadian price level and the Canadian dollar price of the U.S. dollar?

The scope for national monetary independence depends on how fully investors believe that assets that are alike in all attributes except for currency of denomination are close, near, or good substitutes for each other. If investors believe that these assets are close substitutes for each other, then national money markets are integrated. If, in contrast, investors believe they are distant substitutes for each other, then national money markets are segmented. Transactions cost might deter investors from shifting funds among assets denominated in different currencies; similarly, exchange controls might deter these shifts. Such shifts might also be deterred by exchange risk in the form of uncertainty about future exchange rates, or political risk in the form of uncertainty about future changes in exchange controls. Investors are likely to shift funds to profit from differences in interest rates only if they are compensated for these costs and for the associated risks. At most, the differential in interest rates on similar assets denominated in different currencies adjusted for any anticipated changes in exchange rates cannot exceed the sum of these costs and the payments demanded by investors for incurring the risks associated with the movements of funds across the borders between currency areas.

Transactions costs in the foreign exchange market are small or even trivial, especially for large international firms; transactions costs are smaller still for major international banks. Transactions costs have two components: one involves those external to the firm, the actual costs incurred in buying and selling foreign exchange, and the second involves those internal to the firm and incurred in managing its foreign exchange or international monetary investments. Transactions costs to commercial customers are measured by the bid-ask spread—the difference between the prices at which traders and investors could buy and sell a relatively large amount, say, $3 to $5 million, of a particular currency at any moment. The costs encountered by commercial customers in using the foreign exchange market are substantially smaller than those they would incur with transactions of equivalent value in most other markets, for example, the government securities market or the stock market. Depending on the currency, the time, and the maturity of the forward contracts, the cost of a foreign exchange transaction of $1 million would be $100 to $500, or from $1/100$th of 1 percent to $1/20$th of 1 percent. The less volatile the currency is, the smaller are the transactions costs; thus, bid-ask spreads in the Canadian dollar have generally been lower than the bid-ask spreads in the British pound, German mark, and other European currencies, and the Japanese yen. Transaction costs on forward contracts with relatively distant forward maturities—those longer than six months—are larger than those on shorter maturities; transactions costs on spot transactions are lower than those on forward transactions. That transactions costs are so small reflects the technical efficiency of payments, the virtually riskless character of the transactions, and the large size of the transactions.

Transactions costs on interbank transactions in the foreign exchange market are smaller than those on the transactions between banks and customers—much less risk is associated with interbank transactions. The lower level of transactions costs encountered by banks than by their commercial customers means that the banks have an advantage in responding to any potential profit opportunities.

Measuring the payment demanded by investors for carrying exchange risk and political risk is more difficult. One question is whether firms are risk averse, and require payments for bearing these risks. It is sometimes argued that firms are (or should be) risk neutral and seek to maximize profits; if so, they would require no special payments for carrying these risks. Even if firms are risk averse, the cost they would incur in hedging their exposure to foreign exchange is trivial in the long run if not in the short run. Yet firms may nevertheless be deterred from moving funds internationally by uncertainty about this cost.

National financial markets appear segmented to a greater extent than can be readily explained by transactions costs, exchange risk, and political risk. Segmentation provides some opportunity for national monetary independence under pegged exchange rates. If, over time, traders and investors become more knowledgeable about the returns from and the risks and costs of altering the currency mix of their assets and liabilities, so that the segmentation of national money markets declines, changes in monetary policies will be less effective in altering real variables.

THE BALANCE OF PAYMENTS ACCOUNTS

The data on the international transactions of a country are presented in its **balance of payments accounts,** *a record of payments and receipts, organized by major type of transaction, between residents and nonresidents during a particular period* such as a quarter or a year. Table 27.3 summarizes U.S. international transactions for 1984 and 1985.

The approach used in developing such accounts is based on the system of double-entry bookkeeping. All transactions represent exchanges of equal value; for every import of a good, service, or security, there must be a corresponding export of a good, service, or security—so the balance of payments accounts must necessarily balance. When U.S. firms import Scotch whiskey, they export dollars, usually in the form of demand deposits, in payment. The U.S. balance of payments accounts show an increase in U.S. exports of demand deposits and an increase in U.S. commodity imports. The British payments accounts, in contrast, show an increase in commodity exports and an increase in the imports of demand deposits.

The data for the entries in the balance of payments accounts are obtained in various ways. Data on commodity imports and exports are obtained from U.S. tariff collection authorities. Data on tourist expenditures are estimated by questioning travelers. Data on exports of securities are obtained from reports filed by banks and brokerage firms. Because the sum of all recorded receipts and the sum of all recorded payments in a calendar quarter or a calendar year are unlikely to be equal, a statistical discrepancy results, which is shown on Line 63 of the table. The value for this entry is the difference between recorded payments and recorded receipts (this difference between receipts and payments is then added to the smaller figure so that the two values are equal).

The millions of international transactions are summed into three major categories or groups. The trade balance (Line 64) is the difference between the values of commodity exports and commodity imports, usually with imports

Table 27.3   U.S. International Transactions

Line	(Credits + ; debits −)	(millions of dollars) 1984	1985[a]
1	**Exports of goods and services**	**362,021**	**359,702**
2	Merchandise, adjusted, excluding military	219,916	213,990
3	Transfers under U.S. military agency sales contracts	10,086	9,293
4	Travel	11,386	11,655
5	Passenger fares	3,023	2,993
6	Other transportation	13,799	14,342
7	Fees and royalties from affiliated foreigners	6,530	6,817
8	Fees and royalties from unaffiliated foreigners	1,585	1,695
9	Other private services	7,463	7,576
10	U.S. Government misc. services	624	885
	Receipts of income on U.S. assets abroad:		
11	Direct investment	23,078	35,292
12	Other private receipts	59,301	49,883
13	U.S. Government receipts	5,230	5,281
14	**Transfers of goods and services under U.S. military grant programs, net**	**190**	**58**
15	**Imports of goods and services**	**−457,965**	**−462,581**
16	Merchandise, adjusted, excluding military	−334,023	−338,279
17	Direct defense expenditures	−11,851	−11,338
18	Travel	−16,008	−17,043
19	Passenger fares	−6,508	−7,385
20	Other transportation	−14,666	−16,303
21	Fees and royalties to affiliated foreigners	−187	159
22	Fees and royalties to unaffiliated foreigners	−329	−366
23	Private payments for other services	−3,762	−3,967
24	U.S. Government payments for miscellaneous services	−2,133	−2,287
	Payments of income on foreign assets in the United States:		
25	Direct investment	−10,188	−9,013
26	Other private payments	−38,543	−35,453
27	U.S. Government payments	−19,769	−21,306
28	**U.S. military grants of goods and services, net**	**−190**	**−58**

(cont.)

Table 27.3 *(continued)*

Line	(Credits + ; debits −)	(millions of dollars) 1984	1985[a]
29	**Unilateral transfers (excluding military grants of goods and services), net**	−11,413	−14,784
30	U.S. Government grants (excluding military grants of goods and services) ...	−8,522	−11,246
31	U.S. Government pensions and other transfers	−1,591	−1,612
32	Private remittances and other transfers	−1,300	−1,926
33	**U.S. assets abroad, net (increase/capital outflow (−))**	−20,447	−38,183
34	U.S. official reserve assets, net	−3,131	−3,858
35	Gold	—	—
36	Special drawing rights	−979	−897
37	Reserve position in the International Monetary Fund	−995	−908
38	Foreign currencies	−1,156	−3,869
39	U.S. Government assets, other than official reserve assets, net	−5,516	−2,628
40	U.S. credits and other long-term assets ...	−9,619	−7,219
41	Repayments on U.S. loans	4,483	4,435
42	U.S. foreign currency holdings and U.S. short-term assets, net	−380	156
43	U.S. private assets, net	−11,800	−31,697
44	Direct investment	−4,503	−19,091
45	Foreign securities	−5,059	−7,871
46	U.S. claims on unaffiliated foreigners reported by U.S. nonbanking concerns	6,266	n.a.
47	U.S. claims reported by U.S. banks, not included elsewhere	−8,504	−5,926
48	**Foreign assets in the United States, net (increase/capital inflow (+))**	97,319	123,108
49	Foreign official assets in the United States, net	3,424	−1,908
50	U.S. Government securities	4,857	−939
51	U.S. Treasury securities	4,690	−610
52	Other	167	−329
53	Other U.S. Government liabilities	453	148
54	U.S. liabilities reported by U.S. banks, not included elsewhere	663	372
55	Other foreign official assets	−2,549	−1,489
56	Other foreign assets in the United States, net	93,895	125,016

(cont.)

Table 27.3	*(continued)*		

Line	(Credits + ; debits −)	(millions of dollars) 1984	1985[a]
57	Direct investment	22,514	16,254
58	U.S. Treasury securities	22,440	20,910
59	U.S. securities other than U.S. Treasury securities	12,983	50,712
60	U.S. liabilities to unaffiliated foreigners reported by U.S. nonbanking concerns	4,284	n.a.
61	U.S. liabilities reported by U.S. banks, not included elsewhere	31,674	40,610
62	**Allocations of special drawing rights**	—	—
63	**Statistical discrepancy (sum of above items with sign reversed)**	30,486	32,739
	Memoranda:		
64	Balance on merchandise trade (lines 2 and 16)	−114,107	−124,289
65	Balance on goods and services (lines 1 and 15)	−95,945	−102,880
66	Balance on goods, services, and remittances (lines 65, 31, and 32)	−98,836	−106,418
67	Balance on current account (lines 65 and 29)	−107,358	−117,664
	Transactions in U.S. official reserve assets and in foreign official assets in the United States:		
68	Increase (−) in U.S. official reserve assets, net (line 34)	−3,131	−3,858
69	Increase (+) in foreign official assets in the United States (line 49 less line 53)	2,971	−2,056

a: Preliminary.
n.a.: not available.

Source: Bureau of Economic Analysis, *Survey of Current Business* (U.S. Department of Commerce), March 1986.

valued at their landed price, so the value of imports exceeds that reported by the exporting countries by the amount of cargo insurance and freight (CIF) costs. A country has a trade surplus if the value of its commodity exports exceeds the value of its commodity imports. The current-account balance (Line 67) includes all transactions in commodities, together with all transactions in services such as transportation, tourism, royalties and license fees, film rentals, investment income, private remittances such as social security payments, and various gifts, including religious charity, UNICEF, and foreign aid. The characteristic of all international transactions not included in the current-account balance is that they involve transactions in assets or securities with nonresidents, ranging from equities and direct investment to non–interest-bearing demand deposits; transactions in monetary gold, government securities, and bonds are included in the capital-account balance. Lines 33 through 61 summarize various capital-account transactions.

The most important conceptual relationship in the balance of payments accounts is between the current-account balance and the capital-account balance; all international transactions are included in the calculation of one of these balances and no transaction is included in both. (Although purchases of foreign investments are in the capital-account balance and the dividends and interest on these investments are in the current-account balance, these are separate transactions, even in time.) Because of the double-entry character, a surplus on the current account means a deficit on the capital account of the same arithmetic value. Thus, if the United States has a current-account surplus (U.S. exports of goods and services exceed U.S. imports of goods and services) the United States must necessarily—by definition—have a capital-account deficit, and so U.S. imports of securities must exceed U.S. exports of securities. The U.S. net international creditor position is increasing.

The last major group is the payments balance, at one time thought to be a measure of how well a country was doing internationally; this balance is the sum of lines 68 and 69. Payment surpluses were considered indicative of a successful economic performance, and payments deficits of a less successful performance, perhaps because of the association of payments deficits and domestic inflation. Initially payments surpluses were associated with gold inflows, and payments deficits with gold outflows. Subsequently transactions in other types of assets, including liquid assets denominated in the major currencies and claims on the International Monetary Fund, were included in the calculation of the payments balance.

At times, the entry "payments balance" was thought of as the sum of "financing transactions"; all international transactions were segmented either into an autonomous category or into an induced category, and those items in the induced category were considered to be the payments balance. Because of the reliance on the concept of double-entry bookkeeping, the value for the entry for autonomous payments necessarily equals the value for the entry for the induced payments, but with an opposite sign. So if U.S. exports of goods, services, and long-term securities exceed U.S. imports of goods, services, and long-term securities, so that there is a surplus on the U.S. autonomous account, there must be a deficit on the induced account—U.S. imports of monetary gold and foreign exchange reserves exceed U.S. exports of monetary gold and foreign exchange reserves.

An alternative approach considers the payments balance as the sum of transactions in money—liquid assets including gold—by the monetary authorities. A country with payments surplus imports monetary assets. In effect the country has a deficit in the money account: its imports of money exceed its exports of money. The shorthand approach is that a country's payments surplus or deficit should be measured by the change in its central bank's holdings of international money.

Over the last twenty years, various agencies in the U.S. government have debated which transactions are to be included in the measurement of the U.S. payments balance. Prior to 1964, changes in the foreign holdings of liquid dollar assets of foreign commercial banks and foreign private parties as well as of foreign central banks were included in the measurement of the U.S. payments balance. In the 1960s, U.S. authorities took the view that only transactions of foreign monetary authorities should be included. The decision to exclude changes in liquid dollar holdings of foreign commercial banks and of foreign private parties at a time when they were adding to their holdings of liquid dollar assets led to a reduction in the measured U.S. payments deficit. The United States was exporting money because these foreign groups had a continuing demand for dollar assets. With the move to the floating exchange-rate system, U.S. authorities downplayed the significance of the payments balance.

SUMMARY

1 A foreign exchange market is necessary in a multiple currency world. The assets traded in this market are demand deposits denominated in different currencies. The price is the exchange rate.

2 London is the principal center in the world for trading in foreign currency; New York is the next busiest center.

3 Most foreign exchange transactions are either forward contracts, which provide that deposits will be exchanged at specified future days, or swaps, which involve an exchange of a forward contract for a spot exchange contract.

4 Forward exchange contracts are available from banks and should be distinguished from currency futures contracts, which are traded on financial exchanges in Chicago, New York, and London.

5 The interest-rate parity theorem stipulates that the percentage difference between the spot and forward exchange rates will be equal to the difference between interest rates on domestic and foreign securities with maturities equal to that of the forward contract.

6 Some evidence suggests that forward rates may be thought of as the market's "best view" of the spot exchange rates on the dates when the forward contracts mature.

7 The purchasing-power parity theory states that changes in the exchange rates should reflect the difference between changes in the prices of comparable market baskets of goods available in different countries.

8 The Fisher proposition is that domestic interest rates should equal world interest rates plus the anticipated rate of change of the exchange rate.

9 Central bank intervention in the foreign exchange market has been much larger in the period when currencies have been floating than in prior decades with pegged exchange rates.

10 The balance of payments account is the accounting record of transactions in goods, services, and securities between domestic residents and foreign residents.

11 The payments balance measures the purchases and sales of reserve assets by the national monetary authorities.

QUESTIONS AND EXERCISES

1 Discuss why the costs and risks associated with transactions in the foreign exchange market are important for the effective operation of monetary policy in an open economy.

2 Why is the volume of U.S. dollar–British pound foreign exchange transactions in London larger than the volume in New York?

3 Describe how the values for exchange rates for forward exchange contracts of various maturities are related to the spot exchange rate. What are the consequences of an increase in the interest-rate differential on the relationship between the spot exchange rate and the forward exchange rate?

4 Describe the determinants of the level of spot exchange rate. If interest rates on British pound–denominated assets fall, why might the price of the dollar in terms of the British pound increase? Why might the British pound price of the U.S. dollar increase even if the interest-rate differential remains unchanged?

FURTHER READING

ALIBER, ROBERT Z. *Exchange Risk and Corporate International Finance.* New York: Halsted Press, 1979. A systematic guide for analysis of exchange-rate movements.

FEDERAL RESERVE BANK OF BOSTON. *Managed Exchange Rate Flexibility: The Recent Experience.* Boston: Federal Reserve Bank, 1978. A conference volume with numerous essays analyzing the movement of exchange rates in the 1970s.

FRIEDMAN, MILTON. "The Case for Fluctuating Exchange Rates," in his *Essays in Positive Economics.* Chicago: University of Chicago Press, 1953. A classic statement of the case for floating exchange rates.

INTERNATIONAL MONETARY FUND. *Annual Report.* Washington, D.C.: yearly. This report discusses annual developments in the foreign exchange markets.

KUBARYCH, ROGER. *The New York Foreign Exchange Market.* New York: Federal Reserve Bank, 1979. A comprehensive description of the institutional aspects of the foreign exchange markets in the United States.

CHAPTER 28

International Banking and National Monetary Policies

Traditionally, studies in international finance have implicitly assumed that the banking structure in each country is self-contained. In the last several decades, commercial banking has become extensively internationalized in two important, distinct, but related ways: branch systems of U.S. banks have been extended into the domestic markets abroad, and banks headquartered in other countries have established branches in the United States to compete with domestic U.S. banks for dollar deposits and loans. The key concern is how these changes in the institutional structure of banking affect the management of monetary policy in the major countries.

THE INTERNATIONALIZATION OF COMMERCIAL BANKING

The commercial banking systems of the major industrial countries have become internationalized in the last decade and banks headquartered in New York, Chicago, Tokyo, Frankfurt, Zurich, and Toronto have begun to compete aggressively in each other's domestic market. U.S. banks have nearly one thousand branches and subsidiaries in Western Europe, Asia, and Latin America. Banks headquartered in Western Europe and Japan have set up over three hundred banking offices in New York, Chicago, San Francisco, and Los Angeles, and account for 15 percent of the deposits of U.S. banks and 15 percent of the loans.

One consequence of the internationalization of commercial banking is that there is now more extensive competition in the major national financial centers due to the presence of foreign banks that seek to increase their share of markets for loans and for deposits. Banking in Great Britain is dominated by four major banks (National Westminster, Barclays, Midland, and Lloyds); twenty major non-British banks compete for the sterling deposits and loans of major and modest customers. Similarly, the three big German banks (Deutsche, Dresdner, and Commerz) have encountered increased competition for loan and deposit business from forty or fifty branches of foreign banks in Frankfurt, Düsseldorf, and Hamburg.

The Eurodollar Market

The surge in international banking competition has been facilitated by the growth of the external currency market, sometimes called the Eurodollar or offshore banking market. A **Eurodollar deposit** is a *dollar-denominated deposit issued by a banking office located outside the United States.* Similarly, a Euromark deposit is a mark-denominated deposit issued by a banking office located in Luxembourg, London, or any other center outside Germany. These offshore offices engage in an intermediation function virtually identical with that of domestic banks; the major difference is that they sell deposits and buy loans denominated in a currency other than that of the country in which they are located. Thus the London offices of banks in the United States and Germany sell deposits and buy loans denominated in U.S. dollars, German marks, Swiss francs, and perhaps ten currencies other than sterling. Foreign banks with U.S. branches obtain a substantial part of their funds by selling dollar deposits in London and other offshore centers.

At the end of 1984, offshore deposits issued by banks in Western Europe totaled $891 billion. About 70 percent of these deposits were denominated in the U.S. dollar, 14 percent in the German mark, and 7 percent in the Swiss franc. About 25 percent of these deposits were owned by firms and individuals; the rest were owned by banks. The offshore dollar deposits owned by nonbanks were about 27 percent of domestic dollar deposits.

Offshore banking occurs in "monetary havens" such as London, Luxembourg, Singapore, Panama, and the Cayman Islands. Tax havens are an analogy—firms and investors shift funds to tax havens to take advantage of the lower tax rates. Similarly, investors acquire offshore deposits because the interest rates exceed those on domestic deposits by more than enough to compensate for the additional costs, inconvenience, and risks. And offshore banks can pay higher interest rates than domestic banks because they are not subject to interest-rate ceilings and because they are not obliged to hold reserves.

International Banking and Domestic Monetary Policy

The internationalization of banking and the growth of the offshore dollar market raise important questions for the management of U.S. monetary policy. Should offshore dollar deposits be included in the calculation of the U.S. money supply? If so, should the dollar deposits of the offshore offices of U.S. banks be distinguished from the dollar deposits of offshore offices of non-U.S. banks? Should the dollar deposits of U.S. offices of foreign banks be included in the calculation of the U.S. money supply, just as if they were U.S. banks? Should the deposits of the offshore offices of U.S. banks denominated in the German mark, the Swiss franc, and the Japanese yen be included in the measurement of the U.S. money supply? Should the Federal Reserve regulate only the domestic branches of U.S. banks, or should regulation of the offshore branches of U.S. banks be identical with the regulation of domestic branches?

The critical question for monetary analysis is whether the money supply should be measured to include the volume of bank deposits produced within a country (say, the United States or Germany) regardless of currency, or the volume of bank deposits denominated in a particular currency (say, the U.S. dollar or the German mark) regardless of the country in which the deposits are produced, or the volume of deposits produced by banks headquartered in particular countries (say, U.S. banks or German banks) regardless of the currency and the location of the country in which the deposits are produced. The most appropriate answer depends on how well each of these alternative approaches to the measurement of the money supply can explain changes in the level of prices within a country. The narrowest definition of the money supply involves dollar liabilities of U.S.-owned banks produced only by their U.S. offices. This measurement might be expanded in the ownership dimension to include the dollar liabilities produced by the U.S. offices of non–U.S.-owned banks, in the geographic dimension to include the dollar liabilities produced by the foreign offices of U.S. banks, and in the currency dimension to include the nondollar liabilities of U.S. banks.

One view is that the most relevant measure of the U.S. money supply includes the total of dollar-denominated bank liabilities regardless of whether dollar deposits are produced by U.S. banks or by foreign banks, and regardless of whether the deposits are produced in the United States or abroad. The rationale is that the borders between currency areas—between the dollar area and the mark area, for example—are significantly higher than the borders between the domestic and external segments of a particular currency area. The liabilities of foreign-owned banks operating in the United States now are included in the measurement of the U.S. money supply, and there is general agreement that this procedure is appropriate, since households and firms generally view their deposits in foreign-owned banks in the United States as close substitutes for their deposits in U.S. banks; otherwise the branches and subsidiaries of foreign banks would be at a significant competitive disadvantage in selling deposits. However, there is less agreement that offshore deposits denominated in U.S. dollars should be considered part of the U.S. money supply, even though offshore dollars can ultimately only be spent in the United States.

The first issue discussed in this chapter involves the structural differences among countries in the character of banking regulations and the significance of these differences for the management of monetary policy. The second issue involves the relation of the offshore dollar deposits to domestic dollar deposits, and the monetary implications of the development of offshore markets. Attention is given to the implications of the growth of offshore dollar deposits for the management of U.S. monetary policy.

THE STRUCTURE OF INTERNATIONAL BANKING

The traditional approach to the analysis of the structure of international banking examines the market shares within each country for loans and deposits of foreign-owned banks. If data were available, it would be useful to examine the extent to which residents in each country acquire deposits from foreign banks and sell loans to them. Thus, as the costs incurred by residents of any country in acquiring deposits abroad or obtaining loans abroad decline, the size of the market relevant for banks located in a particular center expands.

The growth of international banking is important because foreign-owned banks may have easier access to external funds than domestic banks, and so may be able to sidestep changes in domestic monetary policy, more than domestic banks can. For example, if the Bank of England pursues a more contractive monetary policy, so that British banks find it difficult to extend sterling loans, U.S. and other foreign banks with ready access to dollar funds and mark funds may sell these funds for sterling and then buy more sterling loans. Alternatively, borrowers in London may go to banks in New York and Frankfurt to offset their reduced ability to borrow in London.

One of the striking differences in the comparisons of the domestic banking systems of the major countries is in the size distribution of banks (Tables 28.1 and 28.2). Another is in the form and extent of bank regulation. Although the largest banks in terms of assets are in the United States, the number of banks in the United States is much larger than in any other country. In most other countries, three, four, or five banks, each with hundreds of branches, account for 60 or 70 percent of bank deposits and loans.

That U.S. banks are very large and yet much more numerous than in other countries reflects two factors—one is that the total bank deposits are much larger in the United States than elsewhere because the U.S. economy is much larger. The second is the concern in the United States with maintaining competition in banking, which has led to regulations against expansion of bank branches across state lines (the McFadden Act of 1927) and, in many cases, across political jurisdictions within states, or even across the boundaries between zip code areas.

Paradoxically, in a few cases, the large size of major U.S. banks contributed to the mergers among foreign banks, so they would not be at a size disadvantage relative to the U.S. banks in meeting the financial needs of large multinational firms. Thus, in Great Britain in the early 1970s, National Provincial Bank merged with Westminster Bank while Lloyds merged with British and Overseas Bank. In the Netherlands, Amsterdam Bank and Rotterdam Bank merged.

Most of the foreign offices of U.S. banks are branches; they are not incorporated in the country in which they are located. In a few cases, however, the parents have set up subsidiaries, which have a separate legal status abroad. Frequently, host countries, especially in the developing countries, require that foreign-owned banks have minority domestic ownership, so that the subsidiary form becomes essential. The distinction between branch and subsidiary is

Table 28.1	The Ranking of International Banks, 1983
(billions of dollars in assets, current exchange rates)	
1. Citicorp	125.6
2. Bank America Corp.	115.4
3. Dai Ichi Kangyo Bank	110.3
4. Fuji Bank	103.5
5. Sumitomo Bank	101.1
6. Banque Nationale de Paris	101.0
7. Mitsubishi Bank	98.1
8. Barclays Group	94.1
9. Sanwa Bank	91.3
10. Crédit Agricole	90.2

Source: *The Banker,* London, June 1984.

important for determining U.S. corporate income tax liability, for the income (or losses) of foreign branches is included in U.S. income in the year in which the income is earned, while income of the foreign subsidiaries is subject to U.S. taxation only when the subsidiaries pay dividends to their U.S. parents. Conceivably the subsidiary could close with a loss to its shareholders while the parent remained in business; in contrast, a branch could not fail while the parent remained open for business.[1]

Table 28.2   Distribution of Major Banks by Country, 1983

Country	Top 10	Top 20	Top 50
United States	2	3	8
Japan	5	8	17
France	2	4	5
Great Britain	1	3	5
Germany		1	5
Canada		1	4
Switzerland			2
Netherlands			1
Italy			1
Brazil			1
Hong Kong			1
	10	20	50

Source: *The Banker,* London, June 1984.

---

[1] A subsidiary is a legally incorporated firm that is owned by the parent bank. A branch is an unincorporated extension of the parent bank.

COMPETITION AND REGULATION IN THE BANKING INDUSTRY

The rapid growth of foreign banks in the United States in the last decade focused attention on whether foreign banks had regulatory advantages in the United States relative to U.S. banks. Moreover, their rapid growth led to the concern that the regulations applied by some foreign authorities to the activities of U.S. banks within their jurisdictions were more restrictive than the regulations applied to the activities of foreign banks within the United States —that there may not be reciprocity in the regulation of foreign banks. A key feature of banking regulation within the United States is the multiplicity of regulatory authorities, which was extensively discussed in Chapter 3. The regulatory dilemma is that, if U.S. regulation of foreign banks follows the principle of reciprocity, then the severity of regulations applied to U.S. offices of banks headquartered abroad may vary, depending on the country in which the bank is headquartered.

The growth of offshore banking has facilitated the growth of international banking in several important ways. Branches of U.S. banks established in London to sell dollar deposits could easily compete for British pound deposits and loans at the same time. Similarly, branches established to do offshore banking business in Brussels could sell deposits and buy loans denominated in the Belgian franc. These Brussels branches could obtain funds to make loans by issuing Belgian franc deposits to Belgian residents or by borrowing Belgian francs from the major Belgian banks in the interbank market. Or these branches might have issued Belgian franc deposits in the offshore market, or issued deposits denominated in various foreign currencies in the offshore market and converted the funds to Belgian francs. Because transactions costs encountered by banks are very low, the costs of the currency swap would be insignificant. Similarly, foreign banks that wanted to develop a U.S. loan business could obtain the funds to buy dollar loans by selling dollar deposits in the offshore market in London.

The major expansion of U.S. banks abroad occurred in the 1960s (although a few U.S. banks had established foreign branches in the 1920s and several in the latter part of the nineteenth century) for several reasons. One was to follow the foreign expansion of U.S. firms. A second was to avoid domestic limits on growth, which was especially true for U.S. banks headquartered in New York City. Finally, a large number of U.S. banks went abroad to participate in the offshore money market, and especially to avoid the loss of deposits to the branches of U.S. and foreign banks that were offering higher interest rates on dollar deposits than those that could be paid on domestic dollar deposits. The distribution of foreign offices of U.S. banks matches the pattern of U.S. foreign investment with two major exceptions: U.S. banks are underrepresented in those countries in which entry has been restricted, including Australia, Canada, and Mexico, and overrepresented in London, Luxembourg, the Bahamas, and other monetary havens.

Foreign-owned banks established offices in London, Luxembourg, Singapore, and other monetary havens to participate in the offshore market for deposits denominated in the U.S. dollar, the German mark, and the Swiss franc. Setting up branches abroad to engage in the offshore market was generally less costly or more profitable than setting up additional offices to compete for domestic business. The major expansion of foreign banks in the United States took place in the 1970s, and for several reasons. One was to circumvent the domestic constraints on growth. Another was to participate directly in the dominant international center of finance. A third was to participate in the financing of international trade between their own countries and the United States; because much of the trade was denominated in dollars, foreign banks may have been at a disadvantage in trade financing. A fourth was to serve the particular ethnic markets in the United States, both the expatriate business community and immigrants. Moreover, foreign investment was also increasing in the United States, and the German, Japanese, and British banks did not want to lose their customers to the U.S. banks.

Foreign banks contemplating entry in the United States faced a number of key decisions—one was whether to set up offices in New York or in other cities; a second was whether to enter by starting a new office or through purchase of a U.S. bank; a third was whether to set up a branch, a subsidiary, or an agency. Foreign banks initially had certain advantages in the United States. One was that, although they were not allowed to branch across state lines, they might establish branches in one state and a subsidiary in another (or subsidiaries in several other states). A second was that their U.S. branches were not required to join the Federal Reserve, nor were they required to hold reserves. Their required capital ratios were below those of the U.S. banks; indeed, the U.S. branches of foreign banks had no separate capital of their own.

The International Banking Act of 1978 (IBA) significantly reduced the competitive advantages previously available to foreign banks in the United States by treating them as if they were U.S. banks; the principle of "national treatment" was established. All foreign banks operating in the United States now are to be treated as if they were U.S. banks, regardless of the treatment afforded U.S. banks in their home countries (the national treatment principle has priority over the reciprocity principle). While foreign banks might not join the Federal Reserve, they were required to hold reserves, provided they had deposits in excess of $1 billion, comparable to those held by U.S. banks. The U.S. branches of foreign banks were provided with the option of federal licenses; previously they had only state licenses. Those branches of foreign banks that were involved in retail banking were required to participate in Federal Deposit Insurance. Foreign banks could set up Edge Act corporations, and the powers of the Edge Act corporations of U.S. banks were expanded.[2] The U.S. branches of large foreign banks now are subject to the same supervisory and supervision requirements as comparable U.S. banks.

The impact of the IBA will slow the growth of foreign banks in the United States. Yet these banks are sufficiently numerous and large to increase

---

[2] The Edge Act, which is an amendment to the Federal Reserve Act, relaxes restrictions on U.S. banks engaged in financing international trade and investment. Thus, U.S. banks headquartered in Chicago and San Francisco are permitted to establish subsidiaries in New York to engage in international financial activities. Similarly, New York banks are able to establish subsidiaries in other U.S. cities.

significantly competition in banking, especially in the wholesale market, but also in the retail markets in New York and California. By subjecting foreign-owned banks to reserve requirements, the effectiveness of U.S. monetary control has been increased.

THE GROWTH OF OFFSHORE BANKING

The rapid growth of offshore deposits denominated in U.S. dollars in the 1970s generated considerable controversy about its impact on the rate of world inflation, the stability of the international financial system, and the effectiveness of national monetary control. One assertion is that the growth of offshore dollar deposits led to a surge in the rate of world inflation in the 1970s, largely because offshore banks were not subject to reserve requirements and hence were in a position to create a massive amount of credit on the basis of a modest increase in their reserves. A second concern is that the offshore banking system might collapse along the lines of the failure of banks in the Great Depression. One scenario has one or two poorly managed offshore banks closing due to losses on their loans to high-risk borrowers, much as Bankhaus Herstatt was closed following its losses, triggering the collapse of better managed banks from whom they had borrowed; the metaphor sometimes used is that of a collapsing "house of cards." The third concern is that the growth of the offshore market has reduced the segmentation among national financial markets, so the scope for independent national monetary policies has declined. A variant of this argument is that the weakness of the dollar in the foreign exchange market has resulted from the monies "sloshing about" in the offshore market. Finally, there is concern that the effectiveness of monetary control has declined because U.S. banks can circumvent domestic monetary tightness through their offshore activities.

The rapid growth of offshore deposits denominated in the U.S. dollar reflects investor response to the excess of interest rates on offshore deposits over the interest rates on comparable domestic deposits. Two factors explain this interest-rate differential. One is that offshore banks incur lower costs than domestic banks, largely because they are located in financial centers where they are not obliged to hold reserves against U.S. dollar-denominated deposits. Similar statements can be made about offshore deposits denominated in German marks. Reserve requirements are an implicit tax on deposits. The second factor is that offshore banks are not constrained by ceilings from paying interest rates higher than those that banks can pay on domestic deposits; thus they can pay interest on demand deposits. Both factors reflect that offshore banking is less extensively regulated than banking in domestic financial centers.

Offshore banks are virtually unregulated by the authorities of the countries in which they are located; thus, the British authorities recognize that dollar transactions in London are a matter of geographic convenience and believe these transactions denominated in the U.S. dollar, the German mark, the Swiss franc, and other foreign currencies have no more significance for the management of the British economy than if they had occurred in Luxembourg or New York. Great Britain benefits from exporting more banking services. Indeed, to the extent dollar banking services occur in London, the British have "poached" the banking activities that almost certainly would have occurred in New York or other U.S. cities. Employment in banking and related industries is higher in London and lower in the United States.

Competition for deposits among offshore banks means they pass on to investors or depositors most, if not all, of the cost savings associated with producing deposits in the offshore market. Fifty international banks—the major banks in each industrial country—are important competitors in the London offshore market, while another two hundred banks from various countries also participate. Competition among political jurisdictions such as Great Britain, Luxembourg, the Bahamas, and Singapore for offshore banking business means that each is reluctant to apply any regulations on offshore banks, because these banks might then move to less extensively regulated offshore centers.

Interest Rates in Domestic and Offshore Banks

Once major international banks have established offices to produce and sell offshore deposits, a new set of investment alternatives is available. Investors can buy domestic deposits or, alternatively, they can buy offshore deposits denominated in the same currencies, even from the branches of the same banks from which they can buy domestic deposits. Interest rates on the offshore deposits are higher than those on comparable domestic deposits. If owners of domestic dollar deposits know about the higher interest rates available on offshore deposits, their continued demand for domestic deposits even at the cost of forgone interest income must be explained. One story is that they perceive additional risks with offshore deposits, especially in the form of exchange controls which might be applied to the repatriation of funds from the offshore banks to the domestic banks either by the country in which the deposit is located or by the United States. For these risk-averse investors, the additional interest income is an insufficient return relative to the slight probability of these controls.

To the extent that interest rates on offshore dollar deposits exceed those on comparable domestic deposits by an amount that reflects differences in costs of the two kinds of deposits, each U.S. bank is indifferent between selling an additional offshore deposit and selling an additional domestic deposit. In the absence of exchange controls, banks can use offshore deposits as well as domestic deposits to finance loans to domestic borrowers. There is no necessary link between where a bank sells a deposit and where this bank buys a loan. Interest rates charged to a borrower on an offshore loan are comparable to the interest rates the same borrower would be charged on a domestic loan, for banks have no financial incentive to charge customers lower interest rates on offshore loans. And every borrower has an incentive to compare interest rates they might pay on dollar loans in New York with comparable dollar loans abroad; each has an incentive to borrow in the less expensive center.

Once a bank has decided on the maximum interest rate it can pay on an offshore deposit denominated in U.S. dollars, it can readily determine the maximum interest rate it can pay on offshore deposits denominated in the German mark, the Swiss franc, and other currencies, and still be no worse off than if it had sold an offshore dollar-denominated deposit. Thus, the London branch of a U.S. bank may issue deposits denominated in the German mark and then use the funds to purchase a dollar loan, after first buying U.S. dollars in the foreign exchange market. To reduce or eliminate the exchange risk, the bank would buy the German mark in the forward market at the same time the bank sells the German mark in the spot market. If banks sought to fully cover any possible exchange exposure (or to be compensated for carrying the exposure), differences in interest rates on offshore deposits denominated in various currencies would fully reflect the cost of covering the exchange risk, or the percentage difference between the forward exchange rate and the spot exchange rate.

Some U.S. banks have branches in London, Zurich, Luxembourg, and Paris. At any moment, the branches of a U.S. bank in these centers offer virtually the same interest rate on a U.S. dollar-denominated deposit of a particular maturity. In general, there is no economic incentive for the London branch to offer a higher interest rate on a dollar deposit than the Zurich branch does, especially if the funds realized from issuing the deposits are to be used to finance the purchase of a loan in New York. If investors believe the risk attached to Paris dollar deposits is increasing relative to the risk attached to London dollar deposits, they would shift funds from Paris to London. Nevertheless, the interest rates on London dollar deposits would not change significantly relative to interest rates on Paris dollar deposits.

Occasionally, branches of a bank in a particular center seek to sell offshore deposits there because they wish to buy loans in that country. If investors associate higher risk with offshore deposits available in a particular country because of greater likelihood of exchange controls, then the offshore offices located there must offer higher interest rates on deposits than the offices located in the principal offshore centers. For example, offshore offices in Milan, Italy, have had to pay modestly higher interest rates on dollar deposits than have the London branches of the same banks; investors perceive that a larger risk is attached to offshore deposits in Italy. The banks that sell dollar deposits in Milan use the funds to buy dollar loans from Italian banks. If these banks offered the same interest rate on Milan dollar deposits as on London dollar deposits, they would sell a smaller volume of deposits, or perhaps not sell any at all.

Just as some offshore centers are judged riskier than others, so some offshore banks are judged riskier than others. The riskier banks must pay higher interest rates to sell offshore deposits. The differences in the perceptions of risk reflect several factors, including the size of each bank, measures of its solvency such as the ratio of its capital to its assets, the country of domicile of its parent, and the total of offshore deposits sold by the bank relative to its total domestic deposits. Investors rank offshore banks into three or four major groups, so there is a "tiering" of offshore interest rates (an analogy is the rating of bonds issued by various firms and governments). The spread between the lowest interest rates paid by banks at any time and the highest interest rates paid by other banks has ranged from less than ½ of 1 percent to nearly 2 percent.

At each moment, investors have a large range of deposits available to them. They can choose between domestic deposits and offshore deposits denominated in the U.S dollar, the German mark, the Swiss franc, and other currencies. Moreover, they can choose among offshore deposits denominated in a particular currency in various offshore centers and among offshore deposits and domestic deposits offered by several hundred banks that differ in size and country of domicile.

The much more rapid growth of offshore deposits than of domestic deposits reflects two factors. One is that the interest incentive to shift to off-shore deposits increased as interest rates have increased, since the tax implicit in non–interest-bearing reserves has increased. The second is that the assessment of the risk associated with offshore deposits has decreased.[3]

THE MONETARY IMPLICATIONS OF OFFSHORE DEPOSITS

That the total of offshore deposits increased rapidly in the 1970s at a time when the world inflation rate was also increasing led to the assertion that the growth of offshore deposits caused or intensified increases in the world price level. The analysis of this proposition depends on whether the growth of off-shore deposits has been in addition to the growth of domestic deposits or instead a substitute for the growth of domestic deposits. A related issue is whether the supply of reserves to the commercial banking system has been independent of the growth of offshore deposits.

Two extreme views about the process of credit creation in offshore deposits have led to different conclusions about the inflationary implications of the growth of offshore deposits. One is that the offshore banking system is comparable to the domestic banking system; according to this view, the off-shore banking system bears the same relation to the U.S. banking system as the British banking system does. The major difference is that the offshore banking system lacks a central bank, and, as a result, offshore banks are not subject to reserve requirements. This view implies that a modest increase in the reserves of the offshore banks leads to a substantial expansion of deposits and credit in the offshore banking system, since offshore banks are not required to hold reserves. Thus, the story is that, once an individual shifts funds from a domes-tic bank to an offshore bank, this bank in turn increases its loans to some other individual who buys goods or securities from someone who in turn deposits the receipts in another offshore bank, which in turn lends funds to someone who buys goods, and so on. The size of the fractional-reserve multiplier is much higher in the offshore banking system because these banks aren't required to hold reserves. Those who argue that the growth of offshore

---

[3] The U.S. payments deficit may have contributed modestly to the growth of offshore deposits, to the extent that foreign central banks hold part of their dollar reserves in offshore banks. But such holdings are small. And offshore deposits denominated in the Swiss franc and the German mark have increased, even though Germany and Switzerland have had payments surpluses.

deposits has had a significant impact on the rate of world inflation generally share this view about a segmented and independent offshore banking system.

The competing view is that the offshore market is exclusively an interbank market, the international counterpart of the U.S. federal-funds market. According to this view, no credit is created in the offshore system; rather, the market facilitates more efficient allocation of credit. Thus, banks in countries with balance of payments surpluses extend credit to banks in countries with balance of payments deficits. Extensive interbank transactions in the offshore market support this view.[4] But this view is inconsistent with the data that show that a substantial proportion of liabilities of offshore banks are to private firms and investors, including central banks.

Offshore banks are not part of a segmented financial system but rather are the branches of major international banks located in financial centers where they are not obliged to hold reserves. There are virtually no important offshore banks that are not branches or subsidiaries of major international banks; the offshore offices of major international banks compete with the domestic offices of these banks to sell deposits. If the domestic office of a U.S. bank sells an additional domestic deposit, its required reserve holdings increase; if the offshore office of the same bank sells an additional deposit, its required reserves are unchanged. In effect, any reserves held at an offshore branch of a U.S. bank are mingled with the reserves held against domestic deposits. By selling an additional offshore deposit, a bank is able to reduce the effective or economic level of reserves below the legal level required against domestic deposits. Hence, for any U.S. (or foreign) bank with offshore branches, the ratio of non–interest-earning assets to interest-earning assets declines as offshore deposits increase relative to domestic deposits.

The more rapid growth of offshore deposits than of domestic deposits means that the effective reserve requirements applied to each bank have declined. So there has been a larger than anticipated increase in the supply of dollar credits for a given increase in the supply of reserves to the U.S. banking system because of the increase in the money multiplier. To the extent that growth of offshore deposits has been unanticipated by the Federal Reserve, there has been a more rapid than expected increase in the volume of credit. Estimating the impact of this unanticipated increase in the supply of credit on the U.S. inflation rate and on the world inflation rate is difficult, in part because this source of credit growth may have been a substitute for some other source of credit that otherwise would have grown more rapidly.

The growth of offshore deposits has reduced the effectiveness of monetary control because U.S. monetary authorities can never be confident of the changes in the money supply associated with a given change in bank

---

[4] One reason for the large volume of interbank transactions is that banks that are deemed less risky lend to riskier banks. A second is that banks seek to match maturities of their assets and liabilities to economize on the need for liquidity. A third is that some countries have an advantage in taking deposits while others have an advantage in making loans. A fourth is that offshore banks engage extensively in credit rationing; they have limits on their willingness to acquire loans of individual borrowers, loans of borrowers in a particular country, or loans of borrowers in a particular industry. Once a bank's loans in each category are at its ceilings, it extends credit to banks less able to sell deposits to investors.

reserves. The source of this uncertainty is that the money multiplier changes as the volume of offshore deposits increases relative to the volume of domestic deposits. On a year-to-year basis, the trend has been variable and appears unpredictable.

The growth of offshore deposits has probably decreased the significance of the barriers among currency areas, and complicated the management of monetary policy. Both investors and banks are more conscious of the returns associated with crossing the borders between currency areas. The growth of offshore deposits has increased the willingness of firms to estimate the costs and risks associated with altering their currency exposures, although it has not reduced these costs or risks in any significant way. Thus, the segmentation of currency areas has declined, and so the scope for independent national monetary policies has declined.

Since the major offshore banks are branches of the major international banks, the concern that their failure might trigger the collapse of the banking system is greatly exaggerated. Most offshore banks are unlikely to make riskier loans than their head offices; indeed, the offshore branches of U.S. banks are examined by the same U.S. authorities that examine the domestic offices. Legally, holders of deposits in offshore offices are not likely to incur losses even if these offices make numerous loans that prove faulty. The solvency of these offshore offices is based on the solvency of their head offices. Finally, the various central banks that participate in the activities of the Bank for International Settlements, which was formed in the late 1920s to administer German reparations and now provides various financial and other services to its central bank members, have agreed that each central bank is responsible for the liquidity needs of the offshore offices of its domestic banks.

Reducing the Advantages of Offshore Banks

One proposal to reduce the incentive to export the U.S. banking system is that reserve requirements be applied to offshore deposits. Reserve requirements might be applied to all offshore deposits produced in London. The response to this proposal is that investors would shift funds to other offshore centers which do not apply reserve requirements. Hence, if reserve requirements were applied to offshore deposits in London, owners of offshore deposits would shift their funds to Luxembourg, Paris, and Panama. Alternatively, reserve requirements might be applied by the monetary authorities in each country to the offshore offices of banks headquartered in their jurisdictions; thus, the U.S. authorities could extend domestic reserve requirements to the offshore offices of U.S banks. Similarly, the German authorities might extend their own domestic reserve requirements to the offshore offices of German banks. The response to this proposal is that the owners of offshore deposits would shift their funds to offshore deposits produced by British, French, and Swiss banks. The British could apply requirements, but they have no incentive to do so. A third proposal is to pay market interest rates on reserves held by the central bank. But this proposal, if implemented, would reduce the government's income because interest payments by the central bank would increase.

In 1980 the Federal Reserve permitted banks operating in the United States to establish International Banking Facilities (IBFs)—offices that can issue deposits not subject to reserves. Only nonresidents are permitted to acquire these deposits. Hence, these nonresidents now receive higher interest rates on dollar deposits in the United States than do U.S. residents.

The regulatory problem is that U.S. authorities must choose between reducing the incentive for investors to acquire offshore deposits and adjusting to the more rapid growth of offshore deposits than of domestic deposits. In a period of high interest rates and low-cost communications, banks and their customers have found it easy and profitable to circumvent the tax on domestic deposits implicit in reserve requirements. U.S. authorities must recognize that the structure of U.S. financial regulation cannot be independent of regulations elsewhere; they cannot maintain a level of reserve requirements significantly higher than those abroad, or more U.S. banking business will go abroad.

If U.S. residents were permitted to hold deposits in IBFs, many would shift funds from offshore banks in London and Zurich to IBFs in New York, Chicago, and San Francisco. Yet many holders of domestic deposits in Minneapolis and Salt Lake City and other U.S. cities who were deterred by the possibility of exchange controls from acquiring dollar deposits in London or Zurich also would find it attractive to shift funds to the IBFs in New York, Chicago, and San Francisco. So the potential rush to acquire deposits in the IBFs would mean that banks in each major metropolitan area in the United States would seek to establish an IBF, and reserve requirements would be circumvented, since a smaller and smaller share of deposits would be subject to these requirements. The efforts of the Federal Reserve to maintain high reserve requirements on one class of deposits while virtually identical deposits are not subject to reserve requirements would be readily circumvented. Thus, the implications of establishing free-banking zones in the United States only highlight the problems for monetary management in a world in which similar deposits are subject to different reserve requirements. As long as banks operating in London and other offshore centers are not required to hold reserves, the reserve requirement creates an incentive to export the U.S. banking system.

Bank Regulation and Monetary Policy

The varied approach to the regulation of banks may reduce the effectiveness of monetary policy. Several anomalies are evident. The domestic transactions of U.S. banks are regulated on one basis; their offshore transactions are regulated on another. The offshore transactions of U.S. banks are subject to a set of rules different from those of non-U.S. banks. And the domestic transactions of U.S. banks and the transactions of foreign banks in the countries in which they are headquartered are regulated in different ways.

The question of whether U.S.-owned banks or foreign-owned banks provide banking services to U.S. residents should be distinguished from broader questions about the effectiveness of U.S. monetary policy when national regulations differ. Different regulations have different impacts on the competitive positions of different groups of banks, and on their growth rates. The question of the ownership of the institutions that provide banking services is independent of the monetary implications, with one exception: foreign-owned banks may have easier access to funds at their home offices, and so they may be able to circumvent changes in monetary policy. The significance of this source of funds is an empirical matter. On an a priori basis, the argument would appear to be much more significant for smaller countries than for the United States.

Currently, U.S. monetary control is weakened because of the difference in reserve requirements and the lack of a stable relationship between the growth of offshore dollar deposits and the growth of domestic deposits. In periods of monetary contraction, as interest rates rise and the effective interest cost of reserve requirements applied to U.S. banks increases, the share of U.S. banks in the dollar deposit market declines. To reduce the disadvantage of U.S. banks, either domestic reserve requirements might be lowered to reduce or eliminate the financial incentives in favor of offshore deposits, or interest might be paid on required reserves. The argument for such adjustments demonstrates that U.S. regulatory authorities cannot operate independently of foreign regulations; more severe regulation tends to lead to the export of U.S. financial transactions.

SUMMARY

1 Over the last several decades, commercial banking has become much more international as banks headquartered in the United States, Western Europe, and Japan have established branches and subsidiaries in other countries.

2 The growth in international banking has been facilitated by the expansion of offshore banking—banking offices operating in particular centers sell deposits denominated in a currency other than that of the country in which they are located. Thus, banks in London, including the London branches of U.S. banks, sell deposits denominated in, for example, the U.S. dollar, the German mark, and the Swiss franc.

3 Offshore deposits denominated in the U.S. dollar have grown significantly more rapidly than domestic deposits denominated in the dollar (even after adjustment for the growth of interbank deposits) with the result that the growth in the dollar money supply has been understated.

4 The rapid growth of offshore deposits in the 1970s, like the rapid growth of money-market funds, is a result of the cost of reserve requirements in a period when interest rates increased sharply.

5 The growth of offshore deposits denominated in the U.S. dollar and other currencies has facilitated the integration of national money markets, since banks can sell deposits denominated in one currency, convert the funds into some other currency in which they wish to make the loan, and cover the exchange risk with a forward exchange contract.

6 The growth of offshore deposits denominated in the dollar has meant that the effective reserve requirement applied to dollar deposits is lower; the effective requirement is the weighted average of the reserve requirement applied to domestic deposits and the zero requirement applicable to offshore deposits.

7 The regulatory change that permitted U.S. banks to establish International Banking Facilities (IBFs) will reduce a major incentive for nonresidents to acquire offshore deposits. U.S. residents will continue to acquire offshore dollar deposits as long as they offer higher yields than domestic deposits.

QUESTIONS AND EXERCISES

1 Discuss the conditions necessary for the growth of an external currency market. Why do interest rates on offshore deposits exceed those on comparable domestic deposits? What is the upper limit to this difference? If interest rates on external deposits are higher than those on domestic deposits denominated in the same currency, why does anyone continue to hold domestic deposits?

2 Why might the growth of an offshore market in dollar deposits weaken the effectiveness of monetary control of the Federal Reserve?

3 Is it possible or likely that a financial collapse or disaster might develop in the offshore banking system, and be independent of the domestic banking system?

4 Discuss the ways in which the growth of offshore dollar deposits has contributed to the growth of branches of foreign banks in the United States.

FURTHER READING

FIELEKE, NORMAN. *Key Issues in International Banking*. Boston: Federal Reserve Bank of Boston, 1977. A conference volume with good descriptive material.

LITTLE, JANE SNEDDON. *Eurodollars*. New York: Harper & Row, 1975. A good survey of participants in the offshore money market.

U.S. CONGRESS, HOUSE COMMITTEE ON BANKING, CURRENCY, AND HOUSING. *International Banking*. Washington: Government Printing Office, 1976. A comprehensive survey of international banking, with background material on the International Banking Act of 1979.

CHAPTER 29

The Agenda of International Financial Issues

Over the next several decades, the monetary authorities in the major countries will remain concerned with changes in international financial arrangements. Many will seek methods to reduce the range of movement in exchange rates, and the frequency and severity of the financial disturbances that countries experience from their trading partners. Some will seek to develop arrangements that will enhance the effectiveness of monetary policy without infringing on freer international trade and payments. Some will seek to develop mechanisms to alleviate the debt burdens of the developing countries.

TOWARD A NEW INTERNATIONAL MONETARY SYSTEM

Since the breakdown of the Bretton Woods System of pegged exchange rates, the arrangements for organizing the foreign exchange market and producing international money are seen as being too haphazard to qualify as an international monetary system. To qualify as a system, the arrangements must have more "order," be more systematic, or be based on an international treaty. Some proposals to achieve greater monetary order seek to improve the operation of the floating exchange rates, while others favor a return to pegged exchange rates, on either a global or regional basis. Other proposals seek to alter the assets used as international reserves; one issue is whether gold should continue to be phased out of the international monetary system, or whether gold should again be used as an international reserve asset. The international monetary roles of dollar assets and assets denominated in other currencies would be modified under some proposals.

A key issue is how the changes in these institutional frameworks would affect the management of monetary policy—both the need or demand for monetary independence in the major countries and the ability of U.S. monetary authorities and those in other countries to follow policies appropriate for their domestic objectives with minimal external constraints. The demand for monetary independence arises because the phases of the business cycle are not perfectly correlated across countries; even if they were, however, countries differ in the importance they attach to full employment and to price stability. Even if individual countries decide they wish to pursue greater monetary independence, they may encounter significant external constraints; changes in a country's monetary policy may have significant impacts on the flows of capital or on the foreign exchange value of its currency. In modifying international monetary arrangements, the goal is to enable countries to pursue their domestic objectives without forgoing the advantages of openness and specialization possible in the international economy.

Some of the proposals are ambitious in the extent to which they would modify current arrangements for the organization of the foreign exchange market and the supply of international reserves. A new system implies a set of rules—perhaps based on an international treaty like the Bretton Woods agreement—that would affect the intervention practices of central banks in the foreign exchange market. The participating countries would commit themselves to follow particular practices about exchange-market intervention and international reserve holdings and to refrain from a specified set of measures. Adhering to many of these commitments is likely to have *no* significant cost; even without the treaty, the countries would have behaved much as if they were following the commitments. To the extent adherence to the commitments has a cost in that several of the participating countries are obliged to pursue measures they would not have in the absence of the treaty, the key question is how long they will abide by their commitments, and forgo pursuing their own interests to satisfy their obligations under an international treaty. One issue is how far "in front" of the consensus the treaty can get; treaties that are expensive to domestic interests may, like the Smithsonian Agreement, soon fall by the wayside.

So a major issue involves the impact of changes in international monetary arrangements on national economic policies. The relevant question is how long efforts of central banks to peg or manage the foreign exchange value of their currencies can cause the exchange rate to differ significantly from the values they otherwise would have. Intervention can have a greater impact on the exchange rate in the short run—a period of a few months or even a year —than over a more extended period. In the long run, exchange rates are determined by relative prices and incomes and expectations about changes in relative price levels.

The success in devising an international financial arrangement that will remain viable for some time depends on the relationship between the implied commitments and the prevailing set of monetary and political relationships. An attempt to adopt a system of pegged exchange rates is not likely to be viable in an inflationary period; one characteristic of inflation is that rates of price level increase differ sharply across countries and vary significantly from one year to the next, and so countries are likely to find the domestic economic costs of adhering to their parities for an extended period too high.

If the proposed international financial arrangements are to be viable, they must be consistent with the distribution of political and economic power among nations. Thus, the gold standard succeeded during a period of British economic dominance, and when British policies led to a relatively stable price level. The Bretton Woods System flourished during a period when U.S. economic and political power was dominant, and U.S. economic policies led to a stable price level. As the relative U.S. economic position declined with the resurgence of the German and Japanese economies, the fragility of the Bretton Woods System became more apparent.

The system broke down, however, only when the U.S. price level began to increase at a rate higher than 5 percent a year. Any new set of arrangements must be consistent with a dispersion of economic power among at least three major economic centers—the United States, Germany and other members of the European community, and Japan. Proposals that require extensive centralization of authority are not likely to be viable as long as nationalist pressures remain strong.

Changes in institutional arrangements involve a complicated interplay of interests of various countries. Few central bankers and treasury officials attempt to optimize or maximize a cosmopolitan or universal interest. Rather, in developing positions on these issues, each deals with a national variant on a familiar theme: "What's in it for me?" The policymakers in each country develop an implicit cost-benefit analysis on the impacts that the adoption of each proposal would have on the well-being of their constituents and on the ability of their own governments to realize their objectives. Relatively few national monetary authorities would agree to proposals that might advance the cosmopolitan interest if the cost to their own constituents is high.

International monetary problems develop when national interests diverge. Differences across nations are more extensive, usually, than the differences within nations. Moreover, within countries, there are usually established legal procedures, frequently based on a written constitution, for determining the public interest, or at least for resolving problems, whereas the procedures for determining the cosmopolitan interest of a group of nations are vague. Developing solutions to the questions might be easier if national interests were more malleable or alterable. A frequent proposal is that the national authorities coordinate their policies. But such proposals often ignore the divergence of national interest. Because such interests change only slowly, the problem is to devise a set of international arrangements that will best accommodate the interests of many different countries.

This chapter first traces developments in international monetary arrangements in the last decade. Then attention is given to the modification of exchange-market agreements, the development of reserve arrangements, and the unified currency concept. Three issues are considered—the scope for mergers of national currencies and the optimum currency issue; the choice between pegged rates and floating rates; and the future roles of competing international monies, especially the role of gold, the dollar, and IMF monies.

INTERNATIONAL MONETARY DEVELOPMENTS IN THE LAST DECADE

Change in international monetary arrangements in the last decade was much more extensive than in any previous period. The market price of gold, which had been $35 at the end of the 1960s, exceeded $600 a decade later; in January 1980 the gold price reached $970. The gold price had fallen to $300 in the summer of 1982; by the end of the year, the price had reached $500. In 1985, the price was in the $300 to $350 range, and rose to $400 in 1986.

At the end of the 1960s, the IMF system of adjustable parities came under pressure because of the delay in the necessary changes in exchange parities to the increasing overvaluation of the dollar. The system broke down once in August 1971, was patched and stumbled through 1972, but broke down again at the beginning of 1973. The floating-rate system did not conform to the textbook model, in that the range of movement in exchange rates was much greater than the difference in the increases in national price levels. The national monetary authorities intervened extensively to dampen the amplitude of the movement in exchange rates. Indeed, by the measure of purchases and sales of international reserve assets, intervention was more extensive than in the previous decades with pegged exchange rates.

The changes in the foreign exchange value of the dollar were large and frequently abrupt. When the dollar was weak in the late 1970s, the monetary authorities in many countries sought to diversify their reserves to include relatively more assets denominated in currencies other than the U.S. dollar, especially the German mark, the Swiss franc, and the Japanese yen. In the 1960s, one of the major concerns was the shortage of international reserves, which culminated in the establishment of the special drawing rights (SDRs) arrangement and the production of 10 billion SDRs. In the decade of the 1970s, total reserves minus gold had increased sevenfold, from $40 billion at the end of 1969 to $270 billion at the end of 1979. Total reserves including gold increased from $80 billion to $600 billion if monetary gold is valued at $300 an ounce.

The Impact of Inflation

The factor that relates all of these changes in international financial relationships is the surge in the world inflation rate, from an annual average rate of 4.3 percent in the 1960s to one of 11.1 percent in the 1970s; the U.S. inflation rate increased from an average of 2.3 percent in the 1960s to 7.1 percent in the 1970s. Inflation rates were at their highest-ever levels at the end of the 1970s. While the inflation rate was intensified by the succession of increases in the price of crude petroleum promoted by OPEC in 1973–1974 and then again in 1978–1979, the world inflation rate was already at the double-digit level before the fivefold increase in the price of crude petroleum in 1973–1974. Nevertheless, in 1974 and again in 1979, sharp increases in the price of oil probably caused the annual world inflation rate to be higher by 2 to 3 percentage points. The impact was greater in some countries because the oil price increase triggered increases in the prices of other commodities, and expectations of future price increases.

In periods of accelerating inflation, the private demand for gold increased because investors believed that gold was a hedge against inflation. Those investors with the highest inflationary expectations set the market price of gold. Gold was clearly undervalued at the end of the 1960s, since its price had remained constant since 1934 while the world price level had increased by a factor of 4. The increase in the gold price in the 1970s suggests expectations of continued and accelerating inflation. From time to time, the rules concerning official transactions in gold have been changed. For a while the national monetary authorities agreed not to deal in gold at a price other than the official price. Then the official price was abandoned. A few monetary authorities have raised the valuation attached to their holdings of gold; many monetary authorities consider gold an important component of their international reserves and would be reluctant to agree to proposals to demonetize gold.

OPTIMAL CURRENCY AREAS AND MONETARY UNIONS

One of the central issues in international finance involves the geographic span of the use of particular currencies. Should each country have its own currency, as virtually all now do, or should countries merge their currencies, which is frequently contemplated as the monetary counterpart of integration in the European community? Or would it be worthwhile for certain large countries, say China or Brazil, to develop two or more currencies for distinct regional areas within each country? In the late nineteenth century, currency unification was extensive within Germany, Japan, and Italy—in each case as part of the program of political unification and, in each case, among people who shared the same language and the same culture.

One feature of the last several decades has been an increase in the number of countries and the number of currencies, largely as a result of the breakup of the British, French, Portuguese, and Dutch empires. Thus, the Irish pound, which had been firmly pegged to the British pound since Irish independence in 1922, now floats relative to the British pound. The breakup of various empires and the establishment of new, independent countries has led to a sharp increase in the number of national currencies. Initially these currencies were pegged to those of the countries they were formerly part of. Over time, as the monetary policies in the new countries became more independent and more expansive, these countries have devalued their currencies.

On a more abstract level, the issues about unification of national currencies involve the attributes of countries whose currencies might be merged so as to maximize their economic welfare. The gains from currency unification involve a more efficient allocation of resources and of capital and a reduction in the costs associated with the use of the foreign exchange market. If there were only one currency in the world, these costs would disappear. The United States might be viewed as a unified currency area, comprising twelve Federal Reserve Districts and fifty states. Financial capital flows smoothly and efficiently from high-saving, low-growth areas to low-saving, high-growth areas; one indication of the almost frictionless movement is that interest rates on comparable securities are virtually the same in the capital-rich and the capital-poor areas. Payments can be made on a virtually costless basis from Maine to California by check. Internationally, the segmentation of Western Europe into currency areas incurs costs that would be avoided if the national currency areas were merged into one European currency.

The costs of currency mergers are those associated with the loss of a central bank in one of the areas or countries, and thus with the decline in the ability to manage monetary policy to enhance employment and price-level objectives in the area, country, or region. If the Federal Reserve Bank of Chicago were independent of the other regional Federal Reserve Banks, it might pursue a more expansive monetary policy to counter the higher unemployment rate in the Midwest. The value of having a separate currency area centers on the advantages attached to being able to alter the rate of growth of the money supply. The significance of these costs of unification varies with the choice of countries involved, and with the similarity of their economic structures.

One logical proposition relevant to optimizing the number of currency areas is that there should be no more central banks than there are labor markets. If there were, some of the central banks would be redundant (as eleven of the regional Federal Reserve Banks are) in that the unemployment rates in these labor markets would always be identical with those in other labor markets. A labor market is defined as an area in which excess demand for labor and excess supply of labor of the same type cannot exist at the same time. If labor is perfectly mobile between or among several labor markets, then they effectively are components of one larger labor market, in that the levels of money wages and the changes in these levels cannot differ significantly in the various geographic sectors of this larger labor market. The explanation is straightforward: if the unemployed workers would move to the firms with excess demand for labor and competition among workers maintains reasonable uniformity of wages, no firm would pay a higher wage to attract labor than the prevailing market wage.

Hence the necessary condition for having separate national central banks is that there are segmented labor markets and that labor is not perfectly mobile among them. Economic welfare might be enhanced if the central banks in the areas with high unemployment followed an expansive monetary policy while the central banks in the areas with inflation followed a more contractive policy. However, if financial capital is perfectly mobile between these currency areas, then an independent central bank would be redundant, for one of the central banks could not, by changes in its monetary policy, induce a change in its interest rates relative to world interest rates. In this case where capital mobility negates the efforts at monetary independence, central banks should merge to eliminate the costs of servicing the foreign exchange market. The *sufficient* condition for separate currency areas is that national capital markets are partially segmented.

Even if both labor markets and capital markets are partially segmented, so that independent monetary policies are needed and feasible, the costs of maintaining separate national currencies may exceed the benefits. The trade-off associated with the merger of currencies involves whether the welfare gains from the enhanced flow of goods and securities and the elimination of the costs of servicing the foreign exchange market are larger or smaller than the welfare costs of higher unemployment because of a reduction in the number of central banks.

These general propositions about the economic conditions that should be satisfied if the merger of currencies is to enhance economic welfare must be made operational. One proposal is that, if the several countries' economies are complementary, their currencies should be merged. Another is that their currencies should be merged if their trade patterns are similar. A third is that their currencies should be merged if their business cycles are similar in timing and amplitude; the rationale is that the central banks in these countries would be following similar monetary policies. Small countries have much to gain from mergers of their currencies with each other, or with the currency of a large country as a result of the increased flow of goods and financial capital. Large countries like the United States have already realized these gains, although both Canada and Mexico might gain from merging their currencies with the U.S. dollar because both would have access to the U.S. financial markets on more favorable terms. In addition, currency unification has been suggested for countries that are physically adjacent or share the same language.

The European Community and Currency Unification

The historical experience suggests that currencies are merged to secure political objectives; currency unification is seen as an important step toward political unification. The most ambitious effort to merge national monies in recent years has been that of the European Community. This effort followed the Treaty of Rome (1957), which led to the elimination of tariffs on internal trade among members of the community, to the development of a common external tariff and a common agricultural policy, and to the harmonization of social security, welfare policy, and business taxes in the member countries. So it might seem natural for the member countries to harmonize or coordinate monetary policies, and to move toward a common, communitywide money, a change that would eventually require mergers of their central banks.

One motive for currency unification in Western Europe is that political unification is viewed as a desirable objective. A merger of currencies would be a meaningful step toward this objective. Some note the growth of intra-European trade; an increasing share of the trade of various European countries is with other members of this community. Payments from one country in Europe to another would be facilitated if there were only one currency; then trade within Western Europe would be promoted. Hence, a second motive for the move to a European currency would be to provide a modest amount of trade protection to European firms in competition with U.S. and other non-European firms. A third motive for currency unification is that development of a European currency area might provide a larger center of monetary stability, and better enable the European countries to insulate their economies from monetary shocks generated by the United States.

Once a decision has been reached to merge currencies, the authorities must decide on how to realize this objective. One approach is to harmonize monetary policies and then, if inflation rates are similar, to peg each currency to a common unit of account. An alternative approach involves pegging these currencies in the exchange market, and then harmonizing monetary policies so as to reduce the likelihood of extended payments imbalances at the established parities. The Europeans have been following the second approach.

The likelihood that any large countries outside Western Europe will merge their currencies in the near future is modest. There may also be substantial setbacks in efforts toward currency unification in Western Europe. Nevertheless, the insights gained by the analysis of the costs and benefits of currency unification are applicable to two other questions. The first is whether a country's interests are better served by pegging its currency in the foreign exchange market or by permitting its currency to float. The second is that, if a country decides to peg its currency, it must decide whether its interests are advanced by pegging to the U.S. dollar, the German mark, the Japanese yen, or some other currency.

THE CHOICE BETWEEN FLOATING AND PEGGED EXCHANGE RATES

For most of the last century, the U.S. dollar has been a pegged currency. Prior to World War I, a system of pegged rates resulted because the dollar and other major currencies were pegged to gold. The stylized fact is that central banks were able to maintain their parities because they followed the "rules of the game" for adjustment to payments imbalances, deflating when in deficit and inflating when in surplus.

The 1920s (actually 1919–1926) was the first extensive period with floating currencies. At the outbreak of World War I, the European central banks stopped pegging their currencies at their mint parities; they embargoed gold exports and supported their currencies at levels 5 to 15 percent below their prewar parities. Inflation was extensive, and at quite different rates in various countries. While the dominant objective in most countries was to return to the 1913 parities, this was not immediately feasible at the end of the war because of the large increase in national price levels during the war. Countries permitted their currencies to float, and some attempted to deflate so it would again be possible to peg their currencies to gold at their 1913 parities.

A few countries—Great Britain and the various neutrals, including Switzerland, the Netherlands, and the Scandinavian countries—succeeded in again pegging their currencies at their 1913 parities. The other Allies—France, Belgium, and Italy—eventually pegged their currencies in the late 1920s, after continued inflation and extended depreciation of their currencies, at levels one-third to one-fourth of their previous parities; gold was three to four times as expensive in terms of their currencies than before the war. The defeated countries—Germany, Austria, Hungary, and Russia—also pegged their currencies to gold after hyperinflations forced the adoption of new currencies.

The exchange-rate experience in the 1930s was substantially different from that of the 1920s. Great Britain permitted sterling to float in September

1931; a few countries—Ireland, Denmark, Sweden, and some members of the British Commonwealth—pegged their currencies to sterling, with the result that a sterling currency area was formed; all the currencies in this area floated together in terms of the dollar and other currencies pegged to gold. Then when President Roosevelt took office in early March 1933, he closed all U.S. banks, nationalized private U.S. gold holdings, and eliminated the gold parity for the dollar. For the next ten months, the U.S. dollar price of gold increased; the dollar depreciated in terms of gold and most foreign currencies. At the end of January 1934, the U.S. dollar price of gold was again fixed, this time at $35 an ounce, so the effective increase in the U.S. dollar price of gold was 75 percent. Then speculative pressures developed against currencies that still pegged their currencies to gold, and, in mid-1936, the French franc, the Belgian franc, and the Dutch guilder were devalued.

One conclusion drawn from the operation of floating exchange rates during the interwar period was that international trade and investment would be disrupted because of uncertainty about exchange rates in the future; a second was that speculation would be destabilizing, and that the amplitude of exchange-rate movements would be larger and that speculators would cause the trend value of the exchange rate to follow a path different from the path it would have followed in their absence. Thus, if speculators sold a weak currency, the price of foreign exchange in terms of this currency would increase, and so would the price of imports. The domestic price level would increase more rapidly; in contrast, the domestic price level would increase less rapidly in those countries whose currencies were acquired by speculators. So speculation would be self-justifying. At a later stage, this behavior led to what has been called "vicious and virtuous cycles."

The Litany between Proponents of Pegged and of Floating Exchange Rates

The proponents of floating exchange rates criticized these conclusions, but only after asserting that the primary advantage of a floating exchange-rate system was that countries would be able to achieve greater monetary independence. They claimed that countries would be able to follow monetary policies independent of an external constraint because any tendency toward a payments deficit would automatically lead to a depreciation of their currencies. For example, if a country followed a more expansive monetary policy, one that would be associated with a larger payments deficit than it could readily finance with a pegged exchange-rate system, its currency would depreciate with a floating exchange rate. Similarly, no country would be obliged to purchase large amounts of foreign exchange and hence increase its own money supply to maintain its exchange parity under a floating exchange-rate system; instead, its currency would appreciate and the monetary base would not be affected by its currency flows. The pro-floaters argued that trade and investment would not be disturbed by uncertainty about exchange-rate movements because traders and investors would hedge their foreign exchange commitments through forward contracts. Hence, countries would have greater freedom to follow policies so their price levels would differ from those in other countries; similarly, they would have greater freedom to pursue different employment objectives. The pro-floaters also argued that speculation would not be destabilizing, or that destabilizing speculators would soon go bankrupt because they would be betting against long-run trends.

A litany developed between the critics and the proponents of floating exchange rates. The critics argued that there were inadequate forward exchange-market facilities in most currencies and that, besides, hedging was not a costless activity. They also asserted that monetary independence was a chimera, and that countries would have much less control over their own price and income targets than the proponents of floating exchange rates promised. Moreover, the critics noted that the removal of the exchange parities would eliminate one of the last barriers to domestic inflation, so that countries would use—and abuse—their increased monetary independence, with the consequence that the inflation rate would be higher.

Uncertainty and Independence under a Floating-Rate System

The resolution of the issue between the proponents and the critics of floating rates partly involves the nature and consequences of uncertainty under the floating-rate system. The greater monetary independence under a system of floating exchange rates is possible only because the increased uncertainty about future exchange rates increases the segmentation of national money markets. In the absence of any increase in segmentation, there is no scope for greater monetary independence. The increase in uncertainty necessary for greater monetary independence also deters trade and investment. True, trader and investor uncertainty about future exchange rates can be hedged through the purchase of forward contracts, and hedging may be costless to the extent that forward rates are unbiased predictors—on average—of future spot exchange rates. Yet hedging is not riskless because forward exchange rates individually are not very good predictors of the spot exchange rates on the dates when the forward contracts mature. The benefits of greater monetary independence with floating exchange rates cannot be attained without increased uncertainty, and the cost of this increased uncertainty is a reduced level of trade and investment—or, in a growing world economy, a reduction in the rate of growth of trade and investment. The economic significance of this cost and its value relative to the value of greater monetary independence remain important and unresolved empirical issues.

The critics of floating rates base their assertion that speculation would be destabilizing on the observation that changes in exchange rates have been much larger in amplitude than might be inferred from the difference in contemporaneous changes in national price levels. The proponents of floating rates respond that the period-to-period movement in the exchange rates follows a random walk, that there is no systematic or predictable movement in exchange rates, and hence the exchange market is efficient.[1] There are no

---

[1] A financial market is said to be efficient when market prices of assets adjust immediately and fully to any new information. If "good news" and "bad news" occur randomly, then the changes in the price of the asset should follow a random walk.

"runs" in the time series of exchange-rate movements—periods when the direction of changes in exchange rates can be accurately predicted from past changes. But if the exchange-rate movement follows a trend, then it may do so because the forces "driving" the exchange rate also follow a trend. Alternatively, the monetary authorities may have been "leaning against the wind" when intervening in the foreign exchange market—and retreating. In the last several years, some analysts have concluded that the foreign exchange market is not efficient—that, for brief episodes, day-to-day changes in exchange rates have been serially correlated when the amplitude of movements in exchange rates have been large.

The efforts of national monetary authorities to follow independent monetary policies appear likely to lead to large movements in the spot exchange rate since the current spot exchange rate primarily reflects the anticipated spot exchange rates. Changes in monetary policy affect the current spot exchange because of the impacts of these changes on anticipations of future exchange rates and on price-level developments and on the interest rates at which these future exchange rates are discounted to the present. Thus, a move toward a more expansive monetary policy would be associated with an anticipation of a more rapid increase in the domestic price level and a decline in the domestic interest rate; both factors would cause domestic currency to depreciate. Conversely, a move toward a more contractive monetary policy is associated with appreciation of domestic currency both because of the reduction in the anticipated domestic inflation rate and because of the increase in the interest rate. The large swings in the exchange rates reflect that the changes in monetary policy have been offsetting in time; either a domestic contractive policy is followed by a domestic expansive policy or by contractive policies abroad.

If these swings in exchange rates induced by changes in monetary policy are substantial, then the authorities may be obliged to intervene in the exchange market to limit the swings in the exchange rate; a "would-be" clean float becomes a managed float. Assume that U.S. authorities follow a more expansive monetary policy. If the dollar tends to depreciate, then foreign monetary authorities may buy dollars to limit the appreciation of their own currencies. The purchase of dollars leads to an increase in their money supplies. Unless these sales are offset when the currency movement is reversed, there is upward bias in the growth of the money supplies and in price-level movements. The authorities may have less control over their money supplies in the floating-rate period than in the pegged-rate period because the private capital flows are so much larger.

Problems of Managing an Exchange-Rate System

The proponents of floating exchange rates frequently point to the difficulties of managing a pegged-rate system. Changes in parities almost always occur after too great a delay because the authorities hope that divine providence will intervene so that an almost certain change in a parity will not be necessary. The move to floating exchange rates in the early 1970s did not occur because the proponents of floating exchange rates won the arguments; rather, in a period of increasing inflation and greater divergence among countries in their inflation rates, the authorities were unwilling to incur the domestic political costs associated with the policies necessary to maintain the pegged-rate system. The pegged exchange-rate system might have been maintained if the foreign monetary authorities, especially those in Germany, had been willing to accept the U.S. inflation rate—but the Germans preferred a lower inflation rate.

The evidence of the last hundred years suggests that the monetary system has a tendency to gravitate to pegged rates—as long as such a system is feasible. If inflation rates among major countries are similar and low, a return to pegged rates seems likely. Many countries will peg their currencies to that of a nearby and larger country, which is the pattern of the European Monetary System; the currencies of Belgium, the Netherlands, and other members are effectively pegged to the German mark.[2] Hence, the number of major countries with floating rates will decline, currency blocks will develop, and eventually pegging will reduce the exchange-rate movements among the major currency blocs.

A crawling-peg exchange system has been proposed as an arrangement that combines the advantages of both a pegged- and a floating-rate system. On frequent occasions, perhaps as often as once or twice a month, the authorities change their parities, usually by no more than 2 or 3 percent. Because the changes in parities are frequent, no political trauma is supposed to be associated with these changes. Because the amount of the change is so small, few traders and investors deem it worth their while to attempt to predict the timing of these changes, and to profit from them. Between the time of changes in parities, the monetary authorities would peg the rate; however, because of the frequency of changes in the parity, the domestic monetary implications of pegging the rate would be slight. Many countries in Latin America have followed this approach.

THE SYSTEM OF RESERVE ASSETS

In the 1960s, monetary authorities in many countries were concerned that international reserves were increasing at too slow a rate. In the 1970s, there was an unplanned and unanticipated surge in the level of reserves. The surge in reserves contributed to the increase in the inflation rates in many countries, since their monetary bases expanded. Hence, one of the major concerns is how the growth of reserves might be managed to limit inflationary impacts. A related question involves the components of reserves, and whether gold and liquid assets denominated in the U.S. dollar, the German mark, and other currencies will continue to serve as reserve assets, along with SDRs.

The surprise in the 1970s was the growth in the volume of reserve assets

---

[2] The European Monetary System was established to provide a regime of pegged exchange rates for countries in Western Europe. Much of their trade is with one another and so the motive for pegging the currencies was to reduce the uncertainty associated with payments on intra-European trade.

during a period of floating exchange rates. Foreign central banks acquired dollar assets to limit the appreciation of their currencies when private parties, both American and non-American, "unloaded" their dollar holdings.

At the end of 1965, international reserves totaled $67 billion; when floating began in 1973, reserves totaled $150 billion. Determining the value at the end of 1985 is complicated by the need to place a value on monetary gold holdings. If monetary gold is valued at $300 per ounce, reserves exceed $650 billion. If gold is valued at $250 per ounce, international reserves amount to $600 billion, or about five times the 1970 level. Even after an adjustment for the increase in commodity price levels, the increase in reserves has been substantial. If gold remains in monetary limbo, countries in deficit will be able to sell gold at or near its market price (or else borrow from other countries, using their gold as collateral) to obtain currencies to finance their payments deficits.

A second concern of the 1960s was that the "system" could not produce international reserves without forcing the United States to incur "payments deficits"; the United States was the major supplier of reserves, in the form of both gold and liquid dollar assets. During the sixteen-year period 1950–1965, U.S. gold sales to foreign official institutions were almost as large as new gold production. As foreign holdings of dollars increased and U.S. gold holdings declined, the ability of the United States to maintain its $35 gold parity for an indefinite future appeared increasingly questionable. The conundrum was that, to the extent the United States was successful in reducing its payments deficit, most other countries would no longer be able to increase their holdings of gold and other reserve assets. But unless the United States could reduce its payments deficit, the $35 parity could not be maintained. As U.S. gold holdings declined, numerous other countries became more reluctant holders of dollar assets; they could not readily sell dollar assets to buy gold without jeopardizing the U.S. ability to maintain the gold parity.

A third problem was the asymmetry between the apparent ease with which the United States financed its payments deficits and the difficulties other countries encountered in financing their payments deficits. Other countries "spent" owned reserves and reserves borrowed from international institutions; they had to acquire reserve assets before they could use these assets to finance payments deficits, or, if they borrowed from foreign official institutions to finance deficits, they had to repay these loans. In contrast, the United States financed much of its deficits by "passive borrowing" to the extent that other countries were willing to acquire dollar-denominated assets. Thus, that part of the U.S. deficit not financed by gold sales could be financed "automatically." Such automatic financing led to the concern that the growth of international reserves might be "uncontrolled."

GOLD AS INTERNATIONAL MONEY

Whether gold will again have a role as an international reserve asset depends on the outcome of two forces. One is a continuation of the pressures for economic efficiency that led to the progressive decline in gold's monetary role in the last century. Gold is no longer used as a domestic money, nor do any countries peg their currencies to gold. Gold seems to be a "barbaric relic."

U.S. authorities have sought to reduce the international monetary role of gold—the cliché is "to remove it from the center of the monetary system." They have succeeded, for in the years since the price of gold has been variable central banks have rarely traded gold with each other. Central banks have hoarded their gold, because its market price has been so much higher than the official price.

Gold has been an important monetary asset for centuries; investors and monetary institutions acquired gold because it held its value better than other assets. Moreover, partly because of its underlying commodity value, gold maintained its value over a wider geographic span than any other monetary asset; gold had credibility as a monetary asset that other assets lacked. More important, there was relative price-level stability in the century of the gold standard, if not on a year-to-year basis, then over several decades. Whether price-level stability was a cause or a consequence is arguable. But the period since gold has been shifted from the center of the system is one of much more rapid inflation than that experienced during the previous century. Some U.S. politicians have concluded that there is a persuasive historical case for the return to the gold standard—or at least for pegging national currencies to gold.

The case for reducing the monetary role of gold further is that gold is not readily manageable as a reserve asset. Once a generation, the monetary price of gold might have to be increased, or there would be a cumulative reserve shortage. And investors would continually speculate about the timing and amount of these increases. Such increases, however, are likely to be necessary only if inflation continues; with a stable price level, there is no evidence that the monetary price of gold must be raised.

The competing force involved in the case for maintaining gold as a reserve asset has several elements: gold already is an important monetary asset; gold has a large constituency; and considering gold as an acceptable reserve asset would restore balance to central bank portfolios, now overloaded with assets denominated in the U.S. dollar. The United States would benefit, since U.S. gold holdings approximate the combined gold of the three other largest holders. The importance attached to gold suggests that, once again, a monetary role will develop for gold, because the value of gold in reserves is so large that no substitute can readily be found. Two scenarios for enhancing the monetary role of gold are feasible. One is that central banks will develop arrangements so that countries in deficit will have greater confidence that they will be able to sell gold to other central banks to obtain the foreign exchange necessary to support their currencies in the exchange market. Alternatively, the United States and other countries might agree to a new monetary price for gold in terms of their currencies as part of a complex negotiation involving the roles of gold and other reserve assets.

THE DOLLAR AND OTHER FIAT ASSETS

A major concern in the evolution of the international financial system is the role of the dollar as a reserve asset. While holdings of dollar assets are increasing, holdings of assets denominated in the German mark, the Swiss franc, and the Japanese yen also are likely to increase. International institutions are also likely to continue producing reserve assets. Nevertheless, it seems highly unlikely that the U.S. dollar will be phased out as an international reserve, or that its role will decline significantly. The growth of reserves denominated in various national currencies is a result of the decisions of foreign central banks; almost always each acquires the currencies of the countries with whom it has major trade and financial relations, provided those countries have a reasonable record for commodity price-level stability. Inevitably, only the currencies of a very few countries are acquired as reserve assets.

Over the long run, the growth of reserve assets denominated in different currencies is usually determined by demand; the countries acquiring these assets first decide on the volume of reserves they wish to acquire and then decide on the currency denomination of these assets. On several occasions, however, changes in the volume of reserve assets represent excess production, as with the British pound during World War II, and with the U.S. dollar during the 1969–1971 period. Excess production of reserve assets occurs because countries with the payments surpluses are reluctant to revalue their currencies.

A key policy issue is whether U.S. interests are served by having the U.S. dollar used as an international reserve asset. The dollar became a reserve asset because foreign monetary authorities found it to their advantage to acquire dollar assets; the development of the reserve asset role for the dollar was not the result of a U.S. plan. The United States gains several advantages from being an international banker. One, the seigniorage[3] gain, involves the profit from the production of money—the difference between the cost of producing money and its purchasing power in terms of other assets. In a competitive banking system, such gains would be competed away in the form of higher interest rates on dollar deposits. But U.S. interest rates may be lower, not higher, because of the foreign demand for dollar assets.

A second advantage of being banker is the flexibility that became apparent in the late 1960s. The U.S. payments deficit was financed by the willingness of foreign central banks to add to their holdings of dollar assets. And the third advantage is that there is no effective constraint on the size of the U.S. payments deficit.

In the 1960s, some analysts concluded that the use of the dollar as a reserve-asset currency was *not* in the U.S. national interest. One criticism was that the United States had less control over its monetary policy because there was a greater constraint on changes in U.S. interest rates, due to the concern of the Federal Reserve that shifts of funds to foreign financial centers by private parties would be larger because of the volume of dollars owned by central banks. To the extent that foreign official institutions were buyers of dollar assets rather than of gold, these shifts of private funds presented no problem; the constraint became apparent only if foreign official institutions might sell dollars and buy gold as U.S. interest rates fell. A second criticism was that the United States had less control over the foreign exchange value of the U.S.

---

[3] Seigniorage is the profit derived from the production of money. Thus the difference between the face value of a coin and its cost of production is seigniorage. So is the difference between the face value of currency notes and their cost of production.

dollar than other countries had over the foreign exchange value of their currencies; a U.S. devaluation would be more likely to be followed by comparable devaluations of other countries. The evidence of the early 1970s suggests that the offsetting devaluations probably reflect the unwillingness of other countries to incur the adverse change in their international competitive position due to a U.S. devaluation rather than the possible losses on their holdings of dollar assets. Finally, increases in U.S. exports of securities led to smaller U.S. exports of commodities, which was a cost to the producers of the commodities if not to the U.S. economy.

Now that foreign holdings of dollar assets exceed $300 billion, the question is whether changes in the demand for these assets can have significant impact on the U.S. economy. If foreign holders of dollar assets decide to shift to assets denominated in another currency, the U.S. dollar would depreciate in the foreign exchange market.

When the dollar has been weak in the exchange market, there have been proposals for new arrangements to manage foreign dollar holdings. One proposal is that the United States extend exchange guarantees on foreign dollar holdings; if the dollar depreciated by more than a specified amount, U.S. authorities would make a direct payment to some or all foreign official holders of dollars to compensate them for their exchange losses. Alternatively, some or all of foreign central bank holdings of dollar assets would be transferred to the International Monetary Fund; the Fund in turn would acquire these claims on the United States. U.S. authorities would extend a maintenance-of-value guarantee on these dollar holdings of the Fund, and the Fund in turn would be able to extend a similar guarantee on its liabilities to foreign official institutions. A third proposal is that U.S. authorities begin to support the dollar in the foreign exchange market to limit the variations in the foreign exchange value of the dollar; in this case, U.S. authorities might draw on U.S. reserves and borrow foreign currencies from the International Monetary Fund and from foreign central banks.

The common feature of all these proposals is for U.S. authorities to incur the exchange risk on some or all U.S. liabilities held by foreign official institutions. The presumption is that the United States' willingness to acquire the exchange exposure would limit variations in the foreign exchange value of the dollar. Foreign central banks would be less reluctant to intervene in response to sharp movements in exchange rates that seem out of line with general underlying economic movements.

THE ROLE OF MULTINATIONAL MONETARY INSTITUTIONS

One proposal to resolve the problems resulting from the use of assets denominated in major national currencies as reserve assets is to establish an international institution to produce reserve assets. Member countries would hold reserves in the form of deposits in this institution; when in payments deficits, they would transfer part of their deposits to the countries with the payments surpluses. This type of arrangement has a number of advantages: reserves could be produced without the need for any particular currency to become overvalued; any profit attached to the production of international money could be distributed to all countries; and the rate of growth of international reserves could be managed on a planned basis, so the overproduction of reserves could be limited.

The movement toward an international reserve-providing institution has been slow for several reasons. Since few countries have achieved price-level stability, it doesn't seem likely that the growth of international reserves can be managed to avoid a bias toward inflation. (Indeed, in the domestic context, the evidence is that domestic monetary management has been inflationary.) In the international context, the decisions about the rate of growth of reserves appear likely to be dominated by the inflation-prone countries. Hence, the countries with the strongest commitments to price stability would realize larger-than-desired payments surpluses from acquiring the liabilities of the international institution, and would face the choice of either accepting a higher-than-desired inflation rate or continually revaluing their currencies. If, as seems likely, reserves were produced at too rapid a rate, the surplus countries would be reluctant to acquire deposits in the new institution.

From the point of view of individual countries, the relevant question is whether the attainment of national objectives will be eased by the activities of an international reserve-providing institution. U.S. authorities would necessarily be concerned with the implications for the management of domestic monetary policy of U.S. participation in such an institution. If the United States tended to be in a payments deficit, financing the deficit might be more difficult than under the current arrangement, because foreign official institutions would no longer acquire dollar assets, and so U.S. monetary policy might have to be directed to reduce the deficit. If the United States were in a payments surplus, it would be obliged to extend credit to countries with payments deficits; as a consequence, U.S. authorities might face the choice between monetary expansion to reduce the U.S. payments surplus or monetary contraction to dampen or counter the expansive domestic impacts of the large payments surplus.

National attitudes toward the idea of a central reserve-producing institution generally reflect whether a country is more likely to incur payments deficits or payments surpluses. Those countries with a tendency toward higher inflation and payments deficits generally favor the development of such an institution, since they believe financing their deficits in the future would be easier. Countries with a tendency toward payments surpluses are more skeptical since they would be obliged to extend credit to the countries with the payments deficits.

Developing a new reserve-producing institution does not resolve the problems of accommodating the differences among countries in their inflation rates and their growth rates. Some countries would have payments surpluses, others would have payments deficits, and the problem under the new arrangement, as under previous arrangements, is which group of countries would take the initiative in adopting measures to reduce the payments imbalance.

SUMMARY

1 The source of international monetary problems is that national interests diverge.
2 The Bretton Woods System of pegged exchange rates broke down because of the surge in the world inflation rate, and the efforts of several countries to realize inflation rates lower than those in the United States.
3 If countries were to join a currency or monetary union, they would benefit from the elimination of the various costs of using the foreign exchange market on their transactions with each other; however, their economic welfare might be adversely affected unless their business cycles and trade patterns are similar.
4 For most of the last century, the major industrial countries have pegged their currencies, with the exception of two periods: the first half of the 1920s and from 1973 on.
5 The movements in foreign exchange rates in the 1970s have not conformed with the claims previously advanced by their proponents. Thus, the range of movements in exchange rates has been large, and countries have had much less monetary independence than they would have preferred.
6 In the 1960s, there was almost uniform belief that there would be a shortage of international reserve assets; in contrast, in the 1970s, international reserve assets increased at a very rapid rate.
7 The increase in the market price of gold has had a major impact on the value of central bank holdings of monetary gold. The self-interest of many central banks will be advanced if arrangements develop so they can once again use gold to finance payments deficits.
8 Holdings of dollar-denominated assets are the next largest component of international reserve assets after monetary gold holdings. The United States has almost certainly benefited from the foreign demand for dollar assets.
9 Special Drawing Rights and reserve positions in the International Monetary Fund account for only a small part of international reserves. Because nations must agree before these components can be increased significantly, the likelihood of significant growth in this component of reserve assets is low.

QUESTIONS AND EXERCISES

1 Discuss the costs and benefits of maintaining separate national currencies. Why might the major countries in Western Europe now think the time appropriate to merge their currencies?
2 Discuss the basic arguments for floating exchange rates and the arguments for a system of adjustable parities. What conditions must be satisfied if the major countries are again to peg their currencies?
3 During the 1960s financial officials in the major countries were concerned about the shortage of international reserves. Discuss the conditions that might lead to the conclusion that the volume of international reserves is too small or too large.
4 Why has the relationship between the demand for reserves and the supply of reserves changed in the last decade?

FURTHER READING

MURPHY, J. CARTER. *The International Monetary System: Beyond the First Stages of Reform.* Washington, D.C.: American Enterprise Institute for Public Policy Research, 1976. A liberal's approach to international monetary developments.

SCHMIDT, WILSON E. *The U.S. Balance of Payments and the Sinking Dollar.* New York: New York University Press, 1979. The title tells the story.

INDEX

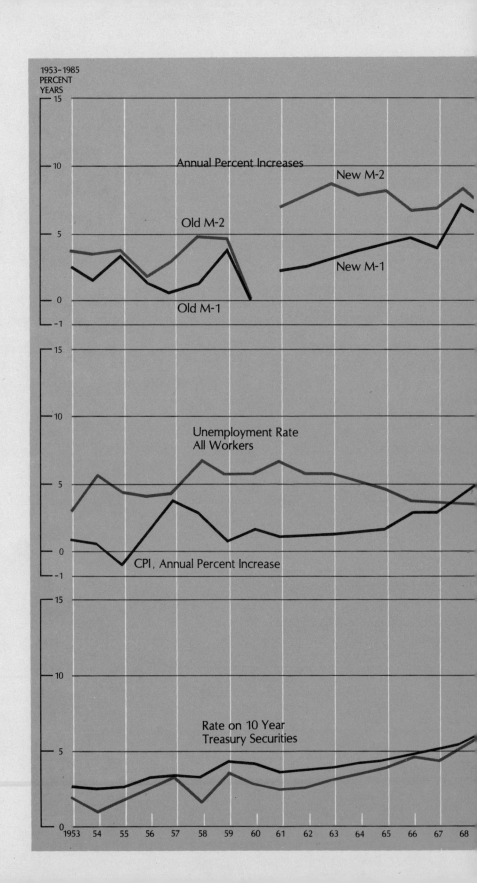